ROUTLEDGE HANDBOOK OF TALENT IDENTIFICATION AND DEVELOPMENT IN SPORT

Identifying athletic talent and developing that talent to its full potential is a central concern in sport. Understanding talent identification and its implications for both positive and negative developmental outcomes is crucial to sporting success. This is the first comprehensive resource for scientists, researchers, students, coaches, analysts and policymakers looking to improve their knowledge of the talent identification and development process.

With contributions from leading researchers and practitioners, this book offers a complete overview of contemporary talent identification and development from in-depth discussion of methodological and philosophical issues through to practical applications. Adopting an international and multi-disciplinary approach, it addresses all key aspects of the talent identification and development process, including skill acquisition and motor learning, psychological factors and family influences, creating optimal environments for performance, and dealing with injury and rehabilitation.

Presenting an unrivalled wealth of research, the *Routledge Handbook of Talent Identification and Development in Sport* is an essential resource for any undergraduate or postgraduate degree course in sport studies, sport science, sport coaching or sport management, as well as for sport policymakers, analysts and coaches.

Joseph Baker is Professor and Head of the Lifespan Health and Performance Laboratory at York University, Canada. He has also held Visiting Researcher/Professor positions in the UK, Australia and Germany. His research examines the varying factors affecting skill acquisition and maintenance across the lifespan. Joe is Past President of the Canadian Society for Psychomotor Learning and Sport Psychology and the author/editor of eight books, four journal special issues and more than 200 peer-reviewed articles and book chapters.

Stephen Cobley is a Senior Lecturer in Motor Control and Skill Acquisition and Sport and Exercise Psychology in the Faculty of Health Sciences at the University of Sydney, Australia. His research interests examine the factors that facilitate or inhibit athlete development from a bio-ecological and multi-disciplinary perspective. His research and applied work has led to the evaluation, modification and writing of athlete development programs and policy for numerous sport organizations. Steve is an Associate Editor for the *Journal of Science and Medicine in Sport*, and previously co-edited *Talent Identification and Development: International perspectives* (Routledge, 2012).

Jörg Schorer is Professor of Sport and Movement Science at the Carl-von-Ossietzky-University in Oldenburg, Germany. He has worked in academia as well as in the applied talent sector. His research focuses on elite sport across the lifespan.

Nick Wattie is an Assistant Professor in the Faculty of Health Sciences at the University of Ontario Institute of Technology, Canada. His research examines various factors related to talent identification and development in sport, with an emphasis on the influence of a range of environmental, individual and task constraints on expertise in sport, skill acquisition and positive youth development, as well as athlete morbidity and mortality.

ROUTLEDGE HANDBOOK OF TALENT IDENTIFICATION AND DEVELOPMENT IN SPORT

Edited by
Joseph Baker, Stephen Cobley, Jörg Schorer and Nick Wattie

LONDON AND NEW YORK

First published 2017 by Routledge

2 Park Square, Milton Park, Abingdon, Oxfordshire OX14 4RN
52 Vanderbilt Avenue, New York, NY 10017

Routledge is an imprint of the Taylor & Francis Group, an informa business

First issued in paperback 2019

British Library Cataloguing in Publication Data
A catalogue record for this book is available from the British Library

Library of Congress Cataloging in Publication Data
A catalog record for this book has been requested

ISBN: 978-1-138-95177-8 (hbk)
ISBN: 978-0-367-87421-6 (pbk)

Typeset in Bembo
by FiSH Books Ltd, Enfield

"To the Kungl Family, with much love"
JB

"Für Lisa und Lukas"
JS

"To Danielle, Natalie & Jessica"
SC

"To Mom and Dad, for their nature and nurture"
NW

CONTENTS

LIST OF FIGURES

xi

LIST OF TABLES

CONTRIBUTORS

Dorothee Alfermann is Full Professor of Sport and Exercise Psychology at the University of Leipzig. Her research topics include: social and psychological influences on athletic careers and career transitions; cross-cultural psychology of sport; effects of sport and exercise on cognitions and on mental health. Dr Alfermann has published numerous journal articles and book chapters on career transitions and dropout in particular. She has served on the board of the International Society of Sport Psychology (ISSP) from 1997 till 2005 and was editor-in-chief of *Psychology of Sport and Exercise*, the official journal of FEPSAC, from 2004 through 2012.

David I. Anderson is a Professor in the Department of Kinesiology at San Francisco State University. He received his PhD in Kinesiology from Louisiana State University in 1994. David's research centers on understanding how motor skills are acquired, how skill acquisition can be facilitated, and how the development of skills in the motor domain influences psychological functioning. David is an Active Fellow in the National Academy of Kinesiology and a long-standing member of the Institute of Human Development at the University of California, Berkeley.

Duarte Araújo is the Director of the Laboratory of Expertise in Sport of the Faculty of Human Kinetics at University of Lisbon, Portugal. Duarte is the President of the Portuguese Society of Sport Psychology and a member of the National Council of Sports of Portugal. His research on sport expertise, team performance and decision-making, and affordances and variability has been funded by the Fundação para a Ciência e Tecnologia (Portuguese Foundation for Science and Technology). Duarte has published more than 100 papers in highly scientific journals, and has been invited worldwide to talk about expert performance behaviours. In his spare time Duarte is a marathon runner.

Joseph Baker is Professor and Head of the Lifespan Health and Performance Laboratory at York University, Canada. He has also held visiting researcher/professor positions in the United Kingdom, Australia and Germany. His research examines the varying factors affecting skill acquisition and maintenance across the lifespan. Joe is Past President of the Canadian Society for Psychomotor Learning and Sport Psychology and the author/editor of 8 books, 4 journal special issues and more than 200 peer reviewed articles and book chapters.

Theresa Beesley is a PhD candidate in the School of Kinesiology and Health Science at York University, Canada. Her research focuses on exploring the factors and process of positive youth development within various sport contexts. She has received a Doctoral Fellowship from the Social Sciences and Humanities Research council of Canada (SSHRC) and Sport Canada and a Sport Canada Research Initiative supplement.

Patrick Belling is a PhD student in Applied Cognitive Science and Human Factors at Michigan Technological University (USA). He earned his Masters degree in this program in 2013. He currently also works as the Lead Cognitive Data Scientist at Axon Sports in Scottsdale, Arizona (USA). Patrick's research and profession has focused on the development and evaluation of simulated and representative tasks for assessing and training perceptual-cognitive skill across several sports.

Dirk Büsch is an Associate Professor and Head of Department of Game and Combat Sports at the Institute for Applied Training Science in Leipzig, Germany. He graduated in Sports Science, received his PhD in Saarbrücken and habilitation (post-doctoral thesis) in Sport Sciences at the University of Bremen, Germany. His research and teaching focus on training and movement science (e.g., muscle strength/power, tactics, laterality), the development, evaluation and implementation of talent programmes (e.g., in handball) and statistical methodology in sports. Dr. Büsch is member of the German Society of Sport Science.

Cordelia W. Carter earned her undergraduate degree from Yale College in 1998, graduating magna cum laude. She returned to Yale University to pursue her medical training and earned her medical degree from that institution in 2004. She then completed orthopaedic surgery residency at New York-Presbyterian Hospital (Columbia University) followed by fellowships in pediatric orthopaedic surgery at Children's Hospital Los Angeles (University of Southern California) and pediatric sports medicine at Children's Hospital Boston (Harvard University). Dr. Carter's interest in pediatric sports medicine has been life-long; in addition to her own participation in athletics – as a student at Yale she was named to the All-Ivy, Academic All-Ivy and Academic All-American Field Hockey teams – she has coached swimming, track and field, lacrosse and field hockey teams at a wide range of scholastic levels. Her academic and research interests have also focused on pediatric sports medicine, and she currently sits on the Board of Directors for the Pediatric Research in Sports Medicine (PRISM) society.

Stephen Cobley is a Senior Lecturer in Motor Control & Skill Acquisition and Sport and Exercise Psychology in the Faculty of Health Sciences at The University of Sydney (Australia). His research interests examine the factors that facilitate or inhibit athlete development from a bio-ecological and multi-disciplinary perspective. His research and applied work has led to the evaluation, modification and writing of athlete development programs and policy for numerous sport organizations. Steve is an Associate Editor for the *Journal of Science & Medicine in Sport*, and previously co-edited "*Talent Identification and Development: International Perspectives*" (Routledge, 2012).

Manuel J. Coelho-e-Silva is a Professor of Pediatric Sport Science in the Faculty of Sport Science and Physical Education at the University of Coimbra, Portugal. The major focus of his teaching and research is pediatric sport science. He served for four years in the Portuguese Society for Physical Education and organized the 2013 Pediatric Work Physiology conference. He presently serves as coordinator of the Master's Program in Youth Sports and also of the

Center for Research on Sport and Physical Activity (Centro de Investigação do Desporto e Actividade Física: uid/dtp/04213/2013), which has a major emphasis on pediatric sport science.

Dave Collins holds a PhD from the University of Surrey and is Professor of Coaching and Performance at the University of Central Lancashire and Director of Grey Matters Performance. He is also a Fellow of the British Association of Sport and Exercise Sciences, an Associate Fellow of the British Psychological Society, and an ex-Royal Marine. From an applied perspective, he has worked with over 60 world or Olympic medalists as well as professional sports teams, performers and business executives. His research interests include performer and coach development, cognitive expertise, and the promotion of peak performance across different challenge environments.

Bob Crudgington is an Associate Lecturer in Sports Coaching in the School of Human Movement and Nutrition Sciences at the University of Queensland. He is an experienced high performance coach and manager and was the medal-winning Head Coach of the Australian Olympic Softball team in Atlanta and Sydney as well as the high performance manager for Diving Australia at the Athens Olympic Games in 2004. Bob originally completed a Bachelor Science with Honours in ecology and is currently engaged in doctoral research investigating the structure and design of digital learning landscapes and its impact on coach learning.

Sean P. Cumming is a Senior Lecturer in Sport and Exercise Sciences in the Department for Health at the University of Bath, UK. Adopting a biocultural perspective, his research examines how psychosocial factors mediate and moderate the impact of biological maturation in the contexts of sport and exercise. Dr. Cumming works in research and consultancy roles with a number of professional clubs and organizations, including the Premier League, Lawn Tennis Association and Bath Rugby.

Keith Davids is Professor of Motor Learning at the Centre for Sports Engineering Research, Sheffield Hallam University, UK. Keith has held professorial positions in the UK, New Zealand, Australia and Finland (Finnish Distinguished Professor 2012–2016). His research programme in ecological dynamics investigates constraints on emergent coordination tendencies in athletes and sports teams. These key ideas have been integrated into a Nonlinear Pedagogy, informed by his work on motor learning design in sport. Keith has conducted research on elite sport programmes at the New Zealand South Island Academy, the Queensland Academy of Sport, the Australian Institute of Sport, Diving Australia, Cricket Australia and the English Institute of Sport.

Rebecca K. Dickinson is a PhD scholar working in the School of Human Movement and Nutrition Sciences at the University of Queensland, Australia. Her research interests broadly include talent identification and development in sport and sport psychology. She is also a practicing psychologist with athletes at all levels, having completed her Honours and Masters degrees at the University of Queensland in Sport and Exercise Psychology.

Lauren Dickler is a Master's candidate in the School of Kinesiology and Health Science, at York University, Canada. Her research examines mental health/illness in high performance/elite athletes. Lauren has worked in the Canadian sport system for over sixteen years. Using the knowledge she has gained from her research as well as her years in sport, she currently provides policy and sport development consulting services at both the provincial and national levels.

Joyce Ehrlinger is Director of the Social Cognition Laboratory and Assistant Professor of Psychology at Washington State University. She is internationally known for her research on antecedents and consequences of confidence and motivation. She has advanced our understanding of how belief systems shape self and others' perceptions. Her work has applications for successful goal pursuit in education, health, business, and relationships. She is Associate Editor for *Social and Personality Compass*, and an editorial Board member for *Social Cognition*. Her research has been published extensively in scientific outlets and popularised by the media, including *New York Times*, *Huffington Post*, and *Atlantic*.

Anne-Marie Elbe is an Associate Professor for Sport and Exercise Psychology at the University of Copenhagen, Denmark. Her previous posts were at Northumbria University, UK and at the University of Potsdam, Germany. Her publications and research interests focus on motivational and self-regulatory aspects of athletic performance, sport psychological diagnostics, doping, health aspects of team sports and sport and integration. She is Past Associate Editor for the *International Journal of Sport and Exercise Psychology* and the *Zeitschrift für Sportpsychologie* and editorial board member of *Psychology of Sport Exercise*. She is President of FEPSAC, the European Federation of Sport Psychology.

Mark Eys is a Professor in the Departments of Kinesiology/Physical Education and Psychology at Wilfrid Laurier University, and a Canada Research Chair in Group Dynamics and Physical Activity. His research interests include role ambiguity and acceptance in sport, cohesion, and social influences in exercise. He is a co-author of *Group Dynamics in Sport* (2005; 2012; FIT) and a co-editor of *Group Dynamics in Exercise and Sport Psychology* (2007; 2014; Routledge). In 2001, he was awarded the Canadian Interuniversity Sport (CIS) Coach of the Year with The University of Western Ontario women's soccer program.

Josef Fahlén is an Associate Professor at the Department of Education, Umeå University, Sweden, where he specializes in issues related to the organizing, management and governance of voluntary sport. His research is concerned with sport policy-making and implementation in general and more specifically with the use of – and consequences of using – voluntary, non-profit and membership-based sport clubs as vehicles for social change.

Damian Farrow holds a joint appointment with Victoria University and the Australian Institute of Sport as a Professor of Skill Acquisition. Damian is responsible for the provision of evidence-based support to Australian coaches seeking to measure and improve the design of the skill learning environment. Damian's research interests centre on understanding the factors critical to developing sport expertise.

Antonio J. Figueiredo is a Professor in the Faculty of Sport Sciences and Physical Education at the University of Coimbra, Portugal. His primary research focus deals with youth ports in the context of interrelationships among growth, maturation and performance relative to talent identification and development. During his career, he has established collaborative research ventures in several European countries and also in Brazil and China.

Christian Fischer is Full Professor in the Educational Sciences with a focus on School Research: Gifted Education and Individual Promotion at the University of Münster, Germany. He is Academic Director of the International Centre for the Study of Giftedness (ICBF) from the Universities of Münster, Osnabrück and Nijmegen (the Netherlands). He also is Vice-

President of the European Council for High Ability (ECHA) and Program Director of the European Advanced Diploma in Educating the Gifted. He is a member of the editorial board of the *Journal for Gifted Education* and his publications focus on gifted education, individual promotion, learning difficulties and self-regulated learning.

Christiane Fischer-Ontrup is a Senior Lecturer in the Institute of Educational Science at the University of Münster, Germany. She is Managing Director of the International Centre for the Study of Giftedness (ICBF) from the Universities of Münster, Osnabrück and Nijmegen (the Netherlands). In research, she focuses on gifted children, underachievement, learning difficulties, motivation and individual promotion.

Paul R. Ford is Senior Lecturer at the University of Brighton, UK. His specialist areas are motor control and learning, expert performance, skill acquisition, learning, and talent development. He has published 30 peer-reviewed articles and 10 book chapters. He has been funded to conduct research by various sport organizations. Paul has supervised 10 PhD students. He is Fellow of the British Association of Sport and Exercise Science and holds their High Performance Sport Accreditation.

Jessica Fraser-Thomas is an Associate Professor in the School of Kinesiology and Health Science at York University, Canada. Her research focuses on children and youths' development through sport with specific foci in positive youth development, psychosocial influences (coaches, family, peers), and withdrawal. Currently, she is examining preschoolers' introductions to organized sport, and program characteristics that facilitate development within special populations. Jessica recently co-edited *Health and Elite Sport: Is High Performance Sport a Healthy Pursuit?* She is a recipient of the Canadian Society for Psychomotor Learning and Sport Psychology Young Scientist Award and the Province of Ontario Volunteer Service Award.

Bill Gerrard is a graduate of the University of Aberdeen, Trinity College, Cambridge and the University of York, and is currently Professor of Business and Sports Analytics at Leeds University Business School. Bill has developed the use of data analysis within an evidence-based approach to coaching in a variety of sports including football, rugby league and rugby union. He worked as the technical analyst at Saracens between 2010 and 2015 during which time they won two Premiership titles and contested 14 domestic and European semi-finals and finals. Bill has also provided statistical analysis for the SkySports coverage of Super League. He has worked with various UK and Dutch football clubs, an Australian rugby league team, a South African rugby union team, and Billy Beane and the Oakland A's ownership group. Bill holds the UEFA B football coaching licence.

Michael Godfrey is a second-year Master's Student at Wilfrid Laurier University. Generally speaking, his research interests revolve around role acceptance and cultural diversity in sport groups. His Master's thesis, funded by the Social Sciences and Humanities Research Council and an Ontario Graduate Scholarship, is examining how parents influence the role acceptance process of youth athletes. Following his Master's, Michael intends on pursuing doctoral studies in the area of group dynamics. Michael completed a Bachelor of Human Kinetics degree at the University of Windsor, where he was also a member of the varsity basketball team.

Adam D. Gorman is a Lecturer in the School of Health and Sport Sciences at the University of the Sunshine Coast in Queensland, Australia. Adam has worked in applied and academic settings and has conducted research into pattern perception, expertise, decision-making, representative practice design, and equipment scaling. He is particularly interested in the factors that contribute to the acquisition of skill in both expert and developing performers, as well as exploring how skill practice sessions can be designed to facilitate learning.

Paul S. Glazier is currently the Head of Biomechanics and Performance Analysis at the National Sports Institute of Malaysia and an Adjunct Research Fellow at the Institute of Sport, Exercise and Active Living at Victoria University in Melbourne. He has expertise in sports biomechanics, motor control, skill acquisition, and performance analysis of sport, and has authored or co-authored over 40 peer-reviewed journal articles, invited book chapters, and published conference papers in these areas. His current research interests include: the biomechanics-motor control interface; the application of dynamical systems theory to movement coordination and control; and the functional role of movement variability. Paul has also provided sport science services to a wide range of athletes and teams, from regional juniors to Olympic and World Champions, in a variety of sports.

Urs Granacher is a Professor and Head of the Division of Training and Movement Sciences, with a research focus on Cognition Sciences at The University of Potsdam, Germany. He graduated in Sports Science and received his PhD and habilitation (post-doctoral thesis) in Training and Movement Sciences at the University of Freiburg, Germany. His research and teaching focus on the assessment of neuromuscular capacities (e.g., muscle strength/power, [dual-task] postural control) as well as the development, evaluation and implementation of exercise programs to improve motor performance and promote physical activity in diverse settings (e.g., schools, workplace) and populations (e.g., children, youth athletes, elite athletes). Dr. Granacher is an editorial board member of *Sports Medicine*.

Arne Güllich is a Professor and Head of the Department of Sport Science at the University of Kaiserslautern, Germany. Until 2008 he worked as the Head of the Department of Talent Development at the German Olympic Sports Confederation (DOSB). Arne also coached international track and field athletes. Some of his research interests focus on talent development and evaluation of talent development programmes, as well as support programmes for elite athletes. Arne recently edited the course book for sport science degree courses at German universities (Springer Spektrum, 2013).

Norbert Hagemann is currently Full Professor for Sport Psychology at the University of Kassel, Germany. He received his PhD from the University of Münster for his thesis "Heuristic problem solving strategies of team coaches". Prof. Hagemann is studying the cognitive processes underlying how athletes perform in training and competitive situations.

Meghan Harlow is a PhD student at York University in the School of Kinesiology and Health Science, Canada. Her research interests include children and youths' development through sport, with a specific focus on early entry into sport and physical activity, with a focus on parents' decisions and families' experiences. She is currently examining sport participation and prolonged engagement within a marginalized youth population.

Kristoffer Henriksen is an Associate Professor at Institute of Sport Science and Clinical Biomechanics at the University of Southern Denmark. His research in sport psychology takes a holistic approach and looks at social relations and their influence on athlete development and performance with an emphasis on successful talent development environments. His employment includes a specialized function as a sport psychology practitioner in Team Denmark (national elite sport institution) including support at World Championships and the Olympic Games with a focus on developing high performance cultures in national teams and mentally strong athletes and coaches.

Tamara John graduated cum laude from Cornell University in 2009 with an emphasis on neurobiology and behavior. She was a formed top-ranked national tennis player and played Division I tennis throughout her undergraduate years. She then attended medical school at the University of Rochester and is currently in her orthopaedic surgery residency training at Yale New Haven Hospital. Since her undergraduate years, Dr. John has had a vested interest in pediatric sports related injury and prevention, which has increased exponentially during her residency training at Yale.

Michael Kellmann is Head of Unit of Sport Psychology at the Faculty of Sport Science at Ruhr-University Bochum (Germany). Prior to his current role, he was Senior Lecturer holding a joint appointment with the Schools of Human Movement Studies and Psychology at The University of Queensland (Australia). He served six years on the Executive Board of the German Association of Sport Psychology and is currently on the editorial board of *The Sport Psychologist* and the *Deutsche Zeitschrift für Sportmedizin*. Michael's research activities include overtraining prevention and recovery enhancement, regeneration management, sport psychological diagnostics and intervention.

Gretchen Kerr is a Professor and Vice-Dean, Academic Affairs, in the Faculty of Kinesiology and Physical Education at the University of Toronto. Her research programme focuses on the psychosocial health of young athletes, maltreatment in sport, and the role of coaches in advancing healthy athlete development. She has served as a harassment officer for provincial and national sport organizations for many years.

Camilla J. Knight is a Senior Lecturer in the Applied Sport, Technology, Exercise and Medicine research centre at Swansea University and the Youth Sport research theme lead for the Welsh Institute of Performance Science. Camilla's research is focused upon enhancing and understanding the psychosocial experiences of children in sport, with a particular focus upon the influence of parents. Camilla is particularly interested in understanding the experiences of parents and how parents can be better supported in the youth sport environment. Camilla works closely with the Child Protection in Sport Unit, as well as a number of national sports organisations to examine and enhance parental involvement within youth sport settings.

Carsten Hvid Larsen is a Visiting Researcher at the Institute of Sport Science and Clinical Biomechanics at the University of Southern Denmark and sport psychology practitioner at Team Denmark (national elite sport institution). His research in sport psychology looks at talent development environments, psychosocial skills and applied sport psychology. His employment at Team Denmark includes support at European, World Championships and the Olympic Games with a focus on culture, peak performance and developing resilient athletes and coaches.

David Lavallee is a Professor at the University of Stirling in Scotland. His academic qualifications include a PhD from the University of Western Australia and a Master's degree from Harvard University. His research focuses on contributing to theoretical developments associated with human lifespan development. For the last 15 years, a central focus of his research has been on the transitions experienced by high performance athletes across their careers.

Srdjan Lemez completed his PhD in the Lifespan Health and Performance Laboratory in the School of Kinesiology and Health Science, at York University, Canada. His research program explores how to maximize individuals' experiences in sport, with a particular focus on incidence, predictors and causes of death in high performance athletes. He has also worked with Wheelchair Basketball Canada and the Canadian Sport Institute – Ontario, where his focus has been to optimize practice and performance environments through sport psychology and motor learning and control principles.

Florian Loffing is a Post-Doctoral Fellow at the Institute of Sports and Sports Sciences of the University of Kassel, Germany. He obtained his PhD from the University of Münster, Germany, for a thesis on handedness in tennis. Florian's research interests focus upon laterality and the perceptual-cognitive processes underlying skilled performance in sports.

Todd M. Loughead is a Professor in the area of sport psychology at the University of Windsor in the Faculty of Human Kinetics. His current research interests include group dynamics in sport with a focus on developing athlete leadership skills, the importance of enhancing cohesion in sport, and the influence of peer-to-peer mentoring in sport and its impact on team functioning. He is a certified practitioner with the Canadian Sport Psychology Association and has extensive experience consulting with athletes who compete at the national, intercollegiate, and professional levels. Dr. Loughead teaches courses in group dynamics, leadership, and applied sport psychology.

Áine MacNamara holds a PhD from the University of Central Lancashire where she is currently a Senior Lecturer in elite performance. Her research, framed by a 'pracademic' perspective, is focused on talent development with a particular interest in the role of psychological characteristics as facilitative of development and the design of talent development systems. Her work involves collaborations with national governing bodies of sport in the UK and Ireland as well as research collaborations across a number of institutions. Her work has been published in peer-reviewed journals in sport, music, and education as well as in over 10 book chapters.

Robert M. Malina is Professor Emeritus in the Department of Kinesiology and Health Education, University of Texas at Austin, and Adjunct Professor in the School of Public Health and Information Sciences at the University of Louisville, KY, USA. A primary area of interest is the biological growth and maturation of children and adolescents with a major focus on youth sports in general, on young athletes and the influence of training for sport. He has worked extensively with the growth and maturation of children in several countries and on youth athletes in several sports including swimming, diving, gymnastics, track and field, basketball, volleyball, American football and soccer among others.

Cliff J. Mallett is with the School of Human Movement and Nutrition Sciences at The University of Queensland, Australia. He is a Professor of Sport Psychology and Coaching. Cliff has published extensively in sport psychology and high performance coaching. He was a successful Olympic coach in track and field and a former registered sport psychologist. Cliff consults with national and international sporting organisations and professional sporting teams.

Anthony M. Mayo is a Lecturer in the Department of Kinesiology at San Francisco State University. He received his PhD in Kinesiology from the University of Minnesota in 2015. Tony's research interests are focused on the effectiveness of various instructional technologies in kinesiology pedagogy, on the way in which posture is regulated to pick up information, and on the development of skill in sport.

Alexandra Mosher is a Masters Candidate in the School of Kinesiology and Health Science at York University, Canada. Her areas of interest include the psychological benefits and determinants of sport for youth. Currently, she is examining factors associated with dropout among youth athletes with intellectual disabilities.

Maximilian Pelka is a Research Associate (and PhD student) in the Unit of Sport Psychology at the Faculty of Sport Science at Ruhr-University Bochum (Germany). Since 2015 he has been part of the Managing Council of the *European Network of Young Specialists in Sport Psychology*. Max's research interests include relaxation techniques in sports, psychology in football and youth development in elite sports. In addition to his academic career he is working in the applied field with an elite youth academy in football.

Erich Petushek is an Assistant Professor in the College of Human Medicine at Michigan State University. Dr. Petushek completed his PhD in Applied Cognitive Science and Human Factors at Michigan Technological University as a National Science Foundation Graduate Research Fellow. He completed his postdoctoral training at the University of Huddersfield in The Applied Cognition & Cognitive Engineering Research (AC2E) Group in collaboration with the English Institute of Sport. His research specializations are in applied expertise, psychological measurement, biomechanics, injury prevention, and movement analysis/judgment. He is founder and lead scientist on the computerized injury prediction skill assessment and outreach project: www.ACL-IQ.org.

Cassidy Preston is a PhD candidate at York University in the School of Kinesiology and Health Science, Canada. His research focuses on coaching elite youth athletes through the lens of positive youth development and athlete-centred coaching. Cassidy also coaches in one of the country's premier minor hockey leagues.

Tracy Rea is currently studying a PhD part time at the University of Stirling under the supervision of David Lavallee. She has worked for a number of years in sport including the **sport**scotland Institute of Sport as well as Performance Director of Scottish Gymnastics. After the Commonwealth Games, Tracy decided to test her own PhD hypotheses of transferring her talent to a different professional environment (banking) as Head of Business Operations within IT.

Ian Renshaw is a Senior Lecturer in the School of Exercise & Nutrition Science at Queensland University of Technology, Australia. His research interests include an ecological dynamics approach to understanding perception and action in sport with particular emphasis on developing effective learning environments. To that end, Ian is particularly interested in the development of a nonlinear pedagogy for talent development, teaching and coaching of sport. Current research projects include; affective learning design in nonlinear pedagogy; the implementation of nonlinear pedagogy in schools and junior sport; principled scaling of junior sport and representative learning design in sporting run-ups.

Fieke Rongen is a Senior Lecturer in Sports Coaching in the Carnegie Faculty at Leeds Beckett University, UK. Fieke has a background in clinical and performance psychology. Her PhD explored the impact of football academy involvement on the development of the youth players using a holistic perspective. Her research placed particular emphasis on exploring the range of outcomes associated with talent development programme involvement as well as what constitutes 'healthy' systems from both a performance and personal development perspective.

Steven B. Rynne is a Senior Lecturer and Program Convenor for Sports Coaching with the School of Human Movement and Nutrition Sciences at The University of Queensland, Australia. Steven has worked and conducted research with a variety of peak domestic and inter-national sporting bodies in the areas of high performance coach learning and Indigenous sport. Steven teaches undergraduate and graduate students, is a registered HPE teacher, and coaches track cyclists.

Jörg Schorer is Professor for Sport and Movement Science at the Carl-von-Ossietzky-University in Oldenburg, Germany. He has worked in academia as well as in the applied talent sector. His research focuses on elite sport across the life-span.

Eivind Åsrum Skille is Professor of Sport Sociology at Hedmark Applied University, Elverum, Norway. Eivind's main research interests are sport policy, sport organization and sport participation – in the span from grassroot sport and sport for all, to elite sport. Three recent projects reflecting his interests are sport policy for Sami sport (sport for indigenous people), the focus on and utilization of young people in the organization of Youth Olympic Games, as well as organizational culture in national federations with a focus on national team coaches.

Richard Shuttleworth is the Head of Professional Coach Development for the England Rugby Football Union. He is responsible for assisting professional coaches with skill acquisi-tion, leadership, innovation, support and development. He has over 20 years of experience of coach education in elite level sport with the Australian Institute of Sport as skill acquisition specialist with Olympic level coaches, and various National Organisations, Super Rugby Franchises, National Rugby League, and Australian Rules Clubs. Currently Richard is completing a PhD at Sheffield Hallam University, UK, investigating adaptive behaviour in team sports focusing on the interpersonal coordination dynamics in elite skill level athletes.

Dean Keith Simonton is Distinguished Professor of Psychology at the University of California, Davis. His more than 500 publications—including 13 books—concern genius, creativity, and leadership. He recently edited *The Wiley Handbook of Genius* (2014). His honors include the William James Book Award, the Sir Francis Galton Award for Outstanding Contributions to the Study of Creativity, the Rudolf Arnheim Award for Outstanding Contributions to Psychology and the Arts, the George A. Miller Outstanding Article Award, the Theoretical Innovation Prize in Personality and Social Psychology, the E. Paul Torrance Award for Creativity, and three Mensa Awards for Excellence in Research.

Natalia Stambulova is a Professor in Sport and Exercise Psychology at School of Health and Welfare at Halmstad University, Sweden. Her professional experiences in sport psychology refer to her work for about four decades as a teacher, researcher, and practitioner in the USSR/Russia and since 2001 in Sweden. Her research and about two hundred publications relate mainly to the athlete career/talent development topic with an emphasis on athletes' career transitions and crises. Dr. Stambulova is a member of editorial boards of several international journals and an associate editor of *Psychology of Sport and Exercise.*

Cecilia Stenling is a Senior Lecturer at the Department of Education, Umeå University, Sweden, where she specializes in issues related to the organizing, management and governance of voluntary sport. Her research is concerned with processes of change in the organizing of voluntary sport, sport policy making and implementation in general and more specifically the use of and consequences of using voluntary, non-profit and membership-based sport clubs as vehicles for social change.

Ashley Stirling is currently an Assistant Professor, Teaching Stream in the Faculty of Kinesiology and Physical Education at the University of Toronto. She has conducted several research projects on high performance athletes' experiences of maltreatment in sport and strategies for athlete protection. Ashley is a recipient of the Thesis Award from the Association for the Advancement of Applied Sport Psychology (AASP), and was also previously awarded the Young Investigator Award by the European College of Sport Science (ECSS) for her research on athlete emotional abuse. Ashley recently co-wrote a coach education module on creating positive and healthy sport experiences for the Coaching Association of Canada. She has presented at numerous international conferences and has several publications in the areas of athlete welfare and high performance sport participation.

Kevin Till is a Senior Lecturer and course leader in Sports Coaching at Leeds Beckett University, UK. He completed his PhD on talent identification and development in rugby league and has since published numerous academic articles on talent identification and development within rugby. Recently his research interests have revolved around monitoring, evaluating and enhancing the physical development of youth athletes where he now co-leads the Carnegie Adolescent Rugby Research (CARR) project. Kevin recently edited the book *The Science of Sport: Rugby* and is also currently working as a Strength and Conditioning Coach at Leeds Rhinos RLFC and Yorkshire Carnegie RUFC.

Andy Van Neutegem has been the High Performance Director for the Canadian National Wheelchair Rugby Team for the past 10 years. Andy led the national wheelchair rugby team to a silver medal at the World Championships in August 2014, and led the preparation for Rio 2016. In 2015–2016, he was also the General Manager with Hockey Canada responsible for the National Sledge Hockey Program. Andy also works part-time for Own the Podium, guiding national teams in player development and technical planning strategies. Andy's academic expertise is sport psychology, adapted sport and research methodology. Andy received his Doctorate in Career Transitions and Long-Term Athlete Development (2007) from the University of Southampton, UK.

Paul Ward is Professor of Applied Cognitive Psychology and Director of The Applied Cognition & Cognitive Engineering (AC2E) Research Group, University of Huddersfield. He is internationally known for his pioneering research on expertise and training. He has published over 100 scientific papers including co-authoring a Psychology Press book entitled *Accelerated Expertise* (2013). He is a Chartered Ergonomist and Human Factors Specialist and Fellow of CIEHF, Chartered Psychologist and Chartered Scientist. He currently serves on the *Human Factors* journal editorial board, is a member of the UK ESRC Peer Review College, and sits on a U.S. National Science Foundation grant review panels.

Nick Wattie is an Assistant Professor in the Faculty of Health Sciences at the University of Ontario Institute of Technology. His research examines various factors related to the influence of environmental, individual and task constraints. These areas include talent identification, development and expertise in sport, skill acquisition, youth development and wellbeing, as well as athlete morbidity and mortality.

Juanita R. Weissensteiner, a physiotherapist by background, is the Acting Head of Department of Athlete Pathways and Development at the Australian Institute of Sport. Juanita is an original co-author of the FTEM Athlete Development Framework and a co-contributor to the recent International Olympic Committee's (IOC) Consensus Statement on Youth Athlete. In her current role, Juanita facilitates the pathway review and refinement of a number of National Sporting Organisations, providing guidance and customised applied solutions utilising an evidence-based, holistic approach featuring contemporary best practice. Juanita has liaised with numerous International sporting bodies including the IOC, UK Sport and the Japanese Institute of Sport.

Johan M. Wikman is an Academic Officer at the Center for Team Sports and Health, University of Copenhagen, Denmark. He completed his PhD on sport psychological training and talent development at the University of Copenhagen. His research interests are in the areas of talent development, sport psychological interventions, motivation for sport and exercise, and questionnaire development. In addition to his academic work, he also works with sport psychology in practice, mostly with young elite athletes.

A. Mark Williams is Professor and Head of Life Sciences Department at Brunel University, London. He has published over 150 peer-reviewed articles, 13 books, and more than 80 book chapters in the areas of motor control and learning, behavioural neuroscience, perceptual-cognitive expertise, talent identification and expert performance. He has been funded to conduct research by numerous sport organizations and research councils. Mark has supervised over 40 PhD students across seven different countries. He is Fellow of the British Association of Sport and Exercise Science and European College of Sports Science. He is a Chartered Psychologist with the British Psychological Society.

Lauren Wolman is a PhD candidate at York University in the School of Kinesiology and Health Science, Canada. Her research area is within sport development, particularly around athlete recruitment and retention. Specifically, she has examined the role of community sports clubs in supporting youth to continue participating in organized sports in adulthood. Currently, she is examining sport participation within marginalized urban communities. For over 20 years, Lauren has been actively involved in women and girls rugby, as a coach and administrator in both Canada and the United Kingdom.

1

TALENT IDENTIFICATION AND DEVELOPMENT IN SPORT

An introduction

Joseph Baker, Stephen Cobley, Jörg Schorer and Nick Wattie

One of the most obvious trends in high performance sport over the past few decades has been the increasing systematization of athlete development and talent identification. There is increasing pressure to identify the most "talented" athletes as early as possible so that they can be placed in "optimal environments." Having a comprehensive understanding of the talent identification and selection process, and its implications for positive and negative developmental outcomes, is critical.

The notion of talent, that is, innate, identifiable factors that affect our long-term development, is well rooted in contemporary and historical social discourses. It is at the heart of the nature vs. nurture debate that has pervaded discussions amongst the lay public and scientists since Francis Galton first used the term in 1864. Indeed, the notion of immutable talents lies at the heart of his 'nature over nurture' perspective. In his paper "Hereditary Talent and Character," Galton (1865) notes that success in most professions is related to several qualities inherited from their parents:

> A man must inherit good health, a love of mental work, a strong purpose and considerable ambition, in order to achieve successes of the high order of which we are speaking. The deficiency of any one of these qualities would certainly be injurious, and *probably be fatal to his chance of obtaining great distinction.*
>
> *(Galton, 1865, p. 318 emphasis added)*

This view has prevailed among many groups, but, perhaps most importantly for the current text, it has been a dominant perspective among many coaches, trainers, parents, and athletes.

In 1998, Howe, Davidson and Sloboda reviewed the wealth of existing evidence for *Innate Talent*, concluding that "evidence … does not support the talent account, according to which excelling is a consequence of possessing innate gifts" (p. 407). However, much has changed since their seminal review. Perhaps most significantly, the human genome has been mapped, an achievement that has changed every aspect of science from medicine (e.g., Rimoin, Pyeritz, & Korf, 2013) to philosophy (e.g., Sloan, 2000). Sport has not been immune to these changes; in fact, given the often obsessive drive for information to foster continued training adaptations, sport has been quick (perhaps too quick) to embrace emerging research suggesting "talent-related" factors have been identified.

The world of high performance sport is one where athletes are constantly evaluated for their potential to succeed at the elite, adult level. In simple terms, talent identification refers to the process of identifying and/or selecting individuals who possess a quality (or qualities) that predicts some form of future attainment, such as in the professional sports drafts where teams have athletes go through a "combine" of tests and then use the scores on these tests to help determine who to select in the draft. Conversely, talent development reflects the range of influences on the process of skill acquisition in the high performance sport setting. These influences may include issues such as how much training is appropriate for children or what type of coach support is required at different levels of development. While, by definition, the process of athlete development is ongoing, sports have regular "check points" in their athlete development systems to systematically evaluate and determine who will be allowed to move forward in the system. These check points can be *passive*, such as when sports programs simply stop due to lack of demand, such as in rural communities that have elite programs at the child and youth levels but nothing further (e.g., ice hockey in Canada) or *active*, such as when athletes are explicitly told they are not selected for advancement at a given point in development (e.g., not being selected for the representative team). Both of these types of selection have different consequences on individual development and sport-system development as a whole.

Although the number of stages or steps in an athlete development program will vary based on the sport, in principle, talent identification and development *should* be an easy task (see Figure 1.1): those who reflect the greatest potential (i.e., far right-hand side of the normal distribution) are selected for development and the rest of de-selected from the high performance system. Unfortunately, research over the past three decades has emphasized two things:

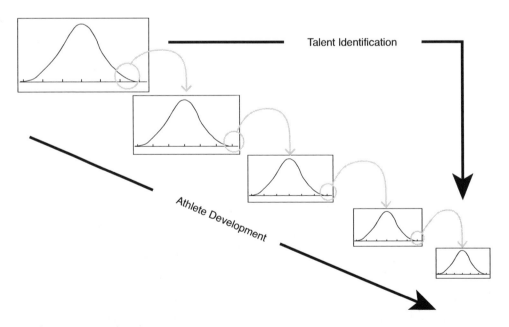

Figure 1.1 The process of talent selection highlighting the distinction between research examining how variables predict future outcomes (Talent Identification) and research on factors facilitating or impeding skill acquisition (Talent Development)

2

first, we know very little about the process of talent identification and what we do know is dominated by studies of physical factors (i.e., very little evaluation of psychological or cognitive elements; see Robinson, Wattie, Schorer, & Baker, 2016) and second, our ability to accurately identify talent seems surprisingly low for the amount of money, time and effort invested (see for example Koz, Fraser-Thomas, & Baker, 2012).

This Handbook emerged out of an increasing demand for evidence to assist practitioners and scientists in understanding the costs and benefits of talent identification initiatives, and the factors influencing the process of athlete development. The aim of this text is to provide a "state of the science" resource for researchers in athlete development, skill acquisition, talent identification and related fields of sport science. Over the past decade, there has been increasing interest in the notion of sporting talent—particularly as it relates to its identification and development. Academic texts such as Baker, Cobley and Schorer's (2012) *Talent Identification and Development in Sport: International Perspectives*, Côté and Lidor's (2013) *Conditions of Children's Talent Development in Sport*, and Aggerholm's (2014) *Talent Development, Existential Philosophy and Sport: On Becoming an Elite Athlete* highlight the emerging importance of this field of sport science and several best-selling popular science books including *Bounce* (Syed, 2010), the *Talent Code* (Coyle, 2009) and *The Sports Gene* (Epstein, 2013) have highlighted the various factors affecting athlete development for a wide readership. However, until now there has not been a comprehensive resource for scientists, practitioners, and students working in this area.

The Routledge Handbook of Talent Identification and Development in Sport

In the Handbook that follows, leading researchers from around the globe summarize their programs of research on talent identification and development. Part I focuses on issues related to *Talent Identification,* ranging from discussions of various theoretical approaches to the validity of talent identification approaches. In this section:

- Dean Keith Simonton (Chapter 2) and Paul Ward, Patrick Belling, Erich Petushek, and Joyce Ehrlinger (Chapter 3) examine the historical roots and evidence concerning "talent," in sport, and the problematic legacy of the nature–nurture debate. Both Simonton and Ward et al. offer distinct but convincing arguments toward the importance of interactive explanations for sporting talent. In doing so, Simonton presents an integrative recursive model to explain talent emergence more comprehensively. Meanwhile, declaring the "nature–nurture debate" as dead, Ward et al. highlights how the development of a combination of domain (task) specific skills, grounded upon "zeal-full practice" and domain-general abilities may be the most predictive factors accounting for accelerated psychomotor and athletic talent development.
- In Chapter 4, Christiane Fischer-Ontrup and Christian Fischer consider the range of definitions for giftedness and talent. This is followed by a discussion of different theoretical models of giftedness and talent development.
- In Chapter 5, Juanita R. Weissensteiner explains how contemporary international research studies have informed the development of Australia's national athletic talent development framework: the Foundational, Talent, Elite and Mastery [FTEM]) framework. The FTEM is now being implemented across sport governing bodies as "best-practice," aiming to coordinate strategies between and within sports systems to better facilitate athlete identification, development and transition.
- Chapter 6 by Nick Wattie and Joseph Baker explores the implications of holding firm nature *or* nurture beliefs about the "origin of talent." They argue that such dichotomized

conceptions are misguided, with potentially important implications for athlete motivation and skill development, and the efficacy of talent identification and development programmes.

- In Chapter 7, Arne Güllich and Stephen Cobley evaluate the efficacy of talent identification and development programmes. Following a review of existing international research, they conclude that there is a low overall efficacy of early identification and development programmed in terms of relating to long-term senior success. They go on to highlight the challenges and implications ahead if such programs are to be improved.
- In the final chapter of the opening section, and with more practitioner emphasis, Dirk Büsch and Urs Granacher consider how talent identification practices are often predicated on subjective, experience-based decisions, rather than by objective statistical assessment. Using an assessment measure from German Handball, they highlight how particular statistical methods could be used, without extra burden, to more accurately and reliably inform identification in various sport contexts.

After the foundational discussions in Part I, Part II focuses on *Talent Development*. This section contains 10 chapters reviewing a range of factors and issues related to the development of high performance athletes. The topics in this section are diverse, reflecting the considerable range of influences on athlete development.

- Chapter 9 by Paul Ford and Mark Williams examines the evidence for an increasingly important issue in athlete development—whether future high performance athletes should specialize in their sport at an early age or whether they should "diversify" their sporting involvement across several different sports.
- In Chapter 10, Juanita R. Weissensteiner gives insight into varying models of talent development. She provides a deeper insight into more sport-specific models of talent development in comparison to Chapter 4. She provides an example from Australia differentiating between foundation, talent, elite, and mastery levels of skill.
- Chapter 11, by Robert Malina, Sean Cumming, Manuel Coelho-e-Silva and Antonio Figueiredo, describes the role of growth, maturation and behavioral development in talent identification and development, as well as the strengths and limitations of contemporary models of talent development with respect to how well they integrate current evidence on growth and maturation.
- The potential and actual role of sport psychology for talent development is described by Anne-Marie Elbe and Johan M. Wikman in Chapter 12. In the first section of their chapter they consider constructs such as motivation and self-regulation while the second section gives insight into how the developmental environment can influence these outcomes.
- In Chapter 13 Camilla J. Knight discusses the role of the family in high performance athlete development. Importantly, she also considers the potential negative consequences of being the family of an elite athlete. This comprehensive chapter highlights the influence of family dynamics across the development process.
- The role of the environment is further considered in Chapter 14, but from a dynamical systems approach. In this chapter, Keith Davids, Arne Güllich, Richard Shuttleworth and Duarte Araújo focus on the macro- and micro-structures of training and development.
- The "next piece of the puzzle" is provided by Florian Loffing, Norbert Hagemann and Damian Farrow in Chapter 15. On the basis of research from the field of perceptual-cognitive expertise, they consider the potential of perceptual learning for the development of athletes.

- In Chapter 16, David I. Andersen and Anthony M. Mayo explore the notion of windows of optimal development for young athletes. They also examine the concept of readiness and discuss its implications for talent development.
- In Chapter 17, Paul S. Glazier argues that talent research has largely neglected the area of biomechanics and movement science. He presents evidence that the failure to incorporate biomechanics may be to the detriment of talent identification and development programmes, with implications for skill development as well as the health and wellbeing of athletes.
- In the final chapter of the section (i.e., Chapter 18), Stephen Cobley and Kevin Till highlight the importance of longitudinal multivariate research to our understanding of athlete development. They synthesize existing longitudinal and multivariate evidence across areas of athlete development (i.e., physical, psychological, technical and tactical), and go on to identify future directions for researchers and practitioners.

Part III focuses on *Creating Optimal Environments*. This section reviews the incredibly diverse assortment of factors influencing the identification of talented athletes and optimal acquisition of sport skill.

- In the first chapter of Part III (Chapter 19), Kristoffer Henriksen and Natalia Stambulova describe the importance of the broad developmental environment (sport and non-sport) for understanding the characteristics of successful and unsuccessful athlete talent development environments and subsequently for applied holistic approaches to athlete development.
- Chapter 20 by Steven B. Rynne, Bob Crudgington, Rebecca K. Dickinson and Cliff J. Mallett describes the multidimensional potential of the coach to positively shape the athlete development environment. They describe coach–athlete relationships in contexts spanning from young children to high performance athletes.
- Chapter 21 by Mark Eys, Todd M. Loughead and Michael Godfrey highlights the importance of group cohesion for individual athlete development outcomes and processes, while acknowledging that both positive and negative outcomes can emerge from group cohesion.
- Using contemporary motor learning principles from nonlinear pedagogy, Adam D. Gorman and Ian Renshaw present evidence (in Chapter 22) that structuring the learning environment and manipulating a range of constraints can optimize skill acquisition in developing athletes.
- In Chapter 23, Carsten Larsen and Dorothee Alfermann discuss dropout from sport. They consider how factors such as coach, parent and environmental characteristics influence the likelihood of dropout before providing suggestions on how to avoid dropout.
- With Chapter 24, Dave Collins and Áine MacNamara expand on their research highlighting the "rocky road" to high performance. This work suggests important distinctions in how coaches deliver challenging training stimuli to promote the development of concepts like resilience.

Part IV considers the possible health and developmental consequences associated with talent identification and high performance athlete development programs.

- In the first chapter in this section (Chapter 25), Maximilian Pelka and Michael Kellmann discuss their research on the concepts of underrecovery, overtraining, and burnout and why understanding differences between these concepts is critical for those working with developing athletes.

- Tamara John and Cordelia W. Carter provide physicians' perspectives on medical issues related to talent development in sport in Chapter 26. Their chapter highlights several critical areas of concern for preventing and treating a range of common acute and chronic athletic injuries.
- Chapter 27 by Jessica Fraser-Thomas, Theresa Beesley, Lauren Dickler, Meghan Harlow, Alexandra Mosher, Cassidy Preston, and Lauren Wolman explores the interaction between elite athlete development and positive youth development through sport, exploring whether these outcomes can co-exist in a high performance athlete development system.
- Srdjan Lemez and Fieke Rongen, in Chapter 28, review the immediate and long-term physical and psychosocial health consequences of high performance sport training. This chapter discusses the health risks associated with involvement in high performance sport and the implications of this research for athlete development.
- In Chapter 29, Gretchen Kerr and Ashley Stirling summarize their research program on athlete maltreatment in sport, with particular attention to how the concept of "mental toughness" might perpetuate maltreatment and its subsequent negative effects on athlete development.

The final section highlights a range of "emerging issues" in this field, providing a perspective on the breadth of research to come in the future. Many of these issues will shape the future of research and practice in athlete selection and development.

- In Chapter 30, Bill Gerrard considers the emerging field of sport analytics for the practice of talent identification and athlete development, and also highlights practical considerations and misconceptions about analytics in sport as it is applied alongside other talent identification and development processes.
- Chapter 31 by Joseph Baker, Srdjan Lemez, Andy Van Neutegem and Nick Wattie examines issues of athlete identification and development in parasport contexts, highlighting the often unique constraints involved when working with athletes with a disability.
- The emerging issue of talent transfer is the focus of Chapter 32 by Tracy Rea and David Lavallee. This chapter presents emerging findings from their research program and notes several areas for further work.
- Many decisions regarding athlete development are made outside of the training environment and in this text's penultimate chapter (Chapter 33), Eivind Åsrum Skille, Cecilia Stenling and Josef Fahlén discuss how a nation's sport policy relates to issues of talent identification and athlete development.

In the final chapter of this Handbook (Chapter 34), we have tried to integrate the range of important issues and limitations highlighted in previous chapters into a road map for future work in talent identification and development in sport.

Our intention with this text was to provide a "state of the science" resource for applied sport scientists, coaches, athletes and other stakeholders; and through the excellent contributors of the chapter authors, we have achieved this goal. The contributors to this volume are among the top scientists working in the fields of talent identification, athlete development and sport training, and without exception the chapters that follow are outstanding. Collectively, this text provides a comprehensive synthesis of a complex field; moreover, it highlights areas where there is good evidence to assist stakeholders in making decisions and illustrates the range of research opportunities available for the next generation of researchers.

References

Aggerholm, K. (2014). *Talent development, existential philosophy and sport: On becoming an elite athlete.* London: Routledge.

Baker, J., Cobley, S., & Schorer, J. (2012). *Talent identification and development in sport: International perspectives.* London: Routledge.

Côté, J., & Lidor, R. (2013). *Conditions of children's talent development in sport.* Morgantown, WV: Fitness Information Technology.

Coyle, D. (2009). *The talent code.* Toronto: Random House.

Epstein, D. (2013). *The sports gene: Inside the science of extraordinary athletic performance.* London: Penguin.

Galton, F. (1865). Hereditary talent and character. *Macmillans Magazine, 12,* 157–166, 318–327.

Howe, M. J. A., Davidson J. W., & Sloboda, J. A. (1998). Innate talents: Reality or myth. *Behavioural and Brain Sciences, 21,* 399–442.

Koz, D., Fraser-Thomas, J., & Baker, J. (2012). Accuracy of professional sports drafts in predicting career potential. *Scandinavian Journal of Medicine and Science in Sports, 22,* e64–e69.

Rimoin, D. L., Pyeritz, R. E., & Korf, B. (2013). *Emery and Rimoin's principles and practice of medical genetics.* Amsterdam: Elsevier.

Robinson, K., Wattie, N., Schorer, J., & Baker, J. (2016). *What predicts talent selection in sport? A systematic review of 25 years of research.* Manuscript under review.

Sloan, P. R. (2000). *Controlling our destinies: Historical, philosophical, ethical, and theological perspectives on the Human Genome Project.* Notre Dame, IN: University of Notre Dame Press.

Syed, M. (2010). *Bounce: Mozart, Federer, Picasso, Beckham, and the science of success.* New York: Harper-Collins.

PART I

Talent identification

2

DOES TALENT EXIST?

Yes!

Dean Keith Simonton

The scientific study of talent is frequently said to begin with Francis Galton's 1869 *Hereditary Genius: An Inquiry into Its Laws and Consequences* (Simonton, 2003). Yet it might be more accurate to say that the explicit study of talent began with an article that he published four years earlier (Galton, 1865). The latter explicitly used the expression "hereditary talent" in place of "hereditary genius." Nonetheless, at this time Galton used talent and genius more or less interchangeably. In addition, the 1865 article can be considered a pilot study for the book-length treatment published in 1869. The latter not only could devote more space to elaborating his theoretical ideas, but also could contain more extensive space to an empirical documentation of those ideas. More specifically, Galton dedicated himself to proving that genius or talent was a very real phenomenon: Eminent achievement in a diversity of domains could be attributed to inherited abilities. This conclusion was demonstrated for achievement domains as varied as politics, religion, law, war, science, literature, painting, music, and sports. In each case, Galton used the family pedigree method—which he was the first to apply in scientific research—to establish that eminent achievers were related to other eminent achievers at incidence rates that far exceeded the population baselines. Genius (or talent) was born, not made.

Galton's own contemporaries raised objections at once. For example, Alphonse de Candolle (1873), who actually came from a distinguished family pedigree, which was explicitly noted in Galton's (1869) work—Candolle was an eminent botanist just like his father—presented his own data implying the critical importance of environmental factors. Galton then retreated somewhat from his extreme biological determinism by conducting a survey of scientists sufficiently eminent to earn election as Fellow of the Royal Society of London, yielding results reported in his 1874 *English Men of Science: Their Nature and Nurture*. As the subtitle implies, Galton introduced some environmental influences that nurture the development of scientific talent. He became thereby the very first researcher to introduce the nature–nurture issue to modern science. Even so, Galton continued to research the genetic basis of achievement, introducing twin studies and parent–child statistical correlations that have become an integral part of behavior genetics (Galton, 1883, 1889). Ultimately, he never relinquished the belief that nature was far more important than nurture—as evinced in his founding of the eugenics movement!

Of course, our understanding of the behavior genetics behind talent has substantially grown since Galton's day. These recent developments have reinforced the case for talent as a very genuine phenomenon (Simonton, 1999, 2001). Talent probably permeates every form of exceptional achievement. That said, current conceptions of talent must necessarily recognize that talent operates in conjunction with environmental factors. Indeed, it will soon become apparent that talent cannot be adequately defined in the absence of those non-genetic influences. As a consequence, I must begin with a discussion of the environmental factors before dealing with how they might work with genetic factors. After dealing with nurture, nature, and the nurture–nature integration, I will then briefly discuss some additional complications in the operation of talent. Although my treatment of these subjects will not be restricted to any particular achievement domain, the sport context will be used to illustrate some main points.

Nurture: Environmental factors

When Candolle (1873) first attacked Galton's (1869) genetic position, the focus was on socio-cultural, political, religious, and economic factors that operated at the national level. Galton's (1874) response, in contrast, scrutinized factors that worked at the individual level, such as family background and education. For example, Galton was the very first to examine the role of birth order in the emergence of eminent achievers. Ordinal position in the family has a special place among environmental factors because it is among the very few that can be claimed totally free of any covert genetic factors (cf. Scarr & McCartney, 1983). In contrast, environmental factors such as socioeconomic class can easily conflate genetic and environmental components (Simonton, 1987). Birth order also leaves an impression on almost every achievement domain. In the case of sports, for instance, later borns are not only likely to participate in physically dangerous sports (Nisbet, 1968), but even in relatively safe sports the later borns tend to be greater risk takers, such as stealing bases in baseball (Sulloway & Zweigenhaft, 2010). Such propensities must then have experiential sources.

Family background factors like ordinal position are generic rather than domain specific. Everybody is born with a birth order. Even so, many of the most variables associated with nurture effects are more specialized with respect to the domain of achievement in which a person attains eminence. A well-researched example are role models and mentors (e.g., Bloom, 1985; Simonton, 1984, 1992a, 1992b; Walberg, Rasher, & Parkerson, 1980). In sports, these would include trainers, coaches, and even highly admired predecessors who set the world records for everyone in the same event to equal and surpass. Closely related to this factor is another that has received considerable attention in recent years, namely, deliberate practice (Ericsson, Krampe, & Tesch-Römer, 1993). Ensuing from early research on the acquisition of expertise in chess and musical performance, this factor was soon extended to all areas that presume domain-specific expertise, such as creativity and sports (Baker & Young, 2014; Ericsson, 2014). To be sure, what it specifically means to engage in deliberate practice depends on the particular domain of achievement, and even in a given domain there often are more than one skill to be practiced. A golfer who only practices on the driving range will not advance very far in professional tours.

Although no contemporary researcher seriously doubts that deliberate practice is essential to acquire the expertise needed for world-class performance in almost any achievement domain, advocates for deliberate practice have often pushed an extreme nurture position (Simonton, 2014; Tucker & Collins, 2012). Deliberate practice is not only necessary but also sufficient. This total rejection of any involvement of nature makes Galton look like he was a moderate advocate of that alternative position. In rejecting the impact of genetic factors, extreme proponents of deliberate practice not only go well beyond their own data, but also are obliged to ignore the well-established findings of behavior genetics.

Nature: Genetic factors

Modern behavior genetics has demonstrated beyond any reasonable doubt that the vast majority of variables on which people can vary feature impressive hereditability coefficients
(Bouchard, 2004; Plomin, DeFries, Knopik, & Neiderhiser, 2016). Those notable heritabilities
hold for physical and cognitive abilities as well as personality traits, interests, and values.
Although the expected magnitude of these heritabilities varies substantially, the size is almost
always large enough to exert an impact on human behavior, thought, and emotion that just
cannot be ignored. Furthermore, the variables that exhibit substantial heritabilities are also associated with exceptional achievement in a multitude of domains, including sports. As an
example, more than half of the population variance in general intelligence can be attributed to
genetic contributions (Bouchard, 2004). Yet general intelligence is ubiquitous as a factor
predicting learning and effectiveness in a wide range of activities (Gottfredson, 1997). Hence,
insofar as general intelligence facilitates the acquisition of expertise or performance given the
expertise acquired, then genetic factors must provide one basis for talent in a given domain.

Now opponents of the involvement of innate talent can object that general intelligence
cannot be considered a domain-specific ability. And that is true. But that criticism misses the
point. Nobody argues today that talent consists of a single gene or set of genes devoted to one
talent and no other. Instead, talent is defined as a portfolio of diverse individual-difference variables that possess non-trivial heritabilities (Simonton, 2007, 2008). Moreover, these variables
will repeatedly show up in numerous talent domains, not just in one. What separates one talent
from another is often the relative weights assigned to various abilities or traits. Thus, general
intelligence likely has more utility in science than it does in most sports. In contrast, a physical
factor like height, which has a high heritability as well, will display far more usefulness in many
sports than in any science. A highly talented person in a given domain will enjoy the optimal
configuration of these genetically influenced traits and abilities.

Because any given talent is defined by a large number of differentially weighted genetically
influenced abilities and traits, the collective impact of the entire set of individual-difference
variables can be quite substantial even if the effect of any single variable is relatively small. To
illustrate, meta-analyses have estimated that genetic endowment may underlie as much as 20
percent of the variance in scientific creativity (Simonton, 2008) and account for about 17
percent of the variance in emergent leadership (Ilies, Gerhardt, & Le, 2004; cf. Simonton, 2007).
If similar figures hold for most sports, then genetic contributions could certainly give highly
endowed athletes a competitive edge. After all, the difference between a gold and silver medal
may be represented by a tiny fraction of second or a mere centimeter. At the same time, it
should be apparent that these estimates suggest that genetic factors most likely explain less than
half of the variance in any achievement criterion. Assuming that much of the remaining variance is accounted by various environmental factors, we then must ask how the two might work
together to produce the end result—a high achiever in a given domain.

Nature–nurture: A formal model

I recently proposed a simple recursive model that incorporates both nature and nurture in a
single causal network (Simonton, 2014). Although the model was originally designed to explain
individual differences in creative performance in the arts and sciences, the model can certainly
be modified to apply to athletic performance. One tentative modification is shown in Figure 2.1.

The model begins with two sets of exogenous variables, namely, genetic factors (GF) and
environmental factors (EF). To simplify discussion, these two sets of factors are assumed to be

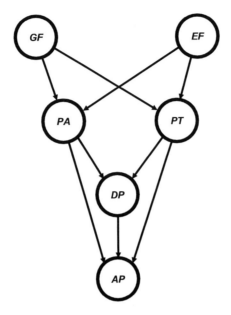

Figure 2.1 Hypothesized recursive model specifying individual differences in athletic performance (*AP*) as a direct function of corresponding individual differences in deliberate practice (*DP*), physical abilities (*PA*), and psychological traits (*PT*), and as an indirect function of genetic factors (*GF*, i.e., "nature") and environmental factors (*EF*, i.e., "nurture"), with *DP*, *PA*, and *PT* providing the mediating variables. Here *GF*, *EF*, *PA*, *PT*, *DP*, and *AP* each indicate entire *sets* of variables rather than single variables, where *PA* and *PT* contain phenotypic variables and *GF* genotypic variables. Accordingly, the arrows linking the sets imply multiple potential direct effects from variables in one set to variables in the other set. The variables themselves in each set may be either observed or latent (as holds for set *GF*). Figure reworked from Simonton (2014) to apply to sports rather than to creativity.

uncorrelated (cf. Scarr & McCartney, 1983; Plomin et al., 2016). An example would be birth order, an environmental factor that could not correlate with any genetic variable. These two sets of factors—nature and nurture—are presumed to underlie two sets of variables further downstream in the causal model: physical abilities (PA) and psychological traits (PT). The former includes all basic physical abilities associated with a given sport (height, strength, endurance, eye–hand coordination, etc.) and the latter includes all psychological traits similarly associated (general intelligence and personality, broadly including risk-taking, interests, values, etc.). In any case, both PA and PT are assumed to be a function of both GF and EF so that both nature and nurture positions are explicitly incorporated.

The next set of variables in the model concern deliberate practice (DP). These concern all knowledge, capacities, and skills that must be mastered in a given sport, including those both psychological and physical (cf. Hodges, Starkes, & MacMahon, 2006; Starkes, Deakin, Allard, Hodges, & Hayes, 1996). The former might include determination and the latter basic endurance (e.g., VO$_2$ max). According to the model, these DP variables are influenced by the variables in sets PA (physical abilities) and PT (psychological traits). Naturally, to keep the model recursive, we must assume that the PA and PT variables are all assessed prior to the onset of deliberate practice, an assumption that I will return to later.

The final set of variables concern various athletic performance criteria relevant for the sport or the athlete's position within a team sport (AP). Thus, a basketball player must be able to shoot both field goals and free throws, pass, rebound, block, guard, steal, dribble, and the like, the relative importance depending on whether the player is a center, forward, or guard (and even these have subcategories, such a shooting versus point guards).

Because GF, EF, PA, PT, DP, and AP all define whole sets of variables rather than single variables, each causal arrow going from one to another actually represent entire sets of causal effects rather than single effects. For instance, the arrow from DP to AP encompasses all ways that certain forms of deliberate practice affect the corresponding performance criteria—such as the degree to which practicing free throws improves actual free throw performance during competitive games. This means that Figure 2.1 implies many more causal effects than the nine depicted arrows might superficially suggest.

So where is talent located in the figure? Clearly, talent is not to be found in any one place, or in any single arrow. Instead, talent is defined by any sequence of variables of the following four kinds: (a) GF → PA → AP, (b) GF → PT → AP, (c) GF → PA → DP → AP, and (d) GF → PT→ DP → AP. In other words, talent consists of all genetic influences that indirectly affect athletic performance, whether mediated by just physical abilities or psychological traits or also mediated by deliberate practice. To disprove the involvement of talent then requires that investigators establish that not a single indirect causal path fits into any of these four categories. Yet if so much as a single path can be so described, then genetic factors must influence athletic performance. The effect may be small, yet it may be big enough to help decide whether an athlete gets a gold or silver medal.

Let us assume that some one- and two-mediator causal chains have been identified. Then these can often be allotted to one of the following two types (cf. Simonton, 2014):

1   *Genetic better-faster effects* entail those two causal sequences—namely (c) and (d)—that involve deliberate practice as a mediating variable after the preceding mediators, physical abilities and psychological traits. These two chains describe instances where deliberate practice is indirectly enhanced by genetic factors, the enhancement frequently taking the form of accelerated expertise acquisition. The talented youth either acquires a given amount of expertise in less time or masters more expertise in the same amount of time. Often when we think of a talented athlete, this is what we mean. In contrast, an untalented youth may not only take longer to show improvement but might even attain some skill ceiling beyond which the would-be athlete may no longer be able to attain competitive levels (Tucker & Collins, 2012). Many amateur athletes have experienced the latter obstacle first-hand. It's why they may have dropped out of the competition.

2   *Genetic more-bang-for-the-buck effects* involve those causal chains—to wit (a) and (b)—that bypass deliberate practice altogether, the effects of physical abilities and psychological traits going directly to athletic performance. This describes the case where one athlete seems to have mastered the same expertise as another athlete, as judged during practice, but manages to exhibit superior performance during competition. Indeed, an athlete might display superior expertise but inferior performance when going from practicing to competing (e.g., the "ball-striker" Moe Norman, who got *less* bang for the buck as a golfer; Starkes et al., 1996). Such indirect causal sequences from GF to PF might help explain why a recent meta-analysis not only found that deliberate practice explained just 18 percent of the variance in athletic performance, but also discovered that the amount of variance accounted for actually shrunk to 1 percent for elite athletes (Macnamara, Moreau, & Hambrick, 2014). Talent may prove more crucial at the highest levels of talent!

One critical feature of the recursive model must be emphasized: Talent is explicitly defined in terms of deliberate practice (Simonton, 2008, 2014). Neither the better-faster effect nor the more-bang-for-the-buck effect has any meaning without the incorporation of deliberate practice into the model. After all, the first effect concerns the indirect effect of genetic factors on deliberate practice, whereas the second effect regards the indirect effect of genetic factors on athletic performance over and above (or "controlling for") the direct effect of deliberate practice. Remove deliberate practice from the model, and both effects cease to have any meaning. Consequently, the formulation of the model outright dismisses the spurious antagonism between nature and nurture.

Discussion

I would be the first to admit that the model of athletic talent sketched in Figure 2.1 is very oversimplified. One problem was already hinted at earlier: It is not always easy to separate genetic and environmental factors. Particularly critical is that many supposedly environmental variables may actually have a partial genetic basis (Plomin et al., 2016). According to Scarr and McCartney (1983), these genetic → environment causal relations can adopt three forms: (a) *passive*, where genetically related parents shape the family environment (e.g., athletic parents who continue to exhibit interests in sports in front of children who are similarly disposed); (b) *evocative*, where the youth's genetically influenced characteristics elicit corresponding responses from others (e.g., tall kids getting chosen for pick-up basketball on the school playground); and (c) *active*, where the youth's genetically shaped interests drive them to shape his or her environment (e.g., a child asking for sports gear on her birthday when the parents were planning on giving her a chemistry set). The last influences help explain why foster children are so much more similar to the biological parents than to their foster parents.

Another oversimplification in the model shown in Figure 2.1 is that it only allows for genetic factors to function in a straightforward additive and static manner (Simonton, 1999). Yet it is far more likely that most complex talents will operate according to multiplicative and dynamic principles (Simonton, 2001). Multiplicative inheritance is associated with *emergenesis*, a form of inheritance which requires that an entire configuration of traits be passed down (Lykken, McGue, Tellegen, & Bouchard, 1992). If any single trait is missing, then the net effect is undermined— such as an exceptionally short would-be basketball player. Dynamic inheritance is associated with *epigenetic growth* (albeit this must not be confused with epigenesis in genetics). Epigenetic growth means that a particular trait does not appear all at once but rather takes many years to unfold. It is for this reason that the heritabilities for some genetic traits will actually increase with age (Bouchard, 2004; Plomin et al., 2016). The important point is that talent becomes more empirically elusive to the extent that it depends on emergenic inheritance and epigenetic growth.

One last oversimplification concerns the recursive nature of the model. More specifically, the model assumes that the crucial variables in the six sets of variables can all be arrayed as causal chains. No two-way causal relations or feedback loops are allowed (cf. Ullén, Hambrick, & Mosing, 2016). Even so, it is highly likely that the true model is non-recursive, at least for most sports. Certainly the relation between deliberate practice and athletic performance would often involve two-way causality. If performance falls short of expectation for a given competition, then any motivated athlete would practice in the areas of weakness before the next competition. Other probable two-way causal relations would exist between deliberate practice and both physical abilities and psychological traits. For example, as athletes gain more confidence before an event, they may practice harder, but as practice increases so may confidence—yielding a positive feedback loop.

Given the current state of our knowledge (as well as my own), I cannot conjecture about all of the possibilities, so may it suffice to say that the model in Figure 2.1 understates the complex ways that genetic factors can yield talent. That means that any empirical tests of that model should be followed by more research on more complex models that implement some of the niceties mentioned earlier. Only after all of the potential conceptions of talent are scrutinized can we even have an informed discussion on whether or not talent exists. Until then, we must acknowledge that a strong prima facie case has been made that talent exists—yes indeed!

References

Baker, J., & Young, B. (2014). 20 years later: Deliberate practice and the development of expertise in sport. *International Review of Sport and Exercise Psychology, 7*, 135–157.

Bloom, B. S. (ed.). (1985). *Developing talent in young people.* New York: Ballantine Books.

Bouchard, T. J., Jr. (2004). Genetic influence on human psychological traits: A survey. *Current Directions in Psychological Science, 13*, 148–151.

Candolle, A. de (1873). *Histoire des sciences et des savants depuis deux siècles.* Geneve: Georg.

Ericsson, K. A. (2014). Creative genius: A view from the expert-performance approach. In D. K. Simonton (ed.), *The Wiley handbook of genius* (pp. 321–349). Oxford, UK: Wiley.

Ericsson, K. A., Krampe, R. T., & Tesch-Römer, C. (1993). The role of deliberate practice in the acquisition of expert performance. *Psychological Review, 100*, 363–406.

Galton, F. (1865). Hereditary talent and character. *Macmillan's Magazine, 12*, 157–166, 318–327.

Galton, F. (1869). *Hereditary genius: An inquiry into its laws and consequences.* London: Macmillan.

Galton, F. (1874). *English men of science: Their nature and nurture.* London: Macmillan.

Galton, F. (1883). *Inquiries into human faculty and its development.* London: Macmillan.

Galton, F. (1889). *Natural inheritance.* London: Macmillan.

Gottfredson, L. S. (1997). Why *g* matters: The complexity of everyday life. *Intelligence, 24*, 79–132.

Hodges, N. J., Starkes, J. L., & MacMahon, C. (2006). Expert performance in sport: A cognitive perspective. In K. A. Ericsson, N. Charness, P. J. Feltovich, & R. R. Hoffman (eds), *The Cambridge handbook of expertise and expert performance* (pp. 471–488). New York: Cambridge University Press.

Ilies, R., Gerhardt, M. W., & Le, H. (2004). Individual differences in leadership emergence: Integrating meta-analytic findings and behavioral genetics estimates. *International Journal of Selection and Assessment, 12*, 207–219.

Lykken, D. T., McGue, M., Tellegen, A., & Bouchard, T. J., Jr. (1992). Emergenesis: Genetic traits that may not run in families. *American Psychologist, 47*, 1565–1577.

Macnamara, B. N., Moreau, D., & Hambrick, D. Z. (2014). The relationship between deliberate practice and performance in sports: A meta-analysis. *Perspectives on Psychological Science, 25*, 1608–1618.

Nisbett, R. E. (1968). Birth order and participation in dangerous sports. *Journal of Personality and Social Psychology, 8*, 351–353.

Plomin, R., DeFries, J. C., Knopik, V. S., & Neiderhiser, J. M. (2016). Top 10 replicated findings from behavioral genetics. *Perspectives on Psychological Science, 2016, 11*, 3–23.

Scarr, S., & McCartney, K. (1983). How people make their own environments: A theory of genotype ® environmental effects. *Child Development, 54*, 424–435.

Simonton, D. K. (1984). Artistic creativity and interpersonal relationships across and within generations. *Journal of Personality and Social Psychology, 46*, 1273–1286.

Simonton, D. K. (1987). Developmental antecedents of achieved eminence. *Annals of Child Development, 5*, 131–169.

Simonton, D. K. (1992a). Leaders of American psychology, 1879–1967: Career development, creative output, and professional achievement. *Journal of Personality and Social Psychology, 62*, 5–17.

Simonton, D. K. (1992b). The social context of career success and course for 2,026 scientists and inventors. *Personality and Social Psychology Bulletin, 18*, 452–463.

Simonton, D. K. (1999). Talent and its development: An emergenic and epigenetic model. *Psychological Review, 106*, 435–457.

Simonton, D. K. (2001). Talent development as a multidimensional, multiplicative, and dynamic process. *Current Directions in Psychological Science, 10*, 39–43.

Simonton, D. K. (2003). Francis Galton's *Hereditary Genius*: Its place in the history and psychology of science. In R. J. Sternberg (ed.), *The anatomy of impact: What has made the great works of psychology great* (pp. 3–18). Washington, DC: American Psychological Association.

Simonton, D. K. (2007). Talent and expertise: The empirical evidence for genetic endowment. *High Ability Studies, 18*, 83–84.

Simonton, D. K. (2008). Scientific talent, training, and performance: Intellect, personality, and genetic endowment. *Review of General Psychology, 12*, 28–46.

Simonton, D. K. (2014). Creative performance, expertise acquisition, individual-differences, and developmental antecedents: An integrative research agenda. *Intelligence, 45*, 66–73.

Starkes, J. L., Deakin, J. M., Allard, F., Hodges, N. J., & Hayes, A. (1996). Deliberate practice in sports: What is it anyway? In K. A. Ericsson (ed.), *The road to expert performance: Empirical evidence from the arts and sciences, sports, and games* (pp. 81–106). Mahwah, NJ: Erlbaum.

Sulloway, F. J., & Zweigenhaft, R. L. (2010). Birth order and risk taking in athletics: A meta-analysis and study of major league baseball players. *Personality and Social Psychology Review, 14*, 402–416.

Tucker, R., & Collins, R. (2012). What makes champions? A review of the relative contribution of genes and training to sporting success. *British Journal of Sports Medicine, 46*, 555–561.

Ullén, F., Hambrick, D. Z., & Mosing, M. A. (2016). Rethinking expertise: A multifactorial gene–environment interaction model of expert performance. *Psychological Bulletin, 142*, 427–446.

Walberg, H. J., Rasher, S. P., & Parkerson, J. (1980). Childhood and eminence. *Journal of Creative Behavior, 13*, 225–231.

3

DOES TALENT EXIST?

A re-evaluation of the nature–nurture debate

Paul Ward, Patrick Belling, Erich Petushek, and Joyce Ehrlinger

Introduction and chapter overview

Throughout history, knowledge and science have often progressed through dialectical debate. Logical arguments from one perspective are posed to counter those from another in the hopes of arriving at a holistic synthesis (e.g., see Sternberg, 1999). The nature–nurture debate has been one of the most enduring, frequently resurrected by the media and scientists alike in an attempt to provide explanation for the fantastic feats of those we call 'talented'. While a central feature of debate is to discuss the pros and cons of opposing views and polarizing stances, relatively few research efforts have sought genuine reconciliation between the extreme positions of nature and nurture (cf. Davids & Baker, 2007). With some exceptions, the modus operandi has been to advocate for one side of the debate while giving little credit to the merits of opposing arguments beyond token gestures.

Debates on the science of talent are almost always theoretically and philosophically entrenched. We argue that perspectives are sometimes taken on one side of the debate to facilitate falsification in a systematic way but, more often, manufactured dichotomies lead to weak tests of a preferred theory, or are used as a guise to promote a preferred perspective incapable of providing unique explanations (see Feynman, 1974). In addition, despite best intentions to conduct 'good science', the tendency has been for research to be piecemeal rather than systematic, and disaggregated rather than systemic (Newell, 1973). Newell (1973) asserted that such practices result in ideological and theoretical differences becoming less clear and conflicting arguments being infrequently resolved. The end product is unlikely to be a mature and cumulative science. The risk here is that the goals of science are relegated in priority and, as a result, science gives way to the process of telling stories based on data ex post facto. Such a path is unlikely to lead to much needed advances in the development of a useful theory of talent and limited capability to improve talent development.

Thankfully, such practices are not unique to the science of talent. Newell's original epiphany about the non-cumulative nature of science resulted from attempts to synthesize the latest research in cognitive science. Numerous researchers over the years have recognized the interplay between science and opinion. Disdain has routinely been expressed by a diverse range of scientists for those 'in the other camp', whose position, purpose, and methods have been described by those holding contrary views as having little scientific or societal value (e.g.,

Gigerenzer, 2004). If we ever want to rise above the 'disaggregated scattering' of research *and* achieve the kind of knowledge synthesis that Newell (1973) described, the science of talent needs to move beyond the mundane polemics portrayed in the typical caricature of nature vs. nurture, in favour of pursuing a much more integrated perspective (Simonton, 2000). Taking an either/or perspective is fundamentally silly (Ackerman, 2007). Both genes and environment (and the interaction between them) are necessary for talent to ensue.

One important question for advancing our understanding of talent is how best to conduct talent research. The research on mono/dizygotic twins provides some insight into Gene × Environment interaction. But, as Ericsson and Ward (2007) have argued, this research only partially informs the development of expertise and of talented individuals who become highly skilled (see Ericsson, 2007). In the meantime, we are left to wait for the necessary accumulation of genetic evidence, make tantalizing leaps of inference from related (e.g., twins) research, or examine the research on nature and nurture independently. The latter approach is likely to lead to a disaggregated body of knowledge! Rather depressingly, it is the approach taken in this chapter, mainly because it reflects the current state of the science – at least as we understand it. Is there any hope? The hope is that we can end this polarizing debate in favour of a more integrative stance – one that embraces and elevates the goals of science above personal perspectives and agendas. The nature vs. nature debate is dead. The issue needs to be reframed.

Let us assume (a) that the scientific evidence in genetics is not yet sufficiently mature to make recommendations about selection or training, and/or (b) that we cannot yet intervene at a genetic level to facilitate performance outcomes in those domains. The questions of primary concern, then, are whether there are any individual differences in domain-general abilities and/or domain-specific skills that affect talent development and whether these can be nurtured. In this chapter we attempt to address these issues (without escaping all polarizing dichotomies) by examining the empirical data on talent and expertise. We provide an overview of research on individual differences in domain-general ability and domain-specific skill,[1] their relative contribution to talent and expertise, and then examine the measurement of talent. Last, we examine issues related to talent development, with a specific focus on practice and preconditions for performance improvement.

From general motor ability to domain-general abilities

Domain-general abilities, such as intelligence and eye–hand coordination, theoretically speaking, are thought to be innate and relatively non-malleable. Arguably, they are the basis on which talent is developed. In one of the first reported investigations of the heritable basis for superior performance, Sir Francis Galton noted that the highest performing individuals were often related to others who were also high performing. He concluded that inherited abilities must be the source of superior performance, and that training culminates in asymptotic levels of performance that are rigidly determined (Galton, 1869/1979). The notion that maximum performance is determined by genetic factors has persisted for over a century.

Much progress was made in our understanding of capability limits around the turn of the twentieth century. This period saw a range of domain-general ability tests being developed for the purposes of assessing physical and motor proficiency, as well as monitoring physical and mental ability, sometimes using verbal, non-verbal and performance-based tests of intelligence. In addition to understanding capability limits, these initiatives were often pragmatically driven, and geared towards improving ability to classify individual differences in all-around psychomotor ability, diagnose performance disabilities, and predict future accomplishment from current levels.

For instance, tests were developed to establish physical efficiency standards (McCurdy, 1923) and to aid in role selection and task assignment for military recruits (Yerkes, 1921).

The concept of a generalized motor ability (GMA) was popularized around the 1920s (see Brace 1927). However, little evidence followed that GMA was capable of predicting psychomotor performance on specialized tasks. For example, GMA did not predict typewriter skill (Walker & Adams, 1934). Only a more focused motor ability – steadiness – predicted rifle marksmanship (Humphreys, Buxton, & Taylor, 1936). Subsequent research confirmed that motor skill was highly task-specific (Henry, 1968); and GMA tests were superseded by those measuring both specific psychomotor (e.g., balance, coordination, etc.) and other non-motor abilities (e.g., intelligence, working memory capacity, etc.; see Fleishman, 1953). Researchers interested in better understanding talent development and training effectiveness adopted similar specific test batteries to address real-world problems of the day; for instance, when McFarland and Franzen (1944) were able to predict successful graduation of naval trainee pilots ($r = .41$) using tests of individual differences in non-motor ability, such as general intelligence, morale, attitudes, and mechanical interests. When psychomotor abilities were included (e.g., Mashburn serial reaction, two hand coordination), prediction capability improved further ($r = .61$).

Similarly, training outcomes in US Army Air Force pilots, navigators, and bombardiers were successfully predicted ($r = .50$) using a battery of mental ability tests (e.g., mechanical comprehension, general intelligence), which improved when performance on specific psychomotor tasks (e.g., Mashburn task) were included ($r = .70$; Melton, 1947). More recently, tests of general cognitive ability (e.g., general intelligence) were shown to be a good predictor of 'trainability' (i.e., potential to improve, $r = .56$), and better than measures of initial performance on tasks that were representative of their future job ($r = .41$) (e.g., Schmidt & Hunter, 1992).

At first glance, whether psychomotor or other abilities are used, these variables appear to do a good job of predicting initial development with training. Considering the (human and resource) costs of making an error in many applied domains (e.g., aviation) however, the predictive value should be considered relatively low (see Fleishman, 1953). Importantly, only training success was predicted in the above studies. The ability to predict advanced training criteria or operational performance was not determined. Fleishman (1953) prognosticated that as individuals become more skilled with training, ability measures are unlikely to predict 'job' performance as well. This prediction has since been borne out (e.g., see Ackerman, 1988). For instance, Wigdor and Green (1991) demonstrated that tests of a range of specific abilities (e.g., Armed Services Vocational Aptitude Battery) – although used to select military personnel for specific roles – did not predict individual differences in on-the-job performance after the first year of service.

In a recent meta-analysis of 20 studies, Voss, Kramer, Basak, Prakash, and Roberts (2010) demonstrated that, while the effects were too small to be detected in any single low-power study, an analysis across studies shows that expert athletes do differ from their lesser skilled counterparts in some aspects of domain-general ability. Rather than psychomotor ability, Voss et al. noted that cognitive processing speed (i.e., ability to quickly and accurately perceive and respond to non-specific environmental stimuli) and varied attentional tests (including measures of spatial and divided attention but not attentional cueing paradigms) yielded significant skill effects between elite and non-elite athletes ($ES = .67$ and $ES = .53$, respectively). Whether skilled athletes possess these capabilities prior to engaging in sport and succeed because of them, or develop these abilities as a consequence of having invested their career in these sports is an empirical question. In the next section, we summarize research that has examined the relative contribution of domain-general abilities and acquired domain-specific skills to the attainment of expertise.

21

From domain-general ability to domain-specific skills

Multidisciplinary research examining the contribution of domain-general abilities and domain-specific skills has featured prominently in talent development research. Numerous physical, physiological, biological and maturational factors have been shown to predict athletic performance in children and young adolescents (e.g., Regnier & Salmela, 1987). However, as individuals mature, psychological factors such as susceptibility to anxiety, perceptual awareness, anticipatory skill and ego-orientation are required (when combined with physical factors) to discriminate across skill levels (e.g., Regnier & Salmela, 1987; Reilly, Williams, Nevill, & Franks, 2000).

Although some talent researchers have taken a multidisciplinary approach to talent, sports expertise researchers have mainly focused on perceptual-cognitive variables. Research by de Groot (1965) and Chase and Simon (1973) in chess drove early interest in the role of perceptual-cognitive abilities and skills in expert performance. Their research demonstrated that (domain-general, short-term) memory for random configurations of chess pieces did not differentiate expert from novice chess players. However, higher skilled chess players were better than less-skilled players at recalling meaningful patterns of chess pieces (i.e., actual game configurations). They concluded that, compared to novices, experts do not possess superior general memory ability. Instead, they have acquired domain-specific memory skills (i.e., can select, encode, index, and organize task-relevant information) that facilitate memory recall and support game play.

The finding that experts have a better memory for domain-specific information in chess and a more accessible knowledge repository – but not better general memory ability – has been extended to other talent domains, such as basketball (e.g., Allard, Graham, & Paarsalu, 1980), field hockey (e.g., Starkes & Deakin, 1984), soccer (e.g., Williams & Davids, 1995), and tennis (e.g., McPherson & French, 1991). Domain-specific memory and expert knowledge are a by-product of skill development that are more representative of on-the-job performance. In sport, those identified skills include anticipation and decision making (for a review, see Ward, Williams, & Hancock, 2006). In a comprehensive meta-analysis of perceptual-cognitive tasks, Mann, Williams, Ward, and Janelle (2007) reviewed 388 effect sizes from 42 studies. Their results indicated that experts were significantly more accurate than novices at anticipating their opponent's actions, made significantly faster decisions and employed a more efficient visual search strategy, suggesting that experts are able to do more with less information. Although the evidence suggests that these representative skills are learned and developed over time, one could argue that such skills have a genetic basis or, at the very least, are sub-served by some foundational abilities (see Voss et al., 2010).

Researchers have pitched the relative contribution of domain-general abilities against domain-specific skills. For instance, Helsen and Starkes (1999) examined expert and intermediate soccer players on domain-general visual, perceptual and cognitive factors (including simple and peripheral reaction time, visual correction time, static, dynamic and mesopic acuity, and horizontal and peripheral visual range) as well as performance on representative tasks requiring perceptual-cognitive skills (i.e., viewing either static images or dynamic first-person perspective video of a soccer game in which they are asked to make a game-related decision). Peripheral visual range was the only domain-general ability measure to discriminate between skill levels, which explained just 3 per cent of the between-group variance. Of the perceptual-cognitive skill measures, experts made faster and more accurate situation-specific decisions than less-skilled players, which explained far more variance than the ability measures (84 per cent vs. 3 per cent). Ward and Williams (2003) conducted a similar study but investigated the relative contribution of similar factors in players aged 9 and 18 years. General visual-perceptual abilities (i.e., dynamic acuity, stereoscopic depth sensitivity, and peripheral awareness) did not discriminate between skill groups at any age, whereas specific perceptual-cognitive skills did (i.e., anticipation, situation assessment, and memory recall). The combination of anticipation and situation assessment skills (i.e., skill at assessing the current situation and predicting the future course of action) yielded the strongest effects across all age groups.

Belling, Suss, and Ward (2015) extended the Ward and Williams (2003) study conceptually by comparing domain-general cognitive abilities with domain-specific perceptual-cognitive skills. The focus on domain-general cognitive abilities (rather than visual-perceptual abilities by Ward & Williams, 2003) was in line with Voss et al. (2010) who showed these are a better predictor of expertise in sport. Cognitive ability was measured using the Berlin Numeracy Test (Cokely, Galesic, Shulz, Ghazal, & Garcia-Retamero, 2012) – a measure of statistical numeracy, highly correlated with intelligence – and a test of spatial ability (i.e., Mental Rotation Test; Vandenberg & Kuse, 1978). Their measure of perceptual-cognitive skill combined the tasks previously identified as most predictive of skilled performance (Ward & Williams, 2003): anticipation and situation assessment. The domain-specific skill measure was a significant predictor of level of expertise, whereas both cognitive ability measures did not contribute significantly to the model.

Across numerous studies, results suggest that only domain-specific perceptual-cognitive skills consistently differentiate between skill groups. When domain-general ability effects are found to contribute significantly to between-group variance, at best, they have minimal prediction capability (e.g., Voss et al., 2010). When direct comparisons are made between the two, perceptual-cognitive skills dwarf the contribution of abilities massively.

Test development as a basis for measuring talent and developing training

The focus of this section is on shifting our direction toward better ways of measuring talent and how we might improve procedures to better predict it. Although some modern-day sports institutions identify talent criteria intuitively, most early researchers adopted a multi-step approach to talent identification and development: delineating the target performance, identifying performance predictors, evaluating performance, and assessing the trainability of these factors (see Durand-Bush & Salmela, 2001). However, this approach has been criticized since criteria that are predictive of early performance success are not necessarily predictive in later years (Geron, 1978). The use of (multiple) one-shot predictors severely underestimates the instability of talent criteria and the non-linearity of the talent development process (Vaeyens, Lenoir, Williams, & Philippaerts, 2008). Bartmus, Neumann and de Marées (1987) suggested that one-shot tests were better used for performance diagnosis than for selection purposes. Their recommendations were consistent with early models of talent in sport that urged the inclusion of assessments of amenability to training, and with more recent progress-monitoring approaches to talent prediction that recommend selection for training based on the rate of performance improvement (Vaeyens et al., 2008; Williams & Reilly, 2000).

Few studies have employed a progress-monitoring approach or have based selection on measures of performance improvement or its rate. A handful of exceptions provide limited evidence of the superiority of this approach (e.g., Pienaar & Spamer, 1998). Hence, much more research is needed in this area before strong recommendations can be made for measuring talent and predicting its development. We argue that the strong recommendations from the extant research – to move away from prediction-based performance measures toward multidisciplinary measures of (the rate of) performance improvement – have, effectively, side-stepped the most important issue in talent science: reliable and valid measurement. Science rests on the adequacy of its measurement. Invalid and unreliable measures provide a weak foundation for research and intervention (Foster & Cone, 1995).

Various means to measure talent exist. Talent researchers have made the positive move towards favouring work-sample/job tests and representative tasks over coach/supervisor subjective evaluations of performance. Despite performance being notoriously difficult to measure and a 'gold standard' assessment task being elusive (Hoffman, Ward, Feltovich, DiBello, Fiore, & Andrews, 2014), talent scientists and expertise researchers have pushed the boundaries in developing representative tasks on which to assess performance (e.g., Ward, Williams, & Hancock, 2006, for a review). However, even those that have implemented systematic approaches to testing and measurement of talent and expert skill (e.g., expert-performance approach) have rarely assessed the psychometric properties of tests employing representative tasks or incorporated established procedures for developing valid and reliable tests (e.g., see Hambleton & Jones, 1993; Lord, 1980). This is the case, even though we have a 100+ year history of using psychometric techniques to measure abilities, as well as psychological traits and states. Formal test development and evaluation procedures can be used to ensure that representative tasks[2] will also provide valid and reliable means to measure talent. This is important, not least when the goal is to objectively measure performance over time or to develop effective training interventions. We argue that integration of these procedures are necessary for the field to make progress in measurement, and hence the development of talent.

Two general theories or approaches have informed methods to analyse and select appropriate test items for inclusion within a test. The classical test theory (CTT) framework – a 'test-based' approach – assumes a linear relationship between test score and ability, whereas item-response theory (IRT) analysis – an 'item-based' approach – assumes a nonlinear relationship between item performance and ability. Item statistics such as difficulty and discriminability, in the case of CTT, are dependent on the specific sample and overall test score. In the case of IRT, the specific item characteristics remain sample independent. IRT also allows a "guessing" factor to be calculated and individual item modelling can be used to describe overall test 'informativeness', which allows for flexibility when selecting items based on the developers' test objectives (e.g., see Hambleton & Jones, 1993; Lord, 1980, for reviews). In general, a test to identify high-performing 'talented' individuals should contain items that have higher discrimination and greater difficulty, but have a low guessing value. To increase efficiency of implementing the test and to minimize response burden, IRT analyses can be used to reduce the number of test items, without reducing its reliability. Once developed, validation is essential to interpret the score meaningfully and to better understand the underlying mechanisms responsible for successful test performance.

One recent example in which these procedures were used to develop a valid and reliable test of observational assessment skill is the Anterior Cruciate Ligament Injury-Risk-Estimation Quiz (ACL-IQ) (e.g., Petushek et al., 2015a, 2015b). The ACL-IQ test was developed to assess an observer's talent at visually estimating an athlete's risk for ACL injury. Put simply, it is a test that determines how good an individual is at diagnosing skilled movement execution – a key skill for any developer of psychomotor talent. In the first instance, we sampled 20 video clips of athletes performing drop vertical jumps – a routine screening test – where we also had concurrent biomechanical assessment of objective risk. Individuals from various athletic and sport medicine disciplines then responded to the clips by rating the athlete's risk for ACL injury. From the responses, we calculated individual item characteristics such as reliability, discriminability, difficulty, and guessing error. The number of test items was reduced to create a short (5-item) test by optimizing these item characteristics and the final test was cross-validated in a larger representative sample. Summary characteristics were consistent across the larger sample, and test-retest reliability was high despite the low numbers of test items.

To provide an estimate of construct validity and to identify the underlying mechanisms supporting skilled performance on the ACL-IQ, we also measured participant performance on various domain-general and domain-specific measures of cognition. General measures included mental rotation and decision making (similar to those used by Belling et al., 2015) as well as a measure of personality. To measure domain-specific skill, we collected measures of ACL knowledge and cue utility ratings (e.g., participant ratings of the importance of particular information cues for risk estimation). Hierarchical and cognitive process modelling results revealed that cue utility and ACL knowledge, rather than domain-general ability measures, were significant predictors of risk estimation ability. Hence, the results suggest that performance on a validated and reliable measure of observational risk assessment skill was better explained by domain-specific measures of performance. Importantly, the measurement, and test development and validation procedures used in the development of the ACL-IQ provide confidence that what is being assessed is actual talent or skill at the task in question, rather than an artefact of the measurement procedure. Moreover, they provide confidence that the underlying factors identified as mediating performance (i.e., cue utility and ACL knowledge) are indicative of how successful performance on the task is and can be attained. Not least, training programs/systems to improve performance that are based on these underlying factors provide a more reliable basis for performance improvement (see Hoffman et al., 2014, for a detailed discussion of training principles and reliable methods to accelerate learning).

Practice, mindset and ability

Undoubtedly, there are certain domains in which genetic predispositions offer considerable advantage. Likewise, it is entirely possible that engagement in particular types of developmental activities, such as diligent and dedicated practice and training not only results in improvements in domain-specific skill and performance improvements, but in the development of domain-general ability. For instance, practice effects have been observed on IQ tests (see Howe, 1990 for a review), though these are not correlated with future performance (Lyons, Hoffman, & Michel, 2009). So what is changed during practice that impacts performance, what influences those changes, and how do they come about?

Numerous researchers have implicated the role of zeal and the capacity to engage in hard work in high levels of proficiency. One of the founders of educational psychology – Edwin Thorndike (1912) – coined the term 'practice with zeal' to capture diligent efforts to improve performance. Engagement in these types of activities was originally studied in domains such as music and sport (e.g., Ericsson, Krampe, & Tesch-Römer, 1993; Hodges & Starkes, 1996). More recently, this notion has been shown to be applicable to many skill and talent development domains, including weather forecasting, piloting, and military command (Hoffman, 2007).

One of the first systematic attempts to examine the developmental activities in which talented athletes engaged en route to expertise was conducted by Bloom (1985). His research highlighted that such individuals initially engaged in their domains through playful activities. Their talent was identified at an early age by parents or coaches and familial support was indicative of athletic success. In subsequent years, dedication increased, practice became serious, competition was more prevalent, their coach played a more demanding and respected role and, ultimately, talented individuals shifted towards greater autonomy and self-regulation.

Inspired by Bloom's (1985) longitudinal research, Ericsson et al. (1993) coined the phrase *deliberate practice*. Consistent with Thorndike (1912), Ericsson et al. suggested that deliberate practice is a highly effortful form of practice in which an individual is focused on monitoring and improving performance. Moreover, they indicated that it is not inherently enjoyable and in some cases involves mentoring or coaching in order to select activities to increase performance. Contrary to Galton, they hypothesized that expert performance is achieved through deliberate practice as opposed to being genetically determined. Their conclusions are based on their observation that the highest performing musicians started training around four or five years of age and logged over 10,000 hours in deliberate practice activities by the time they reached 20. A moderately skilled group spent approximately 8,000 hours and a less skilled group spent 5,000 hours. The authors noted that experts commonly engaged in deliberate practice for 10+ years.

The claims of deliberate practice theory have been assessed in numerous sports, originally in a study of wrestlers (Hodges & Starkes, 1996) and then many times since. The primary deviations from the original theory were that talented sports participants typically engaged in more team and individual practice, participation was both physically and mentally effortful, and often perceived as enjoyable (see also Helsen, Starkes, & Hodges, 1998). Despite these differences in definition, athletes typically had engaged in 10 years of deliberate practice before attaining an elite level of performance.

A study by Ward, Hodges, Starkes, and Williams (2007) also indicated that the number of hours spent in team practice more reliably discriminated between elite and recreational soccer players between 8 and 19 years of age. They showed that elite players spent more time focusing on decision-making activities during practice, were more motivated, and had more support from parents. Moreover, perceptions of enjoyment changed throughout development, with younger players focusing on enjoying participation, and older players focusing on the outcome, especially winning. In a subsequent study, Ford, Ward, Hodges, and Williams (2009) followed up with some of the original participants from the Ward et al. (2007) study. They compared the participation patterns of elite players (when they were aged between 6 to 12 years of age) who either became professionals later in life, or had been at the elite level but did not receive a professional contract. Since both sets of elite players had similar histories in the training academy, their practice profiles were almost identical and no longer discriminated between them. However, the professional elite players had also recorded more hours per year in soccer play activities during the early years. When data were compared to a recreational group, the recreational group had accrued even more play than the professionals, however, they had not received academy-based training or accrued anywhere close to the amount of deliberate practice as either elite group. Accordingly, they proposed the 'early engagement hypothesis', suggesting that both practice and play are important contributors to skill acquisition at a young age (cf. Côté, Baker, & Abernethy, 2007).

Until recently, the literature on deliberate practice has had limited training value. If a coach said to a student, 'go and deliberately practice', they would surely receive the obvious response: 'Doing what?' Although it is quite hard to extract tangible applied implications for training contexts from the research on deliberate practice (see Cobley & Baker, 2010), without additional description of specific practice activities and/or training principles, the mass of research counting hours is unlikely to move talent science forward. Some researchers have identified related practice activities (e.g., engagement in decision making and perceptual-cognitive skill development, see Ward et al., 2007; Côté et al., 2007), and others have identified specific activities in which participants do/should engage (e.g., see microstructure of practice, e.g., Deakin & Cobley, 2003). However, few have increased the training or scientific value of deliberate practice.

In a rare non-retrospective examination of 'deliberate' practice activities, Coughlan, Williams, McRobert, and Ford (2013) followed expert and intermediate Gaelic football players as they practised two types of kicks in a controlled experiment. Expert players spent more time on the challenging kick whereas the intermediate players focused their practice on the less challenging kick. Although experts were better at both kicks, unsurprisingly, both groups improved the most on the kick where they spent the most time. During retention, however, only the expert group maintained their level of performance improvement on both kicks. The cognitive strategies employed during learning, and how players interpreted their engagement may provide some explanation. Experts engaged in more monitoring, evaluative, and planning-type thoughts during training and interpreted engagement as less enjoyable, and more physically and mentally effortful than the intermediate group. This suggests that their greater efforts to improve on more challenging tasks resulted in more marked improvements overall.

One promising strategy for encouraging people to be willing to engage in deliberate practice might be to encourage a growth mindset – a view that talent is a malleable quality that can be developed over time. A wealth of research suggests that growth-mindsets regarding domain-specific talents or abilities predict high levels of motivation and achievement, including in athletic (e.g., Wang & Biddle, 2003), professional (Tabernero & Wood, 1999), and health-relevant domains (e.g., Ehrlinger, Burnette, Park, Harrold, & Orvidas, 2016a). Growth theorists more often choose challenging, effortful tasks (Hong, Chiu, Dweck, Lin, & Wan, 1999), devote more time to practising those tasks (Cury, Da Fonseca, Zahn, & Elliot, 2008; Ehrlinger et al., 2016b), and attend more to negative feedback (Ehrlinger, Mitchum, & Dweck, 2016c) relative to those who hold more fixed views of talent (i.e., fixed theorists). Although researchers have not used the phrase 'deliberate practice' in reference to the benefits of a growth theory, these effects arguably could be defined as such. Unsurprisingly then, growth mindsets predict successful goal achievement. A recent meta-analysis of experimental and correlation studies conducted by Burnette, O'Boyle, VanEpps, Pollack, and Finkel (2013) revealed that growth mindsets lead people to adopt more mastery-oriented goals, to cope more effectively with setbacks and, consequently, to outperform fixed theorists in academics, sports, professional, and health domains. This research has led to successful intervention research that has led to increased adoption of mastery goals (e.g., Spray, Wang, Biddle, Chatzisarantis, & Warburton, 2006), positive views of effort, and higher grades (Blackwell, Trzesniewski, & Dweck, 2007), relative to control conditions.

Beyond individuals' mindsets, past research suggests that managers and coaches who hold growth mindsets may be more effective with respect to both selection and training. Compared to those with more fixed theories, Ehrlinger and Ward (2009) found that growth theorists reported valuing motivation (e.g., willingness to work hard) over 'raw talent' in hiring selections for employees and athletes. After hiring selections have been made, theories of ability held by managers and coaches influence their approach to training and performance evaluation. Managers with stronger growth theories have shown more motivation to provide training (Heslin, Vandewalle & Latham, 2006), and they provide more and higher quality feedback (Heslin & VandeWalle, 2008) to employees than managers with stronger fixed theories. Therefore, managers who believe that their employees can improve are likely to pay closer attention to their performance and provide the feedback needed to help them excel.

To summarize, although attempts have been made to select individuals based on innate abilities and traits, and to count deliberate practice and play hours as a means to predict skilled performance and its development, belief in one's ability to improve and willingness to invest effort in improvement activities may be a more important factor. The research suggests that the beliefs that managers, coaches, employees and athletes hold about their own and others' abilities (and skills) impacts motivation and behaviour (such as deliberate efforts to improve during practice) in ways that have important consequences for talent development.

The theory of deliberate practice (and deliberate play – whichever one advocates) is not without its critics. For instance, Hambrick, Oswald, Altmann, Meinz, Gobet, and Campitelli

(2014) argued that deliberate practice is not nearly as important for determining expertise as Ericsson et al. (1993) claim it is. In particular, the former purported that the latter may have overestimated the role of deliberate practice relative to other individual differences in developing expertise. Persistence in accomplishing long-term goals – or grit – has been shown to predict musical performance – with deliberate practice mediating that relationship (Duckworth, Kirby, Tsukayama, Berstein, & Ericsson, 2012). Likewise, although not mediated through deliberate practice, several variables have been shown to explain some of the variance in performance, including starting age, (e.g., Howard, 2012), global intelligence (e.g., Grabner, Neubauer, & Stern, 2006), verbal and spatial ability (e.g., Hayward & Gromko, 2009), and working memory capacity (e.g., Meinz & Hambrick, 2010). In the latter study, working memory capacity accounted for 7.4 per cent of the variance in pianists' performance, whereas deliberate practice accounted for 45.1 per cent. The correlation between working memory and deliberate practice was near zero. However, when combined with other domain-general factors (e.g., intelligence, music audiation), this combination often explained more of performance variance than does deliberate practice (e.g., Ruthsatz, Detterman, Griscom & Cirullo, 2008). Unfortunately, authors seemingly concerned with debunking the value of deliberate practice have not compared combinations of domain-general abilities (such as those above) with the domain-specific skills acquired through hours of deliberate practice – for example perceptual-cognitive skills. When these comparisons have been made, the contribution of individual differences in general abilities to the development of talent and expertise is typically dwarfed by domain-specific skills. From our perspective, the focus of future research in this area should not be on nature vs. nurture, domain-general abilities vs. domain-specific skills, or even promoting (or demoting) the value of either. Instead, it should be on increasing the training value of the deliberate practice literature (and similar literature in related domains), better understanding for whom specific types of deliberate practice might work best, and gaining a better understanding of how experts learn, and of the types of training that might result in more resilient and adaptive performance in complex and dynamic domains more generally (e.g., Hoffman et al., 2014; Hoffman & Ward, 2015; Ward, Hutton, Hoffman, Gore, Anderson, & Leggatt, 2016).

Summary and commentary on the science of talent

In sum, over the last few decades one might argue that the nature–nurture debate has not always led to advances in talent science that one might have hoped. Rather, there appears to have been an overemphasis on counting practice hours and, compared to other dialectical debates, there has seldom been a push towards a synthesis of perspectives. In our opinion, talent should not and cannot be reduced to one side of the debate versus the other. We hope, no matter how mysterious the media presents it to be, that future talent scientists can embrace and elevate the goals of science above personal perspectives and agendas to pursue a more integrative science in a more systematic, systemic and cumulative manner.

The complete answer to the popular Galtonian question of whether innate traits drive eminence and talent still remains elusive and perhaps it always will. Although some physical traits, such as height and body size may predict expert performance in some sports, there are few domain-general abilities that could be used reliably as a sole predictor of performance in complex domains such as sport – at least to the extent that we could base selection entirely on such factors. Arguably, the antithetical argument is at least partially true too: there are few domain-specific skills that, alone, predict performance in such domains reliably and unequivocally – not without other domain-general skills contributing a small portion of the variance in individual differences in performance. Whether domain-general abilities are improved through engagement in domain-specific deliberate practice remains an empirical question. Likewise, whether some individual differences predispose some people to be able to endure the, arguably, pathological levels of deliberate practice needed to achieve the lofty heights of expertise is open to debate.

What is crucial for advancing the science of talent, however, is reliable and valid measurement, and a better understanding of the context-sensitive nature of expert cognition and performance. Instead of continuing to debate nature versus nurture in talent domains, we call for researchers to focus on the development of methods and representative tasks that capture the complex nature of expertise in context (see Ericsson & Ward, 2007; Hoffman et al., 2014; Hoffman, 2007), and the development of reliable assessment tools that permit valid measurement of talent via the identification of diagnostic test items (Petushek et al., 2015a, 2015b). Following previous recommendations, measurement approaches should also focus on predictors of learning and performance improvement (e.g., see Durand-Bush & Salmela, 2001).

The large body of research evidence now amassed continues to confirm the value of practising with zeal for developing current and future talented performers. The research has also highlighted the value of starting practice at an early age – without overspecialization – and the importance of parenting and coaching to develop expertise (e.g., Côté et al., 2007; Hodges & Starkes, 1996; Helsen et al., 1998; Ward et al., 2007). In addition, recent research suggests that expert mentoring may be a useful vehicle to help scaffold learning, aiding to bridge the divide between current and next proficiency levels (see Hoffman & Ward, 2015; Hoffman et al., 2014).

However, current research also indicates that deliberate practice does not always account for all, or even most of, the variance between expert performers (Hambrick et al., 2014). On average, the data suggest that domain-general abilities (when combined with other abilities) and deliberate practice account for, roughly speaking, the same amount of variance in performance, whereas when one examines the relative contribution of domain-general abilities and domain-specific skills, the latter tend to result in greater discrimination. Although some researchers have identified the specific training activities needed to attain expertise within a domain or have begun to better define the parameters of deliberate practice within a given sport (e.g., Coughlan et al., 2013), the deliberate practice camp has often come up short when providing a meaningful prescriptive contribution to advance the science of training (see Hoffman et al., 2014). Considerable research investment is needed to more clearly articulate the deliberate practice activities, and more importantly, specify the training principles (and how they need to be modified) that drive the acquisition of adaptive and skilled performance in complex domains (see Ward, 2014; Ward et al., 2016). Extant research has tended to focus on one of two areas: (i) adapting traditional classroom-type (and/or laboratory-based) and more exploratory learning methods designed to improve the performance of naive individuals on artificial and/or non-representative tasks, or (ii) on developing simple cue-utilization and recognition methods that focus on a single aspect of perceptual and/or cognitive expertise (e.g., anticipation; see Ward, Farrow, Harris, Williams, Eccles, & Ericsson, 2008; Ward, Suss, & Basevitch, 2009). Neither of these methods accurately reflect how experts learn, nor are they likely to promote the type of understanding needed to develop intuitive skills associated with expert performance. Current evidence suggests that talent can be nurtured but currently, methods to accelerate expertise are being under exploited (see Hoffman et al., 2014).

Finally, a prerequisite for learning may be believing you can improve, and knowing the difference between what you know and what you don't. Individuals that have a growth mindset and those at the higher end of the proficiency continuum typically have more accurate self-assessment (e.g., Ehrlinger et al., 2016c). A wealth of research has shown that viewing one's

..vel of talent as an improvable quality carries benefits in terms of the adoption of mastery-oriented goals, more helpful attributions, and higher achievement compared to viewing talent as more fixed (see Burnette et al., 2013 for a review). A growth mindset seems, in particular, to promote behaviours that could be categorized as deliberate practice, including the increased persistence on (e.g., Ehrlinger et al., 2016b) and attention to (e.g., Ehrlinger et al., 2016c) effortful tasks. Individuals with growth mindsets in sport (Cury et al., 2008), academics (Blackwell et al., 2007), and management (Tabernero & Wood, 1999) outperform those with more fixed views of talent. Perhaps then, one particularly promising avenue for training is to teach growth mindsets in conjunction with clearly specified deliberate practice activities to maximize the opportunities for successful goal pursuit and mastery. Hence, the focus going forward should be on increasing the training value of the deliberate practice by gaining a better understanding of how experts learn, and identifying the training principles and methods that can accelerate the development of resilient and adaptive skill (e.g., Hoffman et al., 2014; Hoffman & Ward, 2015; Ward, 2014; Ward et al., 2016).

Notes

1 Domain-general (DG) abilities typically refer to those underlying, stable and innate characteristics that support performance in, and are generalizable to most, if not all tasks. Examples of DG abilities include cognitive abilities such as intelligence, spatial ability, speed of reaction, and abstract reasoning ability, and psychomotor abilities, such as complex coordination and rotary pursuit. The term domain-general is also used to refer to related characteristics, such as personality traits. Domain-specific (DS) skills, on the other hand, typically refer to particular capabilities that are specific to a particular task or domain and acquired as a consequence of engaging in that specific activity (or engaging in similar activities that rely on a similar problem structure, solution principles, and/or require similar patterns of movement coordination and/or control).
2 Ericsson and Ward (2007) defined a representative task as one that captures the essential characteristics of an expert's superior performance in naturally occurring situations (e.g., low-frequency, challenging tasks that require specific perceptual–cognitive skills and knowledge to complete successfully). This is not dissimilar to Brunswik's (1956) conception of 'representative design' where the recommendation is to include perceptual variables, and their variants, from across the full spectrum of an individual's natural environment to which they have adapted.

References

Ackerman, P. L. (1988). Determinants of individual differences during skill acquisition: Cognitive abilities and information processing. *Journal of Experimental Psychology: General, 117*(3), 288–318.

Ackerman, P. L. (2007). Outgoing editorial: Bridging science and application. *Journal of Experimental Psychology: Applied, 13*(4), 179–181.

Allard, F., Graham, S., & Paarsalu, M. E. (1980). Perception in sport: Basketball. *Journal of Sport Psychology, 2*(1), 14–21

Bartmus, U., Neumann, E., & de Marées, H. (1987). The talent problem in sports. *International Journal of Sports Medicine, 8*, 415–416.

Belling, P. K., Suss, J., & Ward, P. (2015). Advancing theory and application of cognitive research in sport. *Psychology of Sport and Exercise, 16*(1), 45–59.

Blackwell, L., Trzesniewski, K., & Dweck, C. S. (2007). Implicit theories of intelligence predict achievement across an adolescent transition: A longitudinal study and an intervention. *Child Development, 78*, 246–263.

Bloom, B. S. (ed.). (1985). *Developing talent in young people.* New York: Ballantine.

Brace, D. K. (1927). *Measuring motor ability.* New York: A. S. Barnes & Co.

Brunswik, E. (1956). *Perception and the representative design of psychological experiments* (2nd ed.). Oakland, CA: University of California Press.

Burnette, J. L., O'Boyle, E. H., VanEpps, E. M., Pollack, J. M., & Finkel, E. J. (2013). Mind-sets matter: A meta-analytic review of implicit theories and self-regulation. *Psychological Bulletin, 139*(3), 655–701.

Chase, W. G., & Simon, H. A. (1973). Perception in chess. *Cognitive Psychology, 4*(1), 55–81.

Cobley, S., & Baker, J. (2010). Digging it out of the dirt: Ben Hogan, deliberate practice and the secret: A Commentary. *International Journal of Sports Science and Coaching,* 5(Suppl. Annual Review of Golf Coaching), 29–33.

Cokely, E.T., Galesic, M., Schulz, E., Ghazal, S., & Garcia-Retamero, R. (2012). Measuring risk literacy: The Berlin Numeracy Test. *Judgment and Decision Making, 7,* 25–47.

Côté, J., Baker, J., & Abernethy, B. (2007). Practice and play in the development of sport expertise. In G. Tenenbaum and R. C. Eklund (eds), *Handbook of sport psychology* (pp. 184–202). Hoboken, NJ: John Wiley & Sons.

Coughlan, E. K., Williams, A. M., McRobert, A. P., and Ford, P. R. (2013). How experts practice: A novel test of deliberate practice theory. *Journal of Experimental Psychology: Learning, Memory and Cognition, 40,* 449–458.

Cury, F., Da Fonseca, D., Zahn, I., & Elliot, A. (2008). Implicit theories and IQ test performance: A sequential meditational analysis. *Journal of Experimental Social Psychology, 44,* 783–791.

Davids, K., & Baker, J. (2007). Genes, environment and sport performance. *Sports Medicine, 37*(11), 961–980.

de Groot, A. D. (1965). *Thought and choice in chess.* The Hague: Mouton.

Deakin, J., & Cobley, S. (2003). A search for deliberate practice: An examination of the practice environments in figure skating and volleyball. In K. A Ericsson & J. Starkes (eds), *Expert performance in sports advances in research on sport expertise* (pp. 115–136). Champaign, USA: Human Kinetics.

Duckworth, A. L., Kirby, T. A., Tsukayama, E., Berstein, H., & Ericsson, K. A. (2012). Deliberate practice spells success: Why grittier competitors triumph at the National Spelling Bee. *Social Psychological and Personality Science, 2,* 174–181.

Durand-Bush, N., & Salmela, J.H. (2001). The development of talent in sport. In R. R. Singer, C. Hausenblas, & C. J. Janelle (eds), *Handbook of sport psychology* (2nd ed.). New York: Macmillan.

Ehrlinger, J., Burnette, J. L., Park, J., Harrold, M. L., & Orvidas, K. (2016a). Guilty pleasures: Fixed beliefs about weight predict consumption of high calorie, high fat foods. *Manuscript under Review.* Washington State University.

Ehrlinger, J., Hartwig, M., Harrold, M., Vossen, J., Mitchum, A., Biermann, A., & Trzesniewski, K. (2016b). Incremental theories of intelligence predict persistence and, in turn, sustained learning. *Manuscript in Preparation,* Washington State University.

Ehrlinger, J., Mitchum, A. L., & Dweck, C. S. (2016c). Understanding overconfidence: Theories of intelligence, preferential attention, and distorted self-assessment. *Journal of Experimental Social Psychology, 63,* 94–100.

Ehrlinger, J., & Ward, P. (2009). The role of implicit person theories in selection decisions. *Unpublished Data.*

Ericsson, K. A. (2007). Deliberate practice and the modifiability of body and mind: Toward a science of the structure and acquisition of expert and elite performance. *International Journal of Sport Psychology, 38,* 4–34.

Ericsson, K. A., Krampe, R. Th., & Tesch-Römer, C. (1993). The role of deliberate practice in the acquisition of expert performance. *Psychological Review, 100*(3), 363–406.

Ericsson, K. A., & Ward, P. (2007). Capturing the naturally-occurring superior performance of experts in the laboratory: Toward a science of expert and exceptional performance. *Current Directions in Psychological Science, 16*(6), 346–350.

Feynman, R. P. (1974). Cargo Cult Science: Some remarks on science, pseudoscience, and learning how to not fool yourself (Caltech's 1974 commencement address). *Engineering and Science, 37*(7), 11–13.

Fleishman, E. A. (1953). Testing for psychomotor abilities by means of apparatus tests. *Psychological Bulletin, 50,* 241–262.

Ford, P., Ward, P., Hodges, N. J., & Williams, A. M. (2009). The role of deliberate practice and play in career progression in sport: The early engagement hypothesis. *High Ability Studies, 20*(1), 65–75.

Foster, S. L., & Cone, J. D. (1995). Validity issues in clinical assessment. *Psychological Assessment, 7*(3), 248–260.

Galton, F. (1869/1979). *Hereditary genius: An inquiry into its laws and consequences.* London: Julian Friedman Publishers. (Originally published in 1869).

Geron, E. (1978). Psychological assessment of sport giftedness. In U. Simiri (eds), *Proceedings of the international symposium on psychological assessment in sport* (pp. 216–231). Snetanya, Israel: Wingate Institute.

Gigerenzer, G. (2004). Mindless statistics. *The Journal of Socio-Economics, 33,* 587–606.

Grabner, R. H., Neubauer, A. C., & Stern, E. (2006). Superior performance and neural efficiency: The impact of intelligence and expertise. *Brain Research Bulletin, 69,* 422–439.

Hambrick D. Z., Oswald, F. L., Altmann, E. M., Meinz, E. J., Gobet, F., & Campitelli, G. (2014). Deliberate practice: Is that all it takes to become an expert? *Intelligence, 45,* 34–45.

Hambleton, R. K., & Jones, R. W. (1993). Influence of item parameter estimation errors in test development. *Journal of Educational Measurement, 30*(2), 143–155.

Hayward, C. M., & Gromko, J. E. (2009). Relationships among music sight-reading and technical proficiency, spatial visualization, and aural discrimination. *Journal of Research in Music Education, 60,* 81–100.

Helsen, W. F., & Starkes, J. L. (1999). A multidimensional approach to skilled perception and performance in sport. *Applied Cognitive Psychology, 13*(1), 1–27.

Helsen, W. F., Starkes, J. L., & Hodges, N. J. (1998). Team sports and the theory of deliberate practice. *Journal of Sport & Exercise Psychology, 20,* 12–34.

Henry, F. M. (1968). Specificity vs. generality in learning motor skills. In R. C. Brown and G. S. Kenyon (pp. 341–340). Englewood Cliffs, NJ: Prentice Hall.

Heslin, P. A., & Vandewalle, D. (2008). Managers' implicit assumptions about personnel. *Current Directions in Psychological Science, 17*(3), 219–223.

Heslin, P.A., Vandewalle, D., & Latham, G.P. (2006). Keen to help? Managers' implicit person theories and their subsequent employee coaching. *Personnel Psychology, 59,* 871–902.

Hodges, N. J., & Starkes, J. L. (1996). Wrestling with the nature of expertise: A sport specific test of Ericsson, Krampe and Tesch-Römer's (1993) theory of deliberate practice. *International Journal of Sport Psychology, 27,* 400–424.

Hoffman, R. R. (ed.) (2007). *Expertise out of context: Proceedings of the 6th Int'l Conf. on Naturalistic Decision Making.* Boca Raton, FL: Taylor and Francis.

Hoffman, R. R., & Ward, P. (2015). Mentoring: A leverage point for intelligent systems. *IEEE: Intelligent Systems—Human Centered Computing, 15,* 1541–1672.

Hoffman, R. R., Ward, P., Feltovich, P. J., DiBello, L., Fiore, S. M., & Andrews, D. (2014). *Accelerated expertise: Training for high proficiency in a complex world.* New York: Psychology Press.

Hong, Y., Chiu, C., Dweck, C. S., Lin, D. M.-S. S., & Wan, W. (1999). Implicit theories, attributions, and coping: A meaning system approach. *Journal of Personality and Social Psychology, 77*(3), 588–599.

Howard, R. W. (2012). Longitudinal effects of different types of practice on the development of chess expertise. *Applied Cognitive Psychology, 26,* 359–369.

Howe, M. J. A. (1990). *The origins of exceptional abilities.* Oxford, UK: Blackwell.

Humphreys, L. G., Buxton, C. E., & Taylor, H. R. (1936). Steadiness and rifle marksmanship. *Journal of Applied Psychology, 20,* 680–688.

Lord, F. M. (1980). *Applications of item response theory to practical testing problems.* New York: Routledge

Lyons, B., Hoffman, B., & Michel, J. (2009). Not much more than g? An examination of the impact of intelligence on NFL performance. *Human Performance, 22,* 225–245.

Mann, D. Y., Williams, A. M., Ward, P., & Janelle, C. M. (2007). Perceptual-cognitive expertise in sport: A meta-analysis. *Journal of Sport & Exercise Psychology, 29,* 457–478.

McCurdy, J. H. (1923). Physical efficiency standards. *American Physical Education Review, 28,* 109–110.

McFarland, R. A., & Franzen, R. (1944). *The Pensacola study of naval aviators. Final summary report* (Report No. 38). Washington, DC: CAA Division of Research.

McPherson, S. L., & French, K. E. (1991). Changes in cognitive strategies and motor skill in tennis, *Journal of Sport and Exercise Psychology, 13*(1), 26–41.

Meinz, E. J., & Hambrick, D. Z. (2010). Deliberate practice is necessary but not sufficient to explain individual differences in piano sight-reading skill: The role of working memory capacity. *Psychological Science, 21,* 914–919.

Melton, A. W. (Ed.) (1947). *Apparatus tests* (Army Air Forces, Aviation Psychology Program, Research Report 4). Washington, DC: U.S. Government Printing Office.

Newell, A. (1973). You can't play 20 questions with nature and win: Projective comments on the papers of this symposium. In W. G. Chase (ed.), *Visual information processing.* New York: Academic Press.

Petushek, E. J., Cokely, E. T., Ward, P., & Myer, G. D. (2015a). Injury risk estimation expertise: Cognitive-perceptual mechanisms of ACL-IQ. *Journal of Sport & Exercise Psychology, 37,* 291–304.

Petushek, E. J., Cokely, E. T., Ward, P., Durocher, J. J., Wallace, S., & Myer, G. D. (2015b). Injury risk estimation expertise: Assessing the ACL injury risk estimation quiz. *American Journal of Sports Medicine, 43*(7), 1640–1647.

Pienaar, A. E., & Spamer, M. J. (1998). A longitudinal study of talented young rugby players as regards their rugby skills, physical and motor abilities, and anthropometric data. *Journal of Human Movement Studies, 34,* 13–32.

Regnier, G., & Salmela, J. H. (1987). Predictors of success in Canadian male gymnasts. In B. Petiot, J. H. Salmela and T. B. Hoshizaki (eds), *World identification systems for gymnastic talent* (pp. 143–150). Montreal, QC: Sport Psyche Editions.

Reilly, T., Williams, A. M., Nevill, A., & Franks, A. (2000). A multidisciplinary approach to talent identification in soccer. *Journal of Sports Sciences, 18,* 695–702.

Ruthsatz, J., Detterman, D., Griscom, W. S., & Cirullo, B. A. (2008). Becoming an expert in the musical domain: It takes more than just practice. *Intelligence, 36,* 330–338.

Schmidt, F. L., & Hunter, J. E. (1992). Development of causal models of processes determining job performance. *Current Directions in Psychological Science, 1,* 89–92.

Simonton, D. K. (2000). Creative development as acquired expertise: Theoretical issues and an empirical test. *Developmental Review, 20,* 283–318.

Spray, C. M., Wang, C. K. J., Biddle, S. J. H., Chatzisarantis, N. L. D., & Warburton, V. E. (2006). An experimental test of self-theories of ability in youth sport, *Psychology of Sport and Exercise, 7*(3), 255–267.

Starkes, J. L., & Deakin, J. M. (1984). Perception in sport: A cognitive approach to skilled performance. In W. F. Straub & J. M. Williams (eds), *Cognitive Sport Psychology.* Lansing, NY: Sports Science Associates.

Sternberg, R. J. (1999). A dialectical basis for understanding the study of cognition. In R. J. Sternberg (ed.), *The nature of cognition* (pp. 51–78). Boston, MA: MIT Press.

Tabernero, C., & Wood, R. E. (1999). Implicit theories versus the social construal of ability in self-regulation and performance on a complex task. *Organizational Behavior and Human Decision Processes, 78*(2), 104–127.

Thorndike, E. L. (1912). *Education: A first book.* New York: Macmillan.

Vandenberg, S. G., & Kuse, A. R. (1978). Mental rotations, a group test of three-dimensional spatial visualization. *Perceptual and Motor Skills, 69,* 915–921.

Vaeyens, V., Lenoir, M., Williams, A. M., & Philippaerts, R. M. (2008). Talent identification and development programmes in sport: Current models and future directions. *Sports Medicine, 38,* 703–714.

Voss, M. W., Kramer, A. F., Basak, C., Prakash, R. S., & Roberts, B. (2010). Are expert athletes 'expert' in the cognitive laboratory? A meta-analytic review of cognition and sport expertise. *Applied Cognitive Psychology, 24,* 812–826.

Walker, R. Y., & Adams, R. D. (1934). Motor skills: The validity of serial motor tests for predicting typewriter proficiency. *Journal of General Psychology, 11,* 173–186.

Wang, C. K. J., & Biddle, S. J. H. (2003). Intrinsic motivation towards sports in Singaporean students: The role of sport ability beliefs. *Journal of Health Psychology, 8*(5), 515–523.

Ward, P. (2014, May). *Accelerating Expertise via Adaptive Cognitive Engineering (AcE2).* Keynote lecture, Annual Conference of the British Psychological Society-Expertise and Skill Acquisition Network, Sheffield, UK.

Ward, P., Farrow, D., Harris, K. R., Williams, A. M., Eccles, D. W., & Ericsson, K. A. (2008). Training perceptual-cognitive skills: Can sport psychology research inform military decision training? *Military Psychology, 20,* S71–S102.

Ward, P., Hodges, N. J., Starkes, J. L., & Williams, A. M. (2007). The road to excellence: Deliberate practice and the development of expertise. *High Ability Studies, 18*(2), 119–153.

Ward, P., Hutton, R., Hoffman, R. R., Gore, J., Anderson, T., & Leggatt, A. (2016). *Developing skilled adaptive performance: A scoping study. Final Technical Report.* UK Defence Science & Technology Laboratory, Ministry of Defence Report (O-DHCSTC_I2_T_T2_077_005). Yeovil, UK: BAE Systems.

Ward, P., Suss, J., & Basevitch, I. (2009). Expertise and expert performance-based training (ExPerT) in complex domains. *Technology, Instruction, Cognition and Learning, 7*(2), 121–145.

Ward, P., & Williams, A. M. (2003). Perceptual and cognitive skill development in soccer: The multidimensional nature of expert performance. *Journal of Sport & Exercise Psychology, 25*(1), 93–111.

Ward, P., Williams, A. M., & Hancock, P. A. (2006). Simulation for performance and training. In K. A. Ericsson, N. Charness, P. J. Feltovich & R. R. Hoffman (eds), *The Cambridge handbook of expertise and expert performance* (pp. 243–262). New York: Cambridge University Press.

Wigdor, A. K., & Green, B. F. (1991). *Performance assessment for the workplace, Vol. 1 & II.* Washington, DC: National Academy Press.

Williams, A. M., & Davids, K. (1995). Declarative knowledge in sport: A byproduct of experience or a characteristic of expertise? *Journal of Sport & Exercise Psychology, 17*(3), 259–275.

Williams, A. M., & Reilly, T. (2000). Talent identification and development in soccer. *Journal of Sports Sciences, 18*, 657–667.

Yerkes, R. M. (1921). *Psychological examining in the United States Army: Memoirs of the National Academy of Sciences (Volume XV)*. Washington, DC: Government Printing Office.

4

CONCEPTIONS OF GIFTEDNESS AND TALENT

Christiane Fischer-Ontrup and Christian Fischer

Chapter overview

In this chapter, we provide a brief initial overview of the development of giftedness and talent research in different domains. In doing so, we define and compare relevant terms and concepts. This is followed by a survey of the different research approaches in this area, outlined from a psychological and educational perspective. We also highlight the models and factors that have attempted to account for gifted education and talent development in particular contexts. In the final section, we summarize the phenomenology of existing research and attempt to provide an integrated concept of research on gifted education and talent development. Taken together, the chapter provides some insight into why so many different approaches are taken and how unconcise terminology is often used in talent research.

Definitions of giftedness and talent

With regard to the historical development of giftedness research, several milestones can be identified, all of which call for a discussion of the terminology and definitions of high giftedness or special talents. Modern giftedness research was launched at the turn of the twentieth century and was closely linked with the initiation of intelligence research. During that era, the German psychologist Stern (1916) introduced the term 'intelligence quotient' (IQ), which is still the dominating standardized measure to diagnose and assess a person's intellectual capacity. Stern (1928, p. 344) defines intelligence 'as a person's individual ability to employ purposeful cognitive means to confront new challenges'. Stern's IQ formed the basis for one of the first and most extensive and complex longitudinal developmental giftedness studies (Genetic Study of Genius) with more than 1,500 subjects. It began in 1921 and was carried on by Terman and colleagues, using an IQ > 135 as a selection criterion (Terman & Merrill, 1937; Terman & Oden, 1948, 1967) to investigate the influence of high intelligence on the development of excellent performance. For this study, Terman refined the first standardized intelligence test developed by Binet and Simon (1908), which was then used in the survey as the Stanford-Binet Intelligence Scale (1916). Terman and colleagues discovered that a high intelligence score was not enough to predict excellent performance in intellectual domains. In addition, they learned that a distinctive motivation and a stimulating environment were essential to develop expertise that was visible, for example, in Nobel-prize laureates (Ericsson, Prietula, & Cokely, 2007).

As regards the relationship between particular giftedness and high intelligence, two main views are expressed in scientific publications. In the first, one-factorial approaches equate intelligence with giftedness (e.g., Rost, 2000); however, in large part due to the results of the Terman study, most researchers see this concept as more complex (e.g., Sternberg & Davidson, 2005). Representatives of a multi-factorial concept, define high giftedness as high general intelligence plus additional factors. Yet, it should be noted that the understanding and meaning of intelligence differs across different conceptualizations (e.g., fluid versus crystallized intelligence, see Catell, 1963). This also applies to the notion of creativity, which is considered an integral element in the 'Intelligence Structure Concept' (Guilford, 1965) and in the 'Berlin Intelligence Structure Model' (Jäger, 1982). Moreover, Guilford (1967), considered to be the founder of creativity research, makes a difference between convergent and divergent thinking as two mutually complementary processes. A similar differentiation is found rather early in Stern (1928) who distinguishes between reactive and spontaneous intelligence. Guilford's creativity concept (1965) suggests five individual abilities (fluency, flexibility, originality, elaboration, sensibility for problems). These aspects have also received attention in more recent creativity research (Facaoaru, 1985) and have been further differentiated in Urban's (2000) 'Components Model of Creativity'. All this to say that different models use the term 'intelligence' in different ways, and therefore have differing views on the definitions of giftedness and talent. We elaborate on this below.

Various terms for giftedness and talent

Giftedness and talent researchers use different expressions to describe similar terminology, and these differences require explanation. One of the challenges in this area is that many terms are used synonymously (e.g., giftedness, high giftedness, particular giftedness, high ability, talent or genius). When 'particular giftedness' is defined in scientific publications, there is a clear tendency to differentiate between high giftedness and high achievement. In general, talent is defined as individual ability (i.e., potential) for particular achievements (i.e., performance). Stern (1916, p. 110) emphasized that 'talents in themselves, in all instances, just contain the potential for achievements; they are the indispensable precondition, but not the achievement itself'. Heller (2000, p. 241) sees high giftedness as an 'individual's ability potential for excellent achievements', which means that underachievers showing a significantly negative discrepancy between their intelligence and school achievements, can also be considered for high giftedness (Butler-Por, 1987). Ziegler, Ziegler, and Stöger (2012), alluding to the Delphic definition, suggests distinguishing between the following terms: (1) Talent denotes a person who will *possibly* at some point in the future reach achievement excellence; (2) a highly gifted person will *probably* at some point in the future reach achievement excellence; (3) an expert (high performer) is a person who has reached achievement excellence; and (4) an underachiever is a person whose achievement is at present hampered and who lives with the risk of non-intervention leading to unfavourable prognoses for the continuation of his or her achievement development (Ziegler et al., 2012).

The expertise approach

Psychological publications increasingly deal with expertise alongside giftedness research. Gruber and Mandl (1992, p. 59) put it rather provocatively: 'The expert has replaced the gifted person.' In the footsteps of Posner (1988), Schneider (1999, p. 83) defines an expert as 'a person who permanently performs with excellence in a particular field', with comprehensive (previously acquired) knowledge and rich experience in the expertise area (domain) being decisive criteria. Expertise acquisition is, in this context, regarded as experience based on the adaptation to the typical requirements of a domain, and described as the process of the emergence of a person's achievement excellence in a particular, frequently professional area, which typically develops over an extended period of at least ten years (Ericsson et al., 2007). Expertise research largely uses retrospective approaches to explore the decisive conditions of development through expert-novice (or non-expert) comparisons. These factors can also help understand the significant causes of achievement, particularly of the exceptionally gifted. The emergence of achievement excellence can be explained with the help of the performance-oriented 'deliberate practice concept', which regards efficient learning processes as causal mechanisms for a learner's transition from one level of competence to the next (Ericsson et al., 2007).

Different definitions of giftedness

Besides the outlined general definitions of high giftedness, which are still widely accepted, there are other more detailed definitions with different foci. Lucito's (1964) classification summarizes more than 100 definitions of high giftedness published to date. For example, instances of outstanding performance by geniuses serve as social reference points for socially perceived valuable activities. IQ threshold values such as an IQ > 130 (IQ definitions) define intelligence; percentile rankings (e.g., > 98%) describe performance test based definitions; while novelty and uniqueness are used to reflect creative definitions of giftedness. This classification will, however, not always prove selective since the grade of intelligence may be expressed by the IQ as well as by percentile ranking. Another classification of definitions was suggested by Sternberg and Davidson (2005) who used various models as a starting point and used ability potential as a means of orientation, based on psychometric concepts (ability-oriented or trait-oriented models), processes of information processing using concepts of cognitive psychology (cognitive component models), high achievements as found in expertise concepts (achievement-oriented models) and environmental factors for the transformation of giftedness into achievement (socio-culturally oriented models).

In the 'Marland Definition' (Marland, 1972), which was widely influential, especially in the USA, high giftedness is understood to be excellent ability potential to reach notable achievements (see Table 4.1) in the intellectual, creative, social, artistic and psychomotor fields. Thus, this definition is largely in compliance with the mentioned ability-oriented models with a specification of the relevant intellectual and non-intellectual talents.

Table 4.1 Elements of giftedness as noted in the Marland Definition

1. General Intellectual Ability
2. Specific Academic Aptitude
3. Creative or Productive Thinking
4. Leadership Ability
5. Visual and Performing Arts
6. Psychomotor Ability

Source: Marland Report, 1972.

Gardner's theory of intelligences

Gardner's very popular 'Theory of Multiple Intelligences' (1983) is based on an extended notion of intelligence (see Table 4.2), which approximates several multi-factorial intelligence concepts. The intellectual talents (Linguistic, Spatial, Logical-Mathematical) correspond primarily to the content areas of the classical concepts of intelligence (e.g., in the Berlin Intelligence Structure Model). The non-intellectual talents (Bodily-Kinesthetic, Musical, Interpersonal, Intrapersonal) exhibit a specification similar to the corresponding fields of the 'Marland Definition'. In his more recent publications, Gardner (1991) expands his theory by adding one more intelligence (i.e., Naturalistic Intelligence, relating to understanding nature). This notion of multiple intelligences has been debated in the research literature. Whereas Heller (2005) sympathizes with the methodological creation of these relatively autonomous competences, Rost (2000) is doubtful as to the empirical foundation of the non-intellectual intelligences.

Quantitative definitions of giftedness

The operational definition of high giftedness and talent depends largely on the respective theoretical definition. If one follows the ability-oriented concepts of the psychometric tradition, high giftedness is understood to denote the disposition for high achievements. The operationalization of ability potential, as performed by the adherents of a one-factorial giftedness concept, is restricted to the construct of intelligence. Based on the intelligence concepts described above, intelligence is primarily ascertained through the results of standardized intelligence tests. The described IQ or percentage definitions allow further categorization: High (or above average) achievements in intelligence tests with an IQ $\geq$ 130 (or $\geq$ 115) and percentile rank $\geq$ 97.5 (or 85) are considered on a par (Webb, Meckstroth, & Tolan, 1982). In terms of the Gaussian normal distribution curve, these threshold values correspond, for example, to 1 standard deviation above average, which suggests a frequency of 15 per cent in an age group. Too rigid boundaries should, however, be avoided, primarily because intelligence tests are frequently based on different theories of intelligence and because there can be overlapping transitions between particular and normal talents. Supporters of multi-factorial giftedness concepts are also faced with the problem of operationalizing the additional factors, primarily creativity. According to Cropley, McLeod, and Dehn (1988), creativity is a construct that cannot easily be operationalized and, as a consequence, there are hardly any general methods of testing. According to Rost (2000), the same applies to the non-intellectual factors, such as socio-emotional talents.

Table 4.2 Gardner's (1991) Multiple Intelligences

1. Spatial Intelligence
2. Bodily-Kinesthetic Intelligence
3. Musical Intelligence
4. Linguistic Intelligence
5. Logical-Mathematical Intelligence
6. Interpersonal Intelligence
7. Intrapersonal Intelligence
8. Naturalistic Intelligence

Qualitative definitions of giftedness

Whereas the definitions based on psychometric concepts are mainly derived from quantitative differences between particular and normal talents, cognitive psychological concepts assume qualitative differences (Facaoaru & Bittner, 1987). From the cognitive psychological point of view, high giftedness may be defined as a quantitatively accelerated, but qualitatively altered process of information processing (Waldmann & Weinert, 1990). In contrast to classical psychometric (i.e., more status-oriented) giftedness research, more recent cognitive psychological (i.e., more process-oriented) concepts predominantly explore learning and thinking processes. But cognitive psychological test methods, which aim at a systematic inclusion of qualitative changes in problem-solving processes, have so far been unsatisfactorily devised. Psychometric test methods, on the other hand, can only measure quantitative giftedness differences, so that according to Hany (1993) the assessment of qualitative giftedness differences is at present unsatisfactory. This applies to the above mentioned expertise concept too, which assumes quantitative but also qualitative differences in the expert-novice comparison, for instance in problem solving processes. Experts, as opposed to novices, exhibit increased and altered learning and thinking strategies (e.g., accessing knowledge, metacognition), which are relevant for the acquisition of expertise in their specific domain.

Taken together, the sections above highlight the considerable range in definitions of giftedness used in research. Many of the differences in these definitions are explained by the concepts or models underpinning them, but administering the same term for different ideas can become a challenge to our understanding.

Models of giftedness and talent

The outlined definitions of giftedness are closely linked with individual models/conceptions of giftedness and talent. While the mentioned general intelligence models are used for one-factorial giftedness models, multi-factorial giftedness models are more precisely explained by means of special high giftedness models. These models describe the phenomenon of particular talents (or excellent achievements), and explain the origin of high giftedness (or high achievement). Models of giftedness have undergone a historical change, too, not just with regard to the differentiation between giftedness and achievement, but also the transformation of potential into performance.

Multi-component models of giftedness

While multi-dimensional, multi-component models (e.g., Renzulli & Reis, 1997; Mönks, 1996) implicitly consider high giftedness and high achievement to be the same, transformation-oriented moderator models (e.g., Heller, 2005; Gagné, 2008) explicitly regard high giftedness as potential for high achievement. Stern (1916, p. 110) placed emphasis on the question of achievement development: 'For life achievement, [i.e.,] the transformation of subjective capabilities into objective, valuable pieces of work, is essential. That is why psychology must investigate what other mental qualities must be added to giftedness to determine the achievement.' Stern (1916) quotes interest and, more importantly, will as substantial conditions for the transformation of high giftedness into high achievement, which are implicitly taken into account in different giftedness models in the form of motivation.

Renzulli's model of giftedness

In the 1970s, the American psychologist Renzulli (1978) developed the 'Three-Ring Concept of Giftedness' (see Figure 4.1), based on the insight that talent is not only explained by the development of high intellectual abilities. This model defines high giftedness as an intersecting set of three personality characteristics: above-average abilities, task commitment, and creativity. The distinct emergence of these individual components and their successful interaction form a decisive condition for the development of giftedness. According to Renzulli (1986), above-average abilities comprise (1) general abilities in the cognitive area (i.e., general intelligence) and (2) specific abilities in non-cognitive areas (e.g., music, art). Renzulli views task commitment as a focused kind of motivation, which, in the form of intensive engagement (e.g., perseverance, self-confidence), is directed towards a specific domain. Renzulli (1993) defines creativity as a special form of thinking in which fluidity, flexibility and originality excel. This model has been met with some criticism, largely because of the implicit equalization of giftedness and achievement so that underachievers are scarcely considered (Rost et al., 1991a, 1991b). The most important modifications were then made by Renzulli himself (1997), who specified high giftedness as highly gifted behaviour (i.e., high achievement) and attributed its emergence to environmental and personality factors. With this modification, Renzulli (2002) placed emphasis on the relevance of intelligences outside the normal distribution in the form of co-cognitive characteristics (optimism, courage, obsession with a topic or discipline, physical and mental energy, vision and a sense of destiny, and a sense of power to change things), which are of equal importance for the person and society.

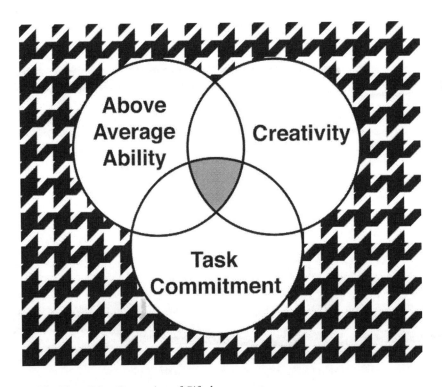

Figure 4.1 The Three-Ring Conception of Giftedness

Source: adapted from Renzulli, 2005 with the permission of Cambridge University Press.

Mönks's model of giftedness

In the 1980s, Renzulli's original model of high giftedness was refined by Mönks (1985) into the 'Multifactor Model of Giftedness' (see Figure 4.2). Similar to Renzulli, it is based on three personality features (i.e., excellent abilities, creativity and task commitment), forming a triad with mutual influence and containing the decisive constituents of high giftedness. Afterwards, Mönks (1996) refined these terms by referring excellent abilities primarily to the domain of intelligence and replacing task commitment by motivation. Thus, he also takes into account, if only partly, Renzulli's criticism of the lack of terminological precision. Due to his background in developmental psychology, Mönks (2000) argues that the development of giftedness is determined by the interaction of environmental and hereditary personality factors. This concept puts into perspective the intensive discussion about the validity of a static (i.e., hereditary) vs. dynamic (i.e., culturally stimulated) conception of giftedness, especially with regard to the interaction of endowment and acquisition. More recently, this debate has been relativized by epigenetics, in particular because the activation of the individual genetic disposition may be strongly controlled by environmental experiences. Mönks (1992) explains that optimal development depends on the known personality features and requires the support of adequate social and environmental features. For Mönks (2000), family, school and peers are the central environmental areas, which, as a second triad, contribute to the realization of the personality

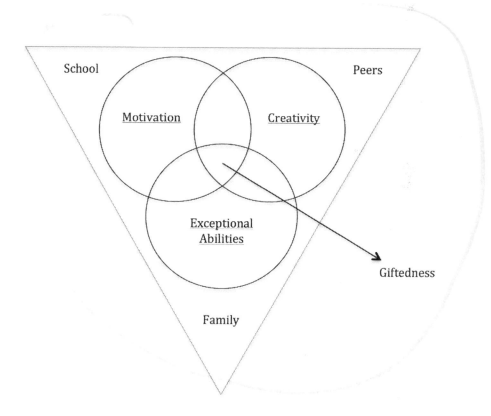

Figure 4.2 The Multifactor Model of Giftedness
Source: adapted from Mönks, 1996.

features. A successful interaction of the two triads presupposes the individual's social competence, which functions as a link between the person and the environment. Like Renzulli's model, this model also has evoked criticism, mainly because of a lack of differentiation between giftedness and achievement and an insufficient specification of the individual environmental factors (Rost, 1991b).

Moderator models of giftedness

Criticism of the implicit equalization of high giftedness and high achievement in multi-component models (Renzulli, 1997; Mönks, 1996) has also been directed towards the lack of differentiation between moderating and constituting factors. Whereas high abilities and creativity can be classified as constituent giftedness factors, motivation and environment can be assigned as factors moderating the relationships between giftedness and achievement. More recent moderator models (Heller, 2005; Gagné, 2008) take this criticism into account and differentiate clearly between forms of giftedness (i.e., potential), achievement areas (i.e., performance) and mediating factors (e.g., motivation). The latter has impact as it can explain the individual learning and development process leading to achievement excellence, but can also account for the causes of learning difficulties. From a certain giftedness threshold in either the intellectual or the creative sphere, this applies, above all, to the role of motivation, which may set the stage for either high achievement or underachievement (Schneider, 1992). More recent giftedness models also contain descriptions of further factors, differentiating between internal personal and external factors caused by the environment. The model of giftedness proposed by Heller, Perleth and Lim (2005), delineates the conditional factors as moderators, whereas Gagné (2005) refers to these as catalysts in his model of giftedness. In both models, the internal and external moderators or catalysts are considered to be trans-sectorally active in the transformation of the different giftedness concepts into the different achievement areas.

Heller's model of giftedness

In the 'Munich Model of Giftedness', Heller (2001) distinguishes between different intellectual and non-intellectual types of giftedness (predictors), which designate excellent in-school and out-of-school achievements (criteria) (see Figure 4.3). This predictor-criterion relationship is systematically influenced by process variables (moderators) in the form of non-cognitive personality and socio-environmental features. Taking these aspects into account, Heller (2001) distinguishes between, among other things, intellectual, creative, social, musical and psychomotor competences, regarding them as individual ability potentials. These individual forms of giftedness, which are as a rule, not always easily distinguishable, can more or less clearly be linked with certain achievement areas (e.g., mathematics, languages, conduct, music, sports). The non-cognitive personality features include, among others, achievement motivation, stress management as well as working and learning strategies, which prove relevant for the acquisition of expertise. Thus, a close link with the environmental factors is established, particularly with regard to the instruction quality in school environments and within the family. This model has undergone significant changes over time, above all with regard to the growing specialization of the predictor, criterion and moderator variables (Heller & Hany, 1986). The 'Munich Process Model of Giftedness' (Perleth & Ziegler, 1997) and the 'Munich Dynamic Achievement Model' (Perleth, 2001) present an interesting expansion of Heller's initial model, which attempts to bridge the gap between giftedness and expertise research, placing emphasis on the active learning processes.

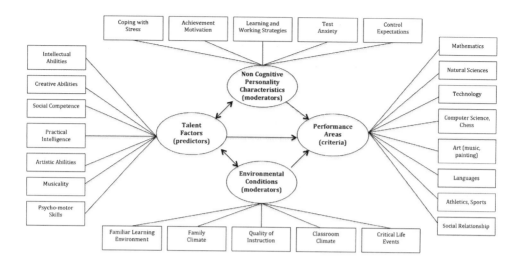

Figure 4.3 The Munich Model of Giftedness

Source: adapted from Heller, Perleth & Lim, 2005.

Gagné's model of giftedness

Gagné's 'Differentiated Model of Giftedness and Talent' (2008) explicitly mentions the transformation of natural abilities (giftedness) into systematically developed skills (talent) as crucial factors for the learning and development process (see Figure 4.4). This process, realized by formal and informal learning and practice, may be affected positively, but also adversely by intrapersonal and environmental catalysts, so that this model also considers underachievers. Gagné also considers the natural abilities factor by distinguishing between mental (intellectual, creative, social, perceptual) and physical (muscular, motor control) abilities, which can be further differentiated (Gagné, 1993). This also applies to achievement areas (e.g., academic, technical, artistic, social, sports and athletic talents), which Gagné (1993, 2000), deviating from other concepts, refers to as talents. Gagné (2000) emphasizes the relevance of intrapersonal catalysts for the transformation of abilities into achievements, mentioning goal-management (motivation, awareness, volition) and traits (physical, mental). With regard to environmental catalysts, Gagné (2005) stresses the relevance of individuals, provisions and the milieu, pointing out that these factors also offer an explanation for the dependence on the specially introduced random factor (i.e., chance). Despite the somewhat vague terminology, Gagné's differentiated model is a suitable tool to assess achievement excellence and also to explain learning difficulties, due to the close interconnection of personality and environmental factors.

Ziegler's model of giftedness

Alongside one-dimensional intelligence models, multi-dimensional multi-component models, transformation-oriented moderator models, and performance-oriented 'deliberate-practice' approaches, the systemic 'Actiotope Concept' remains to be explained. According to Ziegler (2005) an actiotope comprises an individual and the material, social and informational

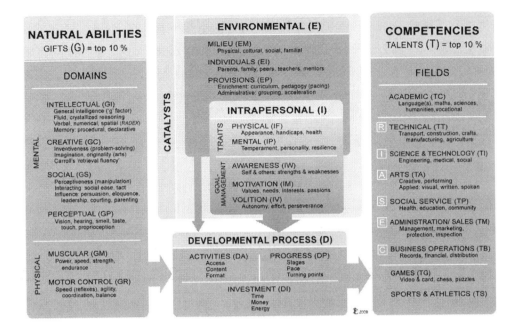

Figure 4.4 The Differentiated Model of Giftedness and Talent

Source: Gagné, 2008.

environment with which he or she 'actively' interacts. Understanding excellence is the central focus of the 'Actiotope Concept', as it attempts to comprehend the person's process of adaptation to special environments, providing functional action repertoires for certain (achievement) domains (Ziegler & Stöger, 2011). The 'Actiotope Model of Giftedness' (see Figure 4.5; Ziegler, 2005) denotes a person as talented if a learning path in a talent domain can be identified for him or her, which bridges the gap between the present action repertoire and the repertoire of achievement excellence. From a systemic point of view, the individual's exogenous and endogenous resources gain relevance, which describe different categories of educational and learning assets (Ziegler & Stöger, 2011). In this model, exogenous resources denote forms of educational assets, which are supplied by society to improve educational and learning processes (i.e., economic, cultural, social, infrastructural, didactic), whereas endogenous resources are exclusively available to an individual, delineate that person's learning assets (organismic, telic, actional, episodic, alternative) (Ziegler & Stöger, 2013).

A potential integration of models

It is beneficial to summarize the various definitions and models of giftedness and talent, and to evaluate their impact on what we understand to be the underpinning of talent. In this respect, the inclusion of non-intellectual alongside intellectual/intelligence factors with regard to the diversity of talent facets within a domain (e.g., in sport and music) is considered. Based on our assessment, it seems that the distinction between potential and performance turns out to be essential (e.g., Gardner, 1991; Heller, et al., 2005). Giftedness may here be understood as

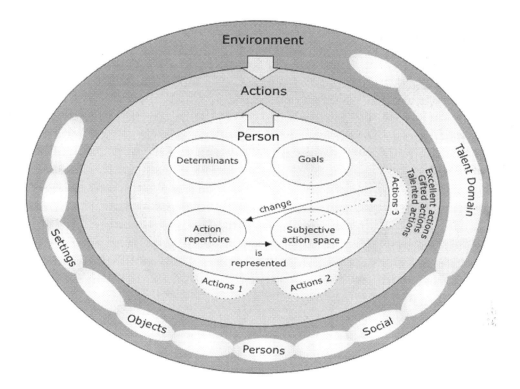

Figure 4.5 The Actiotope Model of Giftedness
Source: Ziegler, 2005.

denoting a *potential ability for particular achievement domains*. As regards the operationalization of (high) talent and giftedness, it seems appropriate to expand their limitations as proposed in the existing models (e.g., Renzulli, 1997; Mönks, 2000), so that the upper 10–15 per cent of a peer group may be included. The transformation of potential into performance is also of great relevance, with the learning process according to Weinert (2000) being the decisive mechanism for the transformation of talent and giftedness into excellent achievements. Also, internal and external conditional factors (i.e., endogenous and exogenous resources) are particularly relevant in identifying (in)efficient learning processes that moderate the occurrence of outstanding or reduced achievements (e.g., high or deficient achievement; Gagné, 2005, Ziegler, 2005).

As a consequence of criticisms of existing approaches to giftedness, the 'Integrative Giftedness and Learning Process Model' (Fischer, 2012) was developed (see Figure 4.6). This model attempts to integrate the strengths of existing giftedness models and to specify – against the background of systemic action models (e.g., Ziegler, 2005) – approaches towards individual giftedness promotion with regard to target-oriented learning activities, performed by the learner in his or her learning environment, relative to his or her achievement development. The circularity of the learning and development process may not only lead to the achievement level being conditioned by the giftedness range, but may also result in potential development being influenced by performance evolvement.

Following propositions of there being multiple intelligences (Gardner, 1991) and the ideas of intelligence structure models (Jäger, 1982), the Integrative Giftedness and Learning Process

Model attempts to systematize the giftedness factors. Taking the criticism of existing giftedness models (Rost, 2000) into account, this model offers a clearer separation of intellectual (e.g., verbal, numeric, visual-spatial) and non-intellectual (e.g., psycho-motor, music-artistic, social-emotional) talents. This applies mainly to the creativity construct, which can be relevant for all domains of giftedness and talent (e.g., verbal/poetry, numeric/architecture, musical/composition, motor/dance). The model then matches these forms of giftedness with corresponding achievement areas (e.g., languages, mathematics, music, sport), allowing further diversifications within a domain (e.g., light athletics, gymnastics, swimming, ball games). The categorization of environmental factors is based on multi-component models (e.g., Renzulli, 1997; Mönks, 1999), followed by further specifications.

Essential social areas (family, pre-school, school, peer group) can exercise a decisive influence on the learning process by way of creating specific learning environments (learning advice, teaching strategies, achievement training). This also holds for personality factors (e.g., achievement motivation, self-management, learning strategies), within which a great deal of the individual features of the moderator models of giftedness (e.g., Munich Model of Giftedness, Differentiated Model of Giftedness and Talent) may also be considered. In this respect, occasional instances of smooth transitions between giftedness types (e.g., socio-emotional talents) and personality factors (e.g., learning motivation, self-management) may become obvious (e.g., Renzulli, 2002), which can result in environmental and personality factors mutually influencing one another in a positive or negative way (e.g., relationship and self-concept). From a systemic point of view, mutual influence (e.g., stimulation and motivation) may occur – not least – in special target groups, for instance gifted children from minorities (e.g., Stamm, 2014) or twice-exceptional children (e.g., Lupart & Toy, 2009).

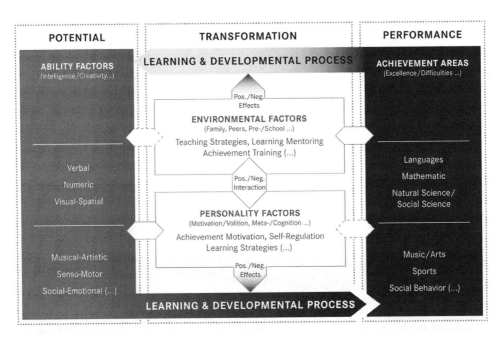

Figure 4.6 Integrative Model of Giftedness and Learning
Source: Fischer, 2012.

Summary

As this review and discussion has highlighted, there continues to be considerable debate and uncertainty about how to define and conceptualize talent and giftedness among researchers in giftedness and talent areas. Although differences in definitions and explanatory models can lead to difficulties in applying these concepts in learning and development environments, they clearly demonstrate that the prevention of underachievement as well as the development of excellence continue to represent major challenges for our development systems (educational and sporting) as well as broader society.

References

Binet, A., & Simon, T. (1908). Le développement de l'intelligence chez les enfants. *Annual Psychology, 14,* 1–94.

Butler-Por, N. (1987). *Underachievers in school. Issues and intervention.* Chichester: John Wiley & Sons Ltd.

Cattell, R. B. (1963). Theory of fluid and crystallized intelligence: A critical experiment. *Journal of Educational Psychology, 54,* 1–22.

Cattell, R. B. (1965). *The scientific analysis of personality.* Chicago: Aldine Pub.

Cropley, A., McLeod, J., & Dehn, D. (1988). *Giftedness and gifted education* (Begabung und Begabungsförderung). Heidelberg: Asanger Roland.

Ericsson, K. A., Prietula, M. J., & Cokely, E. T. (2007). The making of an expert. *Harvard Business Review* (July–August 2007).

Facaoaru, C. (1985). *Creativity in Science and Technology* (Kreativität in Wissenschaft und Technik). Bern: Huber.

Facaoaru, C., & Bittner, R. (1987). Approaches to diagnosis of high giftedness in cognitive psychology (Kognitionspsychologische Ansätze der Hochbegabungsdiagnostik). *Diagnosis of high giftedness. Journal for Differential and Diagnostic Psychology* (Hochbegabungsdiagnostik. Zeitschrift für Differentielle und Diagnostische Psychologie), *3,* 227–233.

Fischer, C. (2012). Individual teaching and learning strategies in gifted education (Individuelle Lehr- und Lernstrategien in der Begabtenförderung). In C. Fischer, C. Fischer-Ontrup, F. Käpnick, F. J. Mönks, H. Scheerer, & C. Solzbacher (eds), *Individual promotion of multiple talents* (Individuelle Förderung multipler Begabungen) (pp. 253–267). Berlin: LIT-Verlag.

Gagné, F. (1993). Constructs and models pertaining to exceptional human abilities. In K. A. Heller, F. J. Mönks & A. H. Passow (eds), *International handbook of research and development of giftedness and talent.* Oxford: Pergamon.

Gagné, F. (2000). Understanding the complex choreography of talent development through DMGT-based analysis. In K. A. Heller, F. J. Mönks, R. J. Sternberg, & R. Subotnik (eds), *International handbook of giftedness and talent* (2nd ed., pp. 67–79). Oxford: Elsevier Science.

Gagné, F. (2005). From gifts to talents: The DMGT as a developmental model. In R. J. Sternberg & J. E. Davidson (eds), *Conceptions of giftedness* (pp. 99–119). New York: Cambridge University Press.

Gagné, F. (2008). The differentiated model of giftedness and talent (DMGT). In J. S. Renzulli, E. J. Gubbins, K. McMillen, R. D. Eckert, & C. A. Little (eds), *Systems and models for developing programs for the gifted and talented* (2nd ed.). Mansfield Center, CT: Creative Learning Press.

Gardner, H. (1983). *Frames of mind: The theory of multiple intelligences.* New York: Basic Books.

Gardner, H. (1991). *Creating minds: An anatomy of creativity seen through the lives of Freud, Einstein, Picasso, Stravinsky, Eliot, Graham and Gandhi.* New York: Basic Books.

Gruber, H., & Mandl, H. (1992). Giftedness and expertise (Begabung und Expertise). In E. A. Hany & H. Nickel (eds), *Giftedness and high giftedness: Theoretical concepts, empirical findings, practical consequences* (Begabung und Hochbegabung. Theoretische Konzepte, empirische Befunde, praktische Konsequenzen) (pp. 125–142). Bern: Huber.

Guilford, J. P. (1965). Creativity. In W. B. Barbe (ed.), *Psychology and education of the gifted: Selected readings* (pp. 455–472). New York: Appleton-Century-Crofts.

Guilford, J. P. (1967). Three aspects of intellectual giftedness (Drei Aspekte der intellektuellen Begabung). In F. Weinert (ed.), *Pedagogical psychology* (Pädagogische Psychologie) (pp. 118–136). Köln: Beltz.

Hany, E. A. (1993). Methodological problems and issues concerning identification. In K. A. Heller, F. J.

Mönks & A. H. Passow (eds), *International handbook of research and development of giftedness and talent* (pp. 209–232). Oxford: Pergamon.

Heller, K. A. (2000). Diagnosing high giftedness (Hochbegabungsdiagnostik). In K. A. Heller (ed.), *Coursebook of giftedness diagnosis for pedagogical educational counselling* (Lehrbuch Begabungsdiagnostik in der Schul- und Erziehungsberatung) (pp. 241–256). Göttingen: Hogrefe.

Heller, K. A. (2001). Project objectives, research results, and practical consequences (Projektziele, Untersuchungsergebnisse und praktische Konsequenzen). In K. A. Heller (ed.), *High giftedness in childhood and adolescence* (Hochbegabung im Kindes- und Jugendalter) (pp. 21–40). Göttingen: Hogrefe.

Heller, K. A. (2005). The Munich Model of Giftedness and its impact on identification and programming. *Gifted and Talented International, 20,* 30–36.

Heller, K. A., & Hany, E. A. (1986). Identification, development, and achievement analysis of talented and gifted children in West Germany. In K. A. Heller & J. F. Feldhusen (eds), *Identifying and nurturing the gifted* (pp. 67–82). Toronto: Huber.

Heller, K. A., Perleth, C., & Lim, T. K. (2005). The Munich Model of Giftedness designed to identify and promote gifted students. In R. J. Sternberg & J. E. Davidson (eds), *Conceptions of Giftedness* (2nd ed., pp. 147–170). New York: Cambridge University Press.

Jäger, A. O. (1982). Multi-dimensional classification of intelligence achievements: An experimentally controlled advancement of an intelligence structure model (Mehrdimensionale Klassifikation von Intelligenztestleistungen. Experimentell kontrollierte Weiterentwicklung eines deskriptiven Intelligenzstrukturmodells). *Diagnostica, 28,* 145–226.

Lucito, L. J. (1964). Gifted children. In L. M. Dunn (ed.), *Exceptional children in the schools* (pp. 179–238). New York: Holt, Rinehart and Winston.

Lupart, J. L., & Toy, R. E. (2009). Twice exceptional: Multiple pathways to success. In L. V. Shavinina (ed.), *International handbook on giftedness: Part one* (pp. 507–525). Niederlande: Springer.

Marland, S. P., Jr. (1972). Education of the gifted and talented: Report to the Congress of the United States by the U.S. *Commissioner of Education and background papers submitted to the U.S. Office of Educations* (2nd ed.). Washington, DC: U.S. Government Printing Office.

Mönks, F. J. (1985). High giftedness: A sketch-map (Hoogbegaafden: een situatieschets). In F. J. Mönks & P. Span (eds), *Highly gifted in society* (Hoogbegaafden in de samenleving) (pp. 17–32). Nijmegen: Gorcum b.v.

Mönks, F. J. (1992). Education of the gifted Europe. Theoretical and research issues. *Report of the Educational Research Workshop held in Nijmegen (The Netherlands)* 23–26 July 1991. Amsterdam: Swets & Zeitlinger.

Mönks, F. J. (1996). The elite debate in the spotlight (Elite-Debatte im Scheinwerfer). *Psychology in education and in the classroom* (Psychology in Erziehung und Unterricht), *43,* 219–224.

Mönks, F. J. (1999). Identifying and promoting gifted learners. In C. Perleth & A. Ziegler (eds), *Pedagogical psychology basics and areas of application* (Pädagogische Psychologie. Grundlagen und Anwendungsfelder) (pp. 65–75). Göttingen: Hogrefe.

Mönks, F. J. (2000). Identifying talents: Promoting the gifted (Begabungen erkennen – Begabte fördern). In H. Joswig (ed.), *Identifying talents: Promoting the gifted.* Contributions during the Scientific Working Days of the ABB e.V. in Rostock 22. – 24.10.1999 (Begabungen erkennen – Begabte fördern. Beiträge anlässlich der Wissenschaftlichen Arbeitstagung des ABB e.V. in Rostock vom 22. – 24.10.1999) (pp. 19–33). Rostock: Universität, Philosophische Fakultät, Institut für Pädagogische Psychologie

Perleth, C. (2001). Procedures for determining relevant features of high giftedness (Verfahren zur Erfassung hochbegabungsrelevanter Merkmale). In K. A. Heller (ed.), *High giftedness in childhood and adolescence* (Hochbegabung im Kindes- und Jugendalter) (2nd ed., pp. 357–446). Göttingen: Hogrefe.

Perleth, C., & Ziegler, A. (1997). Pfüadi Godt Integration – Special education for highly gifted learners (Pfüadi Godt Integration – Sonderschule für Hochbegabte)? In L. Dunkel, C. Enders & C. Hanckel (eds), *School – development – psychology – developmental psychology for schools. Proceedings of the 12th National Conference (Münster, 1996)* (Schule – Entwicklung – Psychologie. Schulentwicklungspsychologie. Kongressbericht der 12. Bundeskonferenz 1996 in Münster) (pp. 143–156). Bonn: Dt. Psychologen-Verlag.

Posner, M. I. (1988). Introduction: What is [it?] to be an expert? In M. T. H. Chi, R. Glaser & M. I. Posner (eds), *The nature of expertise* (pp. 29–36). Hillsdale: Erlbaum.

Renzulli, J. S. (1978). What makes giftedness? Re-examining a definition. *Phi Delta Kappa, 60,* 18–184.

Renzulli, J. S. (1986). The three-ring-conception of giftedness: A developmental model for creative productivity. In R. J. Sternberg & J. E. Davidson (eds), *Conceptions of giftedness* (pp. 53–92). Cambridge: Cambridge University Press.

Renzulli, J. S. (1993). A practical system for identifying highly gifted and talented learners (Ein praktisches System zur Identifizierung hochbegabter und talentierter Schüler). *Psychology in education and schools* (Psychologie in Erziehung und Unterricht), *40*, 217–244.

Renzulli, J. S. (1997). *Interst-A-Lyzer family of instruments: A manual for teachers by Joseph Renzulli*. Wako, TX: Prufrock Press.

Renzulli, J. S. (2002). Expanding the conception of giftedness to include co-cognitive traits and to promote social capital. *Phi Delta Kappan, 84*(1), 33–58.

Renzulli, J.S. (2005). The Three-Ring Conception of Giftedness: A Developmental Model for Promoting Creative Productivity. In R. J. Sternberg & J. E. Davidson (eds), *Conceptions of giftedness* (pp. 246–279). New York: Cambridge University Press.

Renzulli, J. S., & Reis, S. M. (1997). *The schoolwide enrichment model: A how-to guide for educational excellence*. Mansfield: Creative Learning Press.

Rost, D. H. (1991a). Identifying 'high giftedness' (Identifizierung von 'Hochbegabung'). *Journal for Developmental and Pedagogical Psychology* (Zeitschrift für Entwicklungspsychologie und Pädagogische Psychologie), 13/2, 197–231.

Rost, D. H. (1991b). 'Documents', 'models', views, commonplaces, comments on the replies by E. A. Hany, K. A. Heller and F. J. Mönks ('Belege', 'Modelle', Meinungen, Allgemeinplätze. Anmerkungen zu den Repliken von E.A. Hany, K.A. Heller und F. J. Mönks). *Journal for Developmental and Pedagogical Psychology* (Zeitschrift für Entwicklungspsychologie und Pädagogische Psychologie), *13*(3), 250–262.

Rost. D. H. (2000). *Highly gifted and high-performing adolescents: New findings of the Marburg High Giftedness Project* (Hochbegabte und hochleistende Jugendliche: Neue Erkenntnisse aus dem Marburger Hochbegabtenprojekt). Münster: Waxmann.

Schneider, W. (1992). On the acquisition of organisational strategies by children (Zum Erwerb von Organisationsstrategien bei Kindern). In H. Mandl, & H. F. Friedrich (eds), *Learning and thinking strategies: Analysis and intervention* (Lern- und Denkstrategien. Analyse und Intervention) (pp. 80–98). Göttingen: Hogrefe.

Schneider, W. (1999). Expertise (Expertise). In C. Perleth & A. Ziegler (eds), *Pedagogical Psychology. Basics and Areas of Application* (Pädagogische Psychologie. Grundlagen und Anwendungsfelder) (pp. 83–93). Bern: Huber.

Stamm, M. (2014). *Handbook of talent development: theories, methods and practice in psychology and pedagogy* (Handbuch Talententwicklung. Theorien, Methoden und Praxis in Psychologie und Pädagogik). Bern: Huber.

Stern, W. (1916). Psychological giftedness and diagnosis of giftedness (Psychologische Begabung und Begabungsdiagnose). In P. Petersen (ed.), *The rise of the gifted* (Der Aufstieg der Begabten) (pp. 105–120). Leipzig: Teubner.

Stern, W. (1928). *The intelligence of children and adolescents* (Die Intelligenz von Kindern und Jugendlichen). Leipzig: Barth.

Sternberg, R. J., & Davidson, J. E. (2005). *Conceptions of giftedness*. Cambridge: Cambridge University Press.

Terman, L. M., & Merrill, M. A. (1937). *Measuring intelligence*. Boston: Mifflin.

Terman, L. M., & Oden, M. H. (1948). *The gifted child grows up – 25 years' follow-up of a superior group*. Stanford: Stanford University Press.

Terman, L. M., & Oden, M. H. (1967). *The gifted group at mid-life – thirty-five years' follow-up of the superior child*. Stanford: Stanford University Press.

Urban, K. K. (2000). Creativity: From lesson disruption to lesson objectives (Kreativität: Vom Störfaktor zum Unterrichtsziel). In H. Wagner (ed.), *Giftedness and achievement in the classroom: Models for giftedness promotion in theory and practice* (Begabung und Leistung in der Schule. Modelle der Begabtenförderung in Theorie und Praxis) (pp. 117–138). Bad Honnef: Bock.

Waldmann, M. R., & Weinert, F. E. (1990). *Intelligence and thinking: Perspectives of high giftedness research* (Intelligenz und Denken. Perspektiven der Hochbegabungsforschung). Göttingen: Hogrefe.

Webb, J. T., Meckstroth, E. A., & Tolan, S. S. (1982). *Guiding the gifted child*. Dayton: Great Potential Press.

Weinert, F. E. (2000). *Learning as a bridge between high giftedness and excellent achievement* (Lernen als Brücke zwischen hoher Begabung und exzellenter Leistung). Talk Held at the Second International Salzburg Conference on Giftedness Issues and Giftedness Promotion. 13. Oktober 2000 (Vortrag gehalten anlässlich der zweiten internationalen Salzburger Konferenz zu Begabungsfragen und Begabtenförderung. 13. Oktober 2000) (pp. 1–19). Salzburg: MI for Psychological Research.

Ziegler, A. (2005). The actiotope model of giftedness. In R. Sternberg & J. Davidson (eds), *Conceptions of giftedness* (pp. 411–434). Cambridge: Cambridge University Press.

Ziegler, A., & Stöger, H. (2011). The making of an expert as an adaptive and regulative process: The role of educational and learning assets (Expertisierung als Adaptions- und Regulationsprozess: Die Rolle von Bildungs- und Lernkapital). In M. Dresel & L. Lämmle (eds), *Motivation, self-regulation, and achievement excellence* (Motivation, Selbstregulation und Leistungsexzellenz) (pp. 131–152). Münster: LIT-Verlag.

Ziegler, A., & Stöger, H. (2013). Education and learning capitals: A resource-oriented approach (Bildungs- und Lernkapital. Ein ressourcenorientierter Ansatz). *Journal for Gifted Education* (Journal für Begabtenförderung), *13*(2), 4–13.

Ziegler, A., & Stöger, H. (2012). Theoretical issues of underachievement in gifted students. *Roeper Review, 33*.

Ziegler, A., Ziegler A. & Stöger, H. (2012). Shortcomings of the IQ-based construct of underachievement. *Roeper Review, 34*(2), 123–132.

5

HOW CONTEMPORARY INTERNATIONAL PERSPECTIVES HAVE CONSOLIDATED A BEST-PRACTICE APPROACH FOR IDENTIFYING AND DEVELOPING SPORTING TALENT

Juanita R. Weissensteiner

Introduction

The ability to effectively and consistently unearth future Olympic-, Paralympic- and Professional-level athletic talent through talent identification and development (TID) is the prized 'holy grail' of any sporting nation. However, criticism in the literature persists regarding apparent conceptual, methodological and operational shortfalls in TID practice (Bergeron et al., 2015; Suppiah, Low, & Chia, 2015). The recently published International Olympic Committee's (IOC) consensus statement on Youth Athlete Development (Bergeron et al., 2015) and aligned commentary highlight several limitations. These include, a lack of consensus regarding a viable overarching framework to inform TID 'best practice'; a heavy emphasis on non-inclusive, uni-dimensional, low-predictive identification strategies in lieu of effective, individualised, long-term development; a lack of role clarity and expectations between stakeholders; inconsistency in aligned strategy, practice and support and questionable cost effectiveness and success (see also: Abbott & Collins, 2004; Abbott, Button, Pepping, & Collins, 2005; Ackerman, 2013; Buekers, Borry, & Rowe, 2015; Cobley, Schorer, & Baker, 2012; McCarthy & Collins, 2014; Malina, Rogol, Cumming, Coelho-e-Silva, & Figueiredo, 2015; Miller, Cronin, & Baker, 2015; Pinder, Renshaw, & Davids, 2013; Suppiah et al., 2015; Tucker & Collins, 2012; Vaeyens, Lenoir, Williams, & Philippaerts, 2008).

Whilst boasting a rich history of successful programmes and international podium success, a recent review of pre-elite programmes in a number of Australian National Sporting Organisations (Weissensteiner & Medlicott, 2015) also revealed a number of system- and sport-specific level gaps in current TID initiatives. The review outlined a need for ongoing education of all key stakeholders, including coaches and high performance managers regarding evidence-informed best practice approaches for maximising TID; better clarity regarding the coordination, communication and consistency of TID strategies; and further consolidation of

51

talent transfer approaches. Additionally it highlighted the criticality of ongoing athlete monitoring to inform and enhance the individualised, interdisciplinary case management of athletes. Cognisant of these limitations, the need for a theoretical yet practicable overarching framework to inform effective TID strategy and 'best practice' is critical.

In this chapter, contemporary international perspectives and advances in approaches to TID will be showcased. These are then consolidated within a viable, evidence-based, practicable framework and national strategy that is currently guiding TID practice within the Australian sporting system.

Contemporary international perspectives on the identification, confirmation and development of prospective athletic talent

Across the globe, there are exciting approaches that are contributing to and extending the disciplinary knowledge within TID. For example, a notable exemplar is the body of work by Güllich and Emrich (2012, 2014) who have examined the developmental histories and TID experiences of Olympic and Professional athletes. They utilised a retrospective longitudinal approach to examine the biographies, training and competition histories of 1,558 world- and national-level athletes. They revealed that rapidly attained juvenile success was not associated with eventual long term senior elite performance (Güllich & Emrich, 2014). When compared to their less successful national-class counterparts, world-class athletes were characterised by a later onset of training and a later age of specialisation preceded by a greater sampling of other sports. In a further developmental history examination of German footballers, the annual turnover within national junior teams and youth elite academies was 41 per cent and 24.5 per cent respectively (Güllich & Emrich, 2012). Footballers that reached a senior professional level were commonly not involved in early TID programmes, while conversely most early selected youngsters for TID programmes did not reach a senior professional level (Güllich & Emrich, 2012; see Chapter 7).

The implications of this work alone for informing TID practice are numerous. First, it is imperative that overarching TID strategies and planning are 'permeable', catering to an athlete's – at times – chaotic developmental trajectory (Gulbin, Weissensteiner, Oldenziel, & Gagné, 2013b). Second, longitudinally and ideally prospectively, tracking an individual's developmental history is not only a valuable precursor for reviewing and enhancing their ongoing support and management, but also provides valuable metrics for assessing the effectiveness of overarching TID strategies. Third, such findings confirm the limited utility of relying on juvenile performance in TID selection strategies to predict future senior elite performance; and lastly, affirms the importance of sport sampling prior to specialisation, particularly in 'related' or compatible sports (Bergeron et al., 2015; Suppiah et al., 2015).

Toward a better understanding of multi-dimensional and longitudinal talent development: Implications for TID Practice

Contemporary international perspectives offer further insight regarding best TID practice. For instance, it is well accepted in research and practice that the 'profile' underpinning an athlete's sporting development, progression and attainment of elite performance is multi-dimensional and 'multiplicative' (Bailey & Morley, 2006; Elferink-Gemser, Jordet, Coelho-e-Silva, & Visscher, 2011; Fuchslocher, Romann, & Gulbin, 2013; Gulbin & Weissensteiner, 2013; Simonton, 2001; Vaeyens et al., 2008; Williams & Reilly, 2000). Put simply, it is not one athletic component in isolation that leads to performance success, but a complement of interactive factors (i.e., physical, psychological, sport-specific skills and attributes and socio-developmental background) and sub-factors, which are in turn 'modulated' by a choreography of contextual or 'environmental' factors (see Toohey et al., 2015). That said however, uni-dimensional approaches heavily predicated on premature indicators of physicality and confounded by the 'relative age effect' prevail in TID practice.

Until recently, there has been a dearth of empirical research exploring the emergence and relative contribution of these factors to performance considerate of age, maturational status and skill level (Elferink-Gemser, Visscher, Lemminck, & Mulder, 2007; Matthys et al., 2013; Weissensteiner, Abernethy, Farrow, & Müller, 2008; Weissensteiner, Abernethy, & Farrow, 2009; Vaeyens, Güllich, Warr, & Philippaerts, 2009). Research emanating from Belgium, the Netherlands, UK and Australia is now providing valuable multi-dimensional, longitudinal and sport-specific insight with strong implications for TID practice (Elferink-Gemser, Visscher, Lemminck, & Mulder, 2004; Elferink-Gemser et al., 2007, 2011; Elferink-Gemser & Visscher, 2012; Faber, Bustin, Oosterveld, Elferink-Gemser, & van der Sanden, 2015; Huijgen, Elferink-Gemser, Lemmink, & Visscher, 2014; Matthys et al., 2013; Pion et al., 2015a, 2015b; Stoter et al., 2015; Till, Cobley, O'Hara, Brightmore, Cooke, & Chapman, 2011; Till, Cobley, O'Hara, Cooke, & Chapman, 2014; Till, Cobley, O'Hara, Morley, & Chapman, 2015; Vaeyens et al., 2006, 2008; Wierike Te et al., 2015). Together, these contributions emphatically demonstrate that adopting a sport-specific multivariate approach to TID measurement, mindful of an athlete's maturational status, is a more valid and better predictive method for identifying future talent potential.

In better understanding the dynamic nature of talent development, longitudinal studies are powerful. Rather than relying on a 'snapshot' of juvenile performance and physical measures, a full 'complement' of an athlete's attributes (psychological, physical, technical, tactical) are assessed over time relative to age, maturation and skill level. Thus, the examination and determination of which factors are truly predictive and central to future expert performance can be ascertained (see Cobley and Till – Chapter 18, this volume). Through these methodological approaches, it has been demonstrated that an athlete's morphology, functional capacity, strength, power, speed, motor proficiency and sport-specific skills change and interacts with maturation, age and experience (see Matthys et al., 2011; Philippearts et al., 2006; Till et al., 2014; Vaeyens et al., 2006). Consistent with the 'compensation phenomenon' (Williams & Ericsson, 2005), existing longitudinal studies demonstrate that sport performance is not necessarily marked by a standard set of athletic attributes or characteristics, but rather achieved in individualistic or unique ways through different combinations by the 'best compensators' (Vaeyens et al., 2008).

Also of worthy note, is the recent work of Pion et al. (2015a), who tracked the 5-year developmental journeys of pre-elite female gymnasts aged 7–12 years of age. Utilising survival analyses, the Kaplan-Meier estimate revealed that a mere 18 per cent of the original cohort 'survived' (i.e., continued and progressed) within the development programme, reaching a high competition level by the age of 12. The complementary Cox Proportional Hazards metric revealed that gymnasts who scored higher in specific measures of basic motor skills, gross motor coordination as well as shoulder and leg strength increased their 'chances of survival' by 45–129 per cent. Additionally, it was demonstrated that the 'survivors' did not initially score in the best quartile for each of these characteristics at baseline testing. For example, low scores in a quotient of overall gross motor coordination were compensated with higher scores in measures of lower limb flexibility, speed, lower and upper limb power and strength and balance. These findings highlight the imperative of a 'rounded' or fuller complement of 'process measures' of performance for TID selection and strategy within younger cohorts as opposed to 'outcome' performance assessments. Likewise, they highlight the importance of functional movement screening (i.e., measures of joint range of motion, stability, neuromuscular flexibility and integrity, etc.) within TID test batteries to ascertain an athlete's neuro-muscular status and their potential ability to cope with increased training loads. The use of 'survival rate' statistical measures also offers an innovative way to deduce the developmental health of a 'talent pipeline' through conversion assessment. The procedure also provides a better understanding of the factors associated with athlete dropout, retention and progression.

The criticality of psychological factors in pre-elite performance development: The need for inclusion in talent identification and confirmation strategies

A prevailing but justified criticism levelled at past TID strategies is their lack of consideration and incorporation of psychological assessments (Abbott & Collins, 2004; Abbott et al., 2005; McCarthy & Collins, 2014; MacNamara & Collins, 2013). This is at odds with increasing evidence demonstrating emphatically that elite-level athletes are distinguishable by their robust and multi-dimensional psychological profile (Durand-Bush & Salmela, 2002; Gould, Dieffenbach, & Moffett, 2002; Fletcher & Sarkar, 2012; Weissensteiner, Abernethy, Farrow, & Gross, 2012). Possession of a complementary mix of psychological attributes (e.g., high self-regulation, motivation, optimism, mental toughness, resilience, possession of a growth mindset and coping ability etc.) contribute substantially to an athlete enduring their long developmental journey. It is well established that athletes at this level and beyond, are required to 'juggle' numerous competing demands within and outside of their sport, negotiate several key life transitions, cope with negative chance events and stressors, as well as effectively engage and interact with their coaches, support staff, peers and family (Fletcher & Sarkar, 2012; Mountjoy, Rhind, Tiivas, & Leglise, 2015; Stambulova, Engström, Franck, Linnér, & Lindahl, 2015; Toohey et al., 2015; Weissensteiner et al., 2012; Weissensteiner, Warmenhoven, Medlicott, & Gulbin, 2015; Weissensteiner & Cook, 2015; Wylleman & Reints, 2010; Wylleman, De Knop, & Reints, 2011).

To exemplify, effective self-regulation and its complement of practical skills and strategies including the ability to plan and prepare, self-monitor, self-evaluate, reflect and problem solve (Toering, Elferink-Gemser, Jonker, Heuvelen, & Visscher, 2012; Zimmerman, 1986) has been strongly associated with learning ability and performance within sport and academia (Cleary & Zimmerman, 2001; Green & Weissensteiner, 2015; Jonker, Elferink-Gemser, & Visscher, 2010, 2011; Toering, Elferink-Gemser, Jordet, & Visscher, 2009; Wierike Te et al., 2015). In a recent examination of junior to senior elite transition in Australian tennis, successful players who achieved a top 100 ranking internationally were distinguishable through their deployment of self-regulatory skills. These enabled them to effectively negotiate each developmental sub-transition (e.g., transition between futures, satellite, challengers and ATP circuit; Mathews, Farrow, MacMahon, & Weissensteiner, 2012; Toohey et al., 2015) and manage concurrent competing demands on and off the court.

Whilst there is little doubt psychological factors are central to enduring the journey to high performance, further research is required to translate these theoretical underpinnings into valid and reliable practical TID strategies. Recently, in utilising the Self-Regulation of Learning Self-Report scale (SRL-SRS; Toering et al., 2012), Green and Weissensteiner (2015) assessed the self-regulatory skills of over 500 Australian Olympic and Paralympic sport athletes across the developmental spectrum. They identified that elite- and mastery-level athletes were characterised by significantly higher levels of self-efficacy, effort, planning, self-monitoring and reflection, compared to their lower-level counterparts. The study also revealed potential confounding factors and limits to administering psychological inventories within formalised talent identification initiatives, particularly when athletes consider that selection is associated with their questionnaire scores. Inclusion of social desirability items such as the Marlowe-Crowne Questionnaire (Crowne & Marlowe, 1960) within the SRL-SRS, revealed strong association between high self-reporting and social desirability. This finding warrants caution and due consideration when administering psychological inventories in TID contexts. Specific to promoting the effective utility of psychological assessments in TID practice, consolidated enquiry is warranted in regard to viable observational and behaviour-based methods for 'confirming' an athlete's holistic psychological profile (i.e., within the context of training and performance) rather than relying solely on inventory based measures given their potential limitations.

Extending current approaches for identifying talent transfer athletes

In the recent IOC consensus statement, there was also recommendation for greater implementation of mature-aged talent transfer strategies (Bergeron et al., 2015: Suppiah et al., 2015). The foreseeable advantages of such an approach over traditional 'talent selection' strategies include the reduction of uncertainty imposed by maturational differences and the relative age effect. From a system-level perspective, the inclusion of talent transfer athletes can help fill current gaps in a sport's 'talent pipeline' by providing high-calibre athletes a 'second chance' and maximising return on investment (Bullock et al., 2009; Gulbin & Ackland, 2009; Vaeyens et al., 2009). Surprisingly though, despite being a relatively successful strategy in UK and Australian sport systems, a dearth of research exists exploring the theoretical underpinnings of talent transfer and the 'relative' transferability of skills and attributes (e.g., physical, psychological, perceptual, cognitive, motor, social, etc.) between 'donor' and 'recipient' sport contexts (see Rosalie & Müller, 2012 for an exception).

The majority of talent transfer initiatives rely on the compatibility of an athlete's physical characteristics (i.e., physiology and anthropometry) with the assumption that a mature former successful athlete in a donor sport will similarly transfer other necessary (e.g., psychological) skills. However, recent advances in the disciplines of motor control, biomechanics and skill acquisition show great potential for inclusion in future talent transfer strategies. For instance, visualisation of an athlete's 'coordinative signature' (Warmenhoven et al., 2015) through a suite of innovative analytical approaches (see Button, Wheat, & Lamb, 2013; Sacilotto, Warmenhoven, Mason, Ball, & Clothier, 2015; Schöllhorn, Chow, Glazier, & Button, 2014; Warmenhoven et al., 2015) suggests potentially improved accuracy through the provision of more specific and meaningful technical and movement based feedback to athletes and their coaches (Barris, Farrow, & Davids, 2013; Warmenhoven et al., 2015). The ability to 'map' an athlete's coordinative profile along with their perceptual-cognitive abilities (i.e., anticipatory, pattern recall and decision making skills) may provide another overlaying dimension to an athlete's profile, helping ascertain their overall compatibility to a recipient sport in future talent transfer initiatives (see Glazier, Chapter 17 this volume).

Maximising the support and development of pre-elite sporting talent

As a newly identified pre-elite athlete, the developmental journey to senior elite athlete is more typically long and arduous. Successful progression toward the senior elite level is not only dependant on combinations of physical, sport-specific technical skills and psychological 'fortitude', it is also heavily reliant and dependent upon system and environmental support (Davids & Baker, 2007; Fletcher & Sarkar, 2012; Martindale, Collins, & Daubney, 2005; Phillips, Davids, Renshaw, & Portus, 2010; Weissensteiner et al., 2015).

Pre-elite athlete well-being and maintaining effective sport-life balance

The 'Holistic Athletic Career model' developed by Wylleman and colleagues has afforded valuable insight regarding the transitional challenges pre-elite athletes encounter not only specific to their athletic career, but also in regard to the intersections and complexity of their concurrent psychological, psycho-social and academic or vocational development (Wylleman et al., 2011). Consequently, the ongoing monitoring and management of athletes regarding their psychological and psycho-social development, mental well-being, ability to balance competing sport and life demands (i.e., dual career) and negotiate transitional challenges, is critical. Central to effectively managing an athlete's dual career and assisting both normative and non-normative transitions within and outside of their athletic career, it is strongly advocated that athlete-focused education and pre-emptive, tailored interventions are implemented. These include individualised career planning (see e.g., Stambulova's [2010] 'Five step: career planning strategy'), facilitation of an athlete's cognitive readiness and self-regulatory skills, pre-emptive planning for negotiating each key developmental transition, and advice specific to financial management, media and social networking skills.

Towards better social dynamics in pre-elite talent development

The emerging intersections between recognised psychological factors (e.g., self-regulation, resilience), ecological and organisational psychology as well as social network theory, which explain how environmental contexts can be facilitative or debilitative on an athlete's developmental experience, also present exciting recent contributions. For instance, the series of studies conducted by Henriksen, Stambulova, and Roessler (2010a, 2010b, 2011) provide a viable method for 'mapping' and better understanding the impact of talent development environments and their constituents (e.g., coaches, managers, service support providers, peers within and outside of the sport, mentors, family, school, clubs, national culture and organisations, etc.) on athlete development. Such information can greatly assist stakeholders in matching aspects of an athlete's daily training environment with their developmental status and needs. The aligned implementation of innovative diagnostic tools (Cullen-Lester, Palus, & Appaneal, 2014; Hambrick, 2013), which visualise an athlete's support network, shows promise for better understanding the relative impact and dynamics (both facilitative and debilitative) of these environmental factors on an athlete's development, providing valuable information for enhancing individualised athlete support.

Talent transfer and its social and psychological dimensions

Research in Australia indicates that to successfully transfer and make the senior elite ranks, an athlete and their coach, have to negotiate numerous psycho-social and organisational factors and barriers (Dickinson, Mallett, Gulbin, & Weissensteiner, 2012; Gudmundsdottir, Riot, & Auld, 2014; Weissensteiner et al., 2015). The findings of Gudmundsdottir et al. (2014), who utilised a case-study approach including in-depth interviews with athletes, their coaches, and a critical support provider, highlighted emphatically the importance of specialised and matched coaching expertise as well as ongoing organisational commitment and support. The talent transfer coach was identified as a key conduit in the transition process, providing not only specialist expertise, but also possessing strong communication, negotiation, problem-solving and people management skills. These skills supported their athlete through the transition process and effectively brokered the 'triangulated stakeholder relationship' between athlete, coach (themself) and the associated National Sporting Organisation.

Weissensteiner et al. (2015) recently examined the experiences of 117 Paralympic and Olympic talent transfer athletes, including 69 who had competed at a senior International level, using the 'My Sporting Journey' questionnaire. The online questionnaire comprehensively chronicled an athlete's developmental history from an early foundation level to their highest representative level. Findings revealed that for the majority of athletes (74%), their transition into their main sport was difficult due to a number of intrinsic (i.e., psychological, physical, sport-specific skill 'limiters') and extrinsic factors, including a perceived lack of support from their coach and peers, along with imposed unrealistic expectations and time frames. The major- ity of athletes (82%) reported that they were embedded into a mixed cohort whereby they trained alongside talent selected athletes and were not afforded extra individualised support to develop their skills. A third of athletes perceived that they were not accepted by their talent selected training partners reporting incidences of ostracism, negativity and even bullying. These findings highlight the criticality of educating all stakeholders (i.e., coaches, talent pathway and high performance managers, etc.) about the nuances of talent transfer; the importance of shared realistic time frames and expectations; tailored psychological support to assist the talent trans- fer athlete and manage social dynamics; as well as the utility of 'task representative' approaches. The latter referring to maintaining congruence between practice and performance environ- ments through preservation of perception-action coupling in highly relevant task environments to help maximise skill acquisition and performance progression (see Pinder, Davids, Renshaw, & Araújo, 2011; Renshaw, Davids, Phillips, & Kerherve, 2012).

Mindful of the contemporary international perspectives showcased, the chapter now illus- trates how such knowledge and understanding has been considered and consolidated into an effective applied framework for informing best TID practice. This framework is now deployed in the Australian sporting system.

A consolidated system-level approach for promoting effective and sustainable TID in Australia: The FTEM Athlete Development Framework

Since its development in 2011, the FTEM (Foundation, Talent, Elite and Mastery) Athlete Development framework (Gulbin, Croser, Morley, & Weissensteiner, 2013a) has been utilised by the Australian Institute of Sport (AIS). Its aim is to inform the review and refinement of athlete pathways for a number of Australian Olympic, Paralympic and Professional National Sporting Organisations (NSO). Importantly, the FTEM framework and specifically it's comple- ment of 'talent' phases (see Figure 5.1), serves to educate and catalyse a 'system' or national-level understanding of best practice and effective TID with aligned stakeholders (see Chapter 9 for a detailed overview of the FTEM framework including its foundational, elite and mastery phases).

The FTEM framework is adaptable to a sport and sub-discipline specific level and caters for the full complement of TID initiatives (i.e., talent selection, detection, transfer and reintegra- tion) along with their associated pathways and nuances. Informed by prior studies examining the developmental histories of Australian and German senior elite athletes (Gulbin et al., 2013b; Güllich & Emrich, 2012, 2014), the FTEM talent phases and aligned strategies are inclusive and flexible in that they can support a multitude of developmental trajectories and multiple selec- tion (entry) and deselection (exit) points.

The identification and development of pre-elite athletes is a direct fit with the four 'talent' phases of FTEM, Talent Demonstration of Potential (T1), Talent Verification (T2), Talent Practising and Achieving (T3) and Talent Breakthrough and Reward (T4). These four differ- entiated yet integrated phases feature a deliberate complement and coordination of progressive

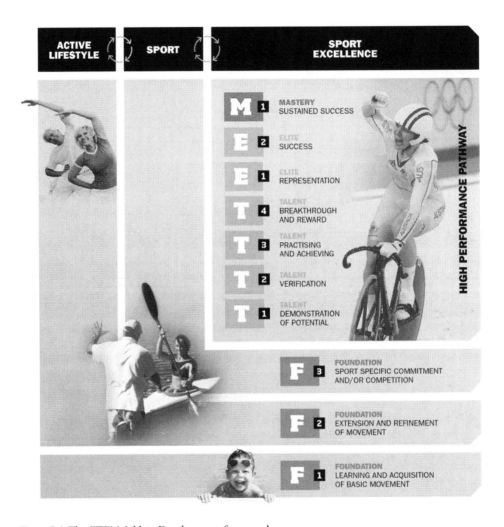

Figure 5.1 The FTEM Athlete Development framework

Source: Image courtesy of the Australian Sports Commission: www.ausport.gov.au

TID strategies. At the start of the High Performance pathway, an athlete's initial identification and future talent potential (T1) is confirmed through their immersion into 'in-situ' training and competition environments (T2). They are then recognised as a 'pre-elite' talent and provided with best practice, holistic developmental support and opportunity (T3), culminating in achievement of a 'breakthrough' performance or milestone (T4), which signals their readiness for transition into the senior elite ranks.

Critical to achieving practical outcomes and ensuring future sustainable international success through effective TID, is adoption of a dedicated 'top-down' approach where evidence-based multi-dimensional athlete profiling directly informs the planning, strategy and allocation of resources for athletes (Weissensteiner, 2015). As depicted within Figure 5.2, consolidated sport-specific (and sub-discipline and gender-specific) elite- and mastery-level athlete profiles

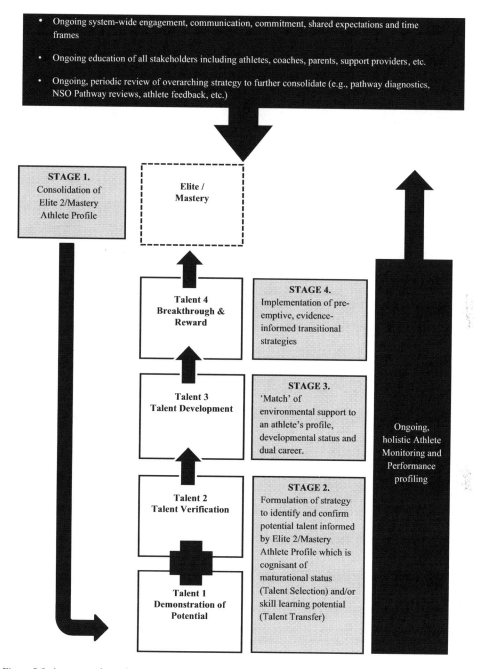

Figure 5.2 An overarching framework utilising the Talent and Elite/Mastery FTEM phases, for informing and coordinating TID best practice

(stage 1) are utilised to inform the review and refinement of current TID and confirmation strategies and assessments (stage 2) as well as maximise a pre-elite athlete's developmental (stage 3) and (stage 4) transitional progression. Such an approach and related decision making is dependent upon the maturational status of an athlete within early talent selection initiatives and their skill learning potential within 'mature-aged' talent transfer initiatives. An ongoing commitment to concurrent, longitudinal holistic athlete monitoring (i.e., inclusive of valid and reliable indicators of well-being, injury and illness status, sport–life balance and impact of environmental and system-level factors, etc.), coupled with effective performance profiling is essential to better supporting the case management of pre-elite athletes.

To minimise potential Type I and II errors and maximise prediction, a deliberate complement of identification and confirmation strategies are utilised. Initial predictions or observations of talent either formally (i.e., valid, reliable, age-appropriate multi-dimensional assessments of talent) or informally (e.g., observation within competition) (T1) are verified, through a dedicated and protracted talent confirmation period. Within the verification phase (T2), athletes are immersed in rich training and competition-like settings along with ecologically relevant scenario-based simulations to confirm their talent potential. Informed initially by a consolidated sport-specific elite/mastery athlete profile (see Figure 5.3), adoption of holistic measures of an athlete's talent are strongly advocated (see Figure 5.4). This includes assessment of an athlete's psychological (e.g., character, learning ability, skills, motivation, commitment, coach-ability, etc.), physical (e.g., physiological capacity, neuromuscular robustness) and sport-specific skills (e.g., technical, perceptual and cognitive components). Specific to talent selected

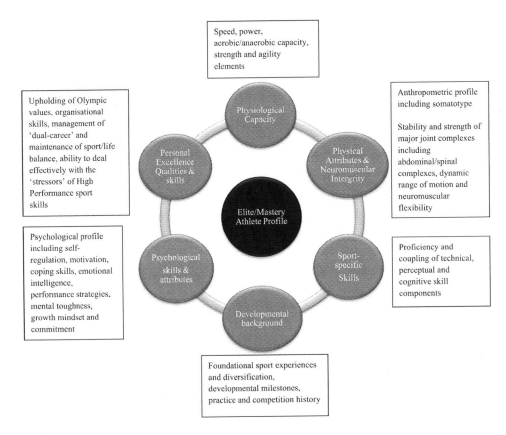

Figure 5.3 A holistic framework for informing Athlete Profiling of Elite (E2) and Mastery (M) athletes

T1: TS & TT: Valid, reliable and age-appropriate physiological assessments and benchmarks measuring aerobic/anaerobic capacity, upper & lower limb strength, power, speed & agility

AND

T2: TS & TT: Confirmation of physiological capacity within training/competition settings e.g., adaptation to training loads

T1: TS & TT: FULL Functional Movement Screening & ISAK Anthropometric Profile considerate of maturational status

AND

T2: TS & TT: Formalised assessments of trainability and adaptation to appropriate training loads within training and competition

T1: TS: Valid, reliable, age-appropriate and ecological sport-specific skill assessments

TT: Basic skill potential/aptitude assessment drawing on 'Coaches Eye'

AND

T2: TS: Utilisation of formalised and ecological assessments of sport-specific skill to ascertain the robustness and adaptability of technical, cognitive and perceptual skill components under fatigue, pressure and environmental constraints.

T1: TS & TT: Consideration of developmental background including:
- Sampling of other sports
- Attainment of developmental milestones in main sport
- Developmental trajectory
- Competition exposure and progression

T2: TS & TT: An athlete exhibits:
- strong character and upholding of Olympic Values
- good life decision making skills
- good self-awareness and management in and out of their sport (e.g., effective sport/life balance, managing dual career, awareness & adoption of recovery, nutrition and injury management strategies
- high coach-ability & receptiveness
- strong commitment

AND

T1: TS & TT: 'Screening' of required psychological skills and characteristics with valid, reliable and age-appropriate inventory-based assessments

AND

T2: TS & TT: Psychological aptitude verified through observed behaviour within training/competition settings environments

T1/T2 Strategies — Physical Attributes & Neuromuscular Integrity — Sport-specific Skills — Developmental background — Psychological skills & attributes — Personal Excellence Qualities & Skills — Physiological Capacity

Figure 5.4 A framework for guiding the formulation of a multi-dimensional and effective approach to talent identification (T1) and confirmation (T2) for talent selection (TS) and talent transfer (TT) initiatives.

athletes, these measures are compared relative to, or normalised with, maturational appropriate benchmarks (see Till et al., 2014, regarding the usage of an estimate of peak height velocity to categorise athletes into 'early', 'average' and 'late' maturation groups). Specific to talent transfer athletes, it is advocated that sport-specific skill tests moderated by experienced coaches are 'task representative' and complemented by 'in-situ' assessments of psychological and physical aptitude to ascertain an athlete's 'skill learning potential'. Functional movement screening tests are likewise utilised to assess an athlete's neuromuscular status and their physical robustness, and if required, be a precursor to the implementation of tailored interventions and subsequent monitoring.

In terms of psychological factors, multi-dimensional assessments (i.e., inventory-based), that match the sport task demands, are valid, and are reliable and age-appropriate, help to provide initial screening of an athlete's psychological aptitude. These initial evaluations are then confirmed, through formalised assessments based on the observable behaviour and character (i.e., personal excellence qualities) of the athlete within scenario-based training and competitive contexts. Screening of psychological aptitude and character leads to prompt follow-up and feedback, customised educational and practical interventions for both the athlete and coach (e.g., incorporation of practical strategies to enhance self-regulation).

In the T3 pre-elite developmental phase, it is strongly advocated that pre-elite athletes are immersed within holistic talent development environments featuring strong 'deliberate programming' (Bullock et al., 2009). As depicted in Figure 5.5, a 'best-practice' talent development environment should align to an athlete's developmental needs. Such an environment coordinated through quality strategic planning, features amongst other things evidence-informed and innovative coaching support (i.e., 'state of the art' skill acquisition, psycho-social load management and injury prevention strategies, task representative approaches, etc.); access to elite peers and mentors; and, best-practice education and interdisciplinary service support including career education and management. Here support is individualised and adaptive, considerate of the relative impact of each aspect of deliberate programming on athlete developmental progression and well-being. Specific to maximising the acquisition and refinement of their skills in their 'new' sport, talent transfer athletes are provided tailored guidance and support from their coaches assisted by state of the art, inter-disciplinary expertise (e.g., skill acquisition, psychology, performance analysis, etc.), and strong system-level commitment expressed through shared and agreed expectations and time frames.

Critical to assisting their ability to manage multiple demands and stressors within and outside of their sport, including their dual career and transition to senior levels, athletes within the T3 and T4 levels are provided proactive educational programmes and self-management strategies delivered through innovative social e-learning platforms (see the AIS's 'myAISPlaybook') supported by mentoring and dedicated academic, vocational and psychological support.

Critical to the effective adoption of this best practice TID approach, is sport and system-level capacity, capability, engagement and commitment. The Athlete Pathways and Development section of the AIS facilitates – via a broadly consultative, evidence-based, educative approach – the development of an NSO's National Athlete Pathway Framework (NAPF). The NAPF is essentially a 'blueprint' for promoting best practice for all components of the athlete pathway inclusive of TID, through the alignment and coordination of strategies, personnel, programmes and resources at a State and National level. Articulating an effective NAPF is now a mandatory requirement of the AIS through its high performance review processes. Aligned metrics and diagnostics (e.g., conversion and 'survival' rates of pre-elite cohorts) in combination with customised 'tools' (e.g., NSO Pathway Healthcheck, 'My Sporting Journey'

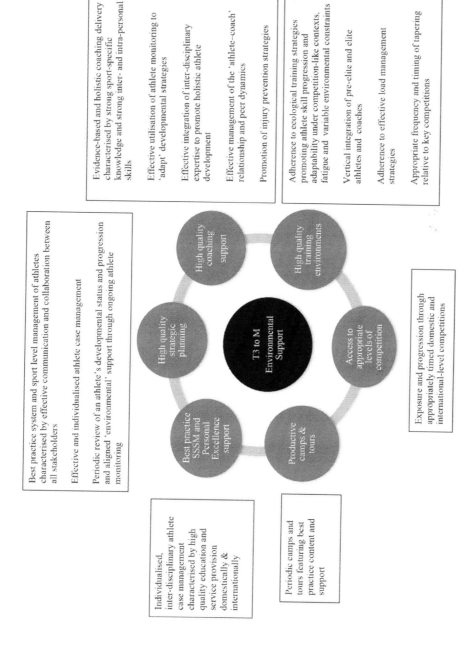

Best practice system and sport level management of athletes characterised by effective communication and collaboration between all stakeholders

Effective and individualised athlete case management

Periodic review of an athlete's developmental status and progression and aligned 'environmental' support through ongoing athlete monitoring

Evidence-based and holistic coaching delivery characterised by strong sport-specific knowledge and strong inter- and intra-personal skills

Effective utilisation of athlete monitoring to 'adapt' developmental strategies

Effective integration of inter-disciplinary expertise to promote holistic athlete development

Effective management of the 'athlete–coach' relationship and peer dynamics

Promotion of injury prevention strategies

Adherence to ecological training strategies promoting athlete skill progression and adaptability under competition-like contexts, fatigue and variable environmental constraints

Vertical integration of pre-elite and elite athletes and coaches

Adherence to effective load management strategies

Appropriate frequency and timing of tapering relative to key competitions

High quality coaching support

High quality training environments

High quality strategic planning

T3 to M Environmental Support

Access to appropriate levels of competition

Best practice SSSM and Personal Excellence support

Productive camps & tours

Exposure and progression through appropriately timed domestic and international-level competitions

Individualised, inter-disciplinary athlete case management characterised by high quality education and service provision domestically & internationally

Periodic camps and tours featuring best practice content and support

Figure 5.5 A generic framework for reviewing and refining the environmental and system support of pre-elite-, elite- and mastery-level athletes

Athlete Questionnaire) help to assess and evaluate the ongoing 'health' of the high performance pathway including its TID components at both a sport and system level.

Whilst still in its relative infancy, adoption of the overarching FTEM framework has led to
the review and refinement of current planning and strategy within a number of Australian
National Sporting Organisations. To date, the framework has informed related stakeholder
knowledge and awareness and has directly informed initiatives such as the AIS Sports Draft a
talent transfer initiative for identifying future Olympic and Paralympic talent. The FTEM
framework has led to better engagement and collaboration between key stakeholders; better
alignment of related strategy and resources; modification and updating of coach education;
better linkage of athlete profiling, and adaptive athlete management informed by prospective
athlete monitoring. To truly verify the efficacy and impact of this system-level approach to TID
requires however, a firm long-term commitment. This can be achieved in part, through the
further consolidation of empirical, sport-specific 'models' of TID that are informed by
'grounded' pluralistic methods (see Weissensteiner et al., 2008, 2009) and confirmed through
longitudinal athlete tracking (see Elferink-Gemser & Visscher, 2012) and best-practice analytical approaches to verify the predictive validity and impact of employed TID assessments and
strategies (see Pion et al., 2015a; Robertson, Burnett, & Wilkie, 2013; Schorer et al., 2012).

Conclusion and future directions

The recently published IOC Consensus statement on Youth Athlete Development (Bergeron
et al., 2015) and supportive commentary (Malina et al., 2015; Mountjoy et al., 2015; Suppiah
et al., 2015; Weissensteiner, 2015) establishes a firm position and call for action in the need to
address prevailing issues affecting pre-elite athletes and their development in TID systems. To
truly advance the discipline and field of practice, unity and commitment between researchers
and practitioners is required to work towards evidence-informed practicable solutions. In this
chapter, advances in contemporary international research were identified, and in this case, have
been used to consolidate and establish an evidence-informed national strategy (i.e., The
FTEM Athlete Development framework) for enhancing TID practice. Through further
consolidation of this system-wide strategic approach, it is anticipated that the 'talent pipelines'
within Australian sport will be healthier in the longer-term, ensuring continued world class
success.

References

Abbott, A., & Collins, D. (2004). Eliminating the dichotomy between theory and practice in talent identification and development: Considering the role of psychology. *Journal of Sports Science, 22,* 395–408.

Abbott, A., Button, C., Pepping, G. J., & Collins, D. (2005). Unnatural selection: Talent identification and
development in sport. *Nonlinear Dynamics, Psychology and Life Sciences, 9,* 61–68.

Ackerman, P. L. (2013). Nonsense, common sense and science of expert performance: Talent and individual differences. *Intelligence, 45,* 6–17.

Bailey, R., & Morley, D. (2006). Towards a model of talent development in physical education. *Sport,
Education, and Society, 11,* 211–230.

Barris, S., Farrow, D., & Davids, K. (2013). Do the kinematics of a baulked take-off in springboard diving
differ from a completed dive? *Journal of Sport Sciences, 31*(3), 305–313.

Bergeron, M. F., Mountjoy, M., Armstrong, N., Chia, M., Côté, J., Emery, C. A., … Engebretsen, L. (2015).
International Olympic Committee consensus statement on youth athletic development. *British Journal
of Sports Medicine, 49,* 843–851.

Buekers, M., Borry, P., & Rowe, P. (2015). Talent in sports: Some reflections about the search for future
champions. *Movement and Sport Sciences – Science & Motricité, 88,* 3–12.

Bullock, N., Gulbin, J. P., Martin, D. T., Ross, A., Holland, T., & Marino, F. (2009). Talent identification and deliberate practice programming in skeleton: Ice novice to winter Olympian in 14 months. *Journal of Sports Sciences, 27,* 397–404.

Button, C., Wheat, J., & Lamb, P. (2013). Why coordination dynamics is relevant for studying sport performance. In K. Davids, D. Araújo, R. Hristovski, N. Balagúe Serre, C. Button & P. Passos (eds), *Complex systems in sport* (pp. 44–61). London: Routledge.

Cleary, T. J., & Zimmerman, B. J. (2001). Self-regulation differences during athletic practice by experts, non-experts, and novices. *Journal of Applied Sport Psychology, 13,* 185–206.

Cobley, S., Schorer, J., & Baker, J. (2012). Identification and development of sport talent. A brief introduction to a growing field of research and practice. In J. Baker, J. Schorer, & S. Cobley (eds), *Talent identification and development in sport: International perspectives* (pp. 1–10). London: Routledge.

Crowne, D. P., & Marlowe, D. (1960). A new scale of social desirability independent of psychopathology. *Journal of Consulting Psychology, 24*(4), 349–354.

Cullen-Lester, K. L., Palus, C. J., & Appaneal, C. (2014). *Developing network perspective: Understanding the basics of social networks and their role in leadership.* Retrieved from Centre for Creative Leadership website: http://insights.ccl.org/articles/white-papers/developing-network-perspective-understanding-the-basics-of-social-networks-and-their-role-in-leadership/

Davids, K., & Baker, J. (2007). Genes, environment and sport performance: Why the nature-nurture dualism is no longer relevant. *Sports Medicine, 37,* 961–980.

Dickinson, R. K., Mallett, C.J., Gulbin, J. P., & Weissensteiner, J. R. (2012). Talent transfer in sport: High level coach insight. *17th Annual Congress of the European College of Sport Science* (p. 159). Belgium.

Durand-Bush, N., & Salmela, J. H. (2002). The development and maintenance of expert athletic performance: Perceptions of world and Olympic champions. *Journal of Applied Sport Psychology, 14*(3), 154–171.

Elferink-Gemser, M. T., Visscher, C., Lemmink, K. A. P. M., Mulder, T. (2004). Relation between multidimensional performance characteristics and level of performance in talented youth field hockey players. *Journal of Sports Sciences, 22,* 1053–1063.

Elferink-Gemser, M. T., Visscher, C., Lemmink, K. A. P. M., & Mulder, T. (2007). Multidimensional performance characteristics and standard of performance in talented youth field hockey players: A longitudinal study. *Journal of Sports Sciences, 25,* 481–489.

Elferink-Gemser, M. T., Jordet, G., Coelho-e-Silva, M. J., & Visscher, C. (2011). The marvels of elite sports: How to get there? *British Journal of Sports Medicine, 45,* 683–684.

Elferink-Gemser, M. T., & Visscher, C. (2012). Who are the superstars of tomorrow: Talent development in Dutch soccer. In J. Baker, S. Cobley, & J. Schorer, (eds), *Talent identification and development in sport: International perspectives* (pp. 95–105). London: Routledge.

Faber, I. R., Bustin, P. M., Oosterveld, F.G., Elferink-Gemser, M. T., & van der Sanden, N. (2015). Assessing personal talent determinants in young racquet sport players: A systematic review. In A. Radmann, S. Hedenborg, & E. Tsolakidis (eds), *20th Annual Congress of the European College of Sport Science* (p. 118), Sweden.

Fletcher, D., & Sarkar, M. (2012). A grounded theory of psychological resilience in Olympic champions. *Psychology of Sport and Exercise, 13,* 669–678.

Fuchslocher, J., Romann, M., & Gulbin, J. (2013). Strategies to support developing talent. *Schweizerische Zeitschrift für Sportmedizin und Sporttraumatologie, 61*(4), 10–14.

Gould, D., Dieffenbach, K., & Moffett, A. (2002). Psychological characteristics and their development in Olympic champions. *Journal of Applied Sport Psychology, 14*(3), 172–204.

Green, D. K., & Weissensteiner, J. R. (2015). The importance of self-regulation in athlete development. In A. Radmann, S. Hedenborg, E. Tsolakidis (eds), *20th Annual Congress of the European College of Sport Science* (p. 33), Sweden.

Gudmundsdottir, E., Riot, C., & Auld, C. (2014). *Talent transfer in high performance sport organisations: Exploring the transition cycle.* Gold Coast, Australia: Griffith University.

Gulbin, J. P., & Ackland, T. R. (2009). Talent identification and profiling. In T. R. Ackland, B. C. Elliott, & J. Bloomfield (eds), *Applied anatomy and biomechanics in sport* (pp. 11–26). Champaign, IL: Human Kinetics.

Gulbin, J. P., & Weissensteiner, J. R. (2013). Functional sport expertise systems. In D. Farrow, J. Baker, & C. MacMahon (eds), *Developing sport expertise: Researchers and coaches put theory into practice* (2nd ed., pp. 45–67). London: Routledge.

Gulbin, J. P., Croser, M. J., Morley, E., & Weissensteiner, J. R. (2013a). An integrated framework for the optimisation of sport and athlete development: A practitioner approach. *Journal of Sports Sciences, 31*(12), 1319–1331.

Gulbin, J. P., Weissensteiner, J. R., Oldenziel, K., & Gagne, F. (2013b). Patterns of performance development in elite athletes. *European Journal of Sport Science, 13*(6), 605–614.

Güllich, A., & Emrich, E. (2012). Individualistic and collectivistic approach in athlete support programmes in the German high-performance sport system. *European Journal for Sport and Society, 9*(4), 243–268.

Güllich, A., & Emrich, E. (2014). Considering long-term sustainability in the development of world class success. *European Journal of Sport Science, 14*(Suppl. 1), S383–S397.

Hambrick, M. E. (2013). Using social network analysis in sport communication research. In P. M. Pedersen (ed.), *The Routledge handbook of sport communication* (pp. 279–288), New York: Routledge.

Henriksen, K., Stambulova, N., & Roessler, K. K. (2010a). Holistic approach to athletic talent development environments: A successful sailing milieu. *Psychology of Sport and Exercise, 11*, 212–222.

Henriksen, K., Stambulova, N., & Roessler, K. K. (2010b). Successful talent development in track and field: Considering the role of environment. *Scandinavian Journal of Medicine & Science in Sports, 20*, 122–132.

Henriksen, K., Stambulova, N., & Roessler, K. K. (2011). Riding the wave of an expert: A successful talent development environment in kayaking. *The Sport Psychologist, 25*, 341–362.

Huijgen, B. C. H., Elferink-Gemser, M. T., Lemmink, K. A. P. M., & Visscher, C. (2014). Multidimensional performance characteristics in selected and deselected talented soccer players. *European Journal of Sport Science, 14*(1), 2–10.

Jonker, L., Elferink-Gemser, M. T., & Visscher, C. (2010). Differences in self-regulatory skills among talented athletes: The significance of competitive level and type of sport. *Journal of Sports Sciences, 28*(8), 901–908.

Jonker, L., Elferink-Gemser, M. T., & Visscher, C. (2011). The role of self-regulatory skills in sport and academic performances of elite youth athletes. *Talent Development & Excellence, 3*(2), 263–275.

McCarthy, N., & Collins, D. (2014). Initial identification & selection bias versus the eventual confirmation of talent: Evidence for the benefits of a rocky road. *Journal of Sport Sciences, 32*(17), 1604–1610.

MacNamara, Á., & Collins, D. (2013). More of the same: Comment on 'An integrated framework for the optimisation of sport and athlete development: A practitioner approach'. *Journal of Sports Sciences, 32*(8), 793–795.

Malina, R. M., Rogol, A. D., Cumming, S. P., Coelho-e-Silva, M. J., & Figueiredo, A. J. (2015). Biological maturation of youth athletes: Assessment and implications. *British Journal of Sports Medicine, 49*, 852–859.

Martindale, R. J. J., Collins, D., & Daubney, J. (2005). Talent development: A guide for practice and research within sport. *Quest, 57*, 353–375.

Mathews, A., Farrow, D., MacMahon, C., & Weissensteiner, J. R. (2012). Examining the barriers and facilitators of the junior to senior transition experience in Australian tennis: An in-depth analysis of the journey towards a professional tennis career. *North American Society for the Psychology of Sport & Physical Activity Conference*. Honolulu, Hawaii.

Matthys, S. P. J., Vaeyens, R., Vandendriessche, J., Vandorpe, B., Pion, J., Coutts, A. J., … & Philippaerts, R. M. (2011). A multidisciplinary identification model for youth handball. *European Journal of Sport Science, 11*(5), 355–363.

Matthys, S. P. J., Vaeyens, R., Fransen, J., Deprez, D., Pion, J., Vandendriessche, J., … Philippaerts, R. M. (2013). A longitudinal study of multidimensional performance characteristics related to physical capacities in youth handball. *Journal of Sport Sciences, 31*, 325–334.

Miller, P. K., Cronin, C., & Baker, G. (2015). Nurture, nature and some very dubious social skills: An interpretative phenomenological analysis of talent identification practices in elite English youth soccer. *Qualitative Research in Sport, Exercise & Health, 7*(5), 642–662.

Mountjoy, M., Rhind, D. J. A., Tiivas, A., & Leglise, M. (2015). Safeguarding the child athlete in sport: A review, a framework and recommendations for the IOC youth athlete development model. *British Journal of Sports Medicine, 49*, 883–886.

Philippaerts, R. M., Vaeyens, R., Janssens, M., Van Renterghem, B., Matthys, D., Craen, R., … Malina, R. M. (2006). The relationship between peak height velocity and physical performers in youth soccer players. *Journal of Sports Sciences, 24*(3), 221–230.

Phillips, E., Davids, K., Renshaw, I., & Portus, M. (2010) Expert performance in sport and the dynamics of talent development. *Sports Medicine, 40*(4), 271–283.

Pinder, R. A., Davids, K., Renshaw, I., & Araújo, D. (2011). Representative learning design and functionality of research and practice in sport. *Journal of Sport & Exercise Psychology, 33*(1), 146–155.

Pinder, R. A., Renshaw, I., & Davids, K. (2013). The role of representative design in talent development: a comment on 'Talent identification and promotion programmes of Olympic athletes'. *Journal of Sports Sciences, 31*(8), 803–806.

Pion, J., Lenoir, M., Vandorpe, B., & Segers, V. (2015a). Talent in female gymnastics: A survival analysis based upon performance characteristics. *International Journal of Sports Medicine, 36,* 935–940.

Pion, J., Segers, V., Fransen, J., Debuyck, G., Deprez, D., Haerens, L., … & Lenoir, M. (2015b). Generic anthropometric and performance characteristics among elite adolescent boys in nine different sports. *European Journal of Sport Science, 15*(5), 357–366.

Renshaw, I., Davids, K., Phillips, E., & Kerherve, H. (2012). Developing talent in athletes as complex neurobiological systems. In J. Baker, S. Cobley & J. Schorer (eds), *Talent identification and development in sport: International perspectives* (pp. 64–80). London: Routledge.

Robertson, S. J., Burnett, A. F., & Wilkie, J. (2013). Tests examining skill outcomes in sport: A systematic review of measurement properties and feasibility. *Sports Medicine, 44*(4), 501–518.

Rosalie, S. M., & Müller, S. (2012). A model for the transfer of perceptual-motor skill learning in human behaviors. *Research Quarterly for Exercise and Sport, 83*(3), 413–421.

Sacilotto, G. B. D., Warmenhoven, J. S., Mason, B. R., Ball, N., & Clothier, P. J. (2015). Investigation of ATM propulsion force-time profiles using functional data analysis on front crawl sprint swimmers. *Scientific Proceedings of the XXXIVth International Symposium on Biomechanics in Sports,* France.

Schöllhorn, W., Chow, J. Y., Glazier, P.S., & Button, C. (2014). Self-organising maps and cluster analysis in elite and sub-elite athletic performance. In K. Davids, D. Araújo, R. Hristovski, N. Balagué Serre, C. Button, & P. Passos (eds), *Complex systems in sport* (pp. 44–61). London: Routledge.

Schorer, J., Büsch, D., Fischer, L., Pabst, J., Reinhoff, R., Sichelschmidt, P., & Strauß, B. (2012). Back to the future: A case report of the ongoing evaluation of the German handball talent selection and development system. In J. Baker, S. Cobley & J. Schorer (eds), *Talent identification and development in sport: International perspectives* (pp. 119–129). London: Routledge.

Simonton D. K. (2001). Talent development as a multidimensional, multiplicative, and dynamic process. *Current Directions in Psychological Science 10,* 39–43.

Stambulova, N. (2010). Counselling athletes in career transitions: The five-step career planning strategy. *Journal of Sport Psychology in Action, 1*(2), 95–105.

Stambulova, N., Engström, C., Franck, A., Linnér, L., & Lindahl, K. (2015). Searching for an optimal balance: Dual career experiences of Swedish adolescent athletes. *Psychology of Sport and Exercise.* Advance online publication. DOI: 0.1016/j.psychsport.2014.08.009

Stoter, I. K., MacIntosh, B. R., Fletcher, J. R., Pootz, S., Zijdewind, I., Hettinga, F. J. (2015). Pacing strategy, muscle fatigue and technique in 1500m speed skating and cycling time-trials. *International Journal of Sports Physiology and Performance.* Advance online publication. DOI: 10.1123/ijspp.2014-0603

Suppiah, H. T., Low, C. Y., & Chia, M. (2015). Detecting and developing youth athlete potential: Different strokes for different folks are warranted. *British Journal of Sports Medicine, 49,* 878–882.

Till, K., Cobley, S., O'Hara, J., Brightmore, A., Cooke, C., & Chapman, C. (2011). Using anthropometric and performance characteristics to predict selection in junior UK Rugby League players. *Journal of Science and Medicine in Sport, 14,* 264–269.

Till, K., Cobley, S., O'Hara, J., Cooke, C., & Chapman, C. (2014). Considering maturation status and relative age in the longitudinal evaluation of junior rugby league players. *Scandinavian Journal of Medicine and Science in Sports, 24,* 569–576.

Till, K., Cobley, S., O'Hara, J., Morley, D., & Chapman, C. (2015). Retrospective analysis of anthropometric and fitness characteristics associated with long-term career progression in Rugby League. *Journal of Science and Medicine in Sport, 18,* 310–314.

Toering, T. T., Elferink-Gemser, M. T., Jordet, G., & Visscher, C. (2009). Self-regulation and performance level of elite and non-elite youth soccer players. *Journal of Sports Sciences, 27,* 1509–1517.

Toering, T. T., Elferink-Gemser, M., Jonker, L., Heuvelen, M., & Visscher, C. (2012) Measuring self-regulation in a learning context: Reliability and validity of the Self-Regulation of Learning Self-Report Scale (SRL-SRS), *International Journal of Sport and Exercise Psychology, 10*(1), 24–38.

Toohey, K., MacMahon, C., Weissensteiner, J. R., Thomson, A., Auld, C., Beaton, A., … Woolcock, G. (2015). *Improving the identification and development of Australia's sporting talent.* Retrieved from www.clearinghouseforsport.gov.au/__data/assets/pdf_file/0005/627080/Improving_the_Identification_and_Development_of_Australias_Sporting_Talent.pdf

Tucker, R., & Collins, M. (2012). What makes champions? A review of the relative contribution of genes and training to sporting success. *British Journal of Sports Medicine, 6,* 555–561.

Vaeyens, R., Malina, R. M., Janssens, M., Van Renterghem, B., Bourgois, J., Vrijens, J., & Philippaerts, R. M. (2006). A multidisciplinary selection model for youth soccer: The Ghent Youth Soccer Project. *British Journal of Sports Medicine, 40,* 928–934.

Vaeyens, R., Lenoir, M., Williams, M. A., & Philippaerts, R. M. (2008). Talent identification and development programmes in sport: Current models and future directions. *Sports Medicine, 38*(9), 703–714.

Vaeyens, R., Güllich, A., Warr, C. R., & Philippaerts, R. (2009). Talent identification and promotion programmes of Olympic athletes. *Journal of Sport Sciences, 27*(13), 1367–1380.

Warmenhoven, J. S., Smith, R., Cobley, S., Draper, C., Harrison, A., & Bargary, N. (2015). The application of functional data analysis techniques for characterizing differences in rowing propulsive-pin force curves. *Scientific Proceedings of the XXXIVth International Symposium on Biomechanics in Sports,* France.

Weissensteiner, J. R. (2015). The importance of listening: Engaging and incorporating the athlete's voice in theory and practice. *British Journal of Sports Medicine, 49,* 839–840.

Weissensteiner, J. R., Abernethy, B., Farrow, D., & Müller, S. (2008). The development of anticipation: A cross-sectional examination of the practice experiences contributing to skill in cricket batting. *Journal of Sport and Exercise Psychology, 30*(6), 663–684.

Weissensteiner, J. R., Abernethy, B., & Farrow, D. (2009). Towards the development of a conceptual model of batting expertise in cricket: A grounded theory approach. *Journal of Applied Psychology, 21*(3), 276–292.

Weissensteiner, J. R., Abernethy, B., Farrow, D., & Gross, J. (2012). Distinguishing psychological characteristics of expert cricket batsmen. *Journal of Science and Medicine in Sport, 15,* 74–79.

Weissensteiner, J. R., & Cook, C. (2015, November). Strive to thrive: Stress and leadership under the test. Presentation at AIS Coach and Athlete Forum, Canberra, Australia.

Weissensteiner, J. R., & Medlicott, R. (2015, June). *Administration of the NSO Pathway Healthcheck: Findings and recommendations for the Australian sporting system.* Presentation at AIS Winning Pathways Workshop, Canberra, Australia.

Weissensteiner, J. R., Warmenhoven, J., Medlicott, R., & Gulbin, J.P. (2015). Giving the athlete a voice: Preliminary findings from the My Sporting Journey Questionnaire. In A. Radmann, S. Hedenborg, E. Tsolakidis (eds), *20th Annual Congress of the European College of Sport Science* (p. 303). Sweden.

Wierike Te, S. C. M, Stoter, I. K., Huijgen, B. C. H., Jonker, L., Elferink-Gemser, M. T., & Visscher, C. (2015). In A. Radmann, S. Hedenborg, E. Tsolakidis (eds), *20th Annual Congress of the European College of Sport Science* (p.116), Sweden.

Williams, A. M., & Ericsson, K. A. (2005). Some considerations when applying the expert performance approach in sport. *Human Movement Science, 24,* 283–307.

Williams, A. M., & Reilly, T. (2000). Talent identification and development in soccer. *Journal of Sport Sciences, 18,* 657–667.

Wylleman, P., De Knop, P., & Reints, A. (2011). Transitions in competitive sports. In N. L. Holt & M. Talbot (eds), *Lifelong engagement in sport and physical activity* (pp. 63–76). New York: Routledge.

Wylleman, P., & Reints, A. (2010). A lifespan perspective on the career of talented and elite athletes: Perspectives on high-intensity sports, *Scandinavian Journal of Medicine and Science in Sports, 20* (Suppl. 2), 101–107.

Zimmerman, B. J. (1986). Becoming a self-regulated learner: Which are the key subprocesses? *Contemporary Educational Psychology, 11,* 307–313.

6

WHY CONCEPTUALIZATIONS OF TALENT MATTER

Implications for skill acquisition and talent identification and development

Nick Wattie and Joseph Baker

As many authors have noted (including several in this Handbook), there is tremendous pressure to identify and develop talented young athletes in many countries around the world. This has resulted in a worldwide sporting culture where significant resources and infrastructure are directed towards selecting athletes who are seen as having the greatest potential for success on the global stage. Perhaps the most extreme example is the 2011 selection of an 18-month-old to a 10-year 'symbolic contract' by a Dutch professional soccer team, largely based on the toddler's performance in a YouTube video.[1] Other examples exist that emphasize the desire for stakeholders in the athlete development system to identify and promote talent as soon as possible, using whatever means available (see 7-year-old Leonel Angel Coira and 10-year-old Ben Lederman who, in 2011, signed development contracts with Real Madrid and FC Barcelona respectively). The pressure and desire to identify and develop talent is also reflected in the tremendous financial investments in talent identification and development (TID) by both stakeholder organizations and the parents of developing athletes (see Campbell & Parcels' [2013] description of the latter).

In light of this emphasis on talent identification and development, we argue that how people think about talent, its origins and how it develops, influence not only the efficacy of TID practices, but more importantly, the youth at the centre of TID. While academic research over the past two decades supports the position that 'the nature-nurture dualism is no longer relevant' (Davids & Baker, 2007), the perpetuation of these beliefs about ability may be a reflection of what evolutionary biologist Richard Dawkins terms 'the tyranny of the discontinuous mind' (Dawkins, 2015, p. 84); our tendency to accept or prefer often arbitrary dichotomies despite evidence to the contrary. Unfortunately, peoples' beliefs about the roles of nature and nurture may still have real relevance 'on the ground'. To borrow a sentiment from Stephen Jay Gould (Harrar, 1984), these things matter because they affect real people. With this in mind, our chapter considers the impacts of two different ways of conceptualizing talent: as something that is relatively stable or as something that can be modified (see Dweck 1999; Wulf & Lewthwaite, 2009). First, we discuss the impact of holding mutually exclusive nature vs. nurture conceptualizations of ability on motivational, affective, and behavioural outcomes, as well as their influence on learning motor skills. We then discuss how a person's beliefs about ability, and the modifiability of those beliefs, may impact *others* (athletes) and the efficacy of TID in sport. We conclude with suggestions for future research and some unique considerations for how to conceptualize the nature of physical abilities.

A world from two mindsets

Social psychology research suggests our beliefs about things like abilities, intelligence and morality tend to fall into one of two opposing paradigms. These two perspectives essentially describe the outdated, but enduring, nature vs. nurture debate that has occupied discourses among both scientific communities and laypeople since Francis Galton first used the term in 1869 (see Davids & Baker, 2007, for a thorough discussion). Generally, this debate reflects the opposing beliefs that an individual's characteristics and potential are innate (unchangeable) *or* solely the product of experiences (changeable). Although the psychology literature refers to these world views as entity and incremental beliefs, respectively, herein we will refer to these beliefs using Wulf and Lewthwaite's (2009) taxonomy, which is somewhat more parsimonious and more relatable to motor learning and skill development in sport settings. Viewing skills as predominantly unchangeable reflects an *inherent ability (IA) belief*, whereas a mindset that views abilities as changeable, for example, through experiences or attention to high-quality training (see Chapter 3) reflects an *acquirable skill (AS) belief*.

Inherent Ability (IA) beliefs

Conceptualizations of ability, which are theoretically and empirically different from perceptions of competence, matter because they ultimately influence individual's attributions for success and failure. In the face of successful performance, believing in IA does not undermine performance. However, research suggests individuals who view intelligence as an IA are more likely to blame failures on their intellectual capacity, or lack thereof (Hong & Dweck, 1992). Indeed, it has been suggested that those who hold an IA perspective are more preoccupied with judgments and appraisals about their traits, and subsequently form goals about their performance outcomes as a strategy to reaffirm judgments about their 'natural ability'. Perhaps not surprisingly, because such individuals ultimately believe that intellectual ability is unchangeable, they often respond to negative feedback with negative self-judgments, negative affect, a lack of persistence (Dweck et al., 1995), and in some instances exhibit depressive symptoms (Dweck, 1999). Such responses to negative feedback or performance by those with an IA perspective have been described as a 'helpless pattern' (Dweck, 1999), which is ultimately not conducive to learning and performance (Dweck et al., 1995).

Although the majority of research on IA vs. AS beliefs has focused on areas such as intelligence and morality (Weiss & Raedeke, 2004), research on physical abilities also supports the premise that people's beliefs about their ability are important, and findings are consistent with the psychology literature. In an early study, for example, youth who held IA beliefs about athletic ability were more likely to have performance (outcome) goal orientations than peers that held AS beliefs (Biddle, Soos, & Chatzisarantis, 1999). In a series of three studies of over 3,000 youth aged 11–19, Biddle and colleagues (Biddle, Wang, Chatzisarantis, & Spray, 2003) assessed the impact of IA and AS beliefs about athletic ability. Believing that athletic ability was predominantly unchangeable (IA) directly predicted amotivation (Biddle et al., 2003). Also consistent with research on intellectual ability, those with an IA perspective of athletic ability were more likely to attribute poor performance to their innate ability level instead of effort, persistence and practice (Spray, Wang, Biddle, Chatzisarantis, & Warburton, 2006).

Similar to research in education, there is also evidence that believing athletic ability to be innate is associated with negative or helpless reaction patterns. For example, regardless of perceived level of ability, secondary school physical education students who have an IA belief of athletic ability had higher levels of anxiety and decreased levels of satisfaction with physical education (Ommundsen, 2001a). This may be a reflection of the importance that IA supporters place on judgments about themselves and the pressure associated with judgments about their abilities. In an interesting addition to research on beliefs about the nature of athletic ability, Ommundsen (2001b) also assessed the degree to which secondary school students self-handicapped, a strategy used to protect one's self-esteem. Self-handicapping is distinct from attributions about ability, in that it attempts to undermine performance in ways that are independent from these attributions. For example, an athlete might self-handicap by arriving to a practice late, unprepared or unrested, and use that self-handicapping strategy to aggrandize good performance or account for poor performance. Interestingly, belief in IA has a direct and positive association with self-handicapping behaviour, while AS beliefs are negatively related to self-handicapping behaviour (Ommundsen, 2001b). This may reflect a desire by individuals with an IA attribution of ability to self-protect in situations where judgments can be readily made about their ability. If poor performance occurs, attention can be directed towards an excuse (i.e., the self-handicapping strategy, such as 'I didn't sleep well last night'); conversely, a good performance that occurs despite self-handicapping can be used to further enhance perceptions about one's IA. Whether or not performance is undermined, self-handicapping behaviours can create barriers to self-regulation (see Chapter 11), future learning, and can decrease the likelihood of successful athlete development. Interestingly, high perceived competence in the absence of failure may buffer the relationship between IA beliefs and self-handicapping, suggesting that less desirable motivational strategies associated with IA beliefs are only probabilistic (Ommundsen, 2001b).

Acquirable Skill (AS) beliefs

In contrast to an IA perspective, believing that skills are predominantly acquirable has been associated with more constructive motivational dispositions and responses to failure. Rather than attribute poor performance to a lack of innate ability, AS believers are more likely to attribute poor performance to a lack of effort or insufficient preparation on their part (Dweck, 1999). AS individuals, therefore, tend to adopt task-oriented motivational strategies rather than performance-oriented motivation strategies. For example, rather than helpless patterns of response to poor performance, AS individuals are more likely to adopt a mastery-oriented behavioural pattern and tend to make process goals, increase their effort, and persist in practice/learning attempts.

Research also suggests that AS beliefs about physical abilities may be related to more positive motivational strategies and characteristics. For example, Biddle et al.'s (2003) study of youths' beliefs about nature of sport/athletic ability observed that AS beliefs were a significant independent predictor of enjoyment. Similarly, youth with AS beliefs were more likely to have higher levels of satisfaction with physical education classes (Ommundsen, 2001a). The importance of these findings is reinforced by the role of enjoyment (and satisfaction) as a determinant of youth sport participation, and the prominent role of enjoyment within theoretical models of sport participation and athlete development (e.g., Developmental Model of Sport Participations: Côté & Fraser-Thomas, 2011; Long-term athlete development/Canadian Sport 4 Life: Balyi & Hamilton, 2004).

While the majority of research on ability beliefs has explored motivational and affective processes and outcomes, a study by Wulf and Lewthwaite (2009) suggested conceptions of ability also impact motor skill acquisition. Prior to practising a balancing task, participants were prompted with a narrative that performance on the upcoming task either reflected a person's IA or that performance was reflective of an AS (a control group, which was not prompted with any narrative, was also included in the study). Although both groups improved their balance over the course of the study practice trials, the AS-prompted group demonstrated a trend for greater performance (i.e., fewer errors in performance) in the retention tests compared to the control and IA-prompted group. In addition, the study also measured the extent of participants' reflexive rapid muscle activation (i.e., mean power frequency). The AS-prompted group demonstrated significantly higher mean power frequency than the control and IA groups in each of the practice trials as well as the retention test. Moreover, while rapid muscle activation remained relatively stable across the practice trials and retention test for the control and IA-prompted groups, the AS-promoted group demonstrated continuous improvement throughout the practice trials and retention test. These results, and the favourable influence of AS beliefs, are notable because a higher frequency of reflexive rapid muscle activation is thought to indicate greater quality of movement control and higher skill level (Wulf & Lewthwaite, 2009).

In an independent but similar study that involved tracking a moving target with a handheld stylus, participants were presented the task as reflecting either AS or IA (Jourden, Bandura, & Banfield, 1991). Participants completed three blocks of trials on the tracing task (there was no control group or retention test). Both groups demonstrated improvements in performance from baseline, however, the AS-prompted group demonstrated significantly greater performance improvements across each of the three blocks of trials with a final per cent change in performance of approximately 400 per cent (compared to an approximately 200 per cent change for the IA-prompted group). In addition, at the completion of the final block of trials the AS-prompted group reported higher levels of self-efficacy, and positive affect related to their performance compared to the IA group. Lastly, after the completion of the three blocks of trials, all participants were told that there were 5 minutes remaining and that they could continue to practise the task if they wished. The authors used willingness to continue the task as a measure of 'interest'. A significantly greater proportion of AS-prompted participants chose to continue the task than IA-promoted participants (72% vs. 21%: Jourden et al., 1991).

While additional research is needed, this research suggests that in addition to having motivational and affective consequences, beliefs about the nature of abilities can also impact the degree of learning in terms of acquiring motor skills, a key component of athlete development. Wulf and Lewthwaite (2009) speculated that an AS-prompt improves performance and learning in a similar way to having an external focus of attention; AS beliefs may direct attention away from the self, whereas IA beliefs may direct attention toward the self and disrupt performance in a way similar to having an internal focus of attention when performing motor skills.

Beyond the self: The influence of ability beliefs on athletes and TID

While there is convincing evidence that ability beliefs influence individual learner responses to failure and motivational strategies, from a TID perspective it is also important to acknowledge how our beliefs might influence others. First, research suggests that a person's beliefs about abilities can influence someone else's beliefs about the nature of their abilities. Second, TID is ultimately a predictive exercise; predictions and judgments are made about how much ability a person has (talent identification) and whether or not an athlete has the potential to develop skills (talent development). In the following section we discuss the interpersonal influence of ability beliefs, and the parallels between research on ability beliefs and predictive accuracy, both with implications for TID.

The interpersonal influence of ability beliefs

While there is convincing evidence that there are personal implications for what an athlete believes about the nature of their abilities, there is also reason to believe that these beliefs are not fixed and may be influenced through interactions with significant others. Most notably, research suggests peoples' ability beliefs (IA vs. AS) can be influenced by external stimuli, as evidenced by experimental studies that have demonstrated their modifiability (see Dweck, 2003; Spray et al., 2006; Wulf & Lewthwaite, 2009). As such, the beliefs of coaches, scouts and parents, and their subsequent behaviour, messages and language can influence the beliefs and experiences of athletes.

Research from motivation studies suggests we have to be careful about the labels and expectations we place on youth athletes, including labelling an athlete as talented. Labelling high-performance youth athletes as talented can attach an expectation that the athlete will be successful at later stages in the athlete development pathway because their 'talent' is innate (natural) and fixed (IA beliefs). As Dweck (2003) describes, praising a learner in a way that reinforces IA beliefs negatively modifies their motivations and reactions to failure: learners 'can be affected by interventions, and when they are, motivation and achievement appear to follow suit' (Dweck, 2003, p. 19). As such, communicating an IA belief to athletes may influence how they view and respond to short- and long-term training as well as poor competitive performances, which may ultimately constrain their development as athletes. In addition, the expectations associated with these beliefs may also be damaging, particularly given that success at one level of sport does automatically lead to success at the next, higher, level of sport (see Barreiros & Fonseca, 2012). It can be damaging to forget that hard work and high-quality training are important to becoming a senior adult high-performance athlete.

It is also important to recognize that viewing talent as entirely malleable (i.e., entirely due to nurture) can likewise be problematic. In recent years the popularized notion that expertise can be accomplished through a sufficient amount of deliberate practice (the colloquial 10,000-hour rule derived from Ericsson et al., 1993 and popularized by Gladwell, 2008) has taken root amongst sport systems, coaches, parents and athletes. To those who believe this notion, the term 'talent development' implies that all athletes have equal amounts of talent to be developed, despite inter-individual differences, and that this is a better approach to athlete development (see Grove, 2016; Syed, 2010). While extensive practice is clearly necessary, it may not be sufficient (see Macnamara, Hambrick & Oswald, 2014): genes, resources and luck are also important (see Bailey 2007; Gagné, 2013). For example, recent research on genes such as COL5A1 (e.g., Posthumus et al., 2009) and ACTN3 (Eynon et al., 2013) reinforces the importance of genetic factors not only in explaining elite athletic performance, but also in providing the biological foundation for the years of training required for exceptional skill acquisition.

Given the different motivational, behavioural and learning outcomes we have described between IA and AS groups, it may be tempting to conclude that deterministic AS beliefs should be nurtured (no pun intended) in young athletes. However, the reality is that IA beliefs do not deterministically result in negative outcomes. Under the right circumstances (e.g., infrequent failure or high perceived competence), a performer with IA beliefs can reach high levels of achievement and not demonstrate maladaptive motivational strategies (Ommundsen, 2001b). Although there may be more risks to this type of ability belief; and while the notion of AS has some appeal, high-performance sport is not a meritocracy and the evidence is clear that not all people have the same potential to develop into high-performance athletes (whether for reasons of probability or propensity).

Therefore, like IA beliefs, those who purely ascribe to the AS belief may also place unfair expectations on themselves and others. Indeed, Dweck (1999) suggests that over-persistence as a result of AS beliefs may be another form of helpless behaviour. Dweck (1999, p. 14) nicely summarizes the potentially serious developmental implication for athletes that believe too fervently in either IA or AS: 'In both cases – either getting out too quickly or staying in too long – the maladaptive response is based on the concern that failure spells serious personal inadequacy.' While youth start to form their ability beliefs during childhood, it appears that these beliefs come together and begin to exert a demonstrable influence on motivation and behaviour around 10–12 years of age, which may start youth on different developmental pathways through adolescence (see Dweck 2003). Coincidentally, the age when ability beliefs coalescence into an influential motivation and behavioural mindset coincides with when many sports take on a more competitive and serious pathway within athlete development.

Foxes vs. Hedgehogs: Ability beliefs and the accuracy of judgments

'The fox knows many things, but the hedgehog knows one big thing.'

(Isaiah Berlin)

While there may be interpersonal implications for the athlete as a result of what a coach, parent, or socio-cultural sport environment espouses, there may also be practical implications of ability beliefs on the effectiveness of talent identification and development practices. In particular, there is an important symmetry between ability beliefs and research on the accuracy of judgments and predictions.

According to Dweck, Chiu, and Hong (1995b) people tend to have one dominant theory of abilities (see below for contradictory evidence), which may be particularly important when considering research on the predictive nature of TID. Philip Tetlock's (for review see Tetlock, 2005) research on expert judgments and predictions led him to playfully describe two types of people: Foxes and Hedgehogs (based on Isaiah Berlin's characterization: Berlin, 2000). True to the quote above, Foxes do not adhere to 'one approach', instead making use of multiple theories, and are unafraid to embrace uncertainty. Foxes will also self-subversively adjust their thinking in the face of convincing evidence. By comparison, Hedgehogs are more likely to ardently adhere to one 'way of thinking' (or theory), fear uncertainty, and interpret new contradictory evidence in such a way that it confirms their existing beliefs. These distinctions in *how* people within an organization (e.g., coaches, administrators) think might have important implications for discussions of talent and development: Hedgehogs tend to make less accurate predictions than Foxes (Tetlock, 2005). For our purposes, *how* people think (i.e., Foxes vs. Hedgehogs) may intersect with *what* people think (i.e., AS beliefs vs. IA beliefs) to ultimately influence talent identification and development practices. For example, when a coach or scout selects an athlete for a team or sport development system they are effectively making a judgment and prediction about the ability and/or potential of that athlete.

Regardless of whether a coach believes ability is modifiable (AS) or non-modifiable (IA), if they hold to their dichotomized theory too strongly it might compromise talent identification and development practices. Both IA *and* AS hedgehogs may be more apt to make false predictions and judgments during TID (see below). Those with strong non-malleable IA beliefs are also more likely to attribute a young athlete's performances to their innate, fixed ability (see Dweck, 1999), and may extend their judgments of other's abilities and characteristics (even after a single observation) to make stronger predictions about future behaviour and performance (Chiu, Hong, & Dweck, 1997). Alternatively, those with strong non-malleable AS beliefs are more likely to attribute performance to environmental circumstances and effort, and make more equivalent predictions of future performance. As we describe above, over-valuing train-ability and the belief that increased effort and practice is sufficient to improve athlete development is unrealistic and may result in an unfair expectations placed on youth athletes.

The fact that our own concepts of ability can influence judgments and predictions of other's ability and behaviour has TID implications for those with single-minded views (i.e., whether IA or AS). An IA Hedgehog may ultimately reject or select talent based on their belief that a performance reflects an innate and fixed level of ability. Alternatively, an AS Hedgehog may fail to reject an athlete believing presently observed lower performance is not necessarily indica-tive of future potential. Both beliefs, too ardently adhered to, may lead to increased probabilities of both Type I and II errors within TID systems (Cobley, Baker, Wattie, & McKenna, 2009). That is, believing talent (or potential) is there when it is not, and rejecting an athlete when they actually have talent (or potential), respectively. We propose that such ability mindsets are asso-ciated with several errors or limitations identified in athlete development research.

Errors in TID: The relative age effect

The relative age effect reflects the increased likelihood of youth who are among the relatively older members of their age cohort to be selected to competitive youth sport team and to become elite athletes (Cobley et al., 2009; Wattie, Schorer, & Baker, 2015). A proposed mech-anism of this effect suggests those involved in talent selection decisions (e.g., coaches, parents, etc.) confound talent with the physical parameters and physiological capacity (e.g., greater height, weight, power, speed etc.; Pearson, Naughton, & Torode, 2006), which result from the probabilistically greater maturation associated with the older chronological age of relatively older youth. Relatively younger peers are often less advanced in terms of growth and matura-tion, which makes them appear less capable (i.e., less talented). One study by our research team (Baker et al., 2010) found that a cohort of elite youth hockey players (9- and 10-year-olds) did not differ in height and weight despite differences of up to one year among the oldest and youngest in the group, suggesting coaches at this level make selection decisions based on phys-ical parameters and performance outcomes rather than valid measures of potential (if such variables exist). The persistence of the relative age effect, despite many years of research high-lighting its negative consequences (Helsen et al., 2012), may reflect robust beliefs among coaches that physical attributes reflect stable predictors of talent. A recent study by Furley and Memmert (2016) examined coaches' implicit associations between size and potential, noting coaches rated taller athletes as being more gifted than smaller athletes despite not knowing anything else about the players other than height. Regardless of whether coaches and scouts believe that talent is predominantly the result of IA or AS, the reliance on physical parameters or physiological capacities (i.e., performance) to reflect either etiology of talent is problematic: Physical parameters and maturation-related performance are not the same thing as talent or the potential to develop elite levels of skill. If such characteristics were indicative of 'talent' then we would probably have much more accurate TID systems (regardless of whether that's conceptu-alized as innate or potential). Abbott and colleagues (Abbott, Button, Pepping, & Collins, 2005) playfully describe reliance on such characteristics for TID as 'unnatural selection' because (among other things) a) discrete performance measures have limited predictive value, b) some of these factors are unstable characteristics, and c) development is non-linear. Relative age effects reflect these limitations, as do fixed IA and AS beliefs.

Errors in TID: Sunk cost effects

Another type of error in action can be seen through 'sunk cost effects' (Staw & Hoang, 1995), which relate to the tendency for individuals to continue to invest in something when the available evidence clearly indicates this continued investment is not warranted. There is evidence of this in the professional sports draft systems where teams, more specifically the managers, owners and coaches who make decisions, continue to devote increased playing time and resources to players who are drafted earlier and therefore represent larger investments for the team. In a study of players in the National Basketball Association (NBA), Staw and Hoang (1995) found that teams gave greater playing time to their most highly drafted players and retained them longer for their franchises, even after controlling for on-court performance, injuries, trade status, and position played. These effects (see also Koz, Fraser-Thomas & Baker, 2012) reflect an error associated with assuming members of a group have greater talent when they do not.

These pervasive effects may partially explain the relatively low levels of success in talent selections (e.g., Koz et al., 2012). They also highlight the potential risk of over-prescribing to certain beliefs about the nature of abilities in predictive TID judgments. However, while research on ability beliefs (IA vs. AS), judgments/predictions of others (see Dweck, 1999) and predictive accuracy of *Foxes vs. Hedgehogs* (Tetlock, 2005) supports their potential influence and importance, future research is needed in sport TID related contexts. While the influence of ability beliefs on physical abilities, reactions to failure, and their motivational strategies have been examined, the same cannot be said for their influence on forecasting and accuracy in TID decisions.

Future directions

Psychological research literature suggests people tend to have a dominant mindset of ability in a particular domain (see Dweck et al., 1995b). However, research on physical abilities (i.e., sport) suggests an 'examination of belief permutations and their motivational correlates' may be necessary (Biddle et al., 2003, p. 986). For example, the result of a cluster analysis revealed groups of youth who were highly motivated and had both high IA and AS beliefs, as well as a less motivated group of youth who had low AS beliefs and high IA beliefs (Wang & Biddle, 2001). This suggests that while some may have a dominant theory of ability, others may consider ability beliefs as a 'continuous spectrum of intermediates' (Dawkins, 2015, p. 84); there are likely Foxes in our midst. Going forward, it will be important to consider whether different permutations of ability belief exist, and if some people have a malleable approach to ability beliefs (i.e., adjusting beliefs based on emerging evidence). Subsequently, it will also be important to study the relationship between the malleability of ability beliefs and how it may influence motivation, skill acquisition, talent identification decisions, as well as coaches' feedback or instruction to their athletes and how coaches structure learning environments. There may also be a need to explore the intersection of ability beliefs with factors such as gender and race/ethnicity. For example, research suggests different ability attributions are often made between white and black athletes, ultimately resulting in positional racial stacking within the National Football League (Rada, 2006; Rada & Wulfemeyer, 2005). Similarly, beliefs about the stability of racial differences may affect individual performance through the mechanism of 'stereotype threat' (see Baker & Horton, 2003; Stone, Lynch, Sjomeling & Darley, 1999). As such, it may be necessary to consider how existing stereotypes correlate or interact with beliefs about the nature of abilities. More generally, in considering all of the above, it may be particularly useful to also consider the role of ability beliefs with respect to the accuracy of TID judgments and predictions, and ultimately the short and long term success of TID programs.

Concluding thoughts

With respect to TID in sport, we suggest that either ability belief perspective, if too ardently adhered to, can be damaging to athletes and counterproductive to TID. Returning to the Fox vs. Hedgehog comparison, coaches, parents, administrators and athletes should be wary of any dichotomy that attempts to explain highly skilled performance from one particular standpoint (i.e., a Hedgehog approach), regardless of whether that factor is nature or nurture. Instead, a more appropriate standpoint for talent selection and development measures might be to consider all evidence available at a given time and choose the best course of action based on these data. The assumption here is that similar decisions in the future will change as new information and new evidence emerges (i.e., a Fox approach).

The persistence of nature vs. nurture beliefs over the past 150 years highlights the enduring nature of these positions. Moreover, these beliefs can be found in many of the policies and institutions governing the structure of sport, both at the grassroots and high-performance levels. For example, when sport systems (or education systems for that matter) stream youth in different ability groups at very young ages, this may reflect the belief that a) innate and stable differences exist between youth, b) these differences can be observed and measured early in life, and c) these initial differences correlate with adult outcomes. The evidence for each of these factors is surprisingly weak (see Howe, Davidson & Sloboda, 1998), yet belief in these factors persist and can have profound effects on youths' experiences in sport, and the efficacy of talent selection and development initiatives.

Note

1   www.youtube.com/watch?v=31pxEs64z9s.

References

Abbott, A., Button, C., Pepping, G-J, & Collins, D. (2005). Unnatural selection: Talent identification and development in sport. *Nonlinear Dynamics, Psychology, and Life Sciences, 9*, 61–88.

Baker, J., & Horton, S. (2003). East African running dominance revisited: A role for stereotype threat? *British Journal of Sports Medicine, 37*, 553–555.

Baker, J., Cobley, S., Montelpare, W. J., Wattie, N., Faught, B., & the Ontario Hockey Research Group (2010). Exploring mechanisms of the relative age effect in Canadian Minor Hockey. *International Journal of Sport Psychology, 41*, 148–159.

Balyi, I., & Hamilton, A. (2004). Long-term athlete development: Trainability in childhood and adolescence. Windows of opportunity. Optimal trainability. Victoria, BC: National Coaching Institute British Columbia & Advanced Training and Performance.

Bailey, R. (2007). Talent development and luck problem. *Sport, ethics and philosophy, 1*, 367–377.

Barreiros, A. N., & Fonseca, A. M. (2012). A retrospective analysis of Portuguese elite athletes' involvement in international competitions. *International Journal of Sport Science and Coaching, 7*, 593–600.

Berlin, I. (2000). The Hedgehog and the Fox. In *The Proper Study of Mankind: An Anthology of Essays*. New York: Farrar, Straus and Giroux.

Biddle, S. J. H., Soos, I., Chatzisarantis, N. (1999). Predicting physical activity intentions using a goal perspectives approach: A study of Hungarian youth. *Scandinavian Journal of Medicine & Science and Sports, 9*, 353–357

Biddle, S. J. H., Wang, C. K. J., Chatzisarantis, N. L. D., & Spray, C. M. (2003). Motivation for physical activity in young people: entity and incremental beliefs about athletic ability. *Journal of Sports Sciences, 21*, 973–989.

Campbell, K., & Parcels, J. (2013). *Selling the dream: How hockey parents and their kids are paying the price for our National obsession.* Toronto: Penguin.

Chiu, C., Hong, Y., & Dweck, C. S. (1997). Lay dispositionism and implicit theories of personality. *Journal of Personality and Social Psychology, 73,* 923–940.

Cobley, S. Baker, J., Wattie, N., & McKenna, J. (2009). Annual Age-Grouping and Athlete Development: A Meta Analytical Review of Relative Age Effects in Sport. *Sports Medicine, 39,* 235–256.

Côté, J., & Fraser-Thomas, J. (2011). Youth involvement and positive youth development in sport. In P. Crocker (ed.), *Sport psychology: A Canadian perspective* (2nd ed., pp. 227–255). Toronto: Pearson.

Davids, K., & Baker, J. (2007). Genes, environment and sport performance: Why the nature–nurture dualism is no longer relevant. *Sports Medicine, 37,* 1–20.

Dawkins, R. (2015). Essentialism. In J. Brockman (ed.), *This idea must die.* New York: Harper, pp. 84–87.

Dweck, C. S. (1999). *Self-theories: Their role in motivation, personality, and development.* Philadelphia, PA: Psychology Press.

Dweck, C. S. (2003). Ability conceptions, motivation and development. *Development and Motivation, 2,* 13–27.

Dweck, C. S., Chiu, C., & Hong, Y. (1995). Implicit theories and their role in judgments and reactions: A world from two perspectives. *Psychological Inquiry, 6,* 267–285.

Ericsson, K. A., Krampe, R. T., & Tesch-Römer, C. (1993). The role of deliberate practice in the acquisition of expert performance. *Psychological Review, 100,* 363–406.

Eynon, N., Hanson, E. D., Lucia, A., Houweling, P. J., Garton, F., North, K. N., & Bishop, D. J. (2013). Genes for elite power and sprint performance: ACTN3 leads the way. *Sports Medicine, 43,* 803–817.

Furley, P., & Memmert, D. (2016). Coaches' implication associations between size and giftedness: Implications for the relative age effect. *Journal of Sports Sciences, 34,* 459–486.

Gagné, F. (2013). The DMGT: Changes within, beneath, and beyond. *Talent Development and Excellence, 5,* 5–19.

Galton, F. (1869). *Hereditary genius: An inquiry into its laws and consequences.* London: Macmillan.

Gladwell, M. (2008). *Outliers: The Story of Success.* New York: Little, Brown and Company.

Grove, J. (2016). Talent development vs. talent identification: Give kids a chance. *Active for Life.com,* retrieved May 12, 2016 from http://activeforlife.com/talent-development-vs-identification/

Harrar, L. (Writer & Director). (1984). Stephan Jay Gould: This view of life. In Apsell, P.S. (Executive Producer), *Nova.* Boston, MA: PBS (WGBH/BBC-TV).

Helsen, W., Baker, J., Micheils, S., Schorer, J., van Wickel, J., & Williams, A. M. (2012). The relative age effect in European professional football: Has anything changed after 10 years of research? *Journal of Sports Sciences, 30,* 1665–1671.

Hong, Y., & Dweck, C. S. (1992). Implicit theories as predictors of self-inference processes. Paper presented at the annual convention of the American Psychological Society, San Diego, CA.

Howe, J. W., Davidson, M. J. A., & Sloboda, J. A. (1998). Innate talent: Reality or myth? *Brain and Behavioral Sciences, 21,* 399–442.

Jourden, F. J., Bandura, A., & Banfield, J. T. (1991). The impact of concepts of ability on self-regulatory factors and motor skill acquisition. *Journal of Sport & Exercise Psychology, 8,* 213–226.

Koz, D., Fraser-Thomas, J., & Baker, J. (2012). Accuracy of professional sports drafts in predicting career potential. *Scandinavian Journal of Medicine and Science in Sports, 22,* e64–e69.

Macnamara, B. N., Hambrick, D. Z., & Oswald, F. L. (2014). Deliberate practice and performance in music, games, sports, education and professions: A meta-analysis. *Psychological Science, 25,* 1608–1618.

Ommundsen, Y. (2001a). Pupils' affective responses in physical education classes: the association of implicit theories of the nature of ability and achievement goals. *European Physical Education Review, 7,* 219–242.

Ommundsen, Y. (2001b). Self-handicapping strategies in physical education classes: the influence of implicit theories of the nature of ability and achievement goal orientations. *Psychology of Sport and Exercise, 2,* 139–156.

Pearson, D. T., Naughton, G. A., & Torode, M. (2006). Predictability of physiological testing and the role maturation in talent identification for adolescent team sports. *Journal of Science and Medicine in Sport, 9,* 277–287.

Posthumus, M., September, A. V., O'Cuinneagain, D., van der Merwe, W., Schwellnus, M. P., & Collins, M. (2009). The COL5A1 gene is associated with increased risk of anterior cruciate ligament rupture in female participants. *American Journal of Sports Medicine, 37,* 2234–2240.

Rada, J. A. (1996). Color blind-sided: Racial bias in network television's coverage of professional football games. *The Howard Journal of Communication, 7,* 231–239.

Rada, J. A., & Wulfemeyer, K. T. (2005). Color coded: Racial descriptors in television coverage of inter-collegiate sports. *Journal of Broadcasting & Electronic Media, 49*, 65–68.

Spray, C. M., Wang, C. K. J, Biddle, S. J. H., Chatzisarantis, N. L. D., & Warburton, V. E. (2006). An experimental test of self-theories of ability in youth sport. *Psychology of Sport and Exercise, 7*, 255–267.

Staw, M. B., & Hoang, H. (1995). Sunk costs in the NBA: Why draft order affects playing time and survival in professional basketball. *Administrative Science Quarterly, 40*, 474–494.

Stone, J., Lynch, C. I., Sjomeling, M., & Darley, J. M. (1999). Stereotype threat effects on black and white athletic performance. *Journal of Personality and Social Psychology, 77*, 1213–1227.

Syed, M. (2010). *Bounce: Mozart, Federer, Picasso, Beckham, and the science of success.* New York: Harper-Collins.

Tetlock, P. E. (2005). *Expert Political Judgment: How Good Is It? How Can We Know?* Princeton: Princeton University Press.

Wang, C. K. J., & Biddle, S. J. H. (2001). Young people's motivational profiles in physical activity: A cluster analysis. *Journal of Sport & Exercise Psychology, 23*, 1–22.

Wattie, N., Schorer, J., & Baker, J. (2015). The relative age effect in sport: A developmental systems model. *Sports Medicine, 45*, 83–94.

Weiss, M. R., & Raedeke, T. D. (2004). Developmental sport psychology: Research status on youth and directions toward a lifespan perspective: A lifespan perspective. In M. R. Weiss (ed.), *Developmental sport and exercise psychology: A lifespan perspective.* (pp. 1–26). Morgantown, WV: Fitness Information Technology.

Wulf, G., & Lewthwaite, R. (2009). Conceptions of ability affect motor learning. *Journal of Motor Behavior, 41*, 461–467.

7

ON THE EFFICACY OF TALENT IDENTIFICATION AND TALENT DEVELOPMENT PROGRAMMES

Arne Güllich and Stephen Cobley

Introduction

Besides the direct competition between athletes, *nations* compete indirectly for *collective* national success (e.g., medal tally) at Olympic Games and other international championships. To facilitate these outcomes, national sport organisations (NSOs) around the world have established organised talent identification (TID) and talent development programmes (TDP), designed to catalyse their most promising young athletes' performance development. Over recent decades, the respective investments in these programmes have increased substantially (e.g., De Bosscher, Bingham, Shibli, & van Bottenburg, 2008; Oakley & Green, 2001).

NSOs face the challenge to structure TID/TDP programmes efficaciously to regularly develop internationally successful athletes. However, analyses from different national sport systems suggest relatively low 'success rates': Only up to 2 per cent of young athletes involved in TDP eventually attain international senior success (e.g., Ackermann, 2013; Gray & Plucker, 2010; Güllich, 2014a; Güllich & Emrich, 2005b, 2012; Höner, Schultz, Schreiner, & Votteler, 2015; Hong, 2008; Ljach, 1997; Malina, 2010; Morris, Dunman, Alvey, Wynn, & Nevill, 2004; Pion, Lenoir, Vandorpe, & Segers, 2015; Sands, 2012; Vaeyens, Güllich, Warr, & Philippaerts, 2009). More or less substantial over-investment is typical of TDP, in terms of athlete numbers selected and interventions applied to them. Also, research-based evidence that definitively informs the design of TID/TDP is still scarce. Policy-makers and researchers alike are thus preoccupied with questions of how to organise TID/TDP efficaciously – for example: At what age to initiate TID/TDP? How many athletes to involve at which age stage? What interventions to apply to them and how intensively; and how to best structure TID/TDP institutions?

To better examine these concerns, the chapter first outlines the central 'idea' and structure of TID and TDP, and crystallizes the fundamental premises underpinning early TID/TDP. Then, we provide an overview of empirical research evidence with reference to these premises. Finally, practical implications and future directions are discussed.

'The idea' and structure of TID and TDP

The central 'idea' of TID is to identify and select the most promising young talents from the general population in order to focus TDP delivery and investments on these promising few.

TDP, in turn, aims to support selected athletes' training and competition process by subsidising resources and applying supportive interventions (i.e., providing 'treatment') to thereby facilitate performance progress, and increase their likelihood of long-term international senior success. TID/TDP is provided mainly by NSOs (and their regional sub-divisions), often utilising elite training centres, athlete service centres (e.g., Australian or English Institutes of Sport, German Olympic Support Centres, China's National Training Centre), youth sport academies (e.g., in artistic gymnastics, soccer, tennis), and/or Elite Sport Schools. Programmes are typically sub-divided in age- and performance-related stages: Some talent search and initial talent development during childhood and early adolescence (often operated at a local/regional level); a junior promotion stage; and senior sub-elite and elite promotion (see Figure 7.1). The typical 'pyramidal' structure implies a larger number of athletes are involved initially, with stepwise reductions at each subsequent stage. Overall, different national structures and elements have been characterised by progressing convergence through recent decades (see Chapter 9); a fact ascribed to the increasing global competition (Houlihan & Green, 2008).

TID usually draws on youngsters' early performance, performance components and/or performance progress over time. They are commonly assessed by the 'coach's eye' that may involve a holistic multidisciplinary perspective (e.g., Christensen, 2009; Vrljic & Mallett, 2008), and/or specifically assessing anthropometrics, performance in competition, motor/physiological performance tests (sometimes evaluated relative to the youngsters' biological maturation), and – less frequently – psychological tests (see Güllich & Emrich, 2005a, for a review; see also Chapters 4 and 5).

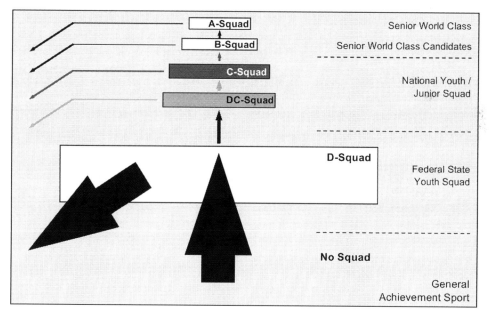

Figure 7.1 Conceptualised squad structure – annual memberships and transitions between squad levels as conceptualised by seven NSOs. The sizes of the rectangles represent the mean annual numbers of members (scale orientation: 'D' n = 6,784; 'A' n = 254), and the widths of the arrows represent the mean numbers of annual individual transitions (scale orientation: 'No Squad' ➔ 'D' n = 1,938 p.a.; 'A' ➔ 'No Squad' n = 42 p.a.)

Source: adapted from Güllich & Emrich, 2012.

TDP ingredients commonly comprise: high-profile coaching, training facilities and equipment; specialist medical, paramedical and scientific service staff; and, support for performance lifestyle and education. Developing outstanding performance requires considerable time investment over many years, and *time* is considered a critical input resource. For this reason, TDP typically aims to select youngsters during *early* career stages, to enable a long period of progressive nurturing until the expected age of peak performance. In addition, when analysing the focus and content of TDP interventions generally (Table 7.1), their primary aim can be summarised as attempting to reinforce *sport-related time economy* (Güllich & Emrich, 2006; Horton, 2012). That is, interventions aim to expand the time available for training and competitions (i.e., *extensive* time-economy) or attempt to achieve efficient time use in terms of increased success gain per time invested (i.e., *intensive* time-economy).

The 'ideal-type' of TID/TDP implies that future high-performers are identified and selected at an early age based on signs or facets of early exceptionality. TDP programming continuously facilitates extensive and intensive time economy of their sport-specific training process. As the duration of involvement extends, training volume and performance increase, the athlete ascends progressively through the consecutive stages of the TDP system, and TDP interventions are gradually intensified. As a consequence, it can be stated that early TID/TDP rests on three fundamental premises:

- Talent can already be identified at a young age.
- Top senior performance results from long-term continuous development within a sport. Success increases with progressive duration of involvement, together with extended training volume and intensified supportive interventions.
- Long-term development of excellence can be positively affected by TDP interventions at a young age, implying expansion and intensification of the time used for sport-specific training and competitions.

However, empirical examinations of world-class athletes' participation histories raise some doubts about the validity of the three premises (see state of research below), and targeted TID/TDP research has begun to examine whether TID and TDP exhibit empirical correspondence to these pre-assumptions. This comprises investigating the questions of: (Q1) To what extent do characteristics assessed in early TID correlate with later performance? (Q2) Does early selection and involvement in TDP correlate with later senior success? This also implies, (Q3) does early TID/TDP preferentially draft (selection) young athletes exhibiting the types of developmental participation patterns likely to benefit long-term development of senior success, and does it facilitate (intervention/socialisation) those patterns?

Individualistic vs. collectivistic approach

From a national-level perspective, it is important to note that the ultimate target of TID/TDP is *collective* success, specifically the *aggregation* of individual athletic attainments compared to other countries' aggregated achievements. Exactly which athletes achieve those attainments is of subordinate relevance. This is significant insofar as a number of future 'top performers' may not have been identified at a young age, and may have developed outside TDP. In the field, talent selection may therefore not be a 'one-off' procedure, but repeated possibly annually through all age ranges. Previous selection may sometimes be revised, in that TDP members are replaced by 'side-entrants' who are now ascribed greater potential (e.g., Cobley, Schorer, & Baker, 2012). In this context, governing bodies can pursue the

Table 7.1 Focus and content of TDP interventions applied to athletes involved in talent development programmes

Provision / support of …	Directionality of effects			Annotations
	Stimulus, incentive (1)	Expansion of training time (extensive time economy)	Intensification of training time (intensive time economy) (3)	
Training and Competition				
Participation in competitions	+	(+)	(+)	Extensive/intensive time-economy if assuming training effects of participation in competitions
Additional training opportunities		+		E.g., training centres, sport academies, training camps, clinics
Training facilities, equipment	(+) (2)	+	(+)	Intensive time-economy only if facilities / equipment benefit success gain per invested time unit
Coaches	(+) (2)	+	+	Expectation of more training and improved performance progress through coached training
Coaches' education	(+) (2)		+	Intensive time-economy if better educated coaches attain more success gain per training time
Athlete Services				
Consulting for performance lifestyle and educational / occupational career		+		Purpose to manage lifestyle and career compatibly to elite sport; possibly also buffering of individual educational / occupational costs / risks
Nutritional consulting		+	+	Appropriate nutrition shall improve load tolerability and adaptation to training stimuli
Medical care		+	+	Health facilitates load tolerability, more activity per training time, adaptation to training stimuli, and avoids training reduction / interruptions
Physiotherapy		+	+	Health as above; improved recovery enables more training and adaptation to training stimuli
Performance assessment (physiology, biomechanics)			+	Purpose to determine whether and how training time could be used more efficiently
Permanent Concentration				
Elite sport school, residential sport school		+		Purpose to adjust educational time demands to sport time demands, save 'dead time' by coordinating school and sport and saving passage time; also provision of extra training

Notes: (1) Incentives may generally benefit motivation and thereby facilitate expansion of training time and effort during training. (2) Coaches, in particular better educated coaches, may exhibit incentives by designing more enjoyable training and/or greater performance progress; likewise, high-quality facilities and equipment may imply incentives. (3) Intensive time economy may imply saving time spent on certain activities and thereby enable expansion of time for other training activities.

Source: Adapted and extended from Güllich & Emrich, 2006.

development of collective success through two complementary but different approaches (Güllich & Emrich, 2012):

- The *individualistic* approach: The future high-performers are identified and selected into TDP at a young age, and a set of TDP interventions are applied to them. The interventions facilitate their performance progress, eventually leading them to increased senior performance. Their enhanced senior performances aggregate across these individuals, leading to improved collective success. According to this approach, future senior elite athletes will have developed exactly from the ranks of the early selected youngsters, while later side-entrants are infrequent. The 'idea' of early TID/TDP along with its fundamental premises rest on this approach.

- The *collectivistic* approach: The collective of the successful senior performers is composed of athletes entering TDP either early or late, where the later entrants develop outside TDP over longer periods. The collective of outstanding senior athletes *emerges* gradually in the course of recurrent procedures of selection, de-selection, and replacement through all age periods and stages. According to this approach, it is essentially irrelevant who exactly become the successful senior performers. There may be considerable fluctuation within the TDP population, and later side-entries may occur quite often. A country's population size, the popularity of a sport, mass participation in competitive sport, and general local training environments are significant social-ecological factors affecting the 'talent pool' that talented athletes can be drawn from.

Based on these approaches, the additional question arises: (Q4) To what extent does the population of senior elite athletes develop from those selected early and their long-term continuous nurturing (*individualistic* approach), or rather emerge via the course of repeated selection, de-selection and replacement across the different age categories (*collectivistic* approach)? We now address these questions, based on the research evidence available.

The state of empirical research

Participation history of top athletes

Generally speaking, the analyses of developmental participation patterns of senior world-class athletes (e.g., Güllich & Emrich, 2014; Rees et al., 2016, for reviews) reveal that many athletes are not involved exclusively in one sport, but engage in various sports across childhood and adolescence. Their age of training initiation and main sport specialisation scatters considerably, across and within the different sports, and success often progresses non-linearly. Remarkably, senior world-class athletes do not differ from their less accomplished peers in more time extensive or intensive sport-specific training during childhood and adolescence. On the other hand, variable experience in different sports and relatively late specialisation are over-represented among world-class athletes. These findings from training and competition histories partly deviate from the premises underpinning early TID/TDP logic.

Predictive accuracy of early TID

Early TID attempts to use individual differences in characteristics assessed at a young age to predict individual differences in future performance exceptionality (i.e., senior success). However, the complex and dynamic nature of talent, and non-linear developmental performance trajectories make the long-term predictive accuracy of early TID extremely diffi-cult. Task demands, performers' characteristics, and environmental factors can all vary; further, they change over time, and they also interact with one another (see Table 7.2 for an overview).

A number of longitudinal studies have actually identified a predictive power of approxi-mately zero for some TID assessment procedures (e.g., Bottoni, Gianfelici, Tamburri, & Faina, 2011; Gee, Marshal, & King, 2010; Kuzmits & Adams, 2008; Lidor, Melnik, Bilkevitz, Arnon, &

Table 7.2 Impediments to the predictive accuracy of early TID

Task	• Success in competition depends on an athlete's / team's performance compared to the competitors' performances, while the latter cannot be influenced.
	• High performance can be attained through different individual combinations of skills and physiological-energetic capacities; i.e., different components of performance may be mutually compensable.
	• The relative influence of different predictors on performance may vary with increasing age and, most notably, from juvenile to senior performance (for example relative significance of stature, physiological capacities, motor and perceptual-cognitive skills etc.; e.g., Vaeyens et al., 2008; Ziv & Lidor, 2014).
	• The structure of performance, the required qualities, and the type of athlete demanded may have changed in the future because the evolution of high-performance sports implies changes in rules (e.g., judgment criteria in gymnastics and figure skating, scoring in basketball, libero in volleyball), material and equipment (carving skies, clap-skate, Nemeth's javelin), movement techniques (Nordic skating technique, ski-jumping V-technique), and playing systems (tempo in soccer).
Performer	• The timing of biological maturation varies inter-individually, in particular during the age range of 12–16 years. Biologically accelerated athletes have hormonal advantages within a calendric age-group inducing advanced growth kinetics, physiological-energetic capacities and performance progress particularly among adolescent boys (Pearson et al., 2006; Malina et al., 2015). However, differential influences of biological maturation on performance disappear by reaching maturity.
	• Within a calendar age year those relatively older have advantages in stature, physiology and performance particularly in adolescent boys (relative age effect, RAE; Cobley et al., 2009; Helsen et al., 2012). However, this advantage decreases at adult elite level (Carling et al., 2012; Gibbs et al., 2012).
	• Psychological qualities relevant to training and competition (such as motivation, resilience, self-regulation) vary over time and inter-individual differences in future development of those qualities are (widely) unknown (e.g., Anshel & Lidor, 2012).
Environment	• Prior training experience influences present performance and the scope for future performance development (e.g., intensified specialised training vs. moderate specialised training with diversified experience). Respective inter-individual differences are usually not ascertained in TID.
	• Configurations of future training, quality of coaching and their effects on performance vary between athletes and within athletes over time. Respective future inter-individual differences are (widely) unknowable.
	• Socio-material environments vary between athletes (coaching, familial support, facilities). Respective future inter-individual differences are (widely) unknowable.
Test quality	• Assessments in TID may be imperfectly objective, reliable and valid.

Falk, 2005a). That said, other studies report methods leading to correct assignment of up to 70 per cent of young athletes to higher and lower performing sub-samples over multiple years (two studies had even higher accuracy rates: Forsman, Blomqvist, Davids, Liukkonen, & Konttinen, 2015; Pion et al., 2015). These studies typically used multi-dimensional approaches including anthropometry, early physiology or skill tests (Falk, Lidor, Lander, & Yang, 2004; Gonaus & Müller, 2012; Höner et al., 2015; Le Gall, Carling, Williams, & Reilly, 2008; Lidor, Melnik, Bilkevitz, Arnon, & Falk, 2005b; Till et al., 2015; Vandorpe et al., 2012), and in some cases also psychological skill/trait assessments (Figueiredo, Goncalves, Coelho-e-Silva, & Malina, 2009; Forsman et al., 2015; Van Yperen, 2009; Zuber, Zibung, & Conzelmann, 2015). Yet, while those findings appear promising at first sight, they do not necessarily reflect the absolute prediction accuracy when transferred to the field. Importantly, the greater mass of both selected and non-selected athletes (compared to limited sub-samples involved in research studies) has to be considered. Thus, two key points need to be considered:

1   Correct assignment is presumably lower at the adjacent margins of the within-group distributions (i.e., between the least promising selected and most promising non-selected athletes).
2   Attempting to predict future high-performers is primarily compromised by the fact that top athletes are extremely rare by definition, relative to the total athletic population, and the relative proportion of young athletes becoming senior top athletes (i.e., the 'base rate') is very low. Ackerman (2013) illustrated the case by a simple calculation. Assuming that 1 out of 1,000 youngsters becomes a world-class athlete ('base rate'), and our TID method classifies 70 per cent of future world-class and non-world-class athletes correctly (which is at the upper margin of evidenced accuracy), the probability that a positively identified and selected talent actually becomes a world-class athlete is then about 0.2 per cent. Even with a 90 per cent correct assignment that proportion would only increase to approximately 0.9 per cent.

The figures correspond to empirical long-term 'success rates' of up to 2 per cent of early selected athletes observed in the field (see Introduction). They suggest that the low prediction rates in TID practice originate from the nature of the subject, rather than from deficient scientific substantiation. They also imply that further extended endeavour to refine the scientific sophistication of TID will presumably only improve the rates of accurate prediction to a minimal degree.

Involvement and development within TDP

Only a few studies in the international literature have addressed athletes' *involvement* and *development within* the TDP system and whether it is related to athletic outcome attainment (Güllich & Richartz, 2015). The following sections draw upon studies from the research programme '*Efficacy of TDP*' (Table 7.3), conducted for about 15 years in Germany, still providing correspondence from available international research.

Stage transitions and member fluctuation within TDP

Transitions between stages within TDP are exemplified in Figure 7.2. The figure illustrates annual transitions within the squad systems of seven NSOs. Stage transitions were by no means always progressive and seamless. In contrast to the notion of continuous linear careers, however,

Table 7.3 Relevant studies within the research programme 'Efficacy of Talent Development Programmes'

Sample, study design	Relevant studied aspects	Reference
20 *national systems* AUS, USA, 18 East-/West-European countries, DA+QA: CS	Sport system, TID criteria, selection age, elite sport schools, athlete services, success	Güllich & Emrich, 2005a
7 *NSOs' squads* (athletics, cycling, field hockey, rowing, table tennis, weightlifting and wrestling; 4,686 athletes), DA: LT 7 y	Member fluctuation, selection age, stage transitions, exit age, success	Güllich & Emrich, 2012
Soccer *national U15-19 squads* (1,059 players), DA: LT 13 y; 13 *youth academies* (1,420 players), DA: LT 13 y; 624 *Bundesliga players*, DA: RS	Member fluctuation, selection age, exit age, success	Güllich, 2014a
1,558 *squad athletes* all Olympic sports, QA: RS; 244 *squad athletes* all Olympic sports, QA: LT 3 y	Selection age, athlete services, training volume, continuity, success	Güllich & Emrich, 2012, 2013; Emrich & Güllich, 2016
39 *Elite Sport Schools*, DA+QA: LT 3 y; 465 *Olympians*, DA: RS; 199 *Olympians*, QA: RS	Member fluctuation, selection age, athlete services, success	Güllich & Emrich, 2005b; Flatau & Emrich, 2013
246 *sports clubs* nominated by their respective NSO for 'exemplary TDP', QA: LT 3 y	Member fluctuation, athlete services, success	Güllich et al., 2005

Notes: DA = document analysis, QA = questionnaire, CS = cross-sectional, LT = longitudinal, RS = retrospective.

downgrades to lower stages, temporary interruptions, 'side-entries' at higher stages, and 'skipping of stages' often occurred (as suggested by Cobley et al., 2012; Gulbin, Weissensteiner, Oldenziel, & Gagné, 2013). Comparisons between more and less successful athletes revealed that 'side-entries', 'skipping of TDP stages', as well as temporary downgrades within TDP, and TDP interruptions were actually more frequent in the highest achieving athletes (Güllich & Emrich, 2012).

Considering the different types of TDPs, they were all consistently characterised by sizeable annual athlete turnover in terms of yearly selections, de-selections, and side-entries across all age ranges (Table 7.4). The probability of still being in a TDP after five years is clearly below 40 per cent in all locally-based TDP sub-divisions, and below 10 per cent in the NSOs' squad systems (see also Hong, 2008; Ljach, 1997; Pion et al., 2015; Sands, 2012; Vaeyens et al., 2009).

Duration and age structure of TDP careers

Most careers within TDPs were relatively short. For example, in eight NSOs' squad systems (the sports mentioned in Figure 7.2 plus soccer) the persistence of approximately 70 per cent of TDP careers lasted ≤ 2 years, and only about 30 per cent persisted in the system for ≥ 3 years (Güllich, 2014a; Güllich & Emrich, 2012); findings consistent with others (e.g., Deprez, Fransen, Philippaerts, & Vaeyens, 2014; Hoare, 1998; Pion et al., 2015; Vaeyens et al., 2009). Consistent across all sports, the age of first entry and the age of exit correlated very closely, specifically '*the younger the entry – the younger the exit*' (Güllich & Emrich, 2012).

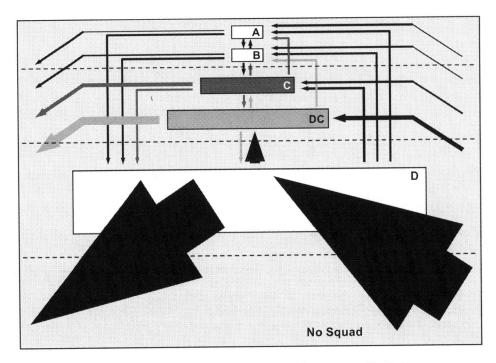

Figure 7.2 Empirical squad structure – mean annual transitions between squad levels (7-year longitudinal observation in athletics, cycling, field hockey, rowing, table tennis, weightlifting, and wrestling). The sizes of the rectangles represent the mean annual numbers of squad members (scale orientation: 'D' n = 6,784; 'A' n = 124), and the widths of the arrows represent the mean numbers of annual individual transitions (scale orientation: 'No Squad' → 'D' n = 3,226 p.a.; 'A' → 'No Squad' n = 55 p.a.). The scale orientation is proportional to Figure 7.1 with the reference size being annual 'D' members.

Source: adapted from Güllich & Emrich, 2012.

Table 7.4 Annual turnover of members in different talent development programmes (TDP)

TDP Programme	Mean annual turnover	Probability of persistence within TDP		Reference
		After 3 y	*After 5 y*	
'Exemplary TDP' sport clubs	19%	*53%*	*35%*	Güllich et al., 2005
Elite Sport Schools	28%	*37%*	*19%*	Güllich & Emrich, 2005b
Soccer youth academies	25%	*43%*	*24%*	Güllich, 2014a
NSOs' squads (7 sports)	44%	*16%*	*5%*	Güllich & Emrich, 2012
NSO's squads (soccer)	41%	*21%*	*7%*	Güllich, 2014a

Notes: Annual turnover = [(Number of annual entries + Number of annual exits)/2]/Total number of members.
Elite Sport Schools and soccer youth academies are local elements of national programmes. They are club-based in that the athletes are members in a sport club that cooperates with a local school.
Generally, turnover rates within TDP programmes may vary depending on the ratio of selected talents per total talent population, number of stages, strength of competition in a sport, magnitude of the difference between selected and non-selected in conditions for talent development, and accuracy of TID.

When comparing athletes who have reached lower or higher squad levels (within the sports defined in Figure 7.2), those who did not exceed the initial squad stage were first selected at 15 ± 3 years, those who reached the national junior squad, but not senior squad were selected at 17 ± 3 years, and senior world-class entered the squad system at 19 ± 4 years. In retrospective analyses of senior elite athletes, all 'top performers' were involved in athlete support programmes at some point of their career, but their entry age varied substantially (e.g., Güllich, 2014a, 2014b; Hardy et al., 2013; Riewald, 2014; Vaeyens et al., 2009). Interestingly, late 'side-entrants' were over-represented among senior world-class athletes across all Olympic sports, compared to their national-class peers. Specifically, world-class athletes consistently entered their respective NSO's squad system about 2 years later than national-class, Olympic Support Centres about 2 years, and Elite Sport Schools (where applicable) about 3 years later (Güllich, 2014b; Güllich & Emrich, 2005b, 2006, 2012, 2013).

When comparing squad members selected younger (<14 years) vs. older (15+ years; see Table 7.5), the former were characterised by starting specialised training and competition 2.5 years younger; reported stronger early intensification of sport-specific training (i.e., 130% more specialised training accumulated until 10 years; 95% more until 14 years); less involvement in other sports; and, 2.4 years earlier specialisation. Earlier selection was associated with greater success at early junior championships, but a reduced likelihood of later international senior success.

Once selected, and when compared to those not yet selected, the athletes involved in the TDP interventions (i.e., physiotherapy, medical care, performance analysis, nutritional consulting, performance lifestyle consulting, Elite Sport School) exhibited another 95 per cent greater *increment* of their annual sport-specific training volume than the non-selected, through the subsequent three years (Emrich & Güllich, 2016). However, participation in athlete services, or their intensity, did not correlate with reduced occurrence or duration of discontinuities in the

Table 7.5 Developmental participation histories, early junior success, and later senior success of athletes from all Olympic sports selected into their NSOs' squad systems at a younger or older age

	Selection age			
	Up to 14 y (n = 429)		At 15+ y (n = 696)	
	M	(SD)	M	(SD)
Age at [years]				
First squad nomination	13.0	(1.0)	16.8	(2.3)
Start training in the main sport	8.5	(2.5)	10.9	(3.9)
Start competitions in the main sport	9.9	(2.4)	12.4	(3.5)
Specialisation in the main sport	10.7	(3.9)	13.1	(5.2)
Training volume until age 14 years				
Hours accumulated in the main sport	2,494	(1,935)	1,279	(1,334)
Sessions accumulated in other sports	228	(496)	350	(653)
Success level until age 14 years				
National / international	65%		33%	
Below	35%		67%	
Later senior success level				
World class (top ten worldwide)	56%		69%	
National class	44%		31%	

Source: Adapted from Emrich & Güllich (2016).

training and competition process, due to injury and/or educational time demands for example (Güllich & Emrich, 2012). Findings were consistent across cgs (centimetre, gram, second), game, martial arts, and artistic composition sports.

Centralisation of TDP

In many sport systems and governing bodies a question often discussed is whether TDP would be more effective if organised with higher or lower degrees of centralisation (Güllich & Emrich, 2005a). The efficacy of centralised TDP is particularly interesting because it constitutes attempts to implement just the 'ideal type' of TID/TDP in its highest form. The 'best talent' together with extensive TDP resources are concentrated in a few centres. Facilities for youngsters' residence are typically provided, and schooling schedules are coordinated with training and competitions by way of Elite Sport Schools or alike (Güllich & Emrich, 2005a; Radtke & Coalter, 2007). The centres possess the capability to organise an entire daily or weekly routine around the sport engagement, and facilitate greater training volumes along with intensified TDP nurture. Their disadvantages however include the inducement of extended individual opportunity costs. Many youngsters may have to leave home, their local school, friends, coach, and training comrades. Also, residence often implies financial costs on parents.

German reunification in 1989/90 brought about a unique opportunity to compare two dissimilar sport systems within one country, now both embedded in an open society (Popper, 1945). The former GDR's TDPs were concentrated in 31 sport clubs with 25 Elite Sport Schools. These were largely conserved after 1990 and integrated into eight Olympic Support Centres with 13 satellite branches and 21 Elite Sport Schools (Güllich & Emrich, 2013). Area-wide development of sport clubs was only re-initiated after 1990. Contrastingly, West-German sport is traditionally more de-centralised, organised in approximately 70,000 sport clubs of which about 35 per cent integrate both mass and competitive sport. Yet, 18 relatively small Elite Sport Schools were established after 1990. In addition, athlete services are provided by twelve Olympic Support Centres with 28 satellite branches.

Ten years after reunification, youth prevalence of sport club membership was still roughly 1.7 times higher in West Germany, while young athletes' probability of involvement in an Elite Sport School was 57 times higher in East Germany (Table 7.6). Eastern Sport Schools also recruited at a significantly younger age and provided much more extensive athlete services (Güllich & Emrich, 2005b). Furthermore, among all youth squad members, the prevalence of involvement in the athlete services of an Olympic Support Centre was 1.6 times higher in East Germany. Eastern athletes participated in the services about 3 years younger (Güllich & Emrich, 2013) and moreover, received 64 per cent more annual service time per athlete.

The organisational differences are also reflected in athletes' dissimilar developmental participation patterns (Güllich & Emrich, 2013). Fewer East German athletes participated in different sports. They specialised in their main sport 2.7 years younger and accumulated 58 per cent more sport-specific training up to 18 years of age. They were more successful only at junior championships, but not in the long-term at international senior levels.

With specific reference to Elite Sport Schools, their overall 'success rate' corresponds to other TDPs, where the prevalence of graduates attaining international senior medals correlates negatively with the proportion of early (≤12 years) selected athletes ($r = -0.41$), and positively with the proportion of late (16+ years) selected athletes ($r = 0.68$). In addition though, members of these schools have reported impaired subjective health and well-being, and achieved comparatively lower educational attainments (Güllich & Emrich, 2005b; Hong, 2008; Van Rens, Elling, & Reijgersberg, 2015; Verkooijen, Van Hove, & Dik, 2012).

Table 7.6 Elite Sport Schools (ESS) in West (n = 16) and East Germany (n = 21): Size (number of elite sport students), recruitment age, and prevalence of international junior and senior success

		West	East	Total
Elite sport students total sum [n]		1,470	9,816	11,286
	Members per ESS [Mean ± SD]	92 ± 68	467 ± 297	305 ± 294
Prevalence of ESS involvement among youth sport club members		0.03%	1.48%	0.18%
Recruitment age	<12 years	44.51%	77.33%	70.03%
	13–15 years	31.25%	18.99%	21.72%
	16+ years	24.24%	3.68%	8.25%
Prevalence of international junior finalists among ESS students		7.07%	2.80%	3.32%
Prevalence of international senior medallists among ESS graduates		4.04%	1.20%	1.55%

Notes: Based on data from Güllich & Emrich (2005b).

When considered together, the findings suggest that centralised approaches to early TID/TDP are actually more associated with economic *inefficiency* when embedded in an open society. They induce larger material and immaterial costs at an individual level (i.e., time, education, psycho-physical health), as well as a system level, which are not necessarily matched by an increased likelihood of senior athletic attainment.

Later-age talent search and transfer

Recent studies have suggested (Güllich & Emrich, 2014; Oldenziel, Gagné, & Gulbin, 2004) that some athletes can successfully switch between sports during late adolescence (or beyond), with sometimes relatively rapid development in their new sport context. Targeted secondary analysis within Güllich & Emrich's (2014) data reveals that 44 per cent of all Olympic and senior world championship medallists reported changing to compete in another sport. For 52 per cent of these, the transition occurred at 15 years plus; to which 89 per cent made their international championship debut in their new sport within three years or less.

While transition often occurs informally, some agencies have launched initiatives to systematically promote the occurrence, supplementing 'mainstream' early TID by establishing later-age talent transfer programmes (see Gulbin, 2008; Vaeyens et al., 2009; see Chapter 35). Vaeyens and colleagues (2009) analysed the first year 'success rate' of the UK's 'Sporting Giants' initiative. Out of 3,010 applicants participating in assessment events (age 19.6 ± 2.9 years), 101 were invited to an 8-week apprenticeship and confirmation phase in canoeing, handball, rowing or volleyball. Of these, 48 were then selected into NSO squads, of which 23 reached national finals or even international representation within one year. While the transferred talents provided an 'injection' of 'only' 4 per cent new talent into the total squad system, the 'success rate' *within* later-age talent transfer (23 out of 101 selected) is appealing, in view of the low efficacy of early TID/TDP.

Summary

The findings evidenced from TID/TDP to date show little empirical correspondence to the fundamental premises that act as central pillars to early TID and TDP. Future outstanding athletes cannot be predicted reliably by way of TID at a young age (cf. Q1). Particularly early

TDP involvement correlates negatively with long-term senior success (cf. Q2). Early TID and TDP preferentially selects (i.e., a selection effect) and further reinforces (i.e., intervention and/or socialisation effects) developmental participation patterns that are partly inconsistent with those developmental patterns likely to benefit long-term international senior success (cf. Q3). Correspondingly, evidence indicates that most TDP careers are short; an earlier age entry correlates with earlier age 'exit; and TDPs generally exhibit high athlete turnover rates. This does not imply that early selection and long-term TDP involvement is not possible, nor that it does not occur, but it is comparatively infrequent. Early TID/TDP primarily proceeds by recruiting great numbers of youngsters and 'trying them out', while expanding the frequency of youngsters 'tried out' through increased athlete turnover. Some are retained while most are de-selected again within short time-periods and new side-entrants are recruited. On the other hand, most world-class athletes were actually only selected at later developmental ages, and late 'side-entrants' were over-represented among world-class. Put another way, most of the many early selected youngsters do not become successful seniors, while most of the successful seniors were not amongst those selected early (see Figure 7.3).

Considered together, these observations suggest that the population of senior top athletes – in the sport contexts examined – predominantly *emerges* in the course of multiple procedures of selection, de-selection, and replacements across the consecutive age and stage categories, rather than originating from early selected youngsters along with the effects of their continuous TDP nurturing (cf. Q4). Potential individualistic TDP effects are obviously 'overwritten' by

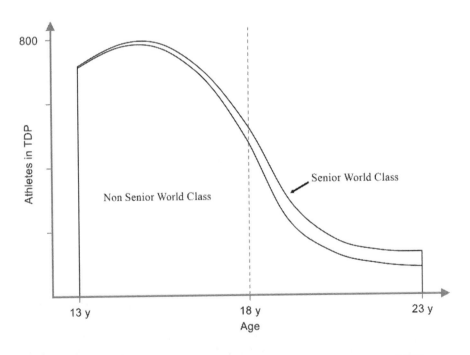

Figure 7.3 Frequency distribution of athletes within talent development programmes (TDP), differentiated within each age category into those who become senior world class and those who do not. Schematic illustration based on data of seven NSOs

Source: Güllich & Emrich, 2012.

collectivistic effects. More precisely, the mass and plurality of non-selected athletes practising competitive sport, together with the diversity of their developmental participation patterns is superior in the probability of bringing out 'high-potentials' in the long-term compared to the comparatively few selected and nurtured at a young age.

Early TID/TDP preferentially selects those young athletes exhibiting – besides higher relative calendric age (RAE) and accelerated biological maturation (see Table 7.2) – earlier specialisation and intensified early sport-specific training (i.e., selection), and in addition reinforces further intensification of specialised training among the selected (i.e., intervention/socialisation). In other words, the 'gift' of subsidised TDP resources leads to greater expenditure of the youngster's individual resources (i.e., youth athlete time, effort, body), and likewise expands their opportunity costs along with increased risks (i.e., compromised enjoyment, health, premature dropout; Butcher, Lindner, & Johns, 2002; Côté, Baker, & Abernethy, 2007; Fraser-Thomas, Côté, J., & Deakin, 2008; Myer et al., 2015; Wiersma, 2000). The alternative approach of moderately intense specific childhood/adolescence training, variable involvement in different sport contexts, and longer development outside TID/TDP (which is over-represented among senior world-class), implies a rather cost-reducing, risk-buffering early sport participation and investment pattern, with greater long-term return (Güllich & Emrich, 2013, 2014).

It should be considered that the ideology and content of TID and TDP across the globe has been widely adopted from the former Eastern bloc's systems; often seen as exemplary (Green & Oakley, 2001). However, they were incommensurable with Western sport systems on multiple aspects; and two key points are particularly relevant here. First, individual decision autonomy was largely delegated to the state, while societal characteristics were extremely 'favourable' for the athlete's motivation and disposition to accept very high individual costs (Güllich & Emrich, 2013). Specifically, the societal scarcity of educational, professional, leisure, and travel opportunities was contrasted by substantial privileges for athletes. For example, they were granted better educational and occupational prospects, and nutrition. Athletes were 'public servants in sport', had material safeguarding, and travelled to Western countries. These extrinsic incentives are less present and potent in Western societies and sport (and gradually cease in Eastern systems), while the larger scope for self-determined decisions about one's allocation of time leads to more careful individual consideration of the balance of one's costs, risks and benefits. Second, achievement sport in the Eastern bloc was stringently restricted to TDP within a few centralised institutions. Practising achievement sport was widely impossible outside TDP, and it was very improbable that non-selected athletes superseded selected athletes or were able to 'side-enter' at later stages. In contrast, Western sport systems cultivate competitive sport in more or less massive area-wide participation (e.g., sport clubs, high-school sport). Among the many initially 'missed' talents, most may still continue competitive sport, with the potential to supersede those selected earlier and to enter TDP in later years.

Practical implications

This chapter suggests some fairly clear implications for policy-makers and practitioners with a view to facilitating national collective senior success. The fact that early TID/TDP is generally not necessary and actually negatively correlates with long-term success is economically relevant. It suggests that particularly early TID/TDP is dispensable and a reallocation of resources may lead to greater utility. Those resources may (1) be shifted to TDP at higher ages, together with (2) proactive later-age talent search and talent transfer, and/or (3) be used to build up and maintain a large talent pool that may 'feed' TDP systems through all age ranges. The latter occurs primarily outside formal TDP, and may comprise: (a) the promotion of general youth participation in competitive sport and strengthening of local training environments; (b) providing opportunities for and encouraging training and competition experience in various sports; and (c) fortifying coaches' education. With a view to the specific design of TDP programming, collective senior success also presumably benefits from lessening individual costs and risks associated with early specialisation and intensified training. The expansion and intensification of specialised training appears only beneficial in late adolescence or later in most sports. Finally, the substantial variation of developmental patterns leading to international senior success highlights the profound individuality of exceptional careers and suggests pronounced *individualisation* in shaping conditions and TDP interventions applied to the individual athlete.

Future directions

The present findings suggest that the low efficacy of early TID/TDP, and the slowed respective growth of knowledge, correlate with the (partial) inaccuracy of the underlying premises. For example, only limited added utility (in terms of improved 'success rates') may presumably be expected from further extended scientific scrutiny of early TID assessment. Besides being near-impossible, early TID is undertaken for the purpose of early selection into TDP, but early TDP has not been evidenced to benefit later senior success. Instead, the subtleties of effective TDP interventions, and the outcomes associated therewith, constitute the need for some clear research priorities. Based on the focus of this chapter: What kinds of conditions and TDP interventions, applied to which athlete at what ages, and in what way, may most optimally benefit long-term performance development; and why?

Finally, the endeavour to investigate and improve TID/TDP systems requires their substantiated *evaluation*. Many evaluation approaches at present typically draw on the *subjective* (i.e., how do participants or stakeholders *subjectively perceive* present TID and TDP) or *normative* quality dimension (i.e., to what extent TID and TDP correspond to a *normative* 'ideal type' defined by a legitimised 'higher authority'; e.g., umbrella organisation). Such thinking and approach rests on the 'gap' notion (Parasuranam, Zeithaml, & Berry, 1985), where 'quality' is defined as the 'discrepancy gap' between the subjective perception of TID and TDP vs. subjective expectations, or normative definitions. Such 'gaps' can be reduced by manipulating expectations, perceptions, or changing the definition of the 'ideal type' of TID and TDP.

By contrast, *instrumental* quality dimension determines to what extent a programme actually contributes to *attaining the objective* to which it was designed. Clearly, the outcome goal is collective senior success (i.e., number of medals). Still, an issue remains: How do you define 'success' of a country's TID and TDP? Two questions require resolution: (1) How many medals are 'good' or 'bad' for a country, in view of different countries' varying success potential relative to socio-economic factors (population size, economic prosperity, state of civil liberties). (2) To what extent does the outcome attainment (medals) rest on TDP effects and/or conditions outside the TDP in a country? A suitable technique may for example be to calculate the linear regression function for how 'population size' and 'GDP per capita' (e.g., Penn Tables) predict the number of medals across the different countries (Bernard & Busse, 2004; Emrich, Klein, Pitsch, & Pierdzioch, 2012; evidently only reasonably applicable within either democratic or authoritarian systems [cf. Freedom House, 2015]). The prediction may then (1) help indicate whether and how far a country is located above or below expected international success. This is combined with (2) analysing to what extent athletes' international success rests on their (earlier) participation in TDP, and on which TDP characteristics.

References

Ackerman, P. L. (2013). Nonsense, common sense, and science of expert performance: Talent and individual difference. *Intelligence, 45,* 6–17.

Anshel, M. H., & Lidor, R. (2012). Talent detection programs in sport: The questionable use of psychological measures. *Journal of Sport Behavior, 35,* 239–266.

Bernard, A. B., & Busse, M. R. (2004). Who wins the Olympic Games: Economic resources and medal total. *The Review of Economics and Statistics, 86,* 413–417.

Bottoni, A., Gianfelici, A., Tamburri, R., & Faina, M. (2011). Talent selection criteria for Olympic distance triathlon. *Journal of Human Sport and Exercise, 6,* 293–304.

Butcher, J., Lindner, K. J., & Johns, D. P. (2002). Withdrawal from competitive youth sport: A retrospective ten-year study. *Journal of Sport Behavior, 25,* 145–163.

Carling, C., Le Gall, F., & Malina, R. M. (2012). Body size, skeletal maturity, and functional characteristics of elite academy soccer players on entry between 1992 and 2003. *Journal of Sports Sciences, 30,* 1683–1693.

Christensen, M. K. (2009). An eye for Talent: Talent identification and practical sense of top-level soccer coaches. *Sociology of Sport Journal, 26,* 365–382.

Cobley, S., Baker, J., Wattie, N., & McKenna, J. (2009). Annual age-grouping and athlete development: A meta-analytical review of relative age effects in sport. *Sports Medicine, 39,* 235–256.

Cobley, S., Schorer, J., & Baker, J. (2012). Identification and development of sport talent: A brief introduction to a growing field of research and practice. In J. Baker, S. Cobley, & J. Schorer (eds), *Talent identification and development in sport: International perspectives,* pp. 1–10. London, New York: Routledge.

Côté, J., Baker, J., & Abernethy, B. (2007). Practice and play in the development of sport expertise. In R. Eklund & G. Tenenbaum (eds), *Handbook of sport psychology,* pp. 184–202. Hoboken, NJ: Wiley.

De Bosscher, V., Bingham, J., Shibli, S., & van Bottenburg, M. (2008). *The global sporting arms race. An international comparative study on sports policy factors leading to international sporting success.* Aachen, Germany: Meyer & Meyer.

Deprez, D., Fransen, J., Philippaerts, R., & Vaeyens, R. (2014). A retrospective study on anthropometrical, physical fitness, and motor coordination characteristics that influence dropout, contract status and first-team playing time in high-level soccer players aged 8–18 years. *The Journal of Strength and Conditioning Research, 29,* 1692–1704.

Emrich, E., Klein, M., Pitsch, W., & Pierdzioch, C. (2012). On the determinants of sporting success: A note on the Olympic Games. *Economics Bulletin, 32,* 1890–1901.

Emrich, E., & Güllich, A. (2016). The production of sporting success [in German: Produktion sportlichen Erfolgs]. In C. Deutscher, G. Hovemann, T. Pawlowski, & L. Thieme (eds), *Handbook of sport economics* [in German: Handbuch Sportökonomik], pp. 135–158. Schorndorf, Germany: Hofmann.

Falk, B., Lidor, R., Lander, Y., & Yang, B. (2004). Talent identification and early development of elite water-polo players: A 2-year follow-up study. *Journal of Sports Sciences, 22,* 347–355.

Figueiredo, A. J., Goncalves, C. E., Coelho-e-Silva, M., & Malina, R. M. (2009). Characteristics of youth soccer players who drop out, persist or move up. *Journal of Sports Sciences, 27,* 883–891.

Flatau, J., & Emrich, E. (2013). Asset specificity in the promotion of elite sports: Efficient institutions of governance for the "production" of long-term future sport success. *International Journal of Sport Finance, 8,* 327–340.

Forsman, H., Blomqvist, M., Davids, K., Liukkonen, J., & Konttinen, N. (2015). Identifying technical, physiological, tactical and psychological characteristics that contribute to career progression in soccer. *International Journal of Sports Science and Coaching, 11,* 505–513.

Fraser-Thomas, J., Côté, J., & Deakin, J. (2008). Examining adolescent sport dropout and prolonged engagement from a developmental perspective. *Journal of Applied Sport Psychology, 20,* 318–333.

Freedom House (2015). *Freedom in the World 2015.* https://freedomhouse.org (10-03-2015).

Gee, C. J., Marshal, J. C., & King, J. F. (2010). Should coaches use personality assessment in the talent identification process? A 15 year predictive study on professional hockey players. *International Journal of Coaching Science, 4,* 25–34.

Gibbs, B. G., Jarvis, J. A., & Dufur, M. J. (2012). The rise of the underdog? The relative age effect reversal among Canadian-born NHL hockey players: A reply to Nolan and Howell. *International Review for the Sociology of Sport, 47,* 644–649.

Gonaus, C., & Müller, E. (2012). Using physiological data to predict future career progression in 14- to 17-year-old Austrian soccer academy players. *Journal of Sports Sciences, 30,* 1673–1682.

Gray, H. J., & Plucker, J. (2010). "She's a natural": Identifying and developing athletic talent. *Journal for the Education of the Gifted, 33,* 361–380.

Green, M., & Oakley, B. (2001). Elite sport development systems and playing to win: uniformity and diversity in international approaches. *Leisure Studies, 20,* 247–267.

Gulbin, J. (2008). Identifying and developing sporting experts. In D. Farrow, J. Baker, & C. MacMahon (eds), *Developing sporting expertise: Researchers and coaches put theory into practice,* pp. 60–72. London, New York: Routledge.

Gulbin, J., Weissensteiner, J., Oldenziel, K., & Gagné, F. (2013). Patterns of performance development in elite athletes. *European Journal of Sport Science, 13,* 605–614.

Güllich, A., Anthes, E., & Emrich, E. (2005). Talent promotion in sport clubs. Part 2: Interventions for talent search and talent promotion [in German: Talentförderung im Sportverein. Teil 2: Interventionen zur Talentsuche und -förderung]. *Leistungssport, 35(6),* 48–55.

Güllich, A., & Emrich, E. (2005a). *Elite Sport and Education in Europe. Technical Report.* Brussels, Belgium: European Commission.

Güllich, A., & Emrich, E. (2005b). *Evaluation of the elite sport schools* [in German: *Bestandsaufnahme Eliteschulen des Sports*]. Frankfurt, Germany: DSB.

Güllich, A., & Emrich, E. (2006). Evaluation of the support of young athletes in the elite sport system. *European Journal for Sport and Society, 2,* 85–108.

Güllich, A., & Emrich, E. (2012). Individualistic and collectivistic approach in athlete support programmes in the German high-performance sport system. *European Journal for Sport and Society, 9,* 243–268.

Güllich, A., & Emrich, E. (2013). Investment patterns in the careers of elite athletes in East and West Germany. *European Journal for Sport and Society, 10,* 191–214.

Güllich, A., & Emrich, E. (2014). Considering long-term sustainability in the development of world class success. *European Journal of Sport Science, 14,* S383–S397.

Güllich, A. (2014a). Selection, de-selection and progression in German football talent promotion. *European Journal of Sport Science, 14,* 530–537.

Güllich, A. (2014b). Many roads lead to Rome: Developmental paths to Olympic gold in men's field hockey. *European Journal of Sport Science, 14,* 763–771.

Güllich, A., & Richartz, A. (2015). High-performance sport [in German: Leistungssport]. In W. Schmidt, N. Neuber, T. Rauschenbach, H.-P. Brandl-Bredenbeck, J. Süßenbach, & C. Breuer (eds), *Third German child and youth sport report* [in German: *Dritter Deutscher Kinder- und Jugendsportbericht*], pp. 140–161. Schorndorf, Germany: Hofmann.

Hardy, L., Laing, S., Barlow, M., Kincheva, L., Evans, L., Rees, T., … & Kavanagh, J. (2013). *A comparison of the biographies of GB serial medal and non-medaling Olympic athletes.* London: UK Sport.

Helsen, W. F., Baker, J., Michiels, S., Schorer, J., Van Winckel, J., & Williams, A. M. (2012). The relative age effect in European professional soccer: Did ten years of research make any difference? *Journal of Sports Sciences, 30,* 1655–1671.

Hoare, D. (1998). Talent search. *Sports Coach Spring 1998,* 32–33.

Höner, O., Schultz, F., Schreiner, R., & Votteler, A. (2015). Prognostic validity of motor diagnostics in the German talent identification and development program. In T. Favero, B. Drust, & B. Dawson (eds), *International research in science and soccer II,* pp. 267–276. London: Routledge.

Hong, F. (2008). China. In B. Houlihan & M. Green (eds), *Comparative elite sport development: Systems, structures and public policy,* pp. 26–52. London: Elsevier.

Horton, S. (2012). Environmental influences on early development in sports experts. In J. Baker, S. Cobley, & J. Schorer (eds), *Talent identification and development in sport: International perspectives,* pp. 39–50. London, New York: Routledge.

Houlihan, B., & Green, M. (2008). Comparative elite sport development. In B. Houlihan & M. Green (eds), *Comparative elite sport development: systems, structures and public policy,* pp. 1–25. London: Elsevier.

Kuzmits, F. E., & Adams, A. J. (2008). The NFL combine: Does it predict performance in the national football league? *Journal of Strength and Conditioning Research, 22,* 1721–1727.

Le Gall, F., Carling, C., Williams, M., & Reilly, T. (2008). Anthropometric and fitness characteristics of international, professional and amateur male graduate soccer players from an elite youth academy. *Journal of Science and Medicine in Sport, 13,* 90–95.

Lidor, R., Falk, B., Arnon, M., Cohen, Y., Segal, G., & Lander, Y. (2005a). Measurement of talent in team-handball: The questionable use of motor and physical tests. *Journal of Strength and Conditioning Research, 19,* 318–325.

Lidor, R., Melnik, Y., Bilkevitz, A., Arnon, M., & Falk, B. (2005b). Measurement of talent in judo using a unique judo-specific test. *The Journal of Sports Medicine and Physical Fitness, 45*, 32–37.

Ljach, W. I. (1997). High-performance sport in childhood in Russia [in German: Kinderhochleistungssport in Russland]. *Leistungssport, 27*(5), 37–40.

Malina, R. M. (2010). Early sport specialization: Roots, effectiveness, risks. *Current Sports Medicine Reports, 9*, 364–371.

Malina, R. M., Rogol, A. D., Cumming, S. P., Coelho-e-Silva, M. J., & Figueiredo, A. J. (2015). Biological maturation of youth athletes: assessment and implications. *British Journal of Sports Medicine, 49*, 852–859.

Morris, J. G., Dunman, N., Alvey, S., Wynn, P., & Nevill, M. E. (2004). *Talent identification in sport: Systems and procedures used around the world.* Loughborough, UK: Loughborough University.

Myer, G. D., Jayanthi, N., Difiori, J. P., Faigenbaum, A. D., Kiefer, A. W., Logerstedt, D., & Micheli, L. J. (2015). Sport specialization, Part I: Does early sports specialization increase negative outcomes and reduce opportunity for success in young athletes? *Sport Health, 7*, 437–442.

Oakley, B., & Green, M. (2001). The production of Olympic champions: International perspectives on elite sport development systems. *European Journal for Sport Management, 8*, 83–105.

Oldenziel, K., Gagné, F., & Gulbin, J. (2004). Factors affecting the rate of athlete development from novice to senior elite: how applicable is the 10-year rule? Paper presented at the Athens 2004 Pre-Olympic Congress. www.cev.org.br/biblioteca/preolymp/download/ O.027.doc (05-20-2008).

Parasuraman, A., Zeithaml, V. A., & Berry, L. L. (1985). A conceptual model of service quality and its implications for future research. *Journal of Marketing, 46* (Fall 1985), 41–50.

Pearson, D. T., Naughton, G. A., & Torode, M. (2006). Predictability of physiological testing and the role of maturation in talent identification for adolescent team sports. *Journal of Science and Medicine in Sport, 9*, 277–287.

Pion, J., Lenoir, M., Vandorpe, B., & Segers, V. (2015). Talent in female gymnastics: a survival analysis based upon performance characteristics. *International Journal of Sports Medicine, 36*, 935–940.

Popper, K. R. (1945). *The open society and its enemies.* London: Routledge.

Radtke, S., & Coalter, F. (2007). *Sport Schools: An international review.* Stirling: University of Stirling.

Rees, T., Hardy, L., Güllich, A., Abernethy, B., Côté, J., Woodman, T., Montgomery, H., … Warr, C. (2016). The Great British Medalists Project: A review of current knowledge on the development of the world's best sporting talent. *Sports Medicine, 46*, 1041–1058

Riewald, S. (ed.). (2014). *The path to excellence: A view on the athletic development of U.S. Olympians who competed from 2000–2012.* Colorado Springs: USOC.

Sands, W. A. (2012). Talent identification and development in women's artistic gymnastics: the talent opportunity program (TOPs). In J. Baker, S. Cobley, & J. Schorer (eds), *Talent identification and development: International perspectives* (pp. 83–94). London, New York: Routledge.

Till, K., Cobley, S., O'Hara, J., Morley, D., Chapman, C., & Cooke, C. (2015). Retrospective analysis of anthropometric and fitness characteristics associated with long-term career progression in rugby league. *Journal of Science and Medicine in Sports, 18*, 310–314.

Vaeyens, R., Lenoir, M., Williams, A. M., & Philippaerts, R. M. (2008). Talent identification and development programmes in Sport: Current models and future directions. *Sports Medicine, 38*, 703–714.

Vaeyens, R., Güllich, A., Warr, C., & Philippaerts, R. (2009). Talent identification and promotion programmes of Olympic athletes. *Journal of Sports Sciences, 27*, 1367–1380.

Vandorpe, B., Vandendriessche, J. B., Vaeyens, R., Pion, J., Lefevre, J. Philippaert, R. M., & Lenoir, M. (2012). The value of a non-sport-specific motor test battery in predicting performance in young female gymnasts. *Journal of Sports Sciences, 30*, 497–505.

Van Rens, F., Elling, A., & Reijgersberg, N. (2015). Topsport talent schools in the Netherlands: A retrospective analysis of the effect on performance in sport and education. *International Review for the Sociology of Sport, 50*, 64–82.

Van Yperen, N. W. (2009). Why some make it and others don't: Identifying psychological factors that predict career success in professional adult soccer. *Sport Psychology, 23*, 317–329.

Verkooijen, K. T., Van Hove, P., & Dik, G. (2012). Athletic identity and well-being among athletes who live at a Dutch elite sport center. *Journal of Applied Sport Psychology, 24*, 106–113.

Vrljic, K., & Mallett, C. J. (2008). Coaching knowledge in identifying football talents. *International Journal of Coaching Science, 2*(1), 63–81

Wiersma, L. D. (2000). Risks and benefits of youth sport specialization: Perspectives and recommendations. *Pediatric Exercise Science, 12*, 13–22.

Ziv, G., & Lidor, R. (2014). Anthropometrics, physical characteristics, physiological attributes, and sport-specific skills in Under-14 athletes involved in early phases of talent development – a review. *Journal of Athletic Enhancement, 3*(6), 1–8.

Zuber, C., Zibung, M., & Conzelmann, A. (2015). Motivational patterns as an instrument for predicting success in promising young football players. *Journal of Sports Sciences, 33,* 160–168.

8

APPLIED STATISTICS FOR PRACTITIONERS AND RESEARCHERS

Dirk Büsch and Urs Granacher

Introduction

Talent identification has historically occurred on the basis of practitioner (e.g., coaches) experience-based decision-making. However, statistics can be utilized to support practitioner and researcher decision-making. The main question determining whether statistics are utilized though is: Can they add extra value without an extra work burden? With these needs in mind, applied statistic methods should always provide practically relevant and meaningful guiding evidence and answers. With the aim to promote adoption of statistical approaches as part of evidence-based practice in talent identification and development, this chapter highlights how statistics can potentially support talent identification and development decision-making (Abbott & Collins, 2002; Meylan & Cronin, 2014; Thomas, Nelson, & Silvermann, 2015). The chapter focuses on the appropriate application, understanding and interpretation of statistical methods in the field. Throughout, examples from coaches' daily work are utilized.

A pragmatic approach

Proficiency levels in sport-specific movement or performance parameters represent key common criteria from which practitioners and researchers decide whether youth athletes are classified as talents (or talented). To accurately determine identification and selection decisions, qualitative (e.g., match performance) and/or quantitative criteria (e.g., 20-metre linear sprint time) are often utilized. In fact, a large variety of tests exists to assess proficiency alongside anthropometric (e.g., body height, mass) as well as psychological attributes (e.g., self-efficacy) and skills (e.g., goal setting). An underlying assumption of these tests is that a given selected form of performance assessment is able to accurately differentiate between athletes with talent potential (i.e., athletes having potential to achieve elite sport) and those with performance potential (i.e., the potential to achieve sub-elite sports). For this purpose, several scientific methods including descriptive and inferential statistics can be used to evaluate *inter-individual differences in performance tests*. These can help to improve the validity and reliability of decisions determining those who have the potential to achieve elite sport. This is of importance as these athletes are likely to be promoted and more likely to receive onward concentrated support for their long-term athletic development. For these reasons, it is recommended that applied statistical methods are adopted to inform and corroborate coaches' decision-making. Key characteristics of an easy-to-administer statistical approach are now illustrated using a data set from the German Handball Federation and their talent identification and development program.

First step: Raw data analysis

When initiating an evaluation of athletic performance on the basis of an objectively measured test or set of performance parameters, it is important to visualize data using graphs or figures. An exemplified scattergram (aka dot plots or bee swarm plots; Curran-Everett, Taylor, & Kafadar, 1998; Drummond & Tom, 2012; Drummond & Vowler, 2011) is presented in Figure 8.1. The figure demonstrates findings from a sport-specific ball-throwing velocity performance test; a test which is a consistent discriminating criterion in female handball (Büsch et al., 2013). Test data should always be initially visually presented, showing the cloud of data points located around the median portion along with smaller clouds at the lower and upper performance levels. In Figure 8.1, the horizontal bar corresponds to the median (*Md*) separating the upper 50 percent of data from the lower 50. The data is indicative of a symmetrical distribution.

After visual inspection, it is recommended that box-plots are created to help ensure that data is not confounded by outliers. When interpreting box-plots, it is important to remember that the box contains 50 percent of data points, with the horizontal bar representing the median and cross reflecting the mean (*M*) value (Figure 8.2). The magnitude of the box is not influenced by outliers, which is why the box is considered to be a robust (i.e., stable) measure of

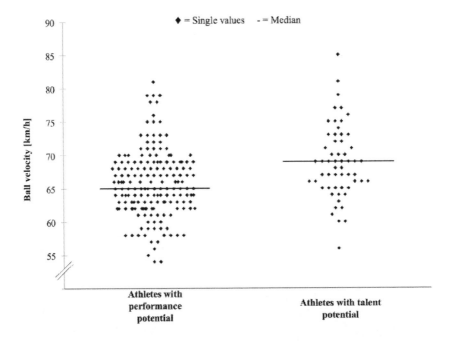

Figure 8.1 Scattergrams illustrating performance in a ball-throwing task for athletes with performance and talent potential

Source: data taken from the talent identification program of the German Handball Federation.

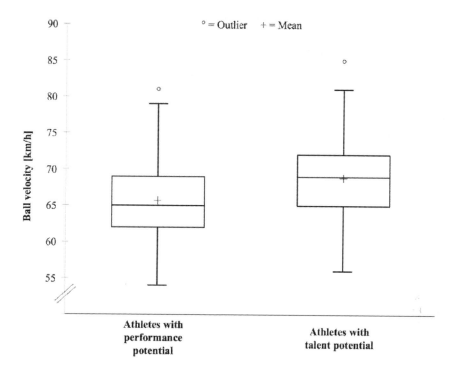

Figure 8.2 Box-plots illustrating performance in a ball-throwing task for athletes with performance and talent potential

Source: data taken from the talent identification program of the German Handball Federation.

statistical dispersion around the median. The two horizontal bars beyond the lower and upper quartiles are called "whiskers" and data points beyond these are denoted as outliers. Given that outliers are unexpected data points, they warrant close examination. In some cases, outliers can be data input errors, but they can, on occasions, be real data points. As a consequence, the specific reason for an outlier has to be clarified before a decision can be made as to whether the data be retained or omitted. Figure 8.2 illustrates an outlier in each group. In this case and upon further examination, outliers were actual true data points.

If the median horizontal bar separates the box in two equally-sized squares, a symmetrical data distribution is identified. In addition, if the mean value (cross) is located close to the median, a unimodal data distribution exists. A normal data distribution (i.e., Gaussian curve) is achieved if median and mean are located close to each other within the data cloud. Normally distributed data has specific advantages. For instance, parametric tests can be applied on normally distributed data, potentially permitting greater ease in finding true differences between experimental groups (i.e., talented athletes vs. a reference group). Further, statistical parameters from parametric tests can be interpreted easier in terms of their practical relevance using effect sizes (see below). Finally, frequency distributions (i.e., histograms) that contain Gaussian curves should also be created. Figure 8.3 demonstrates histograms for athletes with talent potential vs. a group with performance potential.

Second step: Verify essential preconditions for statistical analysis

Besides using graphical methods to examine data distribution, there is also the option to use statistical software packages (e.g., SPSS, Sysstat, R, XLStat, JASP, OpenStat, PSPP, Statistica) or spreadsheet software (e.g., Excel ®) to test for normal data distributions (e.g., Kolmogorov-Smirnov Test, Shapiro-Wilk-Test). In such instances, the statistical output parameters from the Shapiro-Wilk or the Kolmogorov-Smirnov Test can be used to identify whether data significantly deviates (or not) from a theoretically assumed normal distribution. Here any statistical test is based on the assumption that data does not differ from a theoretically assumed distribution, which is always the statistical null hypothesis. In addition, there is the opportunity to analyze samples of athletes with either talent or performance potential. However, these samples are always subsamples of the unknown basic population. Even though the analysis includes a subsample only, conclusions are always drawn for the examined unknown population. Consequently, this approach has two implications for statistical analyses: (i) statistical statements are probability statements because statistical findings from "small" samples are generalized to the unknown basic population; and (ii) even if statistical analyses were conducted with great accuracy, there is always an inherent risk with probability that statements could be erroneous (i.e., acceptance or rejection of the null hypothesis).

Practitioners and researchers may decide that there is a difference between the examined samples even though this difference is not present in the underlying unknown basic population. Statisticians call this misconception a Type I error (α). Type II errors (β) may also be encountered. In other words, it could be erroneously decided that there is no difference between the examined samples, even though the difference actually exists in the unknown population. Both error types are mutually dependent, so that with reference to the actual study hypothesis, a decision has to be made with regards to the specific magnitude of the respective error type that ultimately results in either accepting or rejecting the underlying research hypothesis (Hays, 1994). In the case of the Kolmogorov-Smirnov Test, the study hypothesis corresponds to the statistical null hypothesis, which is indicative of a normally distributed empirical data set. Thus, pragmatic statistical approaches are based on a conventional decision-making rule. For this decision-making process, the p-value (i.e., statistical level of significance or occurrence probability of the null hypothesis) that is generated in spreadsheet or statistical software is compared to a pre-determined limit. The limit is determined a priori to ensure that the null hypothesis will be accepted with high probability. In other words, the data approximately corresponds to normally distributed data. In the empirical sciences (i.e., in sports science), a conventional decision rule has been established that sets the limit for the p-value (i.e., $p > .25$). With reference to the example regarding the Kolmogorov-Smirnov Test (see Table 8.1 and Figure 8.3), a normal distribution of data can be accepted for athletes with talent ($p = .39 \Rightarrow p > .25$) and performance potential ($p = .29 \Rightarrow p > .25$).

Besides normal data distributions, the "level of measurement" or "scale of measure" is another important precondition for the application of parametric tests. Notably, there are three different scales of measurement: nominal (e.g., frequencies), ordinal (e.g., ratings scales), and metric (e.g., interval scales). Metric types include measures like times (e.g., in seconds), distances (e.g., in centimeters) and loads (e.g., in grams), and it is an essential prerequisite to apply parametric tests. An example for metrically scaled data is given when comparing the difference between 1.2 and 1.3 metres (i.e., 10 cm) to the difference between 3.5 and 3.6 metres (i.e., 10 cm). This phenomenon is called equidistance. Metrically scaled data is obtained in various ways according to the performance parameter being tested (e.g., measuring tape, stopwatch, velocity speed-gun).

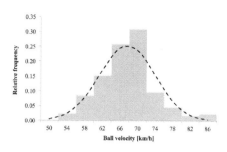 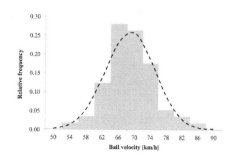

Figure 8.3 Histograms with a normal distribution curve for (a) athletes with performance potential, and (b) athletes with talent potential for ball throwing task performance

Source: data taken from the talent identification program of the German Handball Federation.

Table 8.1 Descriptive statistics illustrating performance in a ball throwing task for athletes with performance and talent potential

Statistics	Athletes with talent potential	Athletes with performance potential
Sample size (*n*)	57	179
Mean (*M*)	68.82	65.69
Median (*Md*)	69	65
Standard deviation (*SD*)	5.43	4.95
Standard error (*SE*)	0.72	0.37
Confidence interval (*CI 95 %*)	67.38–70.26	64.96–66.42
Skewness (*S*)	0.48	0.40
Kurtosis (*E*)	0.71	0.58
Kolmogorov–Smirnov–Test (Z_{K-S})	.89	.98
Significance (p_{K-S})	.39	.29

Source: data taken from the talent identification program of the German Handball Federation.

Visual data inspection is an important first approach to raw data processing. The above described methods can be used as a blueprint (see Figures 8.1 to 8.3 and Table 8.1). However, if data is not normally distributed and data significantly deviates from a Gaussian curve, non-parametric tests have to be applied. Data characteristics that demand the use of non-parametric tests include bimodal data distributions, skewness of data (i.e., large difference between median and mean) or non-metrically-scaled data (e.g., Likert scales in questionnaires). Of note, non-parametric tests do not require any specific preconditions (Siegel & Castellan, 1988). Thus, parametric tests are rather robust but demand minimum requirements like a unimodal data distribution and a sample size equal or larger than 30 athletes. In accordance with Hays (1994), this is called central limit theorem. As with parametric tests, spreadsheet processing software and internet-based statistical calculators (e.g., www.statpages.info) can be used to calculate non-parametric tests.

Third step: Data reduction using confidence intervals

If normal distribution is tested and metric scaling confirmed (i.e., continuous, interval), means and dispersion measures can be calculated, thereafter data needs to be adequately condensed (i.e., reduced). When comparing talent and performance potential athletes, it is assumed that a small number of talent potential athletes exist compared to those with performance potential. Therefore, a statistical measure has to be applied for data condensation (i.e., reduction) that is robust against sample size, such as Confidence intervals (*CI*, Figure 8.4). Standard deviations (i.e., deviations of each data point from the mean, *SD*) are less robust and not suitable for data condensation (Drummond & Tom, 2012). *CI*s are calculated using standard error (*SE*), an estimator for the precision of the sample mean as well as the extreme values from the standard normal data distribution. When translating data into a standard normal form, it is possible to compare different forms of distribution with each other. Furthermore, the translation allows computation of associations (correlations) between test variables. Both, standard error and *CI*s can be calculated with the help of spreadsheet processing or statistical software (Table 8.1).

As compared to the mean value, *CI*s constitute an *interval estimate*, indicating the accuracy of the point estimate *M*. In statistical terms, an appropriate statement to denote the meaning of the 95% *CI* is: "If we were to repeat the experiment over and over, *CI*s contain the true mean in 95% of the repeated experiments." The width of the *CI* (aka—margin of errors) is illustrated in the percent range that should always be presented with the *CI*. The wider the interval, the higher the probability that the mean is located in this interval. By convention, the *CI* is set at a limit of 95%.

*CI*s already contain important information from statistical tests of significance, particularly when illustrated in figures or graphs. According to Cumming and Finch (2005), this is called "inference by eye." Usually, *CI*s are reported in complement to the standard statistical parameters (e.g., *p*-values). *CI*s can contribute to elucidate statistical findings (American Psychological, 2010; Cumming & Finch, 2005; Hoekstra, Morey, Rouder, & Wagenmakers,

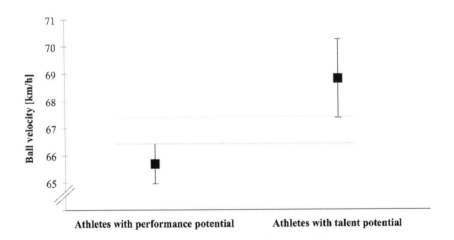

Figure 8.4 Means and 95% confidence intervals for performance in a ball throwing task of athletes with performance and talent potential

Source: data taken from the talent identification program of the German Handball Federation.

2014; Hopkins, 2005, 2007; Hopkins, Batterham, Marshall, & Hanin, 2009a). The most important information that *CIs* provide is the overlapping area of the upper and lower confidence
bounds. If there is little or no overlap in the two confidence bounds, it is likely that statistical
tests will reveal a significant difference. As a rule of thumb, a small overlap or no overlap will
produce small *p*-values (Cumming & Finch, 2005). As an example, Figure 8.4 clearly demonstrates no overlap between *CIs*. Consequently, there is a large difference between the upper and
lower bound of athletes with performance and talent potential, as indicated by the dotted line
(see Figure 8.4). Therefore, it is likely that a statistical test will reveal a statistically significant
between-group difference. In sum, *CIs* can help reveal statistically significant differences
between groups, though visual inspection of *CIs* does not identify the exact *p*-value.

Fourth step: Compute between-group differences

If data is normally distributed and metrically-scaled, differences between two groups (e.g., athletes
with talent vs. performance potential) can be calculated using the t-test for independent samples.
The term "independent samples" or independent variable implies that a person (subject) is only
allocated to one group (e.g., athletes with talent potential) and not both. The test to evaluate
between-group differences is associated with the hypothesis that athletes with talent potential are
better than those classified as performance potential. In our case data, the underlying research
hypothesis is as follows: Mean ball throwing velocity is better in talented athletes (M_T) compared
to athletes with performance potential (M_P). Statisticians and sport scientists denote this hypothesis as follows: $M_T > M_P$. This may appear a trivial point, but it is important in a research context
because the so-called directional hypothesis increases statistical power and represents a theoretically driven hypothesis based on existing knowledge and not speculation. This is more commonly
known as the confirmatory approach to research, as opposed to exploratory research where there
is no foreseeable theoretically driven a priori hypothesis provided. Spreadsheet software (e.g.,
Excel ®, www.sportsci.org/), statistical software (e.g., SPSS, R) or free online calculators (e.g.,
www.quantitativeskills.com/sisa/) can be used to compute t-tests for independent samples (see
Appendix 1). The input parameters required include the mean values, standard deviations and
respective sample size of the two experimental groups (Table 8.2).

Table 8.2 Statistical parameters for t-test and effect size measures of a ball throwing task

Variance homogeneity (Levene test)	
F-value *(F)*	0.36
Significance *(p)*	.55
t-test for independent samples	
t-value *(t)*	4.06
Degrees of freedom *(df)*	234
Two-tailed significance *(p)*	< .001
Test power *(1−)*	.98
Hedges pooled standard deviation	5.07
Effect size (Cohen's d with Hedges adjustment, d_c)	0.62
95% Confidence interval of d_c (lower bound and upper bound)	0.31–0.92
90% Confidence interval of d_c (lower bound and upper bound)	0.36–0.87

Source: data taken from the talent identification program of the German Handball Federation.

After computing the t-test for independent samples, it is important to control for homogeneity of variance to avoid bias, due to potential differences in variance between the two experimental groups (e.g., athletes with talent vs. performance potential). This can be done by applying the F-test or Levene-test before computing *t*-tests for independent samples. The output parameter of the F-test is the *F*-value which is used to calculate the *p*-value. The same decision rule is applied as with tests for normal distribution. In other words, the *p*-value should be larger than .25 ($p > .25$). Our example revealed a *p*-value equal to .55 (i.e., $p > .25$) so that homogeneity of variance can be assumed (Table 8.2). If homogeneity of variance is not given ($p < .25$), standard software packages automatically contain a data adjustment mode to compensate for bias due to differences in variance between groups. When adjusting data for homogeneity of variance, an over-interpretation of marginal differences between two experimental groups can be avoided.

Statistical outcomes from t-tests (Table 8.2) should always be presented with *t*-values and degrees of freedom (*df*). Both values are needed to calculate the *p*-value which corresponds to the empirical probability of error for the null hypothesis (i.e., statistical significance). Given that a directional hypothesis was presented, the previously defined decision rule has to be modified. As a consequence, low *p*-values should be targeted (Cohen, 1994). By convention, the *p*-value is usually set at the 5% limit ($\alpha = .05$) and with reference to our example, *p*-values should be below that limit. Here it is important to recognize the often misunderstood difference between *p* and α. While α corresponds to the a priori determined critical probability of occurrence, *p* corresponds to the actual calculated probability of occurrence of the null hypothesis. Thus, if the goal is to evaluate whether there is a between-group difference, the underlying decision rule is $p < \alpha \Rightarrow p < .05$. In this case, *p* is below .001 and therefore smaller than $\alpha = .05$. Most statistical software programs erroneously report for $p < .001 \Rightarrow p = .000$. However, in mathematical terms, the *p*-value can never equal zero which is why it is important to report $p < .001$ and not $p = .000$.

It is also important to note that the *p*-value simply demonstrates whether there is a between-group difference or not. The *p*-value does not provide any information on the direction of the difference. In other words, it is not possible to deduce whether group 1 is better than group 2 or vice versa. Our example included a directional hypothesis, which is "better performances in athletes with talent as compared to performance potential." With this directional assumption, it is necessary to divide the *p*-value by two because the underlying statistical evaluation is one-sided. Thereafter, Table 8.1 has to be consulted to find out whether the mean value of athletes with talent potential is larger than the mean value of athletes with performance potential. Given the *p*-value is below .001 and in accordance with the limit of $p < .05$, and the mean value of athletes with talent potential is better than those with performance potential, the proposed directional hypothesis can be accepted.

Fifth step: Compute effect sizes

A *p*-value far below the limit of $p < .05$ does not necessarily correspond to a large difference between groups, a point that becomes evident when looking at the two factors that determine the *p*-value. Those are (i) the magnitude of the difference between groups (i.e., effect size [*ES*]) and (ii) sample size (*N*). From this it follows that: $p = ES \times N$. Statistical between-group differences—even if small in magnitude—can always be achieved by simply increasing sample size. Our example is an exception however, as statistical power (aka sensitivity) is high with $1 - \beta = .98$, and is above the limit set by convention (i.e., $1 - \beta \geq .80$; Cohen, 1988). Thus, an increase in sample size would hardly influence (or lower) the *p*-value of the t-test for independent samples to detect between-group differences as statistical power is already saturated. To avoid bias due to an increase in sample size, it is recommended that *ES* is calculated and reported (Batterham & Hopkins, 2006; Buchheit, 2016; Cohen, 1988; Cumming, 2014; Hopkins, Batterham, Marshall, & Hanin, 2009b; Kline, 2005; Page, 2014).

When calculating *ES*, it is important to always report the formula in which it was calculated as there are various types (Baguley, 2009; Morris, 2008; Troncoso Skidmore & Thompson, 2013). The most common *ES* is *Cohen's d* which is calculated according to the following formula: $(M_T - M_p)/SD$. M_T = sample mean of athletes with talent potential; M_p = sample mean for athletes with performance potential; and *SD* = pooled standard deviation of both groups (Cohen, 1988; Rhea, 2004). In our example, between-group differences in sample size have to be considered, demanding the calculation of a pooled standard deviation. Advantages associated with the use of a pooled standard deviation are that (i) it accounts for differences in sample size between groups, and (ii) it is feasible to apply pooled standard deviation even with equal sample sizes. The computation of *ES* with pooled standard deviation is called Hedges *g*, or Cohen's *d* with Hedges adjustment (d_c; (Hedges & Olkin, 1985). Again, online programs (e.g., G*Power: Faul, Erdfelder, Lang, & Buchner, 2007; NDC: Steiger, 2001; Steiger, 2004; Steiger & Fouladi, 1997) and resources (e.g., www.psychometrica.de/effect_size.html) can compute Hedges *g* or Cohen's *d* (see Appendix 1). Also of note, *ES* can also be calculated for parametric and non-parametric methods (Grissom & Kim, 2012).

An explicit advantage of *Cohen's d* and *Hedges g* is that both relate to the examined dependent variable (e.g., throwing velocity in km/h). Sometimes between-group differences are expressed as percentage rates. However, from percentage rates it is impossible to deduce any information on the underlying dependent variable. In addition, relative percentage rates may cause over- or underestimation of the true between-group effect (Gigerenzer, Gaissmaier, Kurz-Milcke, Schwartz, & Woloshin, 2008). If expressed as a relative measure such as percentage rates, it is recommended to additionally and preferentially report effect sizes. In our example, the talent potential group outperformed the performance potential group by 4.8 percent in ball throwing velocity. In other words, the performance potential group attained 95.4 percent of the ball throwing velocity of the talent potential group. The effect size (also called standardized difference between the two groups) amounts to d_c or $g = 0.62$ standard deviations. The pooled standard deviation totals $SD_{pooled} = 5.07$ (km/h). From SD_{pooled} an absolute difference of 3.13 km/h can be identified, which is equal to the mean difference in ball throwing velocity between the talent potential (68.82 km/h = 19.12 m/s) and performance potential group (65.69 km/h = 18.25 m/s; Table 8.1).

Sixth step: Deduce practical significance from effect sizes

How should an $ES = 0.62$ (d_c or g) that corresponds to a difference of 3.13 km/h between groups be interpreted? The easiest and most commonly used method is to apply the classification of *ES*. According to Cohen (1988), effect sizes can be classified as small ($0.20 \leq d \leq 0.49$), medium ($0.50 \leq d \leq 0.79$), and large ($d \geq 0.80$). Thus, a medium-sized effect can be identified between groups in our example. However, this rather crude estimate is of limited help for practitioners and researchers, particularly when performance differences become smaller with increasing expertise. This elite sport-specific phenomenon affords a differentiated and not a generalized effect interpretation. In other words, *ES* have to be interpreted with regards to the specific context and not according to classification models based on agreement (Rhea, 2004; Thompson, 2001). As with the determination of significance α, *ES* have to be established a priori and should be theory-driven (Aiken, 1994; Batterham & Hopkins, 2006; Buchheit, 2016; Kelley & Preacher, 2012; Wilkinson, 2014).

As a consequence, it is important to note that *ES* is not synonymous to practical significance. In fact, practical significance evolves through context-specific interpretations of *ES* (Grissom & Kim, 2012; Kelley & Preacher, 2012). A good example to illustrate the difference between *ES* and practical significance comes from Rhea (2004). After scrutinizing a large number of strength-training studies across different expertise levels, Rhea (2004) proposed a new scale, specific to strength training for determining the magnitude of *ES* according to expertise level (i.e., untrained, recreationally trained, highly trained; Table 8.3). For instance, individuals who have not been consistently training for 1 year (= untrained), *ES* were interpreted as trivial (< 0.50), small (0.50–1.25), moderate (1.25–1.90), large (> 1.90). But for individuals who trained for at least 5 years (highly trained), *ES* were interpreted as trivial (<0 .25), small (0.25–0.50), moderate (0.50–1.00), large (> 1.00). Of note, it is possible to translate the classification for ES according to three graded talent categories (i.e., normative, gifted, talented; Gagné, 1993; Williams, Oliver, & Lloyd, 2014). Thus, the quality of interpretation could be largely improved by (i) presenting a priori directional and theory-driven hypotheses, and (ii) determining the practical significance of *ES* a priori.

When translating Rhea's (2004) classification model to our example, a moderate effect can be established that is indicative of the highest expertise level (e.g., talented female athletes). However, Rhea's approach is still limited in our context because it cannot deduce whether the talent group has a true performance and maturation-related advantage over the performance potential group. In other words, is the observed difference practically relevant? In handball, it is feasible to assume that ball throwing velocity is positively associated with successful goal scoring, particularly for players in backcourt positions. The distance from backcourt area throws to the goal amounts to approximately 8 m (Vila et al., 2012). A female goalkeeper needs at least 500 ms to initiate a save movement and to reach the upper or lower corner of the goal (Gutierrez-Davila, Rojas, Ortega, Campos, & Parraga, 2011). Thus, when throwing a ball from an 8 m distance, an athlete classified as talent potential needs 418 ms (on average) to cover the distance, while an athlete with performance potential needs 438 ms (on average). Mathematically, goalkeepers are successful only if they anticipate the right corner and initiate their defence action in time. From a practical point of view, 20 ms might be decisive for a goalkeeper to successfully make a save. However, when considering the entire time interval for the defence action (i.e., 500 ms), a difference of 20 ms between groups seems to constitute a small-to-moderate significance. In summary, when interpreting single-test item outcomes within a talent test battery, it is important for researchers and practitioners (e.g., coaches) to collectively decide whether a performance difference is of practical significance based on substantive reasoning and not mere convention.

Table 8.3 The practical significance (magnitude) of the effect size *d*

Effect size magnitude	*Untrained*	*Recreationally trained*	*Highly trained*
Trivial	< 0.50	< 0.35	< 0.25
Small	0.50–1.25	0.35–0.80	0.25–0.50
Moderate	1.25–1.9	0.80–1.50	0.50–1.0
Large	> 2.0	> 1.5	> 1.0

Notes: Untrained = Individuals who did not consistently train for 1 year; Recreationally trained = Individuals training consistently from 1–5 years; Highly trained = Individuals trained for at least 5 years.
Source: Rhea (2004, p. 919).

Seventh step: Always compute and report confidence intervals with effect sizes

The recommended determination of *ES* in sports science research represents—as with mean values—a point estimate of the examined population. As a consequence, the empirical *ES* may under or overestimate the true *ES*. To avoid such bias, *CIs* have to be calculated for *ES* as well (Bakker & Wicherts, 2011; Batterham & Hopkins, 2006; Cumming, 2014; Drinkwater, 2008; Nakagawa & Cuthill, 2007; Page, 2014; Thompson, 2007). This can also be achieved using pre-developed macros, internet-based calculators or cost-free software programs (see Appendix 1). What holds true for *CIs* around the mean value is also meaningful in *CIs* for *ES*. That is, if we were to repeat the experiment over and over, in 95 percent of cases the *CIs* contain the true effect size. Here, it is important to note that the true effect could be meaningless if the *CI* includes the null-effect or expands over the zero line (Batterham & Hopkins, 2006; Cumming, 2014). Specifically, if the *CI* includes positive and negative values, the outcome is unclear. However, if the confidence interval includes positive values only, we infer that the true effect has the magnitude of the observed effect (Figure 8.5).

For practical reasons and contrary to the standard convention of 95% *CI*, most statistical textbooks and articles recommend a *CI* range of 90% or even 80% (Cumming, 2012; Drinkwater, 2008; Hopkins et al., 2009b; Mullineaux, Bartlett, & Bennett, 2001).

A distinct advantage of the application of *ES CIs* becomes clear with repeated annual assessments of talent test batteries. If between group differences (i.e., athletes with talent vs. performance potential) are robust and not biased, *CIs* allow one to illustrate a range in which between-group differences are expected. In our example, the 95% *CI* ranges for d_c from 0.31–0.92, corresponding to a range in ball throwing velocity between 1.57–4.66 km/h (lower bound—5.07 [pooled standard deviation] × 0.31 [ES] = 1.57 km/h; upper bound—5.07 [pooled standard deviation] × 0.92 [ES] = 4.66 km/h). For the 90% *CI*, which is of great importance from a practical perspective and which should be applied with directional hypothesis, the *CI* for d_c ranges between 0.36–0.87 (1.83–4.36 km/h, lower bound—5.07 [pooled standard deviation] × 0.36 [ES]; upper bound—5.07 [pooled standard deviation] × 0.86 [ES]). These examples illustrate that the larger the *CI*, the greater the performance enhancement or impairment needed to demonstrate practical significance. In addition, both

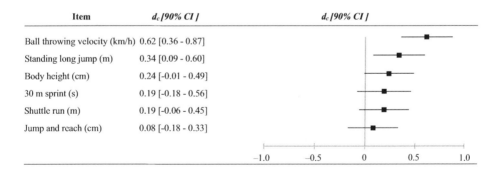

Item	d_c *[90% CI]*	d_c *[90% CI]*
Ball throwing velocity (km/h)	0.62 [0.36 - 0.87]	
Standing long jump (m)	0.34 [0.09 - 0.60]	
Body height (cm)	0.24 [-0.01 - 0.49]	
30 m sprint (s)	0.19 [-0.18 - 0.56]	
Shuttle run (m)	0.19 [-0.06 - 0.45]	
Jump and reach (cm)	0.08 [-0.18 - 0.33]	

Figure 8.5 Forest plot of effect sizes (d_c) and 90% confidence intervals (*90% CI*) of different test items (data taken from the talent identification program of the German Handball Federation). The shuttle run and the ball throwing test are the only two test items in which the 90% *CI* does not expand over the zero line. Therefore, it is possible to infer that the true effect has the magnitude of the observed effect for these two test items

examples demonstrate that *CIs* do not expand over the zero line, indicating a true and replicable difference between the two experimental groups (talent potential vs. performance potential) for ball throwing velocity (Figure 8.5). Therefore, it is recommended that the 90% *CI* is used to evaluate effects in (sub-)elite sports and to obtain practically relevant information. A final theoretical and content-driven evaluation should not follow conventions, but instead consider practical experience of practitioners and researchers as well as data from already existing empirical studies (Fritz, Scherndl, & Kühberger, 2013; Kline, 2005; Thompson, 2001, 2002).

Final considerations

The approach to use *CIs* for the evaluation of between-group differences can be translated to two equally and often reported questions in talent research. The first refers to performance changes over time (i.e., pre-post testing) in the group of talent and/or performance potential. The second implies individual and not group-based performance changes. This is of particular importance in the view of talent being a developmental and individual phenomenon, rather than a general occurrence expressed through a group mean value.

Group-based performance changes over time (e.g., pre- to post-test) are typically assessed using the t-test for dependent samples. The calculation and interpretation of statistical outcomes (i.e., *p*-values, *ES*) is similar to the t-test for independent samples. Again, statistical programs, spreadsheet and websites provide adequate tools for such analysis (see Appendix 1). If performance changes over two or even more test points, or between two or even more experimental groups are of interest, the t-test for dependent samples is no longer an adequate statistical method. In fact, more sophisticated statistical means (e.g., Analysis of Variance [ANOVA]) should be applied. In this specific case, practitioners and researchers are confronted with in-depth statistical analyses that can be prevented if performance differences between two groups or performance changes within one group from pre-post are only evaluated. In addition, it is important that practitioners and researchers determine their expectations on performance changes over time or performance differences between groups prior to the actual evaluation or decisions upon athletes. Statisticians and sport scientists refer to this as more of a "sound statistical approach" as opposed to a "wonky stats approach" (Wagenmakers, Wetzels, Borsboom, van der Maas, & Kievit, 2012).

Performance changes at an individual level can also be examined and assessed using *CIs*. As with the *ES CI*, it is recommended to stick to the 90% *CI* to ensure that performance changes are not biased by individual biological variability. An important precondition for this approach is acceptable reliability of the test instrument that is used to document performance changes. The higher the test-retest reliability ($r \geq .90$), the more sensitive is the test to detect performance changes. Statistically meaningful individual changes can also be evaluated using the Reliable Change Index (*RCI*, Jacobson & Truax, 1991). This instrument is helpful to detect positive or negative performance trends of individual athletes when conducting between-group comparisons.

In summary, this chapter has provided a rationale and exemplification on how statistics can be utilized in talent identification with the aim to substantiate practitioners' and researchers' decision making. A number of data processing steps have been recommended. These included (i) starting with a comprehensive raw data description, (ii) computing between-group differences, and (iii) calculating *ES* and deducing the practical significance of *ES*.

References

Abbott, A., & Collins, D. (2002). A theoretical and empirical analysis of a "State of the Art" talent identification model. *High Ability Studies, 13*(2), 157–178.

Aiken, L. R. (1994). Some observations and recommendations concerning research methodology in the behavioral sciences. *Educational and Psychological Measurement, 54*(4), 848–860. doi:10.1177/0013164494054004001

American Psychological Association. (2010). *Publication manual of the American Psychological Association* (6th ed.). Washington, DC: American Psychological Association.

Baguley, T. (2009). Standardized or simple effect size: What should be reported? *British Journal of Psychology, 100*(3), 603–617. doi:10.1348/000712608x377117

Bakker, M., & Wicherts, J. (2011). The (mis)reporting of statistical results in psychology journals. *Behavior Research Methods, 43*(3), 666–678. doi:10.3758/s13428-011-0089-5

Batterham, A. M., & Hopkins, W. G. (2006). Making meaningful inferences about magnitudes. *International Journal of Sports Physiology and Performance, 1*, 50–57.

Buchheit, M. (2016). The numbers will love you back in return – I promise. *International Journal of Sports Physiology and Performance, 11*, 551–554. doi:10.1123/IJSPP.2016-0214

Büsch, D., Schorer, J., Pabst, J., Strauss, B., Petersen, K.-D., Pfänder, J., & Sichelschmidt, P. (2013). Evaluation of the talent identification programme of the German Handball Federation. In European Handball Federation (ed.), *2nd EHF Scientific Conference. Women and handball: Scientific and practical approaches* (pp. 40–42). Vienna: European Handball Federation.

Cohen, J. (1988). *Statistical power analysis for the behavioral sciences.* Hillsdale, NJ: Lawrence Erlbaum Associates.

Cohen, J. (1994). The earth is round (p < .05). *American Psychologist, 49*(12), 997–1003.

Cumming, G. (2012). *Understanding the new statistics.* New York: Routledge.

Cumming, G. (2014). The new statistics: Why and how. *Psychological Science, 25*(1), 7–29. doi:10.1177/0956797613504966

Cumming, G., & Finch, S. (2005). Inference by eye. *American Psychologist, 60*(2), 170–180. doi:10.1037/0003-066X.60.2.170

Curran-Everett, D., Taylor, S., & Kafadar, K. (1998). Fundamental concepts in statistics: elucidation and illustration. *Journal of Applied Physiology, 85*(3), 775–786.

Drinkwater, E. (2008). Applications of confidence limits and effect sizes in sport research. *The Open Sports Sciences Journal, 1*, 3–4.

Drummond, G. B., & Tom, B. D. M. (2012). Presenting data: Can you follow a recipe? *British Journal of Pharmacology, 165*(4), 777–781. doi:10.1111/j.1476-5381.2011.01735.x

Drummond, G. B., & Vowler, S. L. (2011). Show the data, don't conceal them. *British Journal of Pharmacology, 163*, 208–210. doi:10.1111/j.1476-5381.2011.01251.x

Faul, F., Erdfelder, E., Lang, A.-G., & Buchner, A. (2007). G*Power 3: A flexible statistical power analysis program for the social, behavioral, and biomedical sciences. *Behavior Research Methods, 39*(2), 175–191.

Fritz, A., Scherndl, T., & Kühberger, A. (2013). A comprehensive review of reporting practices in psychological journals: Are effect sizes really enough? *Theory & Psychology, 23*(1), 98–122. doi:10.1177/0959354312436870

Gagné, F. (1993). Constructs and models pertaining to exceptional human abilities. In K. A. Heller, F. J. Monks, & A. H. Passow (eds), *International handbook of research and development of giftedness and talent* (pp. 69–87). Oxford: Pergamon Press.

Gigerenzer, G., Gaissmaier, W., Kurz-Milcke, E., Schwartz, L.M., & Woloshin, S. (2008). Helping doctors and patients make sense of health statistics. *Psychological Science in the Public Interest, 8*(2).

Grissom, R. J., & Kim, J. J. (2012). *Effect sizes for research: Univariate and multivariate applications* (2nd ed.). New York: Routledge Chapman & Hall.

Gutierrez-Davila, M., Rojas, F. J., Ortega, M., Campos, J., & Parraga, J. (2011). Anticipatory strategies of team-handball goalkeepers. *Journal of Sports Sciences, 29*(12), 1321–1328. doi:10.1080/02640414.2011.591421

Hays, W. L. (1994). *Statistics.* Fort Worth: Harcourt Brace College Publishers.

Hedges, L. V., & Olkin, I. (1985). *Statistical methods for meta-analysis.* Orlando, FL: Academic Press.

Hoekstra, R., Morey, R., Rouder, J., & Wagenmakers, E.-J. (2014). Robust misinterpretation of confidence intervals. *Psychonomic Bulletin & Review, 21*(5), 1157–1164. doi:10.3758/s13423-013-0572-3

Hopkins, W. (2005). Making meaningful inferences about magnitudes. *Sportscience, 9*, 6–13. www.sportsci.org/jour/05/ambwgh.htm

Hopkins, W. (2007). A spreadsheet for deriving a confidence interval, mechanistic inference und clinical inference from a p value. *Sportscience, 11,* 16–20. www.sportsci.org/2007/wghinf.htm

Hopkins, W., Batterham, A. M., Marshall, S. W., & Hanin, J. (2009a). Progressive statistics. *Sportscience, 13,* 55–70. www.sportsci.org/2009/prostats.htm

Hopkins, W., Batterham, A. M., Marshall, S. W., & Hanin, J. (2009b). Progressive statistics for studies in sports medicine and exercise science. *Medicine & Science in Sports & Exercercise, 41*(1), 3–12.

Jacobson, N. S., & Truax, P. (1991). Clinical significance: A statistical approach to denning meaningful change in psychotherapy research. *Journal of Consulting and Clinical Psychology, 59*(1), 12–19.

Kelley, K., & Preacher, K. J. (2012). On effect size. *Psychological Methods, 17*(2), 137–152. doi:10.1037/a0028086

Kline, R. B. (2005). *Beyond significance testing* (2nd ed.). Washington, DC: American Psychological Association.

Meylan, C., & Cronin, J. B. (2014). Talent identification. In R. S. Lloyd & J. L. Oliver (eds), *Strength and conditioning for young athletes* (pp. 19–32). Abingdon, UK: Routledge.

Morris, S. B. (2008). Estimating effect sizes from pretest-posttest-control group designs. *Organizational Research Methods, 11*(2), 364–386. doi:10.1177/1094428106291059

Mullineaux, D. R., Bartlett, R. M., & Bennett, S. (2001). Research design and statistics in biomechanics and motor control. *Journal of Sports Sciences, 19*(10), 739–760. doi:10.1080/026404101317015410

Nakagawa, S., & Cuthill, I. C. (2007). Effect size, confidence interval and statistical significance: a practical guide for biologists. *Biological Rewies, 82*(4), 591–605. doi:10.1111/j.1469-185X.2007.00027.x

Page, P. (2014). Beyond statistical significance: clinical interpretation of rehabilitation research literature. *The International Journal of Sports Physical Therapy, 9*(5), 726–736.

Rhea, M. R. (2004). Determing the magnitude of treatment effects in strength training research through the use of the effect size. *Journal of Strength and Conditioning Research, 18*(4), 918–920.

Siegel, S., & Castellan, N. J. (1988). *Nonparametric statistics for the behavioral sciences* (2nd ed.). New York: McGraw Hill.

Steiger, J. H. (2001). NDC: Noncentral distribution calculator [Statistical program]. Vanderbilt University, USA: Department of Psychology and Human Development.

Steiger, J. H. (2004). Beyond the F Test: Effect size confidence intervals and test of close fit in the analysis of variance and contrast analysis. *Psychological Methods, 9*(2), 164–182.

Steiger, J. H., & Fouladi, R. T. (1997). Noncentrality interval estimation and the evaluation of statistical methods. In L. L. Harlow (ed.), *What if there were no significance tests?* (pp. 221–257). London: Routledge.

Thomas, J. R., Nelson, J. K., & Silvermann, S. J. (2015). *Research methods in physical activity* (7th ed.). Champaign: Human Kinetics.

Thompson, B. (2001). Significance, effect sizes, stepwise methods, and other issues: Strong arguments move the field. *Journal of Experimental Education, 70*(1), 80.

Thompson, B. (2002). What future quantitative social science research could look like: Confidence intervals for effect sizes. *Educational Researcher, 31*(3), 25–32. doi:10.3102/0013189x031003025

Thompson, B. (2007). Effect sizes, confidence intervals, and confidence intervals for effect sizes. *Psychology in the Schools, 44*(5), 423–432. doi:10.1002/pits.20234

Troncoso Skidmore, S., & Thompson, B. (2013). Bias and precision of some classical ANOVA effect sizes when assumptions are violated. *Behavior Research Methods, 45*(2), 536–546. doi:10.3758/s13428-012-0257-2

Vila, H., Manchado, C., Rodriguez, N., Abraldes, J. A., Alcaraz, P. E., & Ferragut, C. (2012). Anthropometric profile, vertical jump, and throwing velocity in elite female handball players by playing positions. *Journal of Strength & Conditioning Research, 26*(8), 2146–2155. doi:10.1519/JSC.0b013e31823b0a46

Wagenmakers, E.-J., Wetzels, R., Borsboom, D., van der Maas, H. L. J., & Kievit, R. A. (2012). An agenda for purely confirmatory research. *Perspectives on Psychological Science, 7*(6), 632–638. doi:10.1177/1745691612463078

Wilkinson, M. (2014). Distinguishing between statistical significance and practical/clinical meaningfulness using statistical inference. *Sports Medicine, 44*(3), 295–301. doi:10.1007/s40279-013-0125-y

Williams, C. A., Oliver, J. L., & Lloyd, R. S. (2014). Talent development. In R. S. Lloyd & J. L. Oliver (eds), *Strength and conditioning for young athletes* (pp. 33–46). Abingdon, UK: Routledge.

Appendix 1: List of available helpful online sources

www.sportsci.org/ (spreadsheets for computing effect sizes and confidence intervals)

www.statpower.net/Software.html (NDC, program for computing effect sizes and confidence intervals)

www.gpower.hhu.de/en.html (G*Power, program for computing effect sizes and confidence intervals)

www.psychometrica.de/effect_size.html (internet-based statistical calculator for computing effect sizes and confidence intervals)

www.statpages.info/ (list of web pages which contain statistical calculators)

www.gnu.org/software/pspp/pspp.html (cost-free software for statistical analyses)

https://jasp-stats.org/ (cost-free software for statistical analyses)

PART II

Talent development

9

SPORT ACTIVITY IN CHILDHOOD

Early specialization and diversification

Paul R. Ford and A. Mark Williams

Sport activity in childhood takes place in formal and informal settings. Formal settings involve adults planning, organizing and leading activity for children, such as in coaching or physical education sessions and in competitions. Informal settings involve children leading the sport activities themselves without adult intervention, such as in playgrounds, parks, streets, gardens, car parks, homes, and beaches (Ford, 2016). In some sports in certain countries, children who are considered proficient or with potential are identified to engage in formal, competitive and systematic talent development programmes. In these programmes, children often specialize solely in the sport which has become known as *early specialization* (for a review, see Malina, 2010). Early specialization is defined as starting in the primary sport during childhood (5 to 12 years of age), starting in a talent development programme in childhood, and during that period engaging in one sport only, or at least primarily (Baker, Cobley, & Fraser-Thomas, 2009). Moreover, early specialization involves engaging in a relatively high volume and intensity of training in that sport, as well as in competition in that sport through tournaments, matches and/or leagues (Baker et al., 2009).

Many children engage in sport outside of these formal programmes, such as in informal activity in a single sport, perhaps with some engagement in other sports and/or some formal recreational activity sport, which is known as *early engagement*. Informal playful sports activities are self-directed and are engaged in with the intention of fun and enjoyment (Côté & Hay, 2002). This activity is hypothesized to lead to benefits such as increasing intrinsic motivation (cf. Hendry, Crocker, & Hodges, 2014; Imtiaz, Hancock, & Côté, 2016) and acquiring skills, such as decision-making (e.g., Roca, Williams, & Ford, 2012). Other children engage in sport mainly in formal, recreational settings. At the opposite end of the continuum from early specialization, is a pathway termed *early diversification*. Early diversification is defined as engagement in a number of different sports during childhood in mainly informal, but also formal settings, with late or delayed specialization into formal activity in a single primary sport in adolescence (Côté, Baker, & Abernethy, 2007). In adolescence, these pathways appear to converge to contain increasing specialization for talented athletes in a single sport through a high volume and intensity of training and competition. The predicted characteristics of the early specialization, engagement, and diversification pathways are shown in Table 9.1. The predicted and confirmed outcomes associated with and following early specialization, engagement, and diversification can be found in Table 9.2.

Table 9.1 The predicted characteristics of early specialization, engagement, and diversification

	Early specialization	Early engagement	Early diversification
Childhood			
Start age in primary sport	Childhood	Childhood	Not specified
Start in 'talent programme'	Yes	No	No
Play in primary sport	Low	High	Low to medium
Practice in primary sport	High	Low to medium	Low or no
Competition in primary sport	High	Low or no	Low or no
Other sports	Low	Low to medium	High
Adolescence			
Play in primary sport	Decreases to zero	Decreases to zero	Decreases to zero
Practice in primary sport	High	Increases to high	Increases to high
Competition in primary sport	High	Increases to high	Increases to high
Other sports	Decreases to zero	Decreases to low	Decreases to low

Table 9.2 The predicted and confirmed outcomes associated with and following early specialization, engagement, and diversification

	Early specialization	Early engagement	Early diversification
Positive outcomes in primary sport			
Performance improvement	Yes	Yes	Possibly through transfer
Expert performance	Yes	Yes	Yes
Other positive outcomes			
Continued participation	Some	Yes	Yes
Intrinsic motivation	Lower	Increased	Increased
Enhanced social skills	Lower	Possibly medium	Increased
Negative outcomes			
Overuse injury incidence	Higher	Possibly medium	Lower
Burnout and dropout	Higher	Possibly medium	Lower

Researchers appear to have generally decided that, to paraphrase the renowned English author George Orwell in his book *Animal Farm* (1946), '*early diversification good, early specialization bad*'. The latest incarnation of this idea was forwarded in an International Olympic Committee Consensus Statement on youth athletic development (Bergeron et al., 2016). It states that 'youth should avoid early specialisation, as diverse athletic exposure and sport sampling enhance development and athletic capacity, reduce injury risk and increase the opportunity for a child to discover the sport(s) that he/she will enjoy and possibly excel at' (p. 845). Several other key review papers published in scientific journals have taken a similar position (Baker, 2003; Baker et al., 2009; Côté, Lior, & Hackfort, 2009; Côté & Hancock, 2016; Jayanthi, Pinkham, Dugas, Patrick, & LaBella, 2012; Mostafavifar, Best, & Myer, 2013; Wojtys, 2013). In contrast to this position, coaches and practitioners appear to have decided in Orwell's terms that while '*early diversification is good, early specialization is better*'. In some countries a large industry has been built around youth development programmes that employ thousands of experienced adults to work with children (and adolescents) who specialize in a single sport in well-resourced and expensive facilities.

In this chapter, we present a critical review of research, theory and practice on sport activity in childhood. We support the views of others that childhood sport activities should contain positive features and lead to several positive outcomes (for reviews, see Côté et al., 2009; Côté & Hancock, 2016; Fraser-Thomas, Côté, & Deakin, 2005; Vierimaa, Erickson, Côté, & Gilbert, 2012). However, in this chapter, we mainly limit assessment of the evidence to the development of skill or talent, as is the focus of this book. From this perspective, we seek to identify youth sport activities that cause the development of expert performance at the highest levels of professional sport without the occurrence of any negative consequences, such as overuse injuries or burnout. First, we review evidence for and against early specialization and diversification, which we focus on because these are the two main developmental activity pathways identified by researchers. To our knowledge, there is no single research study that contains children in controlled groups who either specialize or diversify, which measures between-group differences in variables and outcomes of interest at key time points from their current engagement in childhood into adulthood. Such longitudinal research is difficult to undertake for many reasons. Scientists have tended to use case-control and cross-sectional studies from which the quality of evidence is lower because of decreased internal validity when compared to cohort studies or randomized control trials (Petticrew & Roberts, 2006). Nevertheless, in the second part of the chapter, we forward evidence-based recommendations seeking to resolve research and practical issues in this area.

Assessing evidence for early specialization

The main rationale used to support early specialization is the positive relationship repeatedly found between amount of time spent practising a task or domain and level of competence. In this rationale, an earlier start age in a sport coupled with specialization enables a larger accumulation of time spent practising and, thus, higher levels of competence and achievement at a later date when compared to later start ages or not specializing. In addition, the term *practice* is usually used in this argument as a general term to describe engagement in formal sport-specific activities during childhood, including training or coaching sessions. It is beyond the scope of this chapter to review all of the research showing that time spent in practice or training leads to skill acquisition and improved competence, as well as improved physical fitness, but these are generally considered to be scientific laws within certain limits (e.g., Schmidt & Lee, 2011; Kenney, Wilmore, & Costill, 2015).

One of the most influential scientific theories on practice is often cited (e.g., Bullock et al., 2009) as support for early specialization. Deliberate practice theory was introduced by Ericsson, Krampe and Tesch-Römer in 1993. A central part of the theory is the *monotonic benefits assumption*. It holds 'that the amount of time an individual engages in deliberate practice activities is monotonically related to that individual's acquired performance level' (Ericsson et al., 1993, p. 368). As such, they state that 'individuals who start early and practice at higher levels will have a higher level of performance throughout development than those who start later' (p. 392). There is no mention of the term 'early specialization' in the 1993 paper or in Ericsson's subsequent writings on the theory (1996; 2003; 2006; 2007; Ericsson & Towne, 2010). The theory covers all domains of achievement, such as musicians, surgeons or law enforcement, so the earlier start age it refers to does not specify childhood. They do state that 'expert performance is not reached with less than 10 years of deliberate practice' (Ericsson et al., 1993, p. 372) sport, of course, where the attainment of expert performance is most often required in late adolescence or sometimes earlier, such as in gymnastics (Law, Côté, & Ericsson, 2007), the 10-year rule infers a start age in childhood.

One of the main methods used to examine the question of early specialization or diversification was introduced by Ericsson et al. (1993). The retrospective recall method necessitates that expert athletes recall via questionnaires or interviews the number of hours they have spent in practice and other sport activities since they began in their sport. Multiple researchers have shown that hours accumulated by expert adult athletes in practice activities since starting in their sport are greater compared to control groups of lesser-skilled athletes (for recent reviews, see Baker & Young, 2014; Ford, Coughlan, Hodges, & Williams, 2015). In a few of these studies, expert adult or late adolescent athletes reported that they experienced the main characteristics of early specialization in childhood (Ford et al., 2012; Law et al., 2007). Law et al. (2007) used this method to demonstrate that Olympic and international standard adult female rhythmic gymnasts started training in the sport at 6–8 years of age, competing at regional level at age 7–8 years, and started spending all their leisure time training in the sport from 11–12 years of age. During childhood, the Olympic gymnasts accumulated around 2,000 hours of sport-specific training and engaged in one other sport activity. It is likely gymnasts specialized early because expert performance in this sport is required in mid-adolescence, as opposed to in late adolescence or early adulthood in most other sports. Similarly, Ford et al. (2012) showed that late adolescent elite soccer players in Mexico and Sweden started training in the sport around 5 years of age, participated in competitions at age 8 years, and started at an elite academy at 12–13 years of age. During childhood, the elite players accumulated over 1,600 hours of sport-specific training and engaged in one to three other sport activities. However, there was large variation in training hours between players across this period (e.g., *min* = 224 hrs; *max* = 5,680 hrs) and both groups accumulated around 1,200 to 1,400 hours in informal, playful soccer activities during childhood, albeit with large variation in hours between players (e.g., *SD* = 800 hrs). Moreover, late adolescent elite players in England, Brazil, and Portugal demonstrated fewer of the characteristics of childhood specialization in the sport.

Retrospective recall studies have two methodological shortcomings that limit their findings in relation to the question at hand. First, these studies only describe the current youth development system in place in that sport and country and those who stayed in the system. It does not follow that the system is optimal and it may be that many other potential athletes dropped out of the system during their youth or were not selected. Second, retrospective recall studies only show the activities that *preceded* the attainment of expert status in adulthood or late adolescence. They do not show that the early activities *caused* the attainment of expert status. In the next section, we review retrospective recall studies that show how the childhood sports activities that preceded the attainment of expert status in adulthood or late adolescence do not meet the criteria of early specialization. In addition, we review one of the strongest pieces of evidence against early specialization, namely the negative consequences, costs and outcomes of engaging in this pathway.

Assessing evidence against early specialization

been associated with a number of negative outcomes, costs or consequences, such as increased incidence of overuse injuries, burnout, dropout, and decreased social development. Olympic rhythmic gymnasts injuries and lower health across their development when compared to tional gymnasts (Law et al., 2007). Both groups reported more injuries in adolescence compared to childhood. In addition, Olympic gymnasts significantly increased training hours across adolescence, suggesting a positive relationship between training load and injury incidence in this period. Higher workloads and some other aspects of early specialization (e.g., being elite level) have been associated with greater incidence of upper limb overuse injuries in youth gymnasts (DiFiori, Puffer, Mandelbaum, & Mar, 1996) and baseball pitchers (Lyman et al., 2001, 2002; Olsen et al., 2006; for a review, see DiFiori et al., 2014). Similarly, higher training loads and other aspects of early specialization (e.g., frequent intense competition activity, sole-focus) has been associated with greater incidence of burnout, dropout, and overtraining in youth tennis (Gould, Tuffey, Udry, & Lowhr, 1996), gymnastics (Dubuc, Schinke, Eys, Battochio, & Zaichkowsky, 2010), swimming (Fraser-Thomas, Côté, & Deakin, 2008), and golf (Cohn, 1990). These examples of the negative consequences of early specialization led several researchers to recommend early diversification as an alternative pathway (Baker, 2003; Baker et al., 2009; Bergeron et al., 2016; Côté et al., 2009; Côté & Hancock, 2016; Jayanthi et al., 2012; Mostafavifar et al., 2013; Wojtys, 2013).

Further evidence against early specialization can surprisingly be found in deliberate practice theory (Ericsson et al., 1993). The 1993 paper is often misquoted, hence the need for us to use direct quotes from it in this section. In the 1993 paper they outline 'three phases of development toward adult expertise' (p. 369). Of particular interest to this chapter is the first phase of development detailed in the paper. Ericsson et al. state they 'rely on Bloom's (1985) characterization of this (first) period of preparation' (p. 369). They further state that 'from many interviews with international-level performers in several domains, Bloom (1985) found that these individuals start out as children by engaging in playful activities in the domain. After some period of playful and enjoyable experience they reveal 'talent' or promise. At this point, parents typically suggest the start of instruction by a teacher and limited amounts of deliberate practice' (Ericsson et al. 1993, p. 369). They summarize this as follows: 'the first phase of participation in a domain begins with an individual's introduction to activities in the domain and ends with the start of instruction and deliberate practice' (p. 369). The inclusion of this early, pre-deliberate practice stage is often overlooked in reviews of Ericsson et al. (1993). Elsewhere, Ericsson (2003; 2007) uses a version of the 'power law of practice' (Newell & Rosenbloom, 1981) to demonstrate how performance improvement is rapid in the earlier stages of experience in a domain, whereas the rate begins to slow or plateau later in the process. Ericsson clearly states that individuals should begin to engage in deliberate practice once further improvements to performance in the domain start to slow or plateau, suggesting a pre-period of informal activities. We hypothesize that a positive relationship exists in certain domains between the complexity of the domain and the duration of this early period of playful activities. For example, more complex fields, such as certain sport domains, will require longer durations of this first stage of playful activities before performance improvement begins to slow or plateau when compared to less complex domains. In the next section, we review several retrospective recall studies with professional athletes that show they did not engage in the early specialization pathway in childhood, but that they did engage in informal, playful activities during this period.

Assessing evidence for early diversification

Several researchers have advocated early diversification as the pathway that does not lead to the negative consequences of early specialization, but does precede the attainment of professional status in adulthood (Baker, 2003; Baker et al., 2009; Côté et al., 2009; Côté & Hancock, 2016; Fraser-Thomas et al., 2005; Vierimaa et al., 2012; Jayanthi et al., 2012; Mostafavifar et al., 2013;

Wojtys, 2013). The main evidence for early diversification as the activities that precede the attainment of professional status in adulthood is twofold. First, the negative consequences of early specialization support the idea that children should not engage in that pathway. Moreover, as shown in Table 9.2, early diversification is predicted to protect against overuse injures and dropout or burnout and to have other positive outcomes, such as improving social skills. Second, retrospective recall studies examining the developmental activities of athletes are predicted to show early diversification precedes the attainment of later expert status. In the following section we provide a critical review of these retrospective recall studies.

In order to ascertain the sport activities engaged in during childhood, it is necessary to have data on start age in the primary sport and other sports; start age in a talent development programme in the primary sport; the amount of play, practice and competition activity in the primary sport during childhood; and the amount of play, practice and competition activity in other sports during childhood. Table 9.3 (below) uses these criteria and summarizes some studies that have been cited elsewhere as support for early diversification. The criteria for inclusion in Table 9.3 are that the participants in the study are adults playing at the highest level of their professional sport. As such, many papers examining adolescent athletes including those who participate in talent development programmes were excluded because a number of those participants will not achieve the highest professional level and, therefore, their activities create a confounding variable in these data sets that limits their findings (Bridge & Toms, 2013; Côté, 1999; Ford, Ward, Hodges, & Williams, 2009; Ford et al., 2012; Hayman, Borkoles, Taylor, Hemmings, & Polman, 2014; Henriksen, Stambulova, & Roessler, 2010; Leite & Sampaio, 2012; San & Li, 2014; Wall & Côté, 2007; Ward, Hodges, Starkes, & Williams, 2007). In addition, a few studies contain adult participants who *did not* play at the highest level of their professional sport (Hill, 1993; Ford & Williams, 2008, 2012; Roca et al., 2012; Surya, Bruner, MacDonald, & Côté, 2012) and that were excluded from Table 9.3 because their data sets are confounded by this fact. All of these studies have added to knowledge in this area, but for the purposes of this chapter the childhood activities of athletes at the highest level of their professional sport are considered.

We found that no studies provided full data sets on the four aspects of start age in the primary sport; start age in a talent development programme in the primary sport; the amount of play, practice and competition activity in the primary sport during childhood; and the amount of play, practice and competition activity in other sports during childhood. Some studies with professional-level athletes that we wished to include in Table 9.3 had insufficient sets of this data (Coutinho, Mesquita, Fonseca, & De Martin-Silva, 2014; Haugaasen, Toering, & Jordet, 2014; Hodges, Kerr, Starkes, Weir, & Nananidou, 2004; Weissensteiner, Abernethy, Farrow, & Muller, 2008; Young & Salmela, 2010). Moreover, the level of detail required to complete Table 9.3 and answer the key question in this section appeared – on construction of the table – to be available only from studies on athletes from the highest level of *single* sports. Studies that present combined data from professional athletes across multiple sports were excluded from Table 9.3 because they did not contain sufficient amounts of the data we required to be included (Baker, Côté, & Abernethy, 2003a, 2003b; Barreiros & Fonseca, 2012; Hopwood, MacMahon, Farrow, & Baker, 2015; Leite, Baker, & Sampaio, 2009; Memmert, Baker, & Bertsch, 2010; Moesch, Elbe, Hauge, & Wikman, 2011; Moesch, Hauge, Wikman, & Elbe, 2013). These multi-sport studies are addressed in a separate section later in the chapter. Similarly, qualitative studies with professional athletes lacked the details we required for Table 9.3, so were excluded from it and are reviewed in their own section below (Carlson, 1988; Côté, 1999; Durand-Bush & Salmela, 2002; Johnson, Tenenbaum, Edmonds, & Castillo, 2008; Monsaas, 1985; Phillips, Davids, Renshaw, & Portus, 2010; Storm, Kristoffer, & Krog, 2012).

Table 9.3 The findings of key studies examining the developmental activities and pathways of professional athletes

Study	Berry et al. (2008)	Baker et al. (2005)	Law et al. (2007)	Soberlak & Côté (2003)	Hornig et al. (2016)
Country	Australia	Canada	Canada	Canada	Europe (Germany)
Athletes	Australian Rules	Triathlon	Rhythmic gymnasts	Ice Hockey	Soccer
Number of athletes in world	Small	Small	Medium	Medium	Large
Childhood					
Start age in primary sport	Childhood	Adulthood (triathlon) Adolescence (e.g., running)	Childhood	Childhood	Childhood
Start age selected to 'talent programme'	Not available	None	Not available	Early adolescence	Early adolescence
Play in primary sport	Very low	None	No	High	Medium
Practice in primary sport	Low	None	High	Low	Low
Competition in primary sport	Low	None	Not available	Low	Low
Other sports	Low to medium	Low to medium★★	Low	Medium	Low
Adolescence					
Play in primary sport	Low to zero	Not measured★	No	Low	Decreased to low
Practice in primary sport	Increased to high	Increased to medium★	High	High	Medium to high
Competition in primary sport	Not available	None	Yes	Medium	Not available
Other sports	Decreased to zero	Low to medium★★	No	Decreased to low	Low
Notes in addition	Other sports = invasion games	★Running, swimming, cycling ★★Data not separated to age stage	Overuse injuries reported	Other sports = invasion games	Better players > child play in soccer
Childhood pathway followed	Early engagement Early diversification	Early diversification	Early specialization	Early engagement Early diversification	Early engagement

Notes: Low = 0–3 hrs/wk; Medium = 4–7 hrs/wk; High = 8 or more hrs/wk. It should be further noted that hours are usually lower than this average at the start of an age stage and higher at the end.

Finally, studies examining deliberate practice theory in sport from the late 1990s (Helsen et al., 1998; Hodge & Deakin, 1998; Hodges & Starkes, 1996) did not record the amount of time spent in informal activity or in other sports, so were excluded from Table 9.3. It should be noted that these earlier studies do detail start ages in formal activity in the primary sport, with some start ages occurring in childhood preceding a relatively high amount of time in formal sport-specific activities (Helsen et al., 1998) and others in early adolescence (Hodge & Deakin, 1998; Hodges & Starkes, 1996).

Table 9.3 shows that the most common pathway in the studies examining the developmental activities of *team sport* athletes at the highest level of their professional sport is a combination of the early diversification and early engagement pathways (Berry, Abernethy, & Côté, 2008; Hornig, Aust, & Güllich, 2016; Soberlak & Côté, 2003). That is, athletes at the highest level of these team sports started their engagement in childhood and during that stage they engaged in varying amounts of activity in their primary sport. In addition, during childhood they played other sports. Moreover, in most of these studies the most common other sports were other team sports, suggesting the possibility of some transfer of skill occurring between sports (e.g., Causer & Ford, 2014; Smeeton, Ward, & Williams, 2004). A variable that appears to link these team sports is that professional status is attained in late adolescence or early adulthood, probably enabling less specialized engagement in childhood. Australian Football League (AFL) players had the lowest amount of time spent in primary sport activity, albeit the amount of time spent in other sport hours by these players during childhood was low to medium (Berry et al., 2008). In contrast, in childhood, the ice hockey players had the highest amount of time spent in primary sport activity (Soberlak & Côté, 2003), whereas the German soccer players had the lowest amount of time spent in other sports (Hornig et al., 2016).

Table 9.3 shows less coherent findings and less published data for adult athletes at the highest level of *individual sports*. Triathletes in Canada started in their primary sport in adulthood and in running in mid-adolescence, although experts started in these activities earlier compared to lesser-skilled triathletes, with all this preceded in time by some unspecified involvement in other sports (Baker, Côté, & Deakin, 2005). In contrast, as described earlier, Olympic and international standard female rhythmic gymnasts in Canada engaged in an early specialization pathway (Law et al., 2007). It is highly likely that differences in the age that peak performance is required in these sports led to these differences in activities between studies, with triathletes requiring peak performance in adulthood (Baker et al., 2005) and gymnasts in early or mid-adolescence (Law et al., 2007). There is a relatively low amount of data published on the developmental activities of athletes at the highest level of professional individual sports, particularly those meeting the criteria for inclusion in Table 9.3. Athletes at the highest levels of individual sports have been participants in both multi-sport quantitative studies and qualitative studies investigating their developmental activities, which are reviewed in the next sections.

Multi-sport samples

Some researchers have published combined data from professional-level athletes across various sports in single countries (Baker et al., 2003a, 2003b; Barreiros & Fonseca, 2012; Durand-Bush & Salmela, 2002; Leite et al., 2009; Memmert et al., 2010; Moesch et al., 2011, 2013; Storm et al., 2012) or two countries (Hopwood et al., 2015). Some of these studies present insufficient data sets to reliably answer the question at hand, either focusing on the later, elite stage (Barreiros & Fonseca, 2012; Durand-Bush & Salmela, 2002) or by not measuring start age in – or amount of – informal activity (Leite et al., 2009; Moesch et al., 2011). Most of the other studies support the data presented in Table 9.3 showing the most common pattern of childhood sport activities is a combination of the early diversification and early engagement pathways (Memmert et al., 2010; Moesch et al., 2013; Storm et al., 2012). Two studies (Hopwood et al., 2015; Storm et al., 2012) present exceptions to this synthesis of these data sets. Hopwood et al. did not measure other sport involvement in elite athletes across multiple sports in Canada and Australia and found that they had an average start age in the primary sport later than 12 years of age. Storm et al. found a gymnast engaged in the early specialization pathway, supporting the findings for this sport of Law et al. (2007), whereas a rower reported a start age in the sport in mid-adolescence and another rower in adulthood. The findings of Storm et al. and Hopwood et al. may highlight some of the factors that mediate the sport activities engaged in during childhood and early adolescence. These factors include the age at which peak performance is required, the size of the sport in terms of participant numbers, and the athlete attributes required for peak performance.

Of particular importance to this discourse is the Baker et al. (2003a) study because it is often cited as support for the early diversification pathway. Participants were 15 Australian national team players who were selected by coaches as the best decision makers in the sports of female netball ($n = 3$), female field hockey ($n = 4$), male basketball ($n = 4$) and male field hockey ($n = 4$). It appears the players started in their primary sport in childhood, as their current mean age was 27.6 years and they 'had been playing their primary sport for an average of 20.7 years' (p. 15). However, their first involvement in formal activities in their primary sport was an average of 12.9 years prior to their current age, suggesting they engaged in informal activities in their primary sport prior to this during childhood and early adolescence. However, the start age and amount of informal activities in their primary sport in this period is not recorded. The authors do state that the

> ... athletes reported participating in a wide range of sport activities that were not organized by an adult (i.e., activities that might constitute deliberate play). These deliberate play activities (such as backyard games, pick-up games) were performed in informal atmospheres that were not part of an organized sporting system. The most commonly reported deliberate play activities were forms of football, cricket and cycling.
>
> *(Baker et al., 2003a, p. 19)*

The *key finding* presented in this study was a medium-sized negative correlation ($r = -.54$) between the number of sports played during youth and the amount of hours accumulated in practice in the primary sport prior to being selected to the national team. Athletes who had engaged in more other sports in their youth demonstrated less practice hours in their primary sport prior to selection, and vice versa, providing support for early diversification.

The Baker et al. (2003a) study contains participants from three sports and both genders. The published paper contains mean, standard deviation, minimum and maximum descriptive statistics as function of these two variables. At one end of this data set, the male basketball players demonstrated high sport-specific hours and a lower number of other sports, whereas at the other end, the female netball players demonstrated low sport-specific hours and a high number of other sports. In a correlation these differences between these two groups matter when their data are combined because together they contribute to the significant negative correlation. That is, the male basketball players would cause the 'more training hours associated with fewer other sports' and the female netball players would cause the 'fewer training hours associated with more other sports'. In this data set, the hockey players' data is more similar to the netball players than the basketball players, but that group contains both male and female hockey players.

If you were to remove the male basketball players from the data set and re-run the correlation on the more similar data from netball and hockey players, we believe there would be at best a small-sized negative correlation. Moreover, in this data set the female participants demonstrated 'fewer training hours and more other sports' in comparison to male participants who demonstrated 'greater training hours and fewer other sports'. This difference between genders may have fully contributed to the aforementioned significant negative correlations when their data is combined. Therefore, the Baker et al. study appears to show that between-sport and -gender differences exists in the developmental activities of professional-level athletes, rather than providing all-out support for early diversification. It appears that females diversified more than males in this study, possibly because female sports have a lower number of total participants compared to male sports. However, gender differences have not been examined extensively in the literature subsequently.

Qualitative studies

A few researchers have published qualitative studies examining the developmental activities of professional-level athletes (Carlson, 1988; Johnson et al., 2008; Monsaas, 1985; Phillips et al., 2010). All of these studies support the data presented in Table 9.3 that the most common pattern of childhood sport activities was a combination of the early diversification and early engagement pathways (Carlson, 1988; Johnson et al., 2008; Monsaas, 1985; Phillips et al., 2010). Tennis players in Sweden (Carlson, 1988), swimmers (Johnson et al., 2008) and tennis players in North America (Monsaas, 1985) and cricket bowlers in Australia (Phillips et al., 2010) at the highest level of these sports started in their primary sport in childhood. In addition, during childhood they played various other sports. Moreover, the primary sport and other sport activity, certainly in the earliest stage, was mainly either in informal settings or in more recreational-like formal settings. In the main, these athletes specialized in early to mid-adolescence so that they engaged in increasing amounts of more professionalized formal activity solely in their primary sport. The amount of activity is not quantified in these studies, but these athletes do appear to have engaged in a lot of activity in the primary and other sports during childhood and early adolescence.

Assessing evidence against early diversification

The main hypothesis against early diversification is the positive relationship that exists between amount of time spent in domain- or task-specific activity and level of competence in that domain or task. Higher amounts of domain- or task-specific activity are associated with higher levels of competence in that domain or task, suggesting earlier start ages lead to a greater accumulation of activity and the highest levels of competence. In partial support of this hypothesis, Table 9.3 shows that professional athletes in team sports engaged in meaningful amounts of their sport during childhood. However, these athletes engaged in other sports during childhood, which provides partial support for the early diversification pathway. Early diversification is thought to influence skill acquisition in the primary sport through *transfer of learning*. Transfer of learning refers to skill that is acquired in one sport leading to improved performance in ~ sport. Its occurrence is thought to depend upon the amount of similarity in percep- ~nd/or motor elements between the two sports or tasks, with greater similarity ransfer (Schmidt & Lee, 2011). In most of the studies shown in Table 9.3, her sports engaged in had similar elements to the primary sport, suggesting learning could have occurred to the primary sport. For example, expert AFL players spent more time during their youth in other invasion sports compared to time spent in other types of sports, such as net/wall or field/run sports, suggesting the possibility that some transfer of learning could have occurred (Berry et al., 2008).

Engaging in a sport that has different elements to the primary sport is hypothesized to lead to low amounts of transfer of learning. Researchers have suggested that engaging in these other sports may benefit the child in other ways, such as through increasing social skills or protecting against the negative consequences of engaging in the primary sport, perhaps through physical adaptations that protect against overuse injuries (for reviews, see Côté et al., 2009; Côté & Hancock, 2016; Fraser-Thomas et al., 2005; Vierimaa et al., 2012). For example, greater involvement in extracurricular activities including sport was positively associated to academic adjustment, psychological competencies, and a positive peer context in young middle-class adolescents in North America (Fredricks & Eccles, 2006; see also Busseri, Rose-Krasnor, Willoughby, & Chalmers, 2006; Rose-Krasnor, Busseri, Willoughby, & Chalmers, 2006). Further research is required to determine how engaging in other sports enhances these skills in talented youth athletes and protects against overuse injuries as predicted in Table 9.2.

Recommendations for resolving research issues

We are keen for research on this topic to progress and remain open to future findings changing any conclusions we draw from the current literature base. In order for this to occur, we believe four main research issues need to be addressed. These are an increase in the number of research studies conducted; the collection of comprehensive data sets; greater control of independent variables; and the use of newer, more robust research methodologies.

First, several researchers have published multiple review articles on this topic forwarding new hypotheses to be tested (Côté et al., 2009; Côté & Hancock, 2016; Fraser-Thomas et al., 2005; Vierimaa et al., 2012). However, the amount of data on this topic and these hypotheses is relatively low. Therefore, researchers should concentrate future efforts on collecting data to test these hypotheses in order to address the main question of early specialization, engagement and/or diversification.

Second, in order to test these hypotheses and answer this question, researchers using retrospective recall methodologies must ensure they collect comprehensive data sets that include: (i) start age in the primary sport and other sports; (ii) start age in a talent development programme in the primary sport; (iii) the amount of play, practice and competition activity in the primary sport during childhood; and (iv) the amount of play, practice and competition activity in other sports during childhood. It is not possible to draw firm conclusions from data sets that do not include these measures.

Third, researchers must gain greater control over the independent variables that affect data collected in these studies. The main independent variable in these studies is the *skill level* of the participants. Researchers should ensure that participants in the study are adults playing at the highest level of their professional sport. Data collected from youth or lesser-skilled adults limits the conclusions that can be drawn. Another key independent variable is *gender*, with more studies being conducted to date on male as opposed to female participants. A third independent variable is the *country* from which the sample is recruited. Some countries contain adult athletes playing at the highest level of a professional sport, whereas for the same sport the best adult athletes in other countries play at a lower level, with data collected from these lesser-skilled groups again limiting conclusions that can be drawn. Our preferred method in retrospective recall studies is to collect data from adults playing at the highest level of a professional sport in *multiple* key countries (e.g., for a cross-country example, see Ford et al., 2012).

A fourth key independent variable is the *sport* from which the sample is recruited. First, there is a low amount of data from athletes in individual sports, with the majority of studies being conducted on athletes from team sports. Second, the sport influences the data and conclusions through at least three other variables. These are the age at which peak performance is required in the sport, the size of the sport in terms of participant numbers, and the athlete attributes required for peak performance in the sport. We hypothesize that sports with higher ages at which peak performance is required, smaller numbers of participants, and/or lower numbers of mainly physical attributes required would be preceded by greater early diversification (e.g., triathlon, rowing, wrestling). For example, Bullock et al. (2009) report how athletes with a background in sprinting sports were able to start in the minor winter sport of skeleton in young adulthood and compete at World Cups and Olympic Games one year later, providing support for our hypothesis. In contrast, we hypothesize that sports with lower ages at which peak performance is required, high numbers of participants, and/or a high number of more complex technical attributes required would be preceded by greater early engagement (e.g., tennis, soccer). Researchers must gain control over all of these contextual and independent variables and report their results with reference to this larger framework, rather than overstating claims from small data sets sampled from this larger context.

Finally, the retrospective recall methodology introduced by Ericsson et al. (1993) is over 20 years old. There is a need for researchers to develop and use new research methodologies to examine this question and produce higher quality evidence, such as cohort studies or randomized control trials (Petticrew & Roberts, 2006; for an example, see Coughlan, Williams, McRobert, & Ford, 2013).

Recommendations for resolving practical issues

The translation of research into evidence-based practice that positively affects the youths participating in sport and the adults working or volunteering in it is one of our key aims. We believe that three issues in this area must be addressed in children's sport for this to occur. These are: ensuring all children have the opportunity to engage in informal playful activities in safe environments; ensuring adult-led formal activity does not contain the characteristics that constitute the early specialization pathway; and ensuring sports do not function independently of one another. First, adults should ensure that all children have the opportunity to engage in informal playful sports activities in safe environments by creating multiple accessible areas and providing equipment to do so in school playgrounds, parks, and communities. Second, no child should engage in sport activities that constitute the early specialization pathway given the negative consequences associated with this engagement. Adult-led formal sport activity with children should contain the characteristics of informal-playful activity because of its many positive benefits. Educators must equip coaches, physical education teachers and any adults working with children in sport with the knowledge and skills required for them to lead this activity. Educators should consult skill acquisition researchers to help design the content of this educational activity. The recommendations in this chapter only address macro-level activities, whereas adult/child interactions in sport occur as micro-level activities that require an additional set of evidence-based recommendations (e.g., Ford, 2016). Third, formal sports tend to function independently from one another in many countries, such that funding, resources, and expertise are not combined. However, sports must work more closely together to fund, resource, and share expertise at youth level in order for child sport to meet the recommendations outlined in this section.

In summary, the practical recommendations for adults working with children are listed below.

1   No child should engage in sport activities that constitute the early specialization pathway.
2   Children who are highly motivated to play a single sport more so than other sports should be given the opportunity and facilitated to do so through informal playful activities and formal playful-like activities. Those children should be facilitated to engage in some other sports through informal playful activities and formal playful-like activities.
3   Children who are not highly motivated to play a single sport should be given the opportunity and facilitated to sample a variety of sports through informal playful activities and formal playful-like activities.
4   For most sports, across adolescence, the amount of formal training and competition should increase linearly with age until 18 years of age where the athletes should engage full-time in their sport. The amount of informal sport activity across adolescence should decrease linearly with age until 18 years of age where such activity may be ceased.

References

Baker, J. (2003). Early specialization in youth sport: A requirement for adult expertise? *High Ability Studies, 14*, 85–94.

Baker, J., Cobley, S., & Fraser-Thomas, J. (2009). What do we know about early sport specialization? Not much! *High Ability Studies, 20*, 77–89.

Baker, J., Côté, J., & Abernethy, B. (2003a). Sport specific training, deliberate practice and the development of expertise in team ball sports. *Journal of Applied Sport Psychology, 15*, 12–25.

Baker, J., Côté., J., & Abernethy, B. (2003b). Learning from the experts: Practice activities of expert decision makers in sport. *Research Quarterly for Exercise and Sport, 74*, 342–347.

Baker, J., Côté, J., & Deakin, J. (2005). Expertise in ultra-endurance triathletes early sport involvement, training structure, and the theory of deliberate practice. *Journal of Applied Sport Psychology, 17*, 64–78.

Baker, J., & Young, B. (2014). 20 years later: Deliberate practice and the development of expertise in sport. *International Review of Sport and Exercise Psychology, 7*, 135–157.

Barreiros, A. N., & Fonseca, A. M. (2012). A retrospective analysis of Portuguese elite athletes' involvement in international competitions. *International Journal of Sports Science & Coaching, 7*, 593–600.

Bergeron, M. F., Mountjoy M., Armstrong N., et al. (2016). International Olympic Committee consensus statement on youth athletic development. *British Journal of Sports Medicine, 49*, 843–851.

Berry, J., Abernethy, B., & Côté., J. (2008). The contribution of structured activity and deliberate play to the development of expert perceptual and decision-making skill. *Journal of Sport & Exercise Psychology, 30*, 685–708.

Bloom, B. S. (1985). *Developing talent in young people.* New York: Ballantine.

Bridge, M. W., & Toms, M. R. (2013). The specialising or sampling debate: A retrospective analysis of adolescent sports participation in the UK. *Journal of Sports Sciences, 31*, 87–96.

Bullock, N., Gulbin, J. P., Martin, D. T., Ross, A., Holland, T., & Marino, F. (2009). Talent identification and deliberate programming in skeleton: Ice novice to Winter Olympian in 14 months. *Journal of Sports Sciences, 27*, 397–404.

Busseri, M. A., Rose-Krasnor, L., Willoughby, T., & Chalmers, H. (2006). A longitudinal examination of breadth and intensity of youth activity involvement and successful development. *Developmental Psychology, 42*, 1313–1326.

Carlson, R. (1988). The socialization of elite tennis players in Sweden: An analysis of the players' backgrounds and development. *Sociology of Sport Journal, 5*, 241–256.

Causer, J., & Ford, P. R. (2014). 'Decisions, decisions, decisions': Transfer and specificity of decision making skill between sports. *Cognitive Processing, 15*, 385–389.

Cohn, P. C. (1990). An exploratory study on sources of stress and athlete burnout in youth golf. *Sport Psychologist, 4*, 95–106.

Côté, J. (1999). The influence of the family in the development of talent in sport. *The Sport Psychologist, 13*, 395–417.

Côté, J., & Hay, J. (2002). Children's involvement in sport: A developmental perspective. In J. M. Silva & D. Stevens (eds), *Psychological foundations of sport* (pp. 484–502). Boston: Allyn and Bacon.

Côté, J., & Hancock, D. J. (2016). Evidence-based policies for youth sport programmes. *International Journal of Sport Policy and Politics, 8,* 51–65.

Côté, J., Baker, J., & Abernethy, B. (2007). Play and practice in the development of sport expertise. In G. Tenenbaum & R. C. Eklund (eds), *Handbook of sport psychology* (3rd ed., pp. 184–202). New York: Wiley.

Côté, J., Lidor, R., & Hackfort, D. (2009). ISSP Position Stand: To sample or to specialize? Seven postulates about youth sport activities that lead to continued participation and elite performance. *International Journal of Sport and Exercise Psychology, 9,* 7–17.

Coughlan, E. K., Williams, A. M., McRobert, A. P., & Ford, P. R. (2013). How experts practice: A novel test of deliberate practice theory. *Journal of Experimental Psychology: Learning, Memory, and Cognition, 40,* 449–458.

Coutinho P., Mesquita I., Fonseca A. M., & De Martin-Silva, L. (2014). Patterns of sport participation in Portuguese volleyball players according to expertise level and gender. *International journal of Sports Science & Coaching, 9,* 579–592.

DiFiori, J.P., Puffer, J.C., Mandelbaum, B.R., & Mar, S. (1996). Factors associated with wrist pain in the young gymnast. *The American Journal of Sports Medicine, 24,* 9–14.

DiFiori, J. P., Benjamin, H. J., Brenner, J. S., Gregory, A, Jayanthi, N., Landry, G. L. et al. (2014). Overuse injuries and burnout in youth sports: A position statement from the American Medical Society for Sports Medicine. *British Journal of Sports Medicine, 48,* 287–288.

Dubuc, N. G., Schinke, R. J., Eys, M. A., Battochio, R., & Zaichkowsky, L. (2010). Experiences of burnout among adolescent female gymnasts: Three case studies. *Journal of Clinical Sport Psychology, 4,* 1–18.

Durand-Bush, N., & Salmela, J. H. (2002). The development and maintenance of expert athletic performance: Perceptions of world and Olympic champions. *Journal of Applied Sport Psychology, 14,* 154–171.

Ericsson, K. A. (ed.). (1996). *The road to excellence: The acquisition of expert performance in the arts and sciences, sports and games.* Hillsdale, NJ: Lawrence Erlbaum.

Ericsson, K. A. (2003). The development of elite performance and deliberate practice: An update from the perspective of the expert-performance approach. In J. Starkes & K.A. Ericsson (eds), *Expert performance in sport: Recent advances in research on sport expertise* (pp. 49–81). Champaign, IL: Human Kinetics.

Ericsson, K. A. (2006). The influence of experience and deliberate practice on the development of superior expert performance. In K. A. Ericsson, N. Charness, P. Feltovich, & R. R. Hoffman, R. R. (eds),*Cambridge handbook of expertise and expert performance* (pp. 685–706). Cambridge, UK: Cambridge University Press.

Ericsson, K. A. (2007). Deliberate practice and the modifiability of body and mind: Toward a science of the structure and acquisition of expert and elite performance. *International Journal of Sport Psychology, 38,* 4–34.

Ericsson, K. A., Krampe, R. T., & Tesch-Römer, C. (1993). The role of deliberate practice in the acquisition of expert performance. *Psychological Review, 100,* 363–406.

Ericsson, K. A., & Towne, T. J. (2010). Expertise. *WIREs Cognitive Science, 1,* 404–416.

Ford, P. R. (2016). Skill acquisition and learning through practice and other activities. In T. Strudwick (ed.), *Soccer science.* Champaign, IL: Human Kinetics.

Ford, P. R., Carling, C., Garces, M., Marques, M., Miguel, C., Farrant, A., … & Williams, A. M. (2012). The developmental activities of elite soccer players aged under-16 years from Brazil, England, France, Ghana, Mexico, Portugal and Sweden. *Journal of Sports Sciences, 30,* 1653–1663.

Ford, P. R., Coughlan, E. K., Hodges, N. J., & Williams, A. M. (2015). Deliberate practice in sport. In J. Baker & D. Farrow (eds), *The Handbook of Sport Expertise* (pp. 347–362). London: Routledge.

Ford, P. R., Ward, P., Hodges, N. J., & Williams, A. M. (2009). The role of deliberate practice and play in career progression in sport: the early engagement hypothesis. *High Ability Studies, 20,* 65–75.

Ford, P. R., & Williams, A. M. (2008). The effect of participation in Gaelic football on the development of Irish professional soccer players. *Journal of Sport and Exercise Psychology, 30,* 709–722.

Ford P. R., & Williams A. M. (2012). The developmental activities engaged in by elite youth soccer players who progressed to professional status compared to those who did not. *Psychology of Sport and Exercise, 13,* 349–352.

Fraser-Thomas, J., Côté, J., & Deakin, J. (2005). Youth sport programs: An avenue to foster positive youth development. *Physical Education and Sport Pedagogy, 10,* 49–70.

Fraser-Thomas, J., Côté, J., & Deakin, J. (2008). Understanding dropout and prolonged engagement in adolescent competitive sport. *Psychology of Sport and Exercise, 9,* 645–662.

Fredricks, J. A., & Eccles, J. S. (2006). Extracurricular involvement and adolescent adjustment: Impact of duration, number of activities, and breadth of participation. *Applied Developmental Science, 10*, 132–146.

Gould, D., Tuffey, S., Udry, E., & Lowhr, J. (1996). Burnout in competitive junior tennis players: II. Qualitative analysis. *The Sport Psychologist, 10*, 341–366.

Haugaasen, M., Toering, T., & Jordet, G. (2014). From childhood to senior professional football: Elite youth players' engagement in non-football activities. *Journal of Sports Sciences, 32*, 1940–1949.

Hayman, R. J., Borkoles, E., Taylor, J. A., Hemmings, B., & Polman, R. C. (2014). From pre-elite to elite: The pathway travelled by adolescent golfers. *International Journal of Sports Science & Coaching, 9*, 959–974.

Helsen, W. F., Starkes, J. L., & Hodges, N. J. (1998). Team sports and the theory of deliberate practice. *Journal of Sport and Exercise Psychology 20*, 12–34.

Hendry, D. T., Crocker, P. R. E., & Hodges, N. J. (2014). Practice and play as determinants of self-determined motivation in youth soccer players. *Journal of Sports Sciences, 32*, 1091–1099.

Henriksen, K., Stambulova, N., & Roessler, K. K. (2010). Successful talent development in track and field: considering the role of environment. *Scandinavian Journal of Medicine and Science in Sports, 20*, 122–132.

Hill, G. M. (1993). Youth sport participation of professional baseball player. *Sociology of Sport Journal, 10*, 107–111.

Hodge, T., & Deakin, J. (1998). Deliberate practice and expertise in the martial arts: The role of context in motor recall. *Journal of Sport and Exercise Psychology, 20*, 260–279.

Hodges, N. J., & Starkes, J. L. (1996). Wrestling with the nature of expertise: A sport-specific test of Ericsson, Krampe and Tesch-Römer's (1993) theory of 'deliberate practice'. *International Journal of Sport Psychology, 27*, 400–424.

Hodges, N. J., Kerr, T., Starkes, J. L., Weir, P. L., & Nananidou, A. (2004). Predicting performance times from deliberate practice hours for triathletes and swimmers: What, when, and where is practice important? *Journal of Experimental Psychology: Applied, 10*, 219–237.

Hopwood, M. J., MacMahon, C., Farrow, D., & Baker, J. (2015). Is practice the only determinant of sporting expertise? Revisiting Starkes (2000). *International Journal of Sport Psychology, 46*, 631–651.

Hornig, M., Aust, F., & Güllich, A. (2016). Practice and play in the development of German top-level professional football players. *European Journal of Sport Science, 16*, 96–105.

Imtiaz, F., Hancock, D. J., & Côté, J. (2016). Examining young recreational male soccer players' experience in adult- and peer-led structures. *Research Quarterly for Exercise and Sport*. DOI: 10.1080/02701367.2016.1189073

Jayanthi, N., Pinkham, C., Dugas, L., Patrick, B., & LaBella, C. (2012). Sports specialization in young athletes: Evidence-based recommendations. *Sports Health, 5*, 251–257.

Johnson, M. B., Tenenbaum, G., Edmonds, W. A., & Castillo, Y. (2008). A comparison of the developmental experiences of elite and sub-elite swimmers: similar developmental histories can lead to differences in performance level. *Sport, Education and Society, 13*, 453–475.

Kenney, W. L., Wilmore, J., & Costill, D. (2015). *Physiology of Sport and Exercise* (6th ed.). Champaign, IL: Human Kinetics.

Law, M., Côté, J., & Ericsson, K. A. (2007). Characteristics of expert development in rhythmic gymnastics: A retrospective study. *International Journal of Sport and Exercise Psychology, 5*, 82–103.

Leite, N., & Sampaio, J. (2012). Long-term athletic development across different age groups and gender from Portuguese basketball players. *International Journal of Sports Science and Coaching, 7*, 285–300.

Leite, N., Baker, J., & Sampaio, J. (2009). Paths to expertise in Portuguese national team athletes. *Journal of Sports Science and Medicine, 8*, 560–566.

Lyman, S., Fleisig, G. S., Waterbor, J. W. et al. (2001). Longitudinal study of elbow and shoulder pain in youth baseball pitchers. *Medicine and Science in Sports and Exercise, 33*, 1803–1810.

Lyman, S., Fleisig, G. S., Andrews, J. R., et al. (2002). Effect of pitch type, pitch count, and pitching mechanics on risk of elbow and shoulder pain in youth baseball pitchers. *American Journal of Sports Medicine, 30*, 463–468.

Malina, R. M. (2010). Early sport specialization: Roots, effectiveness, risks. *Current Sports Medicine Reports, 9*, 364–371.

Memmert, D., Baker, J., & Bertsch, C. (2010). Play and practice in the development of sport- specific creativity in team ball sports. *High Ability Studies, 21*, 3–18.

Moesch, K., Elbe, A. M., Hauge, M. L. T., & Wikman, J. M. (2011). Late specialization: The key to success in centimetres, grams, or seconds (cgs) sports. *Scandinavian Journal of Medicine & Science in Sports, 21*, e282–e290.

Moesch, K., Hauge, M. L. T., Wikman, J. M., & Elbe, A. M. (2013). Making it to the top in team sports: Start later, intensify, and be determined! *Talent Development & Excellence, 5*, 85–100.

Monsaas, J. A. (1985). Learning to be a world-class tennis player. In B. S. Bloom (ed.), *Developing talent in young people* (pp. 211–269). New York: Ballantine.

Mostafavifar, A. M., Best, T. M., & Myer, G. D. (2013). Early sport specialisation, does it lead to long-term problems? *British Journal of Sports Medicine, 47*, 1060–1061.

Newell, A., & Rosenbloom, P. S. (1981). Mechanisms of skill acquisition and the law of practice. In J. R. Anderson (ed.), *Cognitive skills and their acquisition* (pp. 1–55). Hillsdale, NJ: Erlbaum.

Olsen, S. J., Fleisig, G. S., Dun, S., et al. (2006). Risk factors for shoulder and elbow injuries in adolescent baseball pitchers. *American Journal of Sports Medicine, 34*, 905–912.

Orwell, G. (1946). *Animal Farm.* New York: Harcourt, Brace and Company.

Petticrew, M., & Roberts, H. (2006). *Systematic reviews in the social sciences: A practical guide.* Oxford: Blackwell.

Phillips, E., Davids, K. W., Renshaw, I., & Portus, M. (2010). The development of fast bowling experts in Australian cricket. *Talent Development and Excellence, 2*, 137–148.

Roca, A., Williams, A. M., & Ford, P. R. (2012). Developmental activities and the acquisition of superior anticipation and decision making in soccer players. *Journal of Sports Sciences, 30*, 1643–1652.

Rose-Krasnor, L., Busseri, M. A., Willoughby, T., & Chalmers, H. (2006). Breadth and intensity of youth activity involvement as contexts for positive development. *Journal of Youth and Adolescence, 35*, 365–379.

San, A. T. L., & Li, J. L. F. (2014). Developmental practice activities of elite youth swimmers. *Movement, Health & Exercise, 3*, 27–37.

Schmidt, R. A., & Lee, T. D. (2011). *Motor control and learning* (5th ed.). Champaign, IL: Human Kinetics.

Smeeton, N. J., Ward, P., & Williams, A. M. (2004). Do pattern recognition skills transfer across sports? A preliminary analysis. *Journal of Sports Sciences, 22*, 205–213.

Soberlak, P., & Côté, J. (2003). The developmental activities of professional ice hockey players. *Journal of Applied Sport Psychology, 15*, 41–49.

Storm, L. H., Kristoffer, H., Krog, C. M. (2012). Specialization pathways among elite Danish athletes: A look at the developmental model of sport participation from a cultural perspective. *International Journal of Sport Psychology, 43*, 199–222.

Surya, M., Bruner, M. W., MacDonald, D. J., & Côté, J. (2012). A comparison of developmental activities of elite athletes born in large and small cities. *PHEnex, 4*, 1–8.

Vierimaa, M., Erickson, K., Côté, J., & Gilbert, W. (2012). Positive youth development: A measurement framework for sport. *International Journal of Sports Science and Coaching, 7*, 601–614.

Wall, M., & Côté, J. (2007). Developmental activities that lead to dropout and investment in sport. *Physical Education and Sport Pedagogy, 12*, 77–87.

Ward, P., Hodges, N. J., Starkes, J. L., & Williams, A. M. (2007). The road to excellence: Deliberate practice and the development of expertise. *High Ability Studies, 18*, 119–153.

Weissensteiner, J. R, Abernethy, B., Farrow, D., & Muller, S. (2008). The development of anticipation: A cross-sectional examination of the practice experiences contributing to skill in cricket batting. *Journal of Sport & Exercise Psychology, 30*, 663–684.

Wojtys, E. M. (2013). Sports specialization vs. diversification. *Sports Health, 5*, 212–213.

Young, B. W., & Salmela, J. H. (2002). Perceptions of training and deliberate practice of middle distance runners. *International Journal of Sport Psychology, 33*, 167–181.

Young B. W., & Salmela, J. H. (2010). Examination of practice activities related to the acquisition of elite performance in Canadian middle distance running. *International Journal of Sport Psychology, 41*, 73–90.

10

METHOD IN THE MADNESS

Working towards a viable 'paradigm' for better understanding and supporting the athlete pathway

Juanita R. Weissensteiner

Introduction: Chaos along the athlete pathway!

The developmental journey of an athlete from their 'grass-roots' to international podium, is a long and at times, arduous one. The quest to find the right 'road map' (i.e., developmental framework or model) that adequately captures the nuances of this experience, that can effectively navigate this journey for both the athlete in question and that can guide and coordinate all key stakeholders invested in supporting the 'athlete', continues. Despite a predominance of highly cited and popular concepts and frameworks within the contemporary literature, gaps persist in the athlete pathway and the aligned practice and support of athletes (Bergeron et al., 2015; Gulbin, Croser, Morley, & Weissensteiner, 2013a; Gulbin & Weissensteiner, 2013; Toohey et al., 2015; Weissensteiner & Medlicott, 2015). As depicted in Figure 10.1, within the foundational levels of the athlete pathway, marked declines in the fundamental movement skills (the building blocks for later sporting skill), muscular strength and neuromuscular fitness and coordination of youth participants is occurring in unison with a greater emphasis on earlier, structured sport formats and sports specialization to the detriment of deliberate play and diversified sports sampling (Bergeron et al., 2015; Côté, Lidor, & Hackfort, 2009; Hardy, King, Espinel, Cosgrove, & Bauman, 2010a; Hardy, King, Farrell, Macniven, & Howlett, 2010b; Hardy, Barnett, & Espinel, & Okely, 2013; Jayanthi, LaBella, Fischer, Pasulka, & Dugas, 2015; Lloyd et al., 2015a; Myer et al., 2015; Oakley & Booth, 2004; Telford et al., 2012; Tester, Ackland, & Houghton, 2014). A decline in these foundational competencies are contributing to unrealised talent potential through compromised sport-specific skill development, increased injury risk, burnout and dropout (Bergeron et al., 2015; Côté et al., 2009; Fraser-Thomas, Côté, & Deakin, 2008; Jayanthi et al., 2015; Myer et al., 2015). Questionable and short-sighted coaching and club practices prevail, underpinned by a lack of understanding regarding the holistic nature of athlete development, the impact of biological maturation on adolescent sporting development and performance and the importance of injury prevention (Bergeron et al., 2015; Emery, Thierry-Olivier, Whittaker, Nettel-Aguirre, & van Mechelen, 2015; Malina, Rogol, Cumming, Coelho-e-Silva, & Figueiredo, 2015).

Within the pre-elite levels, uni-dimensional and restrictive talent identification and recruitment strategies predicated on biophysical markers and juvenile performance (shown

Juanita R. Weissensteiner

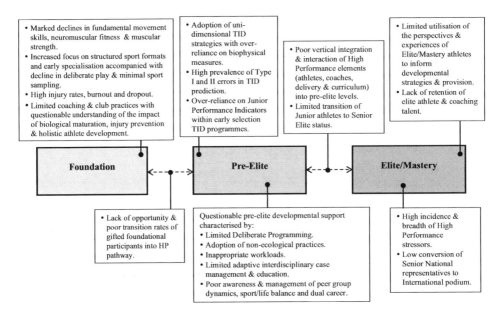

Figure 10.1 Current state of the athlete development pathway

conclusively to be a poor and premature predictor of future elite adult performance) continue to be adopted and the developmental and transitional needs of athletes are not being met (Güllich & Emrich, 2012, 2014; Stambulova, Engström, Franck, Linnér, & Lindahl, 2015; Weissensteiner, Warmenhoven, Medlicott, & Gulbin, 2015; Weissensteiner & Medlicott, 2015; Wyllemann & Reints, 2010.). Additionally, relatively ineffective, non-ecological training practices characterised by low 'task representativeness' continue to be adopted in combination with limited and ineffective case management of athletes (Davids, 2010; Pankhurst, Collins, & MacNamara, 2013; Pankhurst & Collins, 2013; Phillips, Davids, Renshaw, & Portus, 2010; Pinder, Davids, Renshaw, & Araújo, 2011; Pinder, Renshaw, & Davids, 2013).

At the 'pinnacle' of the athlete pathway, conversion rates from national representative to podium are limited, while an inability to negotiate the myriad of high performance stressors and difficulty maintaining a healthy sport–life balance are impacting athletes' well-being and ability to sustain performance on the world stage (Bergeron et al., 2015; Fletcher & Sarkar, 2012; Mountjoy, Rhind, Tiivas, & Leglise, 2015; Weissensteiner & Medlicott, 2015; Weissensteiner et al., 2015).

Working towards a consolidated and unified view of athlete development

As conceptualised in the revised 3D-AD (three dimensional-athlete development) model in Figure 10.2, it is now well established that athlete development is a dynamic and at times 'chaotic' process due to its inherent variability, and that resultant performance is underpinned by a complex and individualistic choreography of athletic attributes and skills (i.e., physical, psychological and sport-specific technical, cognitive and perceptual components) that are in turn, directly impacted upon or 'modulated' by a complement of environmental, system and chance factors (Bailey et al., 2010; Baker & Horton, 2004; Bergeron et al., 2015; Elferink-

134

Gemser, Visscher, Lemmink, & Mulder, 2007; Elferink–Gemser, Visscher, Lemmink, & Mulder, 2011; Gulbin, Oldenziel, Weissensteiner, & Gagné, 2010; Gulbin et al., 2013a; Gulbin & Weissensteiner, 2013; Henriksen, Stambulova, & Roessler, 2010a, 2010b, 2011; Simonton, 2001; Weissensteiner, Abernethy, & Farrow, 2009). The relative contribution of, and relationships within and between, athlete, environmental and system factors, increases and decreases at different times during development, as represented by the changing relative size of and proximity between factors, conceptualised in the bottom of Figure 10.2.

Despite this shared position on athlete development, a large number of existent concepts and at best 'frameworks' (see Carpiano and Daley, 2006 for clarification on what differentiates a 'framework' from a 'model') are predominately subset in focus and application, and subsequently do not fully capture and contribute to a holistic, integrated and longitudinal understanding of the athlete pathway (Abbott & Collins, 2004; Ackerman, 2013; Bailey et al., 2010; Bergeron et al., 2015; Buekers, Borry, & Rowe, 2015; Fuchslocher, Romann, & Gulbin, 2013; Gagné, 2003, 2004; Gulbin & Weissensteiner, 2013; Tucker & Collins, 2012; Vaeyens, Lenoir, Williams, & Philippaerts, 2008). Furthermore, the theoretical and methodological underpinnings and practical utility of some of these frameworks and concepts, have come under question (Ackerman, 2013; Baker & Young, 2014; Bergeron et al., 2015; Ford et al., 2011, Gulbin et al., 2013a; Gulbin & Weissensteiner, 2013; Lang & Light, 2010; Macnamara,

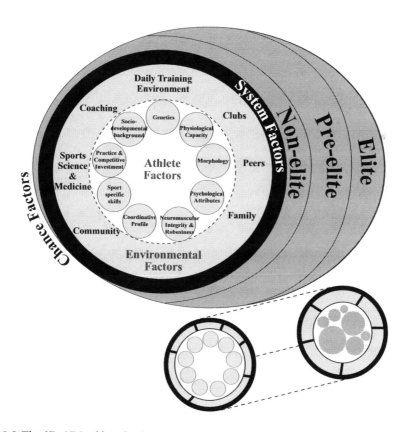

Figure 10.2 The 3D–AD2 athlete development model demonstrating the multidimensional, longitudinal and interactive nature of athlete development

Hambrick, & Oswald, 2014; Malina et al., 2006, 2012, 2015; Tucker & Collins, 2012). Recognised limitations characterising existing athlete development constructs, concepts and frameworks include:

- not spanning the entire athlete pathway from foundation to podium and inclusive of the multiple normative and non-normative transitions that characterise the athlete developmental experience;
- not catering for the complementary outcomes of sport including active lifestyle pursuits, life-long recreational sport involvement and high performance sport;
- being predominately generic and not sensitive and generalizable to sport-specific and individual nuances of athlete development;
- being predicated on chronological age and stringently prescriptive regarding training to competition exposure for specific age ranges;
- not being flexible in catering for the recognised variability of athlete development including reported differences in developmental trajectory, multiple entry and exit points and concurrent investment in junior and senior competition;
- not capturing and catering for the multifactorial, dynamic nature of athlete development including recognised athlete, environmental, system and chance factors;
- not capturing and differentiating between the developmental experiences of Olympic, Paralympic and Professional sport athletes;
- being characterised by inconsistent and non-meaningful nomenclature not readily understood by all sporting stakeholders.

For a comprehensive critique, see Bailey et al. (2010) or Gulbin and Weissensteiner (2013).

Given these prevailing issues, it is therefore not surprising, that at a practical level, sporting stakeholders, those at the day-to-day 'coal face' of sport, find it difficult and confusing to decipher and translate such uncoordinated and, at times, contradictory messages into effective sporting practice and optimised athlete development (Ackerman, 2013; Ford et al., 2011; Gulbin & Weissensteiner, 2013; Güllich & Emrich, 2012, 2014; Pankhurst et al., 2013; Pankhurst & Collins, 2013; Tucker & Collins, 2012).

In addition, the ongoing debate or 'jockeying' of constructs, concepts and frameworks and seeming division between 'research' and 'practice', has to some degree detracted from achieving a robust and stable theoretical 'paradigm' for consolidating our applied understanding of athlete development from foundation to podium, and informing future meaningful and programmatic research. As Carpiano and Daley (2006) advocate, whilst 'theory building' and 'theory testing' are commonly considered separately, to effectively 'identify the problems' and 'design and evaluate the solutions' requires an interplay between the two entities. As Carpiano and Daley (2006, p. 565) write, '… creating theory without testing it, has limited utility for action'.

In response, it has been advocated in the recently published International Olympic Committee (IOC) consensus statement on Youth Athlete Development, that a consolidated and unified approach featuring integrated, holistic, flexible and practical frameworks is necessary for navigating and supporting the athlete pathway (Bergeron et al., 2015). It was argued, that such an approach would better foster the holistic and sustainable development, transition and progression of athletes along the pathway through stronger sport and system connectivity. It was recommended, that adopted frameworks should span the 'trichotomy' of the athlete pathway (Gulbin, 2012) inclusive of its participation (foundational), pre-elite and high performance components and predicated on recognised 'best practice' for each developmental phase rather than age (Bergeron et al., 2015). In addition, they should be flexible to embrace the inherent complexity and non-linearity of athlete development and holistic in embracing the multi-dimensional nature of athlete development.

Cognisant of the 3D-AD conceptualisation of athlete development, recommendations detailed within the IOC consensus statement and recent commentary in the literature (e.g., Ackerman, 2013; Bailey et al., 2010; Gulbin & Weissensteiner, 2013; Pankhurst et al., 2013), recognised that key features of an effective athlete development framework include being:

- inclusive of foundational, pre-elite and elite and mastery components and catering for the full complement of normative and non-normative transitions;
- characterised by consistent and meaningful nomenclature readily understood by all sporting stakeholders including athletes, coaches, sporting organisations, government agencies;
- cognisant of the maturational differences of athletes and predicated on contemporary best practice specific to optimising athlete development and not chronological age;
- flexible in catering for the inherent variability and individualised nature of athlete development;
- holistic and a 'fit' with the recognised multi-dimensional nature of athlete development and performance;
- informed by evidence whereby an initial 'theoretical framework' is consolidated as a practical and effective model through aligned inter-disciplinary and longitudinal research;
- directly translatable to effective sporting practice for all sporting stakeholders and providing an overarching strategy to inform ongoing review and refinement of the athlete pathway and associated strategies and research;
- inclusive and sensitive to differences and commonalities between Olympic, Paralympic and Professional sport athletes.

Vaeyens et al. (2008) touted Gagné's Differentiated Model of Giftedness (DMGT: Gagné 2003, 2004) as a potential holistic and flexible framework for understanding sporting talent development. This framework with its origins in education acknowledges the contribution and interaction of not only intrapersonal and developmental factors but also environmental and contextual factors. Whilst it has been recognised as a potential framework for better understanding talent development and expertise in sport particularly from pre-elite to elite, it is still to be verified empirically within the sporting domain.

An example of an evidence-based, holistic and practical framework for understanding and managing the athlete pathway

Informed by over twenty years of practical insight within the Australian sporting sector and based on an extensive critique of the literature, the FTEM (Foundation, Talent, Elite & Mastery) athlete developmental framework developed by the Australian Institute of Sport (see Figure 5.1 in Chapter 5) has provided an effective 'blueprint' for navigating the athlete pathway (Gulbin et al., 2013a; Gulbin & Weissensteiner, 2013). At a sport and overarching system level, FTEM is now utilised as an operational framework and 'tool' for systematically reviewing and refining the collective athlete pathways of over 30 Australian sporting organisations (including Paralympic disciplines) and directly informing aligned strategy and support (see www.hockey.org.au/AthletePathway for an example).

Central to its design, is FTEM's 'chronology' of ten differentiated yet integrated developmental phases from a foundation to pre-elite, and elite and mastery levels. Implicit with the framework, is its catering for a realistic or fuller complement of 'normative' and 'non-normative' developmental transitions. Unlike the majority of existing frameworks, FTEM is not predicated on age but instead advocates an evidence-informed approach for maximising athlete development, and is adaptable to a sport-specific and sub-discipline level.

Closer in fit to a 'paradigm' (see Carpiano & Daley, 2006), FTEM provides essentially a flexible and broad overarching framework for better understanding and negotiating the athlete pathway through its advocacy of contemporary 'best practice' (i.e., a complement of recognised concepts and strategies as presented within Tables 10.1, 10.2 and 10.3 below). Considerate of the prior learnings afforded from the existent literature and past practice, the key objective of FTEM is to achieve a favourable outcome for each pathway phase, with its 'catchphrase' being to 'provide the right support, at the right time, for the right athletes'. Given these design features, FTEM is arguably 'universal' in its utility and application.

Whilst FTEM appears 'linear' and 'uniform' in its representation of the developmental phases, it is inherently non-linear and flexible in that it can be compressed and extended. An advantage of the framework is its 'permeability' or 'porosity' in catering for the sport-specific and individual nuances of athlete development (Güllich & Emrich, 2012, 2014; Gulbin, Croser, Morley, & Weissensteiner, 2014; Suppiah, Low, & Chia, 2015). It caters for multiple exit and re-entry points into the athlete pathway (i.e., talent transfer and talent reintegration) and the idiosyncratic nature of developmental trajectory including descents and ascents from one competition level to another and concurrent junior and senior competitive experiences (Gulbin, Weissensteiner, Oldenziel, & Gagné, 2013b).

The FTEM framework is inclusive in its shared representation of Active Lifestyle, Recreational and High Performance Sport pathways whereby the collective health of the foundational levels of early sport participation is critical and greatly impactful on the two central outcomes of sport: active, healthy, life-long sport participation and high performance achievement. To assist in promoting better clarity, connectivity and consistency, the framework features meaningful and consistent nomenclature that is translatable and practicable for all sporting stakeholders from the grass roots to a high performance level.

As an overarching operational framework, FTEM has been further consolidated through its association with the 3D-AD model of athlete development, in fostering a committed, evidence-based approach to identifying gaps in the athlete pathway and informing (at a sport and system level) effective strategies and interventions to address these gaps. Cognisant of the holistic and integrated philosophy espoused through the 3D-AD model, coupled with accrued learnings through its theoretical and practical application, adoption of this 'hybrid' approach has contributed to a better understanding and management of athlete development for all pathway stakeholders through its:

- articulation and education of sporting stakeholders regarding adopting a contemporary 'best practice' approach to achieve the desired developmental outcome for each FTEM phase;
- provision of firm evidence relating to the current health of the athlete pathway;
- direct guidance regarding the strategic coordination and management of influential environment and system level 'drivers' and 'enablers' (Gulbin & Weissensteiner, 2013; Weissensteiner, 2015; Weissensteiner & Medlicott, 2015).

The relative success of this approach has been underpinned by embracing an 'action-research' and sport-specific approach whereby the pathway experiences, reflections and perceptions of contemporary athletes (My Sporting Journey Questionnaire: Weissensteiner, 2015) are 'triangulated' with the perspectives and expertise of the governing National sport organisation and their respective stakeholders including coaches, administrators and managers [NSO Pathway Healthcheck] (Weissensteiner & Medlicott, 2015).

The recent findings of the My Sporting Journey questionnaire, have confirmed unequivocally that the journey from grassroots participant to podium medal recipient, is a long and arduous one (Weissensteiner et al., 2015). The questionnaire, which was predicated on the FTEM framework, was administered online to 683 past and current Olympic, Paralympic and Professional Australian athletes including 298 senior elite athletes, to engage their 'voice' (i.e., reflections and experiences) and chronicle their entire sporting developmental history. The findings of this investigation provided valuable insight regarding the foundational antecedents to later sporting expertise and compelling evidence regarding the need for better support and management of athletes specific to the development and refinement of their psychological skills and strategies, managing influential peers and a dual-career, maintaining sport–life balance, preparation for the elite junior to senior transition, first time senior elite experiences and their ability to manage a breadth of concurrent high performance stressors (e.g., financial issues, injury and illness, coach–athlete and peer dynamics, sport–life balance, dual career, family, training and travel demands, expectations of their sporting organisation, etc.).

Recently, the 3D-AD model has been utilised to 'map' the developmental experience of Australian athletes within the sports of AFL, cricket, tennis and kayaking (Toohey et al., 2015, 2015b). Collective evidence of the athlete developmental journey was obtained through the course of a 4-year national government funded project (Australian Research Council) which featured a strong 'transdisciplinary' (i.e., incorporating sports science, sport management, sports psychology, public health and urban geography disciplines) and mixed methodological approach (Toohey et al., 2015). Depicted in Figure 10.3 is a heuristic conceptualisation showing the relative impact, growth and inter-relationships between identified athlete, environmental, system and chance factors across foundational (Figure 10.3a), pre-elite (Figure 10.3b) and elite (Figure 10.3c) levels. It is evidence such as this, coupled with sport-specific insight obtained through administration of the My Sporting Journey survey and NSO Pathway Healthcheck, which is directly informing the review and refinement of current practice and support.

Specific to the foundational, pre-elite and elite and mastery components of the athlete pathway, Tables 10.1, 10.2 and 10.3 present the complement of 'best practice' advocated through the complement of FTEM and 3D-AD. As outlined within Table 10.1, to maximise the acquisition and refinement of foundational sporting skill and promote life-long sports participation, it is advocated that all sporting stakeholders are aware and effectively promote the importance of a full and proficient complement of fundamental movement skills (F1); a complement of deliberate play, exposure to age-appropriate and modified sports and competition formats (F2); and early diversification through sport sampling coupled with best practice coaching and education and flexible competitive formats (F3).

Sport-specific learnings from the My Sporting Journey survey and the NSO Pathway Healthcheck coupled with recognised 'best practice' through FTEM, is also directly assisting the current review and refinement of the Australian Sports Commission's nationwide participation strategies, promoting better parental engagement through customised education and support strategies, stronger linkages between schools and clubs, a review and refinement of the aligned coaching curriculum, and the refinement of age-modified sport formats.

For instance, this 'complement' of best practice foundational strategies and activities, directly informed the development of a 'Top 10 Tips for Parents' resource, which is featured on the website of the Australian Institute of Sport (AIS) (www.ausport.gov.au). Findings emanating from the My Sporting Journey questionnaire demonstrated emphatically the critical role that

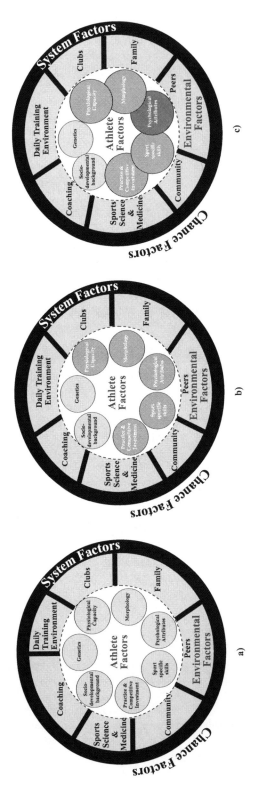

Figure 10.3 Based upon findings from the ARC Linkage project (Toohey et al., 2015b), foundational (a), pre-elite (b) and elite (c) level conceptualisations of the changing contribution and interplay within and between identified athlete, environmental, system level and chance factors on athlete development

Table 10.1 Best practice strategies advocated through the FTEM Athlete framework specific to the foundational levels of the athlete pathway

Foundational phase	Description and outcome	Advocated best practice
Learning & acquisition of basic movement	Learning or re-learning (e.g., acquired disability) and executing a full repertoire of fundamental movement skills (FMS) including locomotor, object control, aquatic and acrobatic skills. Support is primarily provided by parents, caregivers and early childhood educators.	• Awareness of the importance and promotion of a full repertoire of fundmental movement skills at a macro (Sport, Education & Health National agencies), meso (Sport) and micro (parental) level.
Extension & refinement of movement	Further development of FMS, early physical literacy and early acquisition of sport-specific skills through broad exposure to both non-structured (deliberate play) and structured sport formats (age-modified sport formats).	• Promotion of importance of Deliberate Play to all sport outcomes. • Evidence-informed, modified (i.e., age and skill appropriate) formats of sport promoting early sport-specific skill acquisition. • Strong partnership between schools and the sporting club network to assist broader exposure to age-appropriate sport formats. • Awareness of importance of matching sporting equipment to maximise skill acquisition and minimise potential injury.

Commitment to sport and/or active lifestyle	Consolidation of sport-specific skills and physical literacy, expressed through commitment to training and competition within full and alternate formats of sport and active lifestyle pursuits across the lifespan.	• Promotion of early sport diversification through sampling of sports prior to later specialisation.
		• Contemporary and evidence-based coaching curriculum incorporating:
		  ○ understanding the impact of biological maturation on skill development (physical & cognitive);
		  ○ injury prevention & management;
		  ○ coach–athlete dynamics;
		  ○ psychological skill (inc. self-regulation);
		  ○ nutrition, recovery, performance analysis, hydration, strength & conditioning, Olympic values, etc.
		• Age- and skill-appropriate sport and competitive formats (junior to older aged athletes)
		• Flexible competitive formats (e.g., playing vs older peers and adults when appropriate) that foster the skill progression of gifted athletes
		• Strong alliance between schools, universities, national club network and state and national sporting organisations to support transition of gifted F3 athletes into Talent (Pre-elite) levels

Table 10.2 Best practice strategies advocated through the FTEM Athlete framework specific to the pre-elite levels of the athlete pathway

Pre-elite phase	Description and outcome	Advocated best practice
 Demonstration of potential	Initial identification of an athlete's future High Performance (HP) potential through formal (valid, reliable, holistic TID test battery) or informal (Coaches'/Recruiters' eye) methods.	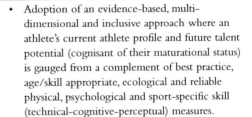 • Adoption of an evidence-based, multi-dimensional and inclusive approach where an athlete's current athlete profile and future talent potential (cognisant of their maturational status) is gauged from a complement of best practice, age/skill appropriate, ecological and reliable physical, psychological and sport-specific skill (technical–cognitive–perceptual) measures. • Complement of talent selection and detection/transfer recruitment strategies.

Talent Verification
	Identified athletes, are immersed into a formalised, observational trial period (e.g., series of camps etc.) to demonstrate their 'full' athletic profile e.g., sport-specific (technical & tactical) and psychological skills (including coach-ability), personal excellence qualities, physical robustness and physiological capacity and adaptability.	• Verification of an athlete's future talent potential through formalised, in-situ, multi-dimensional assessments within training and competition settings specific to:
		  ◦ Psychological skills and character;
		  ◦ Sport-specific skill potential;
		  ◦ Physicality and adaption to training loads;
		  ◦ Coach ability, commitment and motivation.
		• Formalisation of 'Coaches' or Recruiters' eye' assessments, which informs aligned curricula, professional development and provides accountability regarding selection decisions.

Practising & achieving
	Athletes are committed to achieving higher levels of sport performance, with sustained practice and investment through high training volumes and appropriate competition exposure that may lead to the achievement of a key high performance benchmark. At this stage, the coordination and quality of developmental support is critical to reduce dropouts, underachievement and facilitate the transition to senior elite levels.	• Effective overarching strategic planning and commitment featuring strong deliberate programming.
		• Best practice talent development environments informed by state of the art skill acquisition and characterised by:
		  ◦ Ongoing athlete and coach education;
		  ◦ Transitional, relocational and dual career support and management for athletes;
		  ◦ Ecologically valid training strategies;
		  ◦ Effective athlete monitoring and feedback;
		  ◦ Vertical integration with elite athletes.

Table 10.2 continued

Pre-elite phase	Description and outcome	Advocated best practice

T **4**
 	
 Breakthrough & reward
	Athletes attain a significant breakthrough performance and are rewarded for their efforts. For example, they may be selected for a Junior national team or earn a valued sporting scholarship, which often results in a significant increase in ongoing developmental progress and support.	As above for T3 and also including:
		• Preparation and facilitation of athlete transition to elite levels through:
		  ○ Strong understanding of potential barriers;
		  ○ Implementation of proactive strategies to mediate the transition.

Table 10.3 Best practice strategies advocated through the FTEM Athlete framework specific to the elite and mastery levels of the athlete pathway

Elite and mastery phase	Description and outcome	Advocated best practice
E **1** **Senior Elite representation**	Achievement of an elite athlete status through selection and representation at the highest level of Senior international competition or Professional sport.	• Effective deliberate programming including guidance and support prior, during and following early senior elite competition experiences. • Support and management of dual career and significant others (spouse, family). • Support and management of High Performance stressors. • Optimised and individualised athlete case management through effective interdisciplinary service support including dual career.
E **2** **Senior Elite Success**	Achievement of a medal-winning performance at a peak competition such as World championships, Olympics or Paralympics or relevant Professional league accolades.	As E1 above and including: • Preparation for life after sport including formalised and supported coaching/mentor opportunities. • Musculoskeletal maintenance.
M **1** **Sustained Elite success**	Sustained success over multiple HP cycles at the highest level of International or Professional sport.	As E1 and E2 above and including: • Explore potential for re-invention and innovation.

parents play in promoting and supporting early athlete development (Weissensteiner et al., 2015). However, as revealed through the NSO Pathway Healthcheck there is an apparent gap in the education and support of parents. Prioritised by the Australian government to address this issue and to help address marked declines in the fundamental movement skills (FMS) of Australian primary school children (Hardy et al., 2013), the resource was launched in conjunction with a $100 million Australian Government school sport initiative 'Sporting Schools' (www.sportingschools.gov.au) offering best practice foundational sport programmes to primary school children within and after school hours. The parental resource has had a broad national reach through popular mainstream media and is now being featured within the websites of numerous Australian Sporting Organisations. These tips include at an F1 level:

- the importance of a full repertoire of FMS as a platform for sport-specific skill development and perceived competence;
- socio-psychological and health benefits and how to best foster the development of FMS.

at an F2 level:

- the critical role of deliberate play as a necessary adjunct to structured sport formats to promote creativity, adaptability, skill refinement, fun and enjoyment and how to set up diversified and stimulating play environments at home;
- the importance of being a positive role model and how to foster everyday sport activity and playtime at home and be an effective support provider;
- the importance of age-modified formats of sport and matching sporting equipment to minimise injury and promote skill refinement.

and at an F3 level:

- the importance of sports sampling and later specialisation to sport-specific skill development and minimisation of injury, burn out and dropout;
- the utility of adopting an ecological approach to facilitate sport-specific skill development through higher fidelity between training practices and competition;
- the power of observational learning as a useful adjunct for promoting sport-specific skill development;
- the importance of self-regulation in learning and skill development in sport and as a transferable 'life skill' and how a parent can 'facilitate' a child's self-regulatory skills;
- the promotion of accessible AIS produced and endorsed educational resources specific to being an 'athlete' (e.g., nutrition, injury prevention, hydration, etc.);
- the importance of assisting and respecting a child's coach but also finding the right fit of coaching expertise to positively support skill development and engagement in sport.

Specific to the identification, confirmation and development of pre-elite athletes, Table 10.2 outlines a complement of best practice strategies that will arguably lead to a stronger and sustainable 'talent pipeline' up to the elite level. Central to this approach, is the recognised criticality of multi-dimensional, evidence-informed and inclusive talent identification and confirmation strategies; best practice talent development environments characterised by effective deliberate programming (Bullock et al., 2009) and ecological practice (Davids, 2010; Pinder et al., 2011, 2013; Renshaw, Davids, Phillips, & Kerhervé, 2012); aligned athlete and coach education; and pre-emptive, support strategies to assist an athlete's management of their dual career, maintain sport–life balance and transition to elite levels. The coordination of these strategies in promoting more effective talent identification and development are discussed in detail in Chapter 5.

Drawing on 'world's best practice' and further informed by 'triangulated' evidence emanating from a system (Weissensteiner & Medlicott, 2015), sport and athlete perspective (Weissensteiner et al., 2015), Table 10.3 presents the complement of athlete, environmental and system level factors considered integral to converting senior elite representatives into perennial podium winners on the world stage.

Adopting this system-wide and committed long-term approach, utilising FTEM and 3D-AD, has already translated into promising advances within the Australian sporting sector, including but not limited to:

- better system unity through a shared vision of improving the collective health of all athlete pathways;
- at a sport level, better clarity and communication between all pathway stakeholders from a national level down to the grass roots (clubs, parents, coaches etc.), regarding their role and contribution to supporting athlete development;
- better alignment and coordination of sport and system level strategies and resource allocation to maximise athlete development and progression;
- fruitful 'cross-fertilisation' between sports regarding their shared learnings and strategies;
- the refinement of pre-elite identification, development and transitional strategies;
- advances in the education of coaches and other pathway stakeholders, regarding content knowledge specific to developmental best practice, which is complementing existing, innovative approaches led by the AIS which are empowering the intra- and inter-personal skills of coaches and sport leaders;
- innovative, pre-emptive and holistic approaches delivered by the AIS and in partnership with a majority of Australian Sporting Organisations, to assist pre-elite and elite athletes effectively negotiate likely high performance stressors, manage a dual-career and maintain sport-life balance;
- better longitudinal monitoring and individualised case management of athletes to minimise injury and illness and maximise their developmental progression and performance.

Conclusion

In order to enhance the collective health of our athlete pathways from foundation to international podium, related theory and practice must be aligned and expressed within committed, long-term approaches that are evidence-based, translate into effective practice and cater for the individualistic and dynamic nature of athlete development. In this chapter, we provided an example of such a framework, FTEM and its complementary empirical model 3D-AD, which are now heavily adopted within Australia and recognised internationally (Bergeron et al., 2015). Such an approach has translated into sport and system level gains through better clarity, connectivity, communication, education and support of all sporting stakeholders including importantly, the athlete.

To truly ascertain the theoretical and practical 'fit' and contribution of current athlete development frameworks and models to facilitating sustainable and 'healthy' athlete development, such as Gagné's Differentiated Models of Giftedness and Talent (DMGT1 & 2: Gagné, 2003, 2004), Balyi's Long Term Athlete Development model (LTAD: Balyi & Hamilton, 2004), Lloyd et al.'s Composite Youth Development model (Lloyd et al., 2015a, 2015b), McCann's American

Developmental Model (McCann, 2015); Bailey and Morley's (2006) model of Talent Development and Côté's Developmental Model of Sports Participation (DMSP; Côté, 1999; Côté, & Fraser-Thomas, 2007; Côté & Vierimaa, 2014), requires a committed and long-term approach. Future recommendations to this end include, among other things an ongoing commitment to sport-specific, longitudinal action research incorporating trans-disciplinary, pluralistic methodologies (Abernethy, Weissensteiner, & Farrow, 2009; Landers, 1983), featuring individualised developmental histories (See Güllich & Emrich, 2012, 2014, Gulbin, 2012; Gulbin et al., 2013b), which truly engage the 'athlete voice' (Bergeron et al., 2015; Weissensteiner, 2015). It is through this committed approach that the inter-relationships and relative contribution of athlete, environmental and system factors to an athlete's developmental status, well-being and performance can be truly ascertained. Further to this end, the implementation of objective diagnostic assessments that measure the 'health' of the athlete pathway (e.g., retention and developmental conversion rates; see Chapter 5.) and the relative impact and effectiveness of prioritised pathway strategies is critical.

References

Abbott, A., & Collins, D. (2004). Eliminating the dichotomy between theory and practice in talent identification and development: considering the role of psychology. *Journal of Sports Science, 22*, 395–408.

Abernethy, B. A., Weissensteiner, J. R., & Farrow, D. (2009). *Matching research methods to questions: Examples from the skill learning domain.* Symposium on Research Approaches in Sport Psychology. 12th World Congress of Sport Psychology (ISSP), Marrakesh, Morocco.

Ackerman, P. L. (2013). Nonsense, common sense and science of expert performance: Talent and individual differences. *Intelligence, 45*, 6–17.

Australian Institute of Sport. (2015). Top Ten Tips for Parents. Retrieved 2 September, 2015 from www.ausport.gov.au/supporting/top_10_tips_for_parents

Australian Sports Commission. (2015). Sporting Schools. Retrieved 9 September, 2015 from www.sportingschools.gov.au

Baker, J., & Horton, S. (2004). A review of primary and secondary influences on sport expertise. *High Ability Studies, 15*, 211–228.

Baker, J., & Young, B. (2014). 20 years later: deliberate practice and the development of expertise in sport. *International Review of Sport and Exercise Psychology, 7,* 135–157.

Bailey, R., Collins, D., Ford, P., MacNamara, Á., Toms, M., & Pearce, G. (2010). *Participant development in sport: An academic literature review.* Commissioned report for Sports Coach UK. Leeds: Sports Coach UK.

Bailey, R. P., & Morley, D. (2006). Towards a model of talent development in physical education. *Sport Education and Society, 11*, 211–230.

Balyi, I., & Hamilton, A. (2004). *Long-term athlete development: Trainability in childhood and adolescence. Windows of opportunity. Optimal trainability.* Victoria, BC: National Coaching Institute British Columbia & Advanced Training and Performance.

Bergeron, M. F., Mountjoy, M., Armstrong, N., Chia, M., Côté, J., Emery, C. A., Faigenbaum, A., … Engebretsen, L. (2015). International Olympic Committee consensus statement on youth athletic development. *British Journal of Sports Medicine, 49,* 843–851.

Buekers, M., Borry, P., & Rowe, P. (2015). Talent in sports. Some reflections about the search for future champions. *Movement and Sport Sciences – Science & Motricité, 88,* 3–12.

Bullock, N., Gulbin, J. P., Martin, D. T., Ross, A., Holland, T., & Marino, F. (2009). Talent identification and deliberate practice programming in skeleton: Ice novice to winter Olympian in 14 months. *Journal of Sports Sciences, 27,* 397–404.

Carpiano, R, M., & Daley, D. M. (2006). A guide and glossary on post positivist theory building for population health. *Journal of Epidemiology & Community Health, 60,* 564–570.

Côté, J. (1999). The influence of the family in the development of talent in sport. *The Sport Psychologist, 13,* 395–417.

Côté, J., & Fraser-Thomas, J. (2007). Youth involvement in sport. In P. Crocker (ed.), *Sport psychology: A Canadian perspective* (pp. 266–294). Toronto: Pearson.

Côté, J., Lidor, R., & Hackfort, D. (2009). ISSP Position Stand: To sample or to specialise? Seven postulates about youth sport activities that lead to continued participation and elite performance. *International Journal of Sport and Exercise Psychology, 7*, 7–17.

Côté, J., & Vierimaa, M. (2014). The developmental model of sport participation: 15 years after its first conceptualization. *Science and Sports, 29*, S63–S69.

Davids, K. (2010). The constraints-based approach to motor learning: Implications for a non-linear pedagogy in sport and physical education. In I. Renshaw, K. Davids & G. J. P. Savelsbergh (eds), *Motor learning in practice: A constraints-led approach* (pp. 3–16). London: Routledge.

Elferink-Gemser, M. T., Visscher, C., Lemmink, K. A. P. M., & Mulder, T. (2007). Multidimensional performance characteristics and standard of performance in talented youth field hockey players: A longitudinal study. *Journal of Sports Sciences, 25*, 481–489.

Elferink-Gemser, M. T., Jordet, G., Coelho-e-Silva, M. J., & Visscher, C. (2011). The marvels of elite sports: How to get there? *British Journal of Sports Medicine, 45*, 683–684.

Emery, C. A., Thierry-Olivier, R., Whittaker, J. L., Nettel-Aguirre, A., & van Mechelen, W. (2015). Neuromuscular training injury prevention strategies in youth sport: A systematic review and meta-analysis. *British Journal of Sports Medicine, 49*, 865–870.

Fletcher, D., & Sarkar, M. (2012). A grounded theory of psychological resilience in Olympic champions. *Psychology of Sport and Exercise, 13*, 669–678.

Ford, P., De Ste Croix, M., Lloyd, R., Meyers, R., Moosavi, M., Oliver, J., … & Williams, C. (2011). The long term athlete development model: Physiological evidence and application. *Journal of Sports Sciences, 29*(4), 389–402.

Fraser-Thomas, J., Côté, J., & Deakin, J. (2008). Examining adolescent sport drop-out and prolonged engagement from a developmental perspective. *Journal of Applied Sport Psychology, 20*, 318–333.

Fuchslocher, J., Romann, M., & Gulbin, J. (2013). Strategies to support developing talent. *Schweizerische Zeitschrift für Sportmedizin und Sporttraumatologie, 61*(4), 10–14.

Gagné, F. (2003). Transforming gifts into talents: The DMGT as a developmental theory. In N. Colangelo & G. A. Davis (eds), *Handbook of gifted education* (3rd ed., pp. 60–74). Boston, MA: Allyn and Bacon.

Gagné, F. (2004). Transforming gifts into talents: The DMGT as a developmental theory. *High Ability Studies, 15*, 119–147.

Gulbin, J. P., Oldenziel, K., Weissensteiner, J. R., & Gagné, F. (2010). A look through the rear vision mirror: Developmental experiences and insights of high performance athletes. *Talent Development & Excellence, 2*, 149–164.

Gulbin, J. P. (2012). Applying talent identification programs at a system-wide level: The evolution of Australia's national program. In J. Baker, S. Cobley & J. Schorer (eds), *Talent Identification and Development in Sport: International perspectives* (pp. 147–165). London: Routledge.

Gulbin, J. P., Croser, M. J., Morley, E., & Weissensteiner, J. R. (2013a). An integrated framework for the optimisation of sport and athlete development: A practitioner approach. *Journal of Sports Sciences, 31*, 1319–31.

Gulbin, J. P., & Weissensteiner, J. R. (2013). Functional sport expertise systems. In D. Farrow, J. Baker & C. MacMahon (eds), *Developing sport expertise: Researchers and coaches put theory into practice* (2nd ed., pp. 45–67). London: Routledge.

Gulbin, J. P., Weissensteiner, J. R., Oldenziel, K., & Gagné, F. (2013b). Patterns of performance development in elite athletes. *European Journal of Sport Science, 13*, 6, 605–614.

Gulbin, J. P., Croser, M. J., Morley, E., & Weissensteiner, J. R. (2014). A closer look at the FTEM framework. Response to "More of the same? Comment on 'An integrated framework for the optimisation of sport and athlete development: A practitioner approach'". *Journal of Sports Sciences, 32*, 796–800.

Güllich, A., & Emrich, E. (2012). Individualistic and Collectivistic Approach in Athlete Support Programmes in the German High-Performance Sport System. *European Journal for Sport and Society, 9*, 4, 243–268.

Güllich, A., & Emrich, E. (2014). Considering long-term sustainability in the development of world class success. *European Journal of Sport Science, 14*(Suppl. 1), S383–S397.

Hardy, L. L., King, L., Espinel, P., Cosgrove, C., & Bauman, A. (2010a). *NSW Schools Physical Activity and Nutrition Survey (SPANS): Full Report.* Sydney: NSW Ministry of Health.

Hardy, L. L., King, L., Farrell, L., Macniven, R., & Howlett, S. (2010b). Fundamental movement skills among Australian pre-school children. *Journal of Science and Medicine in Sport, 13*, 503–508.

Hardy, L. L., Barnett, L., & Espinel, P., & Okely, A. D. (2013). Thirteen-year trends in child and adolescent fundamental movement skills: 1997–2010. *Medicine and Science in Sports and Exercise, 45*, 1965–1970.

147

Henriksen, K., Stambulova, N., & Roessler, K. K. (2010a). Holistic approach to athletic talent development environments: A successful sailing milieu. *Psychology of Sport and Exercise, 11,* 212–222.

Henriksen, K., Stambulova, N., & Roessler, K. K. (2010b). Successful talent development in track and field: Considering the role of environment. *Scandinavian Journal of Medicine & Science in Sports, 20,* 122–132.

Henriksen, K., Stambulova, N., & Roessler, K. K. (2011). Riding the wave of an expert: A successful talent development environment in kayaking. *The Sport Psychologist, 25,* 341–362.

Jayanthi, N. A., LaBella, C. R., Fischer, D., Pasulka, J., & Dugas, L. R. (2015). Sports-specialized intensive training and the risk of injury in young athletes: A clinical case-control study. *The American Journal of Sports Medicine, 43,* 794–801.

Landers, D. M. (1983). Whatever happened to theory testing in sport psychology? *Journal of Sport Psychology, 5,* 135–151.

Lang, M., & Light R., (2010). Interpreting and implementing the long term athlete development model: English swimming coaches' views on the (swimming) LTAD in practice. *International Journal of Sports Science and Coaching, 5,* 389–402.

Lloyd, R. S., Oliver, J. L., Faigenbaum, A. D, Howard, R, Ste Croix, M. B. A., et al. (2015a), Long-term athletic development- Part 1: A pathway for all youth. *Journal of Strength and Conditioning Research, 29,* 1439–1450.

Lloyd, R. S., Oliver, J. L., Faigenbaum, A. D., Howard, R., De Ste Croix, M. B. A., et al. (2015b). Long-term athletic development, Part 2: Barriers to success and potential solutions. *Journal of Strength and Conditioning Research, 29,* 1451–1464.

Macnamara, B. N., Hambrick, D. Z., Oswald, F. L. (2014). Deliberate Practice and Performance in Music, Games, Sports, Education, and Professions: A Meta-Analysis. *Psychological Science, 25,* 1608–1618.

McCann, D. (2015). Activating the American Development Model. *Olympic Coach, 26*(1), 31–32.

Malina, R. M., Claessens, A. L., Van Acken, K., Thomis, M., Lefevre, J., Philippaerts, R., & Beunen, G. P. (2006). Maturity offset in Gymnasts: Application of a prediction equation. *Medicine and Science in Sports & Exercise, 38,* 1342–1347.

Malina, R. M., Coelho-e-Silva, M. J., Figueiredo, A. J., Carling, C., & Beunen, G. P. (2012). Interrelationships among invasive and non-invasive indicators of biological maturation in adolescent male soccer players. *Journal of Sports Sciences, 30,* 1705–1717.

Malina, R. M., Rogol, A. D., Cumming, S. P., Coelho-e-Silva, M. J., & Figueiredo, A. J. (2015). Biological maturation of youth athletes: Assessment and implications. *British Journal of Sports Medicine, 49,* 852–859.

Mountjoy, M., Rhind, D. J. A., Tiivas, A., & Leglise, M. (2015). Safeguarding the child athlete in sport: A review, a framework and recommendations for the IOC youth athlete development model. *British Journal of Sports Medicine, 49,* 883–886.

Myer, G. D., Jayanthi, N., Difori, J. P., Faigenbaum, A. D., Keifer, A. W., Logerstedt, D., & Micheli, L. J. (2015). Sport Specialization, Part 1: Does early sports specialization increase negative outcomes and reduce the opportunity for success in young athletes? *Sports Health: A Multidisciplinary Approach.* DOI: 10.1177/1941738112464626.

Pankhurst, A., & Collins, D., & MacNamara, Á. (2013). Talent development: Linking the stakeholders to the process. *Journal of Sports Sciences, 31,* 370–380.

Pankhurst, A., & Collins, D. (2013). Talent identification and development: The need for coherence between research, system and process. *Quest, 65,* 83–97.

Phillips, E., Davids, K., Renshaw, I., & Portus, M. (2010) Expert Performance in Sport and the Dynamics of Talent Development. *Sports Medicine, 40,* 271–283.

Pinder, R. A., Davids, K., Renshaw, I., & Araújo, D. (2011). Representative learning design and function-ality of research and practice in sport. *Journal of Sport & Exercise Psychology, 33,* 146–155.

Pinder, R. A., Renshaw, I., & Davids, K. (2013). The role of representative design in talent development: a comment on 'Talent identification and promotion programmes of Olympic athletes'. *Journal of Sports Sciences, 31,* 803–806.

Oakley, A. D., & Booth, M. L. (2004). Mastery of fundamental movement skills among children in New South Wales: Prevalence and sociodemographic distribution. *Journal of Science and Medicine in Sport, 7,* 358–372.

Renshaw, I., Davids, K., Phillips, E., & Kerhervé, H. (2012). Developing talent in athletes as complex neurobiological systems. In J. Baker, S. Cobley, & J. Schorer (eds), *Talent identification and development in sport: International perspectives* (pp. 64–80). New York: Routledge.

Simonton, D. K. (2001). Talent development as a multidimensional, multiplicative, and dynamic process. *Current Directions in Psychological Science, 10,* 39–43.

Stambulova, N., Engström, C., Franck, A., Linnér, L., & Lindahl, K. (2015). Searching for an optimal balance: Dual career experiences of Swedish adolescent athletes. *Psychology of Sport and Exercise.* Advance online publication. DOI:10.1016/j.psychsport.2014.08.009

Suppiah, H. T., Low, C. Y., & Chia, M. (2015). Detecting and developing youth athlete potential: different strokes for different folks are warranted. *British Journal of Sports Medicine, 49,* 878–882.

Telford, R. D., Cunningham, R. B., Fitzgerald, R., Olive, L. S., Prosser, L., Jiang, X., & Telford, R. M. (2012). Physical education, obesity and academic achievement: A 2-year longitudinal investigation of Australian elementary school children. *American Journal of Public Health, 102,* 368–374.

Tester, G., Ackland, T. R., & Houghton, L. (2014). A 30-year journey of monitoring fitness and skill outcomes in physical education: Lessons learned and a focus on the future. *Advances in Physical Education, 4,* 127–137.

Toohey, K., MacMahon, C., Weissensteiner, J. R., Thomson, A., Auld, C., Beaton, A., … Woolcock, G. (2015). *Improving the Identification and Development of Australia's Sporting Talent.* Retrieved from https://secure.ausport.gov.au/__data/assets/pdf_file/0005/627080/Improving_the_Identification_an d_Development_of_Australias_Sporting_Talent.pdf

Tucker, R., & Collins, M. (2012). What makes champions? A review of the relative contribution of genes and training to sporting success. *British Journal of Sports Medicine, 46,* 555–561.

Vaeyens, R., Lenoir, M., Williams, M. A., & Philippaerts, R. M. (2008). Talent identification and development programmes in sport: Current models and future directions. *Sports Medicine, 38,* 703–714.

Weissensteiner, J. R. (2015). The importance of listening: Engaging and incorporating the athlete's voice in theory and practice. *British Journal of Sports Medicine, 49,* 839–840.

Weissensteiner, J. R., Abernethy, B., & Farrow, D. (2009). Towards the development of a conceptual model of batting expertise in cricket: A grounded theory approach. *Journal of Applied Psychology, 21,* 276–292.

Weissensteiner, J. R., & Medlicott, R. (2015, June). *Administration of the NSO Pathway Healthcheck: Findings and recommendations for the Australian sporting system.* Presentation at AIS Winning Pathways Workshop, Canberra, Australia.

Weissensteiner, J. R., Warmenhoven, J., Medlicott, R., & Gulbin, J. P. (2015). Giving the Athlete a voice: Preliminary findings from the My Sporting Journey Questionnaire. In A. Radmann, S. Hedenborg, E. Tsolakidis (eds), *20th Annual Congress of the European College of Sport Science* (p. 303), Sweden.

Wylleman, P., & Reints, A. (2010). A lifespan perspective on the career of talented and elite athletes: Perspectives on high-intensity sports. *Scandinavian Journal of Medicine and Science in Sports, 20* (Suppl. 2), 101–107.

11

TALENT IDENTIFICATION AND DEVELOPMENT IN THE CONTEXT OF "GROWING UP"

Robert M. Malina, Sean P. Cumming,
Manuel J. Coelho-e-Silva and António J. Figueiredo

Introduction

The search for sport talent at relatively young ages is in many ways more prevalent and structured at present compared to the past. An important corollary is the subsequent development of talent in youth as the process is superimposed upon a constantly changing base that comprises the process of "growing up"—the demands of physical growth, biological maturation and behavioral development as youngsters pass from childhood through puberty and adolescence into adulthood. General concepts related to the three dominant processes are briefly considered. Readiness for sport is viewed from the perspective of the characteristics of youth athletes and the demands of the sport environment. Models of talent development are briefly considered with emphasis on areas and issues needing attention. Limitations of available data and assessment protocols are emphasized throughout.

Uniqueness of childhood and adolescence

"Growing up" includes three distinct though related processes—two are biological (growth and maturation) and one is behavioral (development). The processes occur simultaneously and interact to dominate the daily lives of children and adolescents for approximately the first two decades of life (Malina, Bouchard, & Bar-Or, 2004).

Growth

Growth refers to the increase in the size of the body as a whole, and associated changes in body segments, composition, organs and related systems. Different parts of the body grow at different rates and at different times, thus altering proportions. Two organ systems central to physiological performances are related to growth in body size. Heart volume and mass follow a growth pattern like that for body weight, while the lungs and lung functions grow proportionally to height. The brain and nervous system, which are central to the acquisition of movement proficiency, grow very rapidly early in life and then at a more gradual pace.

Maturation

Maturation refers to progress towards the biologically mature state in each body system. Secondary sex characteristics and skeletal age are commonly used markers of maturity status at the time of observation. Maturity timing refers to the chronological age when a specific maturational event occurs; e.g., ages at which stages of secondary sex characteristics appear, age at menarche, and age at maximum rate of growth in height (peak height velocity; PHV). Tempo of maturation refers to the rate at which maturation progresses within a specific system, e.g., how quickly or slowly the youngster passes from initial stages of sexual maturation to the mature state, or how much progress in skeletal age occurs during a calendar year. Estimates of timing and tempo require longitudinal data.

Indicators of growth and maturation are outcomes of biological processes occurring at the cellular level. Both growth and maturation are regulated primarily by interactions of the hypothalamus and several endocrine glands, commonly labeled as the hypothalamic-pituitary-gonadal-adrenal axes. In addition, genetics, nutrition, living conditions and other factors play an important role. Details of biological growth and maturation, and factors which influence these processes have been summarized (Malina et al., 2004). Several issues related to talent models and maturity assessment are considered in a bit more detail later in the chapter.

Development

Development refers to the acquisition of behaviors appropriate for and expected by the culture within which the individual is reared and lives. As children experience life at home, school, church, sport, recreation, and other family/community activities, they develop cognitive, social, emotional, affective, moral, movement and other behaviors. Aspects of behavioral development during childhood and adolescence are well documented (Jones, Bayley, MacFarlane, & Honzik, 1971; Lerner & Steinberg, 2004). The acquisition of proficiency in movement behaviors, often labeled motor development, is a major developmental task of childhood and a major feature in talent identification and development (Malina, 2008; Malina, Cumming, & Coelho-e-Silva, 2016b).

Inter-individual variation in growth, maturation and development *per se* and interactions among the three processes are considerable, especially during the transition into puberty and during sexual maturation and the adolescent growth spurt. Interactions between the biological and behavioral processes vary within and among individuals and during childhood and adolescence, and influence peer and child–adult relationships. Demands of sport are superimposed upon and interact with those associated with growth, maturation and development. The interactions may influence characteristics, skills and behaviors related to a sport or sport discipline, and also athlete–coach relationships. A mismatch between the demands of a sport and those of growth, maturation and development may be a source of stress among talented young athletes and may influence opportunities for success.

Talent

Talent refers to one (or more) special, unique aptitude. In sport, talent is generally framed in the context of potential for success—a medal at international competitions, elite status, professional contract, college scholarship, among others. Not all talented athletes attain success; many factors intervene along the path to the attainment of potential.

Characteristics that reflect outcomes of growth, maturation and development are central to the search for talent:

1   Physical—size, physique, body composition, maturity status and timing
2   Functional capacities—aerobic, anaerobic, speed, power, flexibility, etc.
3   Movement proficiency—general and sport-specific skills
4   Perceptual and cognitive skills—anticipation, reaction time, visual search, and related characteristics
5   Psychological skills—coping, motivation, attention, anxiety … behaviors in general
6   "Game intelligence" or "sport intelligence"—understanding and implementing the nuances of a sport.

The preceding were described in the context of soccer (Williams & Reilly, 2000), but apply to other sports and sport disciplines. Two additional dimensions derived from the theory of multiple intelligences (Gardner, 1993, 1999) can be added to the template: bodily-kinesthetic and spatial awareness. The former refers to the use of the body or body parts to solve problems; the latter refers to the ability to recognize and use patterns of space. Figure skating, artistic gymnastics and diving, for example require control of movements through space. Soccer, basketball, ice and field hockey are fluid and dynamic, and rely on perception, creation, utilization and anticipation of spaces in addition to responses of opponents which are also fluid and dynamic. American football and baseball are also games of spaces, but actions are more intermittent.

Readiness for sport

Readiness for sport can be operationally defined as the "match" or "fit" between the characteristics of the young athlete and the demands of a sport (Malina, 1986, 1993). It is essentially a match between youth and adults. Behavioral readiness for participation in sport (Passer & Wilson, 2002) and readiness to benefit from systematic instruction and practice of motor and sport skills are additional perspectives (Anderson, 2002; Haubenstricker & Seefeldt, 2002).

Characteristics of youth athletes

Characteristics can be framed within the template described above. Information on the growth, maturity and functional capacities of youth athletes in a number of sports is reasonably comprehensive (Beunen & Malina, 2008; Malina, 1994, 1998, 2002, 2006a, 2011, 2016a, 2016b; Malina et al., 2013a; Malina, Coelho-e-Silva, & Figueiredo, 2013b; Malina, Rogol, Cumming, Coelho-e-Silva, & Figueiredo, 2015; Malina & Rogol, 2011). Individual differences are the rule and are magnified by variation in normal growth and in the timing and tempo of sexual maturation and the growth spurt. Information on sport-specific technical skills and perceptual-cognitive skills is somewhat less extensive (Coelho-e-Silva et al., 2010; Di Cagno et al., 2014; Elferink-Gemser, Visscher, Lemmink, & Mulder, 2007; Figueiredo, Gonçalves, Coelho-e-Silva, & Malina, 2009; Ford & Williams, 2013; Huijgen, Elferink-Gemser, Lemmink, & Visscher, 2014; Vandorpe et al., 2012; Williams, Janelle, & Davids, 2004). Data addressing the behavioral development of youth athletes *per se* and in response to sport-specific training are relatively limited; available studies often focus on the influence of peers, parents and home environments (Brustad, 2003; Bruner, Eys, & Turnnidge, 2013; Fraser-Thomas, Strachan, & Jeffery-Tosoni, 2013; Weiss, 2003), and to a lesser extent coaches (Erickson & Gilbert, 2003).

Coaches and trainers presumably understand what is expected of athletes for success in a specific sport; these are rooted in years of experience and tradition, and occasionally sports science. The responsiveness of youth to the sport environment is an additional dimension. This includes responsiveness to specific instructional, training and/or practice protocols ("trainability"), and to the coaching environment—the personal characteristics of coaches/staff, and coaching, teaching, and training style (sometimes labeled "coachability").

The responsiveness of youth to training programs, primarily strength (resistance) and aerobic, has received considerable attention (Malina, 2006b, Malina et al., 2004; Faigenbaum & Myer, 2010; McNarry et al., 2014). Most information is based upon boys. Growth and maturity characteristics of subjects and associated changes during the training program are generally not incorporated into analyses of specific functional changes. As such, it may be difficult to partition training effects from those associated with normal growth and maturation. Results also highlight the specificity of training, but also suggest transfer to other tasks. Transfer of functional improvements to sport-specific technical skills and field-related performances needs systematic study. There is also a need to consider different modes of training over the course of a season or several years during childhood and adolescence.

Individual differences in responses to training among youth are not ordinarily considered. An exception is a 12-week endurance training program in a combined sample of 35 boys and girls 10.9 to 12.8 years at initial observation (Rowland & Boyajian, 1995). Peak VO_2 increased, on average, from 44.7 to 47.6 ml/kg/min (6.5 ± 5.1%), while relative changes among individuals ranged from −2.4% to +19.7%. Given the chronological age range and the interval between initial observation and final testing (24 weeks), some subjects may have begun the growth spurt and/or reached peak height velocity (PHV). Moreover, maximal increments in peak VO_2 occur, on average, concurrent with PHV in both sexes (Geithner et al., 2004; Mirwald & Bailey, 1986).

Genotype is an additional factor. Evidence suggests a genetic dependency of responses to aerobic training but not to strength training (Beunen, Peeters, & Malina, 2011; Bouchard, 2012; Peeters, Thomis, Beunen, & Malina, 2009), although data addressing the genetics of responses to strength training are limited. Data addressing genotypic contributions to the responsiveness to instruction and practice of motor skills in general and sport-specific skills are lacking. Limited data suggest similar rates of learning in monozygotic (identical) and dizygotic (fraternal) twins, variation in estimated genetic contributions during the time course of learning (training) and final level of skill attained, and variation among motor tasks (Skład, 1975; Malina, 2008).

Individual differences in responses of youth athletes to sport-specific training and to systematic instruction/practice of general and technical skills need systematic study. Interactions between characteristics of youth athletes and the training environment, including coaches, should also be addressed. Other relevant questions merit attention. What is unique about youth who experience minimal or no improvement? What is unique about those who experience larger improvements? What are their growth and maturity characteristics? From a more practical perspective, how does one explain lack of improvement with training to an adolescent athlete? What is the influence of lack of improvement on self-perceptions or perhaps persistence in sport? Perceptions of the coach and coaching environment are important components of "coachability". Athlete–coach interactions are obviously critical, but responses of youth athletes to coaches and coaching styles have not received systematic attention. For example, how are athletes and coaches paired? Are talented athletes matched with a talented coach? When is a coach willing to give up an athlete to a better, more experienced coach?

Characteristics of the sport environment

The sport environment comprises two elements: demands of the specific sport, and the environments in which coaching and training occur. The demands of a sport include several interrelated domains: objectives, tasks and rules; techniques and skills; tactics and strategies;

training and preparation; sport-specific requisites—physical, physiological, skill, behavioral, perceptual and cognitive; and competitions. These have been developed over the years by adults—coaches, trainers and sport systems and are often rooted in tradition.

The environments in which sport-specific coaching and training occur reflect the overall atmosphere or culture of specific gymnasia, clubs, academies and/or schools created by coaches, trainers and sport administrators. The environments also include the settings for competitions, the officials and in some sports the judges. The environments vary considerably within and among sports. Of relevance to the present discussion, the potential influence of these environments on youth athletes needs continued study, although information addressing the potential influence of training environments on the behavioral development of youth athletes is limited. (See Chapters 19 and 27 in this Handbook).

The growth and maturity characteristics of youth athletes have a central role in the sport environment from at least two broad perspectives. First, the influence of training for sport on growth and maturation has received considerable attention. Discussions, however, focus more often on potentially negative consequences of training on the growth and maturation of youth athletes in some sports, more so among females than males, for example, "delayed" growth and maturation of artistic gymnasts and later maturation of distance runners. When viewed in the context of the variety of factors that can influence growth and maturation, the selectivity of sport and differential persistence in sport, systematic training has no effect on size attained and rate of growth in height and on maturity status and timing (Malina & Rogol, 2011; Malina et al., 2013a; Malina, 2016b; Malina & Coelho-e-Silva, 2016). Regular training for sport, however, may influence body weight and composition. Training for sport can positively influence adiposity in youth athletes; corresponding data for fat-free or lean tissue mass are suggestive but limited. Bone mineral is the component of fat-free mass that has received considerable attention. Regular training for sport can positively influence bone mineral accrual in youth athletes in many sports, but variable effects of training have been noted in some sports.

Second, the characteristics of youth athletes, including those associated with growth and maturation have high social stimulus value in the context of selection and retention in many sports or disciplines within sport (cf. Wattie, Schorer, & Baker, 2015). Limited attention has been devoted to the influence of the environments in which sport-specific coaching and training occurs on the behavioral development of youth athletes. What do we know about the influence of these environments, either directly or indirectly, on aspects of behavioral development related to sport *per se* and also to life of the youngster outside of sport?

For example, what are the potential consequences of labeling a youngster as talented on his/her behavioral development (see Chapter 6 in this Handbook)? One consequence is apparent in social manipulation, which is perhaps most evident in preferential treatment by the respective sport systems, the media and schools. It is also evident in differential access to resources that favor the elite as in travel, tutors for school work, and access to scholarships. The preferential treatment may also lead to over-dependence on and/or control by coaches and sport organizations, and altered social relationships with peers, parents and family. A potential byproduct of excessive dependence of young athletes upon coaches and sport officials (and often blind faith and trust of parents) is potential for emotional abuse—verbal or non-verbal (see Chapter 29 in this Handbook), physical abuse and sexual abuse and molestation. Elite status in a sport may in fact usurp the youngster's qualities as an individual.

Interactions among harsh coaching methods, an environment of manipulation, control and dependency, elevated stress and disordered eating in youth athletes have received attention (Ryan, 1995). The psychosocial environments of several sports often tacitly or explicitly foster behaviors that function to limit weight gain when accretion of mass is expected with normal

growth. Elite youth female gymnasts are considered at increased risk for disordered eating behaviors (Schwidergall, Weimann, Witzel, Mölenkamp, Brehl, & Böhles, 1998; Davies, Feng, Crisp, Day, & Laidlaw, 1997). Three of 27 elite Swiss adolescent female gymnasts were considered at risk for "manifest mental disorder over time" (Theintz et al., 1994). The same applies to ballet (Mitchell, Haase, Malina, & Cumming, 2016) and other aesthetic activities. Female youth who are elite or approaching elite status, often face challenges related to body size, proportions and composition associated with growth and maturation which may influence performance and coach evaluations. Individual perceptions of changes and reactions and evaluations of others to the changes are significant factors (Cumming, et al., 2012; Hunter Smart et al., 2012).

Studies of fair play and sportsmanship suggest questionable ethical behaviors among coaches. Significant percentages of 5th to 8th grade sport participants (~52% males, 9–15 years) perceived coach behaviors as fostering unethical behaviors—cheating, breaking rules, injuring or getting even with an opponent, among others (Shields, Bredemeier, LaVoi, & Power, 2005). The same is true among high school athletes. Although the overwhelming majority (~90%) of a national sample of both sexes (*n* = 5275) had favorable perceptions of coaches regarding ethics and character, significant numbers perceived their coaches as "teaching negative lessons about cheating and bad sportsmanship" (Josephson Institute, 2007). Examples included faking an injury, using an opponent's stolen play book for American football, illegally altering an ice hockey stick, altering the field of play, throwing at a batter in baseball, not reporting an error in scoring that favored his/her team, among others. Of interest, approval of cheating and other questionable practices was more common among male than female athletes. How do such coach behaviors affect the behavioral development of youth athletes? Systematic data are lacking on the influence of coach behaviors on overall behavioral development and on the behaviors of youth athletes during training and competitions.

Judges are a major component of the environments in several sports—artistic and rhythmic gymnastics, figure skating, diving, and combat sports. Although judges are presumably objective, their behaviors and expectations can impact youth athletes. Although elite female gymnasts are lean and linear in physique (Claessens et al., 1992), performance scores (individual events, overall) were negatively related with skinfold thicknesses and endomorphy (Claessens, Lefevre, Beunen, & Malina, 1999). Do judges have a preference for a specific body form among elite gymnasts? And, within single-year age groups 14–16 years, higher total scores were assigned, on average, to pre-menarcheal than to post-menarcheal gymnasts (Claessens, Lefevre, Beunen, & Malina, 2006). Do pre-menarcheal gymnasts perform better than post-menarcheal gymnasts of the same chronological age? These and other questions regarding judging in aesthetic sports merit attention.

In summary, the environments or more appropriately "cultures" of specific sports, programs and competitions are controlled by adults—coaches, officials, administrators, judges; parents are often complicit. Although optimal training and success are the goals of elite programs, coaching styles, demands and expectations vary considerably. These environments require systematic study in the context of their interactions with growth and maturation and their influence on the overall behavioral development of youth athletes.

Models of talent development

Models generally begin with the screening of potential athletes. The screening commonly includes indicators of growth status and estimates of potential size based on parent heights, and functional characteristics. It occurs at relatively young ages in some sports, largely through primary schools. Children with suitable physical characteristics and movement proficiency, i.e., aptitude for sport, are selected for specialized schools. Alternatively, children interested in a given sport but not possessing the characteristics deemed appropriate would be excluded from the specialized programs. The models also emphasize overall development of movement skills in early and middle childhood (labeled multilateral training), a combination of general and multilateral training and initial specialization during the transition into puberty, a shift to sport-specific skills and functional capacities—power, speed, aerobic, etc., during adolescence, and eventual specialization. Timing of emphasis on sport-specific functional, skill and technical requisites varies with sport. The shift from general to sport-specific training is gradual and generally occurs during the transition into puberty and continues through adolescence.

A comprehensive summary of the many models of talent development is beyond the scope of this chapter (see Chapters 4, 9 and 10 in this Handbook for discussions). However, the growth, maturation and behavioral development of youth athletes have important implications in the models *per se* and their application in the context of specific sports. The subsequent discussion considers issues related to growth, maturation and development relative to early and later specialization with a focus on the Long Term Athlete Development (LTAD) model (Balyi & Hamilton, 2004).

Early entry sports and early specialization

Many of the models differentiated between "early entry" sports and other sports. Artistic and rhythmic gymnastics, figure skating, diving, table tennis and perhaps others are often classified as "early entry" sports. These sports introduce systematic emphasis on instruction and practice (repetition) of sport-specific activities and skills at relatively young ages, e.g., 4–6 years. The LTAD model proposes that each early entry sport develop a model suited to its specific and unique demands (Balyi & Hamilton, 2004). Gymnastics, figure skating and diving demand a unique combination of movement skill and bodily control, balance, rhythmic sensitivity, optical and acoustic reactions, orientation in space, among others. Table tennis presents its own unique perceptual-motor demands (Faber, Nijhuis-van der Sanden, Elferink-Gemser, & Oosterveld, 2015).

Early entry sports are often viewed in the context of early specialization in a specific sport to the exclusion of other sports. The issue of early sport specialization in sport is currently a topic of major discussion (Malina, 2009, 2010). Observations on the development of talented individuals in several fields of endeavor (Bloom, 1985) and the popularity of the expertise model (Ericsson, Krampe, & Tesch-Römer, 1993) have potentially contributed to early specialization in sport and other activities.

The expertise model was largely developed on the basis of non-sport activities, e.g., music and chess, although some observations were based on golf and tennis. The model focuses on deliberate practice over an extended period. Deliberate practice is structured and goal-oriented with emphasis on quality of instruction and correction. Such practice is often repetitious and not necessarily enjoyable, and generally begins in childhood. Biological variables and bio-behavioral interactions were not explicitly considered in early discussions of the expertise model, although the potential role of biological factors, specifically genotypic, is recognized (Ericsson, 2003). As noted above, the LTAD model has adopted the expertise model of deliberate practice.

Early specialization has social consequences. The classic study of talented individuals (Bloom, 1985) and the expertise model of deliberate practice (Ericsson et al., 1993) have likely contributed to a perceived need among parents and coaches, and even among some youth for early specialization in a specific sport to the exclusion of other sports (Malina, 2010). Given the time commitment to a single sport, the young athlete often faces potential for social isolation from age and sex peers, especially during adolescence, and altered social relationships with peers, parents and family. An increasing number of talented young athletes in the United States are being home schooled, thus reducing opportunities for important school-related developmental experiences—peer interactions, social activities, and so on. There is similar risk for youth who attend special sport schools or academies, which focus on a single sport.

Contrary to the expertise model, elite athletes in a variety of sports attained national and international success without 10 years or 10,000 hours of deliberate training (Oldenziel, Gagné, & Gulbin, 2004; Güllich & Emrich, 2006; Moesch, Elbe, Hauge, & Wikman, 2011). Of interest, many successful athletes in "artistic composition sports" (artistic and rhythmic gymnastics, figure skating, diving)—sports that are commonly perceived as early entry and as requiring early specialization—did in fact train and compete in other sports (Güllich & Emrich, 2014). The overwhelming majority of American Junior Olympic divers of both sexes (164 of 189) also participated in a variety of sports in addition to diving (Malina & Geithner, 1993). Such observations and others also contributed to the development of alternative models of talent development (see Bruner, Erickson, McFadden, & Côté, 2009).

Later specialization

The late specialization model of LTAD has received most attention. It identifies six stages, although the four stages spanning childhood through adolescence are relevant to the present discussion (Balyi & Hamilton, 2004):

1   The *fundamental stage* (girls 6–8 years, boys, 6–9 years) emphasizes basic movement skills.
2   The *learning to train stage* (girls 8–11 years, boys 9–12 years) emphasizes refinement of basic motor skills and development of general sport skills. It is viewed as a "window of adaptation to the development of motor coordination."
3   The *training to train stage* (girls 11–15 years, boys 12–16 years) emphasizes development of aerobic and strength capacities and sport specific skills, which "build the 'engine' and consolidate sport-specific skills." Timing of PHV is central to this stage.
4   The *training to compete stage* (girls 15–17 years, boys 15–18 years) focuses on preparation for competition.

Two additional stages span late adolescence and adulthood, and are beyond the scope of this discussion. The *learning to train* and *training to train* stages are viewed as most important. Accordingly, "We *make* or *break* an athlete" during these stages (Balyi & Hamilton, 2004, p. 45, italics added). "We" presumably refers to coaches and sport systems.

Allowing for modifications in labels and suggested chronological age ranges, the stages of the LTAD model are reasonably similar to those described in earlier models (Bompa, 1985, 1995; Drabik, 1995; Rost, & Schon, 1997). Two modifications, however, were introduced into LTAD model (Balyi & Hamilton, 2004): it accepts the tenets of the "ten year rule" of deliberate practice implicit in the expertise model (Ericsson et al., 1993, see above), and it emphasizes the interval of PHV as a period for specific training and perhaps enhanced responsiveness to training (see below). Although the LTAD model has been widely popularized in many countries and applied to a variety of sports, the underlying tenets and assumptions of the model have been questioned (Ford et al., 2011). Assumptions of the LTAD related to growth, maturation and functional milestones are discussed subsequently in the sections dealing with Maturity Assessment and "Windows of Opportunity".

The Developmental Model of Sport Participation (DMSP) is a currently popular alternative model (Côté & Hay, 2002; Côté, Lidor, & Hackfort, 2009; Côté & Vierimaa, 2014). The model emphasizes participation in a variety of sports and child-directed activities (e.g., deliberate play) during childhood as an essential component or foundation for long-term sport outcomes. Although this period of development occurs largely during childhood, it may extend into the pubertal years. It is labeled as the *sampling years*, and provides opportunities and experiences in a variety of sports. The sampling years also serve to open trajectories towards recreational sport participation (recreational years) or elite sport performance (specializing and investment years) during adolescence and continuing into adulthood. Accordingly, youth may or may not decide to specialize in a sport during the adolescent years, whereas others may opt to pursue the path of recreational or leisure sport.

The DMSP is based on a developmental systems approach that features the interactions of variables across time and integrates the various outcomes of sport—performance, participation, and personal development, by focusing on key proximal processes and the environments in which these processes occur (i.e., the roles of coaches, peers, and parents). Although important, attention to specific physical, maturational and functional milestones associated with specific sports, especially during adolescence, is not central to this developmental model.

Maturity assessment

Individual differences in normal growth and in the timing and tempo of sexual maturation and the growth spurt have implications for talent development models and programs, and specifically for tailoring sport-specific training to individual youth. Maturity-related gradients among youth athletes in many sports, which become apparent during the transition into and the course of adolescence, are an additional factor (Malina 2011; Malina et al., 2013b, 2015). Commonly used indicators of maturity status and timing have limitations. Skeletal age and pubertal stages provide valid estimates of maturity status but are often considered "invasive," while longitudinal data are needed to estimate maturity timing (Beunen, 1990; Beunen & Malina, 2008; Malina et al., 2004). These limitations have encouraged the development and application of alternative methods in studies of youth athletes (Malina et al., 2015; Malina, 2016a).

The use of PHV as a reference to individualize and optimize athlete preparation in the *training to train* stage of the LTAD model is problematic. The model recommends quarterly measurements of height to calculate growth velocities in order to monitor the velocity curve (Balyi & Way, 2009). Increments calculated over short intervals are influenced by technical errors of measurement, and also by diurnal and seasonal variation. Height measurements taken after a period of physical activity are likely less than those taken after a period of rest. Increments also need adjustment for the difference between the prescribed and actual intervals between measurements (Malina, 2016a).

The adolescent spurt is more complicated than the preceding would imply. It begins when the rate of growth in height reaches its minimum in late childhood; the acceleration that follows marks the beginning or take-off of the spurt. Rate of growth continues to accelerate until it reaches its maximum (PHV), and then decelerates until growth in height terminates. Age at PHV is an estimate of the point in the time (chronological age) at which the maximal rate of growth in height occurs during the adolescent spurt.

The estimation of PHV requires longitudinal data across adolescence. A variety of methods are available to model serial height records for individuals (Hauspie & Roelarts, 2012). No one model is the standard; all have limitations and underlying assumptions. Although estimated ages at PHV vary somewhat among methods, estimated ages are generally more uniform than estimated peak velocities (cm/yr).

Inter-individual variation in estimated ages at PHV is considerable. Among samples of British, Swiss, Polish, Belgian, Canadian and American youth, ages at PHV span 9.0 to 15.0 years in girls and 10.9 to 17.3 years in boys (Malina et al., 2004, Malina, Chow, Czerwinski, & Chumlea, 2016a; Malina & Kozieł, 2014a, 2014b; Mirwald, Baxter-Jones, Bailey, & Beunen, 2002; Moore et al., 2015). Variation in ages at take-off of the spurt is also considerable and range from 7.0 to 9.8 years and 8.2 to 12.7 years in American girls and boys, respectively (Malina et al., 2016a), and from 6.3 to 12.0 years and 7.0 to 14.1 years in Polish girls and boys, respectively (Malina & Kozieł, 2014a, 2014b). Inter-individual variation in the interval between age at take-off and age at PHV is an additional source of variation.

Predicted time before PHV, labeled maturity offset, and age at PHV estimated as chronological age minus maturity offset are increasingly used in studies of youth athletes. Validation of the sex-specific prediction equations (Mirwald et al., 2002) in longitudinal samples of Polish and American youth, however, highlight major limitations (Malina & Kozieł, 2014a, 2014b; Malina et al., 2016a). Predicted maturity offset and age at PHV are dependent upon chronological age and body size at prediction, and are influenced by individual differences in observed ages of PHV. The latter is especially marked among early and late maturing boys and girls. Among early maturing boys and girls, predicted ages at PHV are later than observed age at PHV, while among late maturing boys and girls, predicted ages are earlier than observed age at PHV. Observations for female artistic gymnasts are consistent with those for late maturing girls (Malina et al., 2006). Intra-individual variation in predicted ages at PHV between 8 and 18 years is also considerable (Kozieł & Malina, 2016; Malina et al., 2016a).

The prediction protocol has been modified and simplified (Moore et al., 2015). Results of the validation of the modified prediction equations for boys in the longitudinal sample of Polish boys are consistent with observations based on the validations of the original equation in American and Polish boys; predictions are affected by chronological age at prediction and by maturity status based on observed age at PHV (Kozieł & Malina, 2016). The modified equations, however, are useful close to the time of observed PHV in average maturing boys, specifically plus/minus one year of observed PHV. Otherwise, the prediction equations have major limitations when applied to early and late maturing boys. Predicted maturity offset and ages at PHV with the modified equations also have reduced ranges of variation compared to predictions with the original equation and especially compared to variation in observed ages at PHV in the validation sample.

Predicted maturity offset and age at PHV are estimates of maturity timing. The predictions are often used to classify cross-sectional samples of youth as pre- and post-PHV, or as pre-, at- and post-PHV. These are maturity status classifications based on predicted maturity timing. Such classifications, however, are variously done in samples of youth spanning relatively broad age ranges, for example, soccer players 11–17 years classified as pre-, circum- and post-PHV (Mendez Villanueva et al., 2010) or sport academy participants 11–15 years classified as pre-, mid- and post-PHV (Meylan, Cronin, Hopkins, & Oliver, 2014). They were also applied independently of chronological age, which is problematic. Chronological age is a predictor in the original and modified equations, and as noted, predicted maturity offset declines with age and predicted age at PHV increases with age.

An alternative method for estimating maturity status is percentage of predicted adult height at the time of observation. Accordingly, adult or mature height is predicted from chronological age, height and weight of the individual and mid-parent height (maternal height + paternal height/2); current height is then expressed as a percentage of predicted adult height. Given two youngsters of the same chronological age, the one closer to adult height is advanced in maturity compared to a youth further removed from adult height (Malina, 2016a). Classifications of maturity status based on percentage of predicted adult height at the time of observation has reasonable concordance with classifications based on skeletal age in male youth participants in American football (Malina, Dompier, Powell, Barron, & Moore, 2007) and soccer (Malina, Coelho-e-Silva, Figueiredo, Carling, & Beunen, 2012).

Maturity matching: Bio-banding

Inter-individual differences in biological maturity status and associated variation in size and functional capacities often prompt discussions of the need to equate groups by size or maturity status to equalize competition and reduce risk of injury during the pubertal years (Malina & Beunen, 1996; Beunen & Malina, 2008). Although matching on the basis of biological charac-teristics for the purpose of equating competitions is often the focus of discussion, the process does not preclude consideration of technical and psychosocial characteristics, i.e., coaches can, and perhaps should, consider the young athletes from a bio-behavioral or holistic perspective before encouraging them to "play up" or "play down" relative to chronological age.

The process of matching players on the basis of growth and/or maturity characteristics in specific chronological age ranges is currently labeled as bio-banding, and has received renewed interest in youth sport. The English Premier League, for example, has organized and evaluated a series of bio-banded soccer tournaments in which players were grouped on the basis of esti-mated biological maturity status rather than age per se. Using percentage of predicted adult height as the indicator of maturity status at the time of observation, teams were restricted to players 11–14 years who have attained 85% to 90% of predicted adult height. The range was viewed as representing late childhood and initial stages of the growth spurt. Initial findings have been supportive of the strategy; both players and coaches rated experiences as positive and encouraged the Premier League to integrate bio-banding within the existing games program. Of interest, early and late maturing players differed in reasons for supporting the initiative. Early maturing players found the competition to be a greater physical challenge, forcing them to adopt a more technical and tactical oriented style of play. In contrast, late maturing players appreciated the greater opportunity to use and demonstrate technical and tactical skills, and to adopt leadership roles. Both early and late maturing players agreed that the tournament chal-lenged them in novel and unique ways and contributed towards a more diverse and positive learning experience (Cumming & Bunce, 2015).

Although the early efforts were restricted to competition, researchers and practitioners are also examining its broader implications, particularly relative to talent identification, develop-ment, and retention. Individual differences in growth and maturation are thus being taken into consideration when scouting, evaluating and training young athletes. As part of the Elite Player Performance Plan (EPPP), the Premier League (2015–2016) has established procedures for the regular assessment of growth and maturation across academy programs. The initiative has enabled clubs to monitor the growth and maturation of youth players and to consider this information when evaluating player fitness, designing and implementing strength and condi-tioning programs, and recognizing periods of rapid growth during which athletes may be more susceptible to certain injuries (e.g., Sever's and Osgood-Schlatter's diseases).

"Windows of opportunity"

"Windows of opportunity" imply enhanced responsiveness to specific instruction, practice and training. Two "windows", one in early- and mid-childhood and another in adolescence are central to many talent development models, including the LTAD model. Emphasis on sport-specific motor skill instruction and practice during childhood characterizes the first "window," while responsiveness to intensive sport-specific functional training during adolescence characterizes the second. Retention in and exclusion from sport also occur during these intervals, but most discussions focus on talent development per se, and generally avoid issues related to exclusion, either systematic or voluntary.

Childhood and movement proficiency

The development of proficiency in a variety of movement skills is a dominant feature of early and middle childhood, and evaluation of movement skills at relatively young ages is central to talent programs. Responsiveness to general instruction and practice is assumed in "early entry" sports, although documentation of the influence of early instruction and practice on sport-specific movement skills has not been extensively reported.

Early childhood is characterized by rapid growth of the brain through 6 or 7 years and associated changes in the central nervous system. Movement skills are outcomes of interactions between neuromuscular maturation and early childhood environments. These environments increasingly include instructional programs in general and sport-specific skills. Successful programs for motor skills among children aged 4–5 years and older typically include guided instruction by specialists and/or qualified coaches, appropriate motor sequences (task analysis), adequate time for practice, and constructive guidance and feedback (Haubenstricker & Seefeldt, 1986, 2002), allowing for inter- and intra-individual variation in development per se and in rates of learning. However, accurate identification of "readiness to learn specific motor skills … through a combination of chronological age, body size, or the various assessments of biological maturation" (Haubenstricker & Seefeldt, 2002, p. 79) is not suggested in the available data.

The dynamical systems framework (Thelen & Smith, 1994; Lewis, 2000) is emphasized in motor development and learning. Dynamical systems are complex and interconnected, have several components, and are characterized by self-organization. Systems continuously change and operate in different time scales and levels with considerable variation in temporal-spatial patterns. Motor development and skill acquisition are viewed as emerging from interactions among the three constraints: child (size, proportions, body composition, biological maturation, cognitive abilities, behaviors, etc.), environment (rearing style, quality of adult instruction/supervision, opportunities, stimulation, object size in manipulative tasks, rules, atmosphere of a gymnasium, etc.), and specific movement tasks (Newell, 1986). Changes in constraints per se and in interactions among constraints guide the neuromuscular system in the development and refinement movement skills.

The development and acquisition of movement proficiency and specific skills are outcomes of interactions among the growing and maturing youngster, environments to which he/she is exposed, and demands of specific motor tasks. Body size, proportions and composition change with growth, the neuromuscular system matures, and motor behaviors develop. These in turn influence interactions with the environments. Children, of course, are dynamic beings who, as they learn to behave within their respective cultures, are capable of making decisions on how they interact with the environments. Children's perceptions of the instructional or sport environments in the context of developing movement skills are not ordinarily considered. There is a need for systematic evaluation of instruction and practice in specific sports on skills and the behavioral development of youth. These programs represent manipulation of environmental constraints aimed at channeling motor behaviors into a finely tuned, controlled system of sport-specific skills.

The preceding is based upon children in general and not on young athletes. There is a need for systematic study of skill acquisition among youth athletes. Can variance in skill acquisition be partitioned among child, coach, specific-sport demands, and their interactions? To what extent does the structure of variance change as skills become finely tuned or approach expert levels?

Adolescence and functional capacities

The second "window" focuses on the responsiveness of functional capacities to training during adolescent growth and maturation. Hormonal changes that underlie pubertal maturation and growth have been proposed as a "trigger" for increased sensitivity of the muscular and cardio-vascular systems to training (Katch, 1983). Although youth respond positively to training (considered earlier), evidence addressing responses of adolescents to aerobic-, strength-, and speed-specific training is not consistent with a "maturation threshold" (McNarry et al., 2014). This makes sense given individual differences in the timing and tempo of growth and matura-tion, and differential timing of spurts in functional capacities. The complexity of the adolescent growth spurt is overlooked in the LTAD model, which focuses on height—specifically PHV. However, body weight, sitting height, estimated leg length, lean tissue mass, bone mineral content, static strength, power and speed also have adolescent growth spurts which vary, on average, relative to the timing of PHV; the spurt in peak VO_2 occurs coincident with PHV (Mirwald & Bailey, 1986; Beunen et al., 1988; Beunen & Malina, 1988; Geithner et al., 2004; Iuliano-Burns, Mirwald, & Bailey, 2001; Malina et al., 2004).

Intra- and inter-individual variation in performances of youth athletes during adolescence needs consideration. The Longitudinal Study of Belgian Boys showed, on average, peak gains in speed of arm movement and a shuttle run prior to PHV, and peak gains in static strength, vertical jump and flexed arm hang after PHV (Beunen et al., 1988). Leg lifts (trunk strength) showed no clear spurt, while sit and reach (lower back-hip flexibility) showed a very small peak prior to PHV. Subsequent analyses identified boys who declined in some but not all perform-ances during the interval of PHV. Boys showing declines in a task (or tasks) had the same or better performance levels in the respective item(s) at the beginning of the interval of PHV than boys whose performances improved. Comparisons of "decliners" and "improvers" during the interval of PHV indicated no differences in peak velocities of growth in height, anthropomet-ric dimensions at the beginning of the interval of PHV and at 18 years of age, and performances at 18 years; the groups also did not differ in an index of sports participation (Beunen & Malina, 1988). Though limited to a single longitudinal study of boys, the results highlight the individuality of adolescent changes in growth and performance, which may influ-ence observations based on short-term studies. Corresponding data for girls are lacking.

The concept of "adolescent awkwardness," specifically in boys, has a long tradition in the adolescent literature (Beunen & Malina, 1988) and may be a confounder in adolescent studies. Popular labels, such as, "first you stretch them and then you fill them out"[1] and "the boy is not as strong as he looks" likely reflect differential timing of growth spurts in height, weight, muscle mass and strength (Malina et al., 2004). Changes in balance may influence impressions of clum-siness. An interval of temporary balance problems during adolescence (no more than six months) that may affect performances on certain tasks has been suggested (Tanner, 1978). It was attributed to the increase in trunk relative to leg lengths before the attainment of full size and muscular strength.

Rapid growth in height has been related to predicted and actual reaching behavior and balance in boys aged 12–13 years (Heffernan & Thomson, 1999). Rapidly growing boys (mean 6-month gain 6.2 cm) showed a greater mismatch between actual and predicted reaching distances, and a tendency to overestimate reaching ability and to lose balance while reaching compared to boys who gained considerably less (mean gain 1.7 cm). Changes in the ability to evaluate one's movement abilities associated with rapid pubertal growth have more recently been labeled "destabilization of movement competence" (Anderson, 2002), which is seemingly another label for adolescent awkwardness.

Overview

The process of talent development is superimposed upon a *constantly changing base*, the demands of physical growth, biological maturation and behavioral development, and their interactions, as children pass from childhood into and through puberty and adolescence, and into adulthood. The processes are dynamic and highly individualized, and include numerous bio-cultural or bio-behavioral interactions.

The talent development process is generally *long term* as youngsters adapt to sport-specific instructional and training programs, the associated social and emotional demands of the sport environment, the adults who direct the programs, and the competitive domain. Nevertheless, the *path to elite status is highly variable* among individuals.

The process is also *exclusive*. Focus is on the "talented" minority, while the majority is excluded or voluntarily withdraws. Moreover, probability of success at the highest levels is highly unlikely.

Note

1   I first heard this description from Dr. Wilton M. Krogman, my major professor in biological anthropology.

References

Anderson, D.I. (2002). Do critical periods determine when to initiate sport skill learning? In F.L. Smoll & R.E. Smith (eds), *Children and Youth in Sport: A Biopsychosocial Perspective* (2nd ed.). Dubuque, IA: Kendall Hunt, pp. 105–148.

Balyi, I., & Hamilton, A. (2004). *Long-Term Athlete Development: Trainability in Childhood and Adolescence – Windows of Opportunity, Optimal Trainability*. Victoria, BC: National Coaching Institute British Columbia and Advanced Training and Performance Ltd.

Balyi, I., & Way, R. (2009). *The Role of Monitoring Growth in Long-Term Athlete Development*. Canadian Sport Centres/Centres Canadiens Multisports: Canadian Sport for Life. http://canadiansportforlife.ca/sites/default/files/resources/MonitoringGrowth%281%29.pdf

Beunen, G. (1990). Biological age in pediatric exercise research. In O. Bar-Or (ed.), *Advances in Pediatric Sport Sciences, Vol III. Biological Issues*. Champaign, IL: Human Kinetics, pp. 1–39.

Beunen, G., & Malina, R.M. (1988). Growth and physical performance relative to the timing of the adolescent spurt. *Exercise and Sports Sciences Reviews*, 16, 503–540.

Beunen, G., & Malina, R.M. (2008). Growth and biological maturation: Relevance to athletic performance. In H. Heberstreit & O. Bar-Or (eds), *The Young Athlete*. Malden, MA: Blackwell, pp. 3–17.

Beunen, G.P., Malina, R.M., Van't Hof, M.A., Simons, J., Ostyn, M., Renson, R., & Van Gerven, D. (1988). *Adolescent Growth and Motor Performance: A Longitudinal Study of Belgian Boys*. Champaign, IL: Human Kinetics.

Beunen, G.P., Peeters, M.W., & Malina. R.M. (2011). Twin studies in sport performance. In C. Bouchard and E.P. Hoffman (eds), *Genetic and Molecular Aspects of Sport Performance*. Chichester, UK: Blackwell, pp. 101–109.

Bloom, B.S. (ed.) (1985). *Developing Talent in Young People*. New York: Ballantine Books.

Bompa, T. (1985). Talent identification. *Sports Science Periodical on Research and Technology in Sport, Physical Testing G1*. Ottawa: Coaching Association of Canada.

Bompa, T. (1995). *From Childhood to Champion Athlete*. Toronto:Veritas Publishing.

Bouchard, C. (2012). Genomic predictors of trainability. *Experimental Physiology*, 97, 347–352.

Bruner, M.W., Erickson, K., McFadden, K., & Côté, J. (2009). Tracing the origins of athlete development models in sport: A citation path analysis. *International Review of Sport and Exercise Psychology*, 2, 23–37.

Bruner, M.W., Eys, M.A., & Turnnidge, J. (2013). Peer and group influences in youth sport. In J. Côté & R. Lidor (eds), *Conditions of Children's Talent Development in Sport*. Morgantown, WV: Fitness Information Technology, pp. 157–178.

Brustad, R.J. (2003). Parental roles and involvement in youth sport: Psychosocial outcomes for children. In R.M. Malina & M.A. Clark (eds), *Youth Sports: Perspectives for a New Century*. Monterey, CA: Coaches Choice, pp. 127–138.

Claessens, A.L., Lefevre, J., Beunen, B., & Malina, R.M. (1999). The contribution of anthropometric characteristics to performance scores in elite female gymnasts. *Journal of Sports Medicine and Physical Fitness*, 39, 355–360.

Claessens, A.L., Lefevre, J., Beunen, G.P., & Malina, R.M. (2006). Maturity-associated variation in the body size and proportions of elite female gymnasts 14–17 years of age. *European Journal of Pediatrics*, 165, 186–192

Claessens, A.L., Malina, R.M., Lefevre, J., Beunen, G., Stijnen, V., Maes, H., & Veer, F.M. (1992). Growth and menarcheal status of elite female gymnasts. *Medicine and Science in Sports and Exercise*, 24, 755–763.

Coelho-e-Silva, M.J., Figueiredo, A.J., Simões, F., Seabra, A., Natal, A, Vaeyens, R., et al. (2010). Discrimination of U-14 soccer players by level and position. *International Journal of Sports Medicine*, 31, 790–796.

Côté, J., & Hay, J. (2002). Children's involvement in sport: A developmental perspective. In J.S. Silva & D. Stevens (eds), *Psychological Foundations of Sport*. Boston: Allyn and Bacon, pp. 484–502.

Côté, J., Lidor, R., & Hackfort, D. (2009). ISSP position stand: To sample or to specialize? Seven postulates about youth sport activities that lead to continued participation and elite performance. *International Journal of Sport and Exercise Psychology*, 9, 7–17.

Côté, J., & Vierimaa, M. (2014). The developmental model of sport participation: 15 years after its first conceptualization. *Science and Sports*, 29S, S63–S69.

Cumming, S.P., & Bunce, J. (2015). Maturation in player development and practical strategies in Premier League Academies. Paper presented at the Rugby Football Union (RFU) Player Development Conference: The Future Player, Twickenham Stadium, UK.

Cumming, S.P., Sherar, L.B., Pindus, D.M., Coelho-e-Silva, M.J., Malina, R.M., & Jardine, P.R. (2012). A biocultural model of maturity-associated variance in adolescent physical activity. *International Review of Sport and Exercise Psychology*, 5, 22–43.

Davies, P.S.W., Feng, J-Y., Crisp, J.A., Day, J.M.E., & Laidlaw, A. (1997). Total energy expenditure and physical activity in young Chinese gymnasts. *Pediatric Exercise Science*, 9, 243–252.

Di Cagno, A., Battaglia, C., Fiorilli, G., Piazza, M., Giombini, A., Faguani, F., et al. (2014). Motor learning as young gymnast's talent indicator. *Journal of Sports Science and Medicine*, 13, 767–773.

Drabik, J. (1996). *Children and Sports Training*. Island Pond, VT: Stadion Publishing Company.

Elfrink-Gemser, M.T., Visscher, C., Lemmink, K.A.P.M., & Mulder, T. (2007). Multidimensional performance characteristics and standard of performance in talented youth field hockey players: A longitudinal study. *Journal of Sports Sciences*, 25, 481–489.

Erickson, K., & Gilbert, W. (2013). Coach-athlete interactions in children's sport. In J. Côté & R. Lidor (eds), *Conditions of Children's Talent Development in Sport*. Morgantown, WV: Fitness Information Technology, pp. 139–156.

Ericsson, K.A. (2003). The development of elite performance and deliberate practice: An update from the perspective of the expert-performance approach. In J. Starkes & K.A. Ericsson (eds), *Expert Performance in Sport: Recent Advances in Research on Sport Expertise*. Champaign, IL: Human Kinetics, pp. 49–81.

Ericsson, K.A., Krampe, R.Th., & Tesch-Römer, C. (1993). The role of deliberate practice in the acquisition of expert performance. *Psychological Review*, 100, 363–406.

Ewing, M.E., & Seefeldt, V. (1988). *Participation and Attrition Patterns in American Agency-Sponsored and Interscholastic Sports: An Executive Summary*. East Lansing: Michigan State University, Institute for the Study of Youth Sports.

Faber, I.R., Nijhuis-van der Sanden, M.W.G., Elferink-Gemser, M.T., & Oosterveld, F.G.J. (2015). The Dutch motor skills assessment as tool for talent development in table tennis: A reproducibility and validity study. *Journal of Sports Sciences*, 33, 1149–1158.

Faigenbaum, A.D., & Myer, G.D. (2010). Resistance training among youth athletes: Safety, efficacy and injury prevention effects. *British Journal of Sports Medicine*, 44, 56–63.

Figueiredo, A.J., Gonçalves, C.E., Coelho-e-Silva, M.J., & Malina, R.M. (2009). Characteristics of youth soccer players who drop out, persist or move up. *Journal of Sports Sciences*, 27, 883–891.

Ford, P., de Ste Croix, M., Lloyd, R., Meyers, R., Moosavi, M., Oliver, J., et al. (2011). The long-term athlete development model: Physiological evidence and application. *Journal of Sports Sciences*, 29, 389–402.

Ford, P.R., & Williams, A.M. (2013). The acquisition of skill and expertise: The role of practice and other activities. In A.M. Williams (ed.), *Science and Soccer: Developing Elite Performers* (3rd ed.). Abington, UK: Routledge, pp. 122–138.

Fraser-Thomas, J., Strachan, L., & Jeffery-Tosoni, S. (2013). Family influences on children's involvement in sport. In J. Côté & R. Lidor (eds), *Conditions of Children's Talent Development in Sport*. Fitness Information Technology: Morgantown, WV, pp. 179–196.

Gardner, H. (1993). *Frames of Mind: The Theory of Multiple Intelligences* (2nd ed.). New York: Basic Books.

Gardner, H. (1999). *Intelligence Reframed. Multiple Intelligences for the 21st Century*. New York: Basic Books.

Geithner, C.A., Thomis, M.A., Vanden Eynde, B., Maes, H.H. M, Loos, R.J.F., Peeters, M., et al. (2004). Growth in peak aerobic power during adolescence. *Medicine and Science in Sports and Exercise*, 36, 1616–1624.

Güllich, A., & Emrich, E. (2006). Evaluation of the support of young athletes in the elite sport system. *European Journal of Sports Sociology*, 3, 85–108.

Güllich, A., & Emrich, E. (2014). Considering long-term sustainability in the development of world class success. *European Journal of Sport Science*, 14, S383–S397.

Haubenstricker, J., & Seefeldt, V. (1986). Acquisition of motor skills during childhood. In V. Seefeldt (ed.), *Physical Activity and Well-Being*. Reston, VA.: American Alliance for Health, Physical Education, Recreation and Dance, pp. 41–101.

Haubenstricker, J.L., & Seefeldt, V. (2002). The concept of readiness applied to the acquisition of motor skills. In F.L. Smoll & R.E. Smith (eds), *Children and Youth in Sport: A Biopsychosocial Perspective* (2nd ed.). Dubuque, IA: Kendall/Hunt, pp. 61–81.

Hauspie, R.C., & Roelarts, M. (2012). Adolescent growth. In N. Cameron & B. Bogin (eds), *Human Growth and Development* (2nd ed.). New York: Elsevier, pp. 57–79.

Heffernan, D., & Thomson, J.A. (1999). Gone fishin': Perceiving what is reachable with rods during a period of rapid growth. In M.A. Grealy & J.A. Thomson (eds), *Studies in Perception and Action V*. Mahwah, NJ: Lawrence Erlbaum Associates, pp. 223–228.

Huijgen, B.C.H., Elferink-Gemser, M.T., Lemmink, K.A.P.M., & Visscher, C. (2014). Multidimensional performance characteristics in selected and deselected talented soccer players. *European Journal of Sport Science*, 14, 2–10.

Hunter Smart, J.E., Cumming, S.P., Sherar, L.B., Standage, M., Neville, H., & Malina, R.M. (2012). Maturity associated variance in physical activity and health-related quality of life in adolescent females: A mediated effects model. *Journal of Physical Activity and Health*, 9, 86–95.

Iuliano-Burns, S., Mirwald, R.L., & Bailey, D.A. (2001). The timing and magnitude of peak height velocity and peak tissue velocities for early, average and late maturing boys and girls. *American Journal of Human Biology*, 13, 1–8.

Jones, M.C., Bayley, N., MacFarlane, J.W., & Honzik, M.P. (eds). (1971). *The Course of Human Development: Selected Papers from the Longitudinal Studies, Institute of Human Development, the University of California, Berkeley*. Waltham, MA: Xerox College Publishing.

Josephson Institute. (2007) *What are Your Children Learning? The Impact of High School Sports on the Values and Ethics of High School Athletes*. Los Angeles, CA: Josephson Institute of Ethics.

Katch, V.L. (1983). Physical conditioning of children. *Journal of Adolescent Health*, 3, 241–6.

Kozieł, S.M., & Malina, R.M. (2016). Validation of the modified maturity offset equations in a longitudinal sample of boys. Manuscript under review.

Lerner, R.M., & Steinberg, L. (2004). *Handbook of Adolescent Psychology* (2nd ed.). Hoboken, NJ: John Wiley and Sons.

Lewis, M.C. (2000). The promise of dynamic systems approaches for an integrated account of human development. *Child Development*, 71, 36–43.

Malina, R.M. (1986). Readiness for competitive sport. In M.R. Weiss & D. Gould (eds), *Sport for Children and Youths*. Champaign, IL: Human Kinetics, pp. 45–50.

Malina, R.M. (1993). Youth sports: Readiness, selection and trainability. In W. Duquet & J.A.P. Day (eds), *Kinanthropometry IV*. London: Spon, pp. 285–301.

Malina, R.M. (1994). Physical growth and biological maturation of young athletes. *Exercise and Sports Sciences Reviews*, 22, 389–433.

Malina, R.M. (1998). Growth and maturation of young athletes – Is training for sport a factor? In K-M. Chan & L.J. Micheli (eds), *Sports and Children*. Hong Kong: Williams and Wilkins Asia-Pacific, pp. 133–161.

Malina, R.M. (2002). The young athlete: Biological growth and maturation in a biocultural context. In F.L. Smoll & R.E. Smith (eds), *Children and Youth in Sports: A Biopsychosocial Perspective* (2nd ed.). Dubuque, IA: Kendall Hunt, pp. 261–292.

Malina, R.M. (2006a). *Growth and Maturation of Child and Adolescent Track and Field Athletes*. Rome: Centro Studi e Ricerche, Federazione Italiana di Atletica Leggera.

Malina, R.M. (2006b). Weight training in youth – growth, maturation, and safety: An evidence based review. *Clinical Journal of Sports Medicine*, 16, 478–487.

Malina, R.M. (2008). Skill: Acquisition and Trainability. In O. Bar-Or & H. Hebestreit (eds), *The Young Athlete*. Oxford, UK: Blackwell Publications, pp. 96–111.

Malina, R.M. (2009). Children and adolescents in the sport culture: The overwhelming majority to the select few. *Journal of Exercise Science and Fitness*, 7 (suppl), S1–S10.

Malina, R.M. (2010). Early sport specialization: Roots, effectiveness, risks. *Current Sports Medicine Reports*, 9, 364–71.

Malina, R.M. (2011). Skeletal age and age verification in youth sport. *Sports Medicine*, 41, 925–947.

Malina, R.M. (2016a). Assessment of biological maturation. In N. Armstrong & W. van Mechelen (eds), *Oxford Textbook of Children's Exercise Science and Medicine*. Oxford: Oxford University Press, in press.

Malina, R.M. (2016b). The influence of physical activity and training on growth and maturation. In N. Armstrong & W. van Mechelen (eds), *Oxford Textbook of Children's Exercise Science and Medicine*. Oxford: Oxford University Press, in press.

Malina, R.M., Baxter-Jones, A.D.G., Armstrong, N., Beunen, G.P., Caine, D., Daly, R.M., et al. (2013a). Role of intensive training in the growth and maturation of artistic gymnasts. *Sports Medicine*, 43, 783–802.

Malina, R.M., & Beunen, G. (1996). Matching of opponents in youth sports. In O. Bar-Or (ed.), *The Child and Adolescent Athlete*. Oxford: Blackwell Science, pp. 202–213.

Malina, R.M., Bouchard, C., & Bar-Or, O. (2004). *Growth, Maturation, and Physical Activity*, 2nd edition. Champaign, IL: Human Kinetics.

Malina, R.M., Chow, A.C., Czerwinski, S.A., & Chumlea, W.C. (2016a). Validation of maturity offset in the Fels Longitudinal Study. *Pediatric Exercise Science*, 28, 439–455.

Malina, R.M., Claessens, A.L., Van Aken, K., Thomis, M., Lefevre, J., Philippaerts, R., & Beunen, G.P. (2006). Maturity offset in gymnasts: Application of a prediction equation. *Medicine and Science in Sports and Exercise*, 38, 1342–1347.

Malina, R.M., & Coelho-e-Silva, M.J. (2016). Physical activity, growth and maturation of youth. In H.C. Lukaski (ed.), *Body Composition: Health and Performance in Exercise and Sport*. Boca Raton, FL: CRC Press/Taylor and Francis Group, in press.

Malina, R.M., Coelho-e-Silva, M.J., & Figueiredo, A.J. (2013b). Growth and maturity status of youth players. In A.M. Williams (ed.), *Science and Soccer: Developing Elite Performers* (3rd ed.). Abingdon, UK: Routledge, pp. 307–332.

Malina, R.M., Coelho-e-Silva, M.J., Figueiredo, M.J., Carling, C., & Beunen, G.P. (2012). Interrelationships among invasive and non-invasive indicators of biological maturation in adolescent male soccer players. *Journal of Sports Sciences*, 30, 1705–1717.

Malina, R.M., Cumming, S.P., & Coelho-e-Silva, M.J. (2016b). Physical activity and movement proficiency: The need for a biocultural approach. *Pediatric Exercise Science*, 28, 233–239.

Malina, R.M., Dompier, T.P., Powell, J.W., Barron, M.J., & Moore, M.T. (2007). Validation of a noninvasive maturity estimate relative to skeletal age in youth football players. *Clinical Journal of Sports Medicine*, 17, 362–368.

Malina, R.M., & Geithner, C.A. (1993). Background in sport, growth status, and growth rate of Junior Olympic Divers. In R.M. Malina & J.L. Gabriel (eds), *U.S. Diving Sport Science Seminar 1993, Proceedings*. Indianapolis, IN: United States Diving, pp. 26–35.

Malina, R.M., & Kozieł, S.M. (2014a). Validation of maturity offset in a longitudinal sample of Polish boys. *Journal of Sports Sciences*, 32, 424–437.

Malina, R.M., & Kozieł, S.M. (2014b). Validation of maturity offset in a longitudinal sample of Polish girls. *Journal of Sports Sciences*, 32, 1374–1382.

Malina, R.M., & Rogol, A.D. (2011). Sport training and the growth and pubertal maturation of young athletes. *Pediatric Endocrinology Review*, 9, 440–454.

Malina, R.M., Rogol, A.D., Cumming, S.P., Coelho-e-Silva, M.J., & Figueiredo, A.J. (2015). Biological maturation of youth athletes: Assessment and implications. *British Journal of Sports Medicine*, 49, 852–859.

McNarry, M., Barker, A., Lloyd, R.S., Buchheit, M., Williams, C., & Oliver, J. (2014). The BASES expert statement on trainability during childhood and adolescence. *The Sport and Exercise Scientist*, 41, 22–23.

Mendez-Villanueva, A., Buchheit, M., Kuitunen, S., Poon, T.K., Simpson, B., & Peltola, E. (2010). Is the relationship between sprinting and maximal aerobic speeds in young soccer players affected by maturation? *Pediatric Exercise Science*, 22, 497–510.

Meylan, C.M., Cronin, J., Hopkins, W.G., & Oliver, J. (2014). Adjustment of measures of strength and power in youth male athletes differing in body mass and maturation. *Pediatric Exercise Science*, 26, 41–48.

Mirwald, R.L., & Bailey, D.A. (1986). *Maximal Aerobic Power: A Longitudinal Analysis*. London, ON: Sports Dynamics, pp. 1–80.

Mirwald, R.L., Baxter-Jones, A.D.G., Bailey, D.A., & Beunen, G.P. (2002). An assessment of maturity from anthropometric measurements. *Medicine and Science in Sports and Exercise*, 34, 689–694.

Mitchell, S.B., Haase, A.M., Malina, R.M., & Cumming, S.P. (2016). The role of puberty in the making and breaking of young ballet dancers: Perspectives of dance teachers. *Journal of Adolescence*, 47, 81–89.

Moesch, K., Elbe, A-M., Hauge, M.L.T., & Wikman, J.M. (2011). Late specialization: The key to success in centimeters, grams, or seconds (cgs) sports. *Scandinavian Journal of Medicine and Science in Sports*, 21, e282–e290.

Moore, S.A., McKay, H.A., MacDonald, H., Nettlefold, L., Baxter-Jones, A.D.G., Cameron, N., and Bracher, P.M.A. (2015). Enhancing a somatic maturity prediction model. *Medicine and Science in Sports and Exercise*, 47, 1755–1764.

Newell, K.M. (1986). Constraints on the development of coordination. In M.G. Wade & H.T.A. Whiting (eds), *Motor Development in Children: Aspects of Coordination Control*. Dordrecht, the Netherlands: Martinus Nijhoff, pp. 341–359.

Oldenziel, K.E., Gagné, F., & Gulbin, J. (2004). Factors affecting the rate of athlete development from novice to senior elite: How applicable is the 10-year rule? Paper presented at the 2004 Pre-Olympic Congress – Sport Science through the Ages. Thessaloniki, Greece, 6–11 August, available at www.ccv.org.br/br/biblioteca/preolymp/download/O.027.doc (accessed 4 September 2008).

Passer, M.W., & Wilson, B.J. (2002). Motivational, emotional, and cognitive determinants of children's age-readiness for competition. In F.L. Smoll & R.E. Smith (eds), *Children and Youth in Sport: A Biopsychosocial Perspective* (2nd ed.). Dubuque, IA: Kendall Hunt, pp. 83–103.

Peeters, M.W., Thomis, M.A., Beunen, G.P., & Malina, R.M. (2009). Genetics and sports: An overview of the pre-molecular biology era. *Medicine and Sport Science*, 54, 28–42.

Premier League. (2015–2016). Bio-banding helping late developers. www.premierleague.com/en-gb/news/news/2015-16/sep/170915-premier-league-bio-banding-helping-late-developers.html.

Rost, K., & Schon, R. (1997). *Talent search for track and field events: Exercise leader and coach's manual for talent selection and basic training of track and field events (Age Class 9 to 14)*. Leipzig, Germany: German Track and Field Association (translated by M. R. Hill, H. Nowoisky, & N.N. Wegink, University of Utah).

Rowland, T.W., & Boyajian, A. (1995). Aerobic response to endurance exercise training in children. *Pediatrics*, 96, 654–658.

Ryan, J. (1995). *Pretty Girls in Little Boxes: the Making and Breaking of Elite Gymnastics and Figure Skaters*. New York: Doubleday.

Schwidergall, S., Weimann, E., Witzel, C., Mölenkamp, G., Brehl, S., & Böhles, H. (1998). Ernährungsverhalten bei weiblichen und männlichen Hochleistungsturnern. *Wiener Medizinische Wochenschrift*, 148, 243–244.

Shields, D.L., Bredemeier, B.L., LaVoi, N.M., & Power, F.C. (2005). The sport behavior of youth, parents, and coaches: The good, the bad, and the ugly. *Journal of Research on Character Education*, 3, 43–59.

Skład, M. (1975). The genetic determination of the rate of learning of motor skills. *Studies in Physical Anthropology*, 1, 3–19.

Tanner, J.M. (1978). *Foetus into Man: Physical Growth from Conception to Maturity*. London: Open Books.

Theintz, G., Ladame, F., Kehre, E., Plichta, C, Howald, H., & Sizonenko, P.C. (1994). Prospective study of psychological development of adolescent female athletes: initial assessment. *Journal of Adolescent Health*, 15, 258–262.

Thelen, E., & Smith, L.B. (1994). *A Dynamic Systems Approach to the Development of Cognition and Action.* Cambridge, MA: The MIT Press.

Vandorpe, B., Vandendriessche, J.B., Vaeyens, R., Pion, J., Lefevre, J., Philippaerts, R.M., et al. (2012). The value of a non-sport-specific motor test battery in predicting performance in young female gymnasts. *Journal of Sports Sciences*, 30, 497–505.

Wattie, N., Schorer, J., & Baker, J. (2015). The relative age effect in sport: A developmental systems model. *Sports Medicine, 45*, 83–94.

Weiss, M.R. (2003). Social influences on children's psychosocial development in youth sports. In R.M. Malina & M.A. Clark (eds), *Youth Sports: Perspectives for a New Century.* Monterey, CA: Coaches Choice, pp. 109–126.

Williams, A.M., Janelle, C.M., & Davids, K. (2004). Constraints on the search for visual information in sport. *International Review of Sport and Exercise Psychology*, 2, 301–318.

Williams, A.M., & Reilly, T. (2000). Talent identification and development in soccer. *Journal of Sports Sciences*, 18, 657–667.

12

PSYCHOLOGICAL FACTORS IN DEVELOPING HIGH PERFORMANCE ATHLETES

Anne-Marie Elbe and Johan M. Wikman

Top-level athletes are often said to have extraordinary personalities and special psychological characteristics (Gould, Dieffenbach & Moffett, 2002). This is not surprising when considering the many years of training needed to achieve athletic success. This long-term engagement in intense training calls for great efforts in dealing with competitive pressure and demands mental strength with regard to endurance, self-motivation and willpower. But while it is somewhat straightforward to specify the physical and physiological skills needed for top performance in a specific sport, it becomes less clear with regard to the psychological skills that are needed. Therefore, the main questions to be addressed in this chapter are: (1) which psychological skills are needed to reach top performance? And (2) (how) can these skills be developed in young talents?

Several approaches can be used to investigate the first main question of this chapter. One is to look at relevant theoretical frameworks that approach the subject of psychological skills required to reach top performance. The Theory of Deliberate Practice (Ericsson, Krampe, & Tesch-Römer, 1993), for example, states that an individual needs up to 10,000 hours of deliberate practice to develop into an expert performer. This deliberate practice underlies three constraints, namely the resource, the effort and the motivational constraint. In order to overcome these constraints and develop into an expert performer, an individual must possess the necessary psychological skills that can help in overcoming these constraints and other challenges he/she might face. The Developmental Model of Sport Participation (Côté, Baker, & Abernethy, 2007) describes an alternate route to expert performance, in which the talented athlete acquires expertise through sampling several sports and deliberate play. Deliberate play is a playful activity, in which the athlete regulates rules and conditions of the game as well as effort to maximize enjoyment. A closer look at the three phases in the Developmental Model of Sport Participation reveals that motivational and self-regulatory skills are important for achieving expertise through the route of sampling and deliberate play. Likewise, the Lifespan Model (Wylleman & Reints, 2010), which describes several phases that the talented athlete passes through, and the Analytical Sports Career Model, which describes normative transitions that the athlete has to go through (Stambulova, 1994), also suggest that motivational and self-regulation skills are needed for successful development. All four theoretical frameworks describe successful talent development and the psychological skills needed to overcome challenges. A communality of all four of these theoretical frameworks is that the developing athlete needs motivational and self-regulatory skills for successful transition through the individual phases and for development into a top-level performer.

Another approach to investigating the first main question of this chapter, namely which psychological skills are needed to reach top-performance, is a cross-sectional investigation of different groups of athletes. In these types of studies, personality characteristics of successful athletes are either investigated alone or compared to those of less successful athletes. Qualitative studies that investigated the psychological characteristics needed to develop excellence in elite sports highlighted the importance of motivational and self-regulatory skills for successful talent development (e.g., Holland, Woodcock, Cumming & Duda, 2010; Larsen, Alfermann & Christensen, 2012; Sarkar & Fletcher, 2014). Gould et al.'s (2002) interviews with 10 Olympic athletes as well as their coaches and parents indicated that the athletes were characterized by a number of psychological characteristics of which the majority also can be summarized as being of motivational and self-regulatory nature (e.g., ability to focus, the ability to set and achieve goals, high dispositional hope, mental toughness, etc.).

Aside from the above-mentioned skills, several other psychological factors that play a role in the talent development process should be mentioned. Wikman (2015) conducted a review of psychological factors related to talent development and came to the conclusion that social skills were among the most frequently mentioned psychological factors. MacNamara, Button, and Collins (2010), Holland et al. (2010) as well as Sarkar and Fletcher (2014) found that confidence is an important factor. Van Yperen (2009) identified that in addition to motivation (goal commitment), engagement in problem-focused coping behaviours, and social support seeking predicted career success in a longitudinal study of young footballers. Coping under pressure was also identified as a key success factor in MacNamara et al.'s (2010) interview study of elite athletes and their parents in addition to factors like imagery, self-belief, and game awareness. Hambrick, MacNamara, Campitelli, Ullén, and Mosing (2016) conclude that susceptibility to performance anxiety and to 'choking' under pressure are personality-type factors that could impact performance development. In short, it seems that talented athletes need a wide array of psychological skills and characteristics in addition in order to develop their full potential. However, motivation and self-regulation seem to be the most important.

But what are motivation and self-regulation actually? Motivation is commonly defined as a force or influence that causes someone to initiate and engage in an action for the expected positive outcome of this action (Heckhausen, 1988). However, motivation alone is not sufficient to maintain athletic training over the long period of time required to achieve expertise. Motivation is a dynamic process, and in some cases competing motivation may work against the completion of an action (Atkinson & Birch, 1970). Meta-motivational processes – which are also described as self-regulatory skills – are required to stabilize motivation in order to maintain the intended action, especially when immediate rewards are not available. These meta-motivational or self-regulatory processes are needed to secure a complete athletic accomplishment and are needed to transform a motivation into an actual action (Kuhl, 1983). So, in sum, motivational plus self-regulatory personality factors are necessary to keep up training over the many years necessary to achieve top-level athletic success.

Earlier quantitative studies (e.g., Gabler, 1995; Gill & Deeter, 1988; White & Duda, 1994) investigated motivational variables and compared those of different groups of athletes. These studies concluded that the achievement motive and achievement motivation are especially relevant for sports performance and that the sport-specific measurement of motivation is superior to a general assessment (Elbe, Beckmann, & Szymanski, 2003b). Gill and Deeter (1988), for example, applied the Sport Orientation Questionnaire and found that competitive orientation is higher in US high-performance athletes than in those athletes who do not participate in competitive sports. White and Duda's (1994) investigation using the Task and Ego Orientation in Sport Questionnaire (TEOSQ) showed that college-level high-performance athletes demonstrate a higher level of ego orientation than competitive high school athletes. However, later studies applying the TEOSQ found that elite athletes have higher task than ego orientation (Elbe, Madsen, & Midtgaard, 2010), and also higher task orientation than their non–elite counterparts (Kavussanu, White, Jowett, & England, 2011), indicating that a high task orientation is important for the development of sport expertise. Recent studies focusing on football found empirical evidence that not only the achievement motives (Zuber & Conzelmann, 2014), but also self-regulatory factors (e.g., Moesch, Hauge, Wikman, & Elbe, 2013; Toering, Elferink-Gemser, Jordet, & Visscher, 2009), and self-referential cognitions (e.g., self-confidence; Reilly, Williams, Nevill, & Franks, 2000) are associated with footballers' performance level. In conclusion, these and numerous other studies indicate that personality factors, especially those connected to motivation and self-regulation, seem to show association with performance at an adult level. They give an indication of which factors could be relevant to develop in young athletes so that they show these personality factors in a later stage of their career.

A caveat of these cross-sectional studies, however, is that they cannot answer the second main question of this chapter, namely if and how these personality characteristics develop. Some authors even question if personality factors can be developed at all and refer to the selection hypothesis. The selection hypothesis assumes that there is a pattern of different personality characteristics that stimulates individuals to participate in sport, and that these personality factors are innate in the individual. Individuals, who demonstrate a favourable – or the most favourable – combination of these personality characteristics, participate in the sport, remain involved and are successful. Those who lack these characteristics either do not initiate a sport activity or rather quickly discontinue their involvement. Following the selection hypothesis, it is assumed that beginners (novices) and successful athletes (experts) have similar personality profiles, since it is these profiles that ultimately determine the particular suitability for the type of sport and also for success in this sport. Only the strength of these characteristics may change over the course of a career. This model ignores environmental influences, since personality is the main focus of attention and interactions are not taken into consideration. However, the selection hypothesis does give justification for selecting talented athletes based on specific personality dispositions (e.g., the achievement motive; Zuber, Zibung, & Conzelmann, 2015).

Other authors clearly favour the socialization hypothesis and believe that social learning and personality development can take place through and in sport. With Ericsson et al.'s (1993) introduction of the Theory of Deliberate Practice in the 1990s, the view has shifted towards expertise as something that can be nourished and developed through training. In their notion of deliberate practice, Ericsson et al. (1993) claim that all the skills needed for top performance, whether they are physical, physiological, psychological or other, should be trained specifically through deliberate practice. The belief that an individual athlete's potential can be developed is also reflected in Abbott and Collins's (2004) as well as in Gagné's (2004) research on talent. Hence, according to the socialization hypothesis, homogeneous personality patterns would not be expected in beginners. Individuals begin with a sport without demonstrating a specific personality pattern corresponding to this particular sport. Those who continue in this type of sport and also achieve success either do so by changing existing and alterable personality characteristics, or by gradually reducing unsuitable patterns (Singer & Haase, 1975) in order to attain more suitable patterns. It is assumed that the existing personality characteristics can change and, in consequence, are not stable. Recently more open and dynamic definitions of talent have been offered (e.g., Seidel & Hohmann, 1999; Abbott & Collins, 2004). Newer definitions incorporate the idea that the development of talent is a dynamic process, and that its development can be influenced by personality and environmental factors. In these definitions, personality is also perceived as a dynamic factor that undergoes developmental changes.

Longitudinal studies investigating the personality development of talented athletes are necessary to investigate to what degree the selection and/or the socialization hypothesis applies to the sport context and whether or not personality characteristics can be developed and enhanced. Looking at motivation, two very early studies – Gabler's (1976) with swimmers and Sack's (1980) with long-distance runners – gave the opportunity to investigate to what extent personality characteristics changed over long-term involvement in sports. The results of both studies confirmed that individuals with certain personality characteristics either remain or drop out of high achievement sports and that competitive sport fails to result in any changes in general personality factors. Gabler's (1995) later investigation of the achievement motive established that 'a greater hope for success and a reduced fear of failure are significant requirements for maintaining the willingness to perform in training over a longer period of time' (Gabler, 1995, p. 90). According to Gabler, the lower the hope for success (the success motive) and the higher the fear of failure (failure motive), the more probable it is that there will be a reduction in or a discontinuation of athletic training. These results highlight the importance of the achievement motive for successful sport performance. In an investigation carried out with young, talented athletes attending an elite sport school, Elbe, Beckmann, and Szymanski (2003b) discovered that students chosen for the sport school at the time of their selection already showed a lower fear of failure than students from a comparable school who were not involved in competitive sports. Furthermore, the achievement motive remained stable over a time period of three years. Feichtinger and Höner's (2015) investigation of young elite footballers aged 12 to 14 years showed that the vast majority of the talented football players' development of achievement motives did not show any reliable change from the under 12 to under 14 age classes. Feichtinger and Höner's study, however, also indicated a decrease in the players' self-efficacy and Elbe, Szymanski and Beckmann (2005) could show a development in the students' self-regulatory skills over time and, hence, contradicted the selection hypothesis.

Turning to self-regulation, in the same six-year project, Elbe, Beckmann, and Szymanski (2003a) compared the volitional development of athletes dropping out of competitive sports despite good performance results to those who remained active. Volition deals with processes that are responsible for initiating an action despite internal and external resistance and for maintaining the action until the goal has been reached (Kuhl, 1983). Volition involves cognitive, motivational and emotional control strategies. Not giving up when things get difficult, not letting oneself be distracted, not losing one's confidence and staying positive, are a few examples of self-regulatory processes. Kuhl (1987) argued that motivational processes lead only to the decision to act. The initiation and the engagement in an action, however, are determined by volitional processes, meaning that volitional processes also determine whether the intention is fulfilled or not. Volition is especially important for performing long, intense training loads during the course of an athletic career or for adhering to regular exercise regimens. In the Elbe et al. (2003a) study numerous volitional skills were combined into the constructs of either *self-optimization*, which includes positive volitional skills necessary for reaching goals like self-motivation and initiative, or *self-impediment*, which on the other hand, addresses skills in stress situations like negative emotionality and procrastination. At the beginning of this study, self-impediment was less developed in the dropout athletes. Until grade nine, self-impediment increased in the dropouts, whereas it remained unchanged in the adhering athletes. The negative development of self-impediment was indicated by lack of energy, procrastination, and intrusions and was associated with an early cessation of a sport career. This longitudinal study therefore gave an indication that certain personality characteristics of talented athletes undergo change. In this case the negative development of volitional skills characterized those athletes dropping out of elite sports. In conclusion, it seems that many personality characteristics important for athletic excellence in sport can change to some extent, favouring the socialization hypothesis, but not completely ruling out the selection hypothesis. The stability vs. changeability of personality factors should be considered in the development of the talented athlete.

Another advantage of longitudinal studies is that they can be used not only to investigate the development of personality variables but also to investigate whether certain personality characteristics are connected to future sport performance. Schneider, Bös, and Rieder's (1993) longitudinal study of talented tennis players found that the personality traits of achievement motivation, concentration, self-regulation and persistence were essential prerequisites for high athletic achievement in young athletes. In another longitudinal investigation focusing on the achievement motives of talented athletes attending a sport school, Seidel (2005) found that high hope for success was related to high athletic performance two years later. A further indication that sport specific achievement orientation seems to be of predictive value are Hellandsig's (1998) results in a longitudinal study with young Norwegian competitive athletes. In this study, sport motivational orientations were measured in top-level male and female athletes, aged 15–16, in a wide range of sports. The results revealed that a high competitiveness and low win orientation predicted future athletic success in all the sports over a period of three years. Most of these and other studies concentrated on individual sports since athletic success can be determined more easily and objectively. Recently there have been a number of longitudinal studies in team sports. One example is Van Yperen's (2009) previously described study of elite football. He found that goal commitment, engagement in problem-focused coping behaviours, and searching for social support distinguished football players who successfully progressed into adult football from those who did not reach this level. The group differences could be identified at data collection fifteen years earlier.

In conclusion, it can be said that both cross-sectional and longitudinal studies with both adult and developing athletes indicate that motivational and self-regulatory personality factors seem to be important for current and future sport performance. The study results seem to suggest that the motivational personality (e.g., the achievement motive) factors are more stable whereas the self-regulatory skills (e.g., volitional skills) seem to show more room for development and enhancement during adolescence.

Several questions arise from the results presented above. These pertain to the questions: How can the development of self-regulatory personality factors be enhanced? How can one develop an athlete's personality in such a way that it will provide a good basis for stable performance? And, might it even be possible to change more stable personality characteristics like the achievement motive? In the next section we will discuss the role that the environment (e.g., an elite sport school) and different environmental agents (e.g., parents, sport psychologists) play in the positive personality development of young elite athletes.

Environmental influences

The role that the environment plays for talent development has received increased interest in the past years. The work of Henriksen and colleagues (Henriksen, Stambulova, & Roessler, 2010a, 2010b, 2011) has moved the focus away from the individual athlete and his or her personal characteristics and towards a holistic perspective focusing on the athlete and his/ her development within the context of the athletic and non-athletic environment. This work has shown how certain environments succeed in producing world-class athletes and how environments can be changed to work better (Larsen, Henriksen, Alfermann, & Christensen, 2014). It can be assumed that optimal environments can contribute to a positive personality development of talented athletes.

Elite sport schools

A very particular environment that has received increased interest in the past years is the school system for elite athletes, and here in particular, the sport boarding school. The question of how a school – specifically catering to talented athletes – affects their personality development was addressed in Beckmann, Elbe, Szymanski, and Ehrlenspiel's (2006) longitudinal elite sport school study. The research results showed that the specific environmental conditions had an influence on the young athlete's personality development. Developmental differences were, for example, determined by whether the athletic talents lived at home with their families or lived in the sport boarding school, where they were nearly constantly influenced by the athletic context. When the living conditions of the two groups of athletic students were compared, it could be shown that those living at the boarding school demonstrated a positive development of their self-regulatory skills (i.e., volition), whereas this was not the case for young athletes living at home. For the latter athletes, their self-regulatory skills decreased over the course of the investigation. Boarding-school students could evidently profit from this environment when it came to developing self-regulation. Interestingly, this socialization effect seemed to emerge directly after school enrolment (Szymanski, Beckmann, Elbe, & Müller, 2004). For the observed developmental advantages in those living at a boarding school, the introductory phase in the new environment of the sport school appeared to play a central role. Just living through and experiencing this period, which is often described as a time of crisis (cf. Cookson & Persell, 1985), is apparently not necessarily negative but, with regard to volition, even beneficial.

Caretakers

Life at the boarding school also offers the opportunity for interaction with further partners, who can contribute to a positive personality development. Here, the role of the caretakers in the boarding schools should not be neglected. Richartz (2002) showed the importance of caretakers in providing support, solving conflicts and developing competencies. Caretakers must be professionally trained and must devote much time to meeting the needs of the young elite athletes. Only under such conditions are they able to contribute to the athletes' personal growth. The caretakers represent valuable social interaction partners who, along with other adults like parents, teachers, and coaches, are important for delivering feedback according to the Systems Conditioning Model (Kuhl & Völker, 1998). The Systems Conditioning Model (Kuhl & Völker, 1998) describes how social interaction should be designed to enhance the development of self-regulation. The interaction needs to occur within a certain time window, and has to be responsive to and in concert with the child's needs. Once the individual expresses sadness or discouragement, for example, the interaction partner needs to address positive feelings and to encourage the child. The feedback has to fit the individual's needs at that certain moment. Only then can the young athlete make a connection between his or her self-system and the self-regulation system. If these specific socialization conditions are present, a favourable self-regulation is most likely developed.

Peers and leisure time

Another explanation for the positive development of volitional skills in those living at the boarding school can be attributed in part to the influence of peers and leisure-time activities with them. Especially when starting at such a school, those students living on campus need to invest more effort on building up new friendships in the boarding school, alongside their efforts in school and in training. They have to prove and assert themselves in the different domains, and evaluate and question their own position in these settings. It takes time and effort until the students can consider the contact with their peers as 'being together with friends'. Precisely during this time, a stronger contact with same-aged peers can be observed among those living in the boarding school. When asked about their leisure-time activities, those students living on campus indicated that they spent significantly more time together with friends than those students living at home with their parents (Elbe & Beckmann, 2002). This means that after joining the new school, those students who lived on campus spent more time with friends, but the students living at home, because of the time it takes to commute between home, school and training facilities, had less time to spend with friends. A relationship between the development of volitional skills and leisure-time activities can therefore be assumed. It seems that the sport boarding school offers the opportunity for spending more time with peers and offers favourable interactional spaces for the development of self-regulation. According to Kuhl and Kraska (1989) these new and challenging situations are the conditions for the development of a conflict-free self that enable efficient self-regulation. Cookson and Persell's (1985) study showed that boarding school inhabitants had a strong desire to find a group of friends rather quickly in order to acquire a feeling of belonging and security. This intense confrontation with one's social role (Sturzbecher & Lenz, 1997), which possibly takes place after entering the boarding school context, is favourable for volitional development. The integration into the new environment of the boarding school, which allowed the athletes to gain experience with social interaction, also included the inherent chance of failure. In addition, the boarding school offers more chances for interaction that is contingent with the athlete's needs. It can be concluded that the leisure-time activities and time with peers at the boarding school offer an opportunity for a favourable development in the area of self-regulation. However, it can also be assumed that both peers and leisure-time activities are also important for those athletes not attending an elite sport school and, in general, offer opportunities for positive personality development. Therefore one needs to ensure that young athletes have enough time for peer interactions and leisure-time activities, which can be a challenge when faced with long commuting times between home and the training facilities.

Parents

Parents are the most important and most influential agents during childhood (see Chapter 12 in this Handbook), and thus play a substantial role in structuring the motivational and self-regulatory personality development of their children (Keegan, Spray, Harwood, & Lavallee, 2014). It is believed, for example, that parents have a strong influence on the development of the achievement motive during early childhood (Heckhausen & Roelofson, 1962) as well as an influence on the achievement climate and overall motivational development (Harwood & Swain, 2002). Providing one's child with feedback according to Kuhl and Völker's (1998) Systems Conditioning Model can further the development of self-regulation. An upbringing that is overprotective or too controlling, on the other hand, can negatively influence personality development. Heim (2002) found that parents' relationship with their competitively active children is generally very supportive. However, he also described a less than optimal situation when the parents' expectations are too high. A 'demanding' parent–child relationship can have negative consequences and hinder the child's personality development. Harwood and Knight (2009) as well as Harwood and Swain (2002) have integrated parent coaching programmes into their consulting work with young athletes in order to enhance parental interactions. These coaching programmes provide parents with information about the challenges and stressors of being a youth sport parent (e.g., Harwood & Knight, 2009; Murray & Blom, 2012) and inform them about potential parent-related stressors for the coaches (Knight & Harwood, 2009). Furthermore, these programmes work on establishing guidelines for parent–coach interactions.

The sport psychologist

A change in personality factors can be brought about not only by good interactions within the social environments but also through systematic sport psychological interventions. A recently conducted literature review (Wikman, 2015) identified 37 studies describing the effects of different types of sport psychological interventions for young athletes. The studies showed a large variation in participants' age and performance level and targeted a wide range of dependent variables such as performance ($n = 19$), motivational variables ($n = 7$), efficacy-related variables ($n = 7$), anxiety ($n = 6$), and goal setting-related variables ($n = 4$) as the most frequent. In general, the studies indicated that training programmes can lead to a change in personality variables and improve sport performance.

Even motivational variables such as sport-specific achievement motives, which are perceived as relatively stable personality factors, can be changed via intervention programmes. Kleine (1980) and Wessling-Lünnemann (1985) showed that through training, a reduction of fear of failure and an increase in the hope for success component can be obtained. Wikman, Stelter, Melzer, Trier Hauge, and Elbe (2014) further demonstrated a significant reduction in fear of failure in young elite athletes by conducting goal-setting training over 12 weeks. Hence, in the case that young talents show high fear of failure, which is not an optimal predisposition for elite sports, systematic sport psychological training can bring about change. However, the study also showed that effects of goal setting decreased once the intervention stopped. It therefore seems that continued psychological skills training is necessary in order to bring about more sustainable change.

In addition to the training of specific personality characteristics, another important role of the sport psychologist is the regular monitoring and regulation of stress and recovery. An important factor for a healthy personality development is the amount and the quality of recovery. Insufficient recovery or too high stress levels can, in the long run, lead to unfavourable personality development. Furthermore, having enough leisure time is important for recovery but also allows time for the above-described important social interactions with peers. In the above-described elite sport school project, Elbe and Beckmann (2002) showed that ninth grade students attending a regular school had an average of 6.2 hours of leisure time during a weekday, whereas young elite athletes attending a sport school had an average of 3.8 hours of free time a day. In addition, the leisure activities that involve social interaction (e.g., spending time with friends, spending time with girlfriend/boyfriend) and which could contribute to personality growth, decreased from grade 7–9. Competitions and longer training sessions limited the young athletes' leisure time on weekends. Even during vacations, young athletes had less free time because they took part in training camps. This was especially the case in sports in which intensive training begins at a very young age (e.g., gymnastics) or in sports with large training loads (e.g., rowing, swimming, and triathlon). Athletes in team sports had more time available. Lack of free time can lead to under-recovery, stress, unfavourable personality development and ultimately to dropping out of competitive sports. The relevance of stress also became evident in the study that investigated young athletes' volitional development and dropout (Elbe et al., 2003a).

Stress and pressure were the main reasons for dropout. It became apparent that by trying to fulfil the demands of school and completing daily training, these athletes were experiencing too much stress. A person able to scientifically monitor the stress levels of young athletes is the sport psychologist. Continuous assessment of stress and recovery, and monitoring of the young athletes' personality development, is crucial in the effort to achieve athletic goals. In this way, negative developments can be identified at an early stage and solutions can be sought. Williams and Reilly (2000) state that, 'the prevention and detection of injury and overuse should be a constant concern in any system of selection and player development' (p. 663). Only this way can over-exertion and burnout be prevented. Long-term training with relaxation techniques can develop greater self-composure with regard to challenging training and competitive situations and can develop the perception that one can effectively deal with these situations (Beckmann & Kellmann, 2004). Even the tendency to ruminate over failures or to have problems in making decisions can be altered through learning programmes (Hartung & Schulte, 1994) and conversation-based interventions such as coaching (Stelter, Nielsen, & Wikman, 2011).

Conclusion

In conclusion, it seems that a wide array of psychological characteristics and skills are needed for successful talent development, in particular those skills falling under the umbrella terms motivation and self-regulation. Following the selection hypothesis, the young athletes that are naturally in possession of abundant motivation and self-regulation skills are the ones that stay in sport and become elite athletes. According to the socialization hypothesis as well as a nurturing approach to talent development, however, these characteristics and skills can be developed, and this should be a priority for those who have influence on the development of the athlete. Many environmental factors including parents, peers and the boarding school environment play roles in the development of young elite athletes and their psychological development. Paying attention to these influential environmental aspects as well as monitoring stress and recovery levels can contribute to healthy personality development, which then also can contribute to athletic performance and aid the long process of developing from a talented to an elite athlete. An optimal way to make sure that attention to the psychological factors of talent development is given is to seek the support of sport psychology consultants who are adequately educated and skilled in talent development.

References

Abbott, A., & Collins, D. (2004). Eliminating the dichotomy between theory and practice in talent identification and development: Considering the role of psychology. *Journal of Sport Sciences, 22,* 395–408.

Atkinson, J. W., & Birch, D. (1970). *A dynamic theory of action.* New York, NY: Wiley.

Beckmann, J., Elbe, A.-M., Szymanski, B., & Ehrlenspiel, F. (2006). *Chancen und Risiken vom Leben im Verbundsystem von Schule und Leistungssport – Psychologische, Soziologische und Leistungsaspekte* [Chances and risks of life in a school system for young elite athletes – Psychological, sociological and achievement aspects]. Köln: Sport und Buch Strauß.

Beckmann, J., & Kellmann, M. (2004). Self-regulation and recovery: Approaching an understanding of the process of recovery from stress. *Psychological Reports, 95,* 1135–1153.

Cookson, P. W., & Persell, C. H. (1985). *Preparing for power – American's elite boarding schools.* New York, NY: Basic Books.

Côté, J., Baker, J., & Abernethy, B. (2007). Practice and play in the development of sport expertise. In R. C. Eklund & G. Tenenbaum (eds), *Handbook of sport psychology* (3rd ed., pp. 184–202). Hoboken, NJ: Wiley.

Elbe, A.-M., & Beckmann, J. (2002). Lebenskonzepte für Sporttalente: Schlussfolgerungen und Perspektiven [Life concepts for athletic talents: Conclusions and perspectives]. In A.-M. Elbe & J. Beckmann (eds), *Dokumentation der 1. Tagung der Eliteschulen des Sports "Lebenskonzepte für Sporttalente"* (pp. 97–102). Frankfurt: DSB–Presse.

Elbe, A.-M., Beckmann, J., & Szymanski, B. (2003a). Das Dropout Phänomen an Eliteschulen des Sports – ein Problem der Selbstregulation? [The drop out phenomenon in young elite athletes – a problem of self-regulation?]. *Leistungssport, 33*(3), 46–49.

Elbe, A.-M., Beckmann, J., & Szymanski, B. (2003b). Entwicklung der allgemeinen und sportspezifischen Leistungsmotivation von SportschülerInnen [Development of the general and sport specific achievement motivation of young elite athletes]. *Psychologie und Sport, 10*, 134–143.

Elbe, A.-M., Madsen, C., & Midtgaard, J. (2010). A cross-cultural comparison of motivational factors in Kenyan and Danish middle and long distance elite runners. *Journal of Psychology in Africa, 20*, 421–428.

Elbe, A.-M., Szymanski, B., & Beckmann, J. (2005). The development of volition in young elite athletes. *Psychology of Sport and Exercise, 6*, 559–569.

Ericsson, K. A., Krampe, R. T., & Tesch-Römer, C. (1993). The role of deliberate practice in the acquisition of expert performance. *Psychological Review, 100*, 363–406.

Feichtinger, P., & Höner, O. (2015). Talented football player's development of achievement motives, volitional components, and self-referential cognitions: A longitudinal study. *European Journal of Sport Science*. Advance online publication.

Gabler, H. (1976). Zur Entwicklung von Persönlichkeitsmerkmalen bei Hochleistungssportlern [Development of personality traits in peak performance athletes]. *Sportwissenschaft, 6*, 247–276.

Gabler, H. (1995). Motivationale Aspekte sportlicher Handlungen [Motivational aspects of sport actions]. In H. Gabler, J. R. Nitsch, & R. Singer (eds), *Einführung in die Sportpsychologie* (pp. 64–102). Schorndorf: Hofmann.

Gagné, F. (2004). Transforming gifts into talents: the DMGT as a developmental theory. *High Ability Studies, 15*(2), 119–147.

Gill, D. L., & Deeter, T. E. (1988). Development of the Sport Orientation Questionnaire. *Research Quarterly for Exercise and Sport, 59*, 191–202.

Gould, D., Dieffenbach, K., & Moffett, A. (2002). Psychological characteristics and their development in Olympic champions. *Journal of Applied Sport Psychology, 14*, 172–204.

Hambrick, D. Z., MacNamara, B. N., Campitelli, G., Ullén, F., & Mosing, M. A. (2016). Beyond born versus made: A new look at expertise. In B. H. Ross (ed.), *The psychology of learning and motivation, 64*, 1–55. Elsevier Academic Press.

Hartung, J., & Schulte, D. (1994). Action- and state-orientations during therapy of phobic disorders. In J. Kuhl & J. Beckmann (eds), *Volition and personality: Action versus state orientation* (pp. 217–232). Seattle, WA: Hogrefe & Huber.

Harwood, C., & Knight, C. J. (2009). Understanding parental stressors: An investigation of British tennis-parents. *Journal of Sport Sciences, 27*, 339–351.

Harwood, C., & Swain, A. (2002). The development and activation of achievement goals within tennis: II. A player, parent, and coach intervention. *The Sport Psychologist, 16*, 111–137.

Heckhausen, H. (1988). *Motivation und Handeln* [Motivation and Action].Berlin, Heidelberg, New York: Springer-Verlag.

Heckhausen, H., & Roelofsen, I. (1962). Anfänge und Entwicklung der Leistungsmotivation. (i) im Wetteifer des Kleinkindes [Origins and development of achievement motivation. (I) The competitiveness of the young child]. *Psychologische Forschung, 26*, 313–397.

Heim, R. (2002). Entwicklung und Perspektiven sportpädagogischer Jugendforschung [Development and perspectives of sport pedagogical youth research]. In G. Friedrich (ed.), *Sportpädagogische Forschung* (pp. 31–50). Hamburg, Germany: Czwalina.

Hellandsig, E. T. (1998). Motivational predictors of high performance and discontinuation in different types of sports among talented teenage athletes. *International Journal of Sport Psychology, 29*, 27–44.

Henriksen, K., Stambulova, N., & Roessler, K. K. (2010a). Holistic approach to athletic talent development environments: A successful sailing milieu. *Psychology of Sport and Exercise, 11*, 212–222.

Henriksen, K., Stambulova, N., & Roessler, K. K. (2010b). Successful talent development in track and field: Considering the role of environment. *Scandinavian Journal of Medicine & Science in Sports, 20*, 122–132.

Henriksen, K., Stambulova, N., & Roessler, K. K. (2011). Riding the wave of an expert: A successful talent development environment in kayaking. *Sport Psychologist, 25*, 341–362.

Holland, M. J. G., Woodcock, C., Cumming, J., & Duda, J. L. (2010). Mental qualities and employed mental techniques of young elite team sport athletes. *Journal of Clinical Sport Psychology, 4,* 19–38.

Kavussanu, M., White, S. A., Jowett, S., & England, S. (2011). Elite and non–elite male footballers differ in goal orientation and perceptions of parental climate. *International Journal of Sport and Exercise Psychology, 9,* 284–290.

Keegan, R., Spray, C. M., Harwood, C. G., & Lavallee, D. E. (2014). A qualitative synthesis of research into social motivational influences across the athletic career span. *Qualitative Research in Sport, Exercise and Health, 6,* 537–567.

Kleine, W. (1980). *Leistungsmotivschulung im Grundschulsport. Eine motivationspsychologische Studie unter sport-pädagogischen Aspekten* [Improving achievement motivation in elementary physical education. A motivation psychological study with a sport pedagogical perspective]. Schorndorf: Hofmann.

Knight, C. J., & Harwood, C. (2009). Exploring parent – related coaching stressors in British tennis: A developmental investigation. *International Journal of Sports Science and Coaching, 4,* 545–585.

Kuhl, J. (1983). *Motivation, Konflikt und Handlungskontrolle* [Motivation, conflict and action control]. Berlin: Springer.

Kuhl, J. (1987). Motivation und Handlungskontrolle: Ohne guten Willen geht es nicht [Motivation and action control: It does not work without good will]. In H. Heckhausen, P. M. Gollwitzer, & F. E. Weinert (eds), *Jenseits des Rubikon: Der Wille in der Humanwissenschaft* [Beyond the Rubicon: The will in human sciences] (pp. 101–120). Berlin, Germany: Springer-Verlag.

Kuhl, J., & Kraska, K. (1989). Self-regulation and metamotivation: Computational mechanisms, development and assessment. In R. Kanfer, P. L. Ackermann, & R. Cudek (eds), *Abilities, motivation, and methodology: The Minnesota symposium on learning and individual differences* (pp. 343–374). Minnesota, MN: Erlbaum.

Kuhl, J., & Völker, S. (1998). Entwicklung und Persönlichkeit [*Development and personality*]. In H. Keller (ed.), *Lehrbuch der Entwicklungspsychologie* [Textbook of Developmental Psychology] (pp. 207–240). Bern: Huber.

Larsen, C. H., Alfermann, D., & Christensen, M. K. (2012). Psychological skills in a youth soccer academy: A holistic ecological perspective. *Sport Science Review, 21,* 51–74.

Larsen, C. H., Henriksen, K., Alfermann, D., & Christensen, M. K. (2014). Preparing footballers for the next step: An intervention program from an ecological perspective. *Sport Psychologist, 28,* 91–102.

MacNamara, Á., Button, A., & Collins, D. (2010). The role of psychological characteristics in facilitating the pathway to elite performance. Part 1: Identifying mental skills and behaviours. *The Sport Psychologist, 24,* 52–73.

Moesch, K., Hauge, M.-L. T., Wikman, J. M., & Elbe, A.-M. (2013). Making it to the top in team sports: Start later, intensify, and be determined! *Talent Development and Excellence, 5,* 85–100.

Murray, M., & Blom, L. C. (2012, March). *Creating effective partnerships with youth sport parents: A coaches' workshop.* Presented at the American Alliance for Health, Physical Education, Recreation and Dance convention, Boston, MA.

Reilly, T., Williams, A. M., Nevill, A., & Franks, A. (2000). A multidisciplinary approach to talent identification in soccer. *Journal of Sports Science, 18,* 695–702.

Richartz, A. (2002). Unterstützen – anregen – Konflikte bewältigen: Grundlagen einer modernen Internatspädagogik [Support – motivate – cope with conflicts: The basics of a modern boarding school pedagogy]. In A.-M. Elbe & J. Beckmann (eds), *Lebenskonzepte für Sporttalente* [Life concepts for sports talents] (pp. 54–66). Frankfurt: DSB Presse.

Sack, H.-G. (1980). *Zur Psychologie des jugendlichen Leistungssportlers* [Psychology of the young competitive athlete]. Schorndorf: Hofmann.

Sarkar, M., & Fletcher, D. (2014). Psychological resilience in sport performers: a review of stressors and protective factors. *Journal of Sport Sciences, 32,* 1419–1434.

Schneider, W., Bös, K., & Rieder, H. (1993). Leistungsprognose bei jugendlichen Spitzensportlern [Performance prediction in young top athletes]. In J. Beckmann, H. Strang, & E. Hahn (eds), *Aufmerksamkeit und Energetisierung. Facetten von Konzentration und Leistung* [Attention and energizing. Facets of concentration and performance] (pp. 277–299). Göttingen: Hogrefe.

Seidel, I. (2005). *Nachwuchsleistungssportler an Eliteschulen des Sports. Analyse ausgewählter Persönlichkeitsmerkmale in der Leichtathletik, im Handball und im Schwimmen* [Junior athletes in elite schools of sport: Analysis of selected personality dispositions in track and field athletics, handball and swimming]. Köln: Sport und Buch Strauß.

Seidel, I., & Hohmann, A. (1999). Ein Forschungsprojekt zum sportlichen Talent [A research project about athletic talent]. In J. Wiemeyer (eds), *Forschungsmethodologie in der trainings- und bewegungsforschung*, [Research methodology in training and movement science research] (pp. 351–355). Hamburg: Czwalina.

Singer, R. N., & Haase, H. (1975). Sport und Persönlichkeit [Sport and personality]. *Sportwissenschaft, 5*, 25–37.

Stambulova, N. B. (1994). Developmental sports career investigations in Russia. A post-perestroika analysis. *The Sport Psychologist, 8*, 221–237.

Stelter, R., Nielsen, G., & Wikman, J. M. (2011). Narrative-collaborative group coaching develops social capital – A randomised control trial and further implications of the social impact of the intervention. *Coaching: An International Journal of Theory, Research and Practice, 4*, 123–137.

Sturzbecher, D., & Lenz, H.-J. (1997). Wir woll'n Spaß, wir woll'n Spaß. Freizeitangebote in Brandenburg und ihre Nutzung [We want to have fun, we want to have fun. Leisure activities in Brandenburg and their utilization]. In D. Sturzbecher (ed.), *Jugend und Gewalt in Ostdeutschland. Lebenserfahrungen in Schule, Freizeit und Familie* [Youth and violence in East Germany. Life experiences in school, free time and family] (pp. 82–110). Göttingen: Verlag für Angewandte Psychologie.

Szymanski, B., Beckmann, J., Elbe, A.-M., & Müller, D. (2004). Wie entwickelt sich die Volition bei Talenten an einer Eliteschule des Sports? [How does volition develop in talents at an elite sport school?]. *Zeitschrift für Sportpsychologie, 11*(3), 103–111.

Toering, T. T., Elferink-Gemser, M. T., Jordet, G., & Visscher, C. (2009). Self-regulation and performance level of elite and non-elite youth soccer players. *Journal of Sports Sciences, 27*, 1509–1517.

Van Yperen, N. W. (2009). Why some make it and others do not: Identifying psychological factors that predict career success in professional soccer. *The Sport Psychologist, 23*, 317–329.

Wessling-Lünnemann, G. (1985). *Motivationsförderung im Unterricht* [Enhancing motivation in the classroom]. Göttingen: Hogrefe.

White, S. A., & Duda, J. L. (1994). The relationship of gender, level of sport involvement, and participation motivation to task and ego orientation. *International Journal of Sport Psychology, 25*, 4–18.

Wikman, J. M. (2015). *Development of an evidence-based sport psychological training program for young elite athletes*. (Doctoral thesis, Department of Nutrition, Exercise and Sports, University of Copenhagen, Copenhagen, Denmark).

Wikman, J. M., Stelter, R., Melzer, M., Trier Hauge, M.-L., & Elbe, A.-M. (2014). Effects of goal setting on fear of failure in young elite athletes. *International Journal of Sport and Exercise Psychology, 12*, 185–205.

Williams, A. M., & Reilly, T. (2000). Talent identification and development in soccer. *Journal of Sports Science, 18*, 657–667.

Wylleman, P., & Reints, A. (2010). A lifespan perspective on the career of talented and elite athletes: Perspectives on high-intensity sports. *Scandinavian Journal of Medicine & Science in Sports, 20*, 88–94.

Zuber, C., & Conzelmann, A. (2014). The impact of the achievement motive on athletic performance in adolescent football players. *European Journal of Sport Science, 14*, 475–483. doi:10.1080/17461391.2013.837513

Zuber, C., Zibung, M., & Conzelmann, A. (2015). Motivational patterns as an instrument for predicting success in promising young football players. *Journal of Sports Sciences, 33*, 160–168. doi:10.1080/02640414.2014.928827.

13

FAMILY INFLUENCES ON TALENT DEVELOPMENT IN SPORT

Camilla J. Knight

In 2013, Andy Murray won Wimbledon; after a 77-year wait, there was once again a British Wimbledon Men's Singles Champion. As Murray sealed his historic victory, the television cameras immediately panned to his supporters' box looking to capture the reactions of his coach, trainers, and now wife. But, most importantly, they wanted to see Andy's mother's reaction. Known as "Tennis's most famous mother," (Brown, 2015), Judy Murray has been Andy's most loyal and visible supporter throughout his professional career. She has been there when he has triumphed and when he has struggled, and her very visible reactions have been shared online and in print media around the world. However, when Andy won Wimbledon and ascended to the supporters' box to embrace his team there was one person he almost forgot. Had it not been for the shouts of "What about your mum!" from the crowd, Andy might well have descended back to the court without acknowledging the enduring and critical support of his mother. In today's society, when many athletes use trophy presentations as a platform from which they can thank their family for their never-ending support and parents are elevated to near celebrity status if their children succeed on the international stage, such a slip from Murray could not go unnoticed. Newspaper article after newspaper article gave space to Andy's "near miss" (e.g., Curtis, 2013) and even a year after the event, as the build up to Murray's title defense began, it was still being discussed (e.g., Malnick, 2014).

Such an intense focus on the interactions between one athlete and his mother are probably a little extreme. However, it does serve to highlight the substantial media attention that is being afforded to the role of the family within elite sport. In the scientific literature, the importance of the family in the development of talented athletes is also well recognized (Lauer, Gould, Roman, & Pierce, 2010a; Wuerth, Lee, & Alfermann, 2004). Family, and particularly parents, are explicitly included or discussed within all the major models of talent development used in sport (e.g., Bloom, 1985; Côté, Baker, & Abernethy, 2003; Gagné, 2000; Henricksen, Stambulova, & Roessler, 2010a, 2010b; Salmela, 1994) and researchers are continually seeking to extend our understanding of their influence (e.g., Gould, Lauer, Rolo, Jannes, & Pennisi, 2006, 2008; Lauer, Gould, Roman, & Pierce, 2010a, 2010b). To put it simply, we know that the "right" family environment, and particularly support from parents, can help talented athletes achieve at the elite level or at least reach their individual sporting potential. If the family support is "wrong" the negative consequences can be so great that talented athletes might burnout or drop out of sport before they have had the opportunity to succeed (e.g., Kay, 2000). Unfortunately, knowing what is "right" and what is "wrong" and, more importantly, being able to act on this knowledge and provide the necessary support to facilitate talent development is anything but simple.

The purpose of this chapter is to unpack the role of the family in the development of talented athletes, focusing on how the family can support or detract from this process. When considering the role of the family in talent development, it is important to note that the majority of literature has focused upon parents' influence rather than considering the influence of siblings or extended family (Horn & Horn, 2007; Partridge, Brustad, & Babkes Stellino, 2008). As such, the majority of this chapter will focus upon parents' involvement. The chapter will start with an overview of the positive and negative influences of parents in sport. Next, a detailed examination of the role of the family throughout the process of athletic development will be provided and the consequences of supporting a talented athlete will be discussed. The chapter will then conclude with suggestions for future research for exploring the complexity of family influence within talent development.

Influence of family involvement on talent development

The development of sporting talent is a complex and dynamic process, which is greatly influenced by the environment in which a young athlete is situated (Abbott & Collins, 2004; Martindale, Collins, & Abraham, 2007). Simply having the necessary attributes to succeed in sport is insufficient. Rather, as Csikszentmihalyi, Rathunde, and Whalen (1993) explained, talent development will only occur if the individual is located in an environment in which their talent is valued by society and also recognized and nurtured by parents, teachers, and coaches. The impact of the immediate environment, as well as the broader cultural and societal influences, on athletic development has received much support in recent years (e.g., Henriksen et al., 2010a, 2010b; Henriksen, Stambulova, & Roessler, 2011; Larsen, Alfermann, Henriksen, & Christensen, 2013). For example, the national value placed on a certain sport, the size of the city or town in which a child is born, the quality and availability of appropriate training and coaching, and the family resources available to invest in sport participation have all been shown to influence athletic development (Kay, 2000; MacNamara & Collins, 2012). In addition to having access to developmental opportunities, young athletes also need to have the necessary resources and capabilities to benefit from these opportunities (MacNamara, Button, & Collins, 2010a, 2010b). Family, and particularly parents, play an important role in facilitating children's access to opportunities and also the development of resources required to optimize their involvement in talent development environments (Pankhurst & Collins, 2013).

Positive consequences of parental involvement

Over the last 30 years, elite athletes and coaches have consistently reinforced the importance of the family in talent development (e.g., Carlson, 1988; Côté, 1999; Kay, 2000; Wuerth et al., 2004). For example, Gould, Dieffenbach, and Moffett (2002) explored the psychological characteristics of US Olympic champions and the sources of influence on the development of these characteristics. A range of psychological characteristics, such as ability to cope with and control anxiety, competitiveness, a hard-work ethic, and optimism, were identified and the development of these characteristics was attributed to numerous influences. Family was seen to be particularly influential, with different family members affecting development in different ways. For example, siblings influenced development by providing support, direct and indirect teaching, and offering feedback and critique as well as teasing and sibling rivalry. Grandparents were seen as important role models for active lifestyles and instilling positive and healthy values and attitudes. Parents' influence ranged from providing encouragement and support, to understanding sport, empathizing with athletes, and creating a positive achievement environment.

Reinforcing the findings of Gould and colleagues (2002), another study of Olympic and World champions revealed that the supportive and nurturing roles of parents and siblings, particularly when facing setbacks, were very important in maintaining an elite status in sport (Durand-Bush & Salmela, 2002). Further, parents' involvement and support has been attributed to the development of mental toughness among elite athletes (Connaughton, Wadey, Hanton, & Jones, 2008), and learning to perceive anxiety as facilitative instead of debilitative (Hanton & Jones, 1999). Parents have also been credited with, among other things, helping to foster intrinsic motivation, supporting the maintenance of self-confidence, developing positive attitudes towards sport including valuing effort and hard work, and enhancing athletes' enjoyment of sport (see Holt & Knight, 2014 for details). Such characteristics have been identified as critical in the development and achievement of an elite status in sport (MacNamara et al., 2010a, 2010b). Through their provision of tangible (e.g., time and money) and informational support, parents also ensure athletes have access to the necessary training, coaching and competition opportunities, are able to manage sporting transitions, feel supported in their sporting endeavors, and maintain balance in their lives (Bloom, 1985; Côté, 1999; Fredricks & Eccles, 2004; Gould et al., 2006, 2008; Wolfenden & Holt, 2005).

Negative consequences of parental involvement

However, although elite athletes frequently describe the positive influence their parents had on their development, some parents have been shown to have a negative or detrimental influence on athletic development (Gould et al., 2006, 2008; Lauer et al., 2010a, 2010b). For example, a survey of 250 US tennis coaches revealed that, although 58.6 percent of coaches thought parents had a positive influence on development, 35.9 percent of parents were perceived to hurt or hinder children's tennis development (Gould et al., 2006). Such a detrimental influence is usually attributed to parental behaviors that result in athletes experiencing pressure (Gould et al., 2006, 2008). Such parental pressure can arise from an excessive emphasis on winning, holding unrealistic expectations for their child, withdrawing love, or using punitive behaviors (e.g., Gould et al., 2006, 2008; Lauer et al., 2010a, 2010b; Woolger, & Power, 2000). When athletes' perceive high levels of parental pressure, it can result in athletes developing a fear of failure, high levels of pre-competitive anxiety and perceived stress, lower self-esteem and self-confidence and negatively influence perceptions of competence and intrinsic motivation (Holt & Knight, 2014). Parents can also negatively influence children's sporting development by interfering in training, being too controlling, and taking sport too seriously (Gould et al., 2006, 2008; Lauer et al., 2010a, 2010b). Further, by encouraging excessive amounts of training and pressuring children to improve and win, children can experience overuse injuries or burnout (Gould, Wilson, Tuffey, & Lochbaum, 1993). Overall, such involvement from parents can lead to children dropping out of sport and not reaching their sporting potential (Harwood & Knight, 2015).

Influence of siblings

When considering the overall influence of siblings within the development of talented athletes, they again appear to have the potential to positively or negatively influence athletes (Harwood, Douglas, & Minniti, 2012; Horn & Horn, 2007). For example, in a number of studies, elite athletes have credited their siblings with being role models to their involvement and effort and encouraging them to participate in sport (e.g., Bloom, 1985; Côté, 1999). Further, some siblings provided support to athletes and celebrated their successes and achievements (Gould et al., 2002). However, due to the need to prioritize athletes' training and competition and invest large amounts of finance into athletes' participation, issues of sibling jealousy and rivalry could arise (Côté, 1999; Taylor & Collins, 2015). Such feelings might detract from athletes' development as they are distracted or concerned about negative interactions with their siblings, but in some instances sibling rivalries further motivate athletes to succeed (Partridge et al., 2008; Harwood et al., 2012). Finally, older sibling's sport participation can also be the "testbed" for young siblings, providing parents with an opportunity to develop an understanding of what is required and how to act in different situations (Knight, Dorsch, Osai, Haderlie, & Sellars, 2016; Knight & Holt, 2013). Thus, parents might be better positioned to support the talent development of their younger children.

Family influence throughout athletic development

As detailed earlier (cf. Chapters 10 and 11 in this Handbook), talent development is a process that is complex, messy, dynamic, and individual (Martindale, Collins, & Daubney, 2005). Similarly, the roles, involvement, and influence of the family in supporting athletes' development are idiographic, changeable, and multi-faceted (Gould et al., 2008; Lauer et al., 2010a, 2010b; Wuerth et al., 2004). The previous section highlighted the overall positive and negative influence of parents and siblings on talent development. However, the specific ways in which the family influences athletic development shift as athlete's progress through different stages of their career (e.g., Bloom, 1985; Côté, 1999; Salmela, 1994; Wylleman & Lavallee, 2004). Managing these changes over the course of their child's development, and fulfilling the appropriate roles at the correct times appears particularly important in helping athletes reach their potential (Harwood & Knight, 2015).

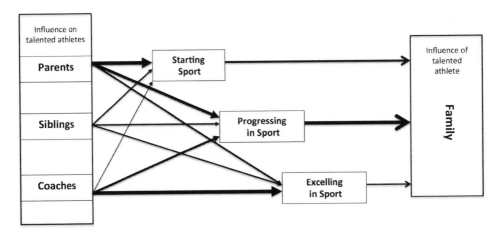

Figure 13.1 Summary of social influences on, and subsequent family consequences of, developing talented athletes. The weight of the arrow provides an estimation of the degree of influence individuals have on the talented athlete as they develop and the subsequent influence their sporting involvement has on the family

Starting sport

The first step in the process of talent development is children becoming involved in sport. During this initial stage (termed, among others, as the initiation or sampling stage; Bloom, 1985; Côté, 1999; Salmela, 1994; Wylleman & Lavallee, 2004), parents are critical. If parents do not value involvement in sport, or do not have the financial means to provide sporting opportunities, the likelihood of children participating is low (Baxter-Jones & Maffuli, 2003; Tranckle & Cushion, 2006). It is important that parents value sport participation, not only because children depend upon their parents to sign them up to play different sports, transport them to training, and fund their participation (Baxter-Jones & Maffulli, 2003; Bloom, 1985, Côté, 1999; Salmela, 1994), but also because parents' attitudes towards sport are often mirrored by children (Jodl, Michael, Malanchuk, Eccles, & Sameroff, 2001). Consequently, if parents do not value sport, it is unlikely children will be provided with opportunities to pursue sport or develop positive attitudes towards participation.

If parents do introduce their children to sport, they must then make a number of decisions that could subsequently enhance or reduce the potential for their children to excel in sport. One of the most important decisions parents are likely to make at the outset of their children's sporting career pertains to what and how many sports their children will participate in (Harwood & Knight, 2015). It is common for parents to introduce their children to the same sports in which they participated (Carlson, 2011; Wuerth et al., 2004). Such a decision can be beneficial because parents will likely be better positioned to understand the system and thus, make more informed decisions regarding training and competition requirements (Knight et al., in press; Knight & Holt, 2014). Similarly, choosing to introduce younger children into the same sport as older siblings can be beneficial because older siblings will act as motivators to participation (Morgan & Giacobbi, 2006; Young & Pearce, 2011) and parents will have started to learn what is needed to help children succeed in these sports (Knight & Holt, 2013). However, introducing children to sports they previously participated in might lead to parents expecting more from their children or struggling to separate their and their child's experience, which might lead to children dropping out (cf. Fraser-Thomas, Côté, & Deakin, 2008).

Parents must also choose how many sports children participate in and the type of training/activities to prioritize (Harwood & Knight, 2015). Most literature points to the importance of children sampling a range of sports for a number of years to reduce the risks of injury or burnout that can arise from early specialization (Baker, 2003). Thus, parents providing opportunities for children to sample a range of sports in an enjoyable and playful manner is most likely to facilitate talent development (Harwood & Knight, 2015; Holt & Knight, 2014). However, parents' decisions will be guided by those around them, particularly coaches and other parents, whose knowledge might vary in accuracy (Knight & Holt, 2013; Pankhurst, Collins, & MacNamara, 2013). Ultimately parents have to decide what information to use and what to discard when making the final decision regarding their children's participation (Martindale et al., 2007).

Having made these decisions, parents must then provide tangible support to help their child participate and progress. This tangible support includes transporting children to different opportunities, purchasing equipment and clothing, paying for coaching, and in some instances coaching their child (Bloom, 1985; Côté, 1999; Wolfenden & Holt, 2005). Parents also play an important role in sharing in their child's excitement and enjoyment (Wuerth et al., 2004), initiating a love of sport (Martindale et al., 2005), and integrating sport within family life (Côté, 1999). Parents also foster important attitudes and behaviors regarding sport in young children (Fredricks & Eccles, 2004), such as appropriate responses to winning, good sportspersonship, the importance of trying one's hardest, and the development of a growth mindset (see Harwood et al., 2012; MacNamara et al., 2010b). Such behaviors and attitudes can be encouraged through parents demonstrating such attitudes themselves and the provision of feedback and support that reinforces these values to children (Fredricks & Eccles, 2004).

Progressing in sport

As child-athletes progress in sport (entering the middle years, Bloom, 1985; specializing stage, Côté, 1999; Developmental stage, Wylleman & Lavellee, 2004), the enduring attitude of their parents towards sport, and particularly the value they place on developing talent, will influence their commitment to their child's sport and athletic development (Jodl et al., 2001). Parents display their commitment to, and support for, their child's athletic endeavors by continuing to provide tangible support in the form of transport and funding (Bloom, 1985; Côté, 1999; Kay, 2000; Lauer et al., 2010a, 2010b). Such tangible support is required to ensure child-athletes can access the necessary training and competitions to develop and have the right equipment and clothing (Wolfenden & Holt, 2005).

One important consideration for parents' pertaining to their provision of tangible (and to a lesser extent emotional) support is how their children perceive such an investment (cf. Clarke, Harwood, & Cushion, 2016). The investment parents make in their children's sport can necessitate changes to their own lifestyle, such as reducing working hours, limiting their social life, spending disproportionate amounts of time with different children, and limiting family holidays (Harwood & Knight, 2009a, 2009b; Kay, 2000; Morgan & Giacobbi, 2006). Such a commitment from parents can inadvertently result in parents' pressuring children (or children perceiving pressure) to succeed so parents gain a return on their investment (Gould et al., 2006, 2008). If children feel such pressure it will likely have detrimental influences on their development. Additionally, the financial and time investment into one child over their siblings can result in jealousy or resentment within the family (Côté, 1999) and feelings of guilt for the parents (Harwood & Knight, 2009a, 2009b). Being aware of such potential issues and developing strategies to manage these concerns will facilitate a smoother development process (Harwood & Knight, 2015).

Parents also increase the emotional support they provide to their child-athlete during this stage (Côté et al., 2003). Such emotional support is particularly important in helping child-athletes maintain their motivation in the face of setbacks (Fraser-Thomas et al., 2008; Gould et al., 2008; Lauer et al., 2010a). However, providing the appropriate types of emotional support to child-athletes is complex (cf. Knight, Boden, & Holt, 2010; Knight, Neely, & Holt, 2011). Recent studies have sought to unpack parental involvement to identify how parents can best support athletic development during early-mid adolescence (e.g., Holt et al., 2009; Knight & Holt, 2014; Knight et al., 2010, 2011). Findings from such research has pointed to the importance of considering not just the individual behaviors parents display or the practices they engage in, but also the broader emotional climate created by parents or the parenting style they adopt (Harwood & Knight, 2015; Knight & Holt, 2014). Further, the importance of parents and children having shared goals for involvement appears fundamental to ensuring the support provided to children is appreciated by, and beneficial for, athletes (Knight & Holt, 2014).

A key component within this stage of talent development is the relationship between parents and coaches (e.g., Côté, 1999; Wolfenden & Holt, 2005). As described, parents are very important and highly engaged in their child-athlete's sporting life during this stage (Harwood et al., 2012). But, coach involvement, feedback, and guidance are also increasingly important (Bloom, 1985; Côté, 1999), and parents need to make space for the coach to do their job (Lauer et al., 2010a, 2010b). Given the importance of the coach during this stage, the parents' role in selecting an appropriate coach who can guide their child's development (cf. Knight & Holt, 2013) and then maintaining an appropriate working relationship with this coach is vital to ensuring the child is receiving the best support and guidance (Harwood & Knight, 2015). If parents are unable to develop a positive relationship with their child's coach it could result in a breakdown in the coach–athlete relationship and negatively impact the child's development (Holt & Knight, 2014). Thus, by committing time and effort to the selection of the coach and the development of a positive working relationship, parents can ensure they maximize opportunities for their child to excel in sport.

Excelling in sport

Once athletes move into the final stage of development (Later years: Bloom 1985; Investment stage: Côté, 1999; Mastery stage: Wylleman & Lavallee, 2004), the influence of the family changes again (Durand-Bush & Salmela, 2002; Morgan & Giacobbi, 2006). Parents continue to be important and impact athletes' development through the provision of emotional and tangible support, but a reduction in direct parental involvement has been noted (Durand-Bush & Salmela, 2002; Morgan & Giacobbi, 2006; Salmela, 1994; Wuerth et al., 2004). Such a reduction in direct involvement may arise due to athletes moving away from home and/or because the coach's leadership role further increases.

Nevertheless, parents still play an important role in helping athletes make decisions regarding the future, particularly relating to decisions about education or work (Christensen & Sørensen, 2009). For some athletes, decisions regarding full-time versus part-time school or moving to academies might have occurred during earlier stages of their career; however, the final stage of athletic development often coincides with the end of compulsory schooling (Wylleman & Lavallee, 2004) so decisions regarding the pursuit of a full-time sporting career or maintaining a dual career (either in a job or education) move to the forefront of athletes and parents' minds (Wylleman & Lavallee, 2004). Family support and guidance is important for helping athletes to make the decisions that will best suit their sporting and holistic development. Such support could take a variety of forms, ranging from providing guidance and sharing information, to understanding and supporting decisions (e.g., Bloom, 1985; Côté, 1999; Durand-Bush & Salmela, 2002).

Managing the transition into elite level or professional sport, which usually occurs during this stage, can also necessitate substantial emotional support from parents. Such a transition can be very difficult for athletes, with data indicating that only 15–35 percent of athletes successfully manage it (Oldenziel, Gagné, & Gulbin, 2003; Vanden Auweele, De Martelaer, Rzewnicki, De Knop, & Wylleman, 2004). Parental and sibling support is likely a key environmental factor influencing the success of this transition, particularly if athletes are facing adversity or setbacks (Giacobbi & Morgan, 2006; Udry, Gould, Bridgers, & Tuffey, 1997).

Impact on families of supporting talented athletes

Supporting the development of talented athletes is not always an easy task (Knight & Holt, 2013). Recognizing the potential impacts of supporting talent athletes, and the need to ensure that families are supported in their attempts to help their children develop, researchers have recently begun to put their focus on the parents themselves (Holt & Knight, 2014). For example, Wiersma and Fifer (2008) identified that parents found providing emotional and instrumental support to their children particularly challenging. The provision of instrumental support was challenging due to the consequences it had on general family life and parents' ability to fulfill other parenting responsibilities (such as organizing dinner, helping with homework, and getting children to bed on time). Challenges associated with providing emotional support arose because parents were unsure of how to support their children in difficult situations, such as when children had been unsuccessful, if they were not as good as the other players on their team, or did not want to commit to a team for an entire season.

Further, Harwood and Knight (2009a, 2009b) surveyed 123 parents and completed interviews with a further 22 parents of tennis-playing children about the stressors they encountered when supporting their children's involvement. Parents reported numerous stressors ranging from competitions, to sibling resentment and inequality of attention, to issues with the organization. Overall, the stressors were categorized into competition stressors (e.g., watching matches, logistical concerns), organizational stressors (e.g., financial concerns, time issues), and developmental stressors (e.g., tennis progression, academic concerns). Different stressors were more prevalent during different stages of athletic development.

The transitions associated with athletes' development appear to be associated with particular challenges for parents (Clarke & Harwood, 2014; Dorsch, Smith, & McDonough, 2009; Lally & Kerr, 2008). For example, Clarke and Harwood (2014) explored parents' experiences of their children's transition into elite football (soccer) academies in the UK. This transition had many positive consequences for parents, such as enhanced parental status due to their child's success in gaining an academy place. However, negative implications for parents were also apparent, including frustration resulting from a decreased sense of agency, limited communication from coaches, and anticipatory fear of their child being cut. Concerns have also been raised by parents once their children leave elite sport (Lally & Kerr, 2008). Parents of former national/international-level gymnasts reported experiencing lingering doubts regarding the long-term impact of negative coach behaviours, their daughters' gymnastics participation on their families, their daughters' limited social interactions outside of gymnastics, and their daughters' experiences of chronic pain. Unfortunately, despite the developing awareness of the consequences parents and families can encounter when supporting talented athletes, strategies to address or minimise such challenges are still limited (Harwood & Knight, 2015).

Areas for future research

There has been a rapid increase in research examining parental involvement in youth sport over the last decade (Holt & Knight, 2014). Such research is beginning to provide an understanding of the complex and intricate nature in which parents can positively and negatively influence the process of talent development. However, there are still many areas that warrant further investigation and application in practice (Taylor & Collins, 2015). With regards to parental involvement in talent development, there is a continuing need to better understand what support parents need in order to be able to help their elite athletes succeed (Knight & Holt, 2013) and how parents can support athletes as they navigate key transition points (Harwood & Knight, 2015). Further, continuing to develop our understanding of the challenges parents encounter and, most importantly, how they deal with these challenges, is of particular importance given the increasing demands parents face (Holt & Knight, 2014).

There is also a desperate need for research considering the influence of the extended family in talent development and particularly the influence of siblings (Horn & Horn, 2007; Taylor & Collins, 2015). Parents are heavily reliant upon their support network to be able to help their children develop (Knight & Holt, 2013), so enhancing our understanding of how the family unit works together to support talented athletes, and how such support can be maximized, is vital to improve the development process. Such an understanding is particularly important when considering the varied structure of families in current society (Kay, 2000; Knight & Holt, 2013). The majority of research considering the family or parent influence in talent development has focused upon nuclear families. However, children may be part of single-parent families or stepfamilies, which, for some, could result in them moving between homes and parents. Further, some children might have no extended family and others might have large families. Exploring how these various family structures influence the talent development process and, most importantly, how these families work to support talented athletes, would provide much needed insight to help ensure all talented athletes, no matter what their family structure, are able to access the necessary support to reach their potential.

References

Abbott, A., & Collins, D. (2004). Eliminating the dichotomy between theory and practice in talent identification and development: Considering the role of psychology. *Journal of Sports Sciences, 22*, 395–408.

Baker, J. (2003). Early specialization in youth sport: a requirement for adult expertise? *High Ability Studies, 14*, 85–94.

Baxter-Jones, A. D. G., & Maffuli, N. (2003). Parental influence on sport participation in elite young athletes. *Journal of Sports Medicine and Physical Fitness, 43*, 250–255.

Bloom, B. (1985). *Developing talent in young people*. New York, NY: Ballantine Books.

Brown, O. (2015). Judy Murray: "I used to enjoy Wimbledon but the pressure on Andy makes it too stressful." Retrieved from www.telegraph.co.uk/sport/tennis/andymurray/11700515/Judy-Murray-I-used-to-enjoy-Wimbledon-but-the-pressure-on-Andy-makes-it-too-stressful.html

Carlson, R. C. (1988). The socialization of elite tennis players in Sweden: An analysis of the players' backgrounds and development. *Sociology of Sport Journal, 5*, 241–256.

Carlson, R. (2011). Talent detection and competitive progress in biathlon – a national example. *Polish Journal of Sport and Tourism, 18*, 290–295.

Christensen, M. K., & Sørensen, J. K. (2009). Sport or school? Dreams and dilemmas for talented young Danish football players. *European Physical Education Review, 15*, 115–133.

Clarke, N. J., & Harwood, C. G. (2014). Parenting experiences in elite youth football: A phenomenological study. *Psychology of Sport & Exercise, 15*, 528–537.

Clarke, N. J., Harwood, C. G., & Cushion, C. J. (2016). A phenomenological interpretation of the parent-child relationship in elite youth football. *Sport, Exercise, and Performance Psychology, 5*, 125–143.

Connaughton, D., Wadey, R., Hanton, S., & Jones, G. (2008). The development and maintenance of mental toughness: Perceptions of elite performers. *Journal of Sports Sciences, 26*, 83–95.

Côté, J. (1999) The influence of family in the development of talent in sport. *The Sport Psychologist, 13*, 395–417.

Coté, J., Baker, J., & Abernethy, B. (2003). From play to practice: A developmental framework for the acquisition of expertise in team sport. In J. Starkes and K. A. Ericsson (eds), *Expert performance in sports: Advances in research on sport expertise* (pp. 89–114). Champaign, IL: Human Kinetics.

Csikszentmihalyi, M., Rathunde, K., & Whalen, S. (1993). *Talented teenagers: The roots of success and failure*. New York: Cambridge.

Curtis, B. (2013). Andy Murray Wimbledon win: Watch champion forget to embrace mum Judy as he jumps into the crowd. Retrieved from www.mirror.co.uk/sport/tennis/andy-murray-wimbledon-win-watch-2036667

Dorsch, T. E., Smith, A. L., & McDonough, M. H. (2009). Parents' perceptions of child-to-parent socialization in organized youth sport. *Journal of Sport and Exercise Psychology, 31*, 444–468.

Durand-Bush, N., & Salmela, J. H. (2002). The development and maintenance of expert athletic performance: Perceptions of World and Olympic champions. *Journal of Applied Sport Psychology, 14*, 154–171.

Fraser-Thomas, J., Côté, J., & Deakin, J. (2008). Examining adolescent sport dropout and prolonged engagement from a developmental perspective. *Journal of Applied Sport Psychology, 20*, 318–333.

Fredricks, J. A., & Eccles, J. S. (2004). Parental influences on youth involvement in sports. In M.R.Weiss (ed.) *Developmental sport and exercise psychology: A lifespan perspective* (pp. 145–164). Morgantown, WV: Fitness Information Technology, Inc.

Gagné, F. (2000). Understanding the complete choreography of talent development through DMGT-based analysis. In K. A. Keller (ed.), *International handbook of giftedness and talent* (2nd ed., pp. 67–79). Oxford, UK: Elsevier Science.

Gould, D., Dieffenbach, K., & Moffett, A. (2002). Psychological talent and their development in Olympic champions. *Journal of Applied Sport Psychology, 14,* 172–204.

Gould, D., Lauer, L., Rolo, C., Jannes, C., & Pennisi, N. (2006). Understanding the role parents play in tennis success: A national survey of junior tennis coaches. *British Journal of Sports Medicine, 40,* 632–636.

Gould, D., Lauer, L., Rolo, C., Jannes, C., & Pennisi, N. (2008). The role of parents in tennis success: Focus group interviews with junior coaches. *The Sport Psychologist, 22,* 18–37.

Gould, D., Wilson, C. G., Tuffey, S., & Lochbaum, M. (1993). Stress and the young athlete: The child's perspective. *Pediatric Exercise Science, 5,* 286–286.

Hanton, S., & Jones, G. (1999). The acquisition and development of cognitive skills and strategies: I. Making the butterflies fly in formation. *The Sport Psychologist, 13,* 1–21.

Harwood, C. G, Douglas, J, & Minniti, A. (2012). Talent development: The role of the family. In S. Murphy (ed.), *The Oxford handbook of sport and performance psychology* (pp. 476–492). New York: Oxford University Press.

Harwood, C.G., & Knight, C.J. (2009a). Stress in youth sport: A developmental examination of tennis parents. *Psychology of Sport and Exercise, 10,* 447–456.

Harwood, C.G., & Knight, C.J. (2009b). Understanding parental stressors: An investigation of British tennis players. *Journal of Sports Sciences, 27,* 339–351.

Harwood, C. G., & Knight, C. J. (2015). Parenting in youth sport: A position paper on parenting expertise. *Psychology in Sport and Exercise, 16,* 24–35.

Henriksen, K., Stambulova, N., & Roessler, K. K. (2010a). A holistic approach to athletic talent development environments: A successful sailing milieu. *Psychology of Sport and Exercise, 11,* 212–222.

Henriksen, K., Stambulova, N., & Roessler, K. K. (2010b). Successful talent development in track and field: considering the role of environment. *Scandinavian Journal of Medicine & Science in Sports, 20,* 122–132.

Henriksen, K., Stambulova, N., & Roessler, K. K. (2011). Riding the wave of an expert: A successful talent development environment in Kayaking. *The Sport Psychologist, 25,* 341–362.

Holt, N. L., & Knight, C. J. (2014). *Parenting in youth sport: From research to practice.* Abingdon: Routledge.

Holt, N. L., Tamminen, K.A., Black, D. E., Mandigo, J. L., & Fox, K. R. (2009). Youth sport parenting styles and practices. *Journal of Sport and Exercise Psychology, 31,* 37–59.

Horn, T. S., & Horn, J. L. (2007). Family influences on children's sport and physical activity participation, behaviour, and psychosocial responses. In Tenenbaum, G., & Eklund, R. (eds). *Handbook of sport psychology* (3rd ed., pp. 685–711). Hoboken, NJ: Wiley & Sons Inc.

Jodl, K. M., Michael, A., Malanchuk, O., Eccles, J. S., & Sameroff, A. (2001). Parents' roles in shaping early adolescents' occupational aspirations. *Child Development, 72,* 1247–1265.

Kay, T. (2000). Sporting excellence: A family affair? *European Physical Education Review, 6,* 151–169.

Knight, C. J., Boden, C. M., & Holt, N. L. (2010). Junior tennis players' preferences for parental behaviors. *Journal of Applied Sport Psychology, 22,* 377–391.

Knight, C. J., Dorsch, T. E., Osai, K. V., Haderlie, K. L., & Sellars, P. A. (2016). Parents' experiences, expectations, and involvement in organized youth sport. *Sport, Exercise, and Performance Psychology, 5,* 161–178.

Knight, C. J., & Holt, N. L. (2013). Strategies used and assistance required to facilitate children's involvement in competitive tennis: Parents' perspectives. *The Sport Psychologist, 27,* 281–291.

Knight, C. J., & Holt, N. L. (2014). Parenting in youth tennis: Understanding and enhancing children's experiences. *Psychology of Sport and Exercise, 15,* 155–164.

Knight, C. J., Neely, K. C., & Holt, N. L. (2011). Parental behaviors in team sports: How do female athletes want parents to behave? *Journal of Applied Sport Psychology, 23,* 76–92.

Lally, P., & Kerr, G. (2008). The effects of athlete retirement on parents. *Journal of Applied Sport Psychology, 20,* 42–56.

Larsen, C. H., Alfermann, D., Henriksen, K., & Christensen, M. K. (2013). Successful talent development in soccer: the characteristics of the environment. *Sport, Exercise, and Performance Psychology, 2,* 190–206.

Lauer, L., Gould, D., Roman, N., & Pierce, M. (2010a). Parental behaviors that affect junior tennis player development. *Psychology of Sport and Exercise, 11,* 487–496.

Lauer, L., Gould, D., Roman, N., & Pierce, M. (2010b). How parents influence junior tennis players' development: Qualitative narratives. *Journal of Clinical Sports Psychology, 4,* 69–92

MacNamara, Á., Button, A., & Collins, D. (2010a). The role of psychological characteristics in facilitating the pathway to elite performance. Part 1: Identifying mental skills and behaviours. *The Sport Psychologist, 24,* 52–73.

MacNamara, Á., Button, A., & Collins, D. (2010b). The role of psychological characteristics in facilitating the pathway to elite performance. Part 2: Examining environmental and stage related differences in skills and behaviours. *The Sport Psychologist, 24,* 74–96.

MacNamara, Á., & Collins, D. (2012). Building talent development systems on mechanistic principles: Making them better at what makes them good. In. J. Baker, S. Cobley, & J. Schorer (eds), *Talent identification and talent development in sport: international perspectives.* Abingdon: Routledge.

Malnick, E. (2014). Why Andy Murray forgot his mother Judy after Wimbledon win. Retrieved from www.telegraph.co.uk/sport/tennis/andymurray/10917337/Why-Andy-Murray-forgot-his-mother-Judy-after-Wimbledon-win.html.

Martindale, R. J. J., Collins, D., & Abraham, A. (2007). Effective talent development: The elite coach perspective in UK sport. *Journal of Applied Sport Psychology, 19,* 187–206.

Martindale, R. J. J., Collins, D., & Daubney, J. (2005). Talent development: A guide for practice and research within sport. *Quest, 25,* 353–375.

Morgan, T. K., & Giacobbi, P. R. (2006). Towards two grounded theories of the talent development and social support process of highly successful collegiate athletes. *The Sport Psychologist, 20,* 295–313.

Oldenziel, K., Gagné, F., & Gulbin, J. (2003). How do elite athletes develop? A look through the 'rearview mirror' [A preliminary report from the National Athlete Development Survey (NADS)]. Canberra: Australian Sports Commission.

Pankhurst, A., & Collins, D. (2013). Talent identification and development: The need for coherence between research, system, and process. *Quest, 65,* 83–97.

Pankhurst, A., Collins, D., & MacNamara, Á. (2013). Talent development: Linking the stakeholders to the process. *Journal of Sports Sciences, 31,* 370–380.

Partridge, J. A., Brustad, R. J., & Babkes Stellino, M. (2008). Social influences in sport. In T. S. Horn (ed.), *Advances in sport psychology* (3rd ed., pp. 269–292). Champaign, IL: Human Kinetics.

Salmela, J. H. (1994). Phases and transitions across sport careers. In D. Hackfort (ed.), *Psych-social issues and interventions in elite sports* (pp. 11–28). Frankfurt: Lang.

Taylor, R. D., & Collins, D. (2015). Reviewing the family unit as a stakeholder in talent development: is it undervalued? *Quest, 67,* 330–343.

Tranckle, P., & Cushion, C. J. (2006). Rethinking giftedness and talent in sport. *Quest, 58,* 265–282.

Udry, E., Gould, D., Bridges, D., & Tuffey, S. (1997). People helping people? Examining the social ties of athletes coping with burnout and injury stress. *Journal of Sport and Exercise Psychology, 19,* 368–395.

Vanden Auweele, Y., De Martelaer, K., Rzewnicki, R., De Knop, P., & Wylleman, P. (2004). Parents and coaches. A help or a harm? Affective outcome for children in sport. In Y. Vanden Auweele (ed.), *Ethics in youth sport.* Leuven, Belgium: Laannoocampus.

Wiersma, L. D., & Fifer, A. M. (2008). "The schedule has been tough but we think it's worth it": The joys, challenges, and recommendations of youth sport parents. *Journal of Leisure Research, 40,* 505–530.

Wolfenden, L.E., & Holt, N. L. (2005). Talent Development in Elite Junior Tennis: Perceptions of players, parents and coaches. *Journal of Applied Sport Psychology, 17,* 108–126.

Woolger, C., & Power, T.G. (2000). Parenting and children's intrinsic motivation in age group swimming. *Journal of Applied Developmental Psychology, 21,* 595–607.

Wuerth, S., Lee, M. J., & Alfermann, D. (2004). Parental involvement and athletes' career in youth sport. *Psychology of Sport and Exercise, 5,* 21–33.

Wylleman, P., & Lavallee, D. (2004). A developmental perspective on transitions faced by athletes. In M. Weiss (ed.), *Developmental sport and exercise psychology: A lifespan perspective,* (pp. 507–527). Morgantown, WV: Fitness Information Technology.

Young, J. A., & Pearce, A. J. (2011). The influence of parents in identifying and developing Australian female tennis talent. *Journal of Medicine and Science in Tennis, 17,* 22–27.

14

UNDERSTANDING ENVIRONMENTAL AND TASK CONSTRAINTS ON TALENT DEVELOPMENT

Analysis of micro-structure of practice and macro-structure of development histories

Keith Davids, Arne Güllich, Richard Shuttleworth and Duarte Araújo

Introduction

A range of personal, task and environmental constraints impinges on performance and learning during athlete development at different, related, timescales. A problem with current research on skill acquisition, expert performance and talent development in sport is that they typically proceed along distinct investigatory strands along different timescales of analysis. These focus separately on: (i) the *macro-structure* of developmental participation histories (e.g., estimating time spent in deliberate practice or unstructured play during prolonged periods of development); and (ii), the contexts of the *micro-structure* of practice (e.g., analysis over shorter timescales on the constraints of the tasks undertaken and the performance goals achieved in each session). Here we consider how the development of an athlete, through sporting activity in practice and competitive performance, has both a macro- and a contextual micro-structure that needs to be analysed at these shorter and longer timescales. Analyses of developmental activities have diverged in current scientific research. Understanding development of expertise in a talented individual requires analysis of larger 'granules' (macro-structure), plotting developmental trajectories of athletes over many years. Analysis of motor learning on the other hand (e.g., performance during and between individual practice sessions) involves a more 'fine-grained' analysis (micro-structure), focusing on the daily and weekly activities of athletes and coaches during training, especially the contexts and functions of practice (Davids, 2000). In this chapter we discuss how the umbrella framework of ecological dynamics can provide theoretical and practical insights from integration of data at these two scales of analysis (differing in granularity and time) for talent development in sport.

Ecological dynamics: A rationale for understanding skill acquisition, expertise and talent development in sport

Ecological dynamics considers athletes and sports teams as complex adaptive systems that need to be understood at an irreducible level of analysis: that of the performer–environment relationship (Davids, Araújo, Seifert, & Orth 2015). In such analyses, talent has been conceptualised as an enhanced and functional relationship developed between a performer and a specific performance environment, for example in different sports like climbing a vertical surface or playing in a team game (Araújo & Davids, 2011). This type of functionality allows an individual athlete to achieve task goals and performance outcomes under pressure in competitive performance environments. From this perspective, conceptualisation of talent in athletes is not predicated on a simplistic notion of expert performance emerging due to a simple aggregation of (genetically bestowed and/or acquired) properties of a young performer. Rather a talented individual in sport can be viewed as an active individual engaged in ongoing dynamical transactions with functionally defined tasks and performance environments. In this respect, talent is not defined by a young athlete's fixed set of genetic or acquired components, but rather *by a dynamically varying relationship captured by the constraints imposed by the tasks experienced, the physical and social environment, and the personal resources of a performer* (Araújo & Davids, 2011). Talented athletes are those who acquire an exceptionally functional relationship with a performance environment after many years of high-quality experiences in practice and performance (Araújo & Davids, 2011). Due to inherent nonlinearities in complex adaptive systems, the amount of time needed to achieve an individual's potential cannot be precisely specified (e.g., due to 10,000 hours of deliberate practice) (Phillips, Davids, Renshaw, & Portus, 2010). An individual's potential is not *static*, but rather is *dynamic*, and continuously open to ongoing influences of task, individual and environmental constraints (e.g., genes, motivation, training, maturation, and availability of facilities and coaching support) (Davids, et al., 2015). Due to nonlinearity of developmental processes in complex adaptive systems, it has been argued that reliable, early *a priori* talent identification is impossible (see Araújo et al., 2010 and Chapter 7 in this Handbook). Accordingly, a more significant emphasis should be placed on the *development* of talent in training programmes (see also Chapter 7 in this Handbook). A key part of this development strategy is to attend to carefully designed contexts and functions in the *micro-structure of practice* to enhance skill acquisition and expertise in sport, through manipulation of task constraints in training environments (Araújo, Davids, Bennett, Button, & Chapman, 2004; Davids, Araújo, Vilar, Pinder, & Renshaw, 2013). Ecological dynamics proposes that the performance progress of talented athletes is, in part, the result of their response to the design, types and modes of playing and training activities undertaken, both structured and unstructured (Coutinho, Mesquita, Davids, Fonseca, & Côté, 2016). An important scientific endeavour, therefore, is to understand the specific nature and composition of activities (undertaken over short and long timescales) that will facilitate development in athletes.

Some previously defined key principles of an ecological dynamics rationale for understanding skill acquisition during talent development include (see Davids, Araújo, Hristovski, Passos, & Chow, 2012; Chow, Davids, Button, & Renshaw, 2016):

• Functional motor solutions emerge from continuous co-adaptations of performers to task and environmental constraints. Through continuous interactions, motor learning facilitates adaptive behaviours in athletes helping them to explore a perceptual-motor landscape of solutions.

- The micro-structure of practice should help athletes develop individualised and contextually functional motor solutions, rather than aim to reproduce a collective 'default technique' or optimal movement 'template', towards which all athletes should aspire (Brisson & Alain, 1996);
- The micro-structure of practice should help athletes become perceptually attuned to affordances (opportunities for action) in a practice landscape and exploit inherent system degeneracy (performance outcomes achieved in different ways);
- Motor learning supports transfer to performance environments, which might be general or specific, depending on the quality of the information designed into practice tasks (Chow et al., 2016).

The scale of co-adaptation to constraints, required by performers, may differ depending on the nature of dynamic performance environments. For example, in football, performers may intentionally constrain their actions, depending on the performance context, deciding to shoot, dribble, or pass the ball. During performance there are variants of each action that emerge during sub-phases of play, constrained by co-positioning and movements of teammates and opponents, weather conditions, field surface, properties of the ball, team strategies and tactics (Davids, Araújo, & Shuttleworth, 2005).

In contrast, in performance of self-paced timing tasks without direct opponent interaction, such as serving a ball in volleyball, tennis or squash, or the athletic jumps, such as long jumping or high jumping, task performance is more stable, and there are only small – but meaningful – variations in conditions of the performance environment. In long jumping these variations include properties of the track, board, and weather conditions like ambient temperature, and wind velocity and direction (Greenwood, Davids, & Renshaw, 2016; Scott, Li, & Davids, 1997). In locomotor pointing in sports like cricket and long jumping (running to place the foot on a target [board or line]), an athlete's kinematics and dynamics of locomotion vary in each attempt, and indeed from stride to stride (speed, stride lengths, lower limb joint angles and dynamics) (Renshaw & Davids, 2006; Greenwood et al., 2016).

Research has shown that co-adaptive behaviours are manifested across refined ranges, with minute performance variations often having substantial effects in terms of functionality. The precise micro-structure of practice should reflect these adaptive requirements of performers in contexts and functions designed by coaches, sport scientists and practitioners. 'Functionality' in practice task design needs to simulate relevant and 'successful' solutions demanded in competitive environments. Functionality is, thus, not absolute but emergent from dynamics of competitive performance environments. Functional performance solutions may vary: (1) contextually; (2) intra-individually during athletic development (through motor learning, changes in strength and conditioning influencing speed and flexibility, or through chronic injuries, or growth and maturation); (3), across expertise levels; and finally, (4), across athlete generations, relative to the dynamics of competitive performance environments including changes in equipment and technology, surfaces, rules and regulations. There have been many examples where performance and the profile of qualities needed to succeed in sport has varied over time, e.g., by changes in rules (3-point-zone in basketball, libero in volleyball, judgement criteria in figure skating and gymnastics), playing systems (tempo of pressing in soccer), technique (Fosbury flop, V-technique in ski-jumping), equipment (tennis racket material, fibreglass in pole vault, carving skis, clap skate), or new disciplines (duel races in slalom skiing, women's steeplechase, bobsled).

These changes require continuous co-adaptations of athletes to changing task and environmental constraints, shaping skill performance, and enhancing the nonlinearity of the relationship between sports and athletes as complex adaptive systems, rendering talent identification virtually impossible (Davids et al., 2012). The literatures on skill acquisition and on long-term talent development have tended to develop separately with few attempts to integrate understanding from them because a comprehensive theoretical framework has been lacking (Phillips et al., 2010).

The macro-structure of elite athletes' developmental participation histories

Childhood and adolescence are significant periods in the long-term development of young talents towards eventual senior performance. The performance of elite athletes has developed – in part – as a response to the developmental activities they have engaged in during expertise development. To investigate the early childhood/adolescence participation patterns of current elite athletes, researchers have typically used the methodology of recording their retrospective recall of their involvement in defined activity types. Different types of activities have been distinguished, based on domain-specificity and formal organisation: involvement in organised (coach-led) practice/training programmes (e.g., in high-school sport, sport clubs, or sport academies) vs. non-organised (peer-led) sporting activity performed in an athlete's main sport vs. in other sports, respectively.

Two contrasting developmental pathway patterns have been discussed most prevalently in the literature: the 'early specialisation' and 'early diversification' pathways (cf. the 'Developmental Model of Sport Participation', DMSP; Côté, Baker, & Abernethy, 2007). They represent the poles of a continuum mainly differing in intensity and exclusivity of early, sport-specific, organised, coach-led practice/training and the volume of involvement in different sports and in non-organised, peer-led sporting play (reviewed in Table 14.1). 'Early specialisation' aligns clearly with the 'deliberate practice' approach (Ericsson, Krampe, & Tesch-Römer, 1993) and has been deemed requisite in sports where peak performance occurs before maturity (e.g., female figure skating, rhythmic gymnastics). But it carries higher risks of reduced enjoyment, burnout, injury, and dropout (Table 14.1). Regarding the 'early diversification' path, despite reduced early sport-specific practice/training, various potential benefits have been hypothesised relating to the athlete's motivation, health, prolonged engagement, skill development, and choice of an appropriate main sport (Table 14.1).

Investigating the relevance of different activity types to elite performance implies comparing more and less accomplished athletes with regard to activities engaged in. In view of so many combinations of amounts of different activities through different age periods, a point of interest is investigation of consistent commonalities within the practice histories of most accomplished performers, and differences in comparisons with less successful peers. Here, we review the outcomes of 20 studies comprising 32 respective group comparisons (Table 14.2). In doing so, it is important to consider the athletes' different age ranges and success levels compared (Rees et al., 2016), while particular interest focuses on activity patterns that distinguish the highest success levels, i.e., senior world-class vs. national-class athletes.

More accomplished *juvenile* athletes had consistently accumulated more sport-specific activity than their less successful peers, particularly involving more organised specific practice/training in all studies, and in some studies also more sport-specific, non-organised play (Ford & Williams, 2012; Güllich & Emrich, 2014; Law, Côté, & Ericsson, 2007; Weissensteiner, Abernethy, Farrow, & Müller, 2008). They did not exhibit more involvement in other sports, rather, in some studies significantly less. By contrast, *adult* world-class athletes consistently did not accumulate more organised sport-specific childhood/adolescence practice/training than their national-class counterparts; rather, they even experienced significantly less early specific

Table 14.1 Characteristics of the 'early specialisation' and 'early diversification' pathways

	Early specialisation	Early diversification
Activities		
Up to ~12 yrs	• Concentration on one sport. • Intensified organised coach-led sport-specific deliberate practice/training. • No/little involvement in other sports. • No/little non-organised peer-led sporting play.	• Involvement in various sports. • Moderate intensity of organised coach-led sport-specific deliberate practice/training. • Extensive non-organised peer-led sporting play.
~13–15 yrs	• Continuous expansion and intensification of specific deliberate practice/training.	• Reduction of participation in various sports and in non-organised play. • Gradual expansion and intensification of specific deliberate practice/training.
16+ yrs	• High volume/intensity of specific deliberate practice/training.	• Concentration on one sport. • High volume/intensity of specific deliberate practice/training. • No/little involvement in non-organised play.
Hypothesized outcomes		
	• Elite performance. • Impaired physical health (Myer et al., 2015), enjoyment and intrinsic motivation, increased risk of premature attrition (Côté et al., 2009, for a review).	• Elite performance. • Cost-reducing, risk-buffering juvenile investment pattern (Güllich & Emrich, 2014), enhanced intrinsic motivation from enjoyment of play (Côté et al., 2007; for dissenting findings, Hendry et al., 2014), reduced overuse injury (Myer et al., 2015), prolonged engagement (Fraser-Thomas et al., 2008). • Specific transfer of common motor elements or physiological capacities between related sports (Côté et al., 2007), facilitation of subsequent skill advancement through later age periods (Güllich & Emrich, 2014; Güllich et al., 2016). • Increased probability of functional matching of the athlete with the sport (Güllich & Emrich, 2014).

practice/training in a number of studies (Carlson, 1988; Güllich, 2013, 2014, 2015; Güllich & Emrich, 2014; Hornig, Aust, & Güllich, 2016; Johnson, Tenenbaum, & Edmonds, 2006; Moesch, Elbe, Hauge, & Wikman, 2011; Moesch, Trier Hauge, Wikman, J., & Elbe, 2013; Van Rossum, 2000). Organised involvement in other sports was consistently over-represented in world-class individuals, and they undertook significantly greater amounts of organised activity

Table 14.2 Differences between more successful compared to less successful athletes within defined age and success ranges with regard to the volumes of different types of activities during childhood and adolescence. Review of 20 studies comprising 32 comparisons between success groups

Age and success	Activities in the athlete's main sport			Activities in other sports		
Levels compared	total	organised	non-org.	total	organised	non-org.
Adult athletes						
World class vs. National class [1]	**less**/*ns*	**less**/*ns*	**more**/*ns*	**more**	**more**	**more**/*ns*
World cl. vs. Regional/below [2], National cl. vs. Regional/below [3]	**more**/*ns*	**more**/*ns*	**more/less**	**more**/*ns*	**more**/*ns*	*ns*
Sub–adult athletes						
World class vs. National class [4], National cl. vs. Regional class [5]	**more**	**more**	**more**/*ns*	**less**/*ns*	**less**/*ns*	*ns*

Notes: **more** = more activity in more successful athletes; *ns* = no significant difference; **less** = less activity in more successful athletes. World class = top ten worldwide. Countries and sports: [1] Carlson (1988, tennis; SWE), Güllich (2013, rowing; 2014, field hockey; 2015, athletics; GER), Güllich & Emrich (2014, cgs, game, combat and artistic composition sports; GER), Hornig et al. (2016, soccer; GER), Johnson et al. (2006, swimming; USA), Moesch et al. (2011, cgs sports; 2013, team game sports; DEN), Van Rossum (2000, field hockey; NED vs. BEL). [2] Baker et al. (2003, team game sports; AUS), Duffy et al. (2004, darts; GBR), Hornig et al. (2016, soccer; GER). [3] Baker et al. (2006, triathlon; CAN), Helsen et al. (1998, field hockey, soccer; BEL), Hodges & Starkes (1996, wrestling; USA), Hodges et al. (2004, swimming, triathlon; USA), Hornig et al. (2016, soccer; GER), Memmert et al. (2010, team game sports; GER), Weissensteiner et al. (2008, cricket; AUS). [4] Law et al. (2007, rhythmic gymnastics; CAN vs. GRE). [5] Ford & Williams (2012, soccer; GBR), Güllich & Emrich (2014, cgs, game, combat, artistic composition sports; GER), Weissensteiner et al. (2008, cricket; AUS). Cgs sports: performance is measured in centimetres, grams or seconds.

volumes in different sports. The world–class athletes mostly engaged in different sports over multi-year periods – typically until late adolescence or beyond – and specialised significantly later than national-class counterparts. Some studies also found more participation of world-class athletes in non-organised play in their main sport and/or in other sports.

Regarding studies comparing adult samples across heterogeneous and/or moderate success levels, the findings are more scattered (Baker, Côté, & Abernethy, 2003; Baker, Côté, & Deakin, 2006; Baluch, & Ericsson, 2004; Helsen, Starkes, & Hodges, 1998; Hornig et al., 2016; Hodges & Starkes, 1996; Hodges, Kerr, Starkes, Weir, & Nananidou, 2004; Memmert, Baker, & Bertsch, 2010; Weissensteiner et al., 2008). In these studies, more successful athletes had accumulated more sport-specific practice/training in some cases, but not in others. Some studies revealed positive, and others negative, correlations between senior success and the amounts of non-organised play in an athlete's main sport. Likewise, some studies found more participation in different sports among more successful performers while numerous others did not.

Across all studies, irrespective of age and success levels, athletes consistently preferred different sports in the same category: e.g., game players preferred other games, 'cgs' athletes preferred other 'cgs' sports, and artistic composition athletes preferred other artistic composition sports. However, a success-differentiating effect of the relatedness of the sports experienced has not been revealed to date.

Developmental participation patterns likely leading to early junior success and to long-term senior success are not identical. Early specialisation, intensification of sport-specific practice/training and reduced involvement in other sports mostly benefit rapid juvenile success. Alternatively, combining moderate early sport-specific practice/training with variable experience in different sports, non-organised sporting play, and late specialisation, facilitates the subsequent long-term development of senior top performance in many athletes.

The findings summarised here do not imply that specific practice/training is not critical to performance progress. All elite athletes similarly accumulated considerable amounts of sport-specific practice/training over longer timescales, and volume of specific practice/training alone does not discriminate between the highest senior success levels. *However, its interaction with (earlier) variable, non-specific activity experiences does.* Notably, senior world-class athletes differed from national-class counterparts, particularly in *organised* practice/training in various sports that typically lasted over multiple years and mostly included participation in competitions (Güllich, 2013, 2014, 2015; Güllich & Emrich, 2014; Hornig et al., 2016). That is, their experience of broadened ranges of motor tasks implied *long-lasting* learning in *dedicated* skill acquisition.

These retrospective studies were extended by a 2-year longitudinal quasi-experiment in youth elite soccer (Güllich, Kovar, Zart, & Reimann, 2016). A matched-pairs design matched player 'twins' identical in age and current match-play performance and equivalent in previous years of soccer practice. Based on higher or lower subsequent performance progress within each pair, they were distinguished into 'strong responders' and 'weak responders' (Dperformance 29% vs. 7% through the next 2 years). Both groups did not differ in their physiological development (speed, power, endurance); i.e., their different match-play progress obviously rested on differential *skill* development. The 'strong responders' exhibited more non-organised soccer play and more organised involvement in other sports, but not more organised soccer practice/training. Within each player pair, the player with more variable previous experience likely displayed superior subsequent performance progress. The study also revealed that each activity type unfolded its effects in *interaction* with the other activities and that diversified learning experiences exhibited *lagged* effects on *subsequent* performance progress.

These data raise questions over how the 'macro-structure' of developmental participation histories, in terms of analysing amounts of activity types defined at a large-scale 'granularity' over long age periods, are 'mapped' onto the micro-structure of practice. When subjected to a more 'fine-grained' lens these findings suggest the need to scrutinize the nature of the specific ways that talented athletes can undergo performance changes through motor learning, and to what extent commonalities are revealed at both scales of 'granularity' of analysis. As discussed next, the findings have implications for the specificity and generality of transfer in motor learning that compose the micro-structure of practice.

The micro-structure of practice: Analysing contexts and functions

Insights of Nikolai Bernstein are important in helping coaches attend to the micro-structure of practice, by focusing on contexts and functions of athletes. He proposed that practice should be considered as 'repetition without repetition' (Bernstein, 1967, p. 204), emphasising the process of athletes finding their own individualised movement solutions to performance problems. He termed this capacity in skilled individuals 'dexterity', defining it as

> the ability to find a motor solution for any external situation, that is, to adequately solve any emerging motor problem correctly (i.e., adequately and accurately), quickly (with respect to both decision making and achieving a correct result), rationally (i.e., expediently and economically), and resourcefully (i.e., quick-wittedly and initiatively).
>
> *(Bernstein, 1967, p. 228)*

His ideas are of enormous significance for practitioners and theoreticians interested in the relations between skill acquisition and talent development. They suggest that, in designing practice contexts, coaches and athletes should focus on the *functions of an action* achieved by an athlete, not on addressing the specific anatomical units involved in reproducing a putative common optimal movement pattern. At a theoretical level, it is apparent that Bernstein's (1967) ideas are aligned with James Gibson's (1979) emphasis on a functional analysis of perception and action. For this reason, constraints of practice environments in training should be designed so that athletes continuously need to adapt their actions to a wide range of information in dynamic performance conditions. Skill acquisition is predicated on learners performing flexibly, constantly adapting actions to variations in task and environmental conditions (Araújo & Davids, 2011).

In designing practice micro-structure, for coaches, the concept of *affordances* is paramount. According to insights of James Gibson (1979), affordances specify the relationship between an individual athlete and a performance environment and can be used to regulate an athlete's behaviours (Chow et al., 2016). Affordances are not environmental *entities* that are perceived, but rather are *functional relationships* formed between an individual performer and a performance environment. This definition emphasises the functional use of information to regulate intentions, decisions, and actions, rather than its structural content (van Dijk, Withagen, & Bongers, 2016). In the micro-structure of practice, coaches can design a landscape of affordances for athletes (Chow et al., 2016; Rietveld & Kiverstein, 2014) relative to properties of a performance environment i.e., considering what an object, surface, or another individual, *offers* an athlete in terms of opportunities for sport-specific actions. Different perceptual variables provide *information for different affordances* that invite specific actions, providing an important principle for designing practice environments in sport (Pinder, Davids, Renshaw, & Araújo, 2011a). Where multiple affordances exist, a manifold or landscape emerges (Chow et al., 2016; Rietveld & Kiverstein, 2014). During practice, learners need to be able to explore the constraints of a performance environment and discover affordances for specific behaviours. A manifold of affordances represents a perceptual-motor workspace created for learners by manipulating task constraints (Davids, 2015).

Together, the concepts of affordance and of adaptive variability have important implications for designing the micro-structure of practice in all sports. The integration of these ideas informs practitioners how learners can be continually challenged to actively explore practice environments to discover affordances for regulating performance behaviours in a functional way (i.e. for goal achievement). This idea was exemplified by data reported by Pinder and colleagues (2011a) who examined the role of ball projection machines for practising dynamic interceptive actions – an integral part of practice micro-structure in many sports from cricket and baseball to volleyball and tennis. Yet questions are raised over the specific nature of the affordances that can be utilised by athletes practising against projection machines. Their over-usage in ball games practice was critically evaluated by Pinder and colleagues in an exemplar investigation of cricket batting performance against a ball projection machine and a real bowler. Their data are relevant for addressing the issue of athletes utilising different affordances in practice (Pinder et al., 2011a). In the micro-structure of practice, a primary role of projection machines is predicated on task repetition, considered traditionally as an essential feature of 'perfecting' a putative 'ideal' technique for hitting, batting and intercepting a ball. Projection machines are designed to place a ball in a specific location to be intercepted, allowing individuals to achieve a high volume of practice by facing more balls in a short period of time. Pinder et al. (2011b) found that prolonged use of ball projection machines led athletes to attune to information sources which are not present during competitive performance (they fixated on the mouth of the projection machine and reacted, rather than perceived affordances of a bowler's run up and delivery actions, which are critical). This practice design led to a predictive (mentally simulated), rather than prospective (perceiving contextual information variables for action) control strategy emerging in learners under the specific task constraints of batting against a projection machine (for an additional example in catching see Stone, Maynard, North, Panchuk, & Davids, 2015). Figure 14.1 shows clearly how these different practice task constraints led to different timing behaviours emerging in cricketers when batting, without any specific instructions to vary these behaviours.

Pinder et al. (2011b) also drew attention to data on the highly distinctive visual search patterns that emerge in experienced cricket batters when practising with projection machines, caused by them fixating their gaze at the mouth of the projection machine, which resulted in a highly reactive action strategy that anticipated trajectory of the ball before release (also observed by Stone et al. (2015) in a study of one-handed catching). Taken together, the data suggest that use of projection machines reduces opportunities for developing batters to utilise affordances offered by relevant sources of information from a bowler/pitcher's movements for coordinating batting actions to anticipate ball trajectory, speed or ball type variations (e.g., different spin rotations), rather than react to a projected ball from the machine.

These results also have implications for understanding the specificity or generality of information for transfer of performance from practice to the competitive environment (reacting vs. anticipating when batting against a machine or person bowling a ball). The data reported by Pinder et al. (2011b) implicated how, through carefully designed practice micro-structure,

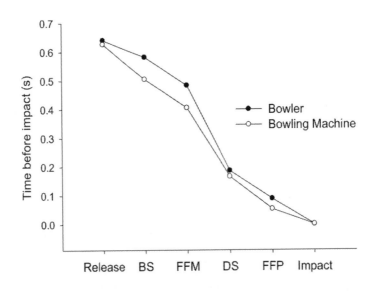

Figure 14.1 Timing during different phases of the front foot drive in cricket, batting against a ball projection machine and a live bowler at a projection speed of ≈27 m s⁻¹.

Notes: Release = point of ball release; BS = backswing; FFM = front foot movement; DS = downswing; FFP: front foot placement; Impact: point of bat-ball contact.

Source: Data from Pinder et al., 2011a.

specificity of transfer can enhance rate of skill and expertise acquisition in developing athletes. These findings are not unique and corroborate results reported on emergent behaviours of boxers (Hristovski, Davids, Araújo, & Passos, 2011) and springboard divers (Barris, Farrow, & Davids, 2013, 2014), as the landscape of affordances are changed during practice.

Implications for talent development

Conceptualising 'talent' as the nature of the functional relationship with a performance environment, underpinning an athlete's potential for developing future excellence, it is fundamental to note that it is not a fixed static trait. Importantly, the insights provided in this chapter clearly suggest how 'talent' can be influenced and built up and expanded. Thus, the *criterion* of the '*functionality of practice*' during childhood/adolescence is: to what extent it contributes to *developing* the athlete's *potential* for *subsequent long-term* skill advancement by enhancing each individual's relationship with a performance environment.

Amplifying early motor experiences, by concerting specific and non-specific learning experiences (macro-structure) with varied task and environmental constraints for each individual within practice (micro-structure), helps young athletes build up a broader and closer-meshed work- and search-space. This facilitates specific and general transfer and promotes both, (a) the expansion of the athlete's potential for subsequent skill advancement during later age periods (i.e., expand 'talent'), and also (b) the realisation of the potential.

From an ecological dynamics viewpoint *specificity of transfer* is predicated on the notion of attunement to specifying information that can be used to regulate actions (Araújo & Davids, 2015). Affordance design is best undertaken in structured practice programmes, and a default mode of practice should not be mere 'rehearsal' of a putative 'common optimal movement pattern' that each individual learner should aspire to (see Figure 14.1). Designing specific information constraints into learning environments will enhance transfer and provide learners with affordances to utilise in achieving their task goals effectively, efficiently and rapidly. Designing more general information sources in practice environments, may still result in transfer and learning, but in a slower, less effective and less efficient manner (Chow et al., 2016). However, this type of practice micro-structure could alleviate issues of early specialisation discussed earlier.

Directed and prescriptive instruction will teach learners what they need to know, but will they learn as efficiently and effectively? *Guided discovery* is likely to help individuals find their own specific movement solutions. And even in less systematically structured and programmed practice environments found in play or peer-led practice, as they search for functional movement solutions, it is possible that learners are attuning to some relevant affordances, via discovery learning (like children in a park practising moves with a skateboard). It is the same for a child kicking a ball against a wall or trying to hit a target or juggling a ball. There may be some functional meta-skills being acquired under these more general task constraints, like information-movement coupling, searching and exploring a performance workspace (Davids et al., 2012; Renshaw et al., 2015).

What do these ideas imply for possible roles of repetitive movement drills and rehearsal of patterns of play during practice? The ecological dynamics framework suggests that they have a role in talent development, but they should not be viewed as *the default method* for teaching/coaching. Their implementation depends on what a coach is seeking to achieve (aim at 'default' of movement execution vs. defining a performance goal, but allowing a functional motor solution to emerge from variations). Indeed, even intending identical repetition of a movement will lead to (slight but meaningful) variations in task execution (Bernstein, 1967).

In conclusion, there appears to be a common principle working at different levels. From an evolutionary perspective, functional (i.e., successful) solutions are more likely to emerge from amplified diversity. For example:

- The development of individually and situationally functional performance solutions emerges from diversified within-skill variation, including variation of task and environmental constraints.
- Contextually embedded decision-making (e.g., decisions to dribble, pass or shoot, including attunement to affordances) emerges from acquiring a variety of adaptive skills and information-movement couplings.
- The probability that an athlete chooses the sport/discipline that he/she is most talented at is increased when the choice emerges from experience in various sports/disciplines.
- At a sport system level, plurality of athlete types and training regimens enhances the chance of the emergence of exceptionally successful athletes; more so in case of (widely unpredictable) changing demands of high-performance sport in the future (e.g., changed rules, equipment, playing system, etc.).

The implication for talent development is that the probability of the emergence of functional solutions can be enhanced by promoting intra-individual variation at within-skill, across-skills and across-sports levels, as well as the inter-individual plurality of athlete profiles.

Future research directions

Analysis of the macro-structure of developmental participation patterns aims at understanding talent development in athletes as a function of the developmental pathways and sport activities they engage in. Current research has typically assigned a set of motor, psychological and social attributes to each activity type, respectively, and activity characteristics were often handled as categorical variables (e.g., high or low playfulness, enjoyment, variability, flexibility, instruction, supervision, etc.; e.g., Coutinho et al., 2016). Those attributes were then ascribed to account for the outcomes of an activity type (e.g., regarding motivation, health, prolonged engagement, skill acquisition, transfer, performance).

The ecological dynamics analysis and data discussed in this chapter suggest that a potential flaw of current macro-structure approaches (e.g., Deliberate Practice and the Developmental Model of Sport Participation) is that particular attributes are proposed to be *correlated* within activity types and distinctive between these categorical types (see Figure 14.2). Integrating these macro-structural approaches with theoretical ideas on skill acquisition that focus on the micro-structure of practice task design reveals that: (a) activity type characteristics are mainly dimensional rather than categorical, (b) may partly correlate, and partly vary independently, and, therefore (c), almost all characteristics can be better understood in combinations (Araújo et al., 2015).

Some examples may serve as an illustration. Top-level soccer players' early organised practice/training time included around 40–50 per cent free soccer play (Hornig et al., 2016). Likewise, top track and field athletes reported that 74 per cent of their organised childhood sessions included game play (Güllich, 2015). Notably, elite track and field adolescents perceived equivalent (or even more) inherent enjoyment from exercising their technique in the various disciplines as from playing games (Güllich, 2015). Furthermore, within organised practice/training sessions there may be more or less prescribed, structured, and/or instructed sequences. On the other hand, peer-led 'kicking around' may be more or less organised; for

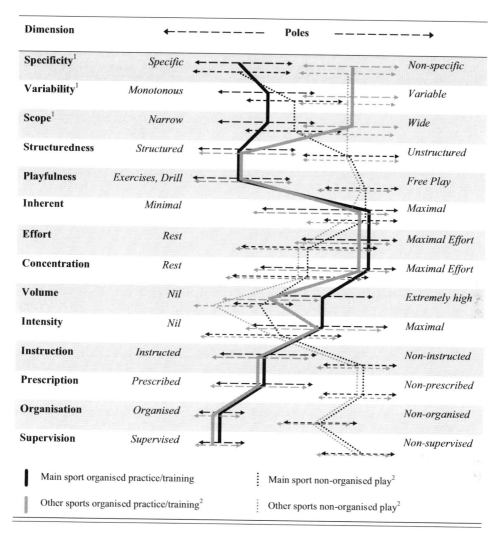

Dimension	← – – – – – – –	Poles	– – – – – – – →

Figure 14.2 Multi–dimensional representation of properties of different types of sporting activities. Schematic illustration exemplified by prototypical activity types described in the literature

Notes: [1] 'Specificity', 'variability' and 'scope' may refer to different dimensions of the activity's properties, e.g., motor, perceptual–cognitive tasks, socio-material environment. [2] In combination with organised practice/training in the main sport.

example the players make appointments as to time and place of playing, rules, and the composition of the teams. They also organise modifications of rules if the game does not 'flow'. Finally, informal uninstructed activity may not necessarily be 'play'; for example, youngsters who go jogging or weightlifting alone. Also, the tennis player arriving at their club 30 minutes before the start of the session in order to hit 100 serves against the wall is actually rather practising than playing. Likewise, the kids in the skateboard park trying a move over and over presumably come close to 'practice' (cf. Côté, Erickson, & Abernethy, 2013: 'spontaneous practice').

These examples may suffice to illustrate that a number of characteristics are only partly correlated at best, and the activity types' characteristics are by no means categorical. It is possible that there are many unexplored 'shades of grey' between activity types that need to be investigated in order to verify in minute detail the nature of the activities experienced by developing athletes that go on to be successful and unsuccessful (carefully defined) in their careers.

Defining these needs for further elaboration is significant for the endeavour to achieve an accurate empirical description of activity properties. Yet most notably, defining an activity type by a *compound* of purportedly correlated attributes impedes analyses concerning which of its characteristics account for potential effects on different outcomes: e.g., motivation, health, prolonged engagement, performance.

In conclusion, investigating which properties or combinations of properties of sport activities benefit which of those outcomes necessitates recording relevant properties *dimensionally* and *individually*. In Figure 14.2 we suggest how potentially relevant characteristics of different activities may be defined and be described on dimensional continua. Drawing on assessments of this kind, each sporting activity can be described on an empirical basis by the profile of its properties. Figure 14.2 illustrates this by way of exemplifying prototypical activity types discussed in the literature. This approach enables: (a) description of the full range of activity modes and their 'shades of grey'; (b) analysis of which of the activities' characteristics (or characteristics' combinations and interactions) differentiate motor learning and performance; and, consequently, (c), better integration of investigations at the macro- and micro-structure level.

References

Araújo, D., Davids, K., Bennett, S.J., Button, C., & Chapman, G. (2004). Emergence of sport skills under constraint. In A.M. Williams & N.J. Hodges (eds), *Skill Acquisition in Sport: Research, Theory and Practice*, pp.409–433. London: Routledge, Taylor & Francis.

Araújo, D., Fonseca, C., Davids, K., Garganta, J., Volossovitch, A., Brandão, R., & Krebs, R. (2010). The role of ecological constraints on expertise development. *Talent Development & Excellence, 2,* 165–179.

Araújo, D., & Davids, K. (2011). Talent development: from possessing gifts, to functional environmental interactions. *Talent Development & Excellence, 3,* 23–26.

Araújo, D., & Davids, K. (2015). Towards a theoretically–driven model of correspondence between behaviours in one context to another: Implications for studying sport performance. *International Journal of Sport Psychology, 46,* 268–280.

Araújo, D., Passos, P., Esteves, P., Duarte, R., Lopes, J., Hristovski, R., & Davids, K. (2015). The micro-macro link in understanding sport tactical behaviours: Integrating information and action at different levels of system analysis in sport. *Movement & Sport Sciences – Science & Motricité, 89,* 53–63.

Baker, J., Côté, J., & Abernethy, B. (2003). Sport-specific practice and the development of expert decision-making in team ball sports. *Journal of Applied Sport Psychology 15,* 12–25.

Baker, J., Côté, J., & Deakin, J. (2006). Patterns of early involvement in expert and nonexpert masters triathletes. *Research Quarterly for Exercise and Sport 77,* 401–407.

Barris, S., Farrow, D., & Davids, K. (2013). Do the kinematics of a baulked take-off in springboard diving differ from a completed dive? *Journal of Sports Science 31,* 305–313.

Barris, S., Farrow, D., & Davids, K. (2014). Increasing functional variability in the preparatory phase of the takeoff improves elite springboard diving performance. *Research Quarterly for Exercise and Sport 85,* 97–106.

Bernstein, N. A. (1967). *The control and regulation of movements.* London: Pergamon Press.

Brisson T.A., & Alain C. (1996). Should common optimal movement patterns be identified as the criterion to be achieved? *Journal of Motor Behavior, 28,* 211–223.

Carlson, R. (1988). The socialization of elite tennis players in Sweden: An analysis of the players' backgrounds and development. *Sociology of Sport Journal, 5,* 241–256.

Chow, J.-Y., Davids, K., Button, C., & Renshaw, I. (2016). *Nonlinear Pedagogy in Skill Acquisition: An Introduction.* Abingdon, UK: Routledge.

Côté, J., Baker, J., & Abernethy, B. (2007). Practice and play in the development of sport expertise. In R. Eklund & G. Tenenbaum (eds), *Handbook of Sport Psychology* (pp. 184–202). Hoboken, NJ: Wiley.

Côté, J., Lidor, R., & Hackfort, D. (2009). ISSP position stand: To sample or to specialize? Seven postulates about youth activities that lead to continued participation and elite performance. *International Journal of Sport and Exercise Psychology, 7,* 7–17.

Côté, J., Erickson, K., & Abernethy, B. (2013). Play and practice in sport development. In J. Côté & R. Lidor (eds), *Conditions of Children's Talent Development in Sport,* pp. 9–20. Morgantown: FIT.

Coutinho, P., Mesquita, I., Davids, K., Fonseca, A. M., & Côté, J. (2016). How structured and unstructured sport activities aid the development of expertise in volleyball players. *Psychology of Sport & Exercise, 25,* 51–59.

Davids, K. (2000). Skill acquisition and the theory of deliberate practice: It ain't what you do it's the way that you do it! Commentary on Starkes, J. 'The road to expertise: Is practice the only determinant?'. *International Journal of Sport Psychology, 31,* 461–465.

Davids, K. (2015). Athletes and sports teams as complex adaptive systems: A review of implications for learning design. *Revista Internacional de Ciencias del Deporte, 39*(11), 48–62. http://dx.doi.org/10.5232/ricyde2015.03904

Davids, K., Araújo, D., Hristovski, R., Passos, P., & Chow, J. Y. (2012). Ecological dynamics and motor learning design in sport. In N. Hodges & M. Williams (eds), *Skill Acquisition in Sport: Research, theory and practice* (2nd ed., pp. 112–130). Abingdon, UK: Routledge.

Davids, K., Araújo, D., Seifert, L., & Orth, D. (2015). Expert performance in sport: An ecological dynamics perspective. In J. Baker & D. Farrow (eds), *Routledge Handbook of Sport Expertise,* pp. 273–303. Abingdon, UK: Routledge.

Davids, K., Araújo, D., & Shuttleworth, R. (2005). Applications of dynamical systems theory to football. In T. Reilly, J. Cabri & D. Araújo (eds), *Science and Football V,* pp. 537–550. London: Routledge.

Davids, K., Araújo, D., Vilar, L., Pinder, R., & Renshaw, I. (2013). An Ecological Dynamics approach to skill acquisition: Implications for development of talent in sport. *Talent Development and Excellence, 5,* 21–34.

Duffy, L.J., Baluch, B., & Ericsson, K.A. (2004). Dart performance as a function of facets of practice amongst professional and amateur men and women players. *International Journal of Sport Psychology, 35,* 232–245.

Ericsson, K. A., Krampe, R. T., & Tesch-Römer, C. (1993). The role of deliberate practice in the acquisition of expert performance. *Psychological Review, 100,* 363–406.

Ford, P. R., & Williams, A. M. (2012). The developmental activities engaged in by elite youth soccer players who progressed to professional status compared to those who did not. *Psychology of Sport and Exercise, 13,* 349–352.

Fraser-Thomas, J., Côté, J., & Deakin, J. (2008). Examining adolescent sport dropout and prolonged engagement from a developmental perspective. *Journal of Applied Sport Psychology, 20,* 318–333.

Gibson, J. J. (1979). *The ecological approach to visual perception.* Boston, MA: Houghton Mifflin.

Greenwood, D., Davids, K., & Renshaw, I. (2016). The role of a vertical reference point in changing gait regulation in cricket run-ups. *European Journal of Sport Science,* First Online: doi.org/10.1080/17461391.2016.1151943

Güllich, A. (2013). Considering long-term sustainability in talent promotion – implications for talent development in rowing. Paper presented at the 18th FISA Youth Coaches Conference, Hamburg, October 25th, 2013.

Güllich, A. (2014). Many roads lead to Rome – Developmental paths to Olympic gold in men's field hockey. *European Journal of Sport Science, 14,* 763–771.

Güllich, A. (2015). Training and competition (in German: Training und Wettkampf). Paper presented at the Youth Athletics Day of the German Athletics Federation (in German: Leichtathletik-Jugendtag des Deutschen Leichtathletik-Verbandes), Kienbaum, November 1, 2015.

Güllich, A., & Emrich, E. (2014). Considering long-term sustainability in the development of world class success. *European Journal of Sport Science, 14(S1),* 383–397.

Güllich, A., Kovar, P., Zart, S., & Reimann, A. (2016). Sporting activities leading to higher or lower improvement of match-play performance in elite youth soccer – a 2-year longitudinal study. *Journal of Sports Sciences 34,* Online First, doi: 10.1080/02640414.2016.1161206

Helsen, W. F., Starkes, J. L., & Hodges, N. J. (1998). Team sports and the theory of deliberate practice. *Journal of Sport and Exercise Psychology 20,* 12–34.

Hendry, D. T., Crocker, P. R., & Hodges, N. J. (2014). Practice and play as determinants of self-determined motivation in youth soccer players. *Journal of Sports Sciences, 32,* 1091–1099.

Hodges, N.J., & Starkes, J.L. (1996). Wrestling with the nature of expertise: A sport specific test of Ericsson, Krampe and Tesch-Römer's (1993) theory of 'deliberate practice'. *International Journal of Sport Psychology, 27*, 400–424.

Hodges, N. J., Kerr, T., Starkes, J. L., Weir, P. L., & Nananidou, A. (2004). Predicting performance times from deliberate practice hours for triathletes and swimmers: What, when, and where is practice important? *Journal of Experimental Psychology: Applied, 10*, 219–237.

Hornig, M., Aust, F., & Güllich, A. (2016). Practice and play in the development of German top-level professional football players. *European Journal of Sport Science, 16*, 96–105.

Hristovski, R., Davids, K., Araújo, D., & Passos, P. (2011). Constraints-induced emergence of functional novelty in complex neurobiological systems: A basis for creativity in sport. *Nonlinear Dynamics, Psychology and the Life Sciences, 15*, 175–206.

Johnson, M., Tenenbaum, G., & Edmonds, W. A. (2006). Adaptation to physically and emotionally demanding conditions: the role of deliberate practice. *High Ability Studies, 17*, 117–136.

Law, M. P., Côté, J., & Ericsson, K. A. (2007). Characteristics of expert development in rhythmic gymnastics: A retrospective study. *International Journal of Sport and Exercise Psychology, 5*, 82–103.

Memmert, D., Baker, J., & Bertsch, C. (2010). Play and practice in the development of sport-specific creativity in team ball sports. *High Ability Studies, 21*(1), 3–18.

Moesch, K., Elbe, A.-M., Hauge, M.-L. T., & Wikman, J. M. (2011). Late specialization: the key to success in centimeters, grams, or seconds (cgs) sports. *Scandinavian Journal of Medicine and Science in Sports, 21*, e282–290.

Moesch, K., Trier Hauge, M.-L., Wikman, J. M., & Elbe, A.-M. (2013). Making it to the top in team sports: Start later, intensify, and be determined! *Talent Development & Excellence, 5*, 85–100.

Myer, G. D., Jayanthi, N, Difiori, J. et al. (2015). Sport specialization, Part 1: Does early sport specialization increase negative outcomes and reduce the opportunity for success in young athletes? *Sports Health*, OnlineFirst, doi: 10.1177/1941738115598747.

Phillips, E., Davids, K., Renshaw, I., & Portus, M. (2010). Expert performance in sport and the dynamics of talent development. *Sports Medicine, 40*, 271–283.

Pinder, R. A., Davids, K., Renshaw, I., & Araújo, D. (2011a). Manipulating informational constraints shapes movement reorganization in interceptive actions. *Attention, Perception & Psychophysics, 73*(4), 1242–1254.

Pinder, R. A., Davids, K., Renshaw, I., & Araújo, D. (2011b). Representative learning design and functionality of research and practice in sport. *Journal of Sport & Exercise Psychology, 33*(1), 146–155.

Rees, T., Hardy, L., Güllich, A., Abernethy, B., Côté, J., Woodman, T., ... Warr, C. (2016). The Great British medallists project: A review of current knowledge on the development of the world's best sporting talent. *Sports Medicine 46*, First Online, doi: 10.1007/s40279-016-0476-2.

Renshaw, I., & Davids, K. (2006). A comparison of locomotor pointing strategies in cricket bowling and long jumping. *International Journal of Sport Psychology, 37*, 38–57.

Renshaw, I., Araújo, D., Button, C., Chow, J.Y., Davids, K., & Moy, B. (2015). Why the constraints-led approach is not teaching games for understanding: A clarification. *Physical Education and Sport Pedagogy*, 1–22.

Rietveld, E., & Kiverstein, J. (2014). A rich landscape of affordances. *Ecological Psychology, 26*(4), 325–352.

Scott, M.A., Li, F.-X., & Davids, K. (1997). Expertise and the regulation of gait in the long jump approach phase. *Journal of Sports Science, 15*, 597–605.

Stone, J., Maynard, I., North, J., Panchuk, D., & Davids, K. (2015). (De)synchronization of advanced visual information and ball flight characteristics constrains emergent information–movement couplings during one-handed catching. *Experimental Brain Research, 233* (2), 449–458. doi:10.1007/s00221-014-4126–3.

Van Dijk, L., Withagen, R., & Bongers, R.M. (2016). Information without content: A Gibsonian reply to enactivists' worries. *Cognition, 134*, 210–214.

Van Rossum, J. H. A. (2000). Deliberate practice and Dutch field hockey: An addendum to Starkes. *International Journal of Sport Psychology, 31*, 452–460.

Weissensteiner, J. R., Abernethy, B., Farrow, D., & Müller, S. (2008). The development of anticipation: A cross-sectional examination of the practice experiences contributing to skill in cricket batting. *Journal of Sport and Exercise Psychology, 30*, 663–684.

15

PERCEPTUAL-COGNITIVE TRAINING

The next piece of the puzzle

Florian Loffing, Norbert Hagemann, and Damian Farrow

The attainment of sporting expertise and stable performance at an elite level are assumed to depend upon a variety of physiological, physical, sociological, and psychological skills (Williams & Reilly, 2000; see also the various chapters in this book). Psychological skills include, but are not limited to, motivation (Crespo & Reid, 2007), emotion regulation and related strategies to cope with stress and performance pressure (Lazarus, 2000) as well as "the ability to identify and acquire environmental information for integration with existing knowledge such that appropriate responses can be selected and executed" (D. T. Y. Mann, Williams, Ward, & Janelle, 2007, p. 457). The latter defines what is usually referred to as *perceptual-cognitive skill* in the sports science literature.

Perceptual-cognitive skill is considered an essential ingredient of talent development and a prerequisite for expert performance (Williams, 2000), particularly in sports requiring precise execution of a motor task under spatiotemporal constraints induced by close distance between competitors, high ball and/or movement speeds or complex sport situations (Müller & Abernethy, 2012; Williams, Davids, & Williams, 1999). Components of perceptual-cognitive skill relate to visual anticipation of an opponent's action intention (e.g., tennis serve direction), decision-making (e.g., where to pass a ball in soccer), visual search or gaze behavior (e.g., during putting in golf or when observing a pitcher in baseball), as well as pattern recall and recognition (e.g., positioning of teammates and opposing players in basketball). Some of these skills are likely to interact and be interdependent (e.g., visual anticipation, decision-making, visual search). Also, these skills' relative contribution to performance is likely to vary with the differing demands of sports.

In past decades, research examining perceptual-cognitive skill has repeatedly demonstrated sports experts have an advantage over novice or less-skilled counterparts in perceptual-cognitive skill components (for reviews, e.g., see Mann et al., 2007; Müller & Abernethy, 2012; Williams, 2009; Yarrow, Brown, & Krakauer, 2009). In view of the findings and assumed relevance of perceptual-cognitive skills for exceptional performance in sports, researchers have become interested in studying whether such skills can be trained and their acquisition be fast-tracked with the ultimate aim to facilitate talent development and the attainment of expert status. In-depth discussions of related efforts and the current level of supporting evidence for such approaches have already been provided in various literature reviews over the past two decades (e.g., Abernethy, Wann, & Parks, 1998; Broadbent, Causer, Williams, & Ford, 2015b; Farrow, 2013;

Jackson & Farrow, 2005; Larkin, Mesagno, Spittle, & Berry, 2015; Schorer, Loffing, Rienhoff, & Hagemann, 2015; Ward et al., 2008; Williams & Grant, 1999; Williams & Ward, 2003).

In this chapter, we will point to the key concepts and findings related to research on perceptual-cognitive training and discuss the potential relevance of such training for talent development. We will conclude with a discussion of open issues and research perspectives that may help better understand whether perceptual-cognitive skill training is an important piece to consider within the puzzling issue of talent development in sport.

Preliminary note

An important question to initially consider when thinking about perceptual-cognitive skill training is what causes the experts' superiority revealed in perceptual-cognitive skill tests (Williams & Grant, 1999)? While the often quasi-experimental nature of research in the area of sport expertise does not permit clear-cut conclusions, there seems considerable consensus in the literature that a large part of the experts' superiority over their less skilled counterparts is not due to better basic perceptual-cognitive functioning (however, see Voss, Kramer, Basak, Prakash, & Roberts, 2010), but rather reflects long-term adaptation to the domain-specific performance demands experienced in extensive training and competition (Williams & Ward, 2003; Yarrow et al., 2009). This view has inspired researchers to assess whether sport-specific perceptual-cognitive training can help lower-skilled athletes acquire the perceptual-cognitive skill set found in experts. In particular, interventions have since focused on visual anticipation, decision-making and gaze control (i.e., quiet eye). This chapter will focus on the two former aspects with the "quiet eye" phenomenon being dealt with in a separate section as an excursus.

Visual anticipation and decision-making

The majority of published interventions have been designed to improve players' ability to perceive, identify and discriminate relevant cues for the correct anticipation of an opponent's action outcome (for recent reviews, e.g., Broadbent et al., 2015b; Schorer et al., 2015). The focus of such training has been on racket sports and standard situations in team sports (e.g., soccer penalty) due to the respective inherent spatiotemporal constraints. Also, from a methodological point of view, researchers could quite easily recreate laboratory-based testing scenarios that are (more or less) representative of the natural on-court demands in those sports or situations (Williams, Ford, Eccles, & Ward, 2011). Positive training effects have been reported in *tennis* (e.g., Farrow & Abernethy, 2002; Farrow, Chivers, Hardingham, & Sachse, 1998; Singer et al., 1994; Smeeton, Williams, Hodges, & Ward, 2005; Williams, Ward, Knowles, & Smeeton, 2002; Williams, Ward, Smeeton, & Allen, 2004), *badminton* (Hagemann & Memmert, 2006; Hagemann, Strauss, & Cañal-Bruland, 2006; Memmert, Hagemann, Althoetmar, Geppert, & Seiler, 2009), *beach volleyball* (Klostermann, Vater, Kredel, & Hossner, 2015), *goalkeeping in soccer* (e.g., McMorris & Hauxwell, 1997; Poulter, Jackson, Wann, & Berry, 2005; Savelsbergh, Van Gastel, & Van Kampen, 2010; Williams & Burwitz, 1993), *team handball* (Abernethy, Schorer, Jackson, & Hagemann, 2012; Schorer, Cañal-Bruland, & Cobley, 2010; Schorer, Loffing, Hagemann, & Baker, 2012) and *field hockey* (Williams, Ward, & Chapman, 2003). Likewise, sport-specific perceptual training was reported to improve decision-making—for example, in youth team-handball players (Hohmann, Obelöer, Schlapkohl, & Raab, 2016), in elite adult Australian Football players (Lorains, Ball, & MacMahon, 2013a), in elite adult women soccer players (Gabbett, Carius, & Mulvey, 2008), and the fielding performance of highly-skilled cricket players (Hopwood, Mann, Farrow, & Nielsen, 2011).

A common approach is that participants watch videos of an opponent performing an action in a particular sport situation recorded from an athlete's classical on-court viewing perspective. Videos are displayed either on a computer monitor or as life-size projections on a large screen. Clips often stop at different time points before or after a critical event (e.g., racket-ball-contact in tennis) and participants are asked to predict the outcome of their opponent's action (e.g., stroke direction or type of stroke) as accurate and/or fast as possible. For example, Farrow et al. (1998) examined the efficacy of a video-based perceptual training on service return performance in tennis. A total of twenty-four novice players were assigned to either a training, placebo, or control group. While the control group did not receive any training between a pre- and post-test, participants from the training and placebo group underwent eight sessions of 15 minutes training each over a 4-week period. During intervention, the training group watched temporally occluded videos and was instructed to visually attend to specific parameters in an opponent's serve stroke movement that were thought to facilitate stroke direction anticipation. The placebo group watched videos of professional tennis matches. Inclusion of that group was considered necessary to counter potential expectancy effects. In both the pre- and post-test, participants watched tennis serves presented on a large screen and they were required to simulate return strokes as accurately and quickly as possible. Analysis of pre- to post-test changes in accuracy and decision-time revealed that, in the post-test, the training group on average decided earlier than the other two groups. That is, unlike the other groups, participants in the training group initiated and executed a return stroke in-time before the ball reached their position. No relevant differences between groups, however, were identified in the prediction of stroke direction. Facilitating effects of perceptual-cognitive skill training on response timing have also been reported by other researchers, for example, in tennis (Smeeton et al., 2005; Williams et al., 2002) and field-hockey (Williams et al., 2003).

Beyond the design used in the exemplar study above, an important question from both a theoretical and applied perspective is whether any recommendations can be given regarding an optimal design of perceptual-cognitive skill training. We will address this issue in the next section.

How to design sport-specific perceptual-cognitive training?

Evidence from the motor learning and control domain, for instance with regard to scheduling practice or the provision of feedback, has inspired scientists to examine whether the concepts revealed may also apply to training of perceptual-cognitive skills. This section summarizes evidence related to instruction and feedback, scheduling of practice, the necessary amount of training, the role of perception–action coupling, the transfer of perceptual training effects to on-court performance and whether there is a particular skill level at which sport-specific perceptual-cognitive training turns out most efficient.

Instruction and feedback

Instructions provided during perceptual-cognitive skill training may vary according to how explicitly participants are informed about the kinematic or situational characteristics likely relevant to anticipation in a particular sport or situation (Jackson & Farrow, 2005). The question of whether there is a superior instruction method that should be used during training has been addressed in different sport situations using different methodologies (e.g., Abernethy et al., 2012; Farrow & Abernethy, 2002; Hagemann et al., 2006; Klostermann et al., 2015; Poulter et al., 2005; Savelsbergh et al., 2010; Smeeton et al., 2005; Williams et al., 2002).

For example, using a pre-post-retention-test design, Farrow and Abernethy (2002) examined the effect of explicit and implicit instructions on tennis serve prediction. Over four weeks, in 12 training sessions with 50 videos presented in each session (showing temporally occluded serves from a receiving player's perspective) an explicit learning group was informed about relations between specific characteristics in a server's movement (e.g., ball toss, service grip, and shoulder rotation) and the direction of the serve. Participants from an implicit learning group watched the same videos; however, they had to estimate the speed of the serve and were not given any specific information comparable to the explicit group. Further, a placebo group (shown excerpts from professional tennis matches) and a control group (no video training at all) were implemented to control for potential expectancy or familiarity effects induced by training. Comparison of pre- to post-test performance revealed that the implicit group significantly improved prediction performance against serves occluded in the time window just before racket–ball contact. No comparable improvement from pre- to post-test was found in the other groups. Prediction performance improvement observed in the implicit learning group, however, was not retained after a retention interval of 32 days without training.

Further research suggests that explicit instruction and guided discovery (i.e., where learners are guided toward anticipation-relevant information to encourage autonomous problem solving) may be similarly beneficial (Williams et al., 2003), with faster learning rates compared to more implicit instruction on the implicit-to-explicit continuum (e.g., discovery learning) (Smeeton et al., 2005). The flip side of explicit training, however, may be that it increases the likelihood for performance deterioration in stressful situations such as under anxiety (Smeeton et al., 2005). Discovery learning may be induced verbally or through the provision of color cues implemented in the videos shown during training to direct the learner's attention toward regions relevant for anticipation or decision-making (Abernethy et al., 2012; Hagemann et al., 2006; Klostermann et al., 2015; Savelsbergh et al., 2010). A positive effect of such visual guidance technique on perceptual-cognitive skill learning has been suggested (Hagemann et al., 2006; Savelsbergh et al., 2010), however, cautionary notes have also been raised as color cues might distract the learner from the critical information behind rather than enhancing its processing as actually intended through application of this method (cf. Klostermann et al., 2015). Despite slower learning rates associated with implicit learning, this approach could prove to be the most beneficial (i.e., sustained improvement) and develop higher resilience under stress (Abernethy et al., 2012). However, when training tactical decision-making in ball games (i.e., handball, basketball, volleyball), implicit learning may only be superior over explicit learning in low-complexity situations, whereas in high-complexity situations, learners may benefit more from explicit than implicit learning (Raab, 2003).

With regard to the provision of feedback during perceptual training, the few studies completed do not suggest a preferred feedback frequency schedule. In badminton, Memmert et al. (2009; Exp. 3) reported that visual anticipation training with novices was almost equally effective irrespective of whether participants were provided with feedback on an opponent's shot outcome on every trial (i.e., 100% feedback rate) or on 66% of trials only. Likewise, team-handball goalkeeping novices' pre-to-post-test learning rates did not markedly differ between groups who received feedback on the directional outcome of temporally occluded seven-meter shots on either 0%, 33%, 66% or 100% of trials (Schorer et al., 2010).

Scheduling practice: Blocked vs. random

According to the motor skill literature, blocked practice (e.g., a block of forehand cross-court shots, then a block of forehand down-the-line shots, then a block of backhand cross-court shots, etc.) is less beneficial for motor skill acquisition compared to random practice (e.g., mixture of forehand and backhand shots with varying directional outcome across trials) (Magill & Hall, 1990). The superiority of a random practice schedule is attributed to contextual interference effects, assuming that variation of task demands on a trial-by-trial basis increases the (cognitive) effort needed to successfully complete a task and consequently results in more stable memorization, albeit at slower rate, of the skill that needs to be acquired to solve the task at hand (Lee, Swinnen, & Serrien, 1994). So far, there is little and inconsistent evidence on contextual interference effects in perceptual-cognitive skill training. Specifically, Memmert et al. (2009; Exp. 2) reported that perceptual learning did not differ between groups of badminton novices practicing according to a blocked vs. random schedule, whereas recent findings by Broadbent, Causer, Ford, and Williams (2015a) in tennis suggest that random practice leads to better perceptual learning compared to blocked practice. Clearly, more evidence is required to allow better conclusions regarding the efficacy of blocked vs. random perceptual-cognitive training. We speculate that learners, and young athletes in particular, might perceive random schedule training as more engaging (e.g., due to trial-by-trial variation in the actions or situations confronted with) as opposed to blocked practice with its more monotonous training demand. Consequently, it may be speculated that random practice of perceptual-cognitive skills will lead to more sustained engagement and in turn greater learning benefits.

Amount of training

Clear-cut recommendations on the (optimal) amount of perceptual-cognitive skill training needed to elicit meaningful improvement in anticipation or decision-making are also difficult to formulate. There is considerable heterogeneity across studies that reported positive training effects, for example, in the intervention period (e.g., six weeks training: Hagemann & Memmert, 2006; one day training: Hagemann et al., 2006; Williams et al., 2002, 2003) as well as in the duration of a single training session (e.g., 10 minutes: Gabbett, Rubinoff, Thorburn, & Farrow, 2007; 45 minutes: Hagemann et al., 2006; Williams et al., 2003) or the number of trials included within (e.g., 30 trials: Gabbett et al., 2007; 200 trials: Hagemann et al., 2006). Recommendations are further complicated by the fact that the domain-specific skill status of learners varies across studies (i.e., from novice to experienced athletes). As a tentative conclusion, it seems that, analogous to the motor domain, the amount of training necessary to induce measureable improvement in perceptual-cognitive skill decreases the lower the learners' skill in the domain of interest (Hagemann et al., 2006). Importantly, perceptual-cognitive skill-training efficacy does not seem limited to novice or less skilled athletes but has also been reported in highly skilled players, for example, in cricket (Hopwood et al., 2011), soccer (Gabbett et al., 2008), and Australian Rules Football (Lorains et al., 2013a). Consequently, when considering perceptual-cognitive skill training as a potential means to foster talent development, how the amount, intensity or duration of such training may be optimally scheduled needs to be based on a thorough diagnosis of an individual's skill status.

Perception–action coupling

Besides the training environment and stimuli being close to the natural performance situation, perceptual-cognitive skill training may demand representativeness in the responses required from learners (Broadbent et al., 2015b). The suggestion of responses ideally being as specific as those required in the natural performance setting is based on evidence suggesting a distinction of functional specialization in the ventral and dorsal visual pathways (Milner & Goodale, 1995).

In essence, though not exclusive, the ventral stream seems specialized for vision-for-perception tasks (e.g., identification of a travelling object as a ball), whereas the dorsal stream is deemed primarily involved in vision-for-action (e.g., using perception of an upcoming ball to guide and control actions towards it such as when batting in cricket or baseball). Since in many sports, demands are assumed to predominantly, but not exclusively, relate to vision-for-action rather than vision-for-perception processes, it could be argued that maintenance of the coupling between perception and action is critical for optimal learning to occur (van der Kamp, Rivas, van Doorn, & Savelsbergh, 2008). Also, considering the important issue of transfer to field performance (see next section below), linking perception and action during perceptual-cognitive skill training appears a reasonable demand. However, the majority of training studies completed to date have required participants to make uncoupled perception–action responses during training (e.g., verbal, key press) and there is limited evidence on potential varying efficacy of training under perception–action coupled vs. uncoupled conditions on perceptual-cognitive skill learning.

Using a pre-post-test design, Williams et al. (2004) compared the efficacy of on-court instructions under a perception–action vs. perception-only condition on novice players' visual anticipation of tennis serve direction. Unlike response accuracy, both groups significantly decreased reaction time compared to another technical instruction group that served as an expectancy control group. No statistical difference was revealed between the perception–action and perception-only groups. Interestingly, RT effect size was larger for the perception–action ($d = 2.44$) than the perception-only group ($d = 1.40$), but it is important to note that the respective group size was small (8 participants each), thus limiting effect size interpretation. Obviously, more substantiated research on perception–action coupled vs. uncoupled training is required before any recommendation on optimal training design can be made.

A final cautionary note seems warranted to those who consider using perception–action coupled training situation in a laboratory setting with presentation of videos or use of virtual environments (for a review see H. C. Miles, Pop, Watt, Lawrence, & John, 2012). In such situations, where learners may only simulate a response, for example, without actual ball interception, the problem may arise that simulated actions are not performed in the same way as on the field. As a consequence, unwanted effects in action execution might be introduced (e.g., false positioning and/or swing towards a ball in tennis return shots) that may ultimately transfer negatively to motor skill execution in the field.

Transfer

As indicated above, another central question relates to whether perceptual-cognitive skill training-induced improvements observed in the laboratory transfer to the field and provide athletes with a measurable benefit (Williams & Ward, 2003). While this issue is not new (e.g., Williams & Grant, 1999) it is still highly topical as appropriate transfer tests have not been regularly included in previous perceptual-cognitive skill training research (cf. Broadbent et al., 2015b; Schorer et al., 2015).

Gabbett et al. (2007) found that a four-week video-based perceptual training (comprising 12 sessions lasting 10 minutes each) improved decision accuracy and time not only in a laboratory setting, but decision accuracy also increased from pre- to post-intervention in a field test. Importantly, these improvements were specific to the video-based training group, with no meaningful changes in the placebo or control group, and were retained over a four-week retention interval without perceptual training. Positive transfer from laboratory-based training to the "field" has also been reported in tennis (Smeeton et al., 2005; Williams et al., 2002) and field hockey (Williams et al., 2003); however, in these studies improvements occurred in decision time, not in accuracy.

Collectively, while research suggests that positive transfer from laboratory to field conditions may occur (Hopwood et al., 2011), more substantiated evidence is needed before properly inferring recommendations on the practical utility of perceptual training. From a methodological viewpoint, this is because some of the field transfer tests used either simplifications of the real performance environment and/or task demands were close to those employed in the respective laboratory settings. Furthermore, based on our narrative review approach in this chapter, it is difficult to exclude a potential publication bias in such a way that training studies where no or even negative transfer from laboratory to the field in experimental groups was found may be kept back from the scientific community ("file-drawer problem"; Rosenthal, 1979).

Another issue that may limit previous findings of positive transfer is that perceptual-cognitive skill training neglected the relevance of contextual information. To exemplify, visual anticipation training focused on conveying the anticipation-relevant kinematic cues in an opponent's movement to learners. However, players do not exclusively rely on such cues for action outcome anticipation, but they may infer predictive information also from contextual factors such as on-court position (Abernethy, Gill, Parks, & Packer, 2001; Loffing & Hagemann, 2014), tactics (Crognier & Féry, 2005), action preferences (D. L. Mann, Schaefers, & Cañal-Bruland, 2014), game score (Farrow & Reid, 2012) or previous events (Gray, 2002; Loffing, Stern, & Hagemann, 2015). Thus, in order to comprehensively assess the utility and field-transfer potential of perceptual-cognitive skill training, interventions may need to consider the richness and complexity of different information sources to promote their pick-up and integration into anticipation or decision-making as required in a real-world competitive environment.

Training gaze control—or the "quiet eye"

Quiet eye is a specific perceptual-motor skill that was initially described by Vickers (1996) and has received much attention from researchers in sports and other behavioral domains over the past two decades (for reviews e.g., see Rienhoff, Tirp, Strauß, Baker, & Schorer, 2015; Vine, Moore, & Wilson, 2014). Vickers (1996) discovered that basketball experts (with mean free throw accuracy of 78%) are characterized by a longer visual fixation on the target (i.e., basket) just before the initiation of a throw movement as opposed to a group of near-experts (mean free throw accuracy of 56%). The "final" visual fixation directed on a target (e.g., basket in basketball, bullseye in darts, hole in golf) prior to the execution of a sport skill has since been termed the "quiet eye" (QE). Following the seminal work by Vickers, numerous studies have suggested that higher skilled athletes are characterized, on average, by longer QE duration than their less skilled counterparts (*inter*-individual differences) and that, within individual athletes, successful attempts are associated with longer QE duration compared to unsuccessful trials (*intra*-individual differences) (Vine et al., 2014).

Longer QE has also been reported for visual anticipation tasks such as goalkeeping in ice-hockey (Panchuk & Vickers, 2006). Here, eight elite goaltenders from college and university teams had a longer final fixation that started earlier before the initiation of a defensive action in successful as opposed to unsuccessful trials (952.3 ms vs. 826.1 ms).

Findings from QE research have been used to develop training programs aiming at an earlier on- and later offset, and thus a prolongation, of the QE period (for reviews see Rienhoff et al., 2015; Schorer et al., 2015; Vine et al., 2014). A core principle of QE training is to convey to the learner when and where to direct the final fixation prior to the initiation of a sport skill (Vine et al., 2014). Demonstration and feedback (e.g., video replays with illustration of a learner's vs. expert model's gaze behavior during execution of a skill) are used to train individuals in applying gaze control strategies of higher skilled or expert athletes in the domain of interest. Positive effects of such intervention have repeatedly been reported in the literature (e.g., Adolphe, Vickers, & Laplante, 1997; Harle & Vickers, 2001). For example, Harle and Vickers (2001) showed that university basketball players benefited from QE training in a laboratory setting (mean free throw accuracy: 62.3% in pre-test vs. 74.3% in post-test; mean QE duration: 783 ms in pre- vs. 981 ms in post-test) and they also improved the proportion of successful free throws during normal match-play by 22.6% after two seasons unlike similar-skilled players from two other teams who did not receive specific QE training.

Training of QE has also been successfully implemented in aiming tasks such as in golf (Moore, Vine, Cooke, Ring, & Wilson, 2012; Moore, Vine, Freeman, & Wilson, 2013), soccer penalties (Wood & Wilson, 2011, 2012), or shotgun shooting (Causer, Holmes, & Williams, 2011). Some of these studies also revealed that QE training may help to counteract performance decrements in pressure situations (e.g., Moore et al., 2012, 2013).

Various mechanisms have been suggested to underlie the QE and its assumed positive training effects (e.g., Klostermann, 2014). Among others, QE training is thought to improve regulation of attentional control mechanisms, thus enabling the maintenance of a more effective goal-driven control strategy and, at the same time, helping to suppress potentially distracting stimuli entering the stimulus-driven attentional system (Corbetta, Patel, & Shulman, 2008; Vine et al., 2014). Also, a longer QE period might allow an almost unhindered transfer of task-relevant visual information to the motor control system, which then could result in more efficient movement execution, or to facilitate the adoption of a potentially performance-enhancing external focus of attention (Vine et al., 2014).

Perceptual-cognitive skill training: A suitable means for young athletes?

The evidence summarized above suggests that perceptual-cognitive skills may be improved through sport-specific training. But is such training equally effective across different age or skill levels? And specifically, is it a suitable means to promote expertise development in young talented athletes? If so, at what "career stage" should it be introduced? So far, systematic investigation of potential facilitating effects of perceptual-cognitive skill training on talent development is missing, but some general issues can be speculated about in combination with recourse to evidence on such training in junior athletes (Williams & Ward, 2003).

At an early stage of an individual's new motor skill acquisition, basic issues related to the proper technical execution of a sport skill are likely to have higher priority over specific perceptual-cognitive skills. With progression in basic skills, other aspects become more relevant, for example, due to an increasing competitive environment and the increasing physiological and psychological demands therein. As a consequence, "it may be that more strategic considerations, such as anticipation and decision making, should be left until intermediate stages of learning" (Williams & Ward, 2003, p. 247). Thus, when considering the implementation of targeted perceptual-cognitive skill training in young or novice athletes, diagnosis of individual players' basic skills might be an important starting point from where to decide about whether or not to actually start such intervention. Apart from this suggestion, more specific research-based guidelines still cannot be formulated.

On a positive note, research indicates that, for example, junior tennis players' visual anticipation may be improved through specific perceptual-cognitive training as reported by Farrow and Abernethy (2002; mean age = 15.0 ± 1.1 years) and Smeeton et al. (2005; mean age ~10.5 years). Also, training of the quiet eye might be an efficient means to improve throw and catch performance in typically developed children (C. A. L. Miles, Vine, Wood, Vickers, & Wilson, 2014; mean age: 10.32 ± 0.57 years) as well as in "special" populations such as children diagnosed with developmental coordination disorder (C. A. L. Miles, Wood, Vine, Vickers, & Wilson, 2015; mean age: 9.07 ± 0.87 years).

Concluding remarks and outlook

Athletes' perceptual-cognitive skills may be improved through specific training, provided that certain prerequisites are met. Direct evidence regarding facilitating effects on talent development, however, is rare to say the least, and likewise, convincing evidence for sustained transfer of training-induced improvements to real-life performance is still warranted. Nonetheless, based on what we know from the literature today, targeted perceptual-cognitive skill training could be one helpful supplemental piece within the big puzzle of how to attain sporting expertise. For example, it could be used as an aid to counter perceptual unfamiliarity with particular type of opponents (e.g., left-handers, Schorer et al., 2012) or be included in rehabilitation programs designed to help athletes recover from injury. Also, the methods identified as likely facilitating perceptual-cognitive skill acquisition and retention (e.g., implicit instruction) could be helpful for practitioners and consequently be adopted in a real field setting.

To broaden the view on the possible relevance of perceptual-cognitive skill training as well as to stimulate future research ideas, we will finally address selected issues.

1   When designing perceptual-cognitive training interventions, researchers and coaches alike may wonder whether to prepare videos in 2D or 3D. The latter type might be assumed to more realistically represent the natural performance situation (Stoffregen, Bardy, Smart, & Pagulayan, 2003), but whether training with 3D videos or even in virtual environments is actually superior to 2D training in all or only some measures (e.g., decision quality vs. decision time) still needs significant investigation (Hohmann et al., 2016; H. C. Miles et al., 2012).

2   It has recently been suggested that playing videos with faster speed in decision-making training (i.e., 1.5 times faster than normal) is more beneficial to learning than normal speeded footage (Lorains et al., 2013a). While the mechanisms underlying that effect still need to be developed, it is speculated that faster videos might induce higher fidelity and provoke more efficient automatic processing particularly in elite sport performers (Lorains, Ball, & MacMahon, 2013b; Lorains, MacMahon, Ball, & Mahoney, 2011).

3   Different athletes are likely to bring in different perceptual-motor skill sets (Bruce, Farrow, Raynor, & Mann, 2012). Consequently, perceptual-cognitive training may not be an issue for each athlete and it may turn out most effective if it takes into account and is adapted to individual athletes' needs. For example, visual anticipation training may be particularly useful for relatively slow as opposed to fast moving soccer goalkeepers in the penalty-kick situation (Dicks, Davids, & Button, 2010). Compared to slow moving goalkeepers, their fast moving colleagues may be allowed to wait somewhat longer for initiating a response towards a penalty-taker's action and thus may base their movement decisions on more reliable predictive cues regarding shot direction. Consequently, visual anticipation of a penalty-taker's intention at an early stage of his or her shot could be particularly relevant to slow moving goalkeepers to help them compensate the possible costs of their need to move earlier to be in the right spot at the right time ("just-in-time"-hypothesis; Schorer

& Baker, 2009). In this regard, careful observation and determination of individual athletes' performance on various measures may be required before instantiating specific perceptual-cognitive skill training.

4   Experimental evidence indicates that an individual's motor expertise for specific actions influences their ability to visually discriminate formerly trained actions when viewing others perform these actions (Casile & Giese, 2006). If this causal relationship also holds outside the laboratory in far more complex sport situations, perceptual-cognitive skills may, at least to some degree, incidentally be improved also through physical training.

5   Recent work suggests that general perceptual-cognitive training such as motion object tracking may benefit athletes' performance in sports (Faubert & Sidebottom, 2012; Romeas, Guldner, & Faubert, 2016). While there has been controversial discussion of this issue for some time with the (preliminary) conclusion that such training appears of little value relative to sport-specific perceptual-cognitive training (Williams & Grant, 1999), nonetheless it seems worthwhile to re-orient perspectives and carefully consider with sound methodological design whether unspecific perceptual training actually is or is not beneficial to athletes.

6   Last but not least, targeted training of perceptual-cognitive skills may not only help talented athletes on their road to expertise. Similarly, talented coaches, judges, umpires or (assistant) referees may also benefit from such intervention. For example, in soccer, perceptual training may help counteract potential biases or fallacies in (assistant) referees' interpretation of one-on-one or offside situations (e.g., Brand, Schweizer, & Plessner, 2009; Catteeuw, Gilis, Jaspers, Wagemans, & Helsen, 2010; Put, Wagemans, Jaspers, & Helsen, 2013; Schweizer, Plessner, Kahlert, & Brand, 2011).

Overall, despite potential positive effects of perceptual-cognitive skill training suggested by the literature, we wish to highlight that an essential component for attaining high sporting expertise remains: that talented athletes gain substantial experience from "real" training and competition within their respective sporting domains (Gabbett et al., 2007) or through positive skill transfer from related areas (e.g., Abernethy, Baker, & Côté, 2005; Baker, Côté, & Abernethy, 2003; Rosalie & Müller, 2012). Consequently, perceptual-cognitive skill training "should only be used as a supplement to actual sport specific practice" (Farrow et al., 1998, p. 241). Moreover, based on our knowledge of the extant literature, and given the complexity of interacting factors likely involved in explaining or predicting expertise (e.g., Davids & Baker, 2007; Ullén, Hambrick, & Mosing, 2016), whether perceptual-cognitive skill training actually provides measureable and sustainable benefit for talent development and the attainment of expertise in sport remains an open question. Elaborate longitudinal randomized controlled designs would ideally be needed to properly tackle this issue. However, besides logistical issues possibly hindering realization of such research (e.g., due to high dropout rates in youth athletes), the necessary inclusion of an experimental control group that does not receive potentially beneficial treatment (i.e., perceptual-cognitive skills training) might be considered an ethical problem. Specifically, athletes from that group might then face a (slight) disadvantage on their path to expertise relative to their peers from the perceptual-cognitive training group. Hence creative experimental solutions, such as the use of a cross-over design (or something similar), need to be considered. With the rapid technological developments in virtual reality and the like, we look forward to the next decades of research on perceptual-cognitive skills training and maybe, at some time, we will better understand the actual relevance of such training for talent development and the attainment of expertise in sport.

References

Abernethy, B., Baker, J., & Côté, J. (2005). Transfer of pattern recall skills may contribute to the development of sport expertise. *Applied Cognitive Psychology, 19*, 705–718.

Abernethy, B., Gill, D. P., Parks, S. L., & Packer, S. T. (2001). Expertise and the perception of kinematic and situational probability information. *Perception, 30*, 233–252.

Abernethy, B., Schorer, J., Jackson, R. C., & Hagemann, N. (2012). Perceptual training methods compared: The relative efficacy of different approaches to enhancing sport-specific anticipation. *Journal of Experimental Psychology: Applied, 18*, 143–153.

Abernethy, B., Wann, J. P., & Parks, S. (1998). Training perceptual-motor skills for sport. In B. C. Elliott (ed.), *Training in sport: Applying sport science* (pp. 1–68). Chichester, UK: Wiley.

Adolphe, R. M., Vickers, J. N., & Laplante, G. (1997). The effects of training visual attention on gaze behaviour and accuracy: A pilot study. *International Journal of Sports Vision, 4*, 28–33.

Baker, J., Côté, J., & Abernethy, B. (2003). Sport-specific practice and the development of expert decision-making in team ball sports. *Journal of Applied Sport Psychology, 15*, 12–25.

Brand, R., Schweizer, G., & Plessner, H. (2009). Conceptual considerations about the development of a decision making training method for expert soccer referees. In D. Araujo, H. Ripoll & M. Raab (eds), *Perspectives on cognition and action in sport* (pp. 181–190). Hauppauge, NY: Nova Science.

Broadbent, D. P., Causer, J., Ford, P. R., & Williams, A. M. (2015). Contextual interference effect on perceptual-cognitive skills training. *Medicine and Science in Sports and Exercise, 47*, 1243–1250.

Broadbent, D. P., Causer, J., Williams, A. M., & Ford, P. R. (2015). Perceptual-cognitive skill training and its transfer to expert performance in the field: Future research directions. *European Journal of Sport Science, 15*, 322–331.

Bruce, L., Farrow, D., Raynor, A., & Mann, D. (2012). But I can't pass that far! The influence of motor skill on decision making. *Psychology of Sport and Exercise, 13*, 152–161.

Casile, A., & Giese, M. A. (2006). Nonvisual motor training influences biological motion perception. *Current Biology, 16*, 69–74.

Catteeuw, P., Gilis, B., Jaspers, A., Wagemans, J., & Helsen, W. (2010). Training of perceptual-cognitive skills in offside decision making. *Journal of Sport & Exercise Psychology, 32*, 845–861.

Causer, J., Holmes, P. S., & Williams, A. M. (2011). Quiet eye training in a visuomotor control task. *Medicine and Science in Sports and Exercise, 43*, 1042–1049.

Corbetta, M., Patel, G., & Shulman, G. L. (2008). The reorienting system of the human brain: From environment to theory of mind. *Neuron, 58*, 306–324.

Crespo, M., & Reid, M. M. (2007). Motivation in tennis. *British Journal of Sports Medicine, 41*, 769–772.

Crognier, L., & Féry, Y. A. (2005). Effect of tactical initiative on predicting passing shots in tennis. *Applied Cognitive Psychology, 19*, 637–649.

Davids, K., & Baker, J. (2007). Genes, environment and sport performance: Why the nature–nurture dualism is no longer relevant. *Sports Medicine, 37*, 961–980.

Dicks, M., Davids, K., & Button, C. (2010). Individual differences in the visual control of intercepting a penalty kick in association football. *Human Movement Science, 29*, 401–411.

Farrow, D. (2013). Practice-enhancing technology: A review of perceptual training applications in sport. *Sports Technology, 6*, 170–176.

Farrow, D., & Abernethy, B. (2002). Can anticipatory skills be learned through implicit video based perceptual training? *Journal of Sports Sciences, 20*, 471–485.

Farrow, D., Chivers, P., Hardingham, C., & Sachse, S. (1998). The effect of video-based perceptual training on the tennis return of serve. *International Journal of Sport Psychology, 29*, 231–242.

Farrow, D., & Reid, M. (2012). The contribution of situational probability information to anticipatory skill. *Journal of Science and Medicine in Sport, 15*, 368–373.

Faubert, J., & Sidebottom, L. (2012). Perceptual-cognitive training of athletes. *Journal of Clinical Sport Psychology, 6*, 85–102.

Gabbett, T. J., Carius, J., & Mulvey, M. (2008). Does improved decision-making ability reduce the physiological demands of game-based activities in field sport athletes? *Journal of Strength and Conditioning Research, 22*, 2027–2035.

Gabbett, T. J., Rubinoff, M., Thorburn, L., & Farrow, D. (2007). Testing and training anticipation skills in softball fielders. *International Journal of Sports Science & Coaching, 2*, 15–24.

Gray, R. (2002). Behavior of college baseball players in a virtual batting task. *Journal of Experimental Psychology: Human Perception and Performance, 28*, 1131–1148.

Hagemann, N., & Memmert, D. (2006). Coaching anticipatory skill in badminton: Laboratory versus field-based perceptual training. *Journal of Human Movement Studies, 50,* 381–398.

Hagemann, N., Strauss, B., & Cañal-Bruland, R. (2006). Training perceptual skill by orienting visual attention. *Journal of Sport & Exercise Psychology, 28,* 143–158.

Harle, S. K., & Vickers, J. N. (2001). Training quiet eye improves accuracy in the basketball free throw. *Sport Psychologist, 15,* 289–305.

Hohmann, T., Obelöer, H., Schlapkohl, N., & Raab, M. (2016). Does training with 3D videos improve decision-making in team invasion sports? *Journal of Sports Sciences, 34,* 746–755.

Hopwood, M. J., Mann, D. L., Farrow, D., & Nielsen, T. (2011). Does visual-perceptual training augment the fielding performance of skilled cricketers? *International Journal of Sports Science & Coaching, 6,* 523–535.

Jackson, R. C., & Farrow, D. (2005). Implicit perceptual training: How, when, and why? *Human Movement Science, 24,* 308–325.

Klostermann, A. (2014). Finale Fixationen, sportmotorische Leistung und eine Inhibitionshypothese. Mechanismen des "Quiet Eye". [Final fixations, motor performance and an inhibition hypothesis. Mechanisms of the "quiet eye"]. *Sportwissenschaft, 44,* 49–59.

Klostermann, A., Vater, C., Kredel, R., & Hossner, E.-J. (2015). Perceptual training in beach volleyball defence: Different effects of gaze-path cueing on gaze and decision-making. *Frontiers in Psychology, 6.*

Larkin, P., Mesagno, C., Spittle, M., & Berry, J. (2015). An evaluation of video-based training programs for perceptual-cognitive skill development. A systematic review of current sport-based knowledge. *International Journal of Sport Psychology, 46,* 555–586.

Lazarus, R. S. (2000). How emotions influence performance in competitive sports. *Sport Psychologist, 14,* 229–252.

Lee, T. D., Swinnen, S. P., & Serrien, D. J. (1994). Cognitive effort and motor learning. *Quest, 46,* 328–344.

Loffing, F., & Hagemann, N. (2014). On-court position influences skilled tennis players' anticipation of shot outcome. *Journal of Sport & Exercise Psychology, 36,* 14–26.

Loffing, F., Stern, R., & Hagemann, N. (2015). Pattern-induced expectation bias in visual anticipation of action outcomes. *Acta Psychologica, 161,* 45–53.

Lorains, M., Ball, K., & MacMahon, C. (2013a). An above real time training intervention for sport decision making. *Psychology of Sport and Exercise, 14,* 670–674.

Lorains, M., Ball, K., & MacMahon, C. (2013b). Expertise differences in a video decision-making task: Speed influences on performance. *Psychology of Sport and Exercise, 14,* 293–297.

Lorains, M., MacMahon, C., Ball, K., & Mahoney, J. (2011). Above real time training for team invasion sport skills. *International Journal of Sports Science & Coaching, 6,* 537–544.

Magill, R. A., & Hall, K. G. (1990). A review of the contextual interference effect in motor skill acquisition. *Human Movement Science, 9,* 241–289. doi: 10.1016/0167-9457(90)90005-x

Mann, D. L., Schaefers, T., & Cañal-Bruland, R. (2014). Action preferences and the anticipation of action outcomes. *Acta Psychologica, 152,* 1–9.

Mann, D. T. Y., Williams, A. M., Ward, P., & Janelle, C. M. (2007). Perceptual-cognitive expertise in sport: A meta-analysis. *Journal of Sport & Exercise Psychology, 29,* 457–478.

McMorris, T., & Hauxwell, B. (1997). Improving anticipation of soccer goalkeepers using video observation. In T. Reilly, J. Bangsbo & M. Hughes (eds), *Science and Football III* (pp. 290–294). London: E & FN Spon.

Memmert, D., Hagemann, N., Althoetmar, R., Geppert, S., & Seiler, D. (2009). Conditions of practice in perceptual skill learning. *Research Quarterly for Exercise and Sport, 80,* 32–43.

Miles, C. A. L., Vine, S. J., Wood, G., Vickers, J. N., & Wilson, M. R. (2014). Quiet eye training improves throw and catch performance in children. *Psychology of Sport and Exercise, 15,* 511–515.

Miles, C. A. L., Wood, G., Vine, S. J., Vickers, J. N., & Wilson, M. R. (2015). Quiet eye training facilitates visuomotor coordination in children with developmental coordination disorder. *Research in Developmental Disabilities, 40,* 31–41.

Miles, H. C., Pop, S. R., Watt, S. J., Lawrence, G. P., & John, N. W. (2012). A review of virtual environments for training in ball sports. *Computers & Graphics, 36,* 714–726.

Milner, A. D., & Goodale, M. A. (1995). *The visual brain in action.* Oxford: Oxford University Press.

Moore, L. J., Vine, S. J., Cooke, A., Ring, C., & Wilson, M. R. (2012). Quiet eye training expedites motor learning and aids performance under heightened anxiety: The roles of response programming and external attention. *Psychophysiology, 49,* 1005–1015.

Moore, L. J., Vine, S. J., Freeman, P., & Wilson, M. R. (2013). Quiet eye training promotes challenge appraisals and aids performance under elevated anxiety. *International Journal of Sport and Exercise Psychology, 11,* 169–183.

Müller, S., & Abernethy, B. (2012). Expert anticipatory skill in striking sports: A review and a model. *Research Quarterly for Exercise and Sport, 83,* 175–187.

Panchuk, D., & Vickers, J. N. (2006). Gaze behaviors of goaltenders under spatial-temporal constraints. *Human Movement Science, 25,* 733–752.

Poulter, D. R., Jackson, R. C., Wann, J. P., & Berry, D. C. (2005). The effect of learning condition on perceptual anticipation, awareness, and visual search. *Human Movement Science, 24,* 345–361.

Put, K., Wagemans, J., Jaspers, A., & Helsen, W. F. (2013). Web-based training improves on-field offside decision-making performance. *Psychology of Sport and Exercise, 14,* 577–585.

Raab, M. (2003). Decision making in sports: Influence of complexity on implicit and explicit learning. *International Journal of Sport and Exercise Psychology, 1,* 406–433.

Rienhoff, R., Tirp, J., Strauß, B., Baker, J., & Schorer, J. (2015). The "quiet eye" and motor performance: A systematic review based on Newell's constraints-led model. *Sports Medicine, 46,* 589–603.

Romeas, T., Guldner, A., & Faubert, J. (2016). 3D-Multiple Object Tracking training task improves passing decision-making accuracy in soccer players. *Psychology of Sport and Exercise, 22,* 1–9.

Rosalie, S. M., & Müller, S. (2012). A model for the transfer of perceptual-motor skill learning in human behaviors. *Research Quarterly for Exercise and Sport, 83,* 413–421.

Rosenthal, R. (1979). The "file drawer problem" and tolerance for null results. *Psychological Bulletin, 86,* 638–641.

Savelsbergh, G. J. P., Van Gastel, P. J., & Van Kampen, P. M. (2010). Anticipation of penalty kicking direction can be improved by directing attention through perceptual learning. *International Journal of Sport Psychology, 41,* 24–41.

Schorer, J., & Baker, J. (2009). An exploratory study of aging and perceptual-motor expertise in handball goalkeepers. *Experimental Aging Research, 35,* 1–19.

Schorer, J., Cañal-Bruland, R., & Cobley, S. (2010). Frequency of knowledge of results does not influence perceptual learning and retention in novices. *International Journal of Sport Psychology, 41,* 107–117.

Schorer, J., Loffing, F., Hagemann, N., & Baker, J. (2012). Human handedness in interactive situations: Negative perceptual frequency effects can be reversed! *Journal of Sports Sciences, 30,* 507–513.

Schorer, J., Loffing, F., Rienhoff, R., & Hagemann, N. (2015). Efficacy of training interventions for acquiring perceptual cognitive skill. In J. Baker & D. Farrow (eds), *Routledge Handbook of Sport Expertise* (pp. 430–438). London: Routledge.

Schweizer, G., Plessner, H., Kahlert, D., & Brand, R. (2011). A video-based training method for improving soccer referees' intuitive decision-making skills. *Journal of Applied Sport Psychology, 23,* 429–442.

Singer, R. N., Cauraugh, J. H., Chen, D., Steinberg, G. M., Frehlich, S. G., & Wang, L. (1994). Training mental quickness in beginning/intermediate tennis players. *The Sport Psychologist, 8,* 305–318.

Smeeton, N. J., Williams, A. M., Hodges, N. J., & Ward, P. (2005). The relative effectiveness of various instructional approaches in developing anticipation skill. *Journal of Experimental Psychology: Applied, 11,* 98–110.

Stoffregen, T. A., Bardy, B. G., Smart, L. J., & Pagulayan, R. (2003). On the nature and evaluation of fidelity in virtual environments. In L. Hettinger & M. Haas (eds), *Virtual and adaptive environments: Applications, implications, and human performance issues* (pp. 111–128). Mahwah, NJ: Lawrence Erlbaum Associates.

Ullén, F., Hambrick, D. Z., & Mosing, M. A. (2016). Rethinking expertise: A multifactorial gene–environment interaction model of expert performance. *Psychological Bulletin, 142,* 427–446.

van der Kamp, J., Rivas, F., van Doorn, H., & Savelsbergh, G. (2008). Ventral and dorsal system contributions to visual anticipation in fast ball sports. *International Journal of Sport Psychology, 39,* 100–130.

Vickers, J. N. (1996). Visual control when aiming at a far target. *Journal of Experimental Psychology: Human Perception and Performance, 22,* 342–354.

Vine, S. J., Moore, L. J., & Wilson, M. R. (2014). Quiet eye training: The acquisition, refinement and resilient performance of targeting skills. *European Journal of Sport Science, 14,* S235–S242.

Voss, M. W., Kramer, A. F., Basak, C., Prakash, R. S., & Roberts, B. (2010). Are expert athletes "expert" in the cognitive laboratory? A meta-analytic review of cognition and sport expertise. *Applied Cognitive Psychology, 24,* 812–826.

Ward, P., Farrow, D., Harris, K. R., Williams, A. M., Eccles, D. W., & Ericsson, K. A. (2008). Training perceptual-cognitive skills: Can sport psychology research inform military decision training? *Military Psychology, 20,* S71–S102.

Williams, A. M. (2000). Perceptual skill in soccer: Implications for talent identification and development. *Journal of Sports Sciences, 18,* 737–750.

Williams, A. M. (2009). Perceiving the intentions of others: How do skilled performers make anticipation judgments? In M. Raab, J. G. Johnson & H. R. Heekeren (eds), *Progress in Brain Research* (Vol. 174, Mind and motion: The bidirectional link between thought and action, pp. 73–83). Amsterdam: Elsevier.

Williams, A. M., & Burwitz, L. (1993). Advance cue utilization in soccer. In T. Reilly, J. Clarys & A. Stibbe (eds), *Science and football II* (pp. 239–243). London: E & FN Spon.

Williams, A. M., Davids, K., & Williams, J. G. (1999). *Visual perception and action in sport.* London: E. & F.N. Spon.

Williams, A. M., Ford, P. R., Eccles, D. W., & Ward, P. (2011). Perceptual-cognitive expertise in sport and its acquisition: Implications for applied cognitive psychology. *Applied Cognitive Psychology, 25,* 432–442.

Williams, A. M., & Grant, A. (1999). Training perceptual skill in sport. *International Journal of Sport Psychology, 30,* 194–220.

Williams, A. M., & Reilly, T. (2000). Talent identification and development in soccer. *Journal of Sports Sciences, 18,* 657–667.

Williams, A. M., & Ward, P. (2003). Perceptual expertise: Development in sport. In J. L. Starkes & K. A. Ericsson (eds), *Expert performance in sports: advances in research on sport expertise* (pp. 219–249). Champaign, IL: Human Kinetics.

Williams, A. M., Ward, P., & Chapman, C. (2003). Training perceptual skill in field hockey: Is there transfer from the laboratory to the field? *Research Quarterly for Exercise and Sport, 74,* 98–103.

Williams, A. M., Ward, P., Knowles, J. M., & Smeeton, N. J. (2002). Anticipation skill in a real-world task: Measurement, training, and transfer in tennis. *Journal of Experimental Psychology: Applied, 8,* 259–270.

Williams, A. M., Ward, P., Smeeton, N. J., & Allen, D. (2004). Developing anticipation skills in tennis using on-court instruction: perception versus perception and action. *Journal of Applied Sport Psychology, 16,* 350–360.

Wood, G., & Wilson, M. R. (2011). Quiet-eye training for soccer penalty kicks. *Cognitive Processing, 12,* 257–266.

Wood, G., & Wilson, M. R. (2012). Quiet-eye training, perceived control and performing under pressure. *Psychology of Sport and Exercise, 13,* 721–728.

Yarrow, K., Brown, P., & Krakauer, J. W. (2009). Inside the brain of an elite athlete: The neural processes that support high achievement in sports. *Nature Reviews Neuroscience, 10,* 585–596.

16

WINDOWS OF OPTIMAL DEVELOPMENT

David I. Anderson and Anthony M. Mayo

A fascinating question in the field of talent identification and development (TID) is whether the physical, technical, tactical, and psychological substrates that underlie expert performance can be developed more effectively and efficiently during certain developmental periods than others. The question is motivated by a fear that if windows of optimal development are not exploited, athletes may never reach their full potential. An equally legitimate fear is that certain developmental stages represent periods of heightened vulnerability to specific experiences. Despite these fears, little evidence supports the existence of such windows in the development of talent in sport. The lack of evidence does not imply that these windows do not exist. Rather, the lack of evidence is a reflection of the glaring lack of research devoted to these intriguing questions and the difficulty of identifying windows of optimal development and vulnerability in an activity as complex, multiply-layered, and multiply-determined as TID in sport.

Although sport-related research is lacking, research in the fields of embryology, ethology, developmental neuroscience, and educational psychology on critical periods in development and readiness for learning offer some important insights about whether and when windows of optimal development and vulnerability are likely to occur for the various subsystems that contribute to TID in sport. In addition, an established body of work on language learning and a rapidly expanding body of research on the learning of musical skills suggest that the age at which children are exposed to complex skills might be incredibly important for later success. Extrapolating from these lines of research provides further insight into potential windows of optimal development and vulnerability in sport.

The purpose of this chapter is to discuss the potential relevance of the windows of optimal development and vulnerability notions to TID in sport. We start by providing a brief overview of the readiness concept and a more extensive introduction to the critical periods concept in human development. Next, we use these concepts to discuss the potential risks of initiating practice or training either too early or too late for the development of the anatomical, physiological, psychological, and perceptual-motor substrates that underlie complex sport skill acquisition. The intent is to provide an introduction to the windows of optimal development and vulnerability phenomenon, knowing full well that it is not possible to cover the entire breadth and complexity of the phenomenon in the space available. Readers are encouraged to consult recent reviews of the critical periods and readiness concepts for more extensive coverage of the issues raised in the chapter (e.g., Anderson, 2002; Anderson, Magill, & Thouvarecq, 2012; Anderson & Mayo, 2015; Hensch, 2004; Werker & Hensch, 2015).

Readiness

The modern origin of the readiness concept is most likely Thorndike's (1913) *law of readiness*, which maintains that learning proceeds most effectively and efficiently when an individual is physically, mentally, and emotionally ready to learn. The concept assumes that development is a constructive process, with higher functions and behaviors emerging via the intercoordination of lower-level components and functions. The idea that developmental complexity emerges as a consequence of the hierarchical integration of subcomponent processes and skills is apparent in contemporary (e.g., Fischer & Bidell, 2006) and traditional (e.g., Bruner, 1966; Hebb, 1949; Gagné, 1968; Piaget, 1954) theories of development. Educational curricula are generally organized with reference to the readiness concept because educators assume that learners must master certain prerequisite skills and knowledge bases before they can acquire more complex skills and knowledge. Unfortunately, however, specifying when children are ready to learn the skills needed to succeed in contemporary society is challenging.

One should not assume that the readiness concept is confined to the learning of complex skills. It has been most frequently applied to complex skill learning, however, it is equally relevant to the development of the various component systems from which skills are assembled. For example, neuroscience research highlights that critical periods for the development of even the most basic neural circuits will not occur until the circuits are mature enough to process the information upon which they will ultimately depend. Thus, critical periods will not open until the system in question is ready to profit from the experiences that define the critical period. Because critical periods depend on adequate readiness, they have been referred to as periods of maximal readiness (Malina, 1993) or periods of optimal readiness (Magill & Anderson, 1996). With that point in mind, we now turn our attention to the critical period concept – the concept most closely associated with the existence of windows of optimal development and vulnerability.

Critical periods

A brief history

The basic idea behind the critical period (CP) concept is that experiences can exert a greater influence at some times during life than at others. Scott, Stewart, and De Ghett (1974) have generically defined a CP as a time during which an organizational process can be most easily altered or modified. The traditional concept has been compared to the opening of a window, with experiences influencing development only while the window is open (Bateson, 1979). The idea has a long history in conventional thinking and some would argue that its origin can be traced back to ancient times (Hess, 1973). The modern evolution of the concept likely began with Freud (1910), who did not explicitly make reference to CPs but who argued that certain neuroses originated in early experiences that occurred at highly constrained times during early development. Embryologists made the first formal reference to the CP concept. Their experiments revealed that cell masses were affected by specific chemicals only during a particular stage in their development and that some cells that were transplanted at one time in their development assumed the characteristics of host location cells and thrived but withered if transplanted at other times (Spemann, 1938; Stockard, 1921). The CP concept is now well established in embryological development (Moore & Persaud, 1998).

The observation that surgical closure of one eye during a brief period after birth causes a severe visual impairment in species such as cats and monkeys when the eye is later reopened is one of the most widely cited examples of a CP in mammalian development (Hubel & Wiesel, 1970; Wiesel & Hubel, 1963). The impairment is much less severe and even negligible if the closure occurs at other times during development. CPs have also been demonstrated for auditory development, tactile development, and vestibular, motor, and neuromuscular development in the rat (Jamon & Serradj, 2009) and a range of sensory processes in human development (Maurer, 2005).

Konrad Lorenz is credited with applying the CP concept to behavioral development via his work on imprinting – the tendency for certain species of birds to fixate and follow the first moving object they see. Lorenz noted that the process of imprinting was confined to a very short period early in life and that once accomplished it was irreversible (Lorenz, 1937). Ensuing discussions of the CP concept in social development associated the concept with Lorenz's idea that CPs were short in duration, irreversible, and occurred early in life. Lorenz's observations inspired an extensive body of research on CPs in imprinting and in other social phenomena, including emotional development in monkeys (Harlow, 1959), social development in dogs and other domestic animals (Scott, 1962), song-bird learning (Bolhuis, Okanoya, & Scharff, 2010), the development of secure attachments between children and their caregivers (Thompson, 2001), language learning (Lenneberg, 1967), and musical development (Habib & Besson, 2009).

Critical periods or sensitive periods?

A number of different types of CP effects have been documented in the literature. For example, periods have been identified in which certain experiences are expected for normal development and periods have been identified in which noxious experiences can irreversibly harm the individual. In addition, periods exist in which certain experiences are not necessary for normal development, but those experiences can nevertheless facilitate development (Moltz, 1973). Moreover, a considerable body of research has shown that CPs rarely conform to the characteristics identified by Lorenz (1937). They are rarely brief and sharply defined and rarely are their effects irreversible (Anderson et al., 2012; Bruer, 2001; Werker & Hensch, 2015), leading some to question the relevance of the CP concept for human behavioral and perceptual development (e.g., Bruer, 1999, 2015; Lerner, 1998; Thelen & Smith, 1998). For example, children can recover from years of severe deprivation (Clarke & Clarke, 1976), children with visual deficits can recover function later in life (Levi, Knill, & Bavelier, 2015), and even kittens deprived of visual experience during the CP defined by Hubel and Wiesel (1970) can improve visual functioning with appropriate visual training (Harwerth, Smith, Crawford, & van Noorden, 1989).

The range of different CP effects has led to considerable controversy about the appropriate label for periods during which developmental processes are most easily modifiable. Many researchers now prefer to use the terms *sensitive phase* or *sensitive period (SP)* when referring to heightened periods of susceptibility to environmental input in behavioral and perceptual development. Knudsen (2004) has defined SPs as those limited periods during which experience has a particularly strong effect on development. He defined CPs as a special and rarer class of SPs in which experiences are essential for normal development and alter performance permanently. The SP concept is much better aligned with the notion of windows of optimal development and so we will use it from here on.

Mechanisms that underlie sensitive periods

The brief history of the SP concept highlights the various fields (from psychology, to embryology, to ethology) that have inspired research on and development of the concept. Most of the current research and theorizing on SPs has occurred in the neurosciences, where the question shifted from whether SPs exist to what process opens them, keeps them open, closes them, and allows them to reopen (Werker & Hensch, 2015). Naturally, in the neurosciences, the focus is on the development of the neural circuitry that underlies behavior, where nature must find a balance between pre-structuring circuits that perform the basic functions necessary to ensure an organism's survival and yet leave enough plasticity in the circuits for behavior to be adapted to the unique characteristics of the local context. Plasticity is also necessary because morphological changes related to growth and maturation, such as in the size and shape of the eye and in the distance between the two eyes, necessitate constant recalibration and fine tuning of the neural circuits that underlie perceptual and motor processes (e.g., Johnson, 2005; Levi, 2005).

Developmental neuroscientists now believe that numerous SPs exist during the development of the brain and behavior. They occur at different times in different regions of the brain and for different functions. Within a particular perceptual system there are multiple SPs for different functions, and more than one SP has been found for specific functions within a perceptual system, like visual acuity (e.g., Lewis & Maurer, 2005). SPs are likely to occur earlier for the most basic functions (or circuits) and later for higher-order functions that are constructed from more basic circuits. For this reason, the development of the neural circuitry underlying behavior can show marked reductions in plasticity across the lifespan (Hensch, 2004; Knudsen, 2004), whereas behavior can exhibit considerable plasticity across the lifespan (e.g., Greenough, Black, & Wallace, 1987; Johnson, 2005). Irreversible changes in a neural circuit do not automatically lead to irreversible changes in behavior because higher-level circuits, which remain plastic for longer periods, can compensate for aberrant circuits at lower levels in the hierarchy or higher-level circuits can derive information from alternate pathways (Knudsen, 2004).

Knudsen (2004) highlighted that SPs in neural development cannot occur until three conditions are met. First, the information that serves as input to the circuit must be sufficiently precise and reliable. Second, the circuit must possess adequate excitatory and inhibitory connections to process the information, and third, mechanisms that enable plasticity must have been turned on. Werker and Hensch (2015) have provided a detailed description of the substrates that underlie SP plasticity. Briefly, precocious plasticity is prevented by various molecular brakes and then enabled by a different set of molecular triggers. However, the timing of SP onset is itself plastic. Though circuits have to mature sufficiently before they are responsive to molecular triggers, the opening of a SP is also determined by outside influences. For example, pharmacological agents can accelerate SP opening, whereas lack of environmental input can delay it. Experience reorganizes circuits via synaptic pruning while the SP is open and then the SP is closed by molecular brakes, which consolidate and stabilize the circuit and limit further plasticity. The SP can be reopened later if the molecular brakes are removed. Werker and Hensch (2015) note that the opening and closing of a SP is like opening and then locking a door. If one has the key to the lock, the SP can be opened again at a later time. Much of the work in neurobiology over the last decade or so has been devoted to discovering those keys.

Windows of optimal development in sport

Earlier we noted that the lack of evidence for windows of optimal development and vulnerability in sport is largely a reflection of the difficulty of identifying these windows in such a multifactorial activity. While windows of optimal development and vulnerability for sport have not been identified, it is possible to extrapolate from research on readiness and critical/sensitive periods in motor and perceptual development to highlight the potential risks of starting practice and training either too late or too early. This research helps to narrow the search for the windows of optimal development and vulnerability. We present a sampling of this research and other relevant research in the following sections.

Risks of starting too late

Anatomical and physiological development

In his work on the development of expertise in sport, Ericsson has maintained that an early start is often necessary because certain anatomical and physiological adaptations necessary for elite performance can be most easily made during SPs that occur during physical maturation (e.g., Ericsson, 2003; Ericsson, Krampe, & Tesch-Römer, 1993). For example, the flexibility needed by ballet dancers seems to be developed most effectively if training begins before puberty (Hutchinson, Sachs-Ericsson, & Ericsson, 2013). Similarly, because flexibility in the ankles and shoulders provides an excellent predictor of swimming speed (Poppleton & Salmoni, 1991), Ericsson et al. (1993) argued that swimmers' flexibility is best developed by intense training at a young age. These suggestions have not been confirmed by more recent research, however. Moreover, Rowland (2015), in a recent review of physiological adaptations that result from early specialized training, concluded that uncertainty still remains as to whether developmental periods exist during which training is more effective. He does note that physiological adaptations to endurance training are greater post-puberty than pre-puberty, suggesting that delaying such training would be advantageous, whereas strength development in response to resistance training is equally effective at all ages.

Development of psychological processes

Perceptual discrimination represents the best illustration of a psychological phenomenon that has an early SP followed by a rapid reduction in plasticity. Scott, Pascalis, and Nelson (2007) noted that perceptual development during the first years of life is characterized by a process referred to as perceptual narrowing, wherein perceptual discrimination is broadly tuned at first and then becomes increasingly selective with experience. The most frequently cited example of perceptual narrowing is the change in phoneme discrimination that occurs as children learn language. Prior to 6 months of age, infants are capable of discriminating all of the speech sounds that comprise all spoken languages, but then experience a rapid decline in sensitivity to non-native phonological speech contrasts between 6 and 12 months of age (Maurer & Werker, 2014). As infants listen to the consonants that characterize their native language, their ability to discriminate those consonants is maintained and sharpened. In contrast, listening to native speech weakens the ability to discriminate non-native consonants.

Is the perceptual narrowing phenomenon relevant to the development of skill in sport? Perhaps so. Because perceptual discrimination is basically a pattern recognition skill, it is interesting to speculate about whether pattern recognition skills relevant to the acquisition of sport skills might be apparent early in life only to disappear because of lack of use. Malcolm Gladwell (1999) recounted a story about Wayne Gretzky that may be relevant to this point. Gretzky is reported to have been mesmerized by ice hockey games on TV before the age of 2. Apparently he would slide across the floor in his socks imitating the players on the ice and then cry when the game was over. Did Gretzky preserve some pattern recognition skill that later contributed to his reputation as one of the greatest readers of the game of ice hockey in history? Did his ability to see scoring opportunities that nobody else saw emerge because he maintained a pattern recognition skill that otherwise would have been lost? We will never know the answer to these questions, of course, but the questions raise the fascinating possibility that certain perceptual substrates that underlie expertise in sport might be most profitably developed very early in life.

Skill acquisition

SPs have been discussed for two perceptual-motor skills, language acquisition and the acquisition of musical skills, which are potentially relevant to our understanding of the risks of late exposure to sports skills. We will provide a brief summary of the relevant work on the acquisition of musical skills, but refer the interested reader to Werker and Hensch (2015) for a comprehensive examination of the research on SPs in language acquisition. Prior to addressing the potential enhancement of motor skills with early training, it is pertinent to point out that early deprivation of expectable experiences can be particularly harmful to general motor skill development. For example, Levin, Zeanah, Fox, and Nelson (2014) reported that children exposed to early physical and psychosocial deprivation as a result of being raised in orphanages, had significantly poorer motor proficiency scores at the age of eight than children who were never institutionalized, even though half of the institutionalized children had been placed in foster homes at an average age of 23 months. Thus, the negative effects of early (and relatively brief) deprivation on motor development persisted even though half of the children had been exposed to a normalized home environment for several years prior to testing.

Returning to the potential enhancing effects of early experience, a number of researchers have argued that children must be exposed to musical training before the age of 7 years to become an expert musician (e.g., Habib & Besson, 2009). The claim is based on the number of differences in brain responses to auditory stimuli observed in musicians who were exposed to musical training before or after the age of 7 years. Watanabe, Savion-Lemieux, and Penhune (2007) have provided the most convincing evidence for an early SP in the motor component of musical training. They matched two groups of musicians who had started practice before or after the age of 7 on years of musical experience, years of formal training, and hours of current practice and then compared them on their ability to learn a rapid, sequential finger-sequencing task that required synchronization with a visual stimulus. Clear differences were seen on the rate and level of learning achieved on the task in favor of the musicians who had begun practice before the age of 7 years. These findings were replicated and extended using an auditory rhythmic synchronization task (Bailey & Penhune, 2010). More recently, Steele, Bailey, Zatorre, and Penhune (2013) showed that the superior motor timing and synchronization skill associated with exposure to musical training before the age of 7 was accompanied by greater white matter connectivity in the corpus callosum. The authors argued that the early musical training was responsible for the structural changes in the brain.

Implications for TID in sport

A clear implication of the aforementioned research on potential SPs for anatomical, physiological, psychological, and motor skill development is that parents need to be educated about the consequences of early environmental enrichment and deprivation for child development to ensure that the pool of potentially talented athletes is as large as possible. Most coaches and scouts will not have opportunities to observe young athletes until after some of the most important SPs for the development of basic perceptual and motor skills have ended. Consequently, it is important that parents understand that lack of environmental input or aberrant input during the first two years of life, in particular, can have deleterious effects on the basic perceptual and motor skills that provide the foundation upon which later sport skills will be developed. The primary implications are 1) that young children with congenital perceptual deficits should be identified early and should have their problems corrected as early as possible to give them the greatest chance to experience success in sports later in life, and 2) young children need exposure to a broad range of motor skills early in life to ensure they will develop the basic motor competence necessary for the development of sport-specific skills later in childhood. Consistent with the evidence suggesting that early-trained musicians show different brain responses to auditory stimuli and acquire perceptual-motor synchronization tasks more rapidly than late-trained musicians, we would advocate that children are given abundant opportunities and encouragement to acquire fundamental motor skills like running, hopping, skipping, jumping, leaping, throwing, catching, and striking well before the age of 7 (Gabbard, 1998, has made a similar recommendation). With respect to augmented experiences, the perceptual narrowing phenomenon suggests that additional "pattern recognition" experiences very early in life could preserve perceptual skills that might be advantageous to athletes later in life. Because it is not at all clear what those experiences might be, research on this topic is sorely needed.

Another implication is that training to develop speed, agility, strength, and flexibility could begin well before the onset of puberty to provide young athletes with a foundation on which to develop sport-specific adaptations during and after puberty, whereas training to develop aerobic or endurance capacity is likely best delayed until after puberty, or at least until after peak height velocity has been reached during puberty. The evidence is quite clear that pre-pubescent children adapt well to resistance training, primarily through neurological adaptations rather than muscle hypertrophy, but show limited adaptation to aerobic training (Bompa & Carrera, 2015; Faigenbaum, Lloyd, & Myer, 2013; Rowland, 2015). Bompa and Carrera (2015) and Faigenbaum et al. (2013) provide excellent suggestions for how to adapt training volumes and intensities to the child's developmental level. It is less obvious when flexibility training should be initiated, despite Ericsson and colleagues' claim that flexibility for dancers and swimmers is most effectively developed before puberty (e.g., Ericsson et al., 1993). The evidence to support these claims is largely anecdotal rather than empirical. The need to develop flexibility at an early age seems to be determined by the age at which athletes who engage in artistic sports that require high degrees of flexibility, like gymnastics, diving, and figure skating, tend to specialize in their sports (e.g., Bompa & Carrera, 2015). More research is certainly needed in this area before definitive recommendations can be made. Despite the uncertainties surrounding the potential windows of opportunities for developing sport skills and their substrates, we have attempted to summarize some of the recommendations we have made in this section in Figure 16.1.

The implications for talent identification are less clear. Because many of the pre-pubertal adaptations to experience and training pertain to the development of basic foundational skills and abilities, whereas sport-specific adaptations are likely to occur post-puberty, it would seem unwise to attempt to identify talent prior to the end of puberty. However, one could also argue that young children who possess a broad and solid foundation of basic competencies are the ones with the greatest potential to develop sport-specific adaptations post-puberty. Consequently, the research discussed in this section could be used to argue for or against early talent identification.

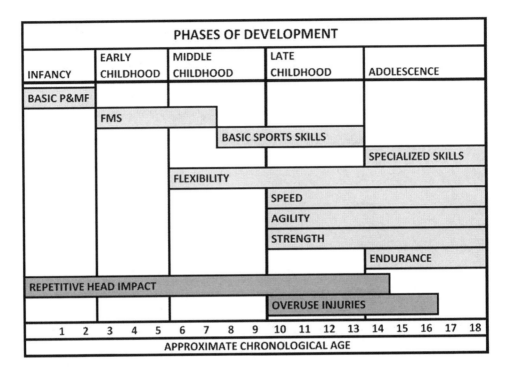

Figure 16.1 Potential windows of opportunity and vulnerability for different aspects and phases in the development of skills in which performance peaks after maturity (i.e., excluding artistic skills like dance, gymnastics, diving, and figure skating). Because the beginning and end points of windows of opportunity are multiply determined and more closely aligned with biological maturity than chronological age, these points are approximations and the end points for many aspects of performance continue past adolescence. Basic P&MF refers to basic perceptual and motor functions that develop rapidly after birth. FMS refers to the fundamental motor skills, like running, jumping, hopping, skipping, throwing, catching, and striking that serve as the foundation upon which sport-specific skills are developed. The optimal window for learning to swim the front crawl appears to be between 5 and 7 years of age. The bottom two bars represent windows of vulnerability.

Risks of starting too early

Anatomical and physiological development

A risk of starting sports skill training too early is overuse injuries, particularly when the child specializes in a single sport (Baker, 2003; Baker, Cobley, & Fraser-Thomas, 2009; LaPrade et al., 2016; Malina, 2009, 2010). Repetitive motions and excessive stress on the developing musculoskeletal system can lead to problems such as elbow or shoulder tendonitis in baseball pitchers and lower limb injuries in ballet dancers and soccer players (Adams, 1965; Bowerman, Whatman, Harris, Bradshaw, & Karin, 2014; Kim & Lim, 2014; Meister et al., 2005; Olsen, Fleisig, Dun, Loftice & Andrews, 2006; Read, Oliver, De Ste Croix, Myer, & Lloyd, 2015). Injuries that occur at or around peak height velocity suggest a window of vulnerability around the adolescent growth spurt. For example, limb length increases rapidly during the adolescent growth spurt, however, muscular strength does not increase simultaneously. Consequently, adolescents can experience traction apophyseal injuries such as Little League elbow and shoulder and Osgood Schlatter's and Sever's Diseases. Olsen et al. (2006) reported that pitchers who experienced elbow and shoulder injuries threw more pitches during the calendar year, threw with high velocity, participated in showcase events, and pitched through pain. Interestingly, injured players were likely to be early maturers. In contrast, van der Sluis, Elferink-Gemser, Brink, and Visscher (2015) reported that late-maturing adolescent soccer players experienced more overuse injuries, before and during peak height velocity, compared to their age-matched early maturing peers. Hall, Barber Foss, Hewett, and Myer (2015) found that adolescent girls who specialized in one sport at an early age were four times more likely to experience Osgood Schlatter's disease than a peer who participated in multiple sports. Changes in coordination that accompany the adolescent growth spurt have also been associated with lower extremity injuries in ballet dancers (Bowerman et al., 2014) and artistic gymnasts (Kim & Lim, 2014).

A current "hot topic" in academia, public health, and the media is sports-related concussion and its effects on cognitive function, mood, and neurological diseases. Much of the current research is driven by the discovery of cognitive decline and neurological diseases like Parkinson's and Alzheimer's in retired National Football League (NFL) players. Stamm et al. (2015a) examined the relationship between age at which retired American professional football players started practicing the sport and post-career cognitive function. Those individuals who began playing organized tackle football between the ages 9 and 12 performed significantly more poorly in tests of executive function, episodic memory, and estimated verbal IQ when compared to individuals who started after age 12. A subsequent study showed that individuals who started prior to the age of 12 had abnormalities in the microstructure of the corpus callosum compared to those who started after age 12 (Stamm et al., 2015b). The investigators proposed that the abnormalities in the brain and deficits in cognitive function were likely due to repetitive head impacts experienced by players during a critical period of neurological development.

Concern over the long-term neurological and psychological consequences of repetitive head impacts has led to the recommendation in a white paper from the Sports Legacy Institute and the Institute of Sports Law and Ethics at Santa Clara University in California to delay the introduction to heading in youth soccer until the age of 14 (Cantu, Nowinski, & Robbins, 2015). The paper reviews evidence showing a link between the frequency of heading and cognitive impairment as well as changes in brain structure, evidence that young people are more susceptible to damage from repetitive concussive and sub-concussive brain trauma, and evidence that greater neck strength significantly reduces head accelerations caused by impact loading. The growing body of evidence linking repetitive head impacts during childhood to neurological and psychological problems later in life will likely have a major influence on when and how children are exposed to sports that have the greatest potential for incurring such impacts.

Development of psychological processes

Two potential risks of starting sport participation too early are the development of bad habits in perceptual and cognitive processes. With respect to perceptual processes, Woollacott, Debû, and Shumway-Cook (1987), after noting a regression in postural control between the ages of 4 and 6, suggested that children go through a period of intersensory integration in which they shift from primarily visual control of movement to an ability to integrate visual, vestibular, and somatosensory information for movement control. According to Woollacott et al. (1987), pressure to specialize in one motor skill or pressure to perform to a criterion before or during this age period could compromise intersensory integration. For example, if a child is forced to perform to a criterion of success the child might continue to rely on visual information to control the movement and fail to integrate other sources of information that would ultimately be needed to refine the movement at later stages of learning. Visual dependence may continue indefinitely, at least for that particular task.

Myrtle McGraw's (1935, 1939) classic training study on the twin boys Johnny and Jimmy provides a good example of the potential to develop bad habits in cognitive processes. Both boys were given early training on a task that required them to manipulate pedestals of varying heights into an arrangement that allowed them to climb upward to obtain a lure that was suspended from the ceiling. Both boys were ultimately able to solve the problem. However, when tested at a later age, the boys used too many pedestals to solve the problem in comparison to age-matched children who had not practiced the task. According to McGraw (1939), the inefficient strategy was a residual of earlier practice when the boys were less discriminating and probably immature in terms of their understanding of spatial relations. The counterintuitive finding that prior experience with the stimuli that characterize a task can interfere with future problem solving is quite common. It is referred to by several terms, including functional fixedness, negative transfer, mental set, and Einstellung (Ellis & Reingold, 2014).

Skill acquisition

Potential downsides of initiating learning too early from the standpoint of skill acquisition are a slower rate of learning, frustrations that are associated with slow progress, and, similar to the perceptual domain, the development of bad habits that can take considerable time to overcome when the child is older. These negative consequences are presumed to be related to inadequate readiness. Much of the evidence for the negative consequences of inadequate readiness was presented in the 1920s and 1930s. For example, McGraw (1935) gave Johnny extensive practice on tricycle riding when he was 11 months old, whereas Jimmy was not exposed to tricycling until he was 22 months old. Johnny struggled for eight months before showing any improvement on the task while Jimmy mastered the task very rapidly. Other researchers from that era found similar consequences of inadequate readiness for motor learning (e.g., Gesell & Thompson, 1929; Hilgard, 1932).

More relevant to the development of sports skills, Barynina and Vaitsekhovskii (1992) found that swimmers on the Russian national team who learned to swim later (females = 10.5 years, males = 9.8) and specialized in intense training later (females = 12.6, males = 12.1) took less time to reach the national team and spent longer on the national team than those who learned to swim earlier (females = 6.8, males = 7.7) and specialized earlier (females = 9.8, males = 10). These findings are consistent with research reporting a negative relation between the age at which formal swimming lessons are started and the number of lessons required to reach specific levels of competence (Anderson & Rodriguez, 2014; Blanksby, Parker, Bradley, & Ong, 1995; Parker & Blanksby, 1997). For example, Anderson and Rodriguez (2014) reported that children who started formal swimming lessons at the age of three required over four times as many lessons to reach level 1 swimming proficiency than children who started lessons at the age of eight (77.7 vs. 18.6). Fewer lessons were also required for the later starters to reach more advanced levels of proficiency than the earlier starters. Anderson and Rodriguez (2014) argued that the optimal window for introducing children to formal swimming lessons was between five and seven years of age.

A potentially devastating effect of premature teaching is that it might result in the child learning not to learn (Scott, 1962) and thus dropping out of the activity. It is important to keep in mind that demonstrating competence is a major motivator for children and adults (Harter, 1985). The development of bad habits in movement control is the other potential risk of participating in an activity too early. Bad habits can be particularly problematic because the foundation upon which learning is built becomes increasingly resistant to change as the earlier-developed skills become hierarchically organized into higher-order skills. The earlier skills become reinforced and stabilized during this process, potentially interfering with the further development of the skill. Anderson and Rodriguez (2014) speculated that their earlier starting swimmers required more lessons than the later starters to progress from a basic front crawl to a more proficient front crawl because they had spent more time swimming the front crawl while breathing by pulling the head directly upward. This pattern of breathing was thought to interfere with the more efficient side-breathing pattern, requiring the habitual pattern to be unlearned before the more efficient pattern could be acquired.

Implications for TID in sport

The primary implication of the aforementioned research is that children who participate in sports should not be treated as if they were miniature adults. The primary risk associated with participating in sports at an early age is not a risk of starting too early per se, but of specializing too early. Children who specialize in one sport too early or who are exposed prematurely to a high volume or intensity of training have the greatest risk of suffering injuries, particularly just before or during the pubescent growth spurt. Though not covered in this chapter, early specializers are also at greatest risk for experiencing psychological burnout and dropping out of sports altogether (LaPrade et al., 2016). These findings further highlight the importance of exposing children to a wide range of sports and activities and helping them to develop a broad fitness base before allowing them to specialize in one sport. In most sports—with artistic sports like gymnastics being a notable exception—specializing in one sport should be delayed until after the pubescent growth spurt. In addition, parents and coaches need to consider the child's readiness to learn before exposing them to any new skill to avoid the frustrations associated with lack of progress and the potential to develop bad habits that may take considerable time and effort to unlearn later on. Unfortunately, clear guidelines for assessing readiness for learning new skills have not been established. More research is desperately needed to establish these guidelines.

With respect to talent identification, it is pertinent to note that early identification of talented athletes may predispose those athletes to the heightened risks for injury and burnout associated with early specialization, undermining the presumed advantage that early identification is thought to give these athletes. These risks can be avoided if talent identification is delayed until after the pubescent growth spurt, or, as mentioned at the end of the previous section of the chapter, if the focus shifts to identifying athletes with a broad foundation of basic skills and competencies rather than specific skills and competencies.

Concluding thoughts

We have attempted to provide an overview of how the notion of windows of optimal development can be applied to TID in sport. It is clear from the foregoing discussion that the notion is broad and complex, with no clear answer to when the windows of optimal development occur for the development of the physical, technical, tactical, and psychological substrates that underlie expert performance. Adding to the complexity, any of the substrates could be potential rate limiters to the broader development of expertise, given the multi-dimensional nature of sport. Different requirements for different sports mean that the windows of optimal development will vary from sport to sport and from skill to skill and substrate to substrate within a sport. Individual differences suggest that the windows will vary from individual to individual, particularly with respect to the timing of physical maturation. Finally, variation can be expected depending on whether windows are sought relative to when a child should be introduced to a sport versus when a child specializes in a sport and whether windows are sought for periods of optimal development or vulnerability.

It is clear, however, that lack of readiness can have serious negative consequences for anatomical/physiological development, the development of psychological processes, and the development of motor skills. Conversely, waiting too long after minimal or optimal readiness to begin practice or training could prevent the child from reaching his or her full potential in sport. We have provided some limited insights into when the windows of optimal development and vulnerability might occur during childhood, but much more research is clearly needed before we can specify these windows with confidence and flesh out their implications for TID. This represents an exciting opportunity for sports science researchers.

References

Adams, J. E. (1965). Injury to the throwing arm: A study of traumatic changes in the elbow joint of boy baseball players. *California Medicine, 102*, 127–132.

Anderson, D. I. (2002). Do critical periods and readiness determine when to initiate sport skill learning? In F. L. Smoll and R. E. Smith (eds), *Children and youth in sport: A biopsychosocial perspective* (2nd ed., pp. 105–148). Dubuque, IA: Kendall/Hunt.

Anderson, D. I., Magill, R. A., & Thouvarecq, R. (2012). Critical periods, sensitive periods, and readiness in motor skill learning. In N. J. Hodges and A. M. Williams (eds), *Skill acquisition in sport: Research, theory and practice* (2nd ed., pp. 211–228). New York: Routledge.

Anderson, D. I., & Mayo, A. M. (2015). A skill acquisition perspective on early specialization in sport. *Kinesiology Review, 4*, 230–247.

Anderson, D. I., & Rodriguez, A. (2014). Is there an optimal age for learning to swim? *Journal of Motor Learning and Development, 2*, 80–89.

Bailey J. A., & Penhune V. B. (2010). Rhythm synchronization performance and auditory working memory in early- and late-trained musicians. *Experimental Brain Research, 204*, 91–101. doi: 10.1007/s00221-010-2299-y

Baker, J. (2003). Early specialization in youth sport: A requirement for adult expertise? *High Ability Studies, 14*, 85–94.

Baker, J., Cobley, S., & Fraser-Thomas, J. (2009). What do we know about early sport specialization? Not much! *High Ability Studies, 20*, 77–89.

Barynina, I. I., & Vaitsekhovskii, S. M. (1992). The aftermath of early sports specialization for highly qualified swimmers. *Fitness and Sports Review International, 27*, 132–133.

Bateson, P. (1979). How do sensitive periods arise and what are they for? *Animal Behaviour, 27*, 470–486.

Blanksby, B. A., Parker, H. E., Bradley, S., & Ong, V. (1995). Children's readiness for learning front crawl swimming. *Australian Journal of Science and Medicine in Sport, 27*, 34–37.

Bolhuis, J. J., Okanoya, K., & Scharff, C. (2010). Twitter evolution: converging mechanisms in birdsong and human speech. *Nature Reviews: Neuroscience, 11*, 747–759.

Bompa, T. O., & Carrera, M. (2015). *Conditioning young athletes*. Champaign, IL: Human Kinetics.

Bowerman, E., Whatman, C., Harris, N., Bradshaw, E., & Karin, J. (2014). Are maturation, growth and lower extremity alignment associated with overuse injury in elite adolescent ballet dancers? *Physical Therapy in Sport, 15*, 234–241.

Bruer, J. T. (1999). *The myth of the first three years: A new understanding of early brain development and lifelong learning*. New York: Free Press.

Bruer, J. T. (2001). A critical and sensitive period primer. In D. B. Bailey, J. T. Bruer, F. J. Symons, & J. W. Lichtman (eds), *Critical thinking about critical periods* (pp. 3–26). Baltimore, MD: Paul H. Brookes.

Bruer, J. T. (2015). Sensitive periods. In S. Robson & S. F. Quinn (eds), *The Routledge international handbook of young children's thinking and understanding* (pp. 238–248). New York: Routledge.

Bruner, J. S. (1966). *Toward a theory of instruction*. Cambridge, MA: Harvard University Press.

Cantu, R., Nowinski, C., & Robbins, C. (2015, February 20). Safer soccer white paper: The neurological consequences of heading in soccer. *Institute of Sports Law and Ethics at Santa Clara University*.

Clarke, A. M., & Clarke, A. D. B. (eds). (1976). *Early experience: Myth and evidence*. New York: Free Press.

Ellis, J. J., & Reingold, E. M. (2014). The Einstellung effect in anagram problem solving: Evidence from eye movements. *Frontiers in Psychology, 5*, 35–41.

Ericsson, K. A. (2003). Development of elite performance and deliberate practice: An update from the perspective of the expert performance approach. In J. L. Starkes & K. A. Ericsson (eds), *Expert performance in sports: Advances in research on sports expertise* (pp. 49–81). Champaign, IL: Human Kinetics.

Ericsson, K. A., Krampe, R. T., & Tesch-Römer, C. (1993). The role of deliberate practice in the acquisition of expert performance. *Psychological Review, 100*, 363–406.

Faigenbaum, A. D., Lloyd, R. S., & Myer, G. D. (2013). Youth resistance training: Past practices, new perspectives, and future directions. *Pediatric Exercise Science, 25*, 591–604.

Fischer, K. W., & Bidell, T. (2006). Dynamic development of action and thought. In W. Damon & R. Lerner (eds), *Handbook of Child Psychology* (6th ed.). *Vol. I: Theoretical models of human development* (pp. 313–399). Hoboken, NJ: John Wiley & Sons.

Freud, S. (1910). *Three contributions to the sexual theory*. New York: Journal of Nervous and Mental Diseases Publishing Company.

Gabbard, C. (1998). Windows of opportunity for early brain and motor development. *Journal of Physical Education, Recreation, & Dance, 69*, 54–61.

Gagné, R. M. (1968). Contributions of learning to human development. *Psychological Review, 75*, 177–191.

Gesell, A., & Thompson, H. (1929). Learning and growth in identical infant twins: An experimental study by the method of co-twin control. *Genetic Psychology Monographs, 6*, 1–124.

Gladwell, M. (1999, August 2). The physical genius: What do Wayne Gretzky, Yo-Yo Ma, and a brain surgeon named Charlie Wilson have in common? *The New Yorker*, 56–65.

Greenough, W. T., Black, J. E., & Wallace, C. S. (1987). Experience and brain development. *Child Development, 58*, 539–559.

Habib, M., & Besson, M. (2009). What do music training and musical experience teach us about brain plasticity? *Music Perception, 26*, 279–285.

Hall, R., Foss, K. B., Hewett, T. E., & Myer, G. D. (2015). Sport specialization's association with an increased risk of developing anterior knee pain in adolescent female athletes. *Journal of Sport Rehabilitation, 24*, 31–35.

Harlow, H. F. (1959). Love in infant monkeys. *Scientific American, 200*, 68–74.

Harter, S. (1985). Competence as a dimension of self-evaluation. Toward a comprehensive model of self-worth. In R. Leahy (ed.), *The development of the self* (pp. 55–122). New York: Academic Press.

Harwerth, R. S., Smith III, E. L., Crawford, M. L. J., & van Noorden, G. K. (1989). The effects of reverse monocular deprivation in monkeys I: Psychophysical experiments. *Experimental Brain Research, 74*, 327–337.

Hebb, D. O. (1949). *The organization of behavior*. London: John Wiley.

Hensch, T. K. (2004). Critical period regulation. *Annual Review of Neuroscience, 27*, 549–579.

Hess, E. H. (1973). *Imprinting*. New York: Van Nostrand Reinhold.

Hilgard, J. R. (1932). Learning and maturation in preschool children. *Journal of Genetic Psychology, 41*, 36–56.

Hubel, D. H., & Wiesel, T. N. (1970). The period of susceptibility to the physiological effects of unilateral eye closure in kittens. *Journal of Physiology, 206*, 419–436.

Hutchinson, C. U., Sachs-Ericsson, N. J., & Ericsson, K. A. (2013). Generalizable aspects of the development of expertise in ballet across countries and cultures: A perspective from the expert-performance approach. *High Ability Studies, 24*, 21–47.

Jamon, M., & Serradj, N. (2009). Ground-based researches on the effects of altered gravity on mice development. *Microgravity Science and Technology, 21*, 327–337.

Johnson, M. H. (2005). Sensitive periods in functional brain development: Problems and prospects. *Developmental Psychobiology, 46*, 287–292.

Kim, K-W., & Lim, B-O. (2014). Effects of menarcheal age on the anterior cruciate ligament injury risk factors during single-legged drop landing in female artistic elite gymnasts. *Archives of Orthopaedic and Trauma Surgery, 134*, 1565–1571.

Knudsen, E. I. (2004). Sensitive periods in the development of brain and behavior. *Journal of Cognitive Neuroscience, 16*, 1412–1425.

LaPrade, R. F., Agel, J., Baker, J., Brenner, J. S., Cordasco, F. A., Côté, J., ... Provencher, M. T. (2016). AOSSM early sport specialization consensus statement. *The Orthopaedic Journal of Sports Medicine, 4*, 1–8.

Lenneberg, E. H. (1967). *Biological foundations of language.* New York: Wiley.

Lerner, R. M. (1998). Theories of human development: Contemporary perspectives. In W. Damon (Editor-in-chief) & R. M. Lerner (Vol. Ed.), *Handbook of child psychology: Vol. 1. Theoretical models of human development* (5th ed., pp. 1–24). New York: John Wiley & Sons.

Levi, D. M. (2005). Perceptual learning in adults with amblyopia: A reevaluation of critical periods in human vision. *Developmental Psychobiology, 46*, 222–232.

Levi, D. M., Knill, D. C., & Bavelier, D. (2015). Stereopsis and amblyopia: A mini-review. *Vision Research, 114*, 17–30.

Levin, A. R., Zeanah, C. H., Fox, N. A., & Nelson, C. A. (2014). Motor outcomes in children exposed to early psychosocial deprivation. *Journal of Pediatrics, 164*, 123–129.

Lewis, T. L., & Maurer, D. (2005). Multiple sensitive periods in human visual development: Evidence from visually deprived children. *Developmental Psychobiology, 46*, 163–183.

Lorenz, K. (1937). The companion in the bird's world. *The Auk, 54*, 245–273.

Magill, R. A., & Anderson, D. I. (1996). Critical periods as optimal readiness for learning sport skills. In F. L. Smoll and R. E. Smith (eds), *Children and youth in sport: A biopsychosocial perspective* (pp. 57–72). Indianapolis: Brown and Benchmark.

Malina, R. M. (1993). Youth sports: Readiness, selection and trainability. In W. Duquet and J. A. P. Day (eds), *Kinanthropometry IV* (pp. 252–266). London: E & FN Spon.

Malina, R. M. (2009). Children and adolescents in the sport culture: The overwhelming majority to the select few [Supplemental material]. *Journal of Exercise Science and Fitness, 7*(2), S1–S10.

Malina, R. M. (2010). Early sport specialization: Roots, effectiveness, risks. *Current Sports Medicine Reports, 9*(6), 364–371.

Maurer, D. (2005). Introduction to the special issue on critical periods reexamined: Evidence from human sensory development. *Developmental Psychobiology, 46*, 155.

Maurer, D., & Werker, J. F. (2014). Perceptual narrowing during infancy: A comparison of language and faces. *Developmental Psychobiology, 56*, 154–178.

McGraw, M. B. (1935). *Growth: A study of Johnny and Jimmy.* New York: Appleton-Century.

McGraw, M. B. (1939). Later development of children specially trained during infancy: Johnny and Jimmy at school age. *Child Development, 10*, 1–19.

Meister, K., Day, T., Horodyski, M, Kaminski, T. W., Wasik, M. P., & Tillman, S. (2005). Rotational motion changes in the glenohumeral joint of the adolescent/Little League baseball player. *The American Journal of Sports Medicine, 33*, 693–698.

Moltz, H. (1973). Some implications of the critical period hypothesis. *Annals of the New York Academy of Sciences, 223*, 144–146.

Moore, K. L., & Persaud, T. V. N. (1998). *The Developing Human: Clinically Oriented Embryology* (6th ed.). Philadelphia: W.B. Saunders.

Olsen, II, S. J., Fleisig, G. S., Dun, S., Loftice, J., & Andrews, J. R. (2006). Risk factors for shoulder and elbow injuries in adolescent baseball players. *The American Journal of Sports Medicine, 34*, 905–912.

Parker, H. E., & Blanksby, B. A. (1997). Starting age and aquatic skill learning in young children: Mastery of prerequisite water confidence and basic aquatic locomotion skills. *The Australian Journal of Science and Medicine in Sport, 29*, 83–87.

Piaget, J. (1954). *The construction of reality in the child.* New York: Basic Books.

Poppleton, W. L., & Salmoni, A. W. (1991). Talent identification in swimming. *Journal of Human Movement Studies, 20*, 85–100.

Read, P., Oliver, J. L., De Ste Croix, M. B. A., Myer, G. D., & Lloyd, R. S. (2015). Injury risk factors in male youth soccer players. *Strength and Conditioning Journal, 37*(5), 1–7.

Rowland, T. W. (2015). Physiological aspects of early specialized athletic training in children. *Kinesiology Review, 4*, 279–291.

Spemann, H. (1938). *Embryonic development and induction.* New Haven: Yale University.

Scott, J. P. (1962). Critical periods in behavioral development. *Science, 138*, 949–958.

Scott, J. P., Stewart, J. M., & De Ghett, V. J. (1974). Critical periods in the organization of systems. *Developmental Psychobiology, 7*, 489–513.

Scott, L. S., Pascalis, O., & Nelson, C. A. (2007). A domain-general theory of the development of perceptual discrimination. *Current Directions in Psychological Science, 16*, 197–201.

Stamm, J. M., Bourlas, A. P., Baugh, C. M., Fritts, N. G., Daneshvar, D. H., Martin, B. M., ... Stern, R. A (2015a). Age of first exposure to football and later-life cognitive impairment in former NFL players. *Neurology, 84*, 1114–1120.

Stamm, J. M., Koerte, I. K., Muehlmann, M., Pasternak, O., Bourlas, A. P., Baugh, C. M., ... Shenton, M. E. (2015b). Age at first exposure to football is associated with altered corpus callosum white matter microstructure in former professional football players. *Journal of Neurotrauma, 32*, 1768–1776.

Steele, C. J., Bailey, J. A., Zatorre, R. J., & Penhune, V. B. (2013). Early musical training and white-matter plasticity in the corpus callosum: Evidence for a sensitive period. *The Journal of Neuroscience, 33*, 1282–1290.

Stockard, C. R. (1921). Developmental rate and structural expression: An experimental study of twins, 'double monsters' and single deformities, and the interaction among embryonic organs during their origin and development. *American Journal of Anatomy, 28*, 115–275.

Thelen, E., & Smith, L. B. (1998). Dynamic systems theories. In W. Damon (Editor-in-chief) & R. M. Lerner (Vol. Ed.), *Handbook of child psychology: Vol. 1. Theoretical models of human development* (5th ed., pp. 563–634). New York: John Wiley & Sons.

Thompson, R. A. (2001). Sensitive periods in attachment? In D. B. Bailey, J. T. Bruer, F. J. Symons, & J. W. Lichtman (eds), *Critical thinking about critical periods* (pp. 83–106). Baltimore, MD: Paul H. Brookes.

Thorndike, E. (1913). *Educational psychology*. New York: Routledge.

van der Sluis, A., Elferink-Gemser, M. T., Brink, M. S., & Visscher, C. (2015). Importance of peak height velocity in terms of injuries in talented soccer players. *International Journal of Sports Medicine, 36*, 327–332.

Watanabe, D., Savion-Lemieux, T., & Penhune, V. B. (2007). The effect of early musical training on adult motor performance: evidence for a sensitive period in motor learning. *Experimental Brain Research, 176*, 332–340.

Werker, J. F., & Hensch, T. K. (2015). Critical periods in speech perception: new directions. *Annual Review of Psychology, 66*, 173–196.

Wiesel, T. N., & Hubel, D. H. (1963). Single-cell responses in striate cortex of kittens deprived of vision in one eye. *Journal of Neurophysiology, 26*, 1003–1017.

Woollacott, M. H., Debû, B., & Shumway-Cook, A. (1987). Children's development of posture and balance control: Changes in motor coordination and sensory integration. In D. Gould & M. R. Weiss (eds), *Advances in pediatric sport sciences: Behavioral issues, Vol. 2* (pp. 211–233). Champaign, IL: Human Kinetics.

17

COULD SPORTS BIOMECHANICS PROVIDE THE MISSING PIECES TO THE TALENT IDENTIFICATION AND DEVELOPMENT PUZZLE?

Paul S. Glazier

Introduction

Over the past 40 years, an increasing number of sports organisations from around the world have adopted talent identification (TI) and talent development (TD) programmes (collectively TID) to help uncover and nurture the next generation of sporting superstars. Professional sports clubs, national governing bodies, high-performance agencies, elite training institutes, and youth development academies, most notably in Australia, the United Kingdom, the United States of America, China, and Qatar, now routinely implement TID programmes in the belief that, by identifying young individuals with sporting potential early, these fledgling prospects can engage in, and accumulate, the 10 years or 10,000 hours of 'deliberate practice' (i.e., highly structured, goal-directed, and effortful activity) thought to be a prerequisite for expert performance in sport (see Ericsson, Krampe, & Tesch-Römer, 1993; Gladwell, 2008). Recently, however, the efficacy of TID programmes has come under scrutiny because, not only do these initiatives have a strong tendency to encourage early specialisation, which may actually hinder progression towards the attainment of sporting excellence by contributing to the development of physical (e.g., overuse injuries) and psychosocial (e.g., burnout, dropout) issues (e.g., Baker, 2003; DiFiori et al., 2014; Feeley, Agel, & LaPrade, 2016), they also typically have a weak scientific basis and lack a sound theoretical rationale, resulting in them having questionable validity and, ultimately, limited predictive power (e.g., Abbott & Collins, 2002; Vaeyens, Lenoir, Williams, & Philippaerts, 2008).

Another reason why TID programmes may not have had the impact they were intended to have is a lack of coverage from the subdiscipline of sports biomechanics. The omission of a formal biomechanics component from the vast majority of TID programmes appears to be a major shortcoming of these initiatives, especially given that, in many sports, one of the strongest indicators of 'talent' is perhaps the technical proficiency with which motor skills integral to those sports are performed. Biomechanics has also been conspicuously absent from almost all scientific discourse on TID in sport (although see Cooke, 2008, for an isolated effort). Although motor/technical skill has featured in schematics of TID in the sport science literature (e.g., see figure 3 of Williams & Reilly, 2000), the facilitative role of biomechanics in the TID process has rarely been considered. Applied empirical studies investigating the biomechanics of sports techniques have occasionally made reference to how results could have ramifications for TID (e.g., Worthington, King, & Ranson, 2013), but, on closer inspection, these claims often prove to be less than convincing. Davids, Lees, and Burwitz (2000) made a number of potentially impactful recommendations about the role biomechanics – supported by contemporary motor control theory – could play in enhancing the understanding of processes of coordination and control in kicking skills, which they suggested could have implications for TID programmes in football (soccer), but, to date, these ideas have not been developed further nor have they been extrapolated and applied to other sports involving similar multiarticular or multijoint actions.

In this chapter, I examine some of the main issues that have prevented biomechanics from occupying a more central role in TID in sport and discuss if, and how, these impediments may be overcome. I begin, however, by critically examining how technical skill has been assessed in TID programmes adopted by different sports organisations and scientific investigations of TID in sport, before arguing a case for the inclusion of a biomechanical component. As there is now a plethora of excellent texts on biomechanical data collection methods and procedures (e.g., Payton & Bartlett, 2008; Robertson, Caldwell, Hamill, Kamen, & Whittlesey, 2013; Winter, 2009), the theory and practice of capturing valid and reliable kinematic, kinetic, and electromyographic data will not be covered here. Interested readers are also directed to Wade and Berg (1991) and Knutzen and Martin (2002) for special consideration of biomechanical measurement issues specifically related to the study of movement in children.

TID in sport: How is technical skill assessed?

Many TID programmes adopted by professional sports clubs have been based on the subjective assessment of factors that are intuitively associated with expert performance in that sport. Technical skill has featured prominently in these assessments alongside other factors such as athleticism, personality, and game intelligence, and in football, for example, these factors have been expressed as acronyms, such as TIPS (Technique, Intelligence, Personality, Speed), TABS (Technique, Attitude, Balance, Speed), SUPS (Speed, Understanding, Personality, Skill), and PAS (Pace, Attitude, Skill) (see Reilly, Williams, & Richardson, 2008). The evaluation of prospective talent against prespecified criteria is usually undertaken by experienced coaches or talent scouts who observe behaviour during formal trials or competitive matches. Although the perceptual abilities of these expert observers should not be underestimated (see the penultimate section of this chapter for a discussion on visual expertise in the perception of action), it is possible that their assessments could be prejudiced by their personal beliefs and opinions about what constitutes 'good technique', thereby potentially introducing bias into the process.

A similar approach has also been adopted by some national governing bodies. For example, in the TI stage of the 'England Cricket Pathway' devised by the England and Wales Cricket Board, schools and clubs nominate promising 9- to 11-year-olds to represent their district and county having shown potential during competitive matches. Again, subjective assessment of technique, amongst other factors, appears to be the main method of identifying talented children, although performance indices, such as runs scored and wickets taken, are also considered. More formal skills testing, in the guise of the 'England Development Programme Talent Test', only occurs, for the first time, at around 12 years of age for those children nominated by their county academy coach. For seam and spin bowlers, these skills tests involve bowling at different areas or 'scoring zones' of the pitch at top pace and imparting as many revolutions on the ball at release as possible whilst maintaining accuracy, respectively. For batters, skills tests involve batting against different speeds of bowling using a narrower than standard bat.

High-performance agencies, often in partnership with elite training institutes (e.g., UK Sport/English Institute of Sport), have implemented more objective tests in their TID or 'performance pathway' programmes. However, owing to the large numbers of potentially talented young adults that present themselves for screening during talent search campaigns, and the diverse requirements of the Olympic and Paralympic sports being recruited for (e.g., rowing, volleyball, skeleton), these tests have tended to be simplistic and somewhat generic in nature, and have typically focused on the collection of anthropometric (e.g., stature, mass, body composition, limb lengths and girths, etc.), physical (e.g., speed, strength, flexibility, etc.), and physiological (e.g., anaerobic and aerobic power, etc.) variables thought to be strong indicators of sporting potential (Gulbin & Ackland, 2009). Technical skill tests have not routinely been implemented, presumably due to this aspect of sports performance being more difficult and time-consuming to assess objectively, and because it is thought that, in most sports being recruited for, technical skill can be developed at a later date with intensive training and specialist coaching providing the basic physical and physiological attributes exist.

The assessment of technical skill has also been inconsistent in scientific investigations of TID in sport. Most empirical studies have tended to focus on anthropometric, physical, physiological, and, to a lesser extent, psychological variables, either in isolation or in combination, with comparatively few attempting to assess technical skill. In the studies that have considered this aspect of sports performance (e.g., Pienaar, Spamer, & Steyn, 1998; Reilly, Williams, Nevill, & Franks, 2000; Keogh, Weber, & Dalton, 2003; Gabbett, Georgieff, & Domrow, 2007), the tests used have typically been simplified versions of tasks integral to the performance of that sport, and the measures produced have been, almost exclusively, outcome-focused. For example, Reilly et al. (2000) used the slalom dribbling and shooting tests summarised in Figure 17.1 to assess talent in young football players. These tests are limited, however, because, not only do

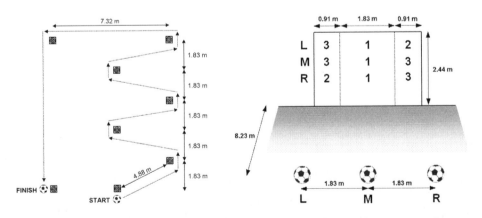

Figure 17.1 Two tests for assessing technical skill in football. In the slalom dribbling test (left), participants are required to dribble the ball between a series of cones, predominantly in a zigzag path, as quickly as possible. In the shooting test (right), participants are required to repeatedly shoot at goal and score as many points as possible (see Reilly & Holmes, 1983, for a full description). These, and other similar, tests have been routinely used in football and other field sports (e.g., hockey) to assess technical skill.

they remove important perceptual information (e.g., the movements of opponents and team-mates) that footballers couple their movements to during competitive matches (i.e., they lack 'task representativeness'; see Phillips, Davids, Renshaw, & Portus, 2010; Vilar, Araújo, Davids, & Renshaw, 2012) and provide no information about the techniques used to perform these tests, their results can be substantially influenced by growth and maturation with physically stronger, more powerful, children able to complete the dribbling task quicker and potentially be more accurate with their shots (see Ali, 2011, for a further critique of skills tests used to assess foot-ball performance).

To summarise, there are several issues surrounding technical skill assessments used in TID programmes and scientific investigations of TID in sport. These include: the inconsistent applica-tion of skills tests across different sports; the potential bias associated with subjective assessments of technical skill; the lack of 'task representativeness' of some skills tests; the confounding effects of physical maturity on outcome measures; and the lack of information provided about the underlying movement patterns that produce the outcomes. In the next section, I examine the role sports biomechanics could have in identifying and developing technical skill in potentially talented young athletes and why it has seldom been used in a TID context previously, before discussing, in the penultimate section of this chapter, what needs to be done to increase the appli-cation and utility of sports biomechanics in TID in sport in the future.

Identifying and developing technical skill in sport: Could sports biomechanics have a role?

The two main aims of sports biomechanics are generally accepted to be the enhancement of sports performance and the reduction of injury risk through the improvement of technique (Bartlett & Bussey, 2012). As one of the goals of TD is to nurture efficient, effective, and safe sports techniques, it would appear, in principle, that sports biomechanics could make a useful contribution to this aspect of TID. Furthermore, given that a necessary prerequisite for devel-oping talent from a biomechanical perspective would appear to be having knowledge about the movement patterns or, more specifically, the coordination and control patterns that characterise efficient, effective, and safe sports techniques, it is possible that this knowledge could, in prin-ciple, be used as a basis for TI. Why, then, has sports biomechanics seldom been used in a TID context previously?

Apart from the prohibitive cost of biomechanical analysis equipment and the specialist tech-nical expertise required to operate it, perhaps the main reason why sports biomechanics has not occupied a central role in TID in sport is the lack of consensus about what constitutes an effi-cient, effective, and safe technique in many sports. A tacit assumption held by many coaching practitioners is that there is one 'best' or 'optimal' technique for each sport usually the one advo-cated in the coaching textbook or exemplified by a champion athlete that all performers should aspire to achieve and coaches can use for comparative purposes to identify faults and prescribe modifications (e.g., Sherman, Sparrow, Jolley, & Eldering, 2001; Irwin, Hanton, & Kerwin, 2005; Jones, Bezodis, & Thompson, 2009). Although this perspective may be tenable in sports such as gymnastics where the task goal often dictates what movement patterns must be adopted, or in sports such as cycling and rowing where movement patterns are greatly constrained by the need to mechanically anchor the pelvis and limbs to the apparatus used, it is perhaps less useful in sports where rules and equipment place no, or very few, restrictions on limb and torso move-ments. Indeed, as the richness and diversity of techniques exhibited by elite sports performers in different sports can attest, it is possible to deviate quite markedly from a putatively 'ideal' movement pattern and still be successful in achieving the task goal (Cavanagh, 1987).

What inferences can be drawn from the scientific literature about the biomechanical characteristics that define efficient, effective, and safe sports techniques? Owing to the experimental paradigms commonly adopted in applied sports biomechanics research, many investigations have only provided very limited information about isolated aspects of sports techniques that are thought to be related to performance and injury. To illustrate some of the main issues and how they impact on the capacity of applied sports biomechanics research to identify efficient, effective, and safe sports techniques for TID purposes, consider the scientific literature on the biomechanics of cricket fast bowling techniques (Glazier & Wheat, 2014). Fast bowling provides an excellent task vehicle for this discussion because a biomechanically 'correct' technique is generally considered to be a prerequisite for producing fast and accurate deliveries and for reducing the likelihood of sustaining lower back injuries, which have been, and continue to be, highly prevalent in aspiring adolescent and young adult fast bowlers (e.g., Johnson, Ferreira, & Hush, 2012). Fast bowling is also one of the few sports skills where sports biomechanists have claimed that biomechanical analyses have been able to make a substantive contribution to the enhancement of technical knowledge by establishing statistical associations between aspects of technique and performance and injury (see Bartlett, 1997, and Elliott & Bartlett, 2006, for commentaries).

How useful is biomechanical information for TID in sport? A cricket fast bowling example

In performance-related biomechanical studies of fast bowling, a common empirical approach has been to correlate time-discrete kinematic variables obtained during the delivery stride (see Figure 17.2 for a description of the key moments and constituent phases of the delivery stride) with ball release speed in a single homogenous skill-level group of fast bowlers (e.g., Glazier, Paradisis, & Cooper, 2000; Loram et al., 2005; Wormgoor, Harden, & McKinon, 2010; Ferdinands, Kersting, & Marshall, 2013). Worthington et al. (2013) extended this correlation approach and used stepwise linear regression to identify four time-discrete kinematic variables that accounted for approximately three-quarters of the variation in ball release speed in a group of young elite fast bowlers. In partial agreement with previous investigations, this study found that the fastest bowlers had a quicker run-up, maintained a straighter front knee and had larger amounts of upper trunk flexion during the front foot contact–ball release (FFC-BR) phase, and delayed the onset of bowling arm circumduction. It was suggested that these results were likely to be useful in a TI context but no further elaboration was provided.

Figure 17.2 Key moments during fast bowling: back foot contact (BFC); front foot contact (FFC); and ball release (BR). The delivery stride is defined as the period between BFC and BR. Images sampled at 20 millisecond intervals.

In injury-related biomechanical studies of fast bowling, a common empirical approach has been to compare mean values of time-discrete kinematic variables obtained during the delivery stride for a sample of fast bowlers retrospectively divided into two or more groups based on injury status (e.g., Foster, John, Elliott, Ackland, & Fitch, 1989; Elliott, Hardcastle, Burnett, & Foster, 1992; Portus, Mason, Elliott, Pfitzner, & Done, 2004). One of the most significant findings to emerge from these studies is that a 'mixed' bowling action, which is characterised by a realignment or counter-rotation of the thorax to a more side-on orientation during the back foot contact–front foot contact (BFC-FFC) phase, has consistently been associated with the occurrence of abnormal radiologic features in the lumbar spine. This finding has profoundly influenced TD in fast bowling over the past 20 years, with many coaching practitioners attempting to minimise the amount of thorax counter-rotation and thereby reduce the incidence of debilitating lower back injuries in adolescent and young adult fast bowlers (see Elliott & Khangure, 2002).

Although these applied studies have provided some useful insights into the biomechanical factors associated with performance and injury in fast bowling, it could be argued that their practical application and utility in a TID context is somewhat limited. Based on their collective findings, it may be concluded that young fast bowlers who have a fast run-up, minimal thorax counter-rotation, delayed bowling arm circumduction, and a straight front knee, and a more flexed upper trunk, at BR, should be targeted in TI programmes as these characteristics have been linked to high ball release speeds and reduced risk of lower back injury. However, group-based research designs only permit probabilistic 'in general' or 'on average' statements being postulated and tend to mask individual differences (see Bouffard, 1993; James & Bates, 1997; Mullineaux, Bartlett, & Bennett, 2001). It is quite feasible, then, that aspiring young fast bowlers may not demonstrate some, or any, of these technical characteristics but still perform to a high level and remain injury free. Indeed, there are many examples of elite fast bowlers who do not display all of these technical characteristics, such as Dennis Lillee and Jeff Thomson, the great Australian duo, who exhibited moderate front knee flexion during the FFC-BR phase and a comparatively slow run-up speed, respectively (Penrose, Foster, & Blanksby, 1976).

A similar problem arises when attempting to apply the results of a group-based analysis to specific individuals in a TD context. Based on the aforementioned findings, it may be concluded that, to improve performance and reduce injury risk in fast bowling, a given fast bowler should attempt to increase run-up speed, minimise thorax counter-rotation, delay bowling arm circumduction, and straighten their front knee, and flex their upper trunk more, at BR. However, caution needs to be applied when interpreting group-based results in this way because, as Bouffard (1993) explained, 'propositions about people cannot necessarily be derived from propositions about the mean of people because the patterns found by aggregating data across people do not necessarily apply to individuals' (p. 371). Indeed, there have been several well-documented cases of elite international fast bowlers, such as James Anderson and Liam Plunkett, who were encouraged to modify their actions based on findings obtained from scientific studies only to lose form and sustain injuries to their lower backs. Only after reverting back to their old, more 'natural', techniques did they recapture previous performance levels, remain relatively injury free, and, in the case of Anderson, become the leading wicket-taker in Test matches for England.

A further issue that compromises the capacity of applied sports biomechanics research to identify efficient, effective, and safe fast bowling techniques for TID purposes is that many studies, paradoxically, do not analyse 'technique', which Lees (2002) defined as 'the *relative* position and orientation of body segments as they *change* during the performance of a sport task' (p. 814, my emphasis). The almost exclusive use of time-discrete kinematic measurements provides, at best, only snapshots of 'technique' and offers very limited information about the underlying patterns of coordination and control (see Glazier, Davids, & Bartlett, 2003; Glazier, Wheat, Pease, & Bartlett, 2006; Glazier & Robins, 2012). For example, it has been shown that the maximum angular velocities of the pelvis and thorax in the transverse plane are both significantly associated with ball release speed (Ferdinands et al., 2013), but this analysis provides no information about how the pelvis and thorax interact with each other or how these two segments interact with preceding and succeeding segments in the kinematic chain to effectively transfer energy and momentum to maximise ball release speed (see Glazier & Wheat, 2014, for further discussion of these issues). Similarly, the reporting of maximum counter-rotation of the thorax during the BFC-FFC phase provides no information about how the pelvis and thorax interact, particularly in the transverse and coronal planes during the FFC-BR phase, which has recently been postulated as a more likely contributory factor to lower back injuries in fast bowlers (e.g., Ranson, Burnett, King, Patel, & O'Sullivan, 2008; Glazier, 2010; Bayne, Elliott, Campbell, & Alderson, 2016).

To summarise, the main aims of sports biomechanics suggest that this subdiscipline of sports science could make an important contribution to TID in sport but the experimental paradigms habitually used in sports biomechanics research currently prevent it from doing so. Although cricket fast bowling has been used here as an exemplar task vehicle, many of the issues highlighted apply to other extant studies on multiarticular actions in sport (see Glazier, Reid, & Ball, 2015). In the penultimate section of this chapter, I underscore the importance of analysing coordination and control in sports skills and its potential significance in TID in sport.

Analysing coordination and control of sports skills: Why is it important and what does it mean for TID in sport?

So far in this chapter, I have described how technical skill has been assessed in TID programmes adopted by different sports organisations and in scientific investigations of TID in sport, and I have proposed that sports biomechanics could have a role in identifying and developing technical skill. To increase the application and utility of sports biomechanics in TID, however, it is recommended that a more process-focused, as opposed to outcome-focused, approach is adopted to gain a better understanding of the underlying patterns of coordination and control that may characterise efficient, effective, and safe sports techniques.

Although the terms 'coordination' and 'control' are often used interchangeably by coaching practitioners when assessing sports techniques (e.g., 'that movement was well coordinated/controlled'), they have distinct meanings in the scientific literature. Based on the framework outlined by Newell (1985), coordination can be operationally defined as the spatiotemporal relationship among body segments, limbs, or limbs and torso, whereas control refers to the absolute magnitude of individual limb, or limb and torso, segment movements. Coordination can be characterised by the topology (shape or form) of the relative motion of the body segments or limbs (i.e., the motion of one body segment or limb with respect to the motion of another body segment or limb), whereas control, which is a product of the tuning, scaling, or parameterisation of this relative motion, can be characterised by the linear and angular kinematics (displacement, velocity, acceleration) and kinetics (force, torque, energy, momentum) of a particular body segment or limb (see Sparrow, 1992). Importantly, coordination precedes control (Meijer, 2001) because coordination is the *organisation of the control* of the motor apparatus (Bernstein, 1967). Figure 17.3 provides further clarification of the distinction between coordination and control, and how they are related, using the motions of limb and torso segments during the performance of a golf swing as a vehicle for this discussion.

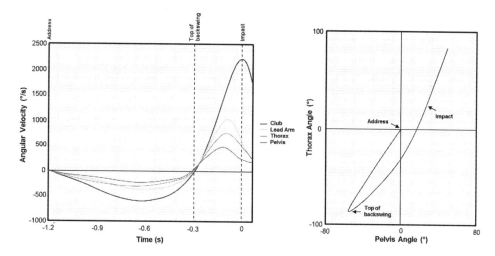

Figure 17.3 As in many other multiarticular throwing, kicking, and hitting actions where the distal-most body segment or hitting implement is required to move at high speed at impact or release, the generation of clubhead speed during the golf swing occurs through a precisely timed sequence of body segment rotations that generally occur in a proximal to distal order. The peak rotational speed of each segment in this linked-segment system or kinematic chain is greater, and occurs closer to impact, than the peak rotational speed of the preceding body segment (left). The amount of energy and momentum transferred between two adjacent body segments (e.g., pelvis → thorax) is dependent on their coupling relationship or relative motion (right), which can be varied according to the amount of clubhead speed required to hit the ball to the target.

In terms of TI, a significant task for sports biomechanists is to identify the patterns of coordination and control that characterise efficient, effective, and safe techniques in different sports against which the techniques of young athletes can be compared. As discussed earlier in this chapter, the amount of variability exemplified in the techniques of elite performers makes this task challenging, particularly if experimental paradigms commonly adopted in applied sports biomechanics research continue to be implemented. Until more robust criteria about what patterns of coordination and control characterise efficient, effective, and safe techniques are established, it may be expedient to use the patterns of coordination and control that are deemed to be harmonious with a mechanically sound technique, such as those described in coaching manuals or exhibited by certain elite performers, as a template on which to base TI. Taken at face value, this proposition may seem at odds with assertions made in the scientific literature questioning the efficacy of 'common optimal movement patterns' in skill acquisition and sports biomechanics (e.g., Brisson & Alain, 1996; Davids, Glazier, Araújo, & Bartlett, 2003; Seifert, Button, & Davids, 2013) and thus may be considered somewhat contentious. However, if *already established* patterns of coordination and control approximate those proven to be effective at the highest level of competition, this approach could be useful in helping to identify talented athletes in certain sports. Indeed, it has been proposed that the close fit between pre-existing coordination and control tendencies (intrinsic dynamics) and those required for the successful completion of a particular task (task dynamics) may explain precocious talent in sport, where young athletes are able to achieve performance excellence at an early age despite receiving limited coaching and/or engaging in minimal practice (e.g., Davids, Button, & Bennett, 2008; Chow, Davids, Button, & Renshaw, 2016).

A further advantage of analysing patterns of coordination and control is that it has been suggested that these aspects of technique may be perceived by coaching practitioners, and athletes themselves, when making subjective assessments about technique (Newell, 1985; Scully & Newell, 1985; Sparrow & Sherman, 2001). Indeed, research on the visual perception of biological motion has demonstrated that observers tend to use relative, as opposed to common, motion of torso and limb segments as their primary source of information (see Scully & Newell, 1985, for a review and discussion of the wider implications for the 'observational learning' of motor skills). In the second section of this chapter, I identified that one of the criticisms often aimed at many TID programmes is that they rely too heavily on subjective evaluation of technique. However, not only is it quite possible that experienced coaches and talent scouts are already highly adept at being able to tacitly identify putatively desirable patterns of coordination and control exemplified by young athletes (i.e., they have a 'good eye' for skilful athletes), it may also be possible to improve the observational skills of less experienced TID personnel. In this way, relative motion information about the coordination and control of sports skills could, in effect, provide a common language with which sports biomechanists, coaching practitioners, and talent scouts can use in their collaborative efforts to identify talented young athletes.

A potentially significant issue that threatens to undermine the efficacy of analysing patterns of coordination and control in TI, however, is the oftentimes rapid changes in key organismic constraints during growth and maturation. As it is now well-established that organismic constraints, in conjunction with environmental and task constraints, act to shape patterns of coordination and control (e.g., Newell, 1986; Araújo, Davids, Bennett, Button, & Chapman, 2004; Glazier & Robins, 2013), any changes in anatomical, morphological, and neurophysiological constraints during periods of accelerated growth are likely to have an impact on technique. One particularly influential morphological constraint is the moment of inertia (MOI) of limb and torso segments (Newell, 1984). The MOI of a body segment represents its resistance to angular acceleration and is the product of its mass and the square of its radius of gyration. To maintain patterns of coordination and control during a growth spurt, any increases in the MOI of body segments need to be matched by concomitant increases in torques produced about the active joints. However, the development of muscular strength typically lags behind increases in MOI of body segments, which has a disequilibrating effect that can destabilise patterns of coordination and control leading to reduced motor performance (Jensen, 1981). So, even though desirable patterns of coordination and control may be identifiable during the prepubescent years, it is far from clear whether they will be maintained during puberty or, if they are 'lost', whether they can be regained during adolescence.

In terms of TD, the role of sports biomechanics is to improve the efficiency, effectiveness, and safety of patterns of coordination and control. Whereas comparing patterns of coordination and control that are *already established* with a mechanically sound model of technique may be a useful strategy for TI, forcing young athletes to approximate the same criterion pattern of coordination and control in an attempt to improve performance and reduce injury risk is ill-advised since organismic constraints can vary considerably between individuals (Brisson & Alain, 1996). One of the main impediments to enhancing sports techniques from a biomechanical perspective is the inability of sports biomechanists to identify athlete-specific optimal techniques in a range of sports (see also Newell & Walter, 1981; Newell & McGinnis, 1985). As already discussed, the experimental paradigms adopted in many applied sports biomechanics studies tend to provide only generalised recommendations, which often have little relevance to facilitating the development of efficient, effective, and safe sports techniques at the individual level. Other statistical and mathematical modelling approaches that have been promoted in the sports biomechanics literature have similar pitfalls. For example, the practice of averaging kinematics across elite performers to establish a normative technique profile (e.g., Mann & Griffin, 1998; Ae, Muraki, Koyama, & Fujii, 2007; Ae, 2008), in effect, perpetuates the view that inter-individual variability represents error or noise and should, therefore, be removed, and the generation of putatively individual-specific optimal sports techniques using computer simulation (e.g., Yeadon & King, 2008; King & Yeadon, 2015) often fails to capture the richness and diversity of techniques exhibited by elite sports performers owing, in large part, to mathematical models of human performers being under-constrained (Glazier & Davids, 2009).

Given that it is not yet possible to objectively identify athlete-specific optimal techniques for different sports and, therefore, criterion templates to help identify faults and prescribe modifications cannot yet be established, other approaches to skill enhancement need to be explored. The application of 'biomechanical principles of movement' (see Lees, 2002, for an elaboration), may facilitate the development of efficient, effective, and safe patterns of coordination and control in young athletes. However, rarely have these principles been subjected to rigorous empirical verification and, on occasions when they have, some have been found to be invalid (e.g., Glazier & Worthington, 2014), whereas others have only been shown to be valid for certain movements and tasks (e.g., Fradet et al., 2004). A potentially more effective approach might be to use biomechanical measurements as augmented information to channel the developing athlete's search towards his or her own optimal movement solution (e.g., Newell, Kugler, van Emmerik, & McDonald, 1989). In golf, for example, shot outcome is directly related to initial launch parameters, which are, in turn, directly related to club delivery parameters (see Tuxen, 2009). However, since different patterns of coordination and control can produce the same club delivery parameters, it is difficult to predict whether a prescribed technical change will lead to improved club delivery for a particular golfer and, if it does, whether this technical adjustment can be reliably performed. To counter this issue, a viable pedagogic strategy might be to manipulate physical and instructional constraints and observe how club delivery parameters (e.g., club speed, swing path, attack and face angle, dynamic loft, etc.), which can be readily measured using launch monitor technology, change with the intervention. Once more desirable club delivery parameters have been achieved, the developing golfer can attempt to iteratively recreate the pattern of coordination and control that produced those more desirable club delivery parameters. This form of 'guided discovery learning' (see Handford, Davids, Bennett, & Button, 1997) has been shown to improve performance in some sports (e.g., Vereijken & Whiting, 1990) and could be instrumental in helping to develop more efficient, effective, and safe techniques in many others.

Concluding remarks

This chapter has provided a very rare exposition of the potential role of biomechanics in TID in sport. Although it is too early to definitively answer the question posed in the title of this chapter, based on the arguments presented above, I speculatively suggest that sports biomechanics could make a valuable contribution to the identification and development of talent in sport but greater attention needs to be given to identifying the underlying patterns of coordination and control that characterise efficient, effective, and safe sports techniques. Further research is required to establish what biomechanical characteristics define expert sports performance and how changes in organismic (e.g., anatomical, morphological, neurophysiological) constraints associated with physical maturation and growth impact on the coordination and control of sports techniques. This research would benefit from adopting an interdisciplinary approach, particularly the integration of biomechanical measurements with motor control theory, and will require the adoption of innovative techniques and methods that have only been fleetingly used in previous biomechanical investigations of sports techniques (e.g., Wheat & Glazier, 2006; Schöllhorn, Chow, Glazier, & Button, 2014). Interestingly, since the same principles governing coordination and control apply across all levels of analysis (see Glazier, 2010, 2015), techniques and methods from the related field of performance analysis could be used to gain a better understanding of how more successful players interact with teammates and/or opposition players, which may also be informative from a TID perspective.

References

Abbott, A., & Collins, D. (2002). A theoretical and empirical analysis of a 'state of the art' talent identification model. *High Ability Studies, 13,* 157–178.

Ae, M. (2008). A biomechanical method for the evaluation of sports techniques by standard motion, motion variability and motion deviation. In Y-H. Kwon, J. Shim, J. K. Shim, & I-S. Shin (eds), *XXVI International Conference on Biomechanics in Sports,* (Seoul, Korea, 14–18 July, 2008), pp. 33–37.

Ae, M., Muraki, Y., & Koyama, H., & Fujii, N. (2007). A biomechanical method to establish a standard motion and identify critical motion by motion variability: With examples of high jump and sprint running. *Bulletin of Institute of Health and Sport Sciences (University of Tsukuba), 30,* 5–12.

Ali, A. (2011). Measuring soccer skill performance: A review. *Scandinavian Journal of Medicine and Science in Sports, 21,* 170–183.

Araújo, D., Davids, K., Bennett, S. J., Button, C., & Chapman, G. (2004). Emergence of sport skills under constraints. In A. M. Williams, & N. J. Hodges (eds), *Skill acquisition in sport: Research, theory and practice* (pp. 409–433). London: Routledge.

Baker, J. (2003). Early specialization in youth sport: A requirement for adult expertise? *High Ability Studies, 14,* 85–94.

Bartlett, R. M. (1997). Current issues in the mechanics of athletic activities: A position paper. *Journal of Biomechanics, 30,* 477–486.

Bartlett, R., & Bussey, M. (2012). *Sports biomechanics: Reducing injury risk and improving sports performance.* London: Routledge.

Bayne, H., Elliott, B., Campbell, A., & Alderson, J. (2016). Lumbar load in adolescent fast bowlers: A prospective injury study. *Journal of Science and Medicine in Sport, 19,* 117–122.

Bernstein, N. A. (1967). *The coordination and regulation of movements.* Oxford: Pergamon Press.

Bouffard, M. (1993). The perils of averaging data in adapted physical activity research. *Adapted Physical Activity Quarterly, 10,* 371–391.

Brisson, T. A., & Alain, C. (1996). Should common optimal movement patterns be identified as the criterion to be achieved? *Journal of Motor Behavior, 28,* 211–223.

Cavanagh, P. R. (1987). The cutting edge in biomechanics. In M. J. Safrit, & H. M. Eckert (eds), *The academy papers: The cutting edge in physical education and exercise science research* (pp. 115–119). Champaign, IL: Human Kinetics.

Chow, J. Y., Davids, K., Button, C., & Renshaw, I. (2016). *Nonlinear pedagogy in skill acquisition: An introduction.* London: Routledge.

Cooke, C. (2008). Biomechanical perspectives on the identification and development of talent in sport. In R. Fisher, & R. Bailey (eds), *Talent identification and development: The search for sporting excellence* (pp. 69–88), Berlin: International Council of Sport Science and Physical Education.

Davids, K., Lees, A., & Burwitz, L. (2000). Understanding and measuring coordination and control in kicking skills in soccer: Implications for talent identification and skill acquisition. *Journal of Sports Sciences, 18,* 703–714.

Davids, K., Button, C., & Bennett, S. J. (2008). *Dynamics of skill acquisition: A constraints-led approach.* Champaign, IL: Human Kinetics.

Davids, K., Glazier, P. S., Araújo, D., & Bartlett, R. (2003). Movement systems as dynamical systems: The functional role of variability and its implications for sports medicine. *Sports Medicine, 33,* 245–260.

DiFiori, J. P., Benjamin, H. J., Brenner, J. S., Gregory, A., Jayanthi, N., Landry, G. L., & Luke, A. (2014). Overuse injuries and burnout in youth sports: A position statement from the American Medical Society for Sports Medicine. *Clinical Journal of Sports Medicine, 24,* 3–20.

Elliott, B., & Bartlett, R. (2006). Sports biomechanics: Does it have a role in coaching? *International Journal of Sports Science and Coaching, 1,* 177–183.

Elliott, B., & Khangure, M. (2002). Disk degeneration and fast bowling in cricket: An intervention study. *Medicine and Science in Sports and Exercise, 34,* 1714–1718.

Elliott, B. C., Hardcastle, P. H., Burnett, A. F., & Foster, D. H. (1992). The influence of fast bowling and physical factors on radiologic features in high performance young fast bowlers. *Sports Medicine, Training and Rehabilitation, 3,* 113–130.

Ericsson, K. A., Krampe, R. T., & Tesch-Römer, C. (1993). The role of deliberate practice in the acquisition of expert performance. *Psychological Review, 100,* 363–406.

Feeley, B. T., Agel, J., & LaPrade, R. F. (2016). When is it too early for single sport specialization? *American Journal of Sports Medicine, 44,* 234–241.

Ferdinands, R. E. D., Kersting, U. G., & Marshall, R. N. (2013). Kinematic and kinetic energy analysis of segmental sequencing in cricket fast bowling. *Sports Technology, 6,* 10–21.

Foster, D., John, D., Elliott, B., Ackland, T., & Fitch, K. (1989). Back injuries to fast bowlers in cricket: A prospective study. *British Journal of Sports Medicine, 23,* 150–154.

Fradet, L., Botcazou, M., Durocher, C., Cretual, A., Multon, F., Prioux, J., & Delamarche, P. (2004). Do handball throws always exhibit a proximal-to-distal segmental sequence? *Journal of Sports Sciences, 22,* 439–447.

Gabbett, T., Georgieff, B., & Domrow, N. (2007). The use of physiological, anthropometric, and skill data to predict selection in a talent-identified junior volleyball squad. *Journal of Sports Sciences, 25,* 1337–1344.

Gladwell, M. (2008). *Outliers: The story of success.* New York: Little, Brown and Company.

Glazier, P. S. (2010). Game, set and match? Substantive issues and future directions in performance analysis. *Sports Medicine, 40,* 625–634.

Glazier, P. S. (2010). Is the 'crunch factor' an important consideration in the aetiology of lumbar spine pathology in cricket fast bowlers? *Sports Medicine, 40,* 809–815.

Glazier, P. S. (2015). Towards a Grand Unified Theory of sports performance. *Human Movement Science.* doi:10.1016/j.humov.2015.08.001

Glazier, P. S., & Davids, K. (2009). Constraints on the complete optimization of human motion. *Sports Medicine, 39,* 15–28.

Glazier, P. S., Davids, K., & Bartlett, R. M. (2003). Dynamical systems theory: A relevant framework for performance-oriented sports biomechanics research. *Sportscience, 7,* (http://sportsci.org/jour/03/psg.htm).

Glazier, P. S., Paradisis, G. P., & Cooper, S. M. (2000). Anthropometric and kinematic influences on release speed in men's fast-medium bowling. *Journal of Sports Sciences, 18,* 1013–1021.

Glazier, P. S., Reid, M. M., & Ball, K. A. (2015). Expertise in the performance of multi-articular sports actions. In J. Baker, & D. Farrow (eds), *Routledge handbook of sport expertise* (pp. 84–94). London: Routledge.

Glazier, P. S., & Robins, M. T. (2012). Comment on "Use of deterministic models in sports and exercise biomechanics research" by Chow and Knudson (2011). *Sports Biomechanics, 11,* 120–122.

Glazier, P. S., & Robins, M. T. (2013). Self-organisation and constraints in sports performance. In T. McGarry, P. O'Donoghue, & J. Sampaio (eds), *Routledge handbook of sports performance analysis* (pp. 42–51). London: Routledge.

Glazier, P. S., & Wheat, J. S. (2014). An integrated approach to the biomechanics and motor control of cricket fast bowling techniques. *Sports Medicine, 44,* 25–36.

Glazier, P. S., Wheat, J. S., Pease, D. L., & Bartlett, R. M. (2006). The interface of biomechanics and motor control: Dynamic systems theory and the functional role of movement variability. In K. Davids, S. Bennett, & K. Newell (eds), *Movement system variability* (pp. 49–69). Champaign, IL: Human Kinetics.

Glazier, P. S., & Worthington, P. J. (2014). The impact of centre of mass kinematics and ground reaction forces on ball release speeds in cricket fast bowling. *Sports Technology, 7,* 4–11.

Gulbin, J. P., & Ackland, T. R. (2009). Talent identification and profiling. In T. R. Ackland, B. C. Elliott, & J. Bloomfield (eds), *Applied anatomy and biomechanics in sport* (2nd ed.) (pp. 11–26), Champaign, IL: Human Kinetics.

Handford, C., Davids, K., Bennett, S., & Button, C. (1997). Skill acquisition in sport: Some applications of an evolving practice ecology. *Journal of Sports Sciences, 15,* 621–640.

Irwin, G., Hanton, S., & Kerwin, D. G. (2005). The conceptual process of skill progression development in artistic gymnastics. *Journal of Sports Sciences, 23,* 1089–1099.

James, C. R., & Bates, B. T. (1997). Experimental and statistical design issues in human movement research. *Measurement in Physical Education and Exercise Science, 1,* 55–69.

Jensen, R. K. (1981). The effect of a 12-month growth period on the body moments of inertia of children. *Medicine and Science in Sports and Exercise, 13,* 238–242.

Johnson, M., Ferreira, M., & Hush, J. (2012). Lumbar vertebral stress injuries in fast bowlers: A review of prevalence and risk factors. *Physical Therapy in Sport, 13,* 45–52.

Jones, R., Bezodis, I., & Thompson, A. (2009). Coaching sprinting: Expert coaches' perception of race phases and technical constructs. *International Journal of Sports Science and Coaching, 4,* 385–396.

Keogh, J. W. L., Weber, C. L., & Dalton, C. T. (2003). Evaluation of anthropometric, physiological, and skill-related tests for talent identification in female field hockey. *Canadian Journal of Applied Physiology, 28,* 397–409.

King, M. A., & Yeadon, M. R. (2015). Advances in the development of whole body computer simulation modelling of sports technique. *Movement & Sport Sciences, 90,* 55–67.

Knutzen, K. M., & Martin, L. (2002). Using biomechanics to explore children's movement. *Pediatric Exercise Science, 14,* 222–247.

Lees, A. (2002). Technique analysis in sports: A critical review. *Journal of Sports Sciences, 20,* 813–828.

Loram, L. C., McKinon, W., Wormgoor, S., Rogers, G. G., Nowak, I., & Harden, L. M. (2005). Determinants of ball release speed in schoolboy fast-medium bowlers in cricket. *Journal of Sports Medicine and Physical Fitness, 45,* 483–490.

Mann, R., & Griffin, F. (1998). *Swing like a pro: The breakthrough scientific method of perfecting your golf swing.* New York: Broadway Books.

Meijer, O. G. (2001). Making things happen: An introduction to the history of movement science. In M. L. Latash, & V. M. Zatsiorsky (eds), *Classics in movement science* (pp. 1–57). Champaign, IL: Human Kinetics.

Mullineaux, D. R., Bartlett, R. M., & Bennett, S. (2001). Research design and statistics in biomechanics and motor control. *Journal of Sports Sciences, 19,* 739–760.

Newell, K. M. (1984). Physical constraints to development of motor skills. In J. R. Thomas (ed.), *Motor development during childhood and adolescence* (pp. 105–120). Minneapolis, MN: Burgess.

Newell, K. M. (1985). Coordination, control and skill. In D. Goodman, R. B. Wilberg, & I. M. Franks (eds), *Differing perspectives in motor learning, memory, and control* (pp. 295–317). Amsterdam: North-Holland.

Newell, K. M. (1986). Constraints on the development of coordination. In M. G. Wade, & H. T. A. Whiting (eds), *Motor development in children: Aspects of coordination and control* (pp. 341–360). Dordrecht: Martinus Nijhoff.

Newell, K. M., Kugler, P. N., van Emmerik, R. E. A., & McDonald, P. V. (1989). Search strategies and the acquisition of coordination. In S. A. Wallace (ed.) *Perspectives on the coordination of movement* (pp. 85–122). Amsterdam: North-Holland.

Newell, K. M., & McGinnis, P. M. (1985). Kinematic information feedback for skilled performance. *Human Learning, 4,* 39–56.

Newell, K. M., & Walter, C. B. (1981). Kinematic and kinetic parameters as information feedback in motor skill acquisition. *Journal of Human Movement Studies, 7,* 235–254.

Payton, C., & Bartlett, R. (eds). (2008). *Biomechanical evaluation of movement in sport and exercise: The British Association of Sport and Exercise Sciences guidelines.* London: Routledge.

Penrose, T., Foster, D., & Blanksby, B. (1976). Release velocities of fast bowlers during a cricket test match. *Australian Journal for Health, Physical Education and Recreation, 71*(suppl), 2–5.

Phillips, E., Davids, K., Renshaw, I., & Portus, M. (2010). Expert performance in sport and the dynamics of talent development. *Sports Medicine, 40,* 271–283.

Pienaar, A. E., Spamer, M. J., & Steyn Jr, H. S. (1998). Identifying and developing rugby talent among 10-year-old boys: A practical model. *Journal of Sports Sciences, 16,* 691–699.

Portus, M. R., Mason, B. R., Elliott, B. C., Pfitzner, M. C., & Done, R. P. (2004). Technique factors related to ball release speed and trunk injuries in high performance cricket fast bowlers. *Sports Biomechanics, 3,* 263–283.

Ranson, C. A., Burnett, A. F., King, M., Patel, N., & O'Sullivan, P. B. (2008). The relationship between bowling action classification and three-dimensional lower trunk motion in fast bowlers in cricket. *Journal of Sports Sciences, 26,* 267–276.

Reilly, T., & Holmes, M. (1983). A preliminary analysis of selected soccer skills. *Physical Education Review, 6,* 64–71. Berlin: International Council of Sport Science and Physical Education.

Reilly, T., Williams, M., & Richardson, D. (2008). Talent identification and development in football. In R. Fisher & R. Bailey (eds), *Talent identification and development: The search for sporting excellence* (pp. 183–199), Germany: H&P Druck.

Reilly, T., Williams, A. M., Nevill, A., & Franks, A. (2000). A multidisciplinary approach to talent identification in soccer. *Journal of Sports Sciences, 18,* 695–702.

Robertson, D. G. E., Caldwell, G. E., Hamill, J., Kamen, G., & Whittlesey, S. N. (eds). (2013). *Research methods in biomechanics* (2nd ed.). Champaign, IL: Human Kinetics.

Schöllhorn, W., Chow, J. Y., Glazier, P. S., & Button, C. (2014). Self-organizing maps and cluster analysis in elite and sub-elite athletic performance. In K. Davids, R. Hristovski, D. Araújo, N. Balagué Serre, C. Button, & P. Passos (eds), *Complex systems in sport* (pp. 145–159). London: Routledge.

Scully, D. M., & Newell, K. M. (1985). Observational learning and the acquisition of motor skills: Toward a visual perception perspective. *Journal of Human Movement Studies, 11,* 169–186.

Seifert, L., Button, C., & Davids, K. (2013). Key properties of expert movement systems in sport: An ecological dynamics perspective. *Sports Medicine, 43,* 167–178.

Sherman, C. A., Sparrow, W. A., Jolley, D., & Eldering, J. (2001). Coaches' perceptions of golf swing kinematics. *International Journal of Sport Psychology, 31,* 257–270.

Sparrow, W. A. (1992). Measuring changes in coordination and control. In J. J. Summers (ed.), *Approaches to the study of motor control and learning* (pp. 147–162). Amsterdam: North-Holland.

Sparrow, W. A., & Sherman, C. (2001). Visual expertise in the perception of action. *Exercise and Sport Sciences Reviews, 29,* 124–128.

Tuxen, F. (2009). The impact of John Jacobs on golf coaching: A commentary. *International Journal of Sports Science and Coaching, 4*(suppl 1), 39–49.

Vaeyens, R., Lenoir, M., Williams, A. M., & Philippaerts, R. M. (2008). Talent identification and development programmes in sport: Current models and future directions. *Sports Medicine, 38,* 703–714.

Vereijken, B., & Whiting, H. T. A. (1990). In defence of discovery learning. *Canadian Journal of Sport Sciences, 15,* 99–106.

Vilar, L., Araújo, D., Davids, K., & Renshaw, I. (2012). The need for 'representative task design' in evaluating efficacy of skills tests in sport: A comment on Russell, Benton and Kingsley (2010). *Journal of Sports Sciences, 30,* 1727–1730.

Wade, M. G., & Berg, W. (1991). How to study movement in children. In J. Fagard, & P. H. Wolff (eds), *The development of timing control and temporal organization in coordinated action* (pp. 261–280). Amsterdam: North-Holland.

Wheat, J. S., & Glazier, P. S. (2006). Measuring coordination and variability in coordination. In K. Davids, S. Bennett, & K. Newell (eds), *Movement system variability* (pp. 167–181). Champaign, IL: Human Kinetics.

Williams, A. M., & Reilly, T. (2000). Talent identification and development in soccer. *Journal of Sports Sciences, 18,* 657–667.

Winter, D. A. (2009). *Biomechanics and motor control of human movement* (4th ed.). Hoboken, NJ: John Wiley & Sons, Inc..

Wormgoor, S., Harden, L., & McKinon, W. (2010). Anthropometric, biomechanical, and isokinetic strength predictors of ball release speed in high-performance cricket fast bowlers. *Journal of Sports Sciences, 28,* 957–965.

Worthington, P. J., King, M. A., & Ranson, C. A. (2013). Relationships between fast bowling technique and ball release speed in cricket. *Journal of Applied Biomechanics, 29,* 78–84.

Yeadon, M. R., & King, M. A. (2008). Biomechanical simulation models of sports activities. In Y. Hong, & R. Bartlett (eds), *Handbook of biomechanics and human movement science* (pp. 367–379). London: Routledge.

18

LONGITUDINAL STUDIES OF ATHLETE DEVELOPMENT

Their importance, methods and future considerations

Stephen Cobley and Kevin Till

Chapter purpose

Based on the propositions and implications from models of human development, coupled with current research design limitations in talent identification and development (TID), the purpose of this chapter is to highlight the significance and benefits from longitudinal multivariate research approaches toward knowledge and understanding of athlete development. To achieve this, we synthesise and overview studies in three sub-disciplinary areas of athlete development (i.e., physical, psychological, technical and tactical) which we feel provide valuable longitudinal and multivariate insight. Afterward, we identify future directions and implications for both researchers and practitioners. All along we accept and acknowledge the challenges in conducting longitudinal multivariate studies, including the time and resources required on researchers, participants and sporting organisations (Matton et al., 2007). Our intention though is to help spur on the TID research field into utilising better research designs, more encompassing measures, and unique analyses. If adopted, we propose that the likelihood of informative unique contributions will increase, potentially helping unravel the complexity of the TID process.

Models of development

Contemporary models of human development and exceptionality (see e.g., Chapter 2 in this Handbook; Ford & Lerner, 1992) emphasise that there are multiple interacting relationships and reciprocal effects that shape (dys)functional development. The implication being that sporting talent and development may reflect the emergenic presence and/or stimulated development of a combination (or set) of psychological, cognitive, technical motor skills (e.g., ballistic and fine motor control) alongside anthropometric (e.g., height, low body-fat) and physiological qualities (e.g., gene allele adaptability, cardio-respiratory fitness). Bronfenbrenner (1979, 2005) and Lerner's (1995) models also consider that forms of development (e.g., psychological) occur in social-ecological contexts (e.g., local sports clubs), recognising that functional relationships between individuals (their attributes) and social processes are central to such development.

To their strength and relevance, developmental models provide multi-disciplinary, multi-dimensional and interactional accounts of athlete development. They can explain how idiosyncratic, oscillatory trajectories and non-linear paths of development occur; handling the variability and diversity of individual to cohort levels of experience and differential outcomes. They also predict that '*functional change*' requires time, emphasising that qualities or capacities evolve, emerge (perhaps later in chronological time) or can be accelerated if key underlying processes that support and sustain self-growth, improvement and plasticity are present. To acknowledge though, there are other predictable (e.g., biological growth; transitions in education) and unpredictable changes over time (e.g., trauma, relationship conflicts) within and outside the sport context, and so functional change can be affected. For instance, Cobley (2016) highlights how in present athlete development systems, athletes often have to meet the sport system requirements at particular ages and stages of performance prior to systems potentially reciprocating their intended forms of functional development (e.g., improved physiological and technical capacities). (Un)predictable change, transitions and events also introduce notions of temporality and instability to individual capacities (e.g., aerobic fitness), sub-qualities (e.g., psychological), the social-ecological context (e.g., coach personnel expertise and programme change) or the system. If negative, these can delay or regress athlete development.

In terms of TID as a research field, developmental models present confronting conceptual, methodological and analytical challenges. For instance, they highlight the need for better research designs and methodologies if we are to (i) improve the efficacy and effectiveness of athlete development programmes, (ii) avoid the negative outcomes and consequences from development programme involvement, and (iii) generally better understand and explain the athlete development process. Yet in the TID field cross-sectional research designs, accompanied by reductionist and isolationist approaches, univariate analyses and mono-disciplinary perspectives predominate; a perennial problem in the sport sciences (Glazier, in press). To confirm, cross-sectional designs cannot detect development change, causal effects, interactions between variables or identify variables associated with onward learning or improvement (i.e., prognostic). As such, athlete development encompasses the need to examine functional or accelerated change over relatively short (e.g., 6 months to 2 years) or longer time periods (e.g., 10 years) depending on the focus of the exact research question(s), necessitating longitudinal (repeated measures) designs.

Athlete development is also multi-factorial including physical, psychological, cognitive skills and capabilities (see e.g., Vaeyens, Lenoir, Williams, & Philippaerts, 2008). Within these areas, variables can also potentially interrelate or constrain to affect each other (Newell; 1986; Phillips, Davids, Renshaw, & Portus, 2010). There is thus a need to more holistically and comprehensively understand the dynamic and non-linear relationships between variables as they change over time. On these grounds, researchers are recommending the need for assessment of multiple variables within and across factorial areas. Collaborative cross-disciplinary longitudinal studies may therefore help better understand the intricacies of functional (de)accelerated change, growth and regression in athletes (e.g., Cobley, Baker, & Schorer, 2012; Unnithan, White, Georgiou, Iga, & Drust, 2012).

Longitudinal studies in athlete development

The following section overviews studies that have examined facets of athlete development longitudinally. Here we define longitudinal studies as those examining some feature of change, and which contain a minimum of three repeated observations over an extended time period (e.g., > 6 months) on at least one substantive construct of interest. Due to space constraints, we review exemplar studies under the headings: (i) *Physical Development*; (ii) *Psychological Development*; and (iii) *Technical and Tactical Development*. Studies are identified for their potential novelty in focus, multivariate nature, methodological approach or knowledge contribution. With the aim to also provide valuable references and resources, accompanying tables summarise longitudinal studies in the three areas highlighting methods and measures utilised.

Physical development

Physical development is the most widely examined area in terms of TID research and practical application (Pyne, Spencer, & Mujika, 2014). Physical assessment archetypally comprises measures of anthropometry, flexibility, speed, agility, (an)aerobic performance as well as lower and upper body strength and power. A collection of measures (or 'test battery') has frequently been used in specific sport contexts, applied either 'in the field' or under 'lab' standardised conditions. There are numerous sport specific reviews identifying the various types of fitness tests and their procedures. For example, there are review articles for: *Soccer* (Hulse et al., 2013), *Tennis* (Fernandez-Fernandez, Ulbricht & Ferrauti, 2014), *Rugby League* (Johnston, Gabbett & Jenkins, 2014), *Cricket* (Johnstone Mitchell, Hughes, Watson, Ford, & Garrett, 2014), *Taekwondo* (Bridge, Santos, Chabene, Pieter, & Franchini, 2013), *Karate* (Chaabene, Hachana, Franchini, Mkaouer, & Chamari, 2012), *Basketball* (Ziv & Lidor, 2009), *Ice-Hockey* (Nightingale, Miller & Turner, 2013) and *Gymnastics* (Sleeper, Kenyon & Casey, 2012). In TID studies, such testing has commonly been used cross-sectionally to differentiate the physical capabilities between individuals or groups at varying skill and selection levels in a given TID system and identify physical characteristics for focus within applied training programmes.

Only recently have longitudinal physical assessments been investigated in TID-related studies (e.g., Till, Cobley, O'Hara, Chapman, & Cooke, 2013b, 2014; Valente-Dos-Santos et al., 2012, 2014). Table 18.1 provides a summary of the range of measures utilised and exemplar studies. Most common measures are those validated and applied in prior studies, though their purpose of use has not been simply for differentiation or (de)selection. Here tests have been used to either track and monitor longer-term development (Philippaerts et al., 2006), help evaluate the effectiveness of training interventions (Buchheit, Mendez-Villanueva, Delhomel, Brughelli, & Ahmaidi, 2010) or assess the effect of normative growth (e.g., maturation status) on physical development (Ford et al., 2011).

Besides demonstrating physical improvements over time, studies of adolescent TID athletes have perhaps most notably shown how the 'physical gap' between athletes of different skill or selection level changes becoming more differentiated over time (i.e., 2–3 years). For example, Mattys et al. (2013) demonstrated significantly enhanced improvements in 10 × 5m shuttle run performance for elite compared to non-elite youth handball players over a two year period (i.e., elite 12–13 years = 18.59 ± 1.14, 14–15 = 16.95 ± 0.66 s vs. non-elite 12–13 = 18.63 ± 1.20, 14–15 = 17.95 ± 1.03 s). Similarly Elferink-Gemser, Visscher, Lemmink, and Mulder (2007) identified how endurance capacity (assessed via the number of runs on an interval endurance test) widened between elite and sub-elite youth field hockey players across three years (i.e., elite – year 1 = 68.8 + 27.8; year 3 = 101.1 + 19.1 runs; sub-elite – year 1 = 70.8 + 22.2, year 3 = 82.9 + 26.1 runs). On face value, findings suggest that change of direction speed (in handball) and endurance capacity (in field hockey) improvement, but not other physical attributes assessed, may be indicative for onward development in these sports. However, understanding the mechanisms for these trajectories is currently limited, with increased training time (i.e., a treatment effect) in elite level players (e.g., 13 vs. 4.5 hours per week in handball; Matthys et al., 2013) the only current explanation. Findings also question whether other physical qualities

Table 18.1 Examples of existing anthropometric and fitness tests used to examine physical variables in athlete development

Physical quality	Measure	Study example
Anthropometry	Height	Till et al. (2013a, b); Valente-dos-Santos et al. (2012, 2014)
	Body Mass	Till et al. (2013a, b); Valente-dos-Santos et al. (2012, 2014)
	Skinfolds	Till et al. (2013a, b); Valente-dos-Santos et al. (2012, 2014)
Maturation	Age at Peak Height Velocity	Matthys et al. (2013); Till et al. (2014)
	Skeletal Age	Valente-dos-Santos et al. (2012)
Flexibility	Sit & Reach	Matthys et al. (2013)
	Shoulder Rotation Test	Matthys et al. (2013)
Speed	Sprints (i.e., 5–60m assessments)	Buchheit & Mendez-Villanueva (2013); Matthys et al. (2013)
Change of Direction or Agility	Agility 505 Test	Till et al. (2013a, b, 2014);
	10 x 5m Agility	Matthys et al. (2013); Valente-dos-Santos et al. (2012, 2014)
Muscular Endurance	Sit up, Hand Grip	Matthys et al. (2013)
Strength	1-RM Bench press, squat and prone row	Till et al. (2015)
Power	Counter-movement Jump	Deprez et al. (2015); Buchheit & Mendez-Villanueva (2013)
	Broad Jump	Valente-dos-Santos et al. (2012)
Endurance or High Intensity Running Ability	Multi-Stage Fitness Test; Yo-Yo IRTL1	Valente-dos-Santos et al. (2014) Deprez et al. (2015a, 2015b); Carvalho et al. (2014)
	Repeated Sprint Ability	Valente-dos-Santos et al. (2012)
Match running performance – Soccer	Global Positioning Systems – Total, Low Speed & High Speed Distance	Saward et al. (2015)
Swim Performance	Times at varying strokes and distances (i.e., freestyle at 100, 200, 400m	Falk et al. (2004); Morais et al. (2015)

should have likewise become more differentiated or whether findings were responses to context specific requirements. Further exploration of physical qualities is necessary to identify whether training or TID program involvement, emergent capabilities or a combination of both can be attributed to performance level development and career attainment. Such questions can only be answered by longitudinal studies that track athletes into adulthood, alongside comparative groups, whilst accounting for numerous developmental factors (e.g., biological growth; training experience; competition load).

TID research has extensively shown how physical capacities are confounded by biological growth and maturation processes (Burgess & Naughton, 2010; Cobley & Till, 2014): A point personified by the benefits of being relatively older and earlier maturing in youth ages and stages of TID systems (Cobley, Baker, Wattie, & McKenna, 2009; Lovell et al., 2015). Recently, Buchheit and Mendez-Villanueva (2013) assessed the stability of anthropometric and physical characteristics across four years in youth soccer players aged 13–18 years old. Findings demonstrated only moderate stability for skinfolds, countermovement jump, 10m sprint and maximum sprint speed. For players who had similar physical performance at 13, large interindividual differences of change occurred in physical performance measures between consecutive testing sessions and across a four-year period. Explanations for such findings were related to the rate of growth and maturation of players during adolescence alongside potential genetic differences, particularly when players were derived from similar teams and had similar training and competition exposures. Till et al. (2014) assessed similar characteristics in youth rugby league players, but classified individuals according to maturation group (i.e., earlier, average and later). Significant time by maturation effects (over two years) were evident for height, sitting height, sum of four skinfolds, medicine ball throw and 60m sprint. Later maturing players demonstrated significantly greater improvements on all physical measures (unless reporting excessive skinfold scores) relative to average and earlier maturing players over the same time period.

These studies (and others) add to present understanding, explaining how potential dynamic and variable physical development trajectories occur during adolescence. They illustrate how growth and maturation need to be considered and controlled; the need to intervene on variables constraining performance (e.g., body fat; fundamental movement control); the need to track athletes beyond maturational stages where such influences diminish, and where the prominence of other physical and non-physical variables may associate with accelerated development. Future work also needs to consider the training and competition load of athletes whilst monitoring physical development to better understand their importance on physical qualities and long-term TID.

Psychological development

By comparison, only pockets of isolated studies have examined psychological variables associated with athlete development in a longitudinal manner (Morris, 2000). This is likely for several reasons. For instance, there are potentially multiple psychological constructs, many of which are latent (e.g., self-regulation, motivation), theoretically driven and multi-faceted, and which makes them challenging to validly and reliably quantify. Many constructs rely on standardised scaling questionnaires for their assessment, though these are limited by response accuracy, bias and reliability concerns. A case in point is the potential limited knowledge and understanding of perceptions and cognitions in young athletes (McCarthy, Jones, Harwood, & Olivier, 2010). To add, psychological variables can be both highly stable and unstable depending on the construct. Some vary according to immediate experiences and events (e.g., emotions), while personality dimensions (e.g., extraversion), self-concept, and attitudes can remain somewhat stable, though evolving temporally. Also, while perceptions, beliefs and cognitions can remain stable or fluctuate, they are amenable to systematic enhancement or regression over shorter time frames (e.g., self-efficacy). These complexities bring added hurdles when attempting to assess functional change longitudinally.

Perhaps the most notable areas where a few longitudinal studies have occurred are associated with the areas of athlete health, stress and recovery (e.g., Brink, Visscher, Arends, Zwerver, Post, & Lemmink, 2010; Brink, Visscher, Coutts, & Lemmink, 2012; Kellman & Kallus, 2001); motivation (e.g., Ames; 1992; Feichtinger & Höner, 2015; Ryan & Deci, 2000; Pelletier et al.,

1995); identity development (Brewer, van Raalte & Linder, 1993; Verkooijen, van Hove, & Dik, 2012); psychological skill development (e.g., Elferink-Gemser et al., 2007; Thomas, Murphy, & Hardy, 1999; Toering, Elferink-Gemser, Jordet, & Visscher, 2009); and, the effects of TID system social conditions and environments upon psycho-social outcomes (e.g., Elbe, Szymanski & Beckmann, 2005; Martindale et al., 2010). Table 18.2 summarises examples of variables and instruments applied to date in longitudinal TID studies. Due to the recurrent concerns of how excessive training loads affect athlete health, and recent developments in understanding how social-ecological contexts affect individual psycho-social outcomes, we now further discuss these topics.

Psychological development: Athlete health and recovery

With progressively intense physical training a core constituent of most TID systems, research and practice has inevitably been concerned with young athlete health, well-being, and recovery. On the basis of prior studies identifying how perceived health, stress and recovery are closely related to biological, hormonal and physical performance (e.g., Jurimae, Maestu, Purge, Jürimäe, & Soot, 2002; Jurimae, Maestu, Purge, & Jürimäe, 2004; Maestu, Jürimäe, Kreegipuu, & Jürimäe, 2006), psychological scales have been utilised as indices for biological health, over-reaching, overtraining and injury. In one early study, which tracked the training and competition schedules of young adult sport competitors over one year, Van Mechelen et al. (1996) examined multiple anthropometric (e.g., BMI) and fitness (e.g., VO_2 max) variables alongside 16 psychological factors, and whether they were predictive of injury. They found injury was more likely in competitive team sport settings, with exposure time and prior injury identified as the strongest predictors, then followed by perceived exhaustion (assessed via the Maastricht Questionnaire – Appels, Höppener, & Mulder, 1987), stressful life events (via Life Events Survey – Sarason, Johnson, & Siegel, 1978) and having a 'social dominance' personality characteristic (via Dutch Personality Inventory – Luteijn, Starren, & van Dijk, 1985).

More recently, Brink et al. (2010) administered the multi-dimensional RESTQ-Sport (Kellman & Kallus, 2001) – which assesses the degree of involvement in general and sport specific stress and recovery related activities – monthly across two competitive seasons in an elite sample (15–18 years old) of Dutch soccer players. Alongside logging weekly physical training, competitive loads, injury and illness events, findings indicated that preceding weeks of monotonously high training load were associated with a heightened risk of traumatic injury and illness in subsequent weeks. Also, general perceived psycho-social stress (e.g., well-being, sleep quality) and sport-stress (i.e., emotional exhaustion; feeling less fit and in shape) were predictive of a heightened risk of illness. Subsequently, Brink et al. (2012) – using a similar sample, method and design – examined perceived stress and recovery overreaching, using a novel submaximal physical test procedure to determine overreaching with broadly similar findings.

Colletively, findings illustrate how training and competition schedules over time affected a combination of frequently monitored psychological characteristics and perceptions, and which subsequently predicted athlete health and functioning. Uniqueness is also reflected in the multi-disciplinary and more holistic assessments adopted. Equally, these studies support integrated multi-disciplinary (i.e., physical and psycho-social) models of health and injury (e.g., Anderson & Williams, 1988; Kenttä & Hassmén, 1998) and recommendations to regularly longitudinally monitor for early signs of compromised psychological and physical responses in order to prevent performance and health decrements (i.e., illness and injury) in the developing athlete (Baker & Cobley, 2008; Brink et al., 2012).

Table 18.2 Examples of existing psychometric tools used to examine psychological constructs in athlete development

Psychological construct	Psychological questionnaire/instrument	Study example
Ind. General Health	Subjective Vitality Scale (SVS – Ryan & Frederick, 1997) General Health Questionnaire-12 (GHQ-12 – Goldberg et al., 1997)	Reinboth & Duda, (2006); Adie et al. (2012). Ivarsson et al. (2015).
Ind. General – Sport Specific Stress & Recovery	The Recovery-Stress Questionnaire for Athletes (RESTQ-Sport – Kellman & Kallus, 2001)★	Brink et al. (2010, 2012).
Ind. Specific Overtraining	Short Overtraining Symptoms Questionnaire (SOSQ – Lemyre et al., 2007) Multi-component Training Distress Scale (MTDS; Main & Grove 2009)	Lemyre et al. (2007). Main et al. (2010).
Burnout	Athlete Burnout Questionnaire (ABQ – Raedeke & Smith, 2001)	Cresswell & Eklund (2006); Quested & Duda (2011).
Sport Motivation	Sport Motivation Scale (SMS – Pelletier et al., 1995) Achievement Goal Scale for Youth Sports (AGSYS; Cumming et al., 2008)	Gaudreau et al. (2009); Vink et al. (2015); Smith et al. (2009).
Athletic Identity	Athletic Identity Measurement Scale (AIMS; Brewer & Cornelius, 2001)	Brewer et al. (2010).
Psychological Skills	Test of Performance Strategies (TOPS – Thomas et al., 1999) Psychological Skills Inventory for Sports (PSIS – Mahoney et al., 1987)	Sheard & Golby (2006); Faggiani et al. (2011); Elferink-Gemser et al. (2004, 2007).
Self-Determination Ind. – Soc. Int-action Psychological Needs	*Perceived Competence* – Competence subscale of Intrinsic Motivation Inventory (IMI – McAuley et al., 1989). *Perceived Autonomy* – Perceived Autonomy (Hollembeak & Amorose, 2005) *Perceived Relatedness* – Feelings of Relatedness Scale (Richer & Vallerand, 1998).	Adie et al. (2012). Kipp & Weiss (2015). Isoard-Gautheur et al. (2012).
Soc. – Environ. Motivational Climate	Perceived Motivational Climate in Sport Questionnaire-2 (PMCSQ-2; Newton et al., 2000) The Motivational Climate for Youth Sports Questionnaire (MCSYS – Smith et al., 2008)	Reinboth & Duda (2006). Ntoumanis et al. (2012).
Environ. Quality Talent Dev. Environment	Talent Development Environment Questionnaire for Sport (TDEQ; Martindale et al., 2010)	Martindale et al. (2013)*; Ivarsson et al (2015).

Notes: *Ind.* = Individual; *Ind. – Soc. Int-action* = Individual–Social Interaction; *Environ.* = Environment; . = Environment; ★ = Instrument also has been been used to assess overtraining; * Not a longitudinal study but shows how TDEQ has discriminated between talent environment quality.

256

Psychological development: The psycho-social environment and athlete development outcomes

Guided by social-ecological theoretical approaches, Talent Development Environments (TDEs) – like other social environments – are predicted to affect individual psychology and psycho-social development (e.g., Henriksen, Stambulova, & Roessler, 2010). Consequently, understanding how social conditions and processes lead to particular outcomes (e.g., health; well-being; motivation; performance; sport withdrawal) and how they can be optimised is significant. To date, there have been some important insights. Generally speaking, TDEs that create and reinforce ego-competitive climates, promote early competition (within TDEs) and exert control over young athlete behaviours have been associated with psychological stress, de-motivation, burnout, and dropout (e.g., Durand-Bush & Salmela, 2002; Isoard-Gautheur, Guillet-Descas, & Lemyre, 2012). Yet, by their distinction, task-based climates that emphasise personal improvement and learning, satisfy individual psychological needs, provide social support networks, and adopt a long-term developmental view are associated with better short- and long-term outcomes.

To illustrate, Reinboth and Duda (2006) examined perceptions of the motivational climate created by coaches, changes in psychological need satisfaction, as well as indices of psychological and physical well-being in a sample of UK University team sport athletes. Though not truly longitudinal according to our definition (i.e., only two time-points of measurement across five months duration), increased perceptions of a task-involving coach climate over time were found to positively predict satisfaction of the psychological needs of competency, autonomy and relatedness. And in turn, autonomy and relatedness significantly predicted perceived psychological well-being. By contrast, those perceiving an ego-involving climate also perceived a lower sense of connection, value, and social support. Elsewhere, Adie, Duda and Ntoumanis (2012) showed in a sample of UK elite youth football players (aged 11–18 years) tracked across two seasons using six measurement time-points, how perceived autonomy support from the coach over two competitive seasons was related to increases and decreases in well- and ill-being respectively. With reference to parent-created social climates, O'Rourke, Smith, Smoll, and Cumming (2011) identified how high parental expectations (i.e., framed as pressure) combined with an ego-orientated climate were associated with higher trait levels of anxiety across a competitive season (measured at three time-points) in a sample of elite swimmers aged 9–14 years. Interestingly, parents with high expectations but who had developed a task-oriented motivational climate were associated with significantly lowered child trait anxiety over the same period.

From an organisational standpoint and based on grounded anecdotal assessments of successful existing TDEs, Martindale et al. (2010; Martindale, Collins, Douglas, & Whike, 2013) recently developed the TDEQ. The TDEQ aims to promote TDE system evaluation, and to encourage implementation of beneficial processes associated with more successful and healthy talent development (i.e., evidenced-based practice). To achieve this, the TDEQ assesses several dimensions of TDE quality including coaching, social support, programme structure, and content. Initial data from TDEQ application suggests accuracy – in alignment with expert evaluations – of being able to discriminate between 'higher' and 'lower quality' TDEs across several sports (Martindale et al., 2013). Recently, Ivarsson et al. (2015) assessed whether TDE quality was predictive of emotional stress (via REST-Q sub-scale) and well-being (via GHQ-12) in a sample of elite Swedish football players (13–16 years) enrolled in development academies over one year using three measurement time-points. They found that higher or lower perceptions of TDE quality at baseline corresponded with higher and lower levels of stress and well-being, with relationships remaining relatively stable over time. Characteristics differentiating TDE initial ratings were linked with (i) the quality of existing relationships between individuals and coaches; (ii) whether developmental goals were set frequently, evaluated, and feedback provided; and (iii) whether relationships between club, coaches, parents and school were supportive, coherent and well-established.

Theoretically and practically driven studies examining psycho-social conditions and processes are beginning to illustrate and explain how types of TDEs and home environments, containing their structural elements and the nature and quality of social relationships therein, affect (or shape) individual and cohort psychology leading to (un)preferred outcomes. The onward logical consequence is that such processes affect athlete decisions and intentions on behavioural participation and investment in TID programmes. The implications for TID practices are to assess, monitor and potentially adapt their psycho-social climates to help preserve and secure psychological health and growth, and help support longer-term TID programme engagement. For researchers, determining the relative importance and contribution of such factors within and across TID is just one future research direction.

Technical and tactical development

By comparison to physical and psychologically TID-related longitudinal studies, studies assessing and examining technical and tactical development have been limited. Yet these same skills are consistently perceived as being equally or more important in given sport performance contexts, and is reflected in the concentration of TID programme delivery (Unnithan et al., 2012). Again, there are reasons for their limited investigation in part due to methodological external and criterion validity related difficulties. Technical skill assessments to date have attempted to use tasks that: isolate and reflect particular skills (e.g., assessing consistency and accuracy); create task representations of actual performance contexts (e.g., time constrained skill performance); quantify assessment meaningfully; and, remove the influence of anthropometric or physical factors (Hendricks, Lambert, Maimala, & Durandt, 2015). However, attempting to satisfy all these requirements in a given technical assessment is challenging, undermining their validity. That said, assessments ranging from the basic to the more intricate have been devised and applied (often in cross-sectional studies) across a range of sports. These include passing, shooting and dribbling in soccer (O'Reilly & Wong, 2012); swing and putting in golf (Barnett, Hardy, Brian, & Robertson, 2015); catch and pass, decision-making and tackling ability in rugby (Hendricks et al., 2015); handling, shooting and dribbling in water polo (Falk, Lidor, Lander, & Yang, 2004); batting in cricket (Portus & Farrow, 2011); as well as dribbling in field hockey (Elferink-Gemser et al., 2007) and handball (Matthys et al., 2013). Table 18.3 provides a summary of the technical and tactical assessments used to date within longitudinal studies.

In longitudinal studies, technical assessments have been relatively simplistic outcome performance measures of accuracy (e.g., hitting a target) and speed of execution (e.g., time elapsed). Nonetheless, Huijgen, Elferink-Gemser, Ali, and Visscher (2013) successfully used the LPST passing test in comparing selected and deselected soccer players aged between 10–18 years in three Dutch development programmes. Their findings showed that test improvements occurred at 8 sec/year between 10–15 years, reducing to 1.5 sec/year at 16–18 years demonstrating the expected improvement in passing accuracy and speed of execution for developing soccer players. Selected players outperformed those deselected, something not originally hypothesised due to perceived group homogeneity. Thus, the improved LSPT score may have validly discriminated players based on passing accuracy and execution speed, reflecting a technical skill associated with TID in youth soccer.

Table 18.3 Examples of existing assessments used to examine technical and tactical skills in athlete development

Sport	Measure	Study example
Technical		
Water Polo	Ball handling – 50m dribble, Throw at goal, throw for distance	Falk et al. (2004)
Soccer	Loughborough Passing Soccer Test (LPST)	Huijgen et al. (2013)
	Ball control with body	Valente-Dos-Santos (2012, 2014)
	Dribbling speed	Valente-Dos-Santos (2012, 2014)
	Shooting accuracy	Valente-Dos-Santos (2012, 2014);
	Wall pass	Francioni et al. (2015)
	Passing accuracy	Valente-Dos-Santos (2012, 2014)
	Dribbling with pass	Francioni et al. (2015)
Field Hockey	Peak shuttle dribble performance, Dribble performance in a repeated shuttle run, and performance in a slalom dribble.	Elferink-Gemser et al. (2007)
Handball	Slalom Dribble test	Matthys et al. (2013)
Tactical		
All	TACSIS	Elferink-Gemser et al. (2007); Kannekens et al. (2009)

To date, tactical knowledge and skill has only (as we are aware) been assessed by the self-report Tactical Skills Inventory for Sports (TACSIS; Elferink-Gemser, Visscher, Lemmink, & Mulder, 2004). The TACSIS assesses four facets including 'Knowing About Ball Actions', 'Knowing About Others', 'Positioning and Deciding' and 'Acting in Changing Situations', although few studies have implemented the TACSIS longitudinally. In their longitudinal study, Kannekens, Elferink-Gemser, Post, and Visscher (2009) assessed the self-reported changes in 256 adolescent soccer players (aged 14–18 years) according to playing positions. Findings showed that defenders and midfielders (e.g., 'Knowing About Ball Actions': 14 = 4.15 ± 0.76 & 18 = 4.31 ± 0.67; 14 = 4.33 ± 0.75 & 18 = 4.36 ± 0.84 respectively) failed to change their TACSIS between 14–18 years relative to attackers (14 = 3.96 ± 0.77, 18 = 4.66 ± 0.63). Kannekens et al. (2009) speculated the finding may be due to attackers being selected based on physical qualities and thus had 'room for improvement' in tactical understanding. Though the only tactical assessment tool available to date, the TACSIS may be limited by its inability to assess the various types of tactical skills and may suffer from self-report bias when completed in isolation (Kannekens et al., 2009).

Overall at this stage, despite strong rationale and relevance, technical and tactical assessment remains an underdeveloped area of TID research, particularly with regard to determining its significance to – and as a composite part of – athlete development. Overcoming assessment challenges, creating new forms of skill-based assessment which address validity concerns; understanding how and when athletes acquire tactical knowledge; understanding how tactical knowledge can be accelerated; and including tactical assessments from coaching observation and perspectives seem to be valuable future directions.

Longitudinal studies: Synthesis and future directions

This broad but concise synthesis of longitudinal research in three areas of TID highlights the existing areas of investigation, research questions examined, methodological approaches adopted, analyses utilised, and provides a current critical assessment of research and applied contributions. There is a growing body of descriptive cohort and prospective longitudinal research (i.e., describing basic linear forms; e.g., mean between-group differences), along with some examples of explanatory prospective longitudinal studies (i.e., identifying causes of change by one or more predictors; see e.g., *athlete health and recovery*). Some existing descriptive studies are multivariate (i.e., often connected to anthropometry and physical testing), though very few are truly cross-disciplinary (e.g., physical, psychological and technical; Elferink-Gemser et al., 2007; Matthys et al., 2013). Overall, perceptible areas of underdevelopment and numerous future research directions have been identified. However, prior to potentially tackling these areas, we now highlight some fundamental methodological considerations for when undertaking longitudinal studies. For more comprehensive overviews of longitudinal research design and analysis, readers are referred to Fitzmaurice, Laird, and Ware (2012); Magnusson and Casaer (2006); Menard (2007); and Twisk (2013).

Future directions: Conceptual considerations

Whether functional change is a predicted or primary outcome, or whether associated performance variables are being examined, ensuring that change is conceptualised appropriately is critical. For instance, depending on the study focus and research question(s), it is theoretically possible for some variables to be more or less stable or volatile to change in an (un)intended manner (see e.g., Feichtinger & Höner, 2015). They may show types of linear, non-linear or discontinuity in change (Ployhart & Vandenberg, 2010). Thus, being able to capture these dynamics within longitudinal research designs (i.e., panel, cohort prospective or retrospective tracking (with controls or reference groups)) with the appropriate time-frames (e.g., from childhood to adulthood) is important. The type of change of interest also has to be considered. Whether between-group mean change (most common in literature currently), intra-unit (within-group; individual) change, the examination of both, or, case/group change relative to standardised or normative values should be identified. Such considerations then influence the decisions as to the variable(s) which need to be assessed, how and when they are assessed (i.e., number, spacing and time points for repeated measurement) and the analysis techniques required.

Future directions: Participant and group characteristic considerations

In terms of participants, longitudinal study involvement can lead to attrition and dropout problems. Similarly, participant characteristics and the sampling frame of those being tracked or in control/reference groups have to be carefully considered. Their characteristics can dictate which variables differentiate or are associated with change and development. For instance, between-group differences are more likely on multiple variables (e.g., anthropometry and physical tests) if participants are heterogeneous in terms of their age, skill and selection level. However as Cobley et al. (2012) proposed and Till et al. (2013b, 2014) identified, when examining already selected or matched (homogenous) athletic groups in terms of anthropometric and physical variables, then it is likely that alternative (other) variables (e.g., technical skill) will differentiate and predict onward progression. Comparative longitudinal designs (e.g., tracking

intervention vs. control) need to reflect both upon the (homo)hetero-geneity between participant group characteristics – and the relative distance between them – as well as within a
participant group at the start of tracking. Likewise, considering which participant characteristics may change over time (confounding or mediating variables) and what might explain
outcome changes is equally important.

Future directions: Measurement and analysis considerations

To help determine genuine longitudinal change, standardised measurement procedures, protocol and analyses are required across measurement time-points. These steps will also help assess
and ensure internal validity and consistency; inter-trial stability, and test-retest reliability (aka –
invariance) on variables of interest. The point is exemplified in Haugen and Buchheit's (2015)
recent sprint monitoring review, which highlighted how large variations in sprint performance
was accounted for by changes in starting position (e.g., standing, 3-point, crouched position),
timing device (e.g., manual, dual beam photocells, video), environmental conditions (e.g.,
humidity, temperatures, wind) and surface (e.g., grass, track, artificial surface). These factors
often exceeded the changes in performance over several years. Thus, absolute standardisation
of procedures is essential across disciplines to minimise types of measurement error. Similarly,
multiple measurement at given time-points, such as within technical skill trials, and multiple
assessors (e.g., when taking anthropometric measures) are steps that help assure data validity and
reliability at a single time-point and across long-term tracking. With reference to physical testing, Roe et al. (2016) and Haugen and Buchheit (2015) illustrate strategies and measures to
help remove and assess measurement error.

Together, the proposed research questions and methodological considerations subsequently
inform the analytical approach adopted. In this regard, Ployhart and Vandenberg (2010) highlight
some common approaches. In brief, if a study focuses upon group mean change, general linear
models (e.g., MANOVA) and trend analysis are generally deemed most appropriate. To assess
between- and within-group (individual) change along with potential predictors, then the utilisation of random coefficient modelling and latent growth modelling (LGM) should be
considered (Singer & Willett, 2003). LGM has the advantages of being more flexible in terms of
analysis options and in being able to handle forms of measurement error. Park and Schutz (2005)
provide an introduction to LGM in sport performance, while Morais, Silva, Marinho, Seifert, and
Barbosa (2015) show a rare example of LGM application in assessing technical performance
change in swimming. Nevertheless like all other statistical approaches, there are strengths and
weaknesses, and their appropriate application has to be carefully contemplated. The potential for
more intricate and advanced techniques are also available (see earlier references).

Integrating together: A theoretically aligned and practically informative approach

To finish, an approach is outlined that is theoretically aligned to holistic developmental models,
practically relevant to TID and is able to handle the various methodological considerations highlighted. Till, Cobley, O'Hara, Chapman, and Cooke (2013a) and Cobley, Till, O'Hara, and
Cooke (2014) investigated how individual intra-athlete variables (e.g., agility) changed over time
relative to a broader cohort and how such variables interacted. They used z-scores and radar
graphs to depict cases of athlete development on a range of anthropometric and physical variables in TID-selected youth rugby players aged 13–15 years. Z-scores utilise a broader data set
of standardised norm values (e.g., age, sex and skill level matched) on given variables to

determine an individual's relative score within that range (McGuigan, Cormack & Gill, 2013). When applied longitudinally, individual change can then be evaluated relative to individual cases, groups or norms over time. In these studies, the type of player who improved or regressed more substantially over time relative to others was assessed to help identify explanatory variables.

Similar to Till, Cobley and colleagues, Figure 18.1 demonstrates a hypothetical example of a longitudinal, multivariate and multi-disciplinary approach to athlete development in soccer. The figure shows how an idiosyncratic (or normative) pattern of development may occur. It likewise, helps illuminate underlying reasons for a particular pattern as well as identify particular strengths and weaknesses in the profile, which may be particularly informative for TID practitioners and programme evaluation. In this case, physical and technical attributes scores are below average in 2013, while psychological and tactical scores are above reference group norms with norms possibly age and skill matched (i.e., homogenous comparison). For 2014 and 2015, there is evidence of physical and technical improvement, though with less change in psychological and tactical indices. Areas of strength and progression across the profile can be utilised to inform TID purposes. Such an approach may be highly informative for effective longitudinal monitoring and for consideration on how to optimise training and accelerate functional change in the developing athlete.

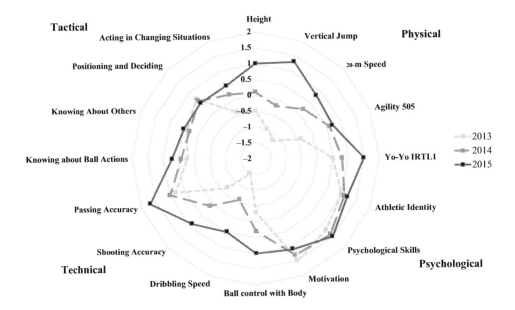

Figure 18.1 Hypothetical longitudinal (over two years) multivariate assessment profile of a soccer academy player relative to others using Z scores

Chapter summary

Contemporary developmental models and sport performance literature indicate that TID is multi-factorial and interactive over time. Functional change requires time, as qualities or capacities emerge, evolve and can be systematically accelerated if the appropriate conditions and processes are present. From a research standpoint, capturing and understanding functional change necessitates longitudinal (higher quality) research designs, with additional benefits from adopting multivariate and multi-disciplinary approaches. The synthesis of longitudinal studies, along with highlighted examples, identifies a growing body of descriptive, prospective and explanatory studies; some of which are also multivariate. Numerous future research directions and areas of potential are identifiable. Nonetheless, there are fundamental conceptual, methodological and analytical concerns to be considered. If done appropriately, substantial enhancement of informative and novel contributions are predicted, benefitting TID research and practice. Such work may also contribute to a broader knowledge and understanding of positive physical and psychological health functioning and development.

References

Adie, J.W., Duda, J. L., & Ntoumanis, N. (2012). Perceived coach–autonomy support, basic need satisfaction and the well-and ill-being of elite youth soccer players: A longitudinal investigation. *Psychology of Sport and Exercise, 13*(1), 51–59.

Ames, C. (1992). Achievement goals, motivational climate, and motivational processes. In G. C. Roberts (ed.), *Motivation in sports and exercise* (pp. 161–176). Champaign, IL: Human Kinetics.

Andersen, M. B., & Williams, J. M. (1988). A model of stress and athletic injury: Prediction and prevention. *Journal of Sport and Exercise Psychology, 10*(3), 294–306.

Appels, A. P. W. M., Höppener, P., & Mulder, P. (1987). A questionnaire to assess premonitory symptoms of myocardial infarction. *International Journal of Cardiology, 17*(1), 15–24.

Baker, J., & Cobley, S. (2008). Does practice make perfect? The role of training in developing the expert athlete. In D. Farrow, J. Baker, & C. MacMahon (eds), *Developing sport expertise: Researchers and coaches put theory into practice* (pp. 29–42). London: Routledge.

Barnett, L. M., Hardy, L. L., Brian, A. S., & Robertson, S. (2015). The development and validation of a golf swing and putt skill assessment for children. *Journal of Sports Science and Medicine, 14*(1), 147–154.

Brewer, B. W., van Raalte, J. L., & Linder, D. E. (1993). Athletic identity: Hercules' muscles or Achilles heel? *International Journal of Sport Psychology, 24*(2), 237–254.

Bridge, C. A., Santos, J., Chabene, H., Pieter, W., & Franchini, E. (2013). Physical and physiological profiles of Taekwondo athletes. *Sports Medicine, 44*, 713–733.

Brink, M. S., Visscher, C., Arends, S., Zwerver, J., Post, W. J., & Lemmink, K. A. (2010). Monitoring stress and recovery: New insights for the prevention of injuries and illnesses in elite youth soccer players. *British Journal of Sports Medicine, 44*(11), 809–815.

Brink, M.S., Visscher, C., Coutts, A.J., & Lemmink, K. A. (2012). Changes in perceived stress and recovery in overreached young elite soccer players. *Scandinavian Journal of Medicine & Science in Sports, 22*(2), 285–292.

Bronfenbrenner, U. (1979). *The ecology of human development: Experiments by nature and design.* Cambridge, MA: Harvard University Press.

Bronfenbrenner, U. (2005). *Making human beings human: Bioecological perspectives on human development.* Thousand Oaks, CA: Sage.

Buchheit, M., Mendez-Villanueva, A., Delhomel, G., Brughelli, M., & Ahmaidi, S. (2010). Improving repeated sprint ability in young elite soccer players: Repeated sprints vs. explosive strength training. *Journal of Strength and Conditioning Research, 24*, 2715–2722.

Buchheit, M., & Mendez-Villanueva, A. (2013). Reliability and stability of anthropometric and performance measures in highly-trained young soccer players: effect of age and maturation. *Journal of Sports Science, 31*(12), 1332–1343.

Burgess, D. J., & Naughton, G.A. (2010) Talent development in adolescent team sports: A review. *International Journal of Sports Physiology and Performance, 5*, 103–116.

Chaabene, H., Hachana, Y., Franchini, E., Mkaouer, B., & Chamari, K. (2012). Physical and physiological profile of elite karate athletes. *Sports Medicine, 41*(10), 829–843.

Cobley, S. (2016). Talent identification and development in youth sport. In A. Smith & K. Green (eds), *Routledge handbook of youth sport* (pp. 476–491). London, UK: Routledge.

Cobley, S., Baker, J., & Schorer, J. (2012). Identification and development of sport talent: A brief introduction to a growing field of research and practice, In J. Baker, S. Cobley, & J. Schorer (eds), *Talent identification & development in sport: International perspectives* (pp. 1–10). London, Routledge.

Cobley, S., Baker, J., Wattie, N., & McKenna, J. (2009). Annual age-grouping and athlete development. *Sports Medicine, 39*(3), 235–256.

Cobley, S., & Till, K. (2014). Talent identification, development and the young rugby player. In C. Twist & P. Worsfold (eds) *The science of rugby*. Abingdon: Routledge.

Cobley, S., Till, K., O'Hara, J., & Cooke, C. (2014). Variable and changing trajectories in youth athlete development: Further verification in advocating a long-term inclusive tracking approach. *Journal of Strength and Conditioning Research. 28*(7), 1959–1970.

Cresswell, S. L., & Eklund, R. C. (2006). Changes in athlete burnout over a thirty-week "rugby year". *Journal of Science and Medicine in Sport, 9*(1), 125–134.

Cumming, S. P., Smith, R. E., Smoll, F. L., Standage, M., & Grossbard, J. R. (2008). Development and validation of the Achievement Goal Scale for Youth Sports. *Psychology of Sport and Exercise, 9*, 686–703.

Deprez, D., Valente-Dos-Santos, J., Coelho-e-Silva, M. J., Lenoir, M., Philippaerts, R., & Vaeyens, R. (2015a). Longitudinal development of explosive leg power from childhood to adulthood in soccer players. *International Journal of Sports Medicine, 36*, 672–679.

Deprez, D., Buchheit, M., Fransen, J., Pion, J., Lenoir, M., Philippaerts, R., & Vaeyens, R. (2015b). A longitudinal study investigating the stability of anthropometry and soccer-specific endurance in pubertal high-level youth soccer players. *Journal of Sports Science and Medicine, 14*, 418–426

Durand-Bush, N., & Salmela, J. H. (2002). The development and maintenance of expert athletic performance: Perceptions of world and Olympic champions. *Journal of Applied Sport Psychology, 14*(3), 154–171.

Elbe, A. M., Szymanski, B., & Beckmann, J. (2005). The development of volition in young elite athletes. *Psychology of Sport and Exercise, 6*(5), 559–569.

Elferink-Gemser, M. T., Visscher, C., Lemmink, K. A., & Mulder, T. (2004). Relation between multidimensional performance characteristics and level of performance in talented youth field hockey players. *Journal of Sports Sciences, 22*, 1053–1063.

Elferink-Gemser, M. T., Visscher, C., Lemmink, K. A., & Mulder, T. (2007). Multidimensional performance characteristics and standard of performance in talented youth field hockey players: A longitudinal study. *Journal of Sports Sciences, 25*(4), 481–489.

Faggiani, F., McRobert, A. P., & Knowles, Z. (2011). Developing pre-performance routines for acrobatic gymnastics: A case study with a youth tumbling gymnast. *Science of Gymnastics Journal, 4*(2), 39–52.

Falk, B., Lidor, R., Lander, Y., & Yang, B. (2004). Talent identification and early development of elite water polo players: A 2 year follow up. *Journal of Sports Science, 22*(4): 347–355.

Feichtinger, P., & Höner, O. (2015). Talented football players' development of achievement motives, volitional components, and self-referential cognitions: A longitudinal study. *European Journal of Sport Science.* Published Online doi: 10.1080/17461391.2015.1051134.

Fernandez-Fernandez, J., Ulbricht, A., & Ferrauti, A. (2014). Fitness Testing of tennis players: How valuable is it? *British Journal of Sports Medicine, 48*, 22–31.

Fitzmaurice, G. M., Laird, N. M., & Ware, J. H. (2012). *Applied longitudinal analysis*. John Wiley & Sons.

Ford, D. L., & Lerner, R. M. (1992). *Developmental systems theory: An integrative approach*. Newbury Park, CA: Sage.

Ford, P., De Ste Croix, M., Lloyd, R., Meyers, R., Moosavi, M., Oliver, J., … Williams, C. (2011). The long-term athlete development model: Physiological evidence and application. *Journal of Sports Sciences, 29*, 389–402.

Francioni, F. M., Figueiredo, A. J., Terribili, M., & Tessitore, A. (2015) Analysis of the intraseasonal stability of field test performances in young academy soccer players. *Journal of Sports Sciences*, http://dx.doi.org/10.1080/02640414.2015.1082612

Gaudreau, P., Amiot, C. E., & Vallerand, R. J. (2009). Trajectories of affective states in adolescent hockey players: Turning point and motivational antecedents. *Developmental Psychology, 45*(2), 307–319.

Glazier, P. S. (in press). Towards a grand unified theory of sports performance. *Human Movement Science.*

Goldberg, D. P., Gater, R., Sartorius, N., Ustun, T., Piccinelli, M., Gureje, O., & Rutter, C. (1997). The validity of two versions of the GHQ in the WHO study of mental illness in general health care. *Psychological Medicine, 27*(1), 191–197.

Haugen, T., & Buchheit, M. (2015). Sprint running performance monitoring: Methodological and practical considerations. *Sports Medicine, 46*(5), 641–656. doi: 10.1007/s40279-015-0446-0.

Hendricks, S., Lambert, M. I., Maimala, H., & Durandt, J. (2015). Measuring skill in rugby union and rugby league as part of the standard team testing battery. *International Journal of Sports Science and Coaching, 10*(5), 949–965.

Henriksen, K., Stambulova, N., & Roessler, K. K. (2010). Holistic approach to athletic talent development environments: A successful sailing milieu. *Psychology of Sport and Exercise, 11*(3), 212–222.

Hollembeak, J., & Amorose, A. J. (2005). Perceived coaching behaviors and college athletes' intrinsic motivation: A test of self-determination theory. *Journal of Applied Sport Psychology, 17*, 20–36.

Huijgen, B. C. H., Elferink-Gemser, M. T., Ali, A., & Visscher, C. (2013). Soccer skill development in talented players. *International Journal of Sports Medicine, 34*, 720–726.

Hulse, M. A., Morris, J. G., Hawkins, R. D., Hodson, A., Nevill, A. M., & Nevill, M. E. (2013). A field test battery for elite, young soccer players. *International Journal of Sports Medicine, 34*(4), 302–311.

Isoard-Gautheur, S., Guillet-Descas, E., & Lemyre, P. N. (2012). A prospective study of the influence of perceived coaching style on burnout propensity in high level young athletes: using a self-determination theory perspective. *The Sport Psychologist, 26*(2), 282–298.

Ivarsson A., Stenling, A., Fallby, J., Johnson, U., Borg, E., & Johansson, G. (2015). The predictive ability of the talent development environment on youth elite football players' well-being: A person-centered approach. *Psychology of Sport and Exercise, 16*, 15–23.

Johnston, R. D., Gabbett, T. J., & Jenkins, D. G. (2014). Applied sport science of rugby league. *Sports Medicine, 44*(8), 1087–1100.

Johnstone, J. A., Mitchell, A. C., Hughes, G., Watson, T., Ford, P. A., & Garrett, A. T. (2014). The athletic profile of fast bowling in cricket: A review. *Journal of Strength and Conditioning Research, 28*(5), 1465–1473.

Jürimäe, J., Maestu, J., Purge, P., Jürimäe, T., & Soot, T. (2002). Relations among heavy training stress, mood state, and performance for male junior rowers. *Perceptual and Motor Skills, 95*(2), 520–526.

Jürimäe, J., Mäestu, J., Purge, P., & Jürimäe, T. (2004). Changes in stress and recovery after heavy training in rowers. *Journal of Science and Medicine in Sport, 7*(3), 335–339.

Kannekens, R., Elferink-Gemser, M. T., Post, W. T., & Visscher, C. (2009). Self assessed tactical skills in elite youth soccer players: A longitudinal study. *Perceptual and Motor Skills, 109*, 459–472.

Kellmann, M., & Kallus, K. W. (2001). *Recovery-stress questionnaire for athletes: User manual.* Champaign, IL: Human Kinetics.

Kenttä, G., & Hassmén, P. (1998). Overtraining and recovery: A conceptual model. *Sports Medicine, 26*, 1–16.

Kipp, L. E., & Weiss, M. R. (2015). Social predictors of psychological need satisfaction and well-being among female adolescent gymnasts: A longitudinal analysis. *Sport, Exercise, and Performance Psychology, 4*(3), 153–169.

Lemyre, P. N., Roberts, G. C., & Stray-Gundersen, J. (2007). Motivation, overtraining, and burnout: Can self-determined motivation predict overtraining and burnout in elite athletes? *European Journal of Sport Science, 7*(2), 115–126.

Lerner, R. M. (1995). *America's youth in crisis: Challenges and options for programs and policies.* Thousand Oaks, CA: Sage.

Lovell, R., Towlson, C., Parkin, G., Portas, M., Vaeyens, R., & Cobley, S. (2015). Soccer player characteristics in English lower-league development programmes: The relationships between relative age, maturation, anthropometry and physical fitness. *PloS One, 10* (9): e0137238.

Luteijn, F., Starren, J., & van Dijk, H. (1985). *Manual for the Dutch Personality Questionnaire* (revised version). Handleiding bij de NPV, herziene uitgave.

Maestu, J., Jürimäe, J., Kreegipuu, K., & Jürimäe, T. (2006). Changes in perceived stress and recovery during heavy training in highly trained male rowers. *Sport Psychologist, 20*(1), 24–39.

Magnusson, D., & Casaer, P. (2006). *Longitudinal research on individual development: Present status and future perspectives* (Vol. 8). Cambridge University Press.

Mahoney, M. J., Gabriel, T. J., & Perkins, T. S. (1987). Psychological skills and exceptional athletic performance. *The Sport Psychologist, 1*(3), 181–199.

Main, L., & Grove, J. R. (2009). A multi-component assessment model for monitoring training distress among athletes. *European Journal of Sport Science, 9*(4), 195–202.

Main, L. C., Landers, G. J., Grove, J. R., Dawson, B., & Goodman, C. (2010). Training patterns and negative health outcomes in triathlon: longitudinal observations across a full competitive season. *The Journal of Sports Medicine and Physical Fitness, 50*(4), 475–485.

Martindale, R. J., Collins, D., Douglas, C., & Whike, A. (2013). Examining the ecological validity of the Talent Development Environment Questionnaire. *Journal of Sports Sciences, 31*(1), 41–47.

Martindale, R. J., Collins, D., Wang, J. C., McNeill, M., Lee, K. S., Sproule, J., & Westbury, T. (2010). Development of the Talent Development Environment Questionnaire for sport. *Journal of Sports Sciences, 28*(11), 1209–1221.

Matthys, S. P. J., Vaeyens, R., Fransen, J., Deprez, S., Pion, J., Vandendriessche, J., … Philippaerts, R. (2013). A longitudinal study of multidimensional performance characteristics related to physical capacities in youth handball. *Journal of Sports Science, 31*, 325–334.

Matton, L., Beunen, G., Duvigneaud, N., Wijndaele, K., Philippaerts, R., Claessens, A., … Lefevre, J. (2007). Methodological issues associated with longitudinal research: Findings from the Leuven longitudinal study on lifestyle, fitness and health (1969–2004). *Journal of Sports Sciences, 25*, 1011–1024.

McAuley, E., Duncan, T., & Tammen, V. V. (1989). Psychometric properties of the Intrinsic Motivation Inventory in a competitive sport setting: A confirmatory factor analysis. *Research Quarterly for Exercise and Sport, 60*(1), 48–58.

McCarthy, P. J., Jones, M. V., Harwood, C. G., & Olivier, S. (2010). What do young athletes implicitly understand about psychological skills? *Journal of Clinical Sport Psychology, 4*(2), 158–172.

McGuigan, M. R., Cormack, S. J., & Gill, N. D. (2013). Strength and power profiling of athletes: Selecting tests and how to use the information for programme design. *Strength and Conditioning Journal, 35*(6), 7–14.

Menard, S. (2007). *Handbook of longitudinal research: Design, measurement, and analysis.* Elsevier.

Morais, J. E., Silva, A. J., Marinho, D.A., Seifert, L., & Barbosa, T. M. (2015). Cluster stability as a new method to assess changes in performance and its determinant factors over a season in young swimmers. *International Journal of Sports Physiology and Performance, 10*(2), 261–268.

Morris, T. (2000). Psychological characteristics and talent identification in soccer. *Journal of Sports Sciences, 18*, 715–726.

Newell, K. M. (1986). Constraints on the development of coordination. In M. G. Wade & H. T. A. Whiting (eds), *Motor development in children: aspects of coordination and control* (pp. 341–360). Dordrecht: Martinus Nijhoff.

Newton, M., Duda, J. L., & ZeNong, Y. (2000). Examination of the psychometric properties of the perceived motivational climate in sport questionnaire-2 in a sample of female athletes. *Journal of Sports Sciences, 18*(4), 275–290.

Nightingale, S. C., Miller, S., & Turner, A. (2013). The usefulness and reliability of fitness testing protocols for ice hockey players: a literature review. *Journal of Strength and Conditioning Research, 27*(6), 1742–1748.

Ntoumanis, N., Taylor, I. M., & Thøgersen-Ntoumani, C. (2012). A longitudinal examination of coach and peer motivational climates in youth sport: Implications for moral attitudes, well-being, and behavioral investment. *Developmental Psychology, 48*(1), 213–223.

O'Reilly, J., & Wong, S. (2012). The development of aerobic and skill assessment in soccer. *Sports Medicine, 42*(12), 1029–1040.

O'Rourke, D. J., Smith, R. E., Smoll, F. L., & Cumming, S. P. (2011). Trait anxiety in young athletes as a function of parental pressure and motivational climate: Is parental pressure always harmful? *Journal of Applied Sport Psychology, 23*(4), 398–412.

Park, I., & Schutz, R. W. (2005). An introduction to latent growth model: analysis of repeated measures physical performance data. *Research Quarterly for Exercise and Sport, 76*(2), 176–192.

Pelletier, L. G., Fortier, M. S., Vallerand, R. J., Tuson, K. M., Briere, N. M., & Blais, M. R. (1995). Toward a new measure of intrinsic motivation, extrinsic motivation, and amotivation in sports: The Sport Motivation Scale (SMS). *Journal of Sport and Exercise Psychology, 17*, 35–53.

Philippaerts, R. M., Vaeyens, R., Janssens, M., Van Renterghem, B., Matthys, D., Craen, D., … Malina, R. M. (2006). The relationship between peak height velocity and physical performance in youth soccer players. *Journal of Sports Science, 24*, 221–230.

Phillips, E., Davids, K., Renshaw, I., & Portus, M. (2010). Expert performance in sport and the dynamics of talent development. *Sports Medicine, 40*, 271–283.

Ployhart, R. E., & Vandenberg, R. J. (2010). Longitudinal research: The theory, design, and analysis of change. *Journal of Management, 36*(1), 94–120.

Portus, M. R., & Farrow, D. (2011). Enhancing cricket batting skill: Implications for biomechanics and skill acquisition research and practice. *Sports Biomechanics, 10*(4), 294–305.

Pyne, D. B., Spencer, M., & Mujika, I. (2014). Improving the value of fitness testing for football. *International Journal of Sports Physiology and Performance, 9*, 511–514.

Quested, E., & Duda, J. L. (2011). Antecedents of burnout among elite dancers: A longitudinal test of basic needs theory. *Psychology of Sport and Exercise, 12*(2), 159–167.

Raedeke, T. D., & Smith, A. L. (2001). Development and preliminary validation of an athlete burnout measure. *Journal of Sport and Exercise Psychology, 23*(4), 281–306.

Reinboth, M., & Duda, J. L. (2006). Perceived motivational climate, need satisfaction and indices of well-being in team sports: A longitudinal perspective. *Psychology of Sport and Exercise, 7*(3), 269–286.

Richer, S., & Vallerand, R. J. (1998). Construction and validation of the perceived relatedness scale. *Revue Européene de Psychologie Appliquée, 48*, 129–137.

Roe, G., Darrall-Jones, D., Till, K., Phibbs, P., Read, D., Weakley, J., & Jones, B. (2016). Between-Day reliability and sensitivity of common fatigue measures in rugby players. *International Journal of Sports Performance and Physiology, 11*(5), 581–586.

Ryan, R. M., & Deci, E. L. (2000). Self-determination theory and the facilitation of intrinsic motivation, social development, and well-being. *American Psychologist, 55*(1), 68–78.

Ryan, R. M., & Frederick, C. (1997). On energy, personality, and health: Subjective vitality as a dynamic reflection of well-being. *Journal of Personality, 65*(3), 529–565.

Sarason, I. G., Johnson, J. H., & Siegel, J. M. (1978). Assessing the impact of life changes: Development of the Life Experiences Survey. *Journal of Consulting and Clinical Psychology, 46*(5), 932–946.

Saward, C., Morris, J. G., Nevill, M. E., Nevill, A. M., & Sunderland, C. (2015). Longitudinal development of match-running performance in elite male youth soccer players. *Scandinavian Journal of Medicine and Science in Sports, 24*. doi: 10.1111/sms.12534

Sheard, M., & Golby, J. (2006). Effect of a psychological skills training program on swimming performance and positive psychological development. *International Journal of Sport and Exercise Psychology, 4*(2), 149–169.

Singer, J. D., & Willett, J. B. (2003). *Applied longitudinal data analysis.* New York: Oxford University Press.

Sleeper, M. D., Kenyon, L. K., & Casey, E. (2012). Measuring fitness in female gymnasts: The gymnastics functional measurement tool. *The International Journal of Sports Physical Therapy, 7*(2), 124–138.

Smith, R. E., Smoll, F. L., & Cumming, S. P. (2009). Motivational climate and changes in young athletes' achievement goal orientations. *Motivation and Emotion, 33*(2), 173–183.

Smith, R. E., Cumming, S. P., & Smoll, F. L. (2008). Development and validation of the Motivational Climate Scale for Youth Sports. *Journal of Applied Sport Psychology, 20*(1), 116–136.

Thomas, P. R., Murphy, S. M., & Hardy, L. (1999). Test of performance strategies: Development and preliminary validation of a comprehensive measure of athletes' psychological skills. *Journal of Sports Sciences, 17*(9), 697–711.

Till, K., Cobley, S., O'Hara, J., Chapman, C., & Cooke, C. (2013a). An individualized longitudinal approach to monitoring the dynamics of growth and fitness development in adolescent athletes. *Journal of Strength & Conditioning Research, 27*(5), 1313–1321.

Till, K., Cobley, S., O'Hara, J., Chapman, C., & Cooke, C. (2013b). A longitudinal evaluation of anthropometric and fitness characteristics in junior rugby league players. *Journal of Science and Medicine in Sport, 16*, 438–443.

Till, K., Cobley, S., O'Hara, J., Chapman, C., & Cooke, C. (2014). Considering maturation and relative age in the longitudinal evaluation of junior rugby league players. *Scandinavian Journal of Science and Medicine in Sport, 24*, 569–576.

Till, K., Jones, B., Darrall-Jones, J., Emmonds, S., & Cooke, C. (2015). The longitudinal development of anthropometric and physical characteristics in academy rugby league players. *Journal of Strength and Conditioning Research. 29*(6), 1713–1722.

Toering, T. T., Elferink-Gemser, M. T., Jordet, G., & Visscher, C. (2009). Self-regulation and performance level of elite and non-elite youth soccer players. *Journal of Sports Sciences, 27*(14), 1509–1517.

Twisk, J. W. (2013). *Applied longitudinal data analysis for epidemiology: A practical guide.* Cambridge: Cambridge University Press.

Unnithan, V., White, J., Georgiou, A., Iga, J., & Drust, B. (2012). Talent identification in youth soccer. *Journal of Sports Sciences, 30*(15): 1719–1726.

Vaeyens, R., Lenoir, M., Williams, A. M., & Philippaerts, R. M. (2008). Talent identification and development programmes in sport: Current models and future directions. *Sports Medicine, 38*, 703–714.

Valente-dos-Santos, J., Coelho-e-Silva, M. J., Simões, F., Figueiredo, A. J., Leite, N., Elferink-Gemser, M. T., … Sherar, L. (2012). Modelling development changes in functional capacities and soccer-specific skills in male players aged 11–17 years. Pediatric Exercise Science, 24(4), 603–621.

Valente-Dos-Santos, J., Coelho-e-Silva, M. J., Vaz, V., Figueiredo, A. J., Capranica, L., Sherar, L. B., … Malina, R. M. (2014). Maturity-associated variation in change of direction and dribbling speed in early pubertal years and 5-year developmental changes in young soccer players. *Journal of Sports, Medicine and Physical Fitness, 54*(3), 307–316.

Van Mechelen, W., Twisk, J., Molendijk, A., Blom, B., Snel, J., & Kemper, H. C. (1996). Subject-related risk factors for sports injuries: A 1-yr prospective study in young adults. *Medicine and Science in Sports and Exercise, 28*(9), 1171–1179.

Verkooijen, K. T., van Hove, P., & Dik, G. (2012). Athletic identity and well-being among young talented athletes who live at a Dutch elite sport center. *Journal of Applied Sport Psychology, 24*(1), 106–113.

Vink, K., Raudsepp, L., & Kais, K. (2015). Intrinsic motivation and individual deliberate practice are reciprocally related: Evidence from a longitudinal study of adolescent team sport athletes. *Psychology of Sport and Exercise, 16*, 1–6.

Ziv, G., & Lidor, R. (2009). Physical attributes, physiological characteristics, on-court performances and nutritional strategies of female and male basketball. *Sports Medicine, 39*(7), 547–568.

PART III

Creating optimal environments

19

CREATING OPTIMAL ENVIRONMENTS FOR TALENT DEVELOPMENT

A holistic ecological approach

Kristoffer Henriksen and Natalia Stambulova

The Norwegian success in kayaking has ... been in spite of the climate and a very small number of paddlers. ... Our talented paddlers have been willing to move to train with the best. This means we have always had a training community with high level athletes and hard competition.

(Norwegian kayak coach; from Henriksen, Stambulova, & Roessler, 2011)

The previous sections of the book have introduced two main perspectives on athletic talent. The *talent discovery approach* is based on the notion that there is an innate reservoir of talent and that systematic assessment and selection of talented athletes results in a more efficient use of resources (Howe, Davidson, & Sloboda, 1998). The *talent development approach* places more emphasis on the quantity and quality of training that athletes need to reach top-level perform-ance (Côté, Lidor, & Hackfort, 2009; Ericsson, Krampe, & Tesch-Römer, 1993). The *holistic ecological approach* (HEA) (Henriksen, 2010; Henriksen, Stambulova, & Roessler, 2010a, 2010b, 2011), which is introduced in this chapter, proposes a shift in research attention from the indi-vidual athletes to the broader developmental context or environment in which they develop. The HEA integrates the somewhat opposing talent discovery and development approaches by focusing on how an environment manages the balance between these two, and how this balance becomes a part of the environment's identity.

Introduction to the holistic ecological approach to talent development

The HEA was developed partly to answer the call for theoretically guided research on ecolog-ical approaches to talent development in sport (Araújo & Davids, 2009; Krebs, 2009). The HEA focuses on the whole environment, and suggests that some environments are superior to others in their capacity to guide talented junior athletes in their transition to elite senior athletes. In this section, we introduce key aspects of HEA, including ecologically inferred definitions of athletic talent and talent development, two working models, a definition of the athletic talent development environment (ATDE), and criteria for its success.

Proposed definitions

The HEA has implications for the way we define core elements of talent research. In the light of the HEA we propose an ecological definition of *athletic talent* as a set of competences and skills developed on the basis of innate potential and of multi-year interactions with the environment – for example training and competitions – as well as the ability to exploit the strengths and compensate for the weaknesses of the environment and to contribute to its development (Henriksen, 2010). Along this line we propose a definition of *athletic talent development* as the progressive mutual accommodation that takes place between an aspiring athlete and a composite and dynamic sporting and non-sporting environment that supports the development of the personal, psycho-social and sport-specific skills required for the pursuit of an elite athletic career (Henriksen, 2010).

The working models

The HEA is built around two working models (Henriksen et al., 2010a) inspired by three background theories. Ecological psychology (Bronfenbrenner, 1979) inspired us to view athletes as embedded in their environment and to depict the environment as a series of nested structures ranging from micro to macro level. Systems theory (Lewin, 1936) encouraged us to view the athletic talent development environment as a complex system with components, structure, functions and development. Cultural psychology (Hofstede, 1997; Si & Lee, 2007) directed our attention to the importance of culture as a 'collective programming of the mind' and to view culture as a multi-level phenomenon ranging from national to group culture.

Figure 19.1 presents the athletic talent development environment (ATDE) working model as a framework for describing the roles and functions of the different components and relations within an environment in the talent development process. The young prospective elite athletes appear at the centre of the model, and other components of the ATDE are structured into two levels (micro- and macro-) and two domains (athletic and non-athletic). The micro-level refers to the environment where the prospective athletes spend a good deal of their daily life. The macro-level refers to social settings, which affect but do not contain the athletes, as well as to the values and customs of the cultures to which the athletes belong. The athletic domain covers the part of the athletes' environment that is directly related to sport, whereas the non-athletic domain presents all the other spheres of the athletes' lives. The outer layer of the model represents the past, present and future of the ATDE, emphasizing that the environment is dynamic.

Figure 19.2 presents the environment success factors (ESF) working model. The model's starting point is the preconditions (e.g., human, material and financial) provided by the environment, all of which are necessary but not sufficient for success. The model then illustrates how the daily routines/process (e.g., training, camps and competitions) have three outcomes: athletes' individual development and achievements (e.g., psycho-social competencies and athletic skills); team achievements (in team sports); and organizational development and culture. *Organizational culture* is central to the ESF model and consists of three levels (Schein, 1990). *Cultural artefacts* include stories and myths told, customs, and physical manifestations such as clothing and organization charts. *Espoused values* are the social principles, goals and standards that the organization shows to the world. *Basic assumptions* are underlying reasons for actions. They consist of beliefs and assumptions that are no longer questioned but are taken for granted. Organizational culture is characterized by integration of key basic assumptions into a cultural paradigm guiding socialization of new members and providing stability. The ESF working model predicts that the ATDE's success is a result of the interplay between preconditions,

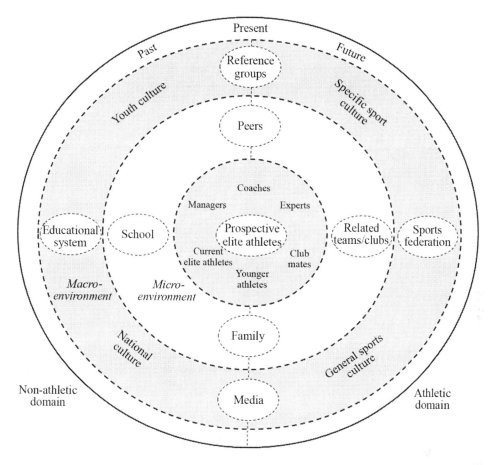

Figure 19.1 The athletic talent development environment (ATDE) working model
Source: Originally published in Henriksen, 2010. Reproduced with permission.

process, individual and team development and achievements, with organizational culture serving to integrate these elements.

Athletic talent development environment: Definition and criterion of success

In continuation of the working models we propose to view the ATDE as a dynamic system comprising a) an athlete's immediate surroundings at the micro-level where athletic and personal development take place, b) the interrelations between these surroundings, c) at the macro-level, the larger context in which these surroundings are embedded, and d) the organizational culture of the sports club or team, which is an integrative factor of the ATDE's effectiveness in helping young talented athletes to develop into senior elite athletes (Henriksen, 2010).

ATDEs have varying degrees of success in nurturing talented athletes. We suggest that successful ATDEs are environments that hold a successful track record of producing elite senior athletes from among their juniors. A key marker of this overall criterion is the environment's

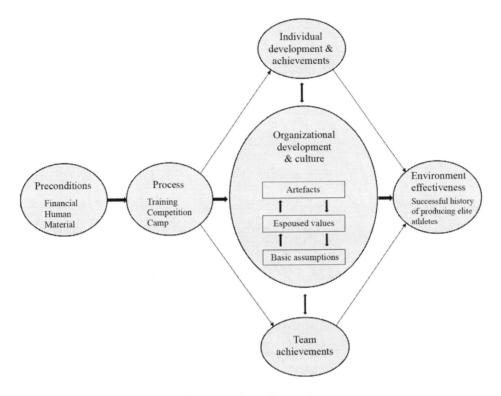

Figure 19.2 The environment success factors (ESF) working model

Source: Originally published in Henriksen, 2010. Reproduced with permission.

success in developing competences and skills that support athletes in meeting the challenges they face both in sport and other spheres of life (Stambulova, 2009).

Successful and less successful athletic talent development environments: Research methodology and major research findings

The HEA promotes a case study design to the investigation of ATDEs. This implies investigating real-life phenomena within their real-life context, using multiple sources of data, and making 'thick descriptions' of particular environments (Flyvbjerg, 2006; Stake, 1995). Whereas most of the research conducted on psychological aspects of athletic talent development has been retrospective in nature, the HEA advocates taking a contemporary – or real-time – view of the functioning of the environment. The working models are instrumental in the research. During data collection, the models guide the researcher's attention through an otherwise over-whelming amount of data. During analysis, the working models serve as a foundation for creating empirical models that capture the unique features of the environment under study and serve as a summary of the case.

The HEA has been tested and developed through empirical investigations of a number of successful environments. These include the Danish national 49'er sailing team (Henriksen et al., 2010a), the IFK Växjö track and field club in Sweden (Henriksen et al., 2010b), the kayak team of the Wang elite sport high school in Norway (Henriksen et al., 2011), the AGF soccer team in Denmark (Larsen, Alfermann, Henriksen & Christensen, 2013) alongside a number of unpublished master theses (e.g., Petersen, 2014; Pyrdol, 2013) that have investigated environments in karate, cycling, soccer, swimming, badminton and more, all in a northern European context. To test our initial ideas about the common features of successful environments, we further studied a less successful golf environment in Denmark (Henriksen, Alfermann, Larsen, & Christensen, 2014).

In the following we present two cases exemplifying the HEA research approach. The first example is based on the study of the flat-water kayak team at Wang School of Elite Sports (Henriksen et al., 2011) – a successful ATDE that was selected due to the impressive results of Norwegian senior elite kayakers, and a steady flow of young paddlers from Wang into the Norwegian senior national team. The second example is based on the study of Seaside golf team in Denmark (Henriksen, Larsen, & Christensen, 2014) that was selected as a less successful ATDE because of its explicit goal of developing young golfers into elite senior athletes, and its lack of success in reaching this goal. In both cases, data were collected from multiple sources (interviews, observations over extended periods and analysis of documents). The results of each case study serve to create empirical versions of both working models that summarize the results and visually depict the environments.

Wang kayak team: A successful environment

Wang School of Elite Sports is a private secondary school located in the heart of Oslo. Wang has been a 'school of elite sports' since 1984 and at the time of the study hosted approximately 360 elite student-athletes. The athletes at Wang receive education and sports training as part of their daily school programme but remain members of their sports clubs. The flat-water kayak team at Wang consisted of 12 paddlers.

Figure 19.3 displays the empirical version of the ATDE model adapted to present the Wang kayak team. Bearing in mind that all the components of the environment are interconnected and affect one another, the empirical model depicts the most important components and relations as well as the structure of the environment. At the centre of the model are the relations between the prospective athletes and a community of current and former elite athletes – a community that includes the school, club, and national team coaches and also a number of mentors. The interaction with this community was the main driver of the prospects' development. The prospects were highly dependent on support from the community, and coaches more often joined training or acted as mentors than they assumed a classic coach-role. The young athletes were very proficient at using the elite athletes as sparring partners. All athletes and coaches mentioned, 'having someone to aspire to' as a central quality of the environment, as explained by an athlete: 'All sports have their role models. What is unique for our environment is that I actually meet these role models every day. I try to beat them in training, I ask questions, and I listen to their advice' (Henriksen et al., 2011, p. 349). With family and non-sporting friends being the only components in the non-athletic domain to which any importance was attributed, the environment was skewed to the athletic side, a fact that was reinforced by the school's elite sport profile. The community of clubs referred to as 'Kayak-Norway' allows the prospective athletes to train in any club in Norway. On the macro-level, acting as a cohesive force, the school management organized relations with the club and with the national Olympic committee's team of experts and worked to assure that everyday school activities were conducive to the talent development process. The time-frame depicts a basic belief in the current state of affairs but also a willingness to develop an even more uncompromising approach to the talent development process (e.g., by organizing training in school holidays).

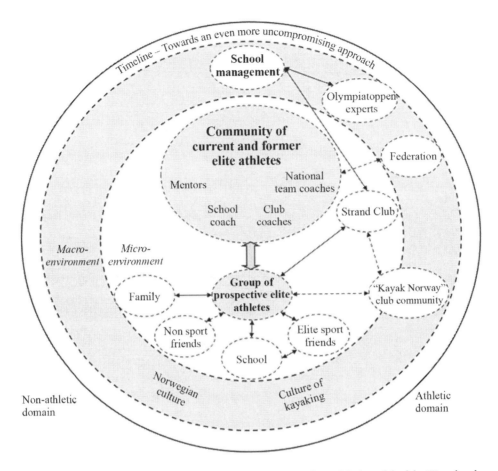

Figure 19.3 The athletic talent development environment (ATDE) empirical model of the Wang kayak
team. 'Olympiatoppen' is an organization that is part of the Norwegian Olympic and
Paralympic Committee and Confederation of Sports with responsibility for training
Norwegian elite sport

Source: Originally published in Henriksen, 2010. Reproduced with permission.

Figure 19.4 presents the empirical version of the ESF model, summarizing the most important factors influencing the success of Wang kayak team. The team had limited financial
resources but benefited from a world-class natural environment in a fjord that provided perfect
conditions for flat-water racing. The daily routines revolved around a large volume of hard
interval-based training and frequent tests and competitions, as dictated by a rooted Norwegian
philosophy about kayaking (e.g., training all-round sport skills and training several sports rather
than focusing on one sport from an early age). The group had a distinct organizational culture
with a strong coherence between artefacts, espoused values and basic assumptions; in other
words with a correspondence between what they say they do and what they actually do. As a
fundamental governing principle, openness and cooperation within an open training community were at the core of the group culture. In the words of the school coach: 'We can see that
medals have always grown out of a community of athletes that train together'. Training was

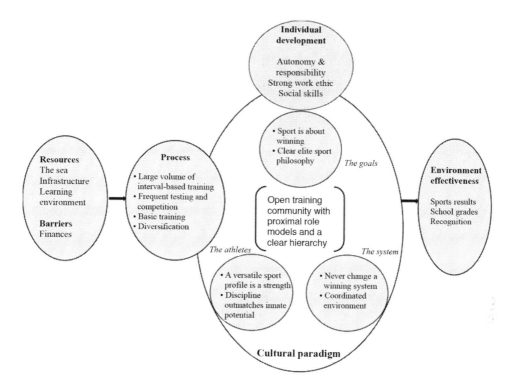

Figure 19.4 The environment success factors (ESF) empirical model of the Wang kayak team
Source: Originally published in Henriksen, 2010. Reproduced with permission.

organized to allow for the prospects to ride the waves of more experienced paddlers. Athletes willingly travelled to the training venues of the best athletes to learn the trade, while former elite athletes remained willing to pass on their knowledge to younger athletes in an informal learning process. Further basic assumptions of the group culture included a conviction that the athletes' discipline and autonomy are more important than their innate potential, and a pragmatic trust in its own system. The daily routines worked in combination with the organizational culture to develop athletes who were autonomous and responsible for their own development and had social skills and a strong work ethic.

In sum, the two empirical models depict a highly integrated environment in which the athletes could expect demands placed on them from different agents (club, school and national teams) to be coordinated, and with a coherent and rooted organizational culture that stimulated the athletes to develop a high work ethic and an ability to effectively exploit the environment's resources.

Seaside golf team: A less successful environment

Seaside International College of Sport and Performance in Denmark combines a solid educational profile with a strong sport and performance (dance, music and film) profile in a boarding school environment for 16- to 19-year-olds. The College provides the student-athletes with academic qualifications and develops talented athletes in many sports. The Seaside golf team (that was considered less successful) volunteered for the HEA-based study (Henriksen et al., 2014).

Figure 19.5 displays the empirical version of the ATDE model adapted to present the Seaside golf team. Considering the model, perhaps the most conspicuous result was the lack of connections between the components in the environment. One key example was the lack of dialogue between the schoolteachers and the coaches, which a student-athlete described as follows: 'My schoolteachers ... do not know my tournament plan. And the coaches know just as little about when I am overloaded with homework. I do not have the impression that they ever talk to each other' (Henriksen et al., 2014, p. 141).

Another example was the lack of dialogue between the school coaches and club coaches. The athletes needed to negotiate the different inputs they got in the two different environments, and sometimes ended up bewildered by conflicting advice and demands. The same was true for a

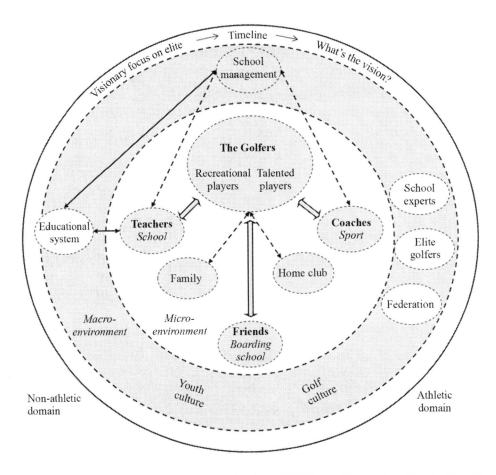

Figure 19.5 The athletic talent development environment (ATDE) empirical model of the Seaside golf team

Source: Originally published in Henriksen, 2014. Reproduced with permission.

lack of dialogue between coaches and experts. The lack of contact with elite golfers left the Seaside golfers with little understanding of the life and culture they aspired to be a part of.

Figure 19.6 presents the empirical version of the ESF model, summarizing the most important factors explaining the lack of success of Seaside golf team as a talent development environment. As regards *preconditions*, the environment benefitted substantially from the fact that school, sport and residences were within close reach and that the school had a number of sport facilities at its disposal, as well as from a healthy eating program and a good social climate. The *process* (daily routines) revolved around balancing the demands of an academic education and a career in golf. Training consisted of few but very long sessions, which the athletes considered a poor organization. Further, the training was characterized by a 'room for everybody' attitude, by being individualized and self-driven to a degree where the athletes felt demotivated and alone, and by being theoretical, formal and fragmented in nature.

The most salient finding regarding the culture of the team was its incoherence across levels. In the interviews, coaches and managers highlighted clear *espoused values*. These included developing 'responsible global citizens' and creating synergy between the students' sport and academic development. During observations, a number of *artefacts* stood out that were in contrast to the espoused values. The athletes were often late for training or did not show up at all. Even the coaches sometimes arrived late for training. The structure of the training was loose, and the coaches neither sanctioned the athletes nor set a good example. Warm-up

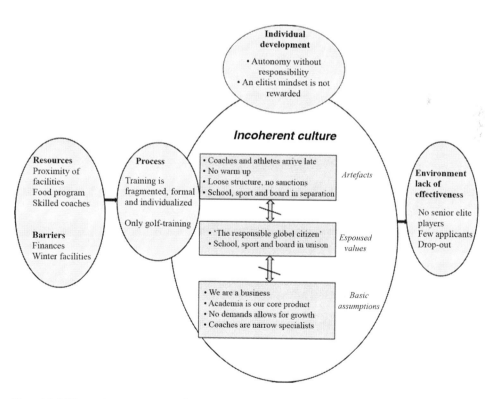

Figure 19.6 The environment success factors (ESF) empirical model of the Seaside golf team

Source: Originally published in Henriksen, 2014. Reproduced with permission.

routines, strength and conditioning training were left up to the athletes and some of them ignored or paid only little attention to these aspects of training. Different parts of the athletes' everyday life (sport, studies, living) were not in synergy, but rather separate. The *basic assumptions* inferred by the researchers helped to understand the discrepancy between the levels of the Seaside golf environment's organizational culture. The central basic assumption stated that 'the school is a business', and therefore, the 'customers' should be kept even if they skip training or arrive too late. Further examples of basic assumptions are that 'academia is our core product' (i.e., not sport), and that 'coaches are narrow specialists' (i.e., knowledgeable in terms of technique, but not expected to lead the way by example). According to the researchers, the athletes in this environment developed autonomy on the one side, but also a lack of responsibility on the other.

In sum, the two empirical models of the Seaside golf team illustrate a disconnected environment with little integration of efforts. The organizational culture with incoherence between artefacts, espoused values and basic assumptions left the members of the environment with a sense of being part of an unclear culture that provided too few supporting guidelines in terms of how to develop as a golfer, a student and a citizen.

Shared features of successful talent development environments

When we compared the case studies of successful environments, we found that each environment was unique. At the same time the successful environments also shared a number of features and in many ways employed the same principles in their work (unlike the less successful golf environment). These principles were, however, not implemented in the same way across the environments. Therefore, the uniqueness of each environment was often expressed in how they implemented the common principles.

The shared features of successful ATDEs and their descriptors are summarized in Table 19.1. The list is provisional and expected to be elaborated and clarified with further research in various cultural and sport contexts. To further clarify the meaning of each feature we include the descriptors' *opposite poles*, meant as examples and inferred logically or grounded in the Seaside study and in the first author's applied experiences. Researchers can use the table as a reference when studying sporting environments, and coaches and sport managers may use it as a lens through which to scan their own environment looking for potential areas of improvement.

From ecological research to ecologically informed practice

As described above, the HEA embraces a set of key concepts, two working models, research guidelines and case examples summarized in the list of common features of successful ATDEs. In this section we are going to complement the HEA description by adding applied principles and providing an example of how they can be used to help ATDEs to improve.

The HEA applied principles (Larsen et al., 2014) stimulate a sport psychology practitioner to: a) conduct the interventions inside the athletes' natural setting rather than in the office, b) involve the athletes' environment (e.g., coaches, managers, teammates) in the intervention, c) even aim to optimize the entire environment around the athlete or team, and d) see the athletes as whole human beings and to facilitate the development of a holistic package of psychosocial resources (e.g., knowledge, skills, attitudes, network) that will be of use for the athletes both in and outside of sport.

Table 19.1 Features of successful athletic talent development environments

Features of successful ATDEs	Descriptors	Opposite poles
Training groups with supportive relationships	Opportunities for inclusion in a training community; supportive relationships and friendships within the group, despite performance level; good communication.	Individualized training programmes at an early stage; training alone; low cohesion in the group; inter-group rivalry; performance as a criterion for inclusion.
Proximal role models	Community of practice includes prospective and current elite athletes; opportunities to train with the elite athletes; elite athletes who are willing to pass on their knowledge.	Airtight boundaries between athletes at different levels. Elite-level athletes keep their secrets and regard prospective athletes as future rivals.
Support of sporting goals by the wider environment	Opportunities to focus on the sport; school, family, friends and others acknowledge and accept the athletes' dedication to sport.	Non-sport environment shows lack of understanding of elite sport and the demands involved.
Support for the development of psychosocial skills	Opportunities to develop skills and competences that are of benefit outside the sporting domain (such as autonomy, responsibility and commitment); considering athletes as 'whole human beings'.	Focus solely on sport and winning at any cost; excessive control from coaches; focus not on personal improvement but on relative performance level, which devalues learning and development.
Training that allows for diversification	Opportunities to sample different sports during early phases; integration of different sports in the daily routines; appreciation of versatile sport profiles and basic sport skills.	Promoting early specialization; focus solely on developing sport-specific skills; considering athletes' interest in trying different sports to be rivalry and a potential threat.
Focus on long-term development	Focus on long-term development of the athletes rather than early success; age-appropriate amount and content of training.	Focus on short-term success; kids are seen as miniature elite athletes; no time to heal when injured.
Strong and coherent organizational culture	Organizational culture characterized by coherence between artifacts, espoused values and basic assumptions; culture provides stability to the group and supports a learning environment.	Fragmented culture in which espoused values do not correspond to actions; uncertainty and confusion among coaches, athletes and others; lack of common vision.
Integration of efforts	Coordination and communication between sport, school, family and other components; athletes experience concordance and synergy in daily life.	Lack of communication; conflicting interests; athletes experience many and contradicting pulls in daily life.

HEA intervention example: Reforming the culture of the Danish national orienteering team

In the following section, the first author shares his HEA intervention experience with the Danish national orienteering team aimed at reforming their existing culture (that guided the team poorly to reach their goals) into a high performance culture (Henriksen, 2015). The team was composed of both male and female athletes with 9 permanent members and 6 athletes who were selected for some but not all camps and competitions, and two coaches. The athletes competed as individual athletes and in relays.

The intervention was designed as an integrated part of the athletes' training and competition environment and included three stages inspired by Schein's (1999) adaptation of Lewin's (1947) theory of change. In the *unfreeze* stage, the members must experience survival anxiety (e.g., from a drop in performance) that outweighs the natural learning anxiety involved in all change processes. This motivates the members to change. In the *change* stage, the members learn new behaviours for example through identifying with role models and developing new solutions. In the *refreeze* stage, the new behaviours are gradually internalized into the members' self-image and incorporated into relationships and habits.

In working with the orienteering team, the *unfreeze stage* consisted of needs assessment and a workshop. In the needs assessment, I interviewed selected athletes and the head coach about their perceptions of the daily training and competition environment. They all described how travelling together was taxing, a disloyal style of communication destroyed focus, and they found themselves competing against each other in an unhealthy manner. In the workshop, I presented the problematic issues that came out of the individual interviews and the coach presented the team's declining medal statistics. The athletes, coaches and staff then interviewed each other in pairs about an episode in which being part of the national team had affected performance in a negative way. In a joint meeting the results were summarized and depicted a less than optimal team culture.

The *change stage* focused on developing new team values through visions of a better future for the team. In a workshop, the athletes, coaches and staff again interviewed each other in pairs, but this time about positive experiences in which being part of the national team helped them perform better than they would have done without the team. The athletes presented their stories in a plenary session and each took notes on what values they could extract from the stories. The athletes further produced videos that portrayed the new culture and how the team overcame obstacles on the rocky road there. During a one-week training camp, the team agreed on five values, which were written on posters, for example, 'We make each other better', 'We discuss strategies and techniques among us', and 'We talk to, rather than about each other'. Designing compelling positive visions served to create a sense of psychological safety and reduce learning anxiety.

The *refreeze stage* aimed to integrate the approved values into the daily life of the team, in other words, to go from espoused to enacted values and to incorporate the new values and behaviours in the team's identity as basic assumptions. I travelled with the team to a number of training camps and competitions and regularly attended daily training, always with a focus on implementing the team values. Specifically we set in motion a number of initiatives. For example, we introduced daily evaluations of one value at a time (how well did we live up to this value today) and encouraged 'the positive story of the day'. In the latter, the task was to speak directly to a teammate about something good that he or she did that day and how the action was an extension of one of the values. Posters displaying the values were hung on the walls of gathering points on every trip and thus served as visible artefacts of the new team culture.

Repeatedly engaging in these strategies in every camp and competition reflected the *refreeze* stage.

During an evaluation meeting after two years, several athletes mentioned that they felt there was a more supportive group culture. This has made it less taxing to travel with the team and allowed the athletes to focus on their performance. Importantly the athletes have also started to perform well and have since medalled in several European and World championships

The intervention reflects the HEA in several ways. First, the intervention did not mainly target the psychological skills of individual athletes but, rather, aspects of the sporting environment. Second, the intervention was set inside the athletes' daily training and competition environment. Third, it involved not only the athletes but also coaches and other staff members. Fourth, it focused on a specific element of the ESF model, namely the organizational culture of the team, and targeted all three levels of culture (artefacts, espoused values and basic assumptions).

Conclusion and future challenges

Inviting researchers to look beyond the individual athlete and mirroring the complexity of talent development in the real world, the HEA constitutes an important supplement to the contemporary literature on athletic talent and career development. The HEA takes an overall and holistic approach to the investigation of ATDEs, but it is still in its developmental phase. The study of few successful ATDEs naturally points to the value of studying further environments, for example, in different sports, different socio-cultural contexts, and different performance domains. We also suggest that future studies should combine the HEA with the *holistic lifespan approach* (Wylleman, Alfermann, & Lavallee, 2004; Wylleman, Reints, & De Knop, 2013) that incorporates talent identification and development into an athlete career context with transitions such as selections for teams and talent programs (Stambulova, 2009; Stambulova, Alfermann, Statler, & Côté, 2009).

The HEA has important implications for sport psychology practice. Suggesting that sport psychology belongs inside the athletes' environment and not in the practitioner's office, the HEA calls for a re-organization of practice. Travelling with teams and regularly attending practices and competitions speak to the advantage of the sport psychology practitioner being a part of the performance staff and hired directly by a club, a sports federation, or a national Olympic committee (rather than as a private contractor). Other implications involve expanding the scope of applied sport psychology to include ways to optimize athletic environments of different performance levels, and more specifically to facilitate the development of organizational cultures that guide the athletes and the staff in their pursuit of excellence.

References

Araújo, D., & Davids, K. (2009). Ecological approaches to cognition and action in sport and exercise: Ask not only what you do, but where you do it. *International Journal of Sport Psychology, 40*(1), 5–37.

Bronfenbrenner, U. (1979). *The ecology of human development.* Cambridge, MA: Harvard University Press.

Côté, J., Lidor, R., & Hackfort, D. (2009). ISSP position stand: To sample or to specialize? Seven postulates about youth sport activities that lead to continued participation and elite performance. *International Journal of Sport and Exercise Psychology, 7*(1), 7–17.

Ericsson, A. K., Krampe, R. T., & Tesch-Römer, C. (1993). The role of deliberate practice in the acquisition of expert performance. *Psychological Review, 100*(3), 363–406.

Flyvbjerg, B. (2006). Five misunderstandings about case study research. *Qualitative Inquiry, 12*(2), 219–245.

Henriksen, K. (2010). *The ecology of talent development in sport: A multiple case study of successful athletic talent development environments in Scandinavia.* Doctoral thesis, Institute of Sport Science and Clinical Biomechanics, University of Southern Denmark.

Henriksen, K. (2015). Developing a high performance culture: A sport psychology intervention from an ecological perspective in elite orienteering. *Journal of Sport Psychology in Action, 6*, 14–153.

Henriksen, K., Larsen, C. H., & Christensen, M. K. (2014). Looking at success from its opposite pole: The case of a talent development golf environment in Denmark. *International Journal of Sport and Exercise Psychology, 12*(2), 134–149. doi: 10.1080/1612197X.2013.853473

Henriksen, K., Stambulova, N., & Roessler, K. K. (2010a). A Holistic approach to athletic talent development environments: A successful sailing milieu. *Psychology of Sport and Exercise, 11*, 212–222. doi: 10.1016/j.psychsport.2009.10.005

Henriksen, K., Stambulova, N., & Roessler, K. K. (2010b). Succesful talent development in track and field: Considering the role of environment. *Scandinavian Journal of Medicine & Science in Sports, 20*, 122–132. doi: 10.1111/j.1600-0838.2010.01187.x

Henriksen, K., Stambulova, N., & Roessler, K. K. (2011). Riding the wave of an expert: A successful talent development environment in kayaking. *Sport Psychologist, 25*(3), 341–362.

Hofstede, G. (1997). *Cultures and organizations: Software of the mind.* New York: McGraw-Hill.

Howe, M. J. A., Davidson, J. W., & Sloboda, J. A. (1998). Innate talents: Reality or myth? *Behavioral and Brain Sciences, 21*(3), 399–442.

Krebs, R. J. (2009). Bronfenbrenner's Bioecological Theory of Human Development and the process of development of sports talent. *International Journal of Sport Psychology, 40*, 108–135.

Larsen, C. H., Alfermann, D., Henriksen, K., & Christensen, M. K. (2013). Successful talent development in soccer: The characteristics of the environment. *Sport Exercise and Performance Psychology, 2*, 190–206. doi: 10.1037/a0031958

Larsen, C. H., Alfermann, D., Henriksen, K., & Christensen, M. K. (2014). Preparing footballers for the next step: An intervention program from an ecological perspective. *The Sport Psychologist, 28*, 91–102. doi: dx.doi.org/10.1123/pes.2013-0015

Lewin, K. (1936). *Principles of topological psychology.* New York: McGraw-Hill.

Lewin, K. (1947). Frontiers in group dynamics: Concept, method and reality in social science; social equilibria and social change. *Human Relations, 1*, 5–41.

Petersen, K. S. (2014). *Talentudviklingsmiljø i cykelsport [A talent development environment in cycling].* Master thesis. University of Southern Denmark.

Pyrdol, N. (2013). *A world class talent factory: A holistic ecological analysis of Ajax Amsterdam Football Academy.* Master thesis. University of Southern Denmark.

Schein, E. H. (1990). Organizational culture. *American Psychologist, 45*(2), 109–119.

Schein, E. H. (1999). *The corporate culture survival guide.* San Francisco, CA: Jossey-Bass.

Si, G., & Lee, H. (2007). Cross cultural issues in sport psychology research. In S. Jowett & D. Lavallee (eds), *Social psychology in sport* (pp. 278–334). Champaign, IL: Human Kinetics.

Stake, R. E. (1995). *The art of case study research.* Thousand Oaks, CA: Sage.

Stambulova, N. (2009). Talent development in sport: The perspective of career transitions. In E. Tsung-Min Hung, R. Lidor & D. Hackfort (eds), *Psychology of sport excellence* (pp. 63–74). Morgantown, WV: Fitness Information Technology.

Stambulova, N., Alfermann, D., Statler, T., & Côté, J. (2009). ISSP position stand: Career development and transitions of athletes. *International Journal of Sport and Exercise Psychology, 7*, 395–412.

Wylleman, P., Alfermann, D., & Lavallee, D. (2004). Career transitions in sport: European perspectives. *Psychology of Sport and Exercise 5*, 7–20.

Wylleman, P., Reints, A., & De Knop, P. (2013). A developmental and holistic perspective on athletic career development. In P. Sotiaradou, & V. De Bosscher (eds), *Managing high performance sport* (pp. 159–182). New York, NY: Routledge.

20

ON THE (POTENTIAL) VALUE OF COACHING

Steven B. Rynne, Bob Crudgington,
Rebecca K. Dickinson, and Clifford J. Mallett

Introduction

There is moderate empirical evidence that supportive families, coaches, and teachers contribute to athlete development (Rees, Hardy, Güllich, et al., 2016). Of these various social actors, athletes and coaches are considered the two key performers in the sporting context (Mallett & Rynne, 2015). Typically, coaches are adults (and in many cases parents) who by age, position, and perceived knowledge assume a position of leadership, and therefore an inherent power differential exists between coach and athlete (Cassidy, Jones, & Potrac, 2015; Coatsworth & Conroy, 2006). Hence, it is logical to assume that in most cases coaches are influential in sport regardless of the setting (e.g., children, emerging, performance, high performance).

This position has received support in the talent literature. For example, Gulbin, Oldenziel, Weissensteiner, and Gagné (2010) found that two-thirds of Australian athletes reported that their coaches were critical and highly influential in their development throughout the athlete pathway. Moreover, athletes reported that coaches increasingly became more important to their development as they progressed to higher competitive levels. They concluded that it was essential to match talented athletes with talented coaches to optimise athlete development. More generally, several researchers in talent development of athletes have argued that expert coaches are foundational to talent identification and development programs (Bullock et al., 2009; Vaeyens, Güllich, Warr, & Philippaerts, 2009).

In this chapter, we consider the potential influence of coaches across various forms of athlete involvement. More specifically we:

- Explicitly deal with why 'value' cannot be assumed with respect to coaching
- Position coaches as architects of the sporting environment and consider the work that coaches undertake
- Consider the knowledge that underpins this work
- Characterise areas of potential impact that coaches can have
- Consider coaching in contexts (different parts of models)

Why the value of coaches cannot be assumed

The coach plays a central role in how athletes experience sport (e.g., attrition, Positive Youth Development, athlete health, and abuse), and this is reported and further explained elsewhere in this Handbook (e.g., Chapters 23, 27, 28, & 29). As a result, it has been argued that coaching in all forms (participation and performance) should be valued for the *potential* contribution it makes to athlete development (Mallett, 2013; Mallett & Rynne, 2015). In addition to variability in the impact of sport experiences on the development of athletes, and more specifically in relation to the work of coaches, there is a paucity of research that has investigated the impact of coaches on the development of athlete talent and it has been argued that what has been published lacks acuity (Rees et al., 2016). An example related to the motivational characteristics created by coaches relates to the findings of Harwood and Swain (2001). These authors found the presence of both positive (task orientation supportive) and negative (ego orientation supportive) environments throughout youth tennis. Even when high-quality coaching exists, there is no assurance that it will be delivered to the 'right' athletes. For example, Gulbin and colleagues (2010) found the formation of coach–athlete dyads to be more often serendipitous in nature rather than planned and systematic. This finding certainly seems problematic in terms of optimising resources to develop athlete talent.

Furthermore, it has been reported that athletes form perceptions of their coaches' behaviours from their own observations (e.g., Gould, Guinan, Greenleaf, Medbery, & Peterson, 1999; Kristiansen & Roberts, 2010). Unsurprisingly, athletes have reported that coaches' behaviours are sometimes helpful and at other times unhelpful for athlete performance (d'Arripe-Longueville, Saury, Fournier, & Durand, 2001; Gould et al., 1999; Kristiansen & Roberts, 2010). Indeed, athletes have been successful in spite of a perceived lack of beneficial support from their coach (e.g., Gould et al., 1999).

The position that we therefore arrive at is that coaches may either foster or thwart athlete development, and in some cases coaches might minimally impact athlete development. Regardless, there is sufficient evidence and associated impetus to consider the coach as playing a potentially pivotal role in athlete development in the sport setting. In other words, coaches have the *potential* to differentially impact athlete development across their sporting careers.

Coaches can be considered to be 'architects' of sport environments

The International Council for Coaching Excellence (ICCE) defined sports coaching as 'a process of guided (athlete and/or team) development in a single sport at identified stages of development' (ICCE, 2013; p. 14). The notion of a 'coaching process' implicitly suggests that the consequences of coaching practice impact athlete development over time (Lyle, 2002). So as to shape and inform potential impact, quality coaching practice is underpinned by coaches' knowledge that operates in specific contexts and seeks to produce specific athlete outcomes (Côté & Gilbert, 2009). To be effective as a coach and therefore positively impact athlete development involves 'the consistent application of integrated professional, interpersonal, and intrapersonal knowledge to improve athletes' competence, confidence, connection and character in specific coaching contexts' (Côté & Gilbert, 2009, p. 316). Hence, effective coaches integrate these three forms of coaching knowledge (professional, interpersonal, and intrapersonal) in various coaching contexts. Furthermore, quality coaches foster athlete development in terms of competence, confidence, connection, and character. Essentially, this definition of coaching effectiveness advocates for consideration of what is needed in specific settings and stages of development. In other words, different learning and development outcomes might be pursued in varying sport settings.

Accordingly, coaches have been viewed as the architects of the sport environment (Mallett, 2005; Mallett & Rynne, 2015), regardless of the reason for involvement (e.g., fun, fitness, skill development, performance) or setting (e.g., training, competition, domestic, international, generalist, specialist). As architects of sport settings, coaches are charged with the responsibility of creating an environment that nurtures learning and development (Mageau & Vallerand, 2003; Rynne & Mallett, 2014). As covered in the previous section, these 'architects' can have variable impact. However, supporting the quality of coaching at all levels necessitates an increasing understanding of the requisite knowledge (noted as being professional, interpersonal, and intrapersonal in nature) and key elements of their work.

A variety of scholars have sought to characterise the work of coaches (e.g., Côté & Salmela, 1996; Cushion, Armour, & Jones, 2006; Lyle, 2002; Rynne, Mallett, & Tinning, 2010). The most obvious aspects of coaches' work relate to direct task behaviours whereby coaches are hands-on with athletes in situations such as training camps, the daily training environment (e.g., teams, squads, pre-season, in-season, recovery), and competitions (e.g., regular, periodic, major, minor). Beyond the obvious face-to-face work that coaches do with athletes, there are a variety of other responsibilities that performance coaches undertake, such as indirect tasks (e.g., planning, managing support staff, talent identification and selection), administrative tasks (e.g., budgets), and public relations tasks (e.g., liaising with stakeholders). Given the focus of this text, we will discuss the indirect tasks further.

Selection

The selection of athletes is an important aspect of the vast majority of coaching environments. While selection trials are often a dominant feature of the pre-season and early in-season activities of coaches, selection occurs at various time points throughout the entire season. For example, coaches may select players from week to week, especially in team sports where the season is characterised by an extended competition schedule. This task can involve selecting a line-up for a particular match or specific opponent and could be based on tactical constraints or simply be a reaction to changes in the 'form' of players. In addition, coaches may seek to select players using a number of other considerations. For example, a coach may provide a less experienced player with an opportunity to develop in a 'less crucial' fixture. The coach may select with a disciplinary rationale so as to embed or reinforce team culture. The coach may seek to send a message to team members regarding complacency. Coaches may also make selections based on players' need for rest, current and future workload, and/or in relation to injuries. The week-to-week selection decisions by the coach have the capacity to impact team dynamics (see Chapter 21) as well as the relationships between team members and the coach (Frontiera, 2010; Schroder, 2010).

In recent times, the scope of coaching work has extended further to encompass special programs such as talent transfer initiatives (see Chapter 32), creating the challenge of novel situations with respect to athlete selection, planning of training, forming relationships, meeting expectations, and the like. While the mechanisms may have changed somewhat over time, the selection processes (incorporating talent identification and selection) enacted by coaches have traditionally and deliberately served to narrow the pool of prospective athletes (i.e., they are generally founded on the notion that coaches need to reduce the number of athletes they work with and limit it to only the best). An issue, however, is that selection processes are often constrained by historical ('this is how many we usually choose'), financial ('this is how many we can afford to have'), and functional ('this is how many we can manage') factors. Moreover, traditional selection processes have tended to maintain a narrow focus on biophysical factors. The application of such narrow principles might inadvertently limit the potential talent pool and exclude potential talent – whereas a stronger appreciation of psychosocial factors may actually serve to 'broaden the net'.

While psychosocial factors are notoriously difficult to quantify (e.g., see Anshell & Lidor, 2012; Hoare & Warr, 2000), recent literature on talent identification has investigated and advocated for consideration of these factors (e.g., MacNamara, 2011; MacNamara, Button, & Collins, 2010; Wattie & Baker, in press). This increased understanding and acknowledgement of the importance of psychosocial factors has contributed to advancing the field, such as a modern trend in TID processes towards the inclusion of 'talent confirmation' phases (an extended period of training and assessment in which an athlete's progress and characteristics such as 'coachability' and adaptation to the environment are monitored by coaches to make final selections for a program) (e.g., Gulbin, Croser, Morley, & Weissensteiner, 2013). Whilst in practice, this process might often be conducted after an initial culling of athletes based primarily on physical factors, it nevertheless represents an attempt to acknowledge and take into account more than just the biophysical. Compounding these constraints is that coaches and a variety of others have (somewhat understandably, given the inherent complexities) failed to appreciate the vagaries of 'talent' and its underpinning factors. For example, a key (and erroneous) assumption in selection might be the notion that current capacity predicts potential (e.g., Barreiros & Fonseca, 2012). Relatedly, there is an increasing acknowledgement that athlete development is influenced by several factors, including socio-economic status (Baker & Wattie, in press; Wattie & Baker, in press; Davids & Baker, 2007), variation in growth and maturation (Till, Cobley, O'Hara, Cooke, & Chapman, 2014), and inherited qualities (Davids & Baker, 2007; Gagné, 2004).

Regardless of the complexities, coaches have been charged with the task of selection (notwithstanding the specific role of the 'scout' or 'talent manager', albeit a role generally performed under direct guidance from the coaching beneficiary). In undertaking this crucial role, a number of scholars (e.g., Christensen, 2009; Vrljic & Mallett, 2008) have noted the role of the 'coaches' eye', and challenge the assumption that selecting is based on rational or objective processes. With increasing acceptance that sports are multi-dimensional, and high-quality players are multifaceted in their characteristics (rather than identified through a few single factors), there has been an associated acknowledgement of the difficult but potentially valuable role that coaches play in selecting athletes. Indeed, researchers from a variety of perspectives have 'stressed that the experience-based judgements of top-level coaches should be a point of departure for understanding talent identification in sport' (Christensen, 2009, p. 367). The subsequent suggestion is that the ability to predict potential with some accuracy might be a special quality of coaches. Moreover, this special quality is seemingly underpinned by significant knowledge (albeit often at a tacit level) regarding influences on performance and selection related to such aspects as relative age and expectancy effects. Such coaches are also skilled synthesisers of evidence, managing other professionals (e.g., sport scientists, performance analysts) in the collection and interpretation of data related to talent (e.g., genetic, anthropometric, physiological, psychological, and sociological factors).

So while coaches are generally cognisant of selection factors (or at least place great importance on them), we might argue that coaches are often less prepared for other aspects associated with selection such as non-selection (what do you do with those who are not selected), de-selection (how do you notify and support those who are no longer selected), re-selection (involvement of those previously not included in teams or squads), athlete transfer (from other sports with different histories), and injured/rehabilitating athletes. This lack of consideration is of concern as potentially these athletes (e.g., non-starters, non-selected) might be required to perform when it counts the most (e.g., through injury to regular starters before or during the game). Another key challenge for coaches is to consider how they engage with 'less able' athletes. These are issues that are broader than the individual coach, of course. Rather, it is about the coaching system. There is a need for capacity in a coaching system so that the most vulnerable, but ultimately important, athletes benefit from ongoing coaching intervention, lest they be lost to the sport. This capacity is somewhat reliant on the fostering of collegiality amongst coaches so that the right coach has contact with the right athlete at the right time. The (potential) value of coaches is further described in the section that follows.

The potential value of coaching

Côté and Fraser-Thomas (2007) proposed three major potential outcomes from engagement in youth sport: (a) improved physical health; (b) psychosocial development; and (c) motor skill development. Nevertheless, Côté, and Fraser-Thomas also underscore the modest achievement of sport programs to achieve these three outcomes. The impact of coaches with regard to improvements in physiological capacities and motor skills is generally assumed and has some empirical support (e.g., Culver, Gilbert, & Trudel, 2003). In this section, we focus on the potential psychosocial impacts of coaching as this is less widely acknowledged and generally poorly understood amongst coaches.

Psychosocial development

Coaches have been highlighted as key social support mechanisms in sport (Fletcher & Sarkar, 2012). Moreover, Gould and colleagues (2002) noted that coaches influence psychosocial development in myriad ways such as employing different styles at different stages of development, encouraging and providing unconditional support, providing challenge and support, individualising approaches, employing direct (e.g., planned session components) and indirect (e.g., modelling) teaching, setting and enforcing standards, providing feedback, and acting as a confidante. Two specific areas of interest within the literature have been (i) the coaches' impact on motivation (e.g., why does the fire burn brightly in some but not others) and (ii) mental toughness (e.g., why do some athletes stand up in difficult circumstances while other crumble).

Motivation

Athlete motivation, and the motivational climate in sport settings created by coaches, has been well researched within Self-Determination Theory (SDT; Deci & Ryan, 1985) and specifically within Mageau and Vallerand's (2003) motivational model of the coach–athlete relationship. A major tenet of SDT is the key role of social actors, such as coaches, in shaping the motivational climate. Essentially, coach behaviours influence psychological need satisfaction (autonomy, competence, and relatedness) that, in turn, fosters different forms or quality of motivation (internal, external) that subsequently has the potential to influence how athletes think, feel, and act. Many studies have shown consistent support for SDT with autonomy-supportive environments linked with adaptive outcomes, such as superior performance, enhanced self-worth, increased effort, persistence, adherence, and self-determined motivation (e.g., Adie, Duda, & Ntoumanis, 2012; Almagro, Sáenz-López, & Moreno, 2010; Amorose & Horn, 2000; Coatsworth & Conroy, 2009; Gillet, Vallerand, Amoura, & Baldes, 2010; Hodge, Henry, &

Smith, 2014; Mallett, 2005; Pelletier, Fortier, Vallerand, & Brière, 2001; Reinboth, Duda, & Ntoumanis, 2004). On the other hand, controlling coaching environments have been linked with increased extrinsic motivation or amotivation and subsequent increased attrition, decreased well-being, increased anxiety, fear of failure, and poorer performance (e.g., Bartholomew, Ntoumanis, & Thøgersen-Ntoumani, 2009; Bartholomew, Ntoumanis, Ryan, Bosch, & Thøgersen-Ntoumani, 2011). In summary, coaches whose pedagogical approach is characterised by autonomy-supportive behaviours support their athletes in many ways, including: (a) satisfying innate psychological needs; (b) sustaining intrinsic motivation; (c) promoting ongoing engagement in sport; and (d) enhancing athletic performance. In contrast, researchers have also demonstrated the negative influence of controlling behaviours on psychological need satisfaction and subsequent negative athlete outcomes (e.g., Bartholomew et al., 2009, 2011).

Mental toughness

For many years 'mental toughness' and other related terms (e.g., resilience, grit) have been extremely popular in characterising successful performance. While this topic of interest has been primarily associated with contact sports and endurance events, it is prevalent in discussions about virtually all sports. However, until fairly recently, such accounts have been largely anecdotal and the area has been rife with vagaries and both conceptual overlap and slippage. The early 2000s signalled the beginning of empirically based investigations into mental toughness as a concept and the impacts of coaches on such capacities. Jones, Hanton, and Connaughton (2002) defined mental toughness as a 'natural or developed psychological edge' (p. 209) that enables mentally tough performers to generally cope better with demands and related pressures and be more consistent in relation to determination, focus, confidence, and control than their sporting opponents.

The ensuing research suggests that mental toughness is developed throughout an athlete's lifespan. As such, it is a lengthy process whereby an athlete may not 'fully' develop until later years (Connaughton, Wadey, Hanton, & Jones, 2008). Coaches play central roles in the social support networks of athletes (e.g., helping them cope, providing encouragement and feedback, creating an optimal motivational climate). Encouragement from significant others (such as coaches) who also act as a resource of knowledge and inspiration (Connaughton et al., 2008), as well as the coach–athlete relationship itself (e.g., Butt, Weinberg, & Culp, 2010) have been identified as important person–environment interactions in the development of an athlete's mental toughness. Appropriate leadership skills from the coach are also central to the development of mental toughness, particularly in the early years. Scaffolding skill development to ensure athletes experience success, providing them with opportunities to learn from more superior/senior athletes, promoting sport/life balance, and providing a motivational climate with friendly rivalry and exposure to competitive stressors are all ways in which coaches contribute to the development of this aspect of sporting performance (Connaughton et al., 2008; Connaughton, Hanton, & Jones, 2010; Coulter, Mallett, & Gucciardi, 2010; Driska, Kamphoff, & Armentrout, 2012; Jones et al., 2002). Recent literature has further suggested that both the direct exploitation of life event challenges and the artificial generation of challenges, when seen to be developmentally appropriate, is an essential feature of the (coach-driven) training environment for both the development of mental toughness and high performance ('talent needs trauma'; e.g., Collins & MacNamara, 2012).

In considering the potential value of coaches with respect to the psychosocial factors described above, as well as the physiological capacities and motor skill development acknowledged earlier, it is clear that athlete development is a long-term project that requires ongoing maintenance. In the section that follows, various models of athlete development are noted with a view to better understanding what the right coach might be at each stage of athlete development.

Coach in context

As previously stated, the coach–athlete relationship is foundational to athlete development, regardless of the context. However, the work of the coach must be differentiated based on the context within which they operate. One way of conceptualising such differentiations is in relation to models of athlete development. Baker and Wattie (in press; see Chapter 9 this book) proposed two broad types of athlete development models: (a) researcher-driven models; and (b) practitioner-based models. The most popular evidence-based models of athlete development are Ericsson and colleagues' notion of *Deliberate Practice* (e.g., Ericsson, 2013; Ericsson, Krampe, & Tesch-Römer, 1993) and Côté and colleagues' *The Developmental Model of Sport Participation (DMSP)* (e.g., Côté, Baker, & Abernethy, 2007; Côté & Fraser-Thomas, 2016). Two models developed and used by coaches and coach developers are Balyi, Way, and colleagues' *Long-Term Athlete Development* (LTAD) and *The Foundations, Talent, Elite & Mastery (FTEM) Model*, which has been recently developed by Gulbin and colleagues at the Australian Institute of Sport (Gulbin et al., 2013). The FTEM was based on both current research and coaches' lived coaching experiences. A detailed critique of these models is beyond the scope of this chapter and can be found in Chapter 10. However, consistent across these four models of athlete development is the central role of the coach in guiding and shaping athlete development.

Coaches, as well as other significant others, serve different purposes during different stages of athlete development (Connaughton et al., 2008, 2010; Gould et al., 2002). A serious concern, however, is that certain coaching approaches are highly desirable in certain contexts but inappropriate in others (Gould et al., 2002; Mallett & Rynne, 2012, 2015). As such, we now consider the work of coaches across the four major contexts in which performance coaches work: (a) young children; (b) emerging athletes; (c) performance athletes; and (d) high-performance athletes. Whilst athletes in performance and especially high-performance contexts might appear to be already highly 'developed', it is our view that athlete development is a continuous process throughout engagement in sport (until such time as an athlete permanently retires). It is suggested that refinement of aspects such as skills and training/performance strategies will continue to occur as athletes progress into higher levels of performance and experience, and therefore the role of the coach, whilst changing, is still crucial to the development, maintenance, and adaptation of athletes' 'talent'. Additionally, athletes in high-performance sport who may be latecomers or enter via alternative (nonlinear/nontraditional) pathways (e.g., dropped from teams/squads and subsequently picked up by another, transferred from other teams/squads, or, in the case of talent transfer, transferred from other sports) may arrive in the high-performance context with talent or potential still to be assessed, nurtured, and developed. Therefore, on the basis of these different contexts in which coaches operate, we consider the potential value of coaching.

Coaching children

Typically, young children's forays into sport are between four and eight years of age. Of course in some instances (e.g., gymnastics), children might commence at an earlier age. There is generally little 'talent identification' occurring at this stage. Rather, it is most often the choice of parents to involve their children in sport(s) based on the potential contribution participation may make to the healthy and holistic development of their children (generally in relation to physical, psychological, social, and emotional aspects) (Trost, 2005). Initiation into sport is aligned with the notion of 'sampling' sports and is also associated with the development of fundamental movement skills (Booth et al., 1999; Côté, 1999; Côté & Hay, 2002; Gulbin et al., 2013). It is argued that access to guided development (e.g., a coach) complements young childrens' free play activities (Côté, 1999) and fosters the acquisition of fundamental motor skills (Davids, Araújo, Hristovski, Passos, & Chow, 2012).

As noted throughout this text, development is inherently complex (e.g., with respect to age-related assumptions and context) (Burrows, 2009; ICCE, 2013). Highly competent coaches, who deliver on a variety of biophysical and psychosocial outcomes, are considered necessary to not only retain young participants in the sport pathways but to develop their capacities, and nurture their love of movement (Côté, Erickson, & Abernethy, 2013). For this reason it is crucial that the child's introduction to sport is associated with the scaffolded development of fundamental motor and manipulative skills within a supportive learning environment (ICCE, 2013). This is the primary function of the coach in this setting.

Potential impact of coaching on children

Coaches are the architects of the learning environment and therefore should take responsibility for creating an environment that fosters healthy and holistic development (Mallett, 2005, 2013). In creating such a supportive learning environment, coaches must be skilled with respect to how they interact with young children and how they explicitly attempt to deliver on the agreed learning outcomes (e.g., the 4Cs of positive youth development) (Vierimaa, Erickson, Côté, & Gilbert, 2012). The subsequent argument is that these learning outcomes become/remain the primary focus of coaches' work as opposed to any explicit focus on performance outcomes (such as wins and losses; acknowledging that both of these represent opportunities for learning).

The outcomes of coaching that have been widely supported relate to the delivery of activities that are enjoyable, challenging, and promote perceptions of competence and belonging (Mageau & Vallerand, 2003; Wall & Côté, 2007). Successful coaches of children typically seek to achieve this through an emphasis on activities that are fun, enjoyable, and engaging (high time on doing the task) (e.g., deliberate play, Côté & Fraser-Thomas, 2007; Wall & Côté, 2007). Similarly, coaches whose feedback is focused on self-referencing rather than normative comparisons are able to better foster internal motivation in the children with whom they work (Fraser-Thomas & Côté, 2006; Mageau & Vallerand, 2003).

These outcomes are particularly important as the lack of fun has been reported as a frequently cited reason for attrition from sport (Butcher, Lindner, & Johns, 2002; Gould, Feltz, Horn, & Weiss, 1982). Coaches shape the environment of children's sport and act as implicit role models for young children. In doing so, they can either foster healthy development or contribute to attrition from sport at an early age (Côté & Gilbert, 2009).

Coaching emerging athletes

As distinct from coaching children involved in participation sport, this section, and those that follow, are more focused on athletes in performance sport. Emerging athletes, the focus of this section, are those who receive specialised, sport-specific training in ways that resemble the 'specialisation stage' of athlete development in Côté and colleagues' (Côté, 1999; Côté & Hay, 2002) DMSP and the transition from 'Foundation 2' to 'Foundation 3' in Gulbin et al.'s (2013)

FTEM model. It is during this time that coaches generally request that athletes spend increasing amounts of time in one sport, generally at the expense of other sporting pursuits or non-sporting interests (Strachan, Côté, & Deakin, 2009; Trudel & Gilbert, 2006).

Even though there is increased attention given to formal practices and competitions in this context, there remains a strong emphasis on fun. Some (e.g., Soberlak & Côté, 2003) have characterised this context as being a combination of deliberate play (Côté, Baker, & Aberbethy, 2003) and deliberate practice (Ericsson et al., 1993). Of particular interest in this text, the emerging athlete context is where the first forays into some kind of sport 'performance pathway' occur. This initiation is generally in the form of selection into representative (junior / regional / academy) sporting squads overseen by one or more designated coaches.

Potential impact of coaching on emerging athletes

The coach's ability to appropriately structure programs for emerging athletes has been shown to have a large bearing on their continued engagement in sport (Fraser-Thomas, Côté, & Deakin, 2008; Smoll & Smith, 2002). Indeed, coaches have a large influence over the most common factors related to dropout including pressure to progress too quickly, too much emphasis on winning, lack of playing time, and showing favouritism (Fraser-Thomas et al., 2008). Conversely, coaches working in the emerging athlete context have a potentially significant role in sustaining the engagement of emerging athletes through offering care and support, demonstrating excellent people skills, and possessing sound technical expertise. To be effective (e.g., facilitate adaptive forms of motivation and enhance perseverance) in this context, coaches must seek to both challenge (technical and skill oriented sessions) and support their athletes (personable, mastery approaches) (Connaughton et al., 2008; Fraser-Thomas et al., 2008; North, 2008).

Problematically, many practices that are taken-for-granted in sports run counter to the aims of long-term athlete engagement and well-being. The emerging athlete context is generally considered to be the sporting context in which arguably the greatest harm can be inflicted on athletes (physically and psychologically) through the inappropriate adoption of high-performance coaching and athletic models (Rynne & Mallett, 2012). Much of this is related to misunderstandings and internal role conflict that some coaches experience between athlete personal development and the desire to produce winning athletes (Gilbert & Trudel, 2004). Compounding these potential issues is the fact that there is often little guidance regarding how best to coach in the emerging athlete context. As such, coaches are generally left to come to their own conclusions about how much emphasis they will place on winning and technical development versus how much they will emphasise fun and the development of psychosocial skills (Gilbert & Trudel, 2004).

Coaching performance athletes

Similar to the emerging athlete context, coaches typically offer specialised, sport-specific training in the performance athlete context. The key difference though, is that the engagement is more prolonged and intense. With respect to the models, it resembles the movement from Côté and colleagues' (Côté, 1999; Côté & Hay, 2002) 'specialising stage' of sport participation to the 'investment stage' and can also be thought of as being across the 'Talent' section of Gulbin et al.'s (2013) FTEM model (especially T2–T3). In general, performance athletes are involved in one sport and are highly committed to sport-specific training (deliberate practice) (including ancillary activities like specialised gym programs) with less emphasis on deliberate play (Côté et al., 2003; Ericsson et al., 1993; Gulbin et al., 2013).

Coaches in this context are generally charged with the responsibility of accelerating the development of performance athletes through highly committed and very stable relationships (indeed, in certain sports the coach that an athlete has in this context may be their coach for the rest of their athletic career). An exception is the representative teams and squads that are a prominent feature of this context where the coaches and athletes may only be together for a relatively short period such as for a state or national championship (Lyle, 2002). In most countries, however, the most common role for coaches in the performance athlete context is in club sport with responsibility for the top teams (variously known as A teams or First teams).

Potential impact of coaching on performance athletes

In the performance athlete context, the emphasis is rightly on performance outcomes achieved through carefully programmed training and scheduled competitions. It is worth noting that, rightly or wrongly, perceptions of coaching quality are closely tied to athlete performance outcomes at this level. Given the increased importance placed on 'talent development' and 'talent acceleration' in the performance athlete context, a factor that has been shown to be important to this group is the issue of expectancy. Those performance athletes who are expected to perform highly tend to view their coaches favourably and, through a variety of mechanisms, tend to perform better in comparison to their low expectancy peers (Trudel & Gilbert, 2006). While this self-fulfilling prophecy effect may be advantageous to some, as alluded to earlier, it problematically serves to limit the performance of the broader pool of potential talent. Coaches in this context who are aware of their expectations are better able to enhance performance more broadly (especially in relation to fringe performers). Similarly, leadership and motivational styles employed by coaches in this context vary somewhat, but as with most forms of coaching, autocratic styles are often favoured (Trudel & Gilbert, 2006; Woodman & Hardy, 2001). Given that autocratic styles have achieved mixed results, the general consensus is that coaches who have a number of styles at their disposal are far more likely to experience longevity of success, with various athletes, across various contexts.

Coaching high-performance athletes

High-performance athletes are firmly in the 'investment stage' of Côté and colleagues' (Côté, 1999; Côté & Hay, 2002) model of sport participation and span the 'Talent', 'Elite', and 'Mastery' sections of Gulbin et al.'s (2013) FTEM model (notably T4–M). In this context, performance is supported by a range of personnel whose sole purpose is advancing the development and achievements of these athletes. Importantly, it is the coaches who are responsible for guiding the continued development of high-performance athletes and coordinating the team of support personnel. In performing this work, coaches employ highly sophisticated planning structures and incorporate a series of clear performance benchmarks (Gulbin et al., 2013; Lyle, 2002; Mallett, 2010; Mallett & Lara-Bercial, 2016). It should also be noted that for coaches in high-performance contexts, the prospects for continued employment (re-appointment) and the performance of their athletes and teams are virtually inseparable.

Potential impact of coaching on high-performance athletes

The coach–high-performance-athlete relationship operates in a highly contested setting, which potentially puts some strain on the partnership at more important events (e.g., major championships). During peak-performance periods, it is highly likely that coaches and athletes in this context will spend more time with each other than with any other person (including partners, children, and friends), which might add to the possible tension between these actors. An effective coach–athlete relationship in this context is likely founded on trust and mutual respect (e.g., Mallett & Lara-Bercial, 2016).

Tellingly, in this context the coach plays a key role in supporting and guiding development as well as assisting high-performance athletes to navigate the many tensions and challenges that are features of elite sport. Regarding development, one of the most important qualities of coaches in this context is a 'strong insistence on perfection' (Gulbin et al., 2010, p. 156; see also Mallett & Lara-Bercial, 2016). Regarding the associated tensions and challenges, coaches are a crucial social support, bolstering aspects such as a sense of competence and self-belief at crucial times (Mallett & Lara-Bercial, 2016). The most obvious example relates to coaches helping high-performance athletes to deal with pre-competition nerves and doubts (Gould et al., 2002; Mallett & Coulter, 2016). Skilled coaches are able to communicate in ways that foster focus and reinforce positive past performances (Mallett & Coulter, 2016; Mallett & Lara-Bercial, 2016; Rees & Hardy, 2000; Woodman & Hardy, 2001).

It is worth noting that because of the importance of athletic performance to future sport funding and coach employment, coaches in this context likely face a variety of dilemmas that challenge their values and beliefs. For some, the incentives to engage in unacceptable and inappropriate ways will be too much, with all too common examples including playing seriously injured athletes, engaging in physical and emotional abuse, and participating in illegal sports betting. In short, for this group of coaches (potentially more than any other described in this chapter) there are far more ethical and moral dimensions to their work because the stakes are so high (Rynne & Mallett, 2014).

Future directions

While there is much rhetoric, a great deal of intuitive support, a large amount of anecdotal evidence, and a growing empirical basis, there is still much to be done in evidencing the actual impact of coaching in a variety of contexts. This rather broad area of inquiry is considered important because of the assumed centrality of the role of coaches. The quality of the athletes' sporting experience, their performance, and the subsequent continued engagement in the sporting pathway may well be premised on the environment that coaches create, but further evidence is required to inform and direct coaching practice. This evidence will also serve to inform the development of these potentially crucial actors in the sporting landscape.

In achieving the aim of evidencing coaching impact, future research might give further consideration to the perspectives of athletes. In foregrounding the 'athlete voice' in investigations into coaching, forthcoming projects may offer new insights into how coaches develop and differentially impact talent and its associated components. In this, and other areas of inquiry, there may be great value in adopting qualitative approaches that are able to offer rich and sophisticated accounts of coaching within the talent development domain.

Adding to this evidentiary sophistication, it may be valuable to offer coaching insights on talent that are more pedagogical (e.g., selecting for development versus performance), psychological (e.g., the role of cultural fit in relation to talented athletes), and/or sociological (e.g., the impact of club owners, media, boards, and high-profile players on the work of coaches) in nature. In effect, it is valuable to shine a variety of spotlights on this complex area of inquiry so that we might develop more comprehensive accounts to inform practice and development.

Summary

This chapter positions coaches as 'architects' of sport environments, and central to the quality of the sporting experience and athlete development – a notion further evidenced by the clear links between material discussed in this chapter, and that covered in other chapters (e.g., Chapter 22: Applied motor learning/skill acquisition; Chapter 23: Dropout; Chapter 27: Positive youth development; Chapter 29: Abuse and exploitation of athletes, to name just a few). Coaches have been found to be influential regardless of the sport setting, and foundational to talent identification and development programmes in sport. However, given the paucity of clear literature pertaining to the impact of coaches on the development of athlete talent, and literature underscoring both positive and negative athlete experiences in sport, it is argued that coaching should be valued for the *potential* contribution it makes to athlete development.

Effective coaches must integrate professional, interpersonal, and intrapersonal coaching knowledge whilst undertaking a variety of tasks – including the selection of athletes. Whilst coaches may be aware that these tasks requires them to have, amongst other skills, knowledge of the multi-dimensional range of factors influencing both athlete performance and selection, and ability to synthesise evidence from a range of sources, they might be less prepared for other aspects associated with their work (such as non-selection, de-selection, and injured/rehabilitating athletes). In addition, the often marginalised value of coaching in psychosocial development has also been illustrated in this chapter using examples of athlete motivation, and the development of mental toughness. In considering the potentially important and highly complicated work that coaches undertake, our suggestion is that there is a need to develop capacity in coaching systems so that the quality of coaching might be advanced for the betterment of the sport. In short, coaches must be supported in fulfilling these significant functions so that potentially important athletes in the future may benefit from ongoing coaching intervention and be retained in sport.

Finally, it is worth re-emphasising that coaches have the ability to differentially impact athlete development across their sporting careers. The potential impact of the coach–athlete relationship across four major contexts of development (young children, emerging athletes, performance athletes, and high-performance athletes) has been discussed in depth in this chapter with the hope that this may act as some guidance for those considering work or research in each of these performance coaching contexts.

References

Adie, J. W., Duda, J. L., & Ntoumanis, N. (2012). Perceived coach-autonomy support, basic need satisfaction and the well- and ill-being of elite youth soccer players: A longitudinal investigation. *Psychology of Sport and Exercise, 13,* 51–59.

Almagro, B., Sáenz-López, P., & Moreno, J. A. (2010). Prediction of sport adherence through the influence of autonomy-supportive coaching among Spanish adolescent athletes. *Journal of Sports Science and Medicine, 9,* 8–14.

Amorose, A., & Horn, T. (2000). Intrinsic motivation: Relationships with collegiate athletes' gender, scholarships status, and perceptions of their coaches' behavior, *Journal of Sport & Exercise Psychology, 22,* 63–84.

Anshell, M.H., & Lidor, R. (2012). Talent detection programs in sport: The questionable use of psychological measures. *Journal of Sport Behavior, 35*(3), 239–266.

Baker, J., & Wattie, N. (in press). Athlete development models. In D. Gould & C. J. Mallett (eds). *Sports Coaching Handbook.* Champaign, IL: Human Kinetics.

Barreiros, A.N., & Fonseca, A.M. (2012). A retrospective analysis of Portuguese elite athletes' involvement in international competitions. *International Journal of Sport Science and Coaching, 7,* 593–600.

Bartholomew, K. J., Ntoumanis, N., & Thøgersen-Ntoumani, C. (2009). A review of controlling motivational strategies from a Self-Determination Theory perspective: Implications for sports coaches. *International Review of Sport and Exercise Psychology, 2*, 215–33.

Bartholomew, K. J., Ntoumanis, N., Ryan, R. M., Bosch, J. A., & Thøgersen-Ntoumani, C. (2011). Self-Determination Theory and diminished functioning: The role of interpersonal control and psychological need thwarting. *Personality and Social Psychology Bulletin, 37*, 1459–1473.

Booth, M. L., Okely, T., McLellan, L., Phongsavan, P., Macaskill, P., Patterson, J., Holland, B. (1999). Mastery of fundamental motor skills among New South Wales schools students: Prevalence and sociodemographic distribution. *Journal of Science and Medicine in Sport, 2*, 93–105.

Bullock, N., Gulbin, J. P., Martin, D. T., Ross, A., Holland, T., & Marino, F. (2009). Talent identification and deliberate programming in skeleton: Ice novice to winter Olympian in 14 months. *Journal of Sports Sciences, 27*, 397–404.

Burrows, L. (2009). Developing' athletes. In, T. Cassidy, R. L. Jones, & P. Potrac, *Understanding sports coaching: The social, cultural, and pedagogical foundations of coaching practice* (2nd ed., pp. 85–92). London: Routledge.

Butcher, J., Lindner, K. J., & Johns, D. P. (2002). Withdrawal from competitive youth sport: A retrospective ten-year study, *Journal of Sport Behaviour, 25*, 145–163.

Butt, J., Weinberg, R., & Culp, B. (2010). Exploring mental toughness in NCAA athletes. *Journal of Intercollegiate Sport, 3*, 316–332.

Cassidy, T., Jones, R., & Potrac, P. (2015). *Understanding sports coaching: The social, cultural and pedagogical foundations of coaching* (3rd ed.). London: Routledge.

Christensen, M. K. (2009). "An eye for talent": Talent identification and the 'practical sense' of top-level soccer coaches. *Sociology of Sport Journal, 26*, 365–382.

Coatsworth, D. E., & Conroy, J. D. (2006). Coach training as a strategy for promoting youth social development. *The Sport Psychologist, 20*, 128–44.

Coatsworth, J. D., & Conroy, D. E. (2009). The effects of autonomy-supportive coaching need satisfaction and self-perceptions on initiative and identity in youth swimmers. *Developmental Psychology, 45*, 320–328.

Collins, D., & MacNamara, Á. (2012). The rocky road to the top. Why talent needs trauma. *Sports Medicine, 42*, 907–914.

Connaughton, D., Hanton, S., & Jones, G. (2010). The development and maintenance of mental toughness in the world's best performers. *The Sport Psychologist, 24*, 168–193.

Connaughton, D., Wadey, R., Hanton, S., & Jones, G. (2008). The development and maintenance of mental toughness: Perceptions of elite performers. *Journal of Sports Sciences, 26*, 83–95.

Côté, J. (1999). The influence of the family in the development of talent in sport. *The Sport Psychologist, 13*, 395–417.

Côté, J., Baker, J., & Abernethy, B. (2003). From play to practice: A developmental framework for the acquisition of expertise in team sports. In J. L. Starkes & K. A. Ericsson (eds), *Expert performance in sports: Advances in research on sport expertise* (pp. 89–114). South Australia: Human Kinetics.

Côté, J., Baker, J., & Abernethy, B. (2007). Practice and play in the development of sport expertise. *Handbook of Sport Psychology, 3*, 184–202.

Côté, J., Erickson, K., & Abernethy, B. (2013). Play and practice in sport development. In J. Côté & R. Lidor (eds), *Conditions of children's talent development in sport* (pp. 9–20). Morgantown: FIT.

Côté, J., & Fraser-Thomas, J. (2007). Youth involvement in sport. In P. R. E. Crocker (ed.), *Introduction to sport psychology: A Canadian perspective* (pp. 266–294). Toronto: Pearson Prentice Hall.

Côté, J., & Gilbert, W. (2009). An integrative definition of coaching effectiveness and expertise. *International Journal of Sports Science & Coaching, 4*, 307–323.

Côté, J., & Hay, J. (2002). Children's involvement in sport: A developmental perspective. In J. M. Silva & D. E. Stevens (eds), *Psychological foundations of sport* (pp. 484–502). Sydney: Allyn and Bacon.

Côté, J., & Salmela, J. H. (1996). The organisational tasks of high-performance gymnastic coaches. *The Sport Psychologist, 10*, 247–60.

Coulter, T., Mallett, C. J., & Gucciardi, D. F. (2010). Understanding mental toughness in Australian soccer: Perceptions of players, parents, and coaches. *Journal of Sports Sciences, 28*, 699–716.

Culver, D. M., Gilbert, W., & Trudel, P. (2003). A decade of qualitative research in sport psychology journals: 1990–1999. *The Sport Psychologist, 17*, 1–15.

Cushion, C. J., Armour, K. M., & Jones, R. L. (2006). Locating the coaching process in practice: Models 'for' and 'of' coaching. *Physical Education and Sport Pedagogy, 11*, 83–99.

d'Arripe-Longueville, F., Saury, J., Fournier, J., & Durand, M. (2001). Coach-athlete interaction during elite archery competitions: An application of methodological frameworks used in ergonomics research to sport psychology. *Journal of Applied Sport Psychology, 13*(3), 275–299.

Davids, K. W, Araújo, D., Hristovski, R., Passos, P., & Chow, J. Y. (2012). Ecological dynamics and motor learning design in sport. In N. Hodges & M. Williams (eds), *Skill acquisition in sport: Research, theory and practice* (2nd ed., pp. 112–130). Abingdon, UK: Routledge.

Davids, K. W., & Baker, J. (2007). Genes, environment and sport performance: Why the Nature-Nurture dualism is no longer relevant. *Sports Medicine, 37*, 961–980.

Deci, E. L., & Ryan, R. M. (1985). *Intrinsic motivation and self-determination in human behavior.* New York: Plenum.

Driska, A. P., Kamphoff, C., & Armentrout, A. M. (2012). Elite swimming coaches' perceptions of mental toughness. *Sport Psychologist, 26*, 189–206.

Ericsson, K. A. (2013). Training history, deliberate practice and elite sports performance: An analysis in response to Tucker and Collins review: What makes champions? *British Journal of Sports Medicine, 47*(9), 533–535.

Ericsson, K. A., Krampe, R. T., & Tesch-Römer, C. (1993). The role of deliberate practice in the acquisition of expert performance. *Psychological Review, 100*, 363–406.

Fletcher, D., & Sarkar, M. (2012). A grounded theory of psychological resilience in Olympic champions. *Psychology of Sport and Exercise, 13*, 669–678.

Fraser-Thomas, J., & Côté, J. (2006, September). Youth sports: Implementing findings and moving forward with research. *Athletic Insight, 8*, Article 2. Retrieved February 1, 2014, from www.athleticinsight.com/Vol8Iss3/YouthSports.htm.

Fraser-Thomas, J., & Côté, J. (2016). *Structured sports and physical activities: Their critical role.*

Fraser-Thomas, J., Côté, J., & Deakin, J. (2008). Understanding dropout and prolonged engagement in adolescent competitive sport. *Psychology of Sport and Exercise, 9*, 645–662.

Frontiera, J. (2010). Leadership and organisational culture transformation in professional sport. *Journal of Leadership & Organisational Studies 17*, 71–86.

Gagné, F. (2004). Transforming gifts into talents: The DMGT as a developmental theory. *High Ability Studies, 15*, 119–147.

Gilbert, W., & Trudel, P. (2004). Role of the coach: How model youth team sport coaches frame their roles. *The Sport Psychologist, 18*, 21–43.

Gillet, N., Vallerand, R. J., Amoura, S., & Baldes, B. (2010). Influence of coaches' autonomy support on athletes' motivation and sport performance: A test of the Hierarchical Model of Intrinsic and Extrinsic Motivation. *Psychology of Sport and Exercise, 11*, 155–61.

Gould, D., Dieffenbach, K., & Moffett, A. (2002). Psychological characteristics and their development in Olympic Champions. *Journal of Applied Sport Psychology, 14*, 172–204.

Gould, D., Feltz, D., Horn, T., & Weiss, M. (1982). Reasons for attrition in competitive youth swimming. *Journal of Sport Behaviour, 5*, 155–165.

Gould, D., Guinan, D., Greenleaf, C., Medbery, R., & Peterson, K. (1999). Applied Research. *Sport Psychologist, 13*, 371–394.

Gulbin, J. P., Oldenziel, K. E., Weissensteiner, J. R., & Gagné, F. (2010). A look through the rear view mirror: Developmental experoences and insights of high peformanc athletes. *Talent Development & Excellence, 2*, 149–164.

Gulbin, J. P., Croser, M. J., Morley, E. J., & Weissensteiner, J. R. (2013). An integrated framework for the optimisation of sport and athlete development: A practitioner approach. *Journal of Sport Sciences, 31*, 1319–1331.

Harwood, C., & Swain, A. B. J. (2001). The development and activation of achievement goals in tennis: I. Understanding the underlying factors. *Sport Psychology, 15*, 319–41.

Hoare, D. G., & Warr, C. R. (2000). Talent identification and women's soccer: An Australian experience. *Journal of Sports Sciences, 18*, 751–758.

Hodge, K., Henry, G., & Smith, W. (2014). A case study of excellence in elite sport: Motivational climate in a world champion team. *The Sport Psychologist, 28*, 60–74.

International Council for Coaching Excellence (ICCE), Association of Summer Olympic International Federations (ASOIF), & Leeds Metropolitan University (LMU) (2013). *International Sport Coaching Framework version 1.2.* Champaign, IL: Human Kinetics.

Jones, G., Hanton, S., & Connaughton, D. (2002). What is this thing called Mental Toughness? An investigation with elite performers. *Journal of Applied Sport Psychology, 14*, 211–224.

Kristiansen, E., & Roberts, G. C. (2010). Young elite athletes and social support: Coping with competitive and organizational stress in "Olympic" competition. *Scandinavian Journal of Medicine & Science in Sports, 20*(4), 686–695.

Lyle, J. (2002). *Sports coaching concepts: A framework for coaches' behaviour.* London: Routledge.

MacNamara, Á. (2011). Psychological characteristics of developing excellence. In D. Collins, H. Richards, & A. Button (eds), *Performance psychology* (pp. 47– 64). Kidlington: Elsevier.

MacNamara, Á., Button, A., & Collins, D. (2010). The role of psychological characteristics in facilitating the pathways to elite performance. Part 1: Identifying mental skills and behaviors. *The Sport Psychologist, 24,* 52–73.

Mageau, G. A., & Vallerand, R. J. (2003). The coach-athlete relationship: A motivational model. *Journal of Sport Sciences, 21,* 883–904.

Mallett, C. J. (2005). Self-determination theory: A case study of evidence-based coaching. *The Sport Psychologist, 19,* 417–429.

Mallett, C. J. (2010). High performance coaches' careers and communities. In J. Lyle & C. Cushion (eds), *Sports coaching: Professionalism and practice* (pp. 119–133). London: Elsevier.

Mallett, C. J. (2013). Roles and responsibilities of the coach. In F. Pyke (ed.), *Coaching excellence* (pp. 3–11). South Australia: Human Kinetics.

Mallett, C. J., & Coulter, T. (2016). The anatomy of a successful Olympic coach: Actor, agent, and author. *International Sport Coaching Journal, 3,* 113–127.

Mallett, C. J., & Lara-Bercial, S. (2016). Serial winning coaches: People, vision and environment. In M. Raab, P. Wylleman, R. Seiler, A-M. Elbe, & A. Hatzigeorgiadis (eds), *Sport and exercise psychology research: Theory to practice* (pp. 289–322). Amsterdam: Elsevier.

Mallett, C. J., & Rynne, S. B. (2012). *Junior Sports Framework Review – Briefing Paper Topic: Role of Adults in Junior Sport.* Prepared for the Australian Sports Commission. St Lucia, Australia: UniQuest Pty Ltd.

Mallett, C. J., & Rynne, S. B. (2015). Changing role of coaches across development. In J. Baker & D. Farrow (eds), *The Routledge handbook of sport expertise* (pp. 394–403). Abingdon: Routledge.

North, J. (2008). Increasing participation in sport: The role of the coach. In *Sports Coach UK.* Sports Coach UK.

Pelletier, L., Fortier, M., Vallerand, R. J., & Brière, N. M. (2001). Associations among perceived autonomy support, forms of self-regulation, and persistence: A prospective study. *Motivation and Emotion, 25,* 279–306.

Rees, T., & Hardy, L. (2000). An investigation of the social support experiences of high-level sports performers. *Sport Psychology, 14*(4), 327–347.

Rees, T., Hardy, L., Güllich, A., Abernethy, B., Côté, J., Woodman, T., … Warr, C. (2016). The Great British Medalists Project: A review of current knowledge on the development of the world's best sporting talent. *Sports Medicine.* doi: 10.1007/s40279-016-0476-2

Reinboth, M., Duda, J. L., & Ntoumanis, N. (2004). Dimensions of coaching behavior, need satisfaction, and the psychological and physical welfare of young athletes. *Motivation and Emotion, 28,* 297–313.

Rynne, S. B., & Mallett, C. J. (2012). Understanding and learning high performance coaches' work. *Physical Education and Sport Pedagogy, 17,* 507–523.

Rynne, S. B., & Mallett, C. J. (2014). Coaches' learning and sustainability in high performance sport. *Reflective Practice, 15,* 12–26.

Rynne, S. B., Mallett, C. J., & Tinning, R. (2010). Workplace learning of high performance sports coaches. *Sport, Education and Society, 15,* 315–330.

Schroeder P.J., (2010). Changing team culture: The perspectives of 10 successful head coaches. *Journal of Sports Behaviour, 33,* 63–87.

Smoll, F. L., & Smith, R. E. (2002). Coaching behavior research and intervention in youth sports. In F. L. Smoll & R. E. Smith (eds), *Children and youth in sport: A biopsycho-social perspective* (2nd ed., pp. 211–233). Dubuque, IA: Kendall/Hunt.

Soberlak, P., & Côté, J. (2003). The developmental activities of elite ice hockey players. *Journal of Applied Sport Psychology, 15,* 41–49.

Strachan, L., Côté, J., & Deakin, J. (2009). "Specializers" versus "samplers" in youth sport: Comparing experiences and outcomes. *The Sport Psychologist, 23,* 77–92.

Till, K., Cobley, S., O'Hara, J., Cooke, C., & Chapman, C. (2014). Considering maturation status and relative age in the longitudinal evaluation of junior rugby league players. *Scandinavian Journal of Medicine and Science in Sports, 24,* 569–576.

Trost, S.G. (2005). *Discussion paper for the development of recommendations for children's and youth's participation in health promoting physical activity*. A report prepared for the Commonwealth Department of Health and Ageing. Canberra: Australian Government.

Trudel, P., & Gilbert, W. (2006). Coaching and coach education. In D. Kirk, D. Macdonald & M. O'Sullivan (eds), *The handbook of physical education* (pp. 516–539). London: Sage.

Vaeyens, R., Güllich, A., Warr, C. R., & Philippaerts, R. (2009). Talent identification and promotion programmes of Olympic athletes. *Journal of Sports Sciences, 27,* 1367–1380.

Vierimaa, M., Erickson, K., Côté, J., & Gilbert, W. (2012). Positive youth development: A measurement framework for sport. *International Journal of Sports Science and Coaching, 7,* 601–614.

Vrljic, K., & Mallett, C. J. (2008). The knowledge of youth performance soccer coaches in identifying talented young soccer players. *International Journal of Coaching Science, 2,* 63–81.

Wall, M., & Côté, J. (2007). Developmental activities that lead to dropout and investment in sport. *Physical Education and Sport Pedagogy, 12,* 77–87.

Wattie, N., & Baker, N. (in press). An uneven playing field: Talent identification systems and the perpetuation of participation biases in high performance sport. In R. Dionigi and M. Gard (eds), *Sport and physical activity across the lifespan: Critical perspectives*. Basingstoke: Palgrave Macmillan.

Woodman. T., & Hardy, L. (2001). A case study of organizational stress in elite sport. *Journal of Applied Sport Psychology, 13,* 207–238.

21

GROUP COHESION AND ATHLETE DEVELOPMENT

Mark Eys, Todd M. Loughead, and Michael Godfrey

The concept of cohesion is, for good reason, considered a group variable. This is for good reason. It is an emergent property of groups resulting from (and influencing) teamwork processes (McEwan & Beauchamp, 2014), and is facilitated by creating an effective structure marked by clear role responsibilities for group members and strong leadership (Carron & Eys, 2012). However, there is ample evidence in the popular media and in the extant academic literature demonstrating links between the team environment, as represented by cohesion, and important *individual* athlete outcomes. For example, in explaining the European Ryder Cup win over the United States in 2004, golfer Colin Montgomerie stated "We're one of the closest teams in international sport. ... It's amazing how well we play for each other" (Shipnuck, 2004, para. 3). Traditionally, golf is not the first sport one thinks of when considering the concept of cohesion. In this example, however, individual performances/behaviors were thought to be enhanced because of the perceived unity and togetherness of this European golf team.

The various sources and levels of interdependence among group members within sport teams (e.g., task, outcome, and resource interdependencies; Evans, Eys, & Bruner, 2012) allow not only for group dynamics to emerge, but also for those group dynamics to reciprocally influence the members (Cronin, Weingart, & Todorova, 2011). The objective of the present chapter, in line with the general purpose of the current text, is to highlight how the group environment affects the development of athletes based on relationships demonstrated between cohesion and individual cognitive, affective, and behavioral outcomes. In essence, after highlighting general principles regarding the concept of cohesion, we make the case that an athlete's development will be inextricably linked to the groups he or she joins.

Cohesion in sport

Cohesion within sport is defined as "a dynamic process which is reflected in the tendency for a group to stick together and remain united in the pursuit of its instrumental objectives and/or for the satisfaction of member affective needs" (Carron, Brawley, & Widmeyer, 1998, p. 213). This definition highlights one overriding distinction pertaining to group cohesion that can be found across domains (e.g., sport, organizations, etc.); specifically, the unity of the group must be considered from both task and social perspectives. This task/social distinction was further reinforced in recent work designed to develop age-appropriate surveys of cohesion for younger athletes (youth, 13–17 years old, and children, 9–12 years old; Eys, Loughead, Bray, & Carron, 2009; Martin, Carron, Eys, & Loughead, 2012; respectively). With adult populations, perceptions of cohesion are also considered from two different orientations that include individuals' assessments of the group as a whole (e.g., degree of group integration) as well as their own personal attractions to task and social aspects of the group.

As would be expected, perceptions revolving around cohesion are related to other group variables. For example, Heuzé, Raimbault, and Fontayne (2006) discussed the positive interrelationships between cohesion and collective efficacy. In other words, the degree to which athletes believe in the team's ability to achieve its desired outcomes is related to their perceptions of group unity. As a second example, group conflict was cited as a potential team-related outcome associated with the disintegration of cohesion and/or the development of cliques (Paradis, Carron, & Martin, 2014). However, the relationship that arguably garners the most interest is the relationship between cohesion and team performance. An oft-cited meta-analysis (Carron, Colman, Wheeler, & Stevens, 2002) found a moderate effect size with respect to the cohesion–performance relationship. Furthermore, this relationship held regardless of type of cohesion (i.e., task vs. social cohesion), type of sport (i.e., team vs. individual sports), and direction of the relationship (i.e., cohesion leading to performance or vice versa). As an aside, the researchers found that gender moderated the relationship (i.e., stronger for females than for males), a finding that was explored further in a qualitative study conducted by Eys and colleagues (2015) with German and Canadian coaches who had experiences leading both male and female sport teams. In this latter study, all of the coaches who were interviewed noted the importance of cohesion for all sport groups. However, subtle differences were raised throughout the study indicating that males and females may differ with respect to how quickly cohesion develops, the direction of the cohesion–performance relationship (i.e., cohesion leading to performance for females vs. performance leading to cohesion for males), the creation of cliques, and the management of roles, status differences, and conflict. While the above represent just a subset of group-related correlates of cohesion, the question under examination in the present chapter is whether the cohesion of a team can also influence the development of *individual* athletes.

Group cohesion and individual outcomes

Our general answer to the above question is a qualified "yes." In the subsequent sections we highlight research that links important cognitive, affective, and behavioral outcomes to the cohesion of the group. These outcomes (e.g., motivation, satisfaction, adherence) all contribute directly or indirectly to the overall development of an athlete. Furthermore, greater participation, quality-directed efforts, and stronger motivation for a task all underpin *deliberate practice* (see Baker & Young, 2014), a concept that is discussed throughout this Handbook as important toward talent development. However, the qualification is that there can be some downsides to high group cohesion, which are presented prior to moving into future research considerations.

Cognitive outcomes

Motivation

Motivation is broadly defined as the various internal processes that energize and direct behavior (Reeve, 2009). There are several theoretical frameworks that have been communicated to understand the motives behind athletes' behaviors. For example, Harwood, Beauchamp, and

Keegan (2014) summarized research pertaining to achievement goal theory (i.e., task and ego orientations; Nicholls, 1984) and noted several links with group-related variables. As it relates specifically to cohesion, they suggested that a "strong task orientation in team members … may foster conditions for achieving optimal team cohesion" (p. 284). Although this represents one side of the ledger regarding the cohesion–motivation link (i.e., achievement goal orientation influencing cohesion), other researchers have provided evidence that one's perceptions of cohesion may subsequently drive motivation. Using Self-Determination Theory as the theoretical base, consistent findings from several studies (e.g., Blanchard, Amiot, Perreault, Valleran, & Provencher, 2009; Taylor & Bruner, 2012) suggest that task cohesion is related directly to more autonomous forms of motivation or indirectly through the satisfaction of psychological needs (i.e., relatedness, autonomy, competence). In a recent study, Heuzé, Eys, Dubuc, Bosselut, and Couture (2015) also emphasized the importance of *social* cohesion toward the motivation of youth athletes. In sum, cohesion is believed to be an important social factor positively predicting psychological need satisfaction and subsequently perceptions of self-determination. This is a critical motivational variable for athletes and one necessary for continued development.

Positive youth development

In promoting positive youth development (PYD), researchers and practitioners stress the potential and strengths of adolescents. Participation in sport groups, as one form of extracurricular activity, has been proposed to directly influence the degree to which youth develop in a positive and healthy manner (Bruner, Eys, & Turnnidge, 2013), and sport also offers a context to explore the antecedents of PYD. Given that a sense of belongingness was proposed as one of eight contextual features likely to promote PYD (Strachan, Côté, & Deakin, 2011), Bruner, Eys, Wilson, and Côté (2014) argued that athletes' perceptions of their team's cohesion should be positively linked to this concept. In Bruner and colleagues' (2014) study, PYD was conceptualized as the degree to which athletes had experiences in their sport team promoting (a) personal and social skills, (b) initiative, (c) cognitive skills, and (d) goal setting, as well as deterring a range of negative experiences (see MacDonald, Côté, Eys, & Deakin, 2012, for further details regarding the measurement of PYD in sport). Overall, Bruner and colleagues (2014) found that perceptions of task cohesion positively predicted youths' perceptions of their development of personal/social skills, initiative, and goal setting, while social cohesion positively predicted personal/social skills, cognitive skills, and goal setting. Increases in task and social cohesion were also related to decreases in the frequency of negative experiences within their teams. Similar to our summary of motivation, integration around task and social aspects of the group appears to set an appropriate context for athlete development.

Understanding role expectations

The roles that individuals occupy in a team can be viewed through cognitive, affective, and behavioral lenses (see Eys, Beauchamp, & Bray, 2006). For example, one could examine an athlete's role *performance* (behavioral) or the degree to which they are *satisfied* with the tasks for which they are responsible (affective). However, there are several cognitions that athletes hold about their roles that include role efficacy, role conflict, role acceptance, and role clarity. With respect to the latter, researchers have provided evidence of a link between group cohesion and role clarity. Generally speaking, more clarity regarding one's role is associated with better perceptions of cohesion (Bosselut, Heuzé, Eys, & Bouthier, 2010; Eys & Carron, 2001). Interestingly, in a longitudinal study with youth athletes, Bosselut, McLaren, Eys, and

Heuzé (2012) found that social cohesion perceptions that athletes' held at mid-season were predictive of their ultimate role clarity at the end of the season. In explaining their results, Bosselut and colleagues (2012) suggested that a more positive social context could increase the likelihood that individual athletes will be receptive to communication conveying role information and/or that more cohesive teams could be engaging in more frequent interactions. Regardless, it would appear that greater levels of cohesion set the stage for a better understanding of one's role.

Pre-competitive appraisals

The ways in which athletes appraise their competitive environment (via primary and secondary appraisals; Lazarus, 1999) can have significant effects on their performance outcomes (Allen, Jones, McCarthy, Sheehan-Mansfield, & Sheffield, 2013). Specifically, assuming that athletes view their upcoming competitions as highly important (i.e., a strong primary appraisal), optimal performance should be possible if athletes perceive good prospects for coping with competitive demands (i.e., a strong secondary appraisal). Alternatively, athletes who anticipate an inability to cope with competitive demands are likely to view these situations as highly threatening. As a result, it is important to understand and control the variables leading to these appraisals. One variable proposed to be important in this regard is cohesion. In a study with approximately 400 intercollegiate athletes, Wolf, Eys, Sadler, and Kleinert (2015) recently found that athletes who perceived higher cohesion in their groups were also more likely to view upcoming competitions as challenging/exciting (i.e., higher primary and secondary appraisals) versus threatening. This finding is congruent with previous research linking cohesion perceptions with the emotional responses (i.e., anxiety) emanating from this appraisal process, which are discussed in the subsequent section.

Affective outcomes

Pre-competitive anxiety

Anxiety is typically viewed as a negative emotion that has the potential to impact sport performance (Raglin & Hanin, 2000). As alluded to above, competitive state anxiety is believed to derive from appraisals concerning the importance of the situation and abilities to cope with situational demands (Burton, 1998). Two forms of anxiety are typically discussed: cognitive anxiety (e.g., feelings of self-doubt) and somatic anxiety (e.g., increased heart rate). Several researchers have been interested in the link between cohesion and this emotional outcome. For example, Stein (1976) proposed that membership in a cohesive team may help reduce competitive state anxiety through the simple effect of being in the comfort of others. In a study of interdependent sport team athletes (e.g., basketball, rugby), Prapavessis and Carron (1996) found one significant relationship between task cohesion (as measured by the Group Environment Questionnaire; GEQ; Carron, Widmeyer, & Brawley, 1985) and competitive state anxiety (as measured by the Competitive State Anxiety Inventory-2 [CSAI-2], Martens, Burton, Vealey, Bump, & Smith, 1990). Specifically, the results demonstrated that higher perceptions of attractions to task aspects of the group (ATG-T) were associated with decreased cognitive anxiety. Building off these results, Borrego, Cid, and Silva (2012) examined the cohesion–anxiety relationship controlling for gender in a sample of soccer players. The results demonstrated no relationships for females. However, for male soccer players, they found that task cohesion was negatively related to both cognitive and somatic anxiety.

Both of the above studies examined *the intensity* of an athlete's competitive state anxiety symptoms and not *the interpretation* of those symptoms. That is, some athletes may interpret their symptoms in a facilitative way (e.g., "I'm feeling prepared for my next match") or in a debilitative way (e.g., "I'm totally not ready to compete"). Consequently, Eys, Hardy, Carron, and Beauchamp (2003) examined how perceptions of task cohesion were related to the interpretation of both cognitive and somatic anxiety symptoms. Generally, the results indicated that athletes who viewed their cognitive and somatic symptoms as facilitative held more positive perceptions of task cohesion. The link between cohesion and the interpretation of pre-competitive symptoms was generally supported more recently by Wolf, Eys, and Kleinert (2015) who also concluded that "enhancing a team's level of cohesion may be a first and efficient way to improve team members' precompetitive feeling states and thus optimize their performance and adherence" (p. 355).

Athlete satisfaction

Chelladurai and Riemer (1997) defined athlete satisfaction as "a positive affective state result-ing from a complex evaluation of the structures, processes, and outcomes associated with the athletic experience" (p. 135). There are well defined links among cohesion, satisfaction, and individual athlete outcomes that make this concept important to consider within the objectives of this chapter. First, athlete satisfaction is thought to be a prerequisite to peak athletic perform-ance (Riemer & Chelladurai, 1998) and, second, athlete satisfaction is also positively associated with cohesion (Paradis & Loughead, 2012). For example, Spink, Nickel, Wilson, and Odnokon (2005) found that elite hockey players who perceived higher levels of task cohesion (i.e., Group Integration-Task) also felt more satisfied with their team. As another example, Paradis and Loughead (2012) examined whether cohesion mediated the relationship between athlete lead-ership and athlete satisfaction. Relevant to this chapter, the results indicated that youth sport athletes from soccer and basketball who perceived themselves to be cohesive with their team-mates on a task level felt more satisfied from a task perspective—a finding similar to Spink et al. However, Paradis and Loughead also found a similar relationship for social cohesion, whereby this type of cohesion was related to social aspects of satisfaction with the team. Taken together, the results from these two studies demonstrate the importance of creating an envi-ronment that is both task and socially cohesive in order to have athletes who feel satisfied with their athletic experience. This is important because satisfied athletes attend more often and expend more effort (Riemer & Chelladurai, 1998); behavioral outcomes that are discussed in the next section.

Behavioral outcomes

Adherence

An important consideration in sport, particularly at the youth level, is the retention of athletes. Retention in sport can be manifested in several ways such as the degree to which team members attend team functions (e.g., games and practices), the degree to which team members maintain their participation across the season, the athletes' intentions to return to their team or sport the following season (Eys, Carron, Bray, & Beauchamp, 2005), or whether athletes actu-ally return the following season (Spink, Wilson, & Odnokon, 2010). Within two investigations, adherence was operationalized as athletes' intentions to return to their sport the following season. Specifically, Spink (1995, 1998) found that ringette players who felt more socially cohesive with their teammates, as reflected by their attractions to social aspects of the group (ATG-S), indicated a greater likelihood to return the following season. In another study, Spink et al. (2010) measured athletes' *actual* return to their team the following season and its relationship to cohesion assessed the year before. Using a sample of elite ice hockey players, the researchers compared perceptions of cohesion of those players who returned to their team versus those who did not return. The results demonstrated that players who actually returned to their team felt more task cohesive (as measured by ATG-T) compared to those who did not.

Effort

Effort is clearly an important behavioral variable in sport since it is related to individual performance, goals, and motivation (Bray & Whaley, 2001). Not surprisingly, this extends to the group level. Individual efforts combine to produce a group outcome. However, group processes also influence how much effort an individual is willing to expend. In one of the first studies to examine effort and cohesion in sport, Prapavessis and Carron (1997) sampled a variety of interdependent team sport athletes and classified them as being lower or higher in task cohesion. Effort was viewed as how hard an athlete worked during a training session relative to how hard the athlete was capable of working; labeled as percentage of maximal VO_2. The results showed that athletes higher in perceptions of task cohesion worked harder than those who were viewed as lower in task cohesion. In discussing their findings, Prapavessis and Carron suggested that effort may mediate the relationship between cohesion and performance.

As a second example, Bray and Whaley (2001) tested the mediational nature of effort with high school basketball teams. The results showed that self-reported effort mediated the relationship between the cohesion and individual basketball performance. Lastly, Gammage, Carron, and Estabrooks (2001) used a scenario protocol that manipulated levels of cohesion, productivity, and individual identifiability to determine the likelihood of effort (measured as the probability of training). The results demonstrated that situations in which there is high cohesion within teams, in conjunction with a high normative expectation to train regularly in the off-season, yielded the highest probability of training.

Potential downsides of cohesion to the individual

Team cohesion is historically considered a positive group attribute. As the previous sections highlight, there is strong evidence to suggest that teams with high levels of cohesion enjoy benefits both collectively and at the individual level. However, researchers in several domains have noted the potential for high cohesion in a group to detract from its overall effectiveness (Carron, Prapavessis, & Grove, 1994; Rovio, Eskola, Kozub, Duda, & Lintunen, 2009; Wise, 2014). Hardy, Eys, and Carron (2005) sought to explore this potential downside of cohesion through open-ended questions on the potential disadvantages of high task and high social cohesion. They found that 56% of the participants expressed high social cohesion disadvantages, while 31% of the participants expressed task cohesion disadvantages. Finally, when combined, only 22% of participants expressed that there could be disadvantages to a team with both high task and high social cohesion. Further, these authors identified the specific disadvantages of high task and social cohesion on sport teams. The disadvantages of cohesion in both of these categories were split into group level and personal level disadvantages. Relevant to the current discussion, individual level disadvantages of having high social cohesion included decreased focus/concentration, reduced task commitment, and social isolation (in the presence of cliques). Disadvantages of high task cohesion at an individual level included negative affect and incompatible attitudes (in cases where the task focus was too high) and perceived pressures to perform because one cares about his/her teammates. These disadvantages, among others, all have the potential to hinder the development of athletes in terms of individual performance, adherence, or development. More recently, Wise (2014) proposed that the relationship between group cohesion and team performance is curvilinear. That is to say that there is an optimal level of group cohesion for performance and that too little or too much cohesion can both lead to negative outcomes. This research was consistent with the results found by Hardy et al. (2005) and qualifies the many advantages outlined regarding group cohesion.

Future considerations

In the previous sections of this chapter, we make the case that group cohesion is important with respect to individual athlete development, evidenced through links with important cognitive, affective, and behavioral outcomes. In the current section, we suggest that research on talent identification could give consideration toward the abilities of athletes to operate within group environments. In essence, the ability to be a team player and/or a leader should be considered alongside other markers of psychological strength and talent identification.

Ability to function within a team environment

In every sport, elite athletes are consistently being recruited to play at higher levels. Despite a large emphasis on physical ability, organizations such as the National Football League (NFL) have been using other tests, such as The Wonderlic Personnel Test, for decades (Batista, 2013). Although this test was deemed extremely unreliable in predicting success in the NFL, its use emphasizes that professional teams recognize there are more factors beyond physical ability in predicting athletes' potential. Realizing the lack of reliability in The Wonderlic Personnel Test, the NFL introduced a new personality test in 2013 to predict individual success through meas- uring aspects such as conscientiousness and learning agility, qualities deemed salient by NFL general managers (Batista, 2013).

A study by Solomon (2008) identified four factors that coaches use in evaluating their athletes including coachability, capacity to be a team player, physical ability, and maturity. The fact that three of these factors involve non-physical related traits stresses the importance of other qualities in talent identification. However, what role these non-physical qualities play when athletes are being recruited to play at higher levels of sport remains to be seen. Despite organizational research by Van Vianen and De Dreu (2001) suggesting the personality traits such as conscientiousness and agreeableness positively contribute to task and social cohesion, it is unknown to what degree coaches or scouts look for specific non-physical qualities when recruiting athletes to play for their teams. Future research should examine whether positive (team player) or negative personality traits (team cancer) play a role in athlete recruitment.

Development of leadership

Effective leadership has long been viewed as critical to success in sport (Chelladurai & Riemer, 1998). While coaches have been historically considered the primary source of leadership within their team (Chelladurai, 1993; Chelladurai & Riemer, 1998), research has also recog- nized the important leadership contributions of athletes (e.g., Bucci, Bloom, Loughead, & Caron, 2012). In fact, research by Crozier, Loughead, and Munroe-Chandler (2013) has shown that athletes believe the majority of teammates should be exhibiting some form of leadership in order to enhance team functioning. Further, when asked how leadership would impact team functioning, the athletes indicated that having effective leadership would result in stronger team cohesion, clearer team norms, enhanced role clarity, and better team communication. Given these benefits to the group, it becomes clear that teams will want to (a) recruit and retain individuals with leadership skills/potential (as part of their talent identification process) and (b) work on developing leadership skills throughout the duration of their involvement.

As it pertains to leadership training, the focus should not only be on developing the leadership capabilities of the individual athlete but also on enhancing the collective capacity of athletes in relation to the team's processes (e.g., enhancing team cohesion). The former is known as human capital, where the emphasis is on intrapersonal development, and the latter is known as social capital, where the importance is on the development of interpersonal factors (Day, 2000). However, it should be noted that leadership training has typically been viewed as an individual skill (Day, 2000), which ignores a large body of research indicating leadership to be a complex interaction between individuals and their task and social environments (Fiedler, 1996). Therefore, an exciting avenue of future research would be the implementation of a comprehensive leadership development program for athletes that contains a focus on developing both human and social capital. In doing so, it would be expected that the team environment (e.g., cohesiveness between team members) and positive characteristics of the athletes would be enhanced concurrently.

Summary

Athlete development is clearly multifaceted. As noted throughout the current text, physiological, biomechanical, motor control, and coaching variables contribute directly to the speed and quality of athlete development. The group environment, however, also plays a vital role with respect to how athletes (a) think about their sport, (b) feel about their involvement and performance, and (c) maintain their effort and participation. Our chapter makes this case by connecting cohesion with several important individual-level variables, while balancing this presentation with information pertaining to potential downsides of high cohesion. Overall, cohesion among group members sets the stage for continued participation and success in sport.

References

Allen, M. S., Jones, M., McCarthy, P. J., Sheehan-Mansfield, S., & Sheffield, D. (2013). Emotions correlate with perceived mental effort and concentration disruption in adult sport performers. *European Journal of Sport Science, 13*, 697–706.

Baker, J., & Young, B. (2014). 20 year later: Deliberate practice and the development of expertise in sport. *International Review of Sport and Exercise Psychology, 7*, 135–157.

Batista, J. (2013, February 21). N.F.L. tries new method for testing mental agility. *The New York Times*. Retrieved from www.nytimes.com/2013/02/22/sports/football/nfl-introduces-new-way-to-test-a-players-mental-agility.html?_r=0

Blanchard, C. M., Amiot, C. E., Perreault, S., Vallerand, R. J., & Provencher, P. (2009). Cohesiveness, coach's interpersonal style and psychological needs: Their effects on self-determination and athletes' subjective well-being. *Psychology of Sport and Exercise, 10*, 545–551.

Borrego, C. C., Cid, L., & Silva, C. (2012). Relationship between group cohesion and anxiety in soccer. *Journal of Human Kinetics, 34*, 119–127. doi: 10.2478/v10078-012-0071-z

Bosselut, G., Heuzé, J., Eys, M. A., & Bouthier, D. (2010). Influence of task cohesion and role ambiguity on cognitive anxiety during a European Rugby Union Championship. *Athletic Insight, 2*, 17–34.

Bosselut, G., McLaren, C. D., Eys, M. A., & Heuzé, J. (2012). Reciprocity of the relationship between role ambiguity and group cohesion in youth interdependent sport. *Psychology of Sport and Exercise, 13*, 341–348.

Bray, C. D., & Whaley, D. E. (2001). Team cohesion, effort, and objective individual performance of high school basketball players. *The Sport Psychologist, 15*, 260–275.

Bruner, M. W., Eys, M., & Turnnidge, J. (2013). Peer and group influences in youth sport. In J. Côté & R. Lidor (eds), *Conditions of children's talent development in sport* (pp. 157–178). Morgantown, WV: Fitness Information Technology.

Bruner, M. W., Eys, M. A., Wilson, K. S., & Côté, J. (2014). Group cohesion and positive youth development in team sport athletes. *Sport, Exercise, and Performance Psychology, 3*, 219–227.

Bucci, J., Bloom, G. A., Loughead, T. M., & Caron, J. G. (2012). Ice hockey coaches' perceptions of athlete leadership. *Journal of Applied Sport Psychology, 24*, 243–259. doi:10.1080/10413200.2011.636416

Burton, D. (1998). Measuring competitive state anxiety. In J. L. Duda (ed.), *Advancements in sport and exercise psychology measurement* (pp. 129–148). Morgantown, WV: Fitness Information Technology.

Carron, A. V., Brawley, L. R., & Widmeyer, W. N. (1998). The measurement of cohesiveness in groups. In J. L. Duda (ed.), *Advancements in in sport and exercise psychology measurement* (pp. 213–226). Morgantown, WV: Fitness Information Technology.

Carron, A. V., Colman, M. M., Wheeler, J., & Stevens, D. (2002). Cohesion and performance in sport: A meta-analysis. *Journal of Sport & Exercise Psychology, 24*, 168–188.

Carron, A. V., & Eys, M. A. (2012). *Group dynamics in sport* (4th ed.). Morgantown, WV: Fitness Information Technology.

Carron, A. V., Prapavessis, H., & Grove, J. R. (1994). Group effects and self-handicapping. *Journal of Sport and Exercise Psychology, 16*, 246–258.

Carron, A. V., Widmeyer, W. N., & Brawley, L. R. (1985). The development of an instrument to assess cohesion in sport teams: The Group Environment Questionnaire. *Journal of Sport Psychology, 7*, 244–266.

Chelladurai, P. (1993). Leadership. In R. N. Singer, M. Murphy, & L. K. Tennant (eds), *Handbook of research on sport psychology* (pp. 647–671). New York: Macmillan.

Chelladurai, P., & Riemer, H. A. (1997). A classification of facets of athlete satisfaction. *Journal of Sport Management, 11*, 133–159.

Chelladurai, P., & Riemer, H. A. (1998). Measurement of leadership in sport. In J. L. Duda (ed.), *Advancements in sport and exercise psychology measurement* (pp. 227–253). Morgantown, WV: Fitness Information Technology.

Cronin, M. A., Weingart, L. R., & Todorova, G. (2011). Dynamics in groups: Are we there yet? *The Academy of Management Annals, 5*, 571–612.

Crozier, A. J., Loughead, T. M., & Munroe-Chandler, K. J. (2013). Examining the benefits of athlete leaders in sport. *Journal of Sport Behavior, 36*, 346–364.

Day, D. V. (2000). Leadership development: A review in context. *The Leadership Quarterly, 11*, 581–613. doi:10.1016/S1048-9843(00)00061-8

Evans, M. B., Eys, M. A., & Bruner, M. W. (2012). Seeing the "we" in "me" sports: The need to consider individual sport team environments. *Canadian Psychology, 53*, 301–308.

Eys, M. A., Beauchamp, M. R., & Bray, S. R. (2006). A review of team roles in sport. In S. Hanton & S. D. Mellalieu (eds), *Literature reviews in sport psychology* (pp. 227–256). Hauppauge, NY: Nova Science Publishers, Inc.

Eys, M.A., & Carron, A.V. (2001). Role ambiguity, task cohesion, and task self-efficacy. *Small Group Research, 32 (3)*, 356–372.

Eys, M. A., Carron, A. V., Bray, S. R., & Beauchamp, M. R. (2005). The relationship between role ambiguity and intention to return the following season. *Journal of Applied Sport Psychology, 17*, 255–261. doi: 10.1080/10413200591010148

Eys, M. A., Hardy, J., Carron, A. V., & Beauchamp, M. R. (2003). The relationship between task cohesion and competitive state anxiety. *Journal of Sport & Exercise Psychology, 25*, 66–76.

Eys, M. A., Loughead, T. M., Bray, S. R., & Carron, A. V. (2009). Development of a cohesion questionnaire for youth: The Youth Sport Environment Questionnaire. *Journal of Sport & Exercise Psychology, 31*, 390–408.

Eys, M. A., Ohlert, J., Evans, B., Wolf, S., Martin, L., VanBussel, M., & Steins, C. (2015). Cohesion and performance for female and male sport teams. *The Sport Psychologist, 29*, 97–109.

Fiedler, F. E. (1996). Research on leadership selection and training: One view of the future. *Administrative Science Quarterly, 41*, 241–250. doi:10.2307/2393716

Gammage, K. L., Carron, A. V., & Estabrooks, P. A. (2001). Team cohesion and individual productivity: The influence of the norm for productivity and the identifiability of individual effort. *Small Group Research, 32*, 3–18.

Hardy, J., Eys, M. A., & Carron, A. V. (2005). Exploring the potential disadvantages of high cohesion in sport teams. *Small Group Research, 36,* 166–187.

Harwood, C., Beauchamp, M. R., & Keegan, R. J. (2014). Group functioning through optimal achievement goals. In M. Beauchamp, & M. Eys (eds), *Group dynamics in exercise and sport psychology* (pp. 279–297). Oxford: Routledge.

Heuzé, J-P., Eys, M., Dubuc, M., Bosselut, G., & Couture, R. (2015). *Cohesion, psychological needs, and intrinsic motivation in youth and adult team sport contexts.* Manuscript submitted for publication.

Heuzé, J-P., Raimbault, N., & Fontayne, P. (2006). Relationships between cohesion, collective efficacy and performance in professional basketball teams: An examination of mediating effects. *Journal of Sports Sciences, 24,* 59–68.

Lazarus, R. S. (1999). *Stress and emotion: A new synthesis.* New York: Springer.

MacDonald, D. J., Côté, J., Eys, M., & Deakin, J. (2012). Psychometric properties of the Youth Experience Survey with young athletes, *Psychology of Sport & Exercise, 13,* 332–340.

Martens, R., Burton, D., Vealey, R. S., Bump, L. A., & Smith, D. E. (1990). The Competitive State Anxiety Inventory-2 (CSAI-2). In R. Martens, R.S. Vealey, & D. Burton (eds), *Competitive anxiety in sport* (pp. 117–190). Champaign, IL: Human Kinetics.

Martin, L. J., Carron, A. V., Eys, M. A., & Loughead, T. M. (2012). Development of a cohesion questionnaire for children's sport teams. *Group Dynamics: Theory, Research, and Practice, 16,* 68–79.

McEwan, D., & Beauchamp, M. R. (2014). Teamwork in sport: A theoretical and integrative review. *International Review of Sport and Exercise Psychology, 7,* 229–250.

Nicholls, J. G. (1984). Achievement motivation: Conceptions of ability, subjective experience, task choice, and performance. *Psychological Review, 91,* 328–346.

Paradis, K. F., Carron, A. V., & Martin, L. J. (2014). Athlete perceptions of intra-group conflict in sport teams. *Sport & Exercise Psychology Review, 10,* 4–18.

Paradis, K. F., & Loughead, T. M. (2012). Examining the mediating role of cohesion between athlete leadership and athlete satisfaction in youth sport. *International Journal of Sport Psychology, 43,* 117–136.

Prapavessis, H., & Carron, A. V. (1996). The effect of group cohesion on competitive state anxiety. *Journal of Sport & Exercise Psychology, 18,* 64–74.

Prapavessis, H., & Carron, A. V. (1997). Cohesion and work output. *Small Group Research, 28,* 294–301.

Raglin, J. S., & Hanin, Y. L. (2000). Competitive anxiety. In Y. L. (ed.), *Emotions in sport* (pp. 93–111). Champaign, IL: Human Kinetics.

Reeve, J. M. (2009). *Understanding motivation and emotion* (5th ed.). Hoboken, NJ: Wiley & Sons.

Riemer, H. A., & Chelladurai, P. (1998). Development of the Athlete Satisfaction Questionnaire (ASQ). *Journal of Sport & Exercise Psychology, 20,* 127–156.

Rovio, E., Eskola, J., Kozub, S. A., Duda, J. L., & Lintunen, T. (2009). Can high group cohesion be harmful? A case study of a junior ice-hockey team. *Small Group Research, 40,* 421–435.

Shipnuck, A. (2004, September). Euro thrash. *Sports Illustrated.* Retrieved from www.si.com/vault/2004/09/27/8186895/euro-thrash.

Solomon, G. (2008). The assessment of athletic ability in intercollegiate sport: Instrument construction and validation. *International Journal of Sports Science and Coaching, 3,* 513–525.

Spink, K. S. (1995). Cohesion and intention to participate of female sport team athletes. *Journal of Sport & Exercise Psychology, 17,* 416–427.

Spink, K. S. (1998). Mediational efforts of social cohesion on the leadership behavior-intention to return relationship in sport. *Group Dynamics: Theory, Research, and Practice, 2,* 92–100.

Spink, K. S., Nickel, D., Wilson, K., & Odnokon, P. (2005). Using a multilevel approach to examine the relationship between task cohesion and team task satisfaction in elite ice hockey players. *Small Group Research, 36,* 539–554. doi:10.1177/1046496405275229

Spink, K. S., Wilson, K. S., & Odnokon, P. (2010). Examining the relationship between cohesion and return to team in elite athletes. *Psychology of Sport and Exercise, 11,* 6–11.

Stein, A. A. (1976). Conflict and cohesion: A review of the literature. *Journal of Conflict Resolution, 20,* 143–172.

Strachan, L. Côté, J., & Deakin, J. (2011). A new view: Exploring positive youth development in elite sport contexts. *Qualitative Research in Sport, Exercise and Health, 3,* 9–32. doi:10.1080/19398441.2010.541483

Taylor, I. M., & Bruner, M. W. (2012). The social environment and developmental experiences in elite youth soccer. *Psychology of Sport and Exercise, 13,* 390–396. doi: 10.1016/j.psychsport.2012.01.008

Van Vianen, A. E., & De Dreu, C. K. (2001). Personality in teams: Its relationship to social cohesion, task cohesion, and team performance. *European Journal of Work and Organizational Psychology, 10,* 97–120.

Wise, S. (2014). Can a team have too much cohesion? The dark side to network density. *European Management Journal, 32,* 703–711.

Wolf, S. A., Eys, M., & Kleinert, J. (2015). Predictors of the precompetitive anxiety response: Relative impact and prospects for anxiety regulation. *International Journal of Sport and Exercise Psychology, 13,* 344–358.

Wolf, S. A., Eys, M., Sadler, P., & Kleinert, J. (2015). Appraisal in a team context: Perceptions of cohesion predict competition importance and prospects for coping. *Journal of Sport & Exercise Psychology, 37,* 489–499.

22

APPLIED MOTOR LEARNING

Optimal environments for successful development

Adam D. Gorman and Ian Renshaw

There are numerous examples to demonstrate the ways in which the principles from motor learning can be successfully applied in the sporting domain (e.g., see Button & Farrow, 2012; Williams, Ford, Causer, Logan, & Murray, 2012; see also Hodges & Williams, 2012; Renshaw, Davids, & Savelsbergh, 2010b). However, there is also evidence to suggest that practitioners are not necessarily taking up this literature, leading to a continued disconnect between academic motor learning scientists and applied practitioners (Ford, Yates, & Williams, 2010; Partington & Cushion, 2013; see also Williams & Ford, 2009; Williams et al., 2012). The lack of take-up of empirical research is exemplified in reported instances of practice sessions containing up to 65% of activities that have been deemed as less relevant for improving the skills required for successful performance in competition (Ford et al., 2010; see also Partington & Cushion, 2013).

Traditional approaches towards skill development typically advocate for the use of repetitive activities in relatively predictable environments, often accompanied by reduced variability and the aim of minimising or eliminating skill errors (for discussions of traditional approaches, see Chow, Davids, Hristovski, Araújo, & Passos, 2011; Davids, Button, & Bennett, 2008; Handford, Davids, Bennett, & Button, 1997; Williams & Hodges, 2005). While such notions may appear quite logical, alternative approaches, supported by evidence-based research and underpinning theoretical frameworks, are becoming more accepted as a means of augmenting the perceptual-motor skills of emerging athletes (Handford et al., 1997; Renshaw, Davids, Shuttleworth, & Chow, 2009; Williams & Hodges, 2005). This chapter is aimed at providing practitioners with an overview of contemporary motor learning principles that can be used in an applied development program to optimise skill acquisition for emerging performers in the sporting domain. The information is complemented by a discussion of pertinent research findings to provide examples of the ways in which many of the key principles can be applied in a practical setting.

Creating an optimal learning environment for skill development

Anecdotally, and in line with our own interactions with practitioners, three of the common skill-related observations reported by coaches working with developmental level athletes (i.e., athletes who are performing at a relatively high level, but who are transitioning towards the highest possible level of their sport) are that: (1) the athletes are talented, but have a limited understanding of the sport in terms of tactical and technical knowledge; (2) the athletes are able to perform quite successfully at lower levels of competition, but have major deficiencies in their technique or decision-making that are likely to prevent further progression to higher competitive levels; and (3) the athletes are able to successfully perform in relatively familiar and stable environments, but are often unable to adapt their skills to suit different performance contexts, particularly those that are likely to be encountered at the highest levels of their sport (see also Partington & Cushion, 2013). Many of the principles from motor learning can provide coaches with a broad range of strategies that can be used to help address these issues (e.g., Williams & Hodges, 2005; Hendry, Ford, Williams & Hodges, 2015). We go into more detail in the following section to outline different strategies that can be used in an applied setting to enhance motor learning in developmental level athletes.

Problem-based coaching and the constraints-led approach

As outlined by Passos, Araújo, Davids, and Shuttleworth (2008), a useful starting point for remedying skill-related issues is to identify the underlying cause of the problem. For example, after observing a number of decision-making errors made by a team-sport athlete over the course of several competitive games, an initial diagnosis may conclude that the player is generally a poor decision-maker. However, without identifying the *specific* underlying issue, the implementation of a generalised intervention may be somewhat hit-and-miss (see Passos et al., 2008), particularly given that decision-making may be affected by a range of potential individual or environmental factors (see Araújo, Davids, & Hristovski, 2006; Williams & Ford, 2008). At the level of the individual, these factors can include physiological influences such as exercise intensity (Royal et al., 2006), psychological factors such as the criticality of the game situation (Bar-Eli & Tractinsky, 2000), or skill-related factors such as tactical knowledge (French & Thomas, 1987; McPherson, 1993) and the capability to actually perform certain skills (French et al., 1996). Whilst environmental factors may seem less obvious, it might be a lack of confidence in a teammate, an inability to adapt to physical environmental factors such as weather conditions, or the culture created by a coach that may be impacting upon the individual's decisions (see Araújo et al., 2006).

Once a better understanding of the specific cause of the problem has been established, the next logical step in the process is to directly address the issue by designing appropriate practice tasks (Passos et al., 2008). A useful strategy for enhancing and/or changing perceptual-motor skills is the constraints-led approach (Araújo, Davids, Bennett, Button, & Chapman, 2004; Davids et al., 2008; Passos et al., 2008; Renshaw et al., 2010b). This approach suggests that human behaviours are influenced by three different categories of constraints including the task itself (e.g., equipment, rules, playing boundaries, state of the game or competition), the environment (e.g., weather conditions, playing surfaces, ambient lighting), and the performer (e.g., height, emotions, fitness level), with the influence of these constraints being either facilitative or restrictive in nature (Araújo et al., 2004; Davids et al., 2008; Newell, 1986).

The application of the constraints-led approach in coaching typically involves the manipulation of one or more categories of constraints in an attempt to encourage the natural emergence of a desired movement behaviour (Araújo et al., 2004; Davids, 2010; Passos et al., 2008). Following on from the example outlined above, if the underlying problem affecting a player's decision-making is related to an inability to rapidly recognise open (unmarked) teammates, small-sided games representative of the situations in a 'proper' game could be created where the attacking team has a numerical advantage in the form of an additional player (see Chow et al., 2009; Davids, 2010; Passos et al., 2008). In these situations, it is likely that at least one teammate will be open for a pass, thereby allowing attacking players to learn to 'read' the important information that specifies a given decision-making option (see Passos et al., 2008). As an increased challenge, an additional defensive player could be called to enter the game at random times (as controlled by the coach) so that, just like in games, the open attacker is only available for brief time periods (see Gorman, 2010; Guadagnoli & Lee, 2004). An important point is that the coach should try to identify the key constraint to manipulate (Chow et al., 2006, 2009); that is, the constraint that is going to lead to a change in performance (Newell & Valvano, 1998). In the constraints-led approach, this factor is known as the 'control parameter' and systematic manipulations should lead to the emergence of new movement patterns (Araújo, Davids, Sainhas, & Fernandes, 2002; Chow et al., 2006; Magill & Anderson, 2014). A simple example of a control parameter that leads to a re-organisation of individual coordination would be increased treadmill speed, which would result in a spontaneous change from walking to running at specific individual speeds (Diedrich & Warren, 1995).

The extant literature contains numerous examples to demonstrate the utility of the constraints-led approach for talent development across a wide range of sports (see Chow et al., 2007; Headrick et al., 2012; Hristovski, Davids, Araújo, & Button, 2006; Passos et al., 2008; Pinder, Davids, & Renshaw, 2012; Renshaw et al., 2010b). For instance, in freestyle swimming, the use of hand paddles with adolescent swimmers has been shown to elicit significant increases in stroke length and mean swimming velocity, while reducing the maximal linear hand velocity during the push phase of the stroke (Gourgoulis, Aggeloussis, Vezos, & Mavromatis, 2006). In this example, the swimmers were simply required to swim at a specified stroke rate using a pull buoy and hand paddles, but there were no other constraints or instructions included in the task (Gourgoulis et al., 2006). Thus, for coaches wishing to address the problem of freestyle swimmers using excessively short stroke lengths, the addition of simple task constraints, in this instance, hand paddles and a pull buoy, could provide the necessary individual–environment interaction to promote the desired changes in technique (see Gourgoulis et al., 2006; Chow et al., 2007; Renshaw et al., 2010b). There are also examples in the literature that demonstrate the utility of manipulating performer constraints to elicit changes in the tactical behaviours of team sport athletes (see Renshaw et al., 2010b). Cordovil et al. (2009, experiment 2) showed that when female defenders in a full-court 1-on-1 contest in basketball were taller than their opponent, the defender tended to entice the attacker closer to the basket. This tactic is likely to allow the defender to use her height advantage to more easily perturb the shooting options of her shorter opponent (Cordovil et al., 2009). Once again, these results demonstrate how the constraints-led approach can be used to specifically address skill-related problems (Chow et al., 2007; Passos et al., 2008; Renshaw et al., 2010b). That is, after identifying the likely cause of the problem (e.g., the ability to adapt to different opponents as shown in the previous example; see Cordovil et al., 2009), practitioners can selectively manipulate key constraints to provide practice opportunities for athletes to refine their technique and/or expand upon their tactical understanding (Passos et al., 2008; Renshaw et al., 2010b; see also Newell & Valvano, 1998). One of the advantages of this strategy is the absence of highly prescriptive or directive instructions provided by a coach (see Chow et al., 2007). Instead, the coach acts as a facilitator by creating learning opportunities for athletes to explore their own movement solutions (Renshaw, Oldham, & Bawden, 2012; Renshaw et al., 2009). This player-centred approach requires creativity on the part of the coach, as well as the use of carefully designed practice activities to guide athletes towards individually optimised solutions (Renshaw et al., 2009, 2012).

Metastability

As highlighted earlier, identification of key control parameters and the subsequent manipulation of these constraints is an important skill for coaches (Araújo et al., 2002; Chow et al., 2006, 2009). At the theoretical level, that is, in ecological dynamics terms, this strategy can be used to create what have been termed 'metastable states' (see Chow et al., 2011; Hristovski, Davids, Araújo, & Passos, 2011; Pinder et al., 2012). When a performer is in a metastable state, there are a range of potentially successful coordination patterns that can emerge, depending upon the nature of the task demands (Davids, Araújo, Hristovski, Passos, & Chow, 2012; Davids et al., 2008; Hristovski et al., 2011; Kelso, 1995, 2008, 2012). In other words, metastability is when the individual is poised between a variety of different options, providing opportunities for the performer to flexibly adapt his/her actions to suit the desired performance goal through adoption of a range of coordination patterns (Chow et al., 2011; Davids et al., 2012; Pinder et al., 2012; see also Kelso, 1995). The potential application of this concept for skill acquisition has been demonstrated in tasks such as boxing (Hristovski et al., 2006) and cricket (Pinder et al., 2012). When a boxer is placed at a distance of 60 cm from a punching bag, the boxer is situated in a metastable region and potential solutions to solve the task are maximised because a large repertoire of punch types (e.g., jabs, uppercuts, and hooks) are able to spontaneously emerge (Hristovski et al., 2006). This encourages the boxer to explore a broad array of action possibilities, allowing the discovery of those that are optimal for the individual, as well as providing opportunities to develop more adaptable movement capabilities (Hristovski et al., 2006; see also Handford et al., 1997; Pinder et al., 2012). In contrast, when the bag is placed either further away or closer to the boxer, the diversity of available options dissipate, thereby limiting the exploratory behaviour of the boxer and the need for the boxer to learn how to select from amongst several available action possibilities (Hristovski et al., 2006).

A similar example of metastability has been observed in cricket batting. Pinder et al. (2012) found that when a batter attempted to hit a ball that bounced in a highly specifying region of the pitch, that is, a location eliciting low amounts of metastability because the type of movement to be executed by the batter was easily identifiable and highly stable, the batters tended to be very consistent in the timing and selection of their shots. In these situations, the landing position of the ball was unambiguously coupled with a certain type of coordination pattern and so the degree of adaptability required on the part of the batter was likely to be minimised (Pinder et al., 2012). In contrast, when the ball bounced in a location that allowed the batters to select between two completely different movement responses (stepping forwards versus stepping backwards), a metastable state was created and so the amount of variability in the batters' movements increased (Pinder et al., 2012). The initial movements of the batters were equally likely to be forward (48%) or backward (52%), and a broader range of shot types were executed (Pinder et al., 2012). Thus, the batters were required to find the optimal balance between identifying a familiar and stable movement pattern that they could execute in a coordinated way, while simultaneously executing that movement pattern in a flexible manner to ensure the final outcome of the movement was successful (Kelso, 2008, 2012; Pinder et al., 2012). These findings have important practical applications (Pinder et al., 2012). For instance, bowling the ball so that it lands in an area of the pitch that provides more action possibilities for the batter may be counterproductive in short-form games (e.g., twenty-over games) where minimising run scoring is typically the most important aim (see Pinder et al., 2012).

The aforementioned examples demonstrate how the manipulation of key constraints, such as the distance a boxer stands from a punching bag (Hristovski et al., 2006), or the bounce location of a cricket ball (Pinder et al., 2012), can be used to create situations where athletes are encouraged to explore and adapt their movement patterns (see Chow et al., 2011; Kello, Anderson, Holden, & Van Orden, 2008). Rather than structuring practice sessions that are highly consistent and predictable, coaches can apply the concept of metastability to create variable performance environments (Chow et al., 2011; Pinder et al., 2012). In the dynamic setting of many sporting competitions, the judicious use of metastability may assist athletes to acquire the necessary skill set to cope with the ever-changing demands of the environment in which they perform (Chow et al., 2011; Headrick, Renshaw, Davids, Pinder, & Araújo, 2015).

Functional variability and individualising motor skill learning

The concept of 'functional variability' suggests that the variability that typically occurs during the execution of a skill may often play an important role in helping to facilitate adaptability (Davids, Glazier, Araújo, & Bartlett, 2003). Functional variability is often observed in elite performers whose coordination patterns have been shown to vary from one trial to the next, suggesting that they are adjusting their movements to adapt to the changing constraints that exist within dynamic performance settings (Bartlett, 2008; Bartlett, Wheat, & Robins, 2007). For example, while performing a basketball shot, skilled players tend to show increased variability within certain joints of the shooting arm, suggesting that the movement is being varied (i.e., adapted) in a functional way, ostensibly to help maintain the consistency of the final release parameters of the shot (Button, MacLeod, Sanders, & Coleman, 2003; see Bartlett et al., 2007; Robins, Wheat, Irwin, & Bartlett, 2006). These movement adaptations may be individually specific and highlight the need to provide learning opportunities that allow the emergence of individualised coordination solutions (see Bartlett et al., 2007; Davids et al., 2012; Morriss, Bartlett, & Fowler, 1997). It is important to note that at the elite level, most athletes possess quite different movement patterns and techniques, even for skills that are performed in a relatively predictable performance environment (Morriss et al., 1997; for reviews, see Bartlett, 2008; Bartlett et al., 2007; see also Glazier, Davids, Renshaw, & Button, 2005). Such evidence suggests that each athlete achieves a given movement outcome in a distinctive manner as a result of the unique interactions between individual, task, and environmental constraints, and argues against the existence of a common 'textbook' technique (Bartlett et al., 2007).

A practical demonstration of the benefits of promoting an individualised program of functional variability to enhance sports performance was recently reported by Barris, Farrow, and Davids (2014) in a study designed to enhance the adaptability of elite female springboard divers. The authors identified that a common problem in the athletes' normal practice sessions was that the divers would frequently choose to prematurely terminate a dive (i.e., baulk) if the diver perceived imperfections in the preparatory phase of her dive. This reduced the overall volume of practice trials, and also discouraged the athletes from learning how to successfully adapt their dives (as would often be required in competition; Barris et al., 2014). To address the issue, the divers were encouraged to avoid baulking during their practice sessions, unless they perceived there to be a safety issue or a risk of injury. The overall intention was to provide opportunities for the divers to learn how to adapt their dives under variable conditions, rather than persisting with their current approach of reducing the variability of their practice attempts by baulking. After a 12-week training program, the results showed an overall decline in the number of baulks, as well as increases in the amount of movement variability, and greater consistency of dive outcomes. It was concluded that the increased movement variability exemplified that the athletes had learned how to functionally adapt their actions to accommodate for variations occurring during the preparatory phases of their dives, and this ultimately led to more consistent performance outcomes (Barris et al., 2014).

Another strategy that further demonstrates the beneficial role of variability during motor skill learning, and that allows athletes to explore and acquire individualised movement patterns, is known as 'differential learning' (see Schöllhorn, Hegen, & Davids, 2012). The strategy is predicated upon the assumption that learning is optimised when the athlete is exposed to a larger perceptual-motor workspace during practice (Schöllhorn, Beckmann, Janssen, & Drepper, 2010; Schöllhorn, Mayer-Kress, Newell, & Michelbrink, 2009). This is achieved through the use of frequently changing and non-repetitive practice trials that are designed to encourage the athlete to explore a broad array of possible movement solutions, thereby promoting the acquisition of more individualised and effective coordination patterns (Schöllhorn et al., 2006, 2009; Schöllhorn, Hegen, & Davids, 2012). The increased fluctuations of practice tasks that occur in a differential learning environment are believed to augment important sources of information regarding the movement, allowing the learner to better differentiate between possible movement solutions for differing circumstances (Savelsbergh, Kamper, Rabius, De Koning, & Schöllhorn, 2010; Schöllhorn et al., 2006, 2010). This increases the capability of the learner to rapidly select a successful coordination pattern for a given situation (Savelsbergh et al., 2010).

The positive impact of differential learning was demonstrated in a study by Schöllhorn et al. (2012) that examined goal shooting and ball control in soccer players. Participants were provided with either a traditional coaching approach, where practice consisted of repetitive activities, corrective feedback, and an emphasis upon achieving an idealised technique, or a differential approach, which included no corrective feedback and avoided using repetitive practice tasks. Examples of the latter tasks included frequent variations in features such as the angles, velocities, and positioning of different body parts when kicking and controlling the ball. After a 4-week training intervention, the differential training group showed significantly greater performance gains than the traditionally trained group (for other examples, see Schöllhorn et al., 2006, 2010). The frequently changing tasks in the differential learning approach essentially amplified the need for the athletes to explore different types of movements to achieve a given outcome goal which, purportedly, encouraged the motor system to self-organise in an attempt to find more stable and effective coordination patterns (Schöllhorn et al., 2012).

In a practical context, rather than mandating that an athlete use a predetermined and idealised technique, the manipulation of key constraints, and/or the judicious application of variability, can provide the necessary freedom for the athlete to explore a broader area of the perceptual-motor workspace to search for an individually optimised movement pattern or tactical behaviour (Davids, Chow, & Shuttleworth, 2005; Renshaw et al., 2009, 2010b; Schöllhorn et al., 2010, 2012). The increased variability within the practice activities, combined with the broadened exploratory behaviour, plays a functional role in motor learning by allowing athletes to self-organise their movements and acquire an adaptable (and therefore more consistently successful) and individualised movement pattern (Davids et al., 2003, 2008; Handford et al., 1997; Renshaw et al., 2009). However, an important consideration for practitioners when applying these concepts is to match the nature of the task to the current needs and capabilities of the performer (Davids et al., 2012; Guadagnoli & Lee, 2004; Milot, Marchal-Crespo, Green, Cramer, & Reinkensmeyer, 2010; Renshaw et al., 2012; Wilson, Simpson, Van Emmerik, & Hamill, 2008). For example, an excessive amount of variability could create a practice environment with such an expansive perceptual-motor workspace that the search process for the athlete becomes not only time-consuming, but also potentially overwhelming and dangerous (Handford et al., 1997; see also Newell, 2003). Additionally, this could have psychological consequences such as declines in confidence and motivation (Handford et al., 1997). This highlights the critical role of the practitioner in terms of designing appropriate practice opportunities to allow athletes to optimise their search for suitable movement solutions in a safe and carefully designed environment (Handford et al., 1997; Renshaw et al., 2012). In addition, although variability may enhance learning (i.e., provide long-term benefits), it may also result in concomitant declines in the immediate performance outputs of the individual (Guadagnoli & Lee, 2004; Handford et al., 1997; Magill & Anderson, 2014; Renshaw et al., 2009). That is, by increasing the variability of the performance context, a more demanding learning environment is created, thereby challenging the athlete to discover more adaptable and efficient coordination patterns (Guadagnoli & Lee, 2004; Handford et al., 1997; Renshaw et al., 2009; Schöllhorn et al., 2010). This discovery process is likely to encourage the performer to explore a variety of both successful *and* unsuccessful solutions, and so it is important for practitioners to recognise that an increase in performance errors is often a functional part of the process of motor development (Cesari & Milanese, 1995; Guadagnoli & Lee, 2004; Handford et al., 1997; Renshaw et al., 2009). With sufficient practice opportunities, combined with the sagacious application of variable practice to promote exploration and adaptation, the ultimate aim is to safely guide athletes towards the development of a broad repertoire of highly functional movement solutions (see Handford et al., 1997; Renshaw et al., 2009, 2012).

Learner-regulated practice environments

The emphasis upon allowing the learner to discover individually appropriate coordination patterns under constraint is a key principle in the constraints-led approach that has been highlighted in the previous sections (e.g., Chow et al., 2006; Handford et al., 1997); but this approach can also be utilised within other elements of the practice environment. For instance, there is growing evidence to suggest that learning may be augmented when individuals are given the opportunity to self-select when they wish to receive feedback or demonstrations during practice sessions (for overviews, see Sanli, Patterson, Bray, & Lee, 2013; Wulf, 2007; see also Renshaw et al., 2012). Similar benefits have also been observed when individuals are given autonomy over certain aspects of their practice schedule such as choosing the number of trials to be performed (Post, Fairbrother, & Barros, 2011), or deciding when to add variability to a practice task (Bund & Wiemeyer, 2004). The increased autonomy and sense of responsibility created by a self-controlled learning environment may elicit benefits in psychological factors such as self-determined motivation, self-efficacy, and may enhance learning through increased levels of cognitive effort (see Andrieux, Danna, & Thon, 2012; Bund & Wiemeyer, 2004; Janelle, Barba, Frehlich, Tennant, & Cauraugh, 1997; Moy, Renshaw, & Davids, 2015; Sanli et al., 2013; Wulf, 2007; see also Guadagnoli & Lee, 2004).

The use of self-controlled strategies may also have the advantage of providing additional opportunities for athletes to use intrapersonal information to guide their actions (Millar, 2014). In research conducted by Millar (2014), experienced rowers were asked to complete sub-maximal rowing bouts while their coaches travelled alongside in a speedboat. Throughout the bouts, rowers and coaches were asked to judge whether the boat was travelling fast by providing a verbal yes/no response. The results showed that the perceptions of boat speed for the rowers were generally more accurate than the coaches, particularly when the changes in speed were marginal. Thus, the rowers' firsthand experience during the task provided them with important information that could not be perceived with the same degree of accuracy by the coach as an external observer (Millar, 2014; see also Knoblich & Flach, 2001). Results such as these suggest that the autonomy afforded by self-controlled learning environments may provide the necessary freedom for athletes to make better use of intrapersonal information to guide their performance during practice, rather than having this information overridden by the external feedback provided by a coach (Millar, 2014). This, in turn, may allow athletes to have a more meaningful and beneficial contribution to the ways in which practice sessions are delivered (Hadfield, 2005; Millar, 2014). These conclusions do not suggest that the role of the coach is redundant, but rather, the emphasis should perhaps be aimed towards increased coach–athlete interactions so that the coach can make better use of the information generated by the athlete (Hadfield, 2005; Millar, 2014).

Representative learning design in the practice environment

Clearly, the role of the sports practitioner is pivotal in creating suitable practice activities to enhance motor learning (Williams & Hodges, 2005). Unfortunately, however, there is evidence to suggest the existence of a considerable gap between the types of activities and behaviours that *should* be implemented within skill practice sessions (based upon existing research findings and theories), and those that *are* being implemented (Ford et al., 2010; Hendry et al., 2015; Partington & Cushion, 2013; see also Williams & Hodges, 2005). Partington and Cushion (2013) examined the practice activities and behaviours of professional youth soccer coaches and found that the sessions tended to contain a large proportion of activities that were deemed as less relevant for enhancing matchplay (see also Ford et al., 2010). They also found that the coaches used relatively high levels of prescriptive instructions, despite the fact that the stated intentions of the coaches were to create more independent players who were capable of making their own decisions. Although the results were limited to a small cohort of coaches and only a sample of practice sessions, the research nonetheless highlights the need for practitioners to understand the importance of creating appropriate practice environments for motor learning (Partington & Cushion, 2013).

The concept of representative learning design suggests that practice activities should ideally include comparable information sources and interacting constraints to those that would typically be experienced in the normal performance setting (Pinder, Davids, Renshaw, & Araújo, 2011a). In simple terms, the activities implemented during practice should closely replicate the demands of competition (Pinder et al., 2011a). This helps to ensure that athletes learn to couple their actions to the key specifying sources of perceptual information that are necessary for guiding behaviour (Pinder et al., 2011a). Thus, practice tasks that alter or remove the close coupling between perception and action can have a significant impact upon the nature of the coordination patterns that emerge during learning (Pinder et al., 2011a; Renshaw et al., 2009; see also Gibson, 1979). For example, when a cricket batter faces a ball delivered by a bowling machine rather than by an actual bowler, significant differences are observed in the timing and movement of the bat, as well as in the stride length of the front foot (Renshaw, Oldham, Davids, & Golds, 2007; see also Pinder, Davids, Renshaw, & Araújo, 2011b). In this situation, the batter's movements are de-coupled from the movements of the bowler, leading to significant changes in the batter's actions (Renshaw et al., 2007). The coach may think that facilitating a practice task where a player hits a ball delivered by a ball projection machine is maintaining the perception–action coupling, however, whilst the batter will indeed couple his or her movements to the flight of the ball, the evidence highlighted above suggests that the coupling will be aligned to different information sources than that used in a 'real' game (Renshaw et al., 2007). Another example to illustrate this point is to consider the behaviours of goalkeepers when saving penalty kicks (Dicks, Button, & Davids, 2010). Measurements of visual search behaviours have shown that goalkeepers scan the scene differently when attempting to save a 'live' penalty kick delivered in a real-world setting compared to when the kick is presented via a video image (Dicks et al., 2010). In other team-sports, the removal of defenders from an action scenario has been shown to elicit changes in the throwing velocity of shots at goal in handball (Rivilla-Garcia, Grande, Sampedro, & van den Tillaar, 2011), and alterations in the movement kinematics of basketball players when executing a jump shot (Rojas, Cepero, Oña, & Gutierrez, 2000). Collectively, the results of such research suggest that removing key sources of perceptual information may elicit significant changes to the behaviours of the performer (Pinder et al., 2011a; Renshaw et al., 2009). This highlights the importance of creating representative practice tasks that maintain the same perception–action couplings that exist in the natural setting (Pinder et al., 2011a).

One of the important, and sometimes neglected factors to consider when designing representative practice tasks is the influence of emotion (Headrick et al., 2015; Pinder, Headrick, & Oudejans, 2015; Renshaw, Headrick, & Davids, 2014; Renshaw et al., 2012). During competition, athletes will typically experience a myriad of emotions that are likely to have at least some influence upon performance (Hanin, 2007; Jones, 2003; Pijpers, Oudejans, & Bakker, 2005; Vast, Young, & Thomas, 2010; see also Cottyn, De Clercq, Crombez, & Lenoir, 2012). It has been postulated that based upon the notion of representative learning design, skill practice sessions should ideally include opportunities for athletes to experience performance environments that not only replicate the motor demands of competition, but also mimic the emotional demands (Headrick et al., 2015; Pinder et al., 2015). This may help to increase the level of engagement of the athletes in the task, and also better prepare those athletes to cope with the various emotions that manifest during competition (Headrick et al., 2015; Jones, 2003; Renshaw et al., 2012; see also LaBar & Cabeza, 2006; Renshaw, Chappell, Fitzgerald, & Davison & McFadyen, 2010a). Researchers investigating the influence of emotions on motor learning have provided empirical support for the inclusion of emotionally representative experiences (termed 'affective learning design') during practice tasks (for overviews, see Headrick et al., 2015; Renshaw et al., 2014). For example, Oudejans and Pijpers (2009; experiment 1) asked expert basketball players to practice free throws under anxiety-provoking conditions during their regular training sessions over a 5-week period. Anxiety was induced using a combination of methods such as penalties for missed shots (e.g., sprints), the placement of cameras on the baseline of the court in clear view of the players, and the use of coaches and other players as spectators. The results showed that despite experiencing relatively high levels of anxiety during the post-tests, the players' free throw performance did not deteriorate to the same extent as that observed prior to the 5-week practice period. In contrast, the free throw performance of a control group who practised under lower levels of anxiety deteriorated when performing under higher levels of anxiety (see also Nieuwenhuys & Oudejans, 2011; Oudejans, 2008; Oudejans & Pijpers, 2009). The use of emotionally representative practice tasks, that are carefully and appropriately implemented, may therefore provide opportunities for athletes to learn how to acclimatise to the emotions that typically occur during normal competition (Headrick et al., 2015).

Concluding remarks

This chapter has discussed a number of the contemporary approaches in motor learning that can be used by practitioners to help design and implement skill practice sessions for developmental level athletes (see Davids et al., 2008; Hendry et al., 2015). As highlighted within the chapter, the intention of these approaches is, among other things, to create an athlete-centred learning environment that not only promotes the acquisition of individualised coordination patterns, but also highly adaptable athletes who are capable of achieving success in the demanding environment of elite level sport (see Davids et al., 2012; Renshaw et al., 2009, 2012).

References

Andrieux, M., Danna, J., & Thon, B. (2012). Self-control of task difficulty during training enhances motor learning of a complex coincidence-anticipation task. *Research Quarterly for Exercise and Sport, 83,* 27–35.

Araújo, D., Davids, K., Bennett, S. J., Button, C., & Chapman, G. (2004). Emergence of sports skills under constraints. In A. M. Williams & N. J. Hodges (eds), *Skill acquisition in sport: Research, theory and practice* (pp. 409–433). London: Routledge.

Araújo, D., Davids, K., & Hristovski, R. (2006). The ecological dynamics of decision making in sport. *Psychology of Sport and Exercise, 7,* 653–676.

Araújo, D., Davids, K., Sainhas, J., & Fernandes, O. (2002). *Emergent decision-making in sport: A constraints-led approach.* Communication to the International Congress on Movement, Attention & Perception, Poitiers, France.

Bar-Eli, M., & Tractinsky, N. (2000). Criticality of game situations and decision making in basketball: A application of performance crisis perspective. *Psychology of Sport and Exercise, 1,* 27–39.

Barris, S., Farrow, D., & Davids, K. (2014). Increasing functional variability in the preparatory phase of the takeoff improves elite springboard diving performance. *Research Quarterly for Exercise and Sport, 85,* 97–106.

Bartlett, R. (2008). Movement variability and its implications for sports scientists and practitioners: An overview. *International Journal of Sports Science & Coaching, 3,* 113–124.

Bartlett, R., Wheat, J., & Robins, M. (2007). Is movement variability important for sports biomechanists? *Sports Biomechanics, 6,* 224–243.

Bund, A., & Wiemeyer, J. (2004). Self-controlled learning of a complex motor skill: Effects of the learners' preferences on performance and self-efficacy. *Journal of Human Movement Studies, 47,* 215–136.

Button, C., & Farrow, D. (2012). Working in the field (Southern Hemisphere). In N. J. Hodges & A. M. Williams (eds), *Skill acquisition in sport: Research, theory and practice* (pp. 367–380). London: Routledge.

Button, C., MacLeod, M., Sanders, R., & Coleman, S. (2003). Examining movement variability in the basketball free-throw action at different skill levels. *Research Quarterly for Exercise and Sport, 74(3),* 257–269.

Cesari, P., & Milanese, C. (1995). What can we learn from mistakes? *Coaching and Sport Science Journal, 1,* 19–28.

Chow, J. Y., Davids, K., Button, C., Renshaw, I., Shuttleworth, R., & Uehara, L. (2009). Non-linear pedagogy: Implications for teaching games for understanding. In T. Hopper, J. Butler, & B. Storey (eds), *TGfU: Simply good pedagogy: Understanding a complex challenge* (pp. 131–157). Ottawa, ON: PHE Canada.

Chow, J. Y., Davids, K., Button, C., Shuttleworth, R., Renshaw, & Araújo, D. (2006). Nonlinear pedagogy: A constraints-led framework for understanding emergence of game play and movement skills. *Nonlinear Dynamics, Psychology, and Life Sciences, 10,* 71–103.

Chow, J. Y., Davids, K., Button, C., Shuttleworth, R., Renshaw, & Araújo, D. (2007). The role of nonlinear pedagogy in physical education. *Review of Educational Research, 77,* 251–278.

Chow, J. Y., Davids, K., Hristovski, R., Araújo, D., & Passos, P. (2011). Nonlinear pedagogy: Learning design for self-organizing neurobiological systems. *New Ideas in Psychology, 29,* 189–200.

Cordovil, R., Araújo, D., Davids, K., Gouveia, L., Barreiros, J., Fernandes, O., & Serpa, S. (2009). The influence of instructions and body-scaling as constraints on decision-making processes in team sports. *European Journal of Sport Science, 9,* 169–179.

Cottyn, J., De Clercq, D., Crombez, G., & Lenoir, M. (2012). The interaction of functional and dysfunctional emotions during balance beam performance. *Research Quarterly for Exercise and Sport, 83,* 300–307.

Davids, K. (2010). The constraints-based approach to motor learning: Implications for a non-linear pedagogy in sport and physical education. In I. Renshaw, K. Davids, & G. J. P. Savelsbergh (eds), *Motor learning in practice: A constraints-led approach* (pp. 3–16). London: Routledge.

Davids, K., Araújo, D., Hristovski, R., Passos, P., & Chow, J. Y. (2012). Ecological dynamics and motor learning in sport. In N. J. Hodges & A. M. Williams (eds). *Skill acquisition in sport: Research, theory and practice* (2nd ed., pp. 112–130). London: Routledge.

Davids, K., Button, C., & Bennett, S. (2008). *Dynamics of skill acquisition: A constraints-led approach.* Champaign, IL: Human Kinetics.

Davids, K., Chow, J. Y., & Shuttleworth, R. (2005). A constraints-based framework for nonlinear pedagogy in physical education. *Journal of Physical Education New Zealand, 38,* 17–29.

Dicks, M., Button, C., & Davids, K. (2010). Examination of gaze behaviors under in situ and video simulation task constraints reveals differences in information pickup for perception and action. *Attention, Perception, & Psychophysics, 72,* 706–720.

Davids, K., Glazier, P., Araújo, D., & Bartlett, R. (2003). Movement systems as dynamical systems: The functional role of variability and its implications for sports medicine. *Sports Medicine, 33,* 245–260.

Diedrich, F. J., & Warren, W. H. (1995). Why change gaits? Dynamics of the walk-run transition. *Journal of Experimental Psychology: Human Perception and Performance, 21,* 183–202.

Ford, P. R., Yates, I., & Williams, A. M. (2010). An analysis of practice activities and instructional behaviours used by youth soccer coaches during practice: Exploring the link between science and application. *Journal of Sports Sciences, 28,* 483–495.

French, K. E., Nevett, M. E., Spurgeon, J. H., Graham, K. C., Rink, J. E., & McPherson, S. L. (1996). Knowledge representation and problem solution in expert and novice youth baseball players. *Research Quarterly for Exercise and Sport, 67,* 386–395.

French, K. E., & Thomas, J. R. (1987). The relation of knowledge development to children's basketball performance. *Journal of Sport Psychology, 9,* 15–32.

Gibson, J. J. (1979). *The ecological approach to visual perception.* Hillsdale, NJ: Lawrence Erlbaum Associates.

Glazier, P., Davids, K., Renshaw, I., & Button, C. (2005). Uncovering the secrets of the Don: Bradman reassessed. *Sport Health, 22,* 16–21.

Gourgoulis, V., Aggeloussis, N., Vezos, N., & Mavromatis, G. (2006). Effect of two different sized hand paddles on the front crawl stroke kinematics. *Journal of Sports Medicine and Physical Fitness, 46,* 232–237.

Gorman, A. D. (2010). Using constraints to enhance decision-making in team sports. In I. Renshaw, K. Davids, & G. Savelsbergh (eds), *Motor learning in practice: A constraints-led approach* (pp. 144–151). London: Routledge.

Guadagnoli, M. A., & Lee, T. D. (2004). Challenge point: A framework for conceptualizing the effects of various practice conditions in motor learning. *Journal of Motor Behavior, 36,* 212–224.

Hadfield, D. (2005). The change challenge: Facilitating self-awareness and improvement in your athletes. In L. Kidman (ed.), *Athlete-centred coaching: Developing inspired and inspiring people* (pp. 31–44). Christchurch, New Zealand: Innovative Print Communications.

Handford, C., Davids, K., Bennett, S., & Button, C. (1997). Skill acquisition in sport: Some applications of an evolving practice ecology. *Journal of Sports Sciences, 15,* 621–640.

Hanin, Y. L. (2007). Emotions in sport: Current issues and perspectives. In G. Tenenbaum & R. C. Eklund (eds), *Handbook of sport psychology* (3rd ed., pp. 31–58). Hoboken, NJ: John Wiley & Sons.

Headrick, J., Davids, K., Renshaw, I., Araújo, A., Passos, P., & Fernandes, O. (2012). Proximity-to-goal as a constraint on patterns of behaviour in attacker-defender dyads in team games. *Journal of Sports Sciences, 30,* 247–253.

Headrick, J., Renshaw, I., Davids, K., Pinder, R. A., & Araújo, D. (2015). The dynamics of expertise acquisition in sport: The role of affective learning design. *Psychology of Sport and Exercise, 16,* 83–90.

Hendry, D. T., Ford, P. R., Williams, A. M., & Hodges, N. J. (2015). Five evidence-based principles of effective practice and instruction. In J. Baker & D. Farrow (eds), *Routledge handbook of sport expertise* (pp. 414–429). London: Routledge.

Hodges, N. J., & Williams, A. M. (2012). *Skill acquisition in sport: Research, theory and practice* (2nd ed.). London: Routledge.

Hristovski, R., Davids, K., Araújo, D., & Button, C. (2006). How boxers decide to punch a target: Emergent behaviour in nonlinear dynamical movement systems. *Journal of Sports Science and Medicine, 5,* 60–73.

Hristovski, R., Davids, K., Araújo, D., & Passos, P. (2011). Constraints-induced emergence of functional novelty in complex neurobiological systems: A basis for creativity in sport. *Nonlinear Dynamics, Psychology, and Life Sciences, 15,* 175–206.

Janelle, C. M., Barba, D. A., Frehlich, S. G., Tennant, L. K., & Cauraugh, J. H. (1997). Maximizing performance feedback effectiveness through videotape replay and a self-controlled learning environment. *Research Quarterly for Exercise and Sport, 68,* 269–279.

Jones, M. V. (2003). Controlling emotions in sport. *The Sport Psychologist, 17,* 471–486.

Kello, C. T., Anderson, G. G., Holden, J. G., & Van Orden, G. C. (2008). The pervasiveness of 1/f scaling in speech reflects the metastable basis of cognition. *Cognitive Science, 32,* 1217–1231.

Kelso, J. A. S. (1995). *Dynamic patterns: The self-organization of brain and behaviour.* Cambridge, MA: MIT Press.

Kelso, J. A. S. (2008). An essay on understanding the mind. *Ecological Psychology, 20,* 180–208.

Kelso, J. A. S. (2012). Multistability and metastability: Understanding dynamic coordination in the brain. *Philosophical Transactions of the Royal Society B, 367,* 906–918.

Knoblich, G., & Flach, R. (2001). Predicting the effects of actions: Interactions of perception and action. *Psychological Science, 12,* 467–472.

LaBar, K. S., & Cabeza, R. (2006). Cognitive neuroscience of emotional memory. *Nature Reviews Neuroscience, 7*, 54–64.

Magill, R. A., & Anderson, D. I. (2014). *Motor learning and control: Concepts and applications* (10th ed.). New York: McGraw-Hill.

McPherson, S. L. (1993). The influence of player experience on problem solving during batting preparation in baseball. *Journal of Sport & Exercise Psychology, 15*, 304–325.

Millar, S.-K. (2014). *Interpersonal and extrapersonal coordination in high-performance rowing* (Doctoral thesis). Auckland University of Technology, Auckland, New Zealand.

Milot, M. H., Marchal-Crespo, L., Green, C. S., Cramer, S. C., & Reinkensmeyer, D. J. (2010). Comparison of error-amplification and haptic-guidance training techniques for learning of a timing-based motor task by healthy individuals. *Experimental Brain Research, 201*, 119–131.

Morriss, C., Bartlett, R., & Fowler, N. (1997). Biomechanical analysis of the men's javelin throw at the 1995 World Championships in Athletics. *New Studies in Athletics, 12*, 31–41.

Moy, B., Renshaw, I., & Davids, K. (2015). The impact of nonlinear pedagogy on physical education teacher education students' intrinsic motivation. *Physical Education and Sport Pedagogy*, 1–22.

Newell, K. M. (1986). Constraints on the development of coordination. In M. G. Wade & H. T. A. Whiting (eds), *Motor skill acquisition in children: Aspects of coordination and control* (pp. 341–360). Dordrecht: Martinus Nijhoff.

Newell, K. M. (2003). Change in motor learning: A coordination and control perspective. *Motriz, Rio Claro, 9*, 1–6.

Newell, K. M., & Valvano, J. (1998). Therapeutic intervention as a constraint in learning and relearning movement skills. *Scandinavian Journal of Occupational Therapy, 5*, 51–57.

Nieuwenhuys, A., & Oudejans, R. R. (2011). Training with anxiety: Short-and long-term effects on police officers' shooting behavior under pressure. *Cognitive Processing, 12*, 277–88.

Oudejans, R. R. D. (2008). Reality based practice under pressure improves handgun shooting performance of police officers. *Ergonomics, 51*, 261–273.

Oudejans, R. R., & Pijpers, J. R. (2009). Training with anxiety has a positive effect on expert perceptual–motor performance under pressure. *The Quarterly Journal of Experimental Psychology, 62*, 1631–1647.

Partington, M., & Cushion, C. (2013). An investigation of the practice activities and coaching behaviors of professional top-level youth soccer coaches. *Scandinavian Journal of Medicine & Science in Sports, 23*, 374–382.

Passos, P., Araújo, D., Davids, K., & Shuttleworth, R. (2008). Manipulating constraints to train decision making in rugby union. *International Journal of Sports Science & Coaching, 3*, 125–140.

Pijpers, J. R., Oudejans, R. R. D., & Bakker, F. C. (2005). Anxiety-induced changes in movement behaviour during the execution of a complex whole-body task. *The Quarterly Journal of Experimental Psychology, 58*, 421–445.

Pinder, R. A., Davids, K., & Renshaw, I. (2012). Metastability and emergent performance of dynamic interceptive actions. *Journal of Science and Medicine in Sport, 15*, 437–443.

Pinder, R. A., Davids, K., Renshaw, I., & Araújo, D. (2011a). Representative learning design and functionality of research and practice in sport. *Journal of Sport & Exercise Psychology, 33*, 146–155.

Pinder, R. A., Davids, K., Renshaw, I., & Araújo, D. (2011b). Manipulating informational constraints shapes movement reorganization in interceptive actions. *Attention, Perception, & Psychophysics, 73*, 1242–1254.

Pinder, R. A., Headrick, J., & Oudejans, R. R. (2015). Issues and challenges in developing representative tasks in sport. In J. Baker & D. Farrow (eds). *The Routledge handbook of sports expertise* (pp. 269–281). London: Routledge.

Post, P. G., Fairbrother, J. T., & Barros, J. A. C. (2011). Self-controlled amount of practice benefits learning of a motor skill. *Research Quarterly for Exercise and Sport, 82*, 474–481.

Renshaw, I., Chappell, G. S., Fitzgerald, D., Davison, J., & McFadyen, B. (2010a). *The battle zone: Constraint-led coaching in action.* Paper presented at the Conference of Science, Medicine, & Coaching in Cricket, Sheraton Mirage, Gold Coast, Queensland: Australia. pp. 181–184.

Renshaw, I., Davids, K., & Savelsbergh, G. J. P. (eds). (2010b). *Motor learning in practice: A constraints-led approach.* London: Routledge.

Renshaw, I., Davids, K., Shuttleworth, R., & Chow, J. Y. (2009). Insights from ecological psychology and dynamic systems theory can underpin a philosophy of coaching. *International Journal of Sport Psychology, 40*, 580–602.

Renshaw, I., Headrick, J., & Davids, K. (2014). *Affective learning design: Building emotions into representative learning design*. Paper presented at the International Conference on Complex Systems and Applications, Le Havre, France.

Renshaw, I., Oldham, A. R. H., & Bawden, M. (2012). Nonlinear pedagogy underpins intrinsic motivation in sports coaching. *The Open Sports Sciences Journal, 5*, 88–99.

Renshaw, I., Oldham, A. R., Davids, K., & Golds, T. (2007). Changing ecological constraints of practice alters coordination of dynamic interceptive actions. *European Journal of Sport Science, 7*, 157–167.

Rivilla-Garcia, J., Grande, I., Sampedro, J., & Van Den Tillaar, R. (2011). Influence of opposition on ball velocity in the handball jump throw. *Journal of Sports Science & Medicine, 10*, 534–539.

Robins, M., Wheat, J., Irwin, G., & Bartlett, R. (2006). The effect of shooting distance on movement variability in basketball. *Journal of Human Movement Studies, 50*, 217–238.

Rojas, F. J., Cepero, M., Oña, A., & Gutierrez, M. (2000). Kinematic adjustments in the basketball jump shot against an opponent. *Ergonomics, 43*, 1651–1660.

Royal, K. A., Farrow, D., Mujika, I., Halson, S., Pyne, D., & Abernethy, B. (2006). The effects of fatigue on decision making and shooting skill performance in water polo players. *Journal of Sports Sciences, 24*, 807–815.

Sanli, E. A., Patterson, J. T., Bray, S. R., & Lee, T. D. (2013). Understanding self-controlled motor learning protocols through the self-determination theory. *Frontiers in Psychology, 3*, 1–17.

Savelsbergh, G. J. P., Kamper, W. J., Rabius, J., De Koning, J. J., & Schöllhorn, W. (2010). A new method to learn to start in speed skating: A differential learning approach. *International Journal of Sport Psychology, 41*, 415–427.

Schöllhorn, W. I., Beckmann, H., Janssen, D., & Drepper, J. (2010). Stochastic perturbations in athletics field events enhance skill acquisition. In I. Renshaw, K. Davids, & G. J. P. Savelsbergh (eds), *Motor learning in practice: A constraints-led approach* (pp. 69–82). London: Routledge.

Schöllhorn, W. I., Beckmann, H., Michelbrink, M., Sechelmann, M., Trockel, M., & Davids, K. (2006). Does noise provide the basis for the unification of motor learning theories? *International Journal of Sport Psychology, 37*, 186–206.

Schöllhorn, W. I., Hegen, P., & Davids, K. (2012). The nonlinear nature of learning: A differential learning approach. *The Open Sports Sciences Journal, 5*, 100–112.

Schöllhorn, W. I., Mayer-Kress, G., Newell, K. M., & Michelbrink, M. (2009). Time scales of adaptive behavior and motor learning in the presence of stochastic perturbations. *Human Movement Science, 28*, 319–333.

Vast, R. L., Young, R. L., & Thomas, P. R. (2010). Emotions in sport: Perceived effects on attention, concentration, and performance. *Australian Psychologist, 45*, 132–140.

Williams, A. M., & Ford, P. R. (2008). Expertise and expert performance in sport. *International Review of Sport and Exercise Psychology, 1*, 4–18.

Williams, A. M., & Ford, P. R. (2009). Promoting a skills-based agenda in Olympic sports: The role of skill-acquisition specialists. *Journal of Sports Sciences, 27*, 1381–1392.

Williams, A. M., Ford, P., Causer, J., Logan, O., & Murray, S. (2012). Translating theory into practice: Working at the 'coal face' in the UK! In N. J. Hodges & A. M. Williams (eds), *Skill acquisition in sport: Research, theory and practice* (pp. 353–366). London: Routledge.

Williams, A. M., & Hodges, N. J. (2005). Practice, instruction and skill acquisition in soccer: Challenging tradition. *Journal of Sports Sciences, 23*, 637–650.

Wilson, C., Simpson, S.E., van Emmerik, R.E.A., & Hamill, J. (2008). Coordination variability and skill development in expert triple jumpers. *Sports Biomechanics, 7*, 2–9.

Wulf, G. (2007). Self-controlled practice enhances motor learning: Implications for physiotherapy. *Physiotherapy, 93*, 96–101.

23

UNDERSTANDING DROPOUT IN THE ATHLETE DEVELOPMENT PROCESS

Carsten Hvid Larsen and Dorothee Alfermann

The path to and transition into the senior elite ranks is successfully mastered by only a tiny minority of athletes. And the question arises: what distinguishes those who make it to the top from those who give up prematurely? Which resources, which abilities, which environmental supports are necessary to cope with the ever increasing demands of elite sports? For a long time, there has been growing interest in talent identification and development in elite sport. Athletic talent was seen from related but different perspectives, namely the biological, psychological, and social. From the biological perspective, talent refers to an athlete's innate potential or giftedness. The psychological perspective views talent as the athlete's acquired abilities, competencies and skills that facilitate athletic performance and help achieve athletic excellence in the chosen sport. Finally, talent can be understood in relation to interactions in the specific talent development environment (Stambulova, 2009). Each of these perspectives guides how coaches or sport psychology practitioners work with athletes and additionally each of these perspectives is related to dropout. Along these lines, dropout is related to how coaches and significant others understand talent. In this chapter, we do not outline a biological perspective related to dropout (for an overview see Martindale & Mortimer, 2011), but instead focus on psychological and social factors.

The talent development process and continuation in elite sport is about handling the diverse challenges of everyday life (Holt & Dunn, 2004). Adolescence is the period of life when investing in great performance should be achieved. These phases of development are especially demanding, and athletes experience a large amount of pressure in school and sport (Brettschneider, 1999). Besides coping with psychological and personal challenges in their careers, young talented athletes are expected to balance what are often conflicting demands of sports and school (Christensen & Sorensen, 2009). Dropout is a phenomenon among athletes in childhood and adolescence due to high demands and expectations in sport from clubs, sporting organizations in elite sport as well as out of sport from parents, peers and school.

The purpose of this chapter is to summarize the research and to broaden our understanding of dropout in the athlete development process. First, we provide a description of different terminologies related to dropout. Second, we describe dropout as a mismatch between resources and demands. Third, we look into personal, lifestyle and sporting reasons associated with dropout. Fourth, we outline athletes' characteristics associated with dropout. Fifth, we describe coaches' and parents' contributions to dropout and subsequently illustrate further environmental factors associated with dropout. Sixth, we provide a summary of factors that prevent dropout and promote continuation; and seventh and finally, we provide strategies, applied perspectives and recommendations for how to prevent dropout of athletes.

Different terminologies of dropout

The transition to senior elite level is considered the hardest in elite sport and young talented athletes need to cope with demands in and out of sport. When reviewing the literature, several different terminologies are used to describe dropout. Therefore, understanding dropout in the athlete development process involves grasping a hold of the many different terminologies and their relationship to discontinuation of the career or dropout. The term *attrition* in sport is the prolonged absence of systematic practice and competition, either in one sport (sport-specific attrition) or all sports and largely social in nature (Balish, McLaren, Rainham, & Blanchard, 2014). The term *burnout* is related to athletes feeling extremely emotionally and physically exhausted which typically leads to affective, cognitive, motivational and behavioral consequences (Gustafsson, Kenttä, Hassmén, & Lundqvist, 2007). The term *retirement* is also commonly used and refers to athletes who voluntarily decide to leave the sport either for having achieved their sport goals or for reasons of having reached a certain age (Alfermann, 1995). Typically retired athletes are older than dropouts in the same sport and the antecedents and the consequences of career termination point to the central role of the time of termination, the preparation for termination, and the athletes' resources like self-concept and well-being. The term *dropout* or *discontinuation* refers to a premature termination of a sport career before the athlete could reach his or her peak performance level in the respective sport (Alfermann & Stambulova, 2007). As the age for peak performance in most sports is in early adulthood, career termination in childhood and adolescence is regarded as premature and the athlete is thus categorized as a dropout (Baron-Thiene & Alfermann, 2015).

Dropout: A mismatch between an athlete's resources and the career demands?

The development of an athlete's career is typically regarded as a sequence of stages where athletes progress from the developmental to the mastery phase (Salmela, 1994) or, as Côté, Baker and Abernethy (2007) put it, from the specializing to the investment years. As emphasized by these and other developmental models of athletic careers (summarized in Alfermann & Stambulova, 2007), the transition from one stage to the next can be facilitated or hindered by internal and external (environmental) factors. Alfermann and Stambulova emphasize that a match between an athlete's resources and the demands of a career transition will allow an athlete to enjoy a successful transition whereas a mismatch is likely to result in a crisis transition and subsequently dropout. Two different categories of dropouts can be differentiated, namely self-controlled (internal) and externally controlled (forced) dropout (Gould, 1987). Resources in the transition are defined as internal and external factors that may facilitate the transition process and help to cope with dropout. Internal resources are, for example, previous coping experiences, skills, and self-esteem, whereas external resources are primarily social, physical and financial support. Barriers for transitions also include all internal and external factors that obstruct the effective management of the transition such as lack of skills and competencies, conflicts with coaches or other athletes, difficulties balancing school and sports. In that sense, when the athletes' resources do not match transition demands it could mean dropout from the sport.

Alfermann and Stambulova emphasized that identifying strategies may be useful for helping athletes to cope with transition demands, and that successful transitions often are related to four S's that influence transitions. These factors are situation, self, support and strategies. 1) *Situation* refers to the characteristics of the event, or non–event, that causes the transition to happen. For example, looking at the different reasons for dropout. Was the transition or withdrawal instigated from the athlete, coach or other? Situation also indicates that stressors and duration of transition (e.g., two weeks or several months) can influence the outcomes. 2) *Self* refers to the personal characteristics and psychological resources that athletes may have and how these influence transition. An example could be which characteristics (e.g., resources, skills) and shortfalls does the athlete have, and what does that mean in terms of how they negotiate the transition? 3) *Support* refers to the environment and thereby who and what assists the athletes through the transition. Support could be from the family, coaches, managers, teammates, friendships outside of sport (e.g., school) or organizations. 4) *Strategies* refer to how the athlete searches for information and prepares for the upcoming transition. Each of the four S's influence transitions and is therefore important for continuation or dropout in sport. In the following, we will provide a description of the four S's related to dropout.

Situation: Reasons and constraints associated to dropout

Dropout is regarded as a complex phenomenon with a multi-causal history (Alfermann, 2014). Research shows that it makes a difference for an athlete if the decision for dropout happens to be voluntary or involuntary. Very often, athletes make an easier transition to the post-career if they see it as the result of a voluntary retreat that they had planned for. Therefore, researchers and practitioners are concerned with the reasons for dropout, its prevention, and athletes' coping efforts. Crane and Temple's (2015) review of dropout in sport recently indicated that intrapersonal and interpersonal constraints are more frequently associated with dropping out than structural constraints, across five major areas: lack of enjoyment, perceptions of competence, social pressures, competing priorities and physical factors (maturation and injuries). Rarely were the interrelationships between factors or the underlying dimensions of factors examined. It is often the case, that dropout is perceived as either a problem related to the athlete (intrapersonal) or the system (interpersonal). However, following the conclusions from Crane and Temple, we like to point to the fact that continuation in the athlete development process and the transition to elite level is related to coordinated efforts in the system (or environment) and not one single person or issue at hand (Henriksen, Stambulova, & Roessler, 2010; Larsen, 2013). Therefore, the following description of the areas (e.g., self, support) should not be perceived individually but as a whole, and reasons for dropout are not necessarily singular but complex and interconnected. Reasons for dropout could be categorized into three areas related to interpersonal and intrapersonal issues: personal, lifestyle, and sporting reasons (Tinsley, 2015).

Personal and lifestyle reasons

During their sporting career, young athletes are developing in four areas (Wylleman & Lavallee, 2004): besides the athletic level there is also the psychological, the psychosocial, and the academic/vocational level that has to be considered. Each of these levels comprises transitions from one stage to another which may result either in successful transitions or alternatively in crisis transitions and subsequent dropout. The developmental model also describes a multitude of demands and expectations from different areas and persons. For instance, an athlete being involved in secondary education would meet demands and expectations to succeed in school and at the same time to succeed in sport. What seems to be an issue for young athletes is the combination of demands and expectations from several areas at the same time, while the athlete is also developing on a personal level (e.g., developing gender role identity). In that sense athletes are doing at least two full-time jobs (e.g., school and sport) while going through a time of their life in which they are about to decide about their future. Some of the personal reasons (both in and out of sport) for dropout also include shifting priorities, as athletes get older, become more mature, develop psychologically or start to ask themselves questions on the meaning of life (e.g., existential issues), which may or may not have something to do with normative or non-normative transitions. For example, for a girl at the age of 16, interests and priorities may have changed compared to prepuberty, and social relationships may now become the number one interest (Tinsley, 2015). Puberty is a very important time in an adolescent's life and developmental tasks like interest stabilization, peer relationships, gender role development, and planning the future have to be solved. There comes a time when the athlete has to decide what to continue and what to give up. If athletes have experiences that would make them doubt the benefits of sport, then sport would lose against other interests, as each person has many interests, but limited time. A study from Sport England (2012) showed that the most significant reasons for dropping out of sport were: time constraints, work commitments or getting older. Alongside these personal issues related to lifestyle, young athletes are no longer able to combine school education with the high demands of sport training and competitions (Alfermann, 2014; Baron-Thiene & Alfermann, 2015). They therefore finish their career in order to give priority to their education. Also, young athletes may realize that they lack the potential to make it to the top and perceive any further investment in their career as a waste of time. This feeling may be heightened by performance slumps—particularly during or after puberty—and by motivational crises, particularly after injuries.

Sporting reasons

Sporting reasons are related to the system surrounding the athlete. This includes persons associated with the sport (e.g., coach, parents) but also demands and expectations from being part of the sport. Fraser-Thomas, Côté, and Deakin (2008a, 2008b) identified several sporting reasons for dropping out of swimming, which included lack of fun and unstructured swimming play, less one-on-one coaching throughout development, and fewer activities besides swimming. In addition, fewer dropouts had taken time off during their careers than engaged athletes, while dropouts had earlier 'top in club' status and started dry land training significantly earlier than engaged athletes. On a more personal and interpersonal level, dropouts experienced competing social pressures, difficulties in coping with the transition from junior to senior, and differences with coach personalities and conflicts with the coaches.

Related to talent identifications and coaches, the relative age effect (RAE) suggests that athletes born in the first two quartiles of a given selection year experience a selection advantage and therefore a greater opportunity for continuation in elite sport. Studies have shown that early-born youth players are more likely to be identified as talented and to be exposed to a higher level of coaching than their late-born counterparts. Along these lines, researchers have established the relationship between relative age and dropout across different sports (e.g., ice hockey: Lemez, Baker, Horton, Wattie, & Weir, 2014) and sport clubs (Wattie et al., 2014). Another sporting reason for dropout could also be associated with involvement and specialization in sport. While early involvement in deliberate practice has been associated with expert performance among some athletes (e.g., Ward, Hodges, Williams, & Starkes, 2004), it has also been linked to dropout (e.g., Wall and Côté, 2007).

All in all, the literature suggests that reasons for dropping out of sport are not necessarily under the control of the individual person. Demographic reasons (relative age), city size (Imtiaz, Hancock, Vierimaa, & Côté, 2014), national reputation of sports, traveling distance to training facilities or just luck may all contribute to an athlete's successful versus unsuccessful sport career.

Self: Personal characteristics and resources associated with dropout

Literature on career transitions highlights that a match between an athlete's resources and the demands of a transition will allow an athlete to enjoy a successful transition whereas a mismatch is likely to result in a crisis transition (Alfermann & Stambulova, 2007; Stambulova, 2009). A key internal factor for career development is the athlete's psychological makeup (e.g., resources or skills) (MacNamara, Button, & Collins, 2010) which allows athletes to cope with the demands of transitions (Alfermann & Stambulova 2007; Stambulova, 2009). Durand-Bush and Salmela (2002) interviewed ten world-class athletes from Canada, all of whom emphasized 'personal attributes such as self-confidence, motivation, and competitiveness' (p. 162) as prerequisites for a successful career. Gould, Dieffenbach, and Moffitt (2002) reported the results of a study that included quantitative measures and interviews with ten US Olympic medalists; motivation (setting and achieving goals; possessing a strong work ethic) and self-confidence were mentioned as essential characteristics for a successful sport career. Bußmann and Alfermann (1994) demonstrated that, compared to non-dropouts, female junior track and field athletes who dropped out not only perceived competitions during their active sport career as less challenging and enjoyable, but they also reported more physical complaints. A recent study in personal characteristics revealed that motivation and volition were contributing factors for adolescent athletes to remain active in their sport (Baron-Thiene & Alfermann, 2015).

Together these studies illustrate that self-confidence and motivation are essential individual characteristics for sport career continuation. However, recently there have been calls for a holistic skills package associated with developing excellence and continuation in sport. Holt and colleagues' study of young talented football players on the verge of making a breakthrough into professional ranks (Holt & Dunn, 2004) and on the verge of not making it into the professional ranks (Holt & Mitchell, 2006) revealed that specific sets of psychological characteristics are associated with making a successful transition into elite football; a set of skills that does not correspond with the skills needed to succeed at the elite level. Moreover, MacNamara et al. (2010) suggest that the delivery of sport psychology services to young athletes should acknowledge that the skills needed to reach the elite level are different from the skills needed to succeed at elite level. They therefore introduced a distinction between psychological characteristics of excellence (PCE, e.g., self regulation, coping under pressure) and psychological characteristics of developing excellence (PCDE, e.g., commitment, social skills, goal setting).

Support: Coaches, parents and environmental factors associated with dropout

Summarizing the literature, reasons for dropping out of sport are not necessarily under control of the individual person; coaches, parents and other environmental factors are associated with dropout. To be able to cope with transitions requires a good support system around the athlete. In that sense, it is important that coaches, parents and peers create a positive environment for the athlete to pursue a dual career as well as make the transitions during the career. Coaches can positively influence an athlete's psychological development by using appropriate reinforcement and encouragement (Côté, 2002). With increasing age and maturity, athletes spend relatively more time with coaches and their relationship is important for the athletes' enjoy-ment and continuation (Côté, 2002) but on the other hand also for dropout. Barnett, Smoll, and Smith (1992) found out that when coaches were trained to increase interaction, intra-team cohesion and to promote participation as an achievement rather than failure, athletes dropped out significantly less than when coaches did not receive training. Fraser-Thomas and colleagues (2008a, 2008b) research in swimming showed that dropouts spoke of coaches ignoring weaker swimmers in favor of top swimmers, while engaged swimmers recognized that subtle favoritism did exist, but everyone still received individualized attention. Boiché and Sarrazin's (2009) study on proximal and more distal psychological antecedents of the dropout revealed that continua-tion and satisfaction were positively predicted by coach's investment and coach's mastery climate, and negatively by conflicts of interest and goal conflict with teammates and the coach. Moreover, a democratic coaching style and mature coach–athlete conversations during adoles-cence may also prevent athletes from dropping out (Pelletier, Fortier, Vallerand, & Brière, 2001; Wright & Côté, 2003).

Looking beyond climate and coaching style, coach personality is also related to dropout. Fraser-Thomas and colleagues (2008a, 2008b) revealed that during the athlete development process coaches may be regarded as being no longer supportive, and athletes would feel forced to leave the training group on the whole. Subsequently, leaving the training group would mean leaving the sport system and financial support may be withdrawn (Alfermann, 2014). The Developmental Model of Sport Participation (DMSP) also suggests the importance of recipro-cal coach–athlete respect during the adolescent years. While engaged athletes often experienced this type of relationship (e.g., their coaches communicated openly with them about their dropout considerations), no dropout athletes remembered similar experiences.

Parents' contribution to dropout

Similar to the coach, the family has an important influence on continuation and dropout. Research on the role of the family in talent development obviously shows that parents' support is positively coherent with joy and enthusiasm (Power & Woolger, 1994) and a high family involvement are related to achieving physical competence (Brustad, 1993) as well as relieving stress (VanYperen, 1995). On the other hand, other studies have shown that parental expecta-tions can become a source of stress and pressure that can interfere with participation and continuation in sport (Weiss, Wiese & Klint, 1989). In that sense, families could create a less positive impact when they become over-involved in their child's sport and put unreasonable pressure on their child to achieve (Barber & Sukhi, 1998; Brown & Branta, 1988; Fraser-Thomas et al., 2008a, 2008b). In addition, family constellation (e.g., one supportive parent in the family) and social class play an important role. Children of lower social class are under-represented at high levels of sports achievement (Duncan, 1997). It can be shown that, in addition to providing essential financial resources, families' abilities to accommodate the activ-ity patterns required by the sport are critical to children's participation and continuation in sport (Kay, 2000).

Further environmental factors associated with dropout

Successful athletic talent development environments in sport are teams or clubs that manage to continually produce senior elite athletes from among their juniors. Within an ecological perspective, researchers have in the recent years expanded our notion of which factors influ-ence the likelihood of a young athlete making it to the elite senior level in individual

(Henriksen, Stambulova, & Roessler, 2010, 2011) and team sports (Larsen, Alfermann, Henriksen, & Christensen, 2013; Storm, 2015). These researchers look beyond the individual athlete's innate preconditions as well as beyond the amount and characteristics of his or her training, and include the entire environment in which the athlete is embedded into their understanding of successful talent development and thereby continuation in sport. On the other hand, less successful environments are teams or clubs that despite favorable conditions rarely if ever manage to help their junior athletes make a successful transition to the senior elite level. Following these lines, a less successful talent development environment does not support the athletes to make the transitions followed by a potential dropout. Recently, Henriksen, Larsen, and Christensen (2014) looked into a golf academy team in Denmark with limited success in producing senior elite athletes from among its juniors. This environment shared a number of features on the opposite pole of successful environments and in particular high-lighting a culture that was incoherent, and whose espoused values did not match actual behavior. Supporting these notions, Le Bars, Gernigon, and Ninot (2009) study on elite young judokas revealed that dropouts perceived the roles of coaches, parents, and peers as less task-involving and less task-oriented. These results stress the importance for all the agents of the athletes' social environment to promote task-involving environments, because such environments appear to be associated to persistence and continuation in elite sport.

Strategies: Applied perspectives and recommendations for preventing dropout

The purpose of this chapter was to unfold different factors and characteristics associated to dropout. Specifically, to look into the different elements that has a consequence for continuation and to illustrate factors or characteristics that prevent the premature termination of a sport career before the athlete reaches his or her peak performance level in the respective sport. The different sections of this chapter highlight several factors that are relevant for continuation in sport and thus actions that could minimize dropout. Table 23.1 summarizes the range of factors that promote continuation in sport.

Research highlights that practitioners should: provide the young athletes with a holistic skills package containing a variety of psychosocial characteristics to enable them stay motivated during the career but also to handle challenges in the transition from junior to senior level; prioritize and plan their daily life; balance sport, school, social life and recovery; and be able to use the professional athletes as a resource. Alongside, staying motivated and handling the transitions during their career, there is a need for acknowledging that the athletes' priorities shift across the career. This extends to the notion that the practitioner, coach and environment should take an interest in the young athlete as a whole person and provide services that help the young athletes to manage the multitude of existential challenges and choices involved in being an athlete, a student, a son or daughter, a boyfriend or girlfriend, and so on (Nesti, 2004).

Looking beyond the athlete's individual resources, researchers highlight that continuation in the athlete development process and the transition to elite level is related to coordinated efforts in the system and reasons for dropout are not necessarily singular but complex and interconnected. Reasons for dropout are related to organizational and structural issues such as RAE, town size and specialization that need to be a focal point for managers and coaches alike. Moving beyond the organization, most career assistance programs aim to build such resources in the athletes, and most programs are also based on the general idea of a practitioner (sport psychologist or other) teaching the athletes skills and preparing them for the adversity to come (see Petitpas & Champagne, 2000). The holistic ecological approach opens new avenues and inspires coaches and practitioners to work with the individual athletes athletic development, as

Table 23.1 Summary of perspectives that promote continuation in sport

Factors related to dropout	Key perspectives to promote continuation (and prevent dropout)
Transition from one stage to the next	Important to create a match between an athlete's resources and the demands of a career transition (a mismatch is likely to result in a crisis transition and subsequently dropout).
Two different categories of dropouts	It is important to be aware that dropout is self-controlled (internal) and/or externally controlled (forced).
4 S's	Successful transitions (and continuation) is related to: (1) *situation* (how is the situation experienced by the athlete); (2) *self* (the athlete's personality); (3) *support* (access to various types of support); and (4) *strategies* (how the athlete searches for information and prepares for the upcoming transition).
Intrapersonal and interpersonal constraints	Intrapersonal and interpersonal constraints are more frequently associated with dropping out than structural constraints across five major areas: lack of enjoyment, perceptions of competence, social pressures, competing priorities and physical factors (maturation and injuries).
Young athletes are developing in four areas	The career is associated with development in the athletic, psychological, psychosocial, and academic/vocational level. Each of these levels comprises transitions from one stage to another, which may result either in successful transitions or alternatively in crisis transitions and subsequent dropout.
Demands and expectations in several areas of life	An athlete being involved in secondary education is confronted with demands and expectations to succeed in school and at the same time to succeed in sport. What seems to be an issue for young athletes is the combination of demands and expectations from several areas at the same time, while the athlete is also developing on a personal level.
Existential issues	Puberty is a very important time in an adolescent's life and developmental tasks like interest stabilization, peer relationships, gender role development and planning the future have to be solved.
Athletes' characteristics	A key internal factor for career development is the athlete's psychological make-up (e.g., resources or skills) which allows athletes to cope with the demands of transitions and continuation in sport. Self-confidence and motivation are essential individual characteristics for sport career continuation.
The relative age effect (RAE)	Athletes born in the first two quartiles of a given selection year experience a selection advantage and therefore a greater opportunity for continuation in elite sport. Therefore it is important to also support athletes born in the final two quartiles of a selection year.
Coaching style and climate	A democratic coaching style and mature coach–athlete conversations during adolescence may also prevent athletes from dropping out. Moreover, continuation and satisfaction is positively predicted by coach's investment and coach's mastery climate, and negatively by conflicts of interest and goal conflict with teammates and the coach.
Parental support	Parents' support is positively correlated with joy and enthusiasm and a high family involvement are related to achieving physical competence as well as relieving stress. Parental expectations can also become a source of stress and pressure that can interfere with participation and continuation in sport if they are over-involved in their child's sport and put unreasonable pressure on their child to achieve.

Table 23.1 continued

Factors related to dropout	Key perspectives to promote continuation (and prevent dropout)
The athletic environment	Less successful talent development environments do not support the athletes to make the transitions and share a number of features on the opposite pole of successful environments. Successful environments in particular represent a culture that is coherent, and whose espoused values match actual behavior.

well as be sensitive to, analyze and work with the athletes, to create an environment that is supportive of the athletes' development (Larsen, Alfermann, Henriksen, & Christensen, 2014); and career assistance programmes could involve the athletes' environment to their advantage.

Understanding dropout in the athlete development process is complex. This chapter has summarized the latest research in dropout. We have clarified the different terminologies associated with dropout and moreover described dropout related to factors such as a mismatch between resources and demands, related to personal, lifestyle and sporting reasons, athletes' characteristics (as well as those of their coaches and parents), environmental factors associated with dropout, and finally illustrated the need for strategies for how to prevent dropout of athletes. In the future, practitioners and researchers need to be aware of the amount of factors (and their interrelatedness) that affect the athlete's development and try to create united strategies that support and provide the athlete, coaches, parents and other agents in the environment with skills to successfully negotiate transitions across the career.

References

Alfermann, D. (1995). Career transitions of elite athletes: Drop-out and retirement. In R. Vanfraechem-Raway & Y. Vanden Auweele (eds), *Proceedings of the 9th European Congress of Sport Psychology* (Part II, pp. 828–833). Brussels: European Federation of Sport Psychology FEPSAC.

Alfermann, D. (2014). Drop-out. In R. Eklund, & G. Tenenbaum (eds), *Encyclopedia of sport and exercise psychology.* (Vol. 4, pp. 216–217). Thousand Oaks, CA: Sage. doi: http://dx.doi.org/10.4135/9781483332222.n88

Alfermann, D., & Stambulova, N. (2007). Career transitions and career termination. In G. Tenenbaum & R. C. Ecklund. (eds). *Handbook of sport psychology* (pp. 712–733). Hoboken, NJ: John Wiley & Sons.

Balish, S. M., McLaren, C., Rainham, D., & Blanchard, C. (2014). Correlates of youth sport attrition: A review and future directions. *Psychology of Sport and Exercise, 15*, 429–439. doi: 10.1016/j.psychsport.2014.04.003

Barnett, N. P., Smoll, F. L., & Smith, R. E. (1992). Effects of enhancing coach-athlete relationships on youth sport attrition. *The Sport Psychologist, 2*, 111–127. Retrieved from http://journals.humankinetics.com/tsp

Barber, H., & Sukhi, H. (1998). The Influence of Parent-Coaches on Participant Motivation and Competitive Anxiety in Youth Sports Participants, *Journal of Sports Behaviour 22*, 162–180.

Baron-Thiene, A., & Alfermann, D. (2015). Personal characteristics as predictors for dual career dropout versus continuation: A prospective study of adolescent athletes from German elite sport schools. *Psychology of Sport and Exercise, 21*, 42–49. dx.doi.org/10.1016/j.psychsport.2015.04.006

Boiché, J., & Sarrazin, P. (2009). Proximal and distal factors associated with dropout out versus maintained participation in organized sport. *Journal of Sports Science and Medicine, 8*, 9–16.

Brettschneider, W. D. (1999). Risks and opportunities: Adolescents in top-level sport – growing up with the pressures of school and training. *European Physical Education Review, 5*, 121–133. doi: 10.1177/1356336X990052004

Brown, E. W., & Branta, C. F. (1988). *Competitive sport for children and youth.* Champaign, IL: Human Kinetics.

Brustad, R. J. (1993). Who will go out and play? Parental and psychological influences on children's attraction to physical activity. *Pediactric Exercise Science, 5,* 210–223.

Bußmann, G., & Alfermann, D. (1994). Drop-out and the female athlete. A study with track and field athletes. In D. Hackfort (ed.), *Psycho-social issues and interventions in elite sports* (pp. 89–129). Frankfurt: Lang.

Christensen, M. K., & Soerensen, J. K. (2009). Sport or school? Dreams and dilemmas for talented young Danish football players. *European Physical Education Review, 15,* 115–133. doi: 10.1177/ 1356336X09105214

Côté, J. (2002). Coach and peer influence on children's development through sport. In J. M. Silva & D. Stevens (eds), *Psychological foundations of sport* (pp. 520–540). Boston, MA: Allyn and Bacon.

Côté, J., Baker, J., & Abernethy, B. (2007). Practice and play in the development of sport expertise. In G. Tenenbaum & R. C. Eklund (eds), *Handbook of sport psychology* (3rd ed., pp. 184–202). Hoboken, NJ: Wiley.

Crane, J., & Temple, V. (2015). A systematic review of dropout from organized sport among children and youth. *European Physical Education Review, 21,* 114–131.

Duncan, J. (1997). Focus group interviews with elite young athletes, coaches and parents. In J. Kremer, K. Trew and S. Ogle (eds), *Young people's involvement in sport* (pp. 217–229). London: Routledge.

Durand-Bush, N., & Salmela, J. H. (2002). The development and maintenance of expert athletic performance: Perceptions of world and Olympic champions. *Journal of Applied Sport Psychology, 14,* 154–171. doi:10.1080/10413200290103473

Fraser-Thomas, J., Côté, J., & Deakin, J. (2008a). Examining adolescent sport dropout and prolonged engagement from a developmental perspective. *Journal of Applied Sport Psychology, 20,* 318–333. doi: 10.1080/10413200802163549

Fraser-Thomas, J., Côté, J., & Deakin, J. (2008b). Understanding dropout and prolonged engagement in adolescent competitive sport. *Psychology of Sport and Exercise, 9,* 645–662.

Gould, D. (1987). Understanding attrition in children's sport. In D. Gould & M. R. Weiss (eds), *Advances in pediatric sport sciences. Vol. 2: Behavioral issues* (pp. 61–85). Champaign, IL: Human Kinetics.

Gould, D., Dieffenbach, K., & Moffitt, A. (2002). Psychological characteristics and their development in Olympic champions. *Journal of Applied Sport Psychology, 14,* 172–204. doi:10.1080/ 10413200290103482

Gustafsson, H., Kenttä, G., Hassmén. P., & Lundqvist, C. (2007). Prevalence of burnout in adolescent competitive athletes. *The Sport Psychologist, 21,* 21–37. Retrieved from http://journals.humankinetics.com/tsp

Henriksen, K., Stambulova, N., & Roessler, K. K. (2010). A holistic approach to athletic talent development environments: A successful sailing milieu. *Psychology of Sport and Exercise, 11,* 212–222. doi: 10.1016/j.psychsport.2009.10.005

Henriksen, K., Stambulova, N., & Roessler, K. K. (2011). Riding the wave of an expert: A successful talent development environment in kayaking. *The Sport Psychologist, 25,* 341–362. Retrieved from http://journals.humankinetics.com/tsp

Henriksen, K., Larsen, C. H., & Christensen, M. K. (2014). Looking at success from its opposite pole: The case of a talent development golf environment in Denmark. *International Journal of Sport and Exercise Psychology, 12,* 134–149. doi: 10.1080/1612197X.2013.853473

Holt, N. L., & Dunn, J. G. H. (2004). Toward a grounded theory of the psychosocial competencies and environmental conditions associated with soccer success. *Journal of Applied Sport Psychology, 16,* 199–219. doi: 10.1080/10413200490437949

Holt, N. L., & Mitchell, T. (2006). Talent development in English professional soccer. *International Journal of Sport Psychology, 37,* 77–98. Retrieved from ISI:000241600700002

Imtiaz, F., Hancock, D. J., Vierimaa, M., & Côté, J. (2014). Place of development and dropout in youth ice hockey, *International Journal of Sport and Exercise Psychology, 12,* 234–244, doi: 10.1080/ 1612197X.2014.880262

Kay, T. (2000). Sporting excellence: A family affair? *European Physical Education Review, 6,* 151–169. doi: 10.1177/1356336X000062004

Larsen, C. H. (2013). *Made in Denmark: Ecological perspectives on talent development and sport psychology in professional football.* (Doctoral thesis). Institute of Sport Science and Clinical Biomechanics, University of Southern Denmark. Retrieved from www.teamdanmark.dk/~/media/Files/PhD%20 Carsten%20Hvid%20Larsen%202013.pdf

Larsen, C. H., Alfermann, D., Henriksen, K., & Christensen, M. K. (2013). Successful talent development in soccer: The characteristics of the environment. *Sport, Exercise and Performance Psychology, 2,* 190–206. doi: 10.1037/a0031958

Larsen, C. H., Alfermann, D., Henriksen, K., & Christensen, M. K. (2014). Preparing footballers for the next step. An intervention program from an ecological perspective. *The Sport Psychologist, 28,* 91–102. Retrieved from http://journals.humankinetics.com/tsp

Le Bars, H., Gernigon, C., & Ninot, G. (2009). Personal and contextual determinants of elite young athletes' persistence or dropping out over time. *Scandinavian Journal of Medicine and Science in Sports, 19,* 274–285. doi: 10.1111/j.1600-0838.2008.00786.x

Lemez, S., Baker, J., Horton, S., Wattie, N., & Weir, P. (2014). Examining the relationship between relative age, competition level, and dropout rates in male youth ice-hockey players. *Scandinavian Journal of Medicine and Science in Sports, 24,* 935–942. doi: 10.1111/sms.12127

MacNamara, Á., Button, A., & Collins, D. (2010). The role of psychological characteristics in facilitating the pathway to elite performance. Part 1: Identifying mental skills and behaviors. *The Sport Psychologist, 24,* 52–73. Retrieved from http://journals.humankinetics.com/tsp

Martindale, R., & Mortimer, P. (2011). Talent development environments: Key considerations for effective practice. In D. Collins, H. Richards, & A. Button (eds), *Performance psychology* (pp. 61–77). Kidlington: Elsevier.

Nesti, M. (2004). *Existential psychology and sport: Theory and applications.* New York: Routledge.

Pelletier, L. G., Fortier, M. S., Vallerand, R. J., & Brière, N. M. (2001). Associations among perceived autonomy support, forms of self-regulations, and persistence: A prospective study. *Motivation and Emotion, 25,* 279–306.

Petitpas, A. J., & Champagne, D. (2000). Practical considerations in implementing sport career transition programs. In D. Lavallee & P. Wylleman (ed.), *Career transitions in sport: International perspectives* (pp. 81–93). Morgantown, WV: Fitness Information Technology.

Power, T. G., & Woolger, C. (1994). Parenting practices and age-group swimming: A correlational study. *Research Quarterly for Exercise and Sport, 65,* 59–66.

Salmela, J. H. (1994). Phases and transitions across sports career. In D. Hackfort (ed.), *Psycho-social issues and interventions in elite sport* (pp. 11–28). Frankfurt: Lang.

Sport England (2012). *Satisfaction survey.* Retrieved from: www.sportengland.org/research/about-our-research/satisfaction-with-the-quality-of-the-sporting-experience-survey/

Stambulova, N. (2009). Talent development in sport: A career transitions perspective. In E. Tsung-Min Hung, R. Lidor, & D. Hackfort (eds), *Psychology of sport excellence* (pp. 63–74). Morgantown, WV: Fitness Information Technology.

Storm, L. K. (2015). *Coloured by culture: Talent development in Scandinavian elite sport as seen from a cultural perspective.* (Doctoral thesis). Institute of Sport Science and Clinical Biomechanics, University of Southern Denmark.

Tinsley, L. (2015). *Investigating reasons for sport drop-out amongst 16–19 year old girls.* Retrieved from: www.englandathletics.org (sport_drop-out_amongst_16–19_year_old_girls.pdf)

Van Yperen, N. W. (1995). Interpersonal stress, performance level and parental support: A longitudinal study among highly skilled young soccer players. *The Sport Psychologist, 9,* 225–241. Retrieved from http://journals.humankinetics.com/tsp

Wall, M., & Côté, J. (2007). Developmental activities that lead to drop out and investment in sport. *Physical Education and Sport Pedagogy, 12,* 77–87.

Ward, P., Hodges, N. J., Williams, A. M., & Starkes, J. L. (2004). Deliberate practice and expert performance: Defining the path to excellence. In A. M. Williams & N. J. Hodges (eds), *Skill acquisition in sport: Research, theory and practice* (pp. 231–258). London: Routledge.

Wattie, N., Tietjens, M., Cobley, S., Schorer, J., Baker, J., & Kurz, D. (2014). Relative age-related participation and dropout trends in German youth sports clubs. *European Journal of Sport Science, 14,* S213–S220. doi: 10.1080/17461391.2012.681806.

Weiss, M. R., Wiese, D. M., & Klint, K. A. (1989). Head over heels with success: The relationship between self-efficacy and performance in competitive youth gymnastics. *Journal of Sport and Exercise Psychology, 11,* 444–451.

Wright, A. D., & Côté, J. (2003). A retrospective analysis of leadership development through sport. *The Sport Psychologist, 17,* 268–291. Retrieved from http://journals.humankinetics.com/tsp

Wylleman, P., & Lavallee, D. (2004). A developmental perspective on transitions faced by athletes. In M. Weiss (ed.), *Developmental sport and exercise psychology: A lifespan perspective* (pp. 507–527). Morgantown, WV: Fitness Information Technology.

24

A SMOOTH SEA NEVER MADE A SKILFUL SAILOR

Optimizing and exploiting the rocky road in talent development

Dave Collins and Áine MacNamara

Talented potential across performance domains can often benefit from, indeed may even need, a variety of challenges to facilitate eventual superior adult performance. In tandem with, or perhaps as a consequence of such challenge, the central importance of psychological competencies and characteristics in negotiating the performance pathway is well established in the literature and gaining traction in the applied domain. Resilience (Seligman, 2011), the growth mind-set (Dweck, 2006), or more comprehensive 'profiles' such as mental toughness (Clough, Earle, & Sewell, 2002; Jones, Hanton, & Connaughton, 2007) or the Psychological Characteristics of Developing Excellence (PCDEs; MacNamara, Button, & Collins, 2010a, 2010b), have been associated positively with both outcome and process on the talent development pathway (MacNamara et al., 2010a). In short, performers high in these and other related constructs seem more able to both negotiate the development pathway *and* realize and sustain successful careers.

However, a common and face-valid philosophy of many pathways is to minimize the number, and certainly the impact, of developmental challenges for best performing youth. Indeed, efforts are often made to make the training environment super-supportive. For example, providing young athletes with financial, coaching, and sport science support in a supportive environment is a common feature of TD pathways. This approach is undertaken in an effort to minimize challenge and allow young athletes to focus on their sporting commitments. Such support to enhance focus is certainly a feature of the working practices commonly established and maintained by top performers (i.e., those already at the top) across a variety of domains. However, as with so many other aspects, the ways by which top performers manage their performing environments are not necessarily equally positive practice for developers. The problem is further compounded since the best performing young athletes may often not encounter many challenges at all during the development years; 'natural' ability can take a performer an awfully long way up the pathway before any naturally occurring setbacks (e.g., defeats, de-selection) are encountered. Indeed, the low transfer of youth to senior success would attest to how smoothness often precedes a fall in talent development terms. This presents a potential conundrum; how do young athletes build and acquire the confidence, resilience and other psychological characteristics needed to achieve at the highest level without experiencing and overcoming adversity and challenge on the way up?

Investigation of elite performers' self-reported progression reveals low points that are influential in their development. Described as a 'Deliberate Experience' (Cleary & Zimmerman, 2001; Durand-Bush & Salmela, 2001; Gould, Dieffenbach, & Moffett, 2010; Ollis, MacPherson, & Collins, 2006), these lows often represent a turning point that results in a refocusing or increasing of effort. These critical episodes can be both chronic and acute, and inevitably interact with the more prescriptively driven developmental stages experienced along the pathway (cf. Bloom, 1985; Côté, Baker, & Abernethy, 2003). Crucially, however, it is the individual's *reaction* to these critical episodes, rather than the mere presence (cf. Savage, Collins, & Cruickshank, 2016), that determines their trajectory; a vital consideration for the design and implementation of a 'rocky road'. Indeed, the manner in which individuals interpret distinct incidents or more chronic experiences as facilitators and debilitators (a process dependent on psychological skills and characteristics – cf. Rosenbaum, 1983; Lazarus, 1993) can significantly influence the trajectory of their developmental pathway (Ollis et al., 2006). For example, a poor performance may be interpreted as a positive growth experience by some athletes, whereby they learn and grow from the experience. For others, however, it can be interpreted in a much more negative light and, as such, can have maladaptive consequences.

The extent to which athletes interpret trauma as a growth opportunity is critical (cf. Collins, MacNamara, & McCarthy, 2016). For less resilient athletes, such experiences are often deeply discouraging, which can precipitate excessive anxiety, injury, retirement or complete withdrawal from participation. Indeed, at this point, it is worth looking carefully at the word 'trauma' in context of talent development (Collins & MacNamara, 2012); our usage seems to raise concerns with some due perhaps to the emotive nature of the word. A definition of trauma would generate the following: 'from Greek, literally wound'; in short, anything from a small cut to losing a limb. Critically, therefore, a focus on pre-emptive preparation that equips aspiring elites with the skills needed to cope with such challenges would seem a sensible strategy. In fact, there is considerable evidence that such 'ups and downs' are important waymarks or transitions of progress. As mentioned earlier, research suggests that an overly smooth linear progression towards the top is often symptomatic of problems and certainly not conducive to sustained progress (Collins, 2011). Similarly, evidence suggests that successful and highly supported young performers are less likely to succeed at adult levels compared to peers who, though less successful at early ages, persevere and continue their involvement (Güllich & Emrich, 2006). Without the early learning and development of skills and confidence that such 'hiccups' can generate, the developing performer can often be knocked back by the sudden, unexpected and rapid increases in challenge that inevitably occur as one nears the top of the performance pyramid.

This evidence is supported by a number of retrospective and prospective investigations differentiating those who do and don't 'make it' to the top level of their performance domain, and interesting parallels can be drawn from other domains such as sport. In one such study, Van Yperen (2009) showed that footballers who eventually made it to the elite level were significantly higher in acknowledged 'challenge' factors such as number of siblings and minority ethnicity. Furthermore, their family backgrounds reflected over three times the divorce rate of peers who failed to reach the highest level. As such, there seems to be a disproportionately high incidence of early trauma, or at least incidents with the potential to traumatize, in the life histories of high-level performers. The knowledge and skills that performers accrued from 'positive life traumas', and their ability to carry over what they learned in that context to novel situations (Fogarty, Perkins, & Barrell, 1992; Savage et al., 2016) certainly appeared to affect their subsequent development and performance (Marini & Genereux, 1995).

The picture certainly seems to point to the importance of challenge in the development of young athletes (e.g., Collins, MacNamara, & McCarthy, 2016). What is less apparent, however, but essential from the practitioner perspective, is how the Talent Development Environment or TDE can be designed and deployed to maximize the benefit of such challenge; in short, some guidelines on how the rocky road can best be designed and exploited. Accordingly, in this chapter we offer some evidence and practice-based guidelines on how psychologists, coaches, administrators and parents can work together to provide an optimal and integrated experience.

We start with a brief critical overview of the major theoretical positions currently apparent. Building from this, we suggest that a proactive, skills-based approach to coach-generated periodized and naturally occurring challenge offers the best route forwards. We then offer some ways in which this can be done before providing data in support of this approach. Our conclusion highlights some useful (and not so useful) directions for future research, once again focused on applied practice.

Theories of development: The current state of play

For the present purpose, we will group the in-vogue approaches into three broad groups: life experience, attitude and skills. While not probably reflective of the original authors' epistemological stance, our structure holds some face/construct validity and facilitates a critical appraisal of each against the needs of the sports practitioner.

Life experiences

The life experience stance sees high achievement as due to the perhaps serendipitous experiences, or perhaps more accurately, misfortunes, experienced by the developing performer. This perspective focuses very much on the role of life experiences, adversity and trauma in particular, in the development of athletes. The current resilience literature of Fletcher, Sarkar and colleagues (Fletcher & Sarkar, 2012; Sarkar & Fletcher, 2014) is a good example of this, using primary data plus autobiographies and biographies of high-level performers to demonstrate the positive results of challenge (e.g., Howells & Fletcher, 2015), as per the title on one of their papers, 'What doesn't kill me makes me stronger' (cf. Sarkar, Fletcher, & Brown, 2014). Our concern here is that the challenge might also kill you! Therefore it is important to understand *how much* stress, of *what kind, when*, and *how dealt with* will generate optimum positive benefit. Furthermore, and especially from an applied perspective, how can the athlete be prepared in advance to benefit from such challenge, or is it *really* just an accident of birth/upbringing? Notably, the relationship between stress and consequent resilience seems to be curvilinear, with optimum growth resulting from moderate levels (too much or too little and benefits seem to dissipate; Seery, 2011). Furthermore, effects can often be due to cumulative rather than single occurrence, acute stress (Seery, Holman, & Silver, 2010). Finally, moderate is a relative, individualized, and often perceptually mediated term. Therefore, it would seem that a trait tendency (such as proactive coping which can be taught) or learnt state (again, taught through a formal skill development process) would be crucial in determining how individuals react, process and learn from these experiences.

Furthering this life experiences approach, and based on interviews with multiple medallists, the UK Sport sponsored report of Great British Medallists (Rees et al., 2016) proposes the early juxtaposition of sporting success and impactful trauma as a universally common feature of developmental experience, discriminating them experientially from less successful peers. The report summarizes that, although a happy childhood may be a good thing, the overcoming of obstacles and difficulties underpins the mental toughness, resilience, and deep-seated need to achieve, which serial gold medallists may possess. We would suggest a number of issues with these findings, especially since they are presented as representative of *every* multi-medallist studied. This seemed to us to be a surprising result, especially against our own working experiences with other similar elites. As an interesting contrast, a parallel study comparing developmental and attitudinal differences in triads of super-champions (multiple medallists or multi-capped, team sport athletes), champions (single medal/low number of caps) and almosts (no senior medals or caps; Collins et al., 2016) found little evidence for this effect. Indeed, almosts reported *more* trauma than super-champions, although even then only as a moderate percentage of the whole sample. What Collins et al.'s study highlights is the importance of the role of functional trauma in development; super champions felt themselves to be almost constantly challenged (albeit in a minor way) in comparison to their less eventually achieving peers (almosts). Notably, in keeping with our earlier contentions, 'almosts' were almost completely characterized by smoother developmental pathways before a catastrophic drop, whilst 'champions' experienced some 'ups and downs' but – significantly and reflecting the importance of active engagement – with less emotional turmoil.

In sum, we contend that the descriptive work that typifies the 'life experience approach' offers comparatively little to the applied field, representing a focus akin to the 'great person' work, leaders are 'born and not made', which characterized the early days of leadership research (Bass, 1990). These doubts relate to a number of concerns, especially from an applied perspective. Should talent identification (TI) be based, at least in part, on an individual's self-reported experience of stress? Furthermore, the existence of challenge is not, in and of itself, a consistent trigger for positive growth. Even if initiated, the process of development is likely to be complex and long term; it is certainly not a static outcome (cf. Tedeschi & Calhoun, 1995).

Attitudes

The second approach centres on the role of attitudes in mediating an individual's responses to challenge and adversity on the pathway to excellence. Considerable attention has been paid to constructs such as growth mindset (Dweck, 2006) and grit (Duckworth, Peterson, Matthews, & Kelly, 2007) within performance domains and they are increasingly used 'buzz words' in talent development. An increasing emphasis is placed on self-discipline, will power, persistence and the ability to defer gratification as key attributes for young athletes. Simply, performers high in these constructs seem more likely to get to the top and achieve more when they get there. For example, grittier individuals, defined as those high in perseverance and passion for long-term goals, seem to achieve more than their less gritty peers across a variety of domains. However, what are less clear from a practitioner perspective are guidelines about the teaching and development of these attitudes as preparation for challenge. Simply, despite the common assumption that these constructs are important for overcoming developmental challenge, there is little consideration of how they are best developed within the TDE. For example, although resilience has been well described as a process, and systemic recommendations offered for education in its broader sense (Winfield, 1994; Doll & Lyon, 1998), approaches for the optimum teaching and structured exercise of resilience skills as a preparation for challenge have been less apparent. Notably, possession of such characteristic(s) is often seen as a given, with little consideration of exactly how they might be developed. Although obliquely acknowledged as significant for development and performance, they are rarely in themselves regarded as discrete foci for structured training with young athletes. This lack of mechanism is a challenge, especially in designing systems which may promote the possession, deployment, and evolution of the characteristic(s).

Beyond the lack of understanding of the mechanisms underpinning these constructs, it is also important to consider the downside to grit; persistence may be counterproductive, termed non-productive persistence (McFarlin, Baumeister, & Blascovich, 1984), especially when this is inappropriate. For example, the rigid form of persistence found in obsessively passionate athletes might be an important explanation of how athletes develop burnout. As such, positive traits, such as grit, may also carry 'dark side' consequences if present or applied in excess. Gritty individuals, especially those on a very competitive developmental pathway, may show persistence at a task, or in overcoming challenge, resulting in remitting failure or inefficient success that could have been surpassed by alternative courses of action such as a change of coaching focus or technique (McFarlin et al., 1984). As such, there seems to be some benefit to knowing when *not* to persist at a task from both an outcome and an individual perspective (e.g., well-being; Hill, MacNamara, & Collins, 2015).

Skills

The third category of work is skills focused and, as such, offers more explicit guidance to the practitioner on what to do. As an example, the work of Toering, Elferink-Gemser, Jordet and Visscher (2009; see also Duckworth, Tsukayama, & May, 2010) shows that self-regulatory skills distinguish between elite and sub-elite academy footballers. Subsequent, more detailed, study suggested that these differences operate, at the least, through the generation of better practice behaviours (Toering et al., 2011). This, and their other work (e.g., Toering, Jordet, & Ripegutu, 2013), suggests that developing such skills in young performers offers them the equipment to make the most of their experiences on the pathway.

A similar picture is provided by the work of MacNamara and colleagues, albeit that their PCDE framework (MacNamara et al., 2010a, 2010b) offers a broader and integrated range of structured skills that can support athletes on the pathway. Once again, however, the crucial point is that skills are taught, tested, refined and redeployed as the athlete progresses along the pathway, using both naturally occurring (e.g., MacNamara & Collins, 2011; MacNamara & Collins, 2014) and constructed challenges (cf. Collins et al., 2012), rather than development being 'left to chance' if and when opportunities occur. A feature of the mechanistic operation of PCDEs is that different combinations of skills are useful for different performance domains and different individuals at different times. The key point however is that a toolbox of skills, with the knowledge to enable appropriate and effective deployment, would seem to offer more potential benefit than a generic skill or set of skills; a portfolio of transferable skills rather than a specific package targeted at a specific issue.

But are these approaches really different?

In order to push progress, it is worth considering the extent to which these different approaches can be reconciled. For example, it may be that the early trauma stressed by the life experience lobby serves to shock the young athlete into active coping; after all, the naivety of young performers is a feature of our experience and also supported by research (e.g., Mortensen, Henriksen, & Stelter, 2013). But if this is so, where do the skills originate, unless from the home/school background? This is certainly tenable, especially as the makeup of the British team on which the trauma research was focused (Rees et al., 2016) is usually disproportionately drawn from private schools (Vasagar, 2012), in itself both a stressor and a source of arguably better education. If this were the case, however, it would certainly place restrictions on the TI process, limiting the talent pool by focusing on conditions of talent identification in much the same way as suggesting that early trauma is essential to future success (cf. Rees et al.,

2016). It certainly does not help the increasing number of youth sport coaches to build their developmental agendas on a firm evidence base.

In fairness, some researchers who espouse other approaches (e.g., Sarkar et al., 2014) do also see the importance of skill development and appropriate practice opportunities. They state:

> It is important to encourage athletes to actively engage with challenging situations … Setbacks and failures that are encountered on the pathway to sporting excellence could be used as a focus for learning, reflection, and praxis.
>
> *(Sarkar et al., 2015, p. 8)*

This is almost exactly what the skill approach is built around, so maybe some of the approaches *are* compatible. In our applied field, however, it is the 'what to do, why and how' that is of interest; as we said earlier, studies based only around continued description and correlation without action seem a bit of a waste, especially since such studies have already been done, published and integrated into practice.

Structuring and periodizing challenge along the pathway

Reflecting the best elements of the approaches discussed in the previous section, it is important to consider how coaches and psychologists should be supporting the next generation of super champions. First, our experience and research are strongly supportive of a systematic teaching, challenging, evaluating and refining cycle that matches Kolb's traditional experiential learning model (Kolb, 1984). Through this medium, young athletes experience a gradual development of skills, which are then tested against realistic (rather than contrived) challenges. After the challenge, coaches and other practitioners engage the athletes in review, developing their own capacity to evaluate and self-manage in tandem with structured feedback. Essentially, skills need to be taught, exercised, and supported against real-life challenges, if genuine and transferrable benefits are to accrue: 'for newly acquired skills to have real power to enhance developmental outcomes over time, they must be integrated into a system of behaviour that serves some functional purpose' (Pianta & Walsh, 1998; p. 412). As a result, performers learn generalizable skills, how to deploy them and build confidence in their capacity to do so.

Second, there is strong evidence from a variety of sources that these skills have a causative influence on the performer's ability to cope with challenge, most notably for individuals following a developmental pathway. Once again, the need for informed and proactive teaching, then supported deployment, and then facilitated self-reflection is important. Work must be one-on-one as much as possible, to help the individual to explore, discover and build confidence in the particular blend which works best for them in each particular environment. This, in turn, raises the need for regular and ongoing refinement or even revision as people grow and situations change, a factor which seems to have been ignored by some of the life experience research cited in the previous section, even though their work also supports this.

Of course, how much challenge and of what types can be employed for optimum development is an important question. For example, there is good evidence that too great a challenge in childhood can 'limit' adult achievement and adjustment (Breslau, Chilcoat, Kessler, & Davis, 1999). Furthermore, constructs such as learned helplessness (Seligman, 1972; Maier & Seligman, 1976) show that solely positive outcomes from the imposition of pressure are hardly inevitable. Consequently, and as with so much in performance psychology, the 'with who, how much and when' decisions are likely to be very individualized, impacted by a variety of characteristics and prior experiences. For example, Mineka and Zinbarg (2006) show how early learning and individual vulnerabilities can affect later responses to stress, both in the long- and short-term. In simple terms, the degree of control perceived on early stressors has a significant influence on the individual's perceived ability to control challenges in later life. As such, appropriate attention to individual differences and understanding the performance context is key. Supporting this, the need for such individualization to cater for all aspects of the bio-psychosocial situation of each performer is also well documented (Collins, Bailey, Ford, MacNamara, Toms, & Pearce, 2012).

Evidence in support of the skills-based approach to periodized challenge

There is significant evidence that the skills described in the previous sections can be taught, impacting a performer's ability to cope with developmental challenges. Given the positive implications for the application of these skills, building these into TDEs should be a feature of effective programs. Indeed, there are examples of the impact of such skill-based developmental programs. For example, the Developing the Potential of Young People in Sport (DPYPS; Collins, Martindale, Button & Sowerby, 2010) pilot program is one example that used physical challenge and taught PCDEs in an integrated approach to young school children. PCDEs were formally taught, encouraged, modelled and refined, then transferred and tested using a variety of means in both curricular physical education and extra-curricular sport. Results from this intervention showed that young participants were able to apply PCDEs to a wide range of challenges, from both within and outside their sporting environment, which helped them maintain progress and development. Indeed, they spontaneously deployed the skills to other challenges outside sport, with a virtuous spiral of benefits.

Of course, these skills and psychological robustness may also be developed by virtue of the pathway. McCarthy and colleagues (McCarthy, Collins, & Court, 2015; McCarthy & Collins, 2014) suggest that the attritional journey experienced by relatively younger athletes within a year-group acts as a catalyst for the development and deployment of coping strategies, psychological resilience and 'mental toughness'. It would seem that overcoming high levels of challenge due to the physical and cognitive loads experienced by relatively young athletes is actually beneficial for long-term development as it provides opportunities to develop, deploy and refine the PCDEs required for long-term development.

There are also several strands of, perhaps, parallel research that support the skills approach. For example, levels of hardiness (i.e., commitment, belief in control and enjoyment of challenge) discriminate successful athletes (Sheard & Golby, 2010), so it is likely that any intervention that builds these would support the pursuit of higher levels of achievement. The tendency for initial appraisal of stress as a challenge (how can I handle it) as opposed to threat is also concomitant (e.g., Kassam, Kostov, & Mendes, 2009), or maybe even causative (cf. Greenglass & Fiksenbaum, 2009) of a positive outcome. Once again, the development of these attitudes through skills training, challenge, support and reassurance would seem desirable.

Of course, we should stress that no one answer, including the one tendered here, can represent the total solution. Clearly, the provision of support to athletes is a subtle and complex issue; certainly not just a case of teach them some skills and watch them grow! Indeed, as Güllich and Emrich (2006) show in an important and rare large-scale quantitative survey, certain support structures and procedures may lose or even reverse effects over time. In similar fashion, there are a range of individual differences which mediate the impact of mental skills training on performance (Geukes, Mesagno, Hanrahan, & Kellmann, 2013; Roberts, Woodman, Hardy, Davis, & Wallace, 2013), and some subtle differences exist between facilitative and debilitative versions of the same construct (e.g., perfectionist strivings versus concerns; Stoeber, 2011).

These complicating factors underpin our earlier insistence on an individualized treatment to the development and deployment of skills.

In acknowledging these complexities, however, we would still suggest that a concentration on the possession of, confidence in, and ability to deploy skills against increasingly varied types of challenge offers the best-applied focus for practitioners. Indeed, even the post-traumatic stress literature implies the deployment of skills, many of which are taught by the therapist to the client, to facilitate the transformation of stress into growth. As Joseph, Murphy and Regel (2012, p. 319) state 'affective–cognitive processing takes place via the cycle of event cognitions appraisal, emotional state, and coping as the person attempts to reconcile pre-trauma-related assumptions with the new trauma-related information'. Their model also highlights the complexity of this process, stating that a variety of methods may work, or even be required, both between and within the individual. In other words, the transformation from stress to growth is far from automatic, and seems dependent on the input of well-trained and well-informed practitioners.

Conclusion

The argument presented in this chapter suggests that attention should be paid to the early experiences of talented youth, to ensure that individuals are prepared for the challenges that are inherent in the development pathway and can then maintain their involvement. As such, overly 'smooth' and successful early involvement may not be the best preparation for long-term and adult success. It is increasingly acknowledged that individuals who have had some adversity in their past are better prepared for future adverse events, suggesting that some level of challenge or trauma develops the resilience and associated skills that allow an individual to cope with future challenges. In fact, there is considerable empirical evidence that documents the positive changes possible following trauma and adversity (e.g., Joseph & Linley, 2005; Tedeschi & Calhoun, 1995). It is hypothesized that struggling with adversity can lead to a higher level of functioning than had been experienced before the event. Often termed 'adversarial growth' (Joseph & Linley 2005), individuals appear to learn and benefit from these experiences and, therefore, rather than avoiding adversity, there appears to be a strong argument for ensuring that the most talented young athletes must experience challenge and trauma early in their development. It is of course essential that young athletes also have the opportunity to develop psycho-behavioural and coping skills, and have adequate social support, so as to ensure that adversity is interpreted as a positive growth experience. Tedeschi and Calhoun (1995) for example suggest that individuals with few coping skills are unlikely to benefit from adversity experiences. As such, the importance of preparing young athletes for challenges, supporting them through the experience, and then encouraging positive evaluation and reflection is key to successful outcome.

In summary, there appears to be a strong case for both the direct exploitation of life event challenges and the artificial generation of challenge when this is seen to be developmentally appropriate. Indeed, the inclusion of artificial 'speed bumps' for those high potential individuals who are experiencing little or no challenge from their pathway (as evidenced, for example, by a smooth and positive linear development) is a deliberate feature of those talent pathways with which we consult, across a broad range of domains. The talent pathway should not be a comfortable place; rather, it should offer a variety of lessons to be learnt through both explicit and implicit means. The provision of skills, formally taught but also developed through a variety of parallel interacting routes is essential; this area of development should not just be left to chance or the serendipity of supportive home backgrounds. Finally, support through the early challenges, with confidence- and skill-building debriefs afterwards, will help to optimize development, although the importance of doing this on an individual basis is clearly critical. Without this implementation and exploitation of a 'rocky road', talented young athletes may be less likely to convert to superior adult performers.

References

Bass, B. M. (1990). *Bass and Stodgill's handbook of leadership*. New York: The Free Press.

Bloom, B. S. (ed.). (1985). *Developing talent in young people*. New York: Ballantine Books.

Breslau, N., Chilcoat, H. D., Kessler, R. C., & Davis, G. C. (1999). Previous exposure to trauma and PTSD effects of subsequent trauma: results from the Detroit Area Survey of Trauma. *American Journal of Psychiatry*, 156(6), 902–907.

Cleary, T., & Zimmerman, B. J. (2001). Self-regulation differences during athletic practice by experts, non-experts and novices. *Journal of Applied Sport Psychology*, 31, 461–466.

Clough, P., Earle, K., & Sewell, D. (2002). Mental toughness: The concept and its measurement. In I. Cockerill (ed.), *Solutions in sport psychology*. London: Thomson, pp. 32–45.

Collins, D. (2011). *Talent Development: The game between the ears*. Invited keynote presentation. Science for Success, KIHU, Jyväskylä, Finland.

Collins, D., Bailey, R., Ford, P. A., MacNamara, Á., Toms, M., & Pearce, G. (2012). Three worlds: New directions in participant development in sport and physical activity. *Sport, Education and Society*, 17(2): 225–243.

Collins, D., & MacNamara, Á. (2012). The rocky road to the top: Why talent needs trauma. *Sports Medicine*, 42(11): 907–914. http://dx.doi.org/10.1007/BF03262302

Collins, D., MacNamara, Á., & McCarthy, N. (2016). Super Champions, champions, and almosts: Important differences and commonalities on the rocky road. *Frontiers in Psychology and Movement Science*, 11(6); 2009. doi: 10.3389/fpsyg.2015.02009.

Collins, D., Martindale, R. J. J., Button, A., & Sowerby, K. (2010). Building a physically active and talent rich culture: An educationally sound approach. *European Physical Education Review*, 16(1), 7–28.

Côté, J., Baker, J., & Abernethy, B. (2003). From play to practice: A developmental framework for the acquisition of expertise in team sport. In J. Starkes & K. A. Ericsson (eds), *Recent advances in research on sport expertise* (pp. 89–114). Champaign, IL: Human Kinetics.

Doll, B., & Lyon, M. A. (1998). Risk and resilience: Implications for the delivery of educational and mental health services in schools. *School Psychology Review*, 27(3), 348–263.

Duckworth, A. L., Peterson, C., Matthews, M. D., & Kelly, D. R. (2007). Grit: perseverance and passion for long-term goals. *Journal of Personality and Social Psychology*, 92(6), 1087–101. http://dx.doi.org/10.1037/0022-3514.92.6.1087

Duckworth, A. L., Tsukayama, E., & May, H. (2010). Establishing causality using longitudinal hierarchical linear modelling: an illustration predicting achievement from self-control. *Social Psychology and Personality Science*, 1(4): 311–7. http://dx.doi.org/10.1177/1948550609359707

Durand-Bush, N., & Salmela, J. H. (2001). The development of talent in sport. In R. N. Singer, H. A. Hausenblas, & C. Janelle (eds), *Handbook of sport psychology* (2nd ed., pp. 269–289). New York: John Wiley.

Dweck, C. S. (2006) *Mindset: The new psychology of success*. New York, NY: Random House.

Fletcher, D., & Sarkar, M. (2012). A grounded theory of psychological resilience in Olympic Champions. *Psychology of Sport and Exercise*, 13(5), 669–678. http://dx.doi.org/10.1016/j.psychsport.2012.04.007

Fogarty, R., Perkins, D., & Barrell, J. (1992). *The mindful school: How to teach for transfer*. Highett, Australia: Hawker Brownlow Education.

Gould, D., Deieffenbach, K., & Moffett, A. (2010). Psychological characteristics and their development in Olympic champions. *Journal of Applied Sport Psychology*, 14(3), 172–204. doi: 10.1080/10413200290103482

Greenglass, E. R., & Fiksenbaum, L. (2009). Proactive coping, positive affect, and well-being: Testing for mediation using Path Analysis. *European Psychologist*, 14(1), 29–39. doi: 10.1027/1016-9040.14.1.29

Geukes, K., Mesagno, C., Hanrahan, S. J., & Kellmann, M. (2013). Performing under pressure in private: Activation of self-focus traits. *International Journal of Sport and Exercise Psychology*, 11, 11–23.

Güllich, A., & Emrich, E. (2006). Evaluation of the support of young athletes in the elite sport system. *European Journal of Sports Sciences*, 3, 85–108.

Hill A., MacNamara Á., Collins D. (2015). Psycho-behaviourally based features of effective talent development in rugby union: a coach's perspective. *The Sport Psychologist*. 29, 201–212. http://dx.doi.org/10.1123/tsp.2014-0103

Howells, K., & Fletcher, D. (2015). Sink or swim: Adversity- and growth-related experiences in Olympic swimming champions. *Psychology of Sport and Exercise*, 16, 37–48. http://dx.doi.org/10.1016/j.psychsport.2014.08.004

Jones, G., Hanton, S., & Connaughton, D. (2007). A framework of mental toughness in the world's best performers. *The Sport Psychologist*, 21, 243–264.

Joseph, S., & Linley, P. A. (2005). Positive adjustment to threatening events: An organismic valuing theory of growth through adversity. *Review of General Psychology*, 9, 262–280.

Joseph, S. Murphy, D., & Regel, S. (2012). An affective–cognitive processing model of post-traumatic growth. *Clinical Psychology and Psychotherapy*, 19, 316–325. http://dx.doi.org/10.1002/cpp.1798

Kassam, K., Koslov, K., & Mendes, W. B. (2009). Decisions under distress: Stress profiles influence anchoring and adjustment. *Psychological Science, 20,* 1394–1399.

Kolb, D. A. (1984). *Experiential learning: Experience as the source of learning and development* (Vol. 1). Englewood Cliffs, NJ: Prentice-Hall.

Lazarus, R. S. (1993). Coping theory and research: Past, present and future. *Psychosomatic Medicine, 55,* 234–247.

MacNamara, Á., Button, A., & Collins, D. (2010a). The role of psychological characteristics in facilitating the pathway to elite performance. Part 1: Identifying mental skills and behaviours. *The Sport Psychologist,* 24, 52–73.

MacNamara, Á., Button, A., & Collins, D. (2010b). The role of psychological characteristics in facilitating the pathway to elite performance. Part 2: Examining environmental and stage related differences in skills and behaviours. *The Sport Psychologist,* 24, 74–96.

MacNamara, Á., & Collins D. (2011). Development and initial validation of the psychological characteristics of developing excellence questionnaire. *Journal of Sport Sciences,* 29, 1273–1286. doi: 10.1080/02640414.2011.589468

MacNamara, Á., & Collins, D. (2014). Staying with the 'force' and countering the 'dark side': Profiling, exploiting and countering psychological characteristics in talent identification and development. *The Sport Psychologist,* 29(1), 73–81.

Maier, S. F., & Seligman, M. E. P. (1976). Learned helplessness: Theory and evidence. *Journal of Experimental Psychology: General,* 105, 3–46.

Marini, A., & Genereux, R. (1995). The challenge of teaching for transfer. In A. McKeough (ed.), *Teaching for transfer: Fostering generalization in learning.* Mahwah, NJ: Lawrence Erlbaum Associates, pp. 1–19.

McCarthy, N., & Collins, D. (2014). Initial identification & selection bias versus the eventual confirmation of talent: evidence for the benefits of a rocky road? *Journal of Sport Sciences,* 32(17), 1604–1610.

McCarthy, N., Collins, D., & Court, D. (2015). Start hard, finish better: Further evidence for the reversal of the RAE advantage. *Journal of Sport Sciences,* doi: 10.1080/02640414.2015.1119297

McFarlin, D. B., Baumeister, R. F., & Blascovich, J. (1984). On knowing when to quit: Task failure, self-esteem, advice, and non-productive persistence. *Journal of Personality,* 52, 138–155.

Mineka, S., & Zinbarg, R. (2006). A contemporary learning theory perspective on the etiology of anxiety disorders: It's not what you thought it was. *American Psychologist,* 61(1), 10–26.

Mortensen, J., Henriksen, K., & Stelter, R. (2013). Tales from the future. *Sport Science Review,* 22(5–6), 305–327. doi: 10.2478/ssr-2013-0015

Ollis, S. MacPherson, A., & Collins, D. (2006). Expertise and talent development in rugby referees: An ethnographic enquiry. *Journal of Sports Sciences,* 24(3), 309–322.

Pianta, R. C., & Walsh, D. J. (1998). Applying the construct of resilience in schools. *School Psychology Review,* 27(3), 207–217.

Rees, T., Hardy, L., Abernathy, B., Güllich, A., Côté, J., Woodman, T., … Warr, C. (2016). The Great British Medallists Project: A review of current knowledge on the development of the world's best sporting talent. *Sports Medicine,* Feb 03. doi: 10.1007/s40279-016-0476-2

Roberts, R., Woodman, T., Hardy, L., Davis, L., & Wallace, H. M. (2013). Psychological skills do not always help performance: The moderating role of narcissism. *Journal of Applied Sport Psychology,* 25, 316–325. doi: 10.1080/10413200.2012.731472

Rosenbaum, M. (1983). Learned resourcefulness as a behavioural repertoire for the self-regulation of internal events: Issues and speculations. In M. C. M. Rosenbaum, C. M. Franks, & J. Jaffe (eds), *Perspectives in behaviour therapy in the eighties.* New York: Springer, pp. 54–73.

Sarkar, M., & Fletcher, D. (2014). Psychological resilience in sport performers: A review of stressors and protective factors. *Journal of Sports Sciences*, 32(15), 1419–1434.

Sarkar, M., Fletcher, D., & Brown, D. J. (2014). What doesn't kill me: Adversity-related experiences are vital in the development of superior Olympic performance. *Journal of Science and Medicine in Sport*, http://dx.doi.org/10.1016/j.jsams.2014.06.010

Savage, J., Collins, D., & Cruickshank, A. (2016). Exploring traumas in the development of talent: What are they, what do they do, and what do they require? *Journal of Applied Sport Psychology*, 29(1), 101–117.

Seery, M. D. (2011). Challenge or threat? Cardiovascular indexes of resilience and vulnerability to potential stress in humans. *Neuroscience and Biobehavioral Reviews*, 35, 1603–1610.

Seery, M. D., Holman, E. A., & Silver, R. C. (2010). Whatever does not kill us: Cumulative lifetime adversity, vulnerability, and resilience. *Journal of Personality and Social Psychology*, 99, 1025–1041.

Seligman, M. E. P. (1972). Learned helplessness. *Annual Review of Medicine*, 23, 407–412.

Seligman, M. E. P. (2011). *Flourish: A visionary new understanding of happiness and well-being*. New York: Simon & Schuster.

Sheard, M., & Golby, J. (2010). Personality hardiness differentiates elite level sport performers. *International Journal of Sport and Exercise Psychology*, 8, 160–169.

Stoeber, J. (2011). The dual nature of perfectionism in sports: Relationships with emotion, motivation, and performance. *International Review of Sport and Exercise Psychology*, 4(2), 128–145. doi:10.1080/1750984X.2011.604789.

Tedeschi, R. G., & Calhoun, L. G. (1995). *Trauma and transformation: Growing in the aftermath of suffering*. Thousand Oaks, CA: Sage.

Toering, T. T., Elferink-Gemser, M. T., Jordet, G., & Visscher, C. (2009). Self-regulation and performance level of elite and non-elite youth soccer players. *Journal of Sports Sciences*, 27, 1509–1517.

Toering, T. T., Elferink-Gemser, M. T., Jordet, G., Pepping, G. J., Jorna, C., & Visscher, C. (2011). Self-regulation of practice behavior among elite youth soccer players: An exploratory study. *Journal of Applied Sport Psychology*, 23, 110–128.

Toering, T, Jordet, G., & Ripegutu, A. (2013). Effective learning among elite football players: The development of a football-specific self-regulated learning questionnaire. *Journal of Sports Sciences*, 31, 1412–1420.

Van Yperen, N. (2009). Why some make it and others do not: Identifying psychological factors that predict career success in professional adult soccer. *The Sport Psychologist*, 23, 317–29.

Vasagar, J. (2012, August 13). Olympics 2012: Third of Team GB medallists came from private schools. *The Guardian*. Retrieved from www.theguardian.com/education/2012/aug/13/olympics-2012-gb-medallists-private-schooling

Winfield, L. F. (1994). *Developing resilience in urban youth*. Oak Brook, IL: Urban.

PART IV

Health and development concerns

25

UNDERSTANDING UNDERRECOVERY, OVERTRAINING, AND BURNOUT IN THE DEVELOPING ATHLETE

Maximilian Pelka and Michael Kellmann

Demands of youth sports

Seeking elite status as a youth athlete and competing at elite levels require athletes to invest a large amount of time and intense effort in training (Gustafsson, Davis, Skoog, Kenttä, & Haberl, 2015). Young athletes have to dedicate significant resources to deliberate practice and maintain this level of dedication over several years in order to achieve their goals (Ward, Hodges, Starkes, & Williams, 2007). This is a challenging endeavour and the experience of aspiring athletes who undertake it can differ considerably. For some athletes, this process can be psychologically rewarding and place them on a path to long-term sport participation (Jowett, Hill, Hall, & Curran, 2016). For others, the psychological and physical demands can prove too great, fostering an experience laden with self-doubt and frustration that places them on a path to extreme disaffection (Jowett et al., 2016). That might lead to detrimental consequences such as underrecovery, overtraining, injuries, and burnout (Gustafsson, Hassmén, Kenttä, & Johansson, 2008) and more severe mental health problems (Hughes & Leavey, 2012). Curran, Appleton, Hill, and Hall (2013) indicated that aspiring young athletes may be at particular risk. This risk increases when elite athletes are injured, face career termination, or experience performance difficulties (Rice et al., 2016). As a result, in many sports, negative consequences such as burnout and subsequent dropout are a common occurrence (Crane & Temple, 2015; Dubuc, Schinke, Eys, Battochio, & Zaichowsky, 2010; Cresswell & Eklund, 2007; Harris & Watson, 2014; Strachan, Côté, & Deakin, 2009).

The emphasis on competitive success at young ages, early elite-level team selection, collegiate scholarships, becoming an Olympic and national team member and getting professional contracts as early as possible have become widespread (Gould & Dieffenbach, 2002; DiFiori et al., 2014) and more important than 30 years ago (Gould, Feltz, & Weiss, 1985). Competition calendars in youth football reflect this pattern; while European and World Championships for under 17-year-olds were introduced in 1982 and 1985 respectively, in 2011 a club-level European Cup was added to competition calendars (NextGen Series; from 2014 on UEFA Youth League). With these changes, the developing athletes' competition calendars are similar to those of players from the German soccer club Borussia Dortmund's Under-17 squad during the 2014/15 season (Transfermarkt, 2015). During that season, these elite athletes had to perform on 26 match days during the regular season, on 20 match days for the Germany Under-17 squad, on four match days in the county cup, and in additional eight friendlies during summer and winter pre-season on average. In total, that sums up to around 66 matches within a single season. In other words, it seems as if many programmes have focused primarily on the early identification of talent, often in order to select the best youngsters in the hope that they will be the most likely to become the best adults. While competition and training load are two considerable stressors that young athletes face, additional factors such as interpersonal relationships, school and work demands as well as competitive pressure also need to be considered (Arnold & Fletcher, 2012; Gustafsson et al., 2015; Gustafsson, Kenttä, & Hassmén, 2011; Sarkar & Fletcher, 2014). The pressure exerted by sports organizations, sponsors, and, in some countries, by governmental bodies (e.g., Sport Authorities, Olympic Training Centers) on young athletes to be successful is greater than ever (Anshel & Lidor, 2012; Rice et al., 2016). Therefore, managing psychosocial stressors might be as important as managing training load to avoid negative consequences, including burnout (Appleton, Hall, & Hill, 2009; Rumbold, Fletcher, & Daniels, 2012).

Stress and other emotional responses are part of a complex interplay of physiological, psychological, and behavioural reactions to environmental and situational stimuli. When young athletes engage in regular training and competition, they actively challenge their natural homeostatic balance to elicit adaptions and performance gains (Folland &Williams, 2007; Main & Landers, 2012; Meeusen et al., 2013). However, stressors outside of sport may also compromise this balance (Gustafsson et al., 2011). Contributors to that complex environment include: coaches, parents, peers, officials, sponsors, and agents (among others) that all interact with each other (Cresswell, 2009; Gustafsson et al., 2011). For example, parental pressure to compete and succeed, which potentially leads to goals skewed towards parental intentions and not towards the development of the child (Lauer, Gould, Roman, & Pierce, 2010), financial issues brought in by sponsors or agents (Hanton, Fletcher, & Coughlan, 2005), or lack of conversation between athletes and coaches or team managers (Hanton et al., 2005).

Issues that play crucial roles and negatively influence the development of youth athletes are often indicated by the inappropriate and unrealistic demands and expectations to which these young athletes are exposed (Bergeron et al., 2015). These interacting factors of young athletes' developmental courses can result in extreme stress for youth athletes. However, stressors alone are not the only reasons why underrecovery, overtraining, and burnout are developed; it depends on how athletes and their environment perceive and react to them (Lazarus, 2000; Nicholls & Polman, 2007). Following Lazarus (1999) the situations could be appraised as, harm/loss, a threat, a challenge, or beneficial (primary appraisal) and then followed by the decision to respond to the situation (secondary appraisal). For example, one athlete might perceive the struggle with a teammate as challenging and therefore invests more effort into practice to be better; however, another one might perceive it as threat and as a consequence act more restrained. Probably one of the most important issues is balancing academics, sports, and leisure time (Gould, Tuffey, Udry, & Loehr, 1996; Hanton et al., 2005; Rice et al., 2016). Young athletes have to coordinate school with its demands (e.g., nine-to-five school days, recent changes in the schooling system, e.g., going from nine to eight years of secondary school), sports life with its frequent competitions and training demands, and leisure time, which may be limited given the tough schedules of the two aforementioned factors. Therefore, determining how these areas can be balanced to optimize development is key. The following sections describe the importance of the interplay between the above-mentioned stressors and recovery as they relate to the development of underrecovery, overtraining, and burnout syndromes.

Recovery

Optimal performance is only achievable if athletes recover appropriately after training and competition, and optimally balance stress with adequate recovery (Kellmann, 2010; Kuipers, 1998). The same applies for talent development: if young athletes are not capable of dealing with new encounters because they are in an imbalanced recovery-stress state, they will not proceed to the next steps. As Meeusen et al. (2013) stated, successful training most likely involves overload but also avoids the combination of excessive overload and inadequate recovery. Therefore, it is essential to implement appropriate regeneration phases in training regimens that aim for development and competitive success. Research has established relationships between training intensity, frequency, and duration and their consequences for performance and health. For example, Aagaard and Jørgensen (1996) found that during the decade preceding their study, overuse injury rates increased from 16% to 47% in elite volleyball. They suggested this was due to a 50% increase in training activity during this period. Since then, training and competition frequency has increased even more. Research has shown that inadequate recovery between matches because of congested match calendars can lead to fatigue and increase the risk of injury associated with overuse and poor performance during subsequent performance (Dupont et al., 2010; Nédélec et al., 2012, 2013). The importance of regaining an adequate working state for consistently successful performance and steady development is widely recognized by athletes and their coaches but nevertheless overtraining syndrome and burnout syndrome are still among the relevant problems encountered in competitive sports (Kellmann & Günther, 2000).

Kallus and Kellmann (2000) described the recovery process as an inter- and intra-individual multilevel process for the re-establishment of performance abilities, which includes an action-oriented component and self-initiated activities that can be systematically used to optimize situational conditions to build and restore personal resources and buffers. Similar to the construct of stress, this multilevel process has several dimensions (i.e., physiological, mood-related, psychological, behavioural, social, and emotional recovery; Kallus & Kellmann, 2000). Essentially, recovery depends on a reduction of, a change of, or a break from stress, and is a gradual and cumulative process that is dependent on previous activities (Kellmann, 2002). In addition, recovery is tightly linked to environmental circumstances; for example, if an athlete is disturbed in his preparation or sleeping habits, it influences the entire process.

Interrelations between stress and recovery

The complexity of fine-tuning the training process can be recognized when considering all factors that influence performance and development both inside and outside of the sport domain, such as training (e.g., extent, intensity, training techniques, periodization), lifestyle (e.g., sleep, nutrition, recreational activities), state of health (e.g., cold, infections), or environment (e.g., family, team members, school/university; Beckmann & Elbe, 2015). All of these factors need to be considered when targeting optimal and appropriate talent development as all are potential stressors athletes have to react to. In his model, Kellmann (2002; see Figure 25.1) described the interplay between stress states and recovery demands of an individual, based on the assumption that an athlete has limited resources to compensate for and cope with stressors (Hampel & Petermann, 2006). Under increased stress and the inability to meet increased recovery demands (i.e., quality of necessary recovery activities to level-out the current recovery-stress state), a young athlete experiences more stress. At this point, athletes may be stressed to the point that they fail to find or invest time to adequately recover, or to consider better ways of coping with

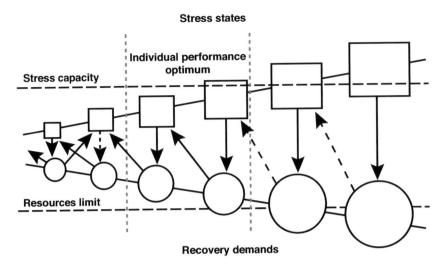

Stress states

Figure 25.1 The scissors model of the interrelation of stress states and recovery demands

Source: Reprinted, with permission, from K.W. Kallus and M. Kellmann, 2000, Burnout in athletes and coaches. In *Emotions in sport*, edited by Y. Hanin (Champaign, IL: Human Kinetics), 212.

their situations. Failing to adapt has the potential to lead to even more stress, leading to the need for more recovery time. This situation can be handled until the recovery demands surpass the resource limit or the stress states exceed the stress capacity. Beyond these points, an athlete cannot meet recovery demands without additional recovery measures. Stress will accumulate and, without intervention, underrecovery and/or overtraining are more likely to occur.

Stress states can be seen on a continuum of increasing training load ranging from no training to overtraining. With additional training loads, recovery demands increase proportionally along the recovery axis. A short-term planned sacrifice of recovery (e.g., a day off following a practice session that was more strenuous than expected while planning the training regimen), however, enhances long-term effects. If training load and intensity increase over a longer time with inadequate or inappropriate recovery, the individual experiences long-term underrecovery that may result in overtraining. At each stage of the model, recovery can work as a regulation mechanism; the higher a person's stress state the higher the demand for recovery to reach individual optimal recovery-stress states. It has to be stated, however, that being high on stress does not necessarily imply negative consequences as long as recovery demands are met accordingly. Thus, if young athletes lack the necessary coping strategies, stress can become chronic, with overtraining and burnout as inevitable consequences (Gustafsson et al., 2008).

Consequences of lack of recovery

When an athlete's or coach's focus is on dysfunctional actions, such as inappropriate time management or training load, and priorities are set incorrectly, decisive disadvantages arise quickly. At this point three potential consequences of imbalances in recovery versus stress are introduced (i.e., underrecovery, the overtraining syndrome, and the burnout syndrome) that differ in intensity, severity, and longevity, and are likely to affect the development of young athletes. The relationship between these three concepts could be conceptualized with underrecovery as the antecedent of overtraining and burnout in terms of individual well-being, performance decrements, and influence on short- and long-term development. It has to be stated that these three topics are not as thoroughly investigated in youth as in adults. Thus, it would be beneficial to intensify research in this area if we want to avoid talented athletes dropping out the sporting system too early (Crane & Temple, 2015).

Underrecovery and disturbed recovery

If recovery time is too short or disturbed by any circumstances, underrecovery may occur. *Underrecovery* is defined as the imbalance of recovery periods and daily life demands of a person. These demands can be intensive practice, competitions, as well as other stressors linked to the sport and everyday life of an athlete. For example, distance from family because of extensive travel can be an important stressor disturbing adequate recovery before and after games. Other potential risk factors include monotonous training programmes, training sessions that are too long, ignoring training principles, or periodization (not including rest days or periods of lower intensity; Kenttä & Hassmén, 2002). While short periods of underrecovery can be compensated by the athletes' use of recovery strategies (e.g., relaxation techniques), chronic underrecovery can have both short-term and long-term consequences. Short-term consequences include increased feelings of tiredness, exhaustion, and lethargy, decreased motivation, as well as development of negative cognitions towards upcoming activities, all of which negatively influence future performance and may lead to early dropout (Kellmann & Altfeld, 2014a). Less concentration and body tension can also increase the risk of injuries and therefore affect the career development of youth athletes by resulting in long periods without practice during the most crucial learning stages in youth development. Additionally, in contrast to the overtraining syndrome, underrecovery affects athletes' daily routines. Reduced energy levels during daily activities can reinforce long-term consequences, including feelings of depression, emotional instability, weight loss, increased resting heart rate, hormonal changes, disturbed sleep, and increased vulnerability to injuries and respiratory diseases (Kellmann & Altfeld, 2014a).

Unpredictable events and changing conditions are also likely to occur in daily routines. These can vary and might include variability in the environmental conditions (e.g., noise, heat, problems with facilities), self-related issues such as tension, disturbing cognitions or inner conflicts, or even domestic issues (e.g., family problems, extra workload), which could have a deep impact on recovery. This phenomenon is termed *disturbed recovery* (Kellmann, 2002) and is present when conditions for optimal recovery are given, but the process is interrupted by environmental issues (Kellmann, Altenburg, Lormes, & Steinacker, 2001). During these moments of deep concentration and attempted relaxation, any disturbance could be experienced as a stressor and lead to underrecovery.

Overtraining

If an athlete reaches the state of chronic underrecovery, small periods of regeneration or spontaneous interventions are ineffective, requiring longer rest periods (from several weeks to months) and professional help from doctors or psychologists. This condition is termed *overtraining* and can be viewed as the result of too much training and stress with insufficient recovery (Meeusen et al., 2013). Therefore, underrecovery syndrome (insufficient and/or lack of recovery time) can be characterized as a longer-lasting pre-condition to overtraining syndrome. Overtraining develops over time and occurs when athletes are unable to refill their energy stores adequately and continue to practise in a tired state (Kellmann & Altfeld, 2014b). Research has revealed that the most frequent causes of overtraining are (1) too much stress and pressure, (2) too much practice and physical training, (3) boredom because of too much repetition, and (4) poor rest and lack of proper sleep. In addition to training load, non-training factors have a tremendous influence on the young athlete but are not yet fully integrated in the overtraining concept (Gustafsson et al., 2011). As already mentioned, performance abilities are influenced by many factors, such as state of health (e.g., infections), lifestyle (e.g., sleep), environment (e.g., family, friends, school), and psychological and physiological development (e.g., puberty). Emotional worries (e.g., troubles at home or with team dynamics) can also highly affect the developing athlete. Similarly, being seen as an elite athlete in early stages of development (e.g., gymnasts) can be an obstacle (Dubuc et al., 2010), as the demands (performance and otherwise) may not be appropriate for younger age groups' level of cognitive and social development.

Overtraining can have both short- and long-term effects. Besides the short-term consequences of tiredness and exhaustion, the long-term consequences include psychological, physiological, and/or hormonal changes that could be (a) directly related to performance, in terms of decreased or stagnating sports and school performance, or (b) indirectly through other symptoms. Physiological changes include chronic muscle or joint pain, and elevated resting heart rate (Small, 2002). In addition, personality or mood changes can occur. Increased impressions/feelings of fatigue could arise frequently as well as a general lack of enthusiasm or ambition (Lazarus, 2000). Furthermore, difficulties in completing daily routines, changes in sleep patterns, or decreased appetite probably resulting in weight loss are frequently reported by athletes suffering from overtraining syndrome (Gustafsson, Kenttä, Hassmén, Lundqvist, & Durand-Bush, 2007; Gustafsson et al., 2008; Kenttä & Hassmén, 2002). Often, individuals can cope with these situations, but when heavy training load is added to already high stress, young athletes' resources may be depleted quickly, as highlighted by research indicating that injuries, illness, or infections appear more frequently during these times than during optimal recovery-stress states (Gustafsson et al., 2011). Considering all these factors, young athletes may be especially susceptible to overtraining. Due to their incomplete development, the variability of psychological and physiological characteristics is higher than that of other athletes.

Burnout

Overtraining has been primarily associated with physiological stress; on the contrary, *burnout syndrome* considers psychological factors to a greater extent (Gustafsson et al., 2011), although the boundaries between those two concepts are blurred. After Maslach and Jackson (1984) intensified research on burnout in organizational settings, different models were proposed in sport settings and developed over time. At first, Smith (1986) imbedded burnout in a cognitive-affective model with emphasis on imbalances between demands, coping resources and the cognitive appraisal of these imbalances. He defined four stages: (1) the young athlete is placed in a situation that involves varying demands; (2) the demands are perceived as excessive; (3) the young athlete experiences varying physiological responses; and (4) varying burnout consequences develop. Silva (1990) defined burnout as an endpoint of excessive physical training and Coakley (1992) operationalized it as the physical withdrawal from sports following an intense investment of effort and high achievements in sports. A much more recent integrated framework was developed by Gustafsson et al. (2011) for the purpose of directing future research. They proposed that burnout consists of major antecedents, early signs, entrapment, personality, coping and environment, key dimensions and consequences, including fully developed burnout and in many cases withdrawal and exit from sport (Gustafsson et al., 2008).

Burnout denotes a negative emotional reaction to sports participation, and while it is known that overtrained athletes can still maintain their performance motivation to keep training, a burned-out athlete will commonly have no motivation to pursue his/her activity (Fry, Morton, & Keast, 1991). Similarly, burnout has been defined as an exhaustive psychophysiological response to massive chronic stress that develops gradually (Gustafsson et al., 2007). Burnout has also been shown to lead to affective, cognitive, motivational, and behavioural consequences with chronic emotional and physical exhaustion as key components (Goodger, Gorely, Lavallee, & Harwood, 2007). The symptoms of burnout resemble those of the overtraining syndrome and can be linked to three indicators suggested by Raedeke (1997): (1) physical and emotional exhaustion; (2) reduced sense of personal accomplishment; and (3) sport devaluation. In the end, it often requires a long break from organized sport-related activities to recover from chronic stress. Repeated episodes of overtraining appear to increase the risk of burnout, with the motivation to continue training being the essential factor to differentiate between the seriousness of the overtraining syndrome and the likelihood of dropout (Raglin, Sawamura, Alexiou, Hassmén, & Kenttä, 2000). In this context, young athletes withdraw from sports because they perceive it is not possible to meet the psychological and physiological demands of the sport (Matos, Winsley, & Williams, 2011). Furthermore, athletes who specialize early in their careers were found to have higher physical and emotional exhaustion self-ratings than those who did various sports in the beginning of their careers (Strachan et al., 2009). Frequently, the early specializers drop out of the sport before having achieved top levels. It is important to recognize that not all young athletes who drop out are burned out; however, the incident of dropping out may still have detrimental effects on the child participating in sports as a lifelong healthy activity (Crane & Temple, 2015; Harris & Watson, 2014). The prevalence of burnout is still on the rise due to increasing training loads and pressure in elite sports (Gould & Dieffenbach, 2002).

Suggestions for prevention and intervention

Being able to react to/prevent underrecovery, overtraining, and burnout syndromes requires an appreciation of the interconnectivity of factors contributing to the complex system of youth sports development (Dubuc et al., 2010). Therefore, a holistic training approach to these syndromes may reflect the best solution, where (1) training must be balanced and varied, and (2) non-training time has to be considered as a major influence on training and competition (Gustafsson et al., 2011; Le Bars, Gernigon, & Ninot, 2008). All factors outside the realm of training sessions (e.g., competitive and organizational stressors; Hanton et al., 2005), therefore, need to be evaluated as to their possible negative influences on overall fatigue.

However, priority should lie on the education of all stakeholders on the importance of recovery and how appropriate recovery can be implemented. To prevent the extreme states of physical and emotional exhaustion, coaches and athletes need to incorporate sufficient and high-quality periods of regeneration into training regimens, ensuring that recovery periods are long enough, with minimal disturbances. Recovery can be divided into active, passive, and proactive methods (Kellmann, 2002). Active recovery involves moderate exercise during the recovery process to eliminate the results of fatigue through target-oriented physical activity (e.g., low-intensity cycling for a certain amount of time on an ergometer after a Tour de France stage). The passive approach consists of hot and cold baths, massages, steam baths, sauna or even sitting and lying quietly. It works through the initiation of physiological reactions to physiological stimuli such as heat, cold, or pressure and includes psychological and biological processes to restore pre-task/performance states. Whenever recovery includes a purposeful, self-initiated and self-determined action, it can be seen as proactive recovery (e.g., stretching to overcome a long wait for a medal ceremony when there is competition on the following day). If the perception of the whole process is positive, crucial changes in outcomes are likely (Botterill &

Wilson, 2002). While there is a range of recovery strategies, individuals will respond to them differently and athletes need to find a set of appropriate strategies that suits their unique needs. This implies conscientious selection and consistent training of those strategies.

Having appropriate recovery strategies is a crucial part of a successful recovery process, and includes a variety of ways to achieve a state of well-being and potentially prevent underrecovery, overtraining, and burnout syndromes from occurring (Kaur, Agarwal, & Babbar, 2014; Kudlackova, Eccles, & Dieffenbach, 2013; Pelka et al., 2016). People sleep, nap, read, or meditate to calm down from various stressors they were exposed to. Even running, dancing or other strenuous exercises could be declared relaxing if they are appraised as relaxation. One common recovery strategy involves systematic relaxation techniques and previous research has divided these techniques into two separate groups. *Muscle-to-mind techniques* focus on the training of one's sensitivity to muscle tension (e.g., progressive muscle relaxation, breathing techniques) while *mind-to-muscle techniques* focus on the cognitive processes involved in relaxation (e.g., autogenic training, hypnosis). Strategies with predominant cognitive components are associated with decreases in amounts of worrying, self-assessments of anxiety or pain, and an increase in the ability to concentrate (Jain et al., 2007). Strategies with predominant skeletal muscle components tend to produce greater muscular effects (i.e., a decrease in heart rate and blood pressure and an increase in finger pulse volume). Different versions of progressive muscle relaxation, biofeedback, yoga, and breathing are also prominent in this domain.

Interpersonal relationships play a role as well (Curran, Appleton, Hill, & Hall, 2013; Curran, Hill, Hall, & Jowett, 2015). A good athlete–coach relationship seems to have a preventive effect when the athlete can talk about stressors, disturbances during recovery periods, or other problems that occur during or outside of practice. Coaches need to take care that each youth athlete is different, because what is too much for one could be just right for another. Consequently, well-structured training and competition schedules are an important step to preventing monotonous training. Relating to that, lack of enjoyment has been shown to be the most influential predictor of burnout in youth athletes (Crane & Temple, 2015; Harris & Watson, 2014). Fraser-Thomas, Côté, and Deakin (2005) hypothesized that early specialization in one sport leads to a lack of self-determined behaviour and thereby to absence of enjoyment. This development then increases the likelihood of burnout.

Regarding the considerable individual differences between athletes on the issue of how much training and non-training stress is too much, monitoring protocols could be a possible solution. The Recovery-Stress Questionnaire for Athletes (RESTQ-Sport, 76 items; Kellmann & Kallus, 2016) was developed to measure the frequency of current stress symptoms along with the frequency of recovery-associated activities and states in athletes. This allows the current recovery-stress state to be evaluated based on the previous three days. Among others (e.g., the Profile of Mood States; McNair, Lorr, & Droppleman, 1981; and The Emotional Recovery Questionnaire; Lundqvist & Kentta, 2010), the RESTQ-Sport is considered an important tool for monitoring training in the applied field (Meeusen et al., 2013) and was implemented to investigate the influence of the recovery-stress balance on the injury risk in professional soccer players (Laux, Krumm, Diers, & Flor, 2015), in overreached young soccer players (Brink, Visscher, Coutts, & Lemmink, 2012) or on floorball performance (van der Does et al., 2015). Other options are the recently developed Acute Recovery and Stress Scale (ARSS, 32 items; Kellmann, Kölling, & Hitzschke, 2016) and the Short Recovery Stress Scale (SRSS, 8 items; Kellmann et al., 2016), two instruments developed to measure the acute recovery-stress state of athletes and evaluated during training camps of the German U21 field hockey team (Kölling et al., 2015). Additionally, the SRSS was implemented to monitor the sleep–wake patterns of the German U19 rowing team in preparation for the World Rowing Junior Championships (Kölling et al., 2016).

Final recommendations

Research in the area of recovery and stress in sports reflects that all three syndromes, underrecovery, overtraining, and burnout have a great influence on the career of an athlete and avoiding these syndromes requires individualized and proactive planning. Young athletes, in particular, are at a high risk, whenever situational circumstances are paired with high training loads and high academic demands. Consequently, research has to expand its efforts on examining the onset and development of underrecovery, overtraining and burnout to prevent their occurrence. Currently, talent development may be supported by thoroughly considering the following recommendations.

- Tailor schedules in a way that adequate rest and sleep is ensured
- Ensure that recovery is individual-specific
- Let athletes prepare different recovery/relaxation methods to react to stressors
- Take time off from organized or structured sports participation one to two days per week to allow the body to rest or participate in other activities
- Permit longer scheduled breaks from training and competition every 2 to 3 months, while focusing on other activities and cross-training to prevent loss of skill or level of conditioning
- Monitor the impact of training
- Focus on well-being and teaching athletes to be in tune with their bodies for cues to slow down or alter training methods
- Include parents and peers in your planning/consideration
- Communicate regularly with your athlete
- Consider the advantages and disadvantages of early sports specialization
- Keep workouts interesting with age-appropriate games and training
- Keep practice fun

Conclusion

In the developing young athlete, a balance between academia, sports, and leisure time should be the key ingredient to a successful and fulfilling career. Without de-emphasizing the demanding role of competition, environmental stressors in terms of organizational stresses will affect young athletes increasingly more throughout their careers. Therefore, emphasis should be placed on these issues early on. However, research has to address the interconnection of different stressors and how they influence the development of young athletes. Considering the key foci of high performance youth sport – that is, talent identification and development – research supports the conclusion that greater emphasis should be on the development of young athletes with less on identification issues. Moreover, a set of standardized, state-of-the-science measures collected when entering elite sports programmes could prove invaluable to monitor and accompany athletes on their path to sporting success.

References

Aagaard, H., & Jørgensen, U. (1996). Injuries in elite volleyball. *Scandinavian Journal of Medicine and Science in Sports, 6*, 228–232.

Anshel, M. H., & Lidor, R. (2012). Talent detection programs in sport: The questionable use of psychological measures. *Journal of Sport Behaviour, 35*(3), 239–266.

Appleton, P. A., Hall, H. K., & Hill, A. P. (2009). Relations between multidimensional perfectionism and burnout in junior-elite male athletes. *Psychology of Sport and Exercise, 10*, 457–465.

Arnold, R., & Fletcher, D. (2012). A research synthesis and taxonomic classification of organisational stressors encountered by sport performers. *Journal of Sport and Exercise Psychology, 34*, 397–429.

Beckmann, J., & Elbe, A-M. (2015). *Sport psychological intervention in competitive sports.* Newcastle upon Tyne, UK: Cambridge Scholars Publishing.

Bergeron, M. F., Mountjoy, M., Armstrong, N., Chia, M., Côté, J., Emery, C. A., ... Engebretsen, L. (2015). International Olympic Committee consensus on youth athletic development. *British Journal of Sports Medicine, 49*, 843–851. doi:10.1136/bjsports-2015-094962

Botterill, C., & Wilson, C. (2002). Overtraining: Emotional and interdisciplinary dimensions. In M. Kellmann (ed.), *Enhancing recovery: Preventing underperformance in athletes* (pp. 143–160). Champaign, IL: Human Kinetics.

Brink, M. S., Visscher, C., Coutts, A. J., & Lemmink, K. A. P. M. (2012). Changes in perceived stress and recovery in overreached young elite soccer players. *Scandinavian Journal of Medicine and Science in Sports, 22*(2), 285–292.

Coakley, J. (1992). Burnout among adolescent athletes: A personal failure or social problem. *Sociology of Sport Journal, 9*(3), 271–285.

Curran, T., Appleton, P. R., Hill, A. P., & Hall, H. K. (2013). The mediating role of psychological need satisfaction in relationships between types of passion for sport and athlete burnout. *Journal of Sports Sciences, 31*(6), 597–606.

Curran, T., Hill, A. P., Hall, H. K., & Jowett, G. E. (2015). Perceived coach behaviours and athletes' engagement and disaffection in youth sport: The mediating role of the psychological needs. *International Journal of Sport Psychology, 45*(6), 559–580.

Crane, J., & Temple, V. (2015). A systematic review of dropout from organized sport among children and youth. *European Physical Education Review, 21*(1), 114–131. doi:10.1177/1356336X14555294

Cresswell, S. L. (2009). The early signs of burnout: A prospective study. *Journal of Science and Medicine in Sports, 12*, 393–398.

Cresswell, S. L., & Eklund, R. C. (2007). Athlete burnout: A longitudinal qualitative study. *The Sport Psychologist, 21*(1), 1–20.

DiFiori, J. P., Benjamin, H. J., Brenner, J. S., Gregory, A., Jayanthi, N., Landry, G. L., & Luke, A. (2014). Overuse injuries and burnout in youth sports: A position statement from the American medical society for sports medicine. *British Journal of Sports Medicine, 48*, 287–288. doi:10.1136/bjsports-2013-093299

Dubuc, N. G., Schinke, R. J., Eys, M. A., Battochio, R., & Zaichkowsky, L. (2010). Experiences of burnout among adolescent female gymnasts: Three case studies. *Journal of Clinical Sport Psychology, 4*, 1–18.

Dupont, G., Nédélec, M., McCall, A., McCormack, D., Berthoin, S., & Wisløff, U. (2010). Effect of 2 soccer matches in a week on physical performance and injury rate. *The American Journal of Sports Medicine, 38*(9), 1752–1758.

Folland, J. P., & Williams, A. G. (2007). The adaptions to strength training: Methodological and neurological contributions to increased strength. *Sports Medicine, 47*, 145–168.

Fraser-Thomas, J. L., Côté, J., & Deakin, J. (2005). Youth sport programs: An avenue to foster positive youth development. *Physical Education and Sport Pedagogy, 10*(1), 19–40.

Fry, R. W., Morton, A. R., & Keast, D. (1991). Overtraining in athletes. *Sports Medicine, 12*(1), 32–65.

Goodger, K., Gorely, T., Lavallee, D., & Harwood, C. (2007). Burnout in sport: A systematic review. *The Sport Psychologist, 21*(2), 127–151.

Gould, D., & Dieffenbach, K. (2002). Overtraining, underrecovery, and burnout in sport. In M. Kellmann (ed.), *Enhancing recovery: Preventing underperformance in athletes* (pp. 25–35). Champaign, IL: Human Kinetics.

Gould, D., Feltz, D., & Weiss, M. (1985). Motives for participating in competitive youth swimming. *International Journal of Sports Psychology, 16*, 126–140.

Gould, D., Tuffey, S., Udry, E., & Loehr, J. (1996). Burnout in competitive junior tennis players: I. A quantitative psychological assessment. *The Sport Psychologist, 10*, 322–340.

Gustafsson, H., Davis, P., Skoog, T., Kenttä, G., & Haberl, P. (2015). Mindfulness and its relationship with perceived stress, affect, and burnout in elite junior athletes. *Journal of Clinical Sport Psychology, 9*, 263–281. doi:10.1123/jcsp-2014-0051

Gustafsson, H., Hassmén, P., Kenttä, G., & Johansson, M. (2008). A qualitative analysis of burnout in elite Swedish athletes. *Psychology of Sport and Exercise, 9*(6), 800–816.

Gustafsson, H., Kenttä, G., & Hassmén, P. (2011). Athlete burnout: An integrated model and future research directions. *International Review of Sport and Exercise Psychology, 4*(1), 3–24.

Gustafsson, H., Kenttä, G., Hassmén, P., Lundqvist, C., & Durand-Bush, N. (2007). The process of burnout: A multiple case study of three elite endurance athletes. *International Journal of Sport Psychology, 38*(4), 388–416.

Hampel, P., & Petermann, F. (2006). Perceived stress, coping, and adjustment in adolescents. *Journal of Adolescent Health, 38*(4), 409–415.

Hanton, D., Fletcher, G., & Coughlan, J. (2005). Stress in elite sport performers: A comparative study of competitive and organizational stressors. *Journal of Sports Sciences, 23*(10), 1129–1141.

Harris, B. S., & Watson, J. C. (2014). Developmental consideration in youth athlete burnout: A model for youth sport participants. *Journal of Clinical Sport Psychology, 8*, 1–18. doi:10.1123/jscp.2014-0009

Hughes, L., & Leavey, G. (2012). Setting the bar: Athletes and vulnerability to mental illness. *British Journal of Psychiatry, 200*(2), 95–96.

Jain, S., Shapiro, S. L., Swanick, S., Roesch, S. C., Mills, P. J., Bell, I., & Schwartz, G. E. (2007). A randomized controlled trial of mindfulness meditation versus relaxation training: Effects on distress, positive states of mind, rumination, and distraction. *Annals of Behavioral Medicine, 33*(1), 11–21.

Jowett, G. E., Hill, A. P., Hall, H. K., & Curran, T. (2016). Perfectionism, burnout and engagement in youth sport: The mediating role of basic psychological needs. *Psychology of Sport and Exercise, 24*, 18–26. doi:10.1016/j.psychsport.2016.01.001

Kallus, K. W., & Kellmann, M. (2000). Burnout in athletes and coaches. In Y. L. Hanin (ed.), *Emotions in sport* (pp. 209–230). Champaign, IL: Human Kinetics.

Kaur, S., Agarwal, N., & Babbar, R. (2014). Effectiveness of relaxation techniques in reducing stress levels by measuring heart rate variability. *International Journal of Physiology, 2*(1), 26–30.

Kellmann, M. (2002). Underrecovery and overtraining: Different concepts – similar impact? In M. Kellmann (ed.), *Enhancing Recovery: Preventing underperformance in athletes* (pp. 3–24). Champaign, IL: Human Kinetics.

Kellmann, M. (2010). Preventing overtraining in athletes in high-intensity sports and stress/recovery monitoring. *Scandinavian Journal of Medicine and Science in Sports, 20*(Suppl 2), 95–102. doi: 10.1111/j.1600-0838.2010.01192.x

Kellmann, M., & Altfeld, S. (2014a). Underrecovery syndrome. In R. C. Eklund & G. Tenenbaum (eds), *Encyclopedia of sport and exercise psychology* (Vol. 2, pp. 773–775). New York: Sage.

Kellmann, M., & Altfeld, S. (2014b). Overtraining syndrome. In R. C. Eklund & G. Tenenbaum (eds), *Encyclopedia of sport and exercise psychology* (Vol. 2, pp. 510–512). New York: Sage.

Kellmann, M., Altenburg, D., Lormes, W., & Steinacker, J. M. (2001). Assessing stress and recovery during preparation for the World Championships in Rowing. *The Sport Psychologist, 15*, 151–167.

Kellmann, M., & Günther, K. D. (2000). Changes in stress and recovery in elite rowers during preparation for the Olympic Games. *Medicine and Science in Sports and Exercise, 32*(3), 676–683.

Kellmann, M., & Kallus, K. W. (2016). The Recovery-Stress Questionnaire for Athletes. In K. W. Kallus & M. Kellmann (eds), *The Recovery-Stress Questionnaires: User manual* (pp. 89–134). Frankfurt: Pearson.

Kellmann, M., Kölling, S., & Hitzschke, B. (2016). *Das Akutmaß und die Kurzskala zur Erfassung von Erholung und Beanspruchung im Sport – Manual* [The Acute Measure and the Short Scale of Recovery and Stress for Sports – Manual]. Hellenthal: Sportverlag Strauß.

Kenttä, G., & Hassmén, P. (2002). Underrecovery and overtraining: A conceptual model. In M. Kellmann (ed.), *Enhancing recovery: Preventing underperformance in athletes* (pp. 57–79). Champaign, IL: Human Kinetics.

Kölling, S., Hitzschke, B., Holst, T., Ferrauti, A., Meyer, T., Pfeiffer, M., & Kellmann, M. (2015). Validity of the Acute Recovery and Stress Scale: Training monitoring of the German junior national field hockey team. *International Journal of Sports Science and Coaching, 10*, 529–542.

Kölling, S., Steinacker, J., Endler, S., Ferrauti, A., Meyer, T., & Kellmann, M. (2016). The longer the better: Sleep-wake patterns during preparation of the World Rowing Junior Championships. *Chronobiology International, 33*(1), 73–84.

Kuipers, H. (1998). Training and overtraining: An introduction. *Medicine and Science in Sports and Exercise, 30*(7), 1137–1139.

Kudlackova, K., Eccles, D. W., & Dieffenbach, K. (2013). Use of relaxation skills in differentially skilled athletes. *Psychology of Sport and Exercise, 14*(4), 468–475.

Lauer, L., Gould, D., Roman, N., & Pierce, M. (2010). Parental behaviours that affect junior tennis player development. *Psychology of Sport and Exercise, 11*(6), 487–496.

Laux, P., Krumm, B., Diers, M., & Flor, H. (2015). Recovery-stress balance and injury risk in professional football players: A prospective study. *Journal of Sports Sciences, 33*(20), 2140–2148.

Lazarus, R. S. (2000). How emotions influence performance in competitive sports. *The Sport Psychologist, 14*(3), 229–252.

Lazarus, R. S. (1999). *Stress and emotion: A new synthesis.* New York: Springer.

Le Bars, H., Gernigon, C., & Ninot, G. (2009). Personal and contextual determinants of elite young athletes' persistence or dropping out over time. *Scandinavian Journal of Medicine and Science in Sports, 19*(2), 274–285.

Lundqvist, C., & Kenttä, G. (2010). Positive emotions are not simply the absence of the negative ones: Development and validation of the Emotional Recovery Questionnaire (EmRecQ). *The Sport Psychologist, 24,* 468–488.

Main, L., & Landers, G. (2012). Overtraining or burnout: A training and psycho-behavioural case study. *International Journal of Sports Science and Coaching, 7*(1), 23–32.

Maslach, C., & Jackson, S. E. (1984). Burnout in organizational settings. *Applied Social Psychology Annual, 5,* 133–153.

Matos, N. F., Winsley, R. J., & Williams, C. A. (2011). Prevalence of nonfunctional overreaching/overtraining in young English athletes. *Medicine and Science in Sports and Exercise, 43*(7), 1287–1294.

McNair, D. M., Lorr, M., & Droppleman, L. F. (1981). *Profile of Mood States POMS.* San Diego, CA: Educational and Industrial Testing Service.

Meeusen, R., Duclos, M., Foster, C., Fry, A., Gleeson, M., Nieman, D., … Urhausen, A. (2013). Prevention, diagnosis, and treatment of the overtraining syndrome: Joint consensus statement of the European College of Sport Science and the American College of Sports Medicine. *Medicine and Science in Sports and Exercise, 45*(1), 186–205. doi: 10.1249/MSS.0b013e318279a10a

Nédélec, M., McCall, A., Carling, C., Legall, F., Berthoin, S., & Dupont, G. (2012). Recovery in soccer: Part I – post-match fatigue and time course of recovery. *Sports Medicine, 42*(12), 997–1015.

Nédélec, M., McCall, A., Carling, C., Legall, F., Berthoin, S., & Dupont, G. (2013). Recovery in soccer: Part II – recovery strategies. *Sports Medicine, 43*(1), 9–22.

Nicholls, A. R., & Polman, R. C. J. (2007). Coping in sport: A systematic review. *Journal of Sports Sciences, 25*(1), 11–31.

Pelka, M., Kölling, S., Ferrauti, A., Meyer, T., Pfeiffer, M., & Kellmann, M. (2016). Acute effects of psychological relaxation techniques between two physical tasks. *Journal of Sports Sciences,* doi:10.1080/02640414.2016.1161208

Raedeke, T. D. (1997). A sport commitment perspective. *Journal of Sport and Exercise Psychology, 19,* 396–417.

Raglin, J., Sawamura, S., Alexiou, S., Hassmén, P., & Kenttä, G. (2000). Training practices and staleness in 13–18-year-old swimmers: A cross-cultural study. *Pediatric Exercise Science, 12*(1), 61–70.

Rice, S. M., Purcell, R., De Silva, S., Mawren, D., McGorry, P., & Parker, A. G. (2016). The mental health of elite athletes: A narrative systematic review. *Sports Medicine, 46*(9), 1333–1353. doi:10.1007/s40279-016-0492-2

Rumbold, J. L., Fletcher, D., & Daniels, K. (2012). A systematic review of stress management interventions with sport performers. *Sport, Exercise, and Performance Psychology, 1*(3), 173–193.

Sarkar, M., & Fletcher, D. (2014). Psychological resilience in sport performers: A review of stressors and protective factors. *Journal of Sports Sciences, 32*(15), 1419–1434. doi:10.1080/02640414.2014.901551

Silva III, J. M. (1990). An analysis of the training stress syndrome in competitive athletics. *Journal of Applied Sport Psychology, 2*(1), 5–20.

Small, E. (2002). Chronic musculoskeletal pain in young athletes. *Pediatric Clinics of North America, 49*(3), 655–662.

Smith, R. E. (1986). Toward a cognitive-affective model of athletic burnout. *Journal of Sport Psychology, 8*(1), 36–50.

Strachan, L., Côté, J., & Deakin, J. (2009). An evaluation of personal and contextual factors in competitive youth sport. *Journal of Applied Sport Psychology, 21*(3), 340–355.

Transfermarkt (2015). Player profiles. Retrieved from www.transfermarkt.co.uk/ felixpasslack/leistungsdatenspieler/274461/plus/0?saison=2014.

van der Does, H. T., Brink, M. S., Visscher, C., Huijgen, B. C., Frencken, W. G., & Lemmink, K. A. P. M. (2015). The effect of stress and recovery on field-test performance in floorball. *International Journal of Sports Medicine, 36*(6), 460–465.

Ward, P., Hodges, N. J., Starkes, J. I., & Williams, M. A. (2007). The road to excellence: Deliberate practice and the development of expertise. *High Ability Studies, 18*(2), 119–153.

26

MEDICAL PERSPECTIVES ON TALENT DEVELOPMENT IN YOUTH SPORTS

Tamara John and Cordelia W. Carter

While much attention is paid to the identification and cultivation of athletic talent in children and adolescents, it is essential to remember that the benefits of youth talent development are only realized if young athletes are able to stay healthy and injury-free as they mature and develop. Having a basic understanding of the specific risks of injury and illness that young athletes face is critical to ensuring their continued health, optimal performance, and athletic longevity. The primary goal of health care providers who interact with young athletes is therefore to *protect* talent by identifying those young athletes at risk for sports-related injuries—both acute and chronic—and taking steps to mitigate or avoid entirely the impact that such injuries may ultimately have on present and future athletic performance.

Child-specific risk factors for sport participation

The adage that "children aren't little adults" is never truer than when applied to the young athlete. Children and adolescents who participate in sports may certainly suffer from similar illnesses and injuries as their adult counterparts; however, there are several child-specific risk factors for injury that deserve special mention.

Physical growth

Unlike adults, who have reached their definitive height and body composition, child and adolescent athletes are still actively growing: linear height acquisition continues in females until roughly age 14, and in males until age 16 (Adirim & Cheng, 2003). There is a sex difference in the timing and tempo of muscular strength acquisition, with males exhibiting accelerated increases in muscular strength throughout late adolescence and ultimately greater peak strength than females (Beunen & Malina, 1988).

While there are differences between males and females in terms of when and at what speed musculoskeletal growth occurs, the dynamic nature of these changes is common to all young athletes. Rapid elongation of the long bones may put extra stress on adjacent joints as the muscles and tendons adapt; pain in the knees, hips, and lower back may be reported during periods of skeletal growth. Additionally, the rapid increases in height and weight that occur during the peri-pubertal period change the body's center of gravity dramatically. There is a corresponding temporary decline in coordination and balance observed during this time as the athlete adjusts to the body's physical changes—the result is the "clumsy teenager" (Michaud, 2001). The adolescent growth spurt can further interfere with progression of sports skills until the body has adjusted and can be especially noticeable in sports that require tremendous balance and body control such as figure skating, diving, and gymnastics. Furthermore, newly elongated limbs can affect precision when catching and hitting a ball with a bat or racquet. The observed decline in sports performance can be challenging for the young athlete. The key is for parents, coaches, and athletes to recognize that this is a temporary component of growth and development. Focusing attention on stretching, strengthening and nutrition during periods of rapid growth may be useful for optimizing a young athlete's mental and physical health during this time (Tursz & Crost, 1986).

Heat-related illness

It is generally accepted that young athletes have a greater risk of suffering from heat-related illness than adults. This theory is based upon the observation that children have higher body surface area-to-mass ratio, with the potential for greater heat transfer from the environment to the child. This proposed physiological vulnerability may then be coupled with a child's poor judgment in seeking adequate hydration during sports participation, a situation that may lead to exertional heat illness (Bergeron, Devore, & Rice, 2011).

Exertional heat illness includes a spectrum of disorders, with heat exhaustion and heat stroke representing the most extreme. Young athletes with heat exhaustion may initially complain of muscle cramps; other common symptoms include profuse sweating, rapid breathing, weakness and dizziness. If heat exhaustion goes untreated, it may progress to heat stroke, which is characterized by a core body temperature elevated above 105°F, dry skin, rapid pulse, agitation, confusion, seizures, and in its most extreme, coma (Pretzlaff, 2002). Paying special attention to heat exposure and protection against heat-related illness is critical for health maintenance in the young athlete. A summary of recommendations for prevention of heat-related illness is presented in Table 26.1.

Medical factors that may preclude sports participation

One essential way to protect a young athlete from illness and injury is to identify any disorders that may place him or her at an unacceptably high risk for having a devastating complication if allowed to participate in sports. In some cases, knowledge of a medical condition (e.g., sickle cell disease) allows coaches, trainers, and other personnel involved in the care of the athlete to employ preventative measures (such as hydration and heat-control strategies, in the case of sickle cell disease) that allow continued safe sport participation. However, the presence of other pre-existing conditions, such as certain cervical spine abnormalities, may preclude safe participation for the young athlete in collision sports due to the increased risk of catastrophic spinal cord injury. Although not exhaustive, the discussion that follows reviews representative medical and musculoskeletal conditions that may require modification of, or exclusion from, sports activities.

Abnormalities of the cervical spine

The cervical spine consists of the uppermost seven vertebrae, which connect the spinal column to the skull and serve to protect the spinal cord. In general, abnormalities of the cervical spine

Table 26.1 Summary of recommendations to prevent heat-related illness in young athletes

- **Fluid replacement**
  - Adequate and readily accessible fluids should be available at each game and practice to allow fluid consumption at regular intervals before, during, and after sports participation.
  - 9 to 12-year-old athletes should consume 100–250 milliliters of water every 20 minutes and older adolescents should consume 1–1.5 liters per hour to sufficiently minimize sweating-induced body-water deficits sustained during exercise.
- **Education**
  - Children, coaches and all personnel involved with young athletes should be educated on the merits of proper sports preparation including ample hydration and sufficient recovery and rest.
- **Training**
  - Young athletes must be allowed and encouraged to gradually adapt to pre-season practice and conditioning, sport participation, or other physical activities in heat
- **Equipment modification**
  - American Youth Football recommends limiting football practice gear to light- colored, lightweight cotton or mesh shorts and helmets with shoulder pads. Athletes should also be given chances to remove their helmets whenever possible.
- **Special circumstances**
  - Young athletes should limit or avoid sport participation when recovering from a gastrointestinal illness, where large amounts of body fluids may be lost.

that narrow the space available for the spinal cord or that put the bones that encase the spinal cord at risk for fracture are associated with sports-related spinal cord injuries. As a result, young persons who are identified as having such an abnormality of the cervical spine are considered "high risk" for participation in contact and collision sports such as rugby, lacrosse, and American football.

Conditions of the cervical spine may be divided into three categories: congenital, developmental, and post-traumatic. One example of a congenital cervical spine condition is atlanto-occipital fusion (an abnormal connection of the first cervical vertebra to the skull), which places the adjacent spinal segments at risk for fracture. Atlantoaxial instability (abnormally increased motion between the first two cervical vertebrae) is another contraindication to sport participation, as this condition may result in impingement to the spinal cord (see Figure 26.1). This condition is particularly common amongst athletes with ligamentous laxity, similar to what might be seen in those with Down's syndrome (Goldenring, 1994).

In contrast to congenital conditions, which are present from the time of birth, development conditions of the cervical spine, as their name implies, develop over time. A common example of this is "spear-tackler's spine." Spear tackler's spine is a syndrome of cervical stenosis (narrowing of the spinal canal) caused by repetitive microtrauma theorized to be due, in part, to improper tackling techniques (Torg, Sennett, Pavlov, Leventhal, & Glasgow, 1993). Young athletes with developmental cervical stenosis require evaluation by a medical specialist to determine whether participation in contact and collision sports may be safely continued without undue risk of spinal cord injury. Finally, the most familiar example of traumatic cervical spine abnormality precluding sport participation is fracture. Athletes with acute spinal fractures are typically unable to participate in sports. Athletes with healed fractures should be evaluated by a medical specialist prior to resumption of sports. The decision to return a young athlete to

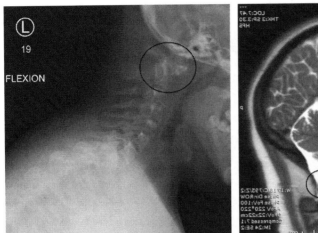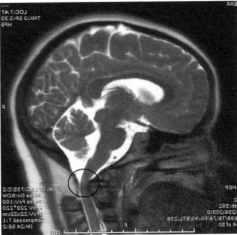

Figure 26.1 Atlantoaxial instability. Panel A (left) is a sagittal radiograph of the cervical spine of a 16-year-old female with Down's syndrome and atlantoaxial instability (abnormal motion between the 1st and 2nd cervical vertebrae; black circle). Panel B is the MRI of the same patient, demonstrating impingement of the spinal cord in the cervical spine (black circle)

play is typically made after consideration of patient-specific factors such as age, experience, ability, level of participation, position played, and sport, in addition to the fracture appearance on diagnostic imaging such as X-ray, magnetic resonance imaging (MRI), and computed tomography (CT) scan (Torg & Ramsey-Emrhein, 1997).

Cardiovascular conditions

Hypertrophic cardiomyopathy (HCM) is the quintessential example of a heart condition that is considered an absolute contraindication to sports participation for young athletes. HCM is a rare genetic myocardial disease in which a portion of the heart muscle is abnormally thickened, which impairs the heart's ability to function properly. When people with HCM exercise strenuously, the stress placed on the abnormal heart muscle may result in cardiac arrest (heart attack) and sudden death. Not infrequently, these young athletes may not have exhibited any symptoms (e.g., shortness of breath, chest pain, palpitations) prior to experiencing heart attack (Corrado, Basso, Schiavon, & Thiene, 1998). HCM is implicated as the principal cause of cardiac arrest in younger competitive athletes in the US, accounting for about one third of fatal cases (Maron, Haas, Ahluwalia, Murphy & Garberich, 2016). HCM may be detected by electrocardiogram (EKG) and echocardiogram, although there is currently no mandatory pre-season screening policy for HCM in the United States. Other cardiac conditions that preclude participation in sports include long QT syndrome, acute myocarditis and pericarditis (Goldenring, 1994).

Neurologic conditions

Concussion is the most common example of a neurologic condition that may present a contraindication to sport participation. Concussion may be defined as a head injury that is associated with a biomechanical insult to the brain, which initiates a destructive neurometabolic cascade; the end result is a temporary loss of brain function. Concussed athletes may exhibit a variety of symptoms, including headache, dizziness, nausea, disorientation, and poor balance. Changes in mood, cognition, and sleep patterns may also be observed (Majerske et al., 2008). Because young athletes who have sustained one concussion are at higher risk for sustaining a second—especially in the immediate post-concussion period—return-to-play guidelines for concussed athletes have evolved over time to be increasingly stringent.

In general, young athletes with an acute concussion are removed from play immediately. Physical and cognitive rest is recommended until symptoms have resolved. Once the young athlete has recovered symptomatically while at rest, a gradual progression of sport skills is introduced; successful completion of one skill without symptom recurrence is required for advancement to the next level. Athletes are progressed from performing easier skills (i.e., walking) to increasingly more difficult skills (i.e., jogging, running, sport-specific drills and ultimately to practice and competition) in a supervised fashion (McCrory et al., 2009).

Because concussions, and particularly recurrent concussions, have been linked to long-term cognitive dysfunction, it is of paramount importance to adhere to current return-to-play guidelines in order to protect young athletes who have sustained a concussion. For some young athletes, concussion may be a season-ending injury; the occurrence of multiple concussions in a young athlete may be a career-ender.

Hematologic conditions

Sickle cell trait is the classic example of a condition affecting the blood that affects a young athlete's participation in sport. Like the more severe sickle cell disease, sickle cell trait is an inherited condition that results in the formation of red blood cells with atypical, "sickle" shapes (Thompson, 2013). Unlike people with sickle cell disease, people with sickle cell trait are generally asymptomatic during activities of daily living. However, with physical exertion, athletes with sickle cell trait may develop exertional rhabdomyolysis. This syndrome is characterized by muscle pain, cramping, fatigue, and the production of dark urine—consequences of the abnormal breakdown of skeletal muscle due to the impaired function of the sickled red blood cells. In its most extreme iteration, exertional rhabdomyolysis may lead to sudden death (Gallagher, Finison, Guyer, & Goodenough, 1984).

In 2010, the National Collegiate Athletic Association (NCAA) implemented a universal mandatory sickle cell trait screening of all Division I student athletes. Athletes who are found to have sickle cell trait are still allowed to participate in sports but are encouraged to focus on appropriate pre-season and in-season conditioning. Because exercise-induced dehydration and exhaustion may bring about a sickling episode in these athletes, the NCAA has recommended multiple preventative hydration and temperature-monitoring strategies that have proven to be effective in this specific population (Tarini, Brooks, & Bundy, 2011).

Solitary organs

Coaches, trainers, and health care personnel are encouraged to inquire of their athletes about the presence of a single paired organ (e.g., eye, testis, kidney), as loss of the remaining organ might have more dire medical consequences than would be expected for an athlete with a full organ complement. The decision to allow athletes to participate in sports with only one of a paired organ is controversial, especially for athletes with only one kidney. For example, a survey of 438 American Medical Society for Sports Medicine members showed that 54.1% would allow an asymptomatic patient with a normally functioning solitary kidney to participate in collision or contact sports. Of the 44.7% who would not allow sports participation, 63.3%

reported that this decision was based upon medical liability concerns (Grafe, Paul, & Foster, 1997).

Patients with one eye should have an ophthalmology evaluation prior to sport participation, although these athletes can usually safely participate in sports that do not involve projected objects and that permit protective eyewear, such as swimming, track and field, and gymnastics. There are no limitations for athletes who have one testicle, but the use of a protective cup is strongly encouraged with participation in contact sports (Grafe et al., 1997).

Acute illness

Medical conditions causing splenomegaly (enlarged spleen) are considered relative contraindications to participation in sport, due to the risk of splenic rupture with the concomitant potential for massive internal bleeding. Infectious mononucleosis (IM) is one example of this. In brief, IM is a common medical condition that afflicts thousands of young athletes each year. It is a disease transmitted by the Epstein-Barr virus (EBV), usually through exchange of saliva. Symptoms include malaise, headache, fever, fatigue, and sore throat.

Splenomegaly occurs commonly with EBV infection and the concern for splenic rupture drives the debate surrounding an athlete's participation in contact sports. Splenic rupture can either occur spontaneously or as a result of trauma; the overall incidence rate has been reported as 0.1%. The spleen appears to be most vulnerable to rupture in the first 3–4 weeks of illness. Although the appropriate time for safe return to contact play is unclear, given the increased risk of splenic rupture within weeks one to three, a time frame of at least three weeks is commonly recommended (Putukian et al., 2008). Additionally, return to play should only be allowed once the athlete is asymptomatic.

Common sports-related injuries of the young athlete

As increasing numbers of children and adolescents participate in athletics, health care practitioners have seen corresponding increases in the incidence of sports-related injuries, which may be broadly characterized as acute (generally, traumatic) and chronic (generally atraumatic, or overuse-related) in nature.

Acute injuries

Concussion, discussed in the previous section, is one example of an acute sports-related injury. Other non-musculoskeletal injuries include traumatic injuries of the eye or of other solid organs such as the spleen, liver, or kidneys. More common, however, are acute injuries involving the musculoskeletal system. These may affect bones, joints, ligaments, tendons, muscles or some combination thereof. A comprehensive assessment of all sports-related musculoskeletal injuries is beyond the scope of this chapter; rather, representative examples of frequently occurring acute musculoskeletal injuries will be reviewed.

Perhaps the most familiar traumatic injury affecting young athletes is fracture, and fracture of the clavicle (e.g., the collarbone) is one example of this (Figure 26.2A). In general, acute, displaced fractures such as the one depicted here require a period of immobilization (4–6 weeks) to ensure that adequate healing has occurred prior to resumption of activity, and may therefore be season-ending injuries (Maffulli & Baxter-Jones, 1995). Some fractures may require more than simple immobilization in a cast, splint, or sling to achieve adequate healing; depending upon the bone involved, the fracture pattern, the age and physiologic

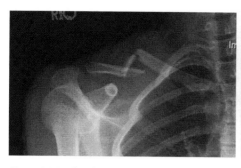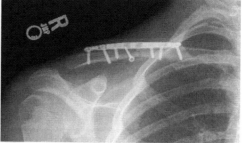

Figure 26.2 Clavicle fracture. Panel A (left) is an anteroposterior (AP) radiograph of the right clavicle of a 15-year-old male with a displaced, comminuted mid-shaft clavicle fracture sustained during soccer practice. Panel B (right) demonstrates the same fracture following open reduction and internal fixation (ORIF)

maturity of the athlete, and the sport played, operative treatment may be indicated (Figure 26.2B).

Joints, too, may be primarily affected by injury. In the young athletic population, shoulder dislocation is a well-known example. In the vast majority of cases, primary traumatic shoulder instability is anterior in direction (i.e., the shoulder comes out of place in the front, Figure 26.3A) and requires manipulation to achieve relocation (Figure 26.3B). Males are affected more frequently than females, and are also more likely to have recurrent instability after a first-time dislocation event (Wasserlauf & Paletta, 2003). In fact, young male athletes are at highest risk for repeated dislocations, with rates of recurrent instability estimated to be as high as 85% for 15-year-old males (Mariscalco & Saluan, 2011). Traditionally, initial treatment for isolated shoulder dislocation has been a brief period of immobilization in a sling, followed by formal rehabilitation. Return-to-play decisions are guided by the athlete's symptoms, as well as by the

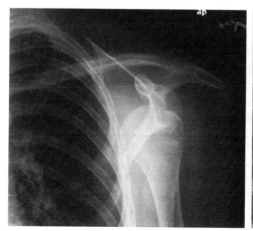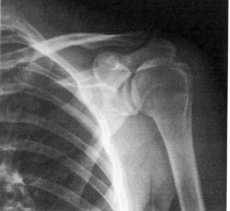

Figure 26.3 Shoulder instability. Panel A (left) is an AP radiograph of the left shoulder of a 17-year-old male who sustained a shoulder dislocation during football practice. Panel B (right) is the same patient, following reduction of the shoulder in the emergency room

sport and the timing of the injury within the athlete's season. Because of the high risk of recurrent instability, some young athletes with primary traumatic anterior shoulder instability are candidates for surgical stabilization (Wasserlauf & Paletta, 2003). Surgical stabilization is routinely recommended for athletes with recurrent instability.

Injury of the anterior cruciate ligament (ACL) is the quintessential ligamentous injury of the young athlete. The mechanism of injury for ACL injury is frequently reported to be a non-contact injury in which the athlete's foot is planted and the knee twists around it. An injured athlete might report the sensation of a "pop" in the knee followed by the appearance of swelling and difficulty bearing weight through the affected limb (Mariscalco & Saluan, 2011). Physical examination may be adequate for diagnosis of ACL rupture, although magnetic resonance imaging (MRI) of the knee may be helpful for identification of additional injuries of the collateral ligaments and meniscus (see Figure 26.4; Gornitzky et al., 2015). Female athletes have a greater than 2-fold increased risk of sustaining an ACL injury than their male peers (Beynnon et al., 2014). Rupture of the ACL is generally a season-ending injury, with most athletes requiring surgical reconstruction of the ligament followed by extensive rehabilitation in order to safely return to sport. Because of the tremendous financial, social, and emotional costs associated with ACL injuries, primary prevention strategies such as the FIFA 11+ program have become increasingly popular (FIFA, nd).

Ankle sprain is another common ligamentous injury amongst adolescent athletes. A typical injury mechanism for a lateral ankle sprain is inversion and plantarflexion of the ankle, which occurs when the foot rolls inward with the toes pointed down. This type of injury can be seen when an athlete lands awkwardly on another player's shoe while playing basketball, for example, or when a person steps on uneven ground. The most commonly injured ligament in this

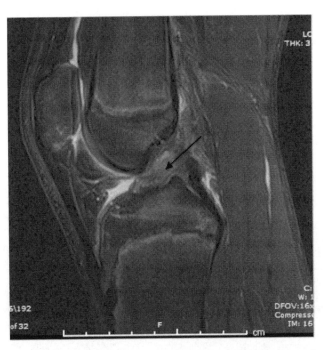

Figure 26.4 Anterior cruciate ligament (ACL) rupture. The figure shows a sagittal MRI of the knee of a 12-year-old female, demonstrating a mid-substance tear of the ACL (black arrow)

setting is the anterior talofibular ligament (Omey & Micheli, 1999). Athletes with lateral ankle sprains have varying degrees of swelling, bruising, localized tenderness, and difficulty bearing weight. Treatment begins with rest, ice, compression and elevation. Athletes with an ankle sprain can usually bear weight as tolerated in a supportive ankle brace or walking boot. Rehabilitation begins early after injury, with the primary goals of rehabilitation including: decreasing swelling, regaining motion, and restoring normal kinematics to the affected limb. Low-grade ankle sprains may only require minimal time away from sport participation, while higher-grade injuries may take weeks or, in some cases, months to heal. A return to sport before ankle proprioception is restored may result in recurrent instability and long-term dysfunction. Prevention programs for ankle injuries have been described and studied, with most demonstrating a positive effect (Smith & Reischl, 1986).

While injury of a ligament (the fibrous tissue that connects two bones together in a joint) is termed a "sprain", the nomenclature used to describe injury of muscles and tendons (the cord-like soft tissues that attach muscles to bones) is a "strain" (Maffulli & Bruns, 2000). A common example of an acute sports-related strain involves the musculotendinous unit of the hamstrings, the primary flexors of the knee. Usually an athlete with an acute hamstring strain will report the onset of sharp pain in the back of the thigh, often associated with a rapid acceleration maneuver, such as the start of a sprint. Low-grade strains generally involve a stretch of the muscle, without disruption of fibers and may be treated simply according to the mnemonic RICE: rest, ice, compression and elevation. Athletes with low-grade strains typically have a rapid return to sport participation, on the order of days to weeks. High-grade strains, by contrast, involve frank tearing of the muscle and/or tendon and have a slower course of healing; in some cases, surgical repair may be required (Guzzanti, 2013).

Chronic (overuse) injuries

In contrast to acute injuries, which may be quite dramatic when they occur, chronic sports-related injuries typically develop gradually, with symptoms appearing in an insidious fashion. Repetition of the same activity over time (e.g., throwing a baseball, long-distance running, kicking a soccer ball) without adequate time for recovery is the causative factor. Stages of overuse injuries have been the described by Brenner (2007): the initial stage is characterized by pain in the affected area after physical activity. With continued use, pain becomes present both during and after physical activity, which may or may not restrict sport performance; left untreated, pain may progress until it becomes constant. Just as acute sports injuries may affect any part of the musculoskeletal system, chronic overuse injuries may affect bone, ligament, tendon, and/or muscle.

The classic example of overuse injury is stress fracture (see Figure 26.5). Unlike traumatic fractures, which occur as the result of a fall or direct blow, stress fractures result from repetitive mechanical stress. Stress fractures occur more frequently in the lower extremities, although sites of injury may be sport-specific: rowers, for example, may develop stress fractures of the ribs, gymnasts are commonly afflicted with stress fractures of the spine (e.g., spondylolysis), and runners typically present with stress fractures of the foot, tibia, and femur. Cessation of the offending activity is a necessary first step in the treatment of stress fractures, usually for a period not shorter than 4–6 weeks (Hulkko & Orava, 1987). For injuries of the lower extremities, the addition of crutches may be helpful. Once the athlete is pain-free, activities may be gradually reintroduced, with progression to more difficult skills allowed only if the athlete remains asymptomatic. Some stress fractures require surgical treatment to prevent progression to catastrophic injury; stress fractures of the anterior tibial cortex and femoral neck are examples

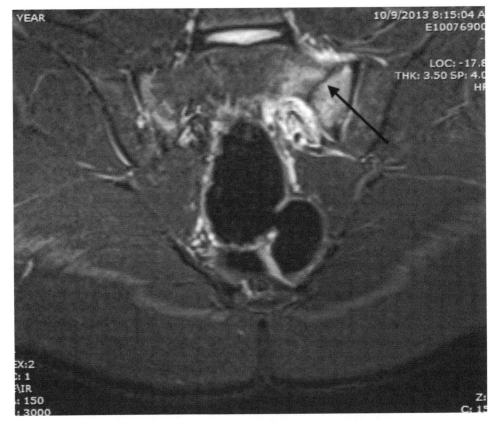

Figure 26.5 Stress fracture. The figure shows a coronal MRI image of the pelvis of an 11-year-old premenarchal female who developed atraumatic posterior hip pain during her cross-country season. A left-sided sacral stress fracture is present (black arrow)

of this (Brenner, 2007). Finally, investigation into a young athlete's training regimen, injury history, nutritional status, and menstrual status (for female athletes) may provide clues about additional factors contributing to the development of this overuse injury. Identification and treatment of contributing factors such as the presence of an eating disorder and menstrual dysfunction are essential for prevention of future injury.

The growth plate and articular cartilage

The presence of growth plates renders young athletes fundamentally different from older adolescents and adults. In brief, growth plates are areas of cartilage typically located at either end of the long bones, such as the femur and tibia, that are characterized by robust growth and cellular turnover; this combination renders the growth plate the "weakest link" in the musculoskeletal unit, and therefore most prone to injury (Caine, 2006). The inherent vulnerability of the growth plate (also called the physis) is further exacerbated during periods of rapid growth (i.e., the adolescent "growth spurt"). Injuries of the growth plate may be acute or chronic in nature.

Acute injuries of the growth plate

Acute injuries of the physis occur commonly in young athletes. One example of this is a fracture that traverses the growth plate, the so-called "Salter-Harris" type of fracture, which represents roughly 15% of all fractures in the pediatric population (see Figure 26.6). Such fractures differ from other fractures in that these injuries may cause subsequent premature closure of the growth plate; limb-length discrepancy and/or angular deformity may result. Just as with fractures through other parts of the bone, fractures through growth plates are typically season-ending injuries for young athletes, requiring 4–6 weeks of immobilization for fracture healing followed generally by formal rehabilitation prior to resumption of sporting activities (Caine, 2006). Not infrequently, surgical treatment is necessary. One common example of acute physeal injury in the skeletally immature population is the Salter-Harris injury of the distal fibula (the ankle). While older children and adolescents typically sustain ankle sprains with an inversion injury of the ankle, this mechanism of injury in a younger athlete may result instead in a non- or minimally-displaced fracture through the cartilaginous growth plate of the fibula (Smith & Reischl, 1986). The diagnosis is made by identifying the area of maximal tenderness over the lateral ankle. Treatment is similar to that for other physeal injuries, outlined above.

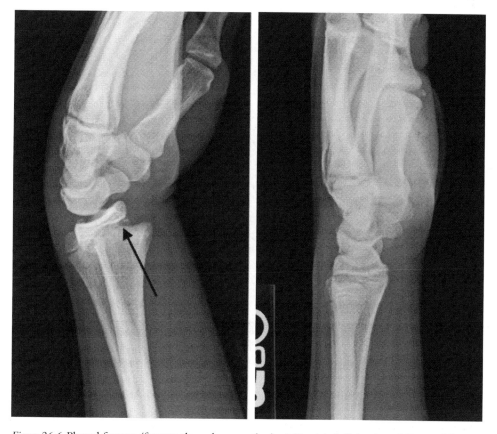

Figure 26.6 Physeal fracture (fracture through a growth plate). Panel A (left) is a lateral X-ray of the wrist of a 14-year-old male with complete translation through the radial growth plate (black arrow). Panel B (right) is a lateral X-ray following fracture reduction

A second type of acute growth plate injury involves the apophysis—a growth plate to which a musculotendinous unit is attached. Unlike regular growth plates, apophyses are not responsible for longitudinal growth. Acute injuries of the apophysis are generally avulsion fractures; powerful contraction of the attached muscle exerts a traction force through the growth plate, which ultimately fails. Common examples of apophyseal avulsion fractures include the tibial tubercle (the knee, where the quadriceps tendon inserts, Figure 26.7); the medial epicondyle of the humerus (the elbow, where the wrist flexor tendons insert); and the base of the fifth metatarsal (the foot, where the peroneus brevis tendon inserts) (Caine, 2006). Treatment for apophyseal avulsion fractures is similar to that of other growth plate fractures: non- and minimally-displaced fractures are treated with a period of immobilization (e.g., a cast or brace), followed by rehabilitation and gradual return to sport. Displaced fractures are treated surgically.

Finally, acute injury of the articular (joint) cartilage may also occur in the young, athletic population. While they do not technically involve the "growth cartilage", it is nonetheless essential to diagnose and appropriately treat injuries involving the joint; loss of articular congruity with displacement of greater than 2mm at the level of the cartilaginous joint surface is believed to be associated with the subsequent development of premature osteoarthritis (Guzzanti, 2013). One example of an acute intra-articular injury is the osteochondral fracture that often occurs with patellar dislocation. Patients who sustain injuries of the joint cartilage not infrequently undergo surgical treatment, with the goal of restoring the anatomic alignment of the articular surface (Maffulli & Baxter-Jones, 1995). Due to the need for prolonged immobilization followed by rehabilitation for patients with acute fractures through the growth plate and/or articular cartilage, these are typically season-ending injuries.

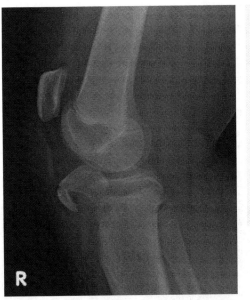
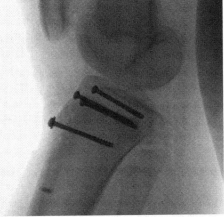

Figure 26.7 Apophyseal avulsion fracture. Panel A (left) is a lateral radiograph of the knee of a 14-year-old male who sustained a displaced tibial tubercle avulsion fracture while playing basketball. He underwent open reduction and internal fixation of his injury, demonstrated in the fluoroscopic image in Panel B (right)

Chronic injuries of the growth plate

Painful overuse injuries of the growth plates occur commonly amongst young athletes, and it is essential to distinguish between injury of the physis and injury of the apophysis, as treatment and outcomes are vastly different for these two different clinical entities. For example, a common repetitive overuse injury of the growth plate is "gymnast's wrist"—injury to the distal radial physis (growth plate of the wrist). In this scenario, repeated forceful weight-bearing through the wrist, such as that which occurs during tumbling, results in abnormalities of the growth plate, and in its most extreme iteration, premature closure of the physis (Tursz & Crost, 1986). "Little Leaguer's shoulder," in which damage to the proximal humeral physis is sustained by the stress of repeated throwing, is another example of chronic physeal injury (Adirim & Cheng, 2003). Patients with this type of repetitive overuse injury require modification of activities (e.g., restrictions on tumbling, throwing) until symptoms have resolved, followed by gradual reintroduction of sports and radiographic monitoring to ensure that long-term sequelae of physeal injury (growth disturbance, limb-length inequality, and angular deformity) do not occur.

By contrast, repetitive overuse injuries of the apophyses, while painful, do not require the restriction of a young athlete's activities and are not associated with long-term problems with longitudinal growth (Adirim & Cheng, 2003). The quintessential apophyseal overuse injury in this population is Osgood-Schlatter's disease—inflammation, or apophysitis, of the proximal tibial tubercle growth plate at the site of attachment of the patellar tendon. Another eponymous traction apophysitis is Sever's disease, inflammation of the growth plate of the heel at the insertion of the Achilles tendon (Figure 26.8). While these injuries may be painful, it is important to note that they are unlikely to cause long-term dysfunction due to physeal arrest (growth

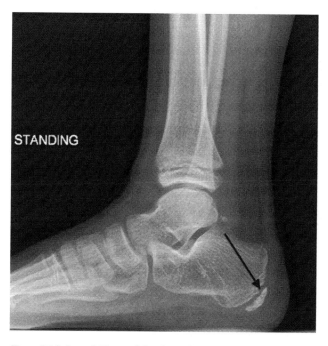

Figure 26.8 Lateral X-ray of the foot of a 10-year-old male with calcaneal apophysitis (Sever's disease). Black arrow points to normal growth plate of the heel

plate disturbance). Patients with traction apophysitis may benefit from treatment aimed at reduction of inflammation (e.g., stretching, bracing, icing, non-steroidal anti-inflammatory medication (NSAIDs) but unlike patients with injury of the growth cartilage or the articular cartilage, young athletes with traction apophysitis may "play through" the injury, without the risk of long-term problems (Caine, 2006).

Finally, the articular (joint) cartilage may be negatively affected by repetitive overuse. Osteochondritis dissecans (OCD) best exemplifies this phenomenon. In brief, OCD is a poorly understood condition seen in young athletes in which it is believed that repetitive overuse results in injury to the blood supply to normal bone and joint cartilage; over time, the loss of blood supply causes the bone and cartilage to fragment, producing vague pain and, in its later stages, mechanical symptoms such as locking and popping of the affected joint Maffulli & Baxter-Jones, 1995). OCD lesions are evaluated by X-rays and often with additional imaging such as MRI (see Figure 26.9). Treatment for OCD generally begins with activity modification—removal of the athlete from the offending activity (e.g., running, throwing, tumbling) for a period of 6–12 weeks Adirim & Cheng, 2003). Return-to-play decisions are made based upon a combination of factors, including resolution of an athlete's symptoms as well as evidence of healing on X-ray. OCD lesions that do not heal generally require surgical treatment. Although the symptoms associated with OCD may be mild and young athletes feel comfortable "playing through" the pain, the dire consequence of unhealed OCD—presumptive progression to premature osteoarthritis—mandates aggressive treatment. As a result, OCD is frequently a season-ending injury.

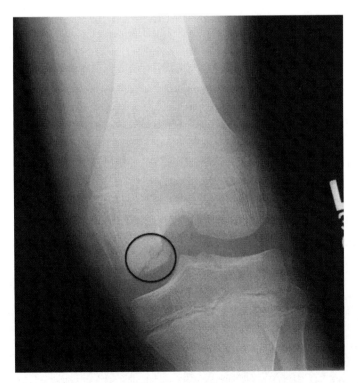

Figure 26.9 Osteochondritis dissecans. The figure shows an AP radiograph of the knee of a 15-year-old male who participates avidly in soccer and lacrosse and presented with knee pain, swelling, and locking. An osteochondritis dissecans (OCD) lesion is present (black circle)

Conclusions

The successful development of youth sports talent requires young athletes to remain healthy and injury-free. It is therefore essential that coaches, trainers, and other persons who work with young competitors be well informed about the possible medical hazards of sport participation, so that at-risk athletes may be identified early and appropriate measures may be taken to prevent catastrophic harm. Similarly, a basic understanding of common youth sports injuries such as those outlined above is vital so that when injuries do occur, they may be recognized and treated in a timely fashion. In this way, young athletic talent may be protected, ensuring optimal present and future athletic performance.

References

Adirim, T. A., & Cheng, T. L. (2003). Overview of injuries in the young athlete. *Sports Medicine, 33*, 75–81.

Bergeron, M. F., Devore, C., & Rice, S. G. (2011). American Academy of Pediatrics. Policy Statement— Climatic Heat Stress and Exercising Children and Adolescents. *Pediatrics, 128*, e741–e747.

Beunen, G., & Malina, R. M. (1988). Growth and physical performance relative to the timing of the adolescent spurt. *Exercise and Sport Sciences Reviews, 16*, 503–540.

Beynnon, B. D., Vacek, P. M., Newell, M. K., Tourville, T. W., Smith, H. C., Shultz, S. J., Johnson, R. J. (2014). The effects of level of competition, sport, and sex on the incidence of first-time noncontact anterior cruciate ligament injury. *The American Journal of Sports Medicine, 42*, 1806–1812.

Brenner, J. S. (2007). Overuse injuries, overtraining, and burnout in child and adolescent athletes. *Pediatrics, 119*, 1242–1245.

Caine, D. (2006). Physeal injuries in children's and youth sports: Reasons for concern? *British Journal of Sports Medicine, 40*, 749–760.

Corrado, D., Basso, C., Schiavon, M., & Thiene, G. (1998). Screening for Hypertrophic Cardiomyopathy in young athletes. *New England Journal of Medicine, 339*, 364–369.

FIFA 11 Website. (n.d.). http://f-marc.com/11plus/home/

Gallagher, S. S., Finison, K., Guyer, B., & Goodenough, S. (1984). The incidence of injuries among 87,000 Massachusetts children and adolescents: Results of the 1980–81 Statewide Childhood Injury Prevention Program Surveillance System. *American Journal of Public Health, 74*, 1340–1347.

Goldenring J. (1994). Athletic Preparticipation Examinations for Adolescents. *Archives of Pediatrics & Adolescent Medicine, 148*, 997–998.

Gornitzky, A. L., Lott, A., Yellin, J. L., Fabricant, P. D., Lawrence, J. T., & Ganley, T. J. (2015). Sport-specific yearly risk and incidence of anterior cruciate ligament tears in high school athletes: A systematic review and meta-analysis. *The American Journal of Sports Medicine*. pii: 0363546515617742. [Epub ahead of print].

Grafe, M. W., Paul, G. R., & Foster, T. E. (1997). The Preparticipation Sports Examination for High School and College Athletes. *Clinics in Sports Medicine, 16*, 569–591.

Guzzanti, V. (2013). *Pediatric and adolescent sports traumatology* (pp. 52–53). Milan: Springer.

Hulkko, A., & Orava, S. (1987). Stress fractures in athletes. *International Journal of Sports Medicine, 8*, 221–226.

Maffulli, N., & Baxter-Jones, A. D. (1995). Common skeletal injuries in young athletes. *Sports Medicine, 19*, 137–149.

Maffulli, N., & Bruns, W. (2000). Injuries in young athletes. *European Journal of Pediatrics, 159*, 59–63.

Majerske, C. W., Mihalik, J. P., Ren, D., Collins, M. W., Reddy, C. C., Lovell, M. R., & Wagner, A. K. (2008). Concussion in sports: Postconcussive activity levels, symptoms, and neurocognitive performance. *Journal of Athletic Training, 43*, 265–274.

Mariscalco, M. W., & Saluan, P. (2011). Upper extremity injuries in the adolescent athlete. *Sports Medicine and Arthroscopy Review, 19*, 17–26.

Maron, B. J., Haas, T. S., Ahluwalia, A., Murphy, C. J., & Garberich, R. F. (2016). Demographics and epidemiology of sudden deaths in young competitive athletes: From the United States National Registry. *The American Journal of Medicine*. doi: 10.1016/j.amjmed.2016.02.031. [Epub ahead of print]

McCrory, P., Meeuwisse, W., Johnston, K., Dvorak, J., Aubry, M., Molloy, M., & Cantu, R. (2009). Consensus Statement on Concussion in Sport: The 3rd International Conference on Concussion in Sport held in Zurich, November 2008. *British Journal of Sports Medicine, 43*(Suppl. 1), 176–184.

Michaud, P. (2001). Sports activities related to injuries? A survey among 9–19 year olds in Switzerland. *Injury Prevention, 7*(1), 41–45.

Omey, M. L., & Micheli, L. J. (1999). Foot and ankle problems in the young athlete. *Medicine & Science in Sports & Exercise, 31*, S470–S486.

Pretzlaff, R. K. (2002). Death of an adolescent athlete with sickle cell trait caused by exertional heat stroke. *Pediatric Critical Care Medicine, 3*, 308–310.

Putukian, M., O Connor, F. G., Stricker, P., Mcgrew, C., Hosey, R. G., Gordon, S. M., … Landry, G. (2008). Mononucleosis and athletic participation: An evidence-based subject review. *Clinical Journal of Sport Medicine, 18*, 309–315.

Smith, R. W., & Reischl, S. F. (1986). Treatment of ankle sprains in young athletes. *The American Journal of Sports Medicine, 14*, 465–471.

Tarini, B. A., Brooks, M. A., & Bundy, D. G. (2011). A policy impact analysis of the mandatory NCAA Sickle Cell Trait Screening Program. *Health Services Research, 47*.

Thompson, A. A. (2013). Sickle cell trait testing and athletic participation: A solution in search of a problem? *Hematology, 2013*, 632–637.

Torg, J. S., Sennett, B., Pavlov, H., Leventhal, M. R., & Glasgow, S. G. (1993). Spear tackler's spine: An entity precluding participation in tackle football and collision activities that expose the cervical spine to axial energy inputs. *The American Journal of Sports Medicine, 21*, 640–649.

Torg, J. S., & Ramsey-Emrhein, J. A. (1997). Management guidelines for participation in collision activities with congenital, developmental, or post-injury lesions involving the cervical spine. *Clinics in Sports Medicine, 16*, 501–530.

Tursz, A., & Crost, M. (1986). Sports-related injuries in children: A study of their characteristics, frequency, and severity, with comparison to other types of accidental injuries. *The American Journal of Sports Medicine, 14*, 294–299.

Wasserlauf, B. L., & Paletta, G. A. (2003). Shoulder disorders in the skeletally immature throwing athlete. *Orthopedic Clinics of North America, 34*, 427–437.

27

DEVELOPING TALENT WHILE PROMOTING POSITIVE YOUTH DEVELOPMENT

A balancing act

Jessica Fraser-Thomas, Theresa Beesley, Lauren Dickler,
Meghan Harlow, Alexandra Mosher, Cassidy Preston,
and Lauren Wolman

In recent years, a growing interest in talent identification and development among high performance athletes has trickled down to children and youth in grassroots-level sports. With this has come an increased focus on fostering talent among children and youth, leading to concerns surrounding children's physical, psychological, social, and cognitive development. While many models of talent development embrace a simplistic physiological approach, frameworks are evolving to integrate the developing child into broader sport structural and organizational processes (Harwood & Johnston, 2016; Vierimaa, Erickson, & Côté, 2016). Cobley (2016) proposes that youth talent be conceptualized as a combination of youths' particular skills and qualities, grounded in the complex interaction of their individual characteristics, specific sport tasks, social environment, and policy priorities that underpin elite sport. However, despite the commonly held assumption that sport (at any level) is as a vehicle of psychosocial development (e.g., character-building), many have argued that the act of participation in sport alone is insufficient to produce identifiable outcomes (Fraser-Thomas, Côté, & Deakin, 2005; Holt & Neely, 2011). Further, the potential conflict between the goals of talent development (i.e., optimal performance), and youths' overall healthy development (i.e., positive youth development; PYD) has garnered growing attention as an issue of concern (Fraser-Thomas & Strachan, 2015; Gould, Collins, Lauer, & Chung, 2007).

Personal Assets Framework

While several definitions of PYD have been put forward over the past two decades, fundamental to PYD is a strength-based approach to youths' development, focused on youths' 'engagement in pro-social behaviours and avoidance of health compromising behaviours and future jeopardizing behaviours' (Roth, Brooks-Gunn, Murray, & Foster, 1998, p. 426). Broadly, PYD focuses on youth as assets to be developed, exploring youths' optimal developmental potential (Damon, 2004). The Personal Assets Framework (PAF) was recently proposed as a conceptual model that 'accounts for the mechanisms and outcomes that constitute PYD in sport' (Côté, Turnnidge, & Evans, 2014; Côté, Turnnidge, & Vierimaa, 2016). Three outcomes are identified which include *participation* (i.e., continued sport or physical activity participation throughout the lifespan), *performance* (i.e., sport expertise), and *personal development* (i.e., healthy psychological, emotional and social outcomes) (i.e., the 3Ps; Côté, Strachan, & Fraser-Thomas, 2008). In this chapter, we focus specifically on two of these outcomes – performance and personal development – and address the concern that an overemphasis on one of these outcomes, may compromise the emergence of the other. Throughout, we aim to explore the potential to mediate and balance these potentially conflicting outcomes.

In framing our discussion, we focus on the three key dynamic elements shaping youths' sport experiences, as outlined within the PAF (Côté et al., 2016): (1) personal factors (i.e., the 'what' – personal engagement in activities), (2) relational factors (i.e., the 'who' – quality relationships), and (3) organizational environments (i.e., the 'where' – appropriate settings). The PAF further outlines how interactions between the three dynamic elements of activities, relationships, and contexts, shape youths' sport experiences, which over time leads to the development of personal assets identified as the 4Cs of PYD (Côté, Burner, Erickson, Strachan, & Fraser-Thomas, 2010; originally proposed as the 5Cs of PYD; Lerner et al., 2005). The 4Cs comprise (1) *competence* in diverse domains including social, academic, cognitive, and vocational, (2) *confidence*, conceptualized as self-efficacy and global self-regard, (3) *connections*, which include positive exchanges between peers, family, school, and community, and (4) *character*, expressed as respect for societal and cultural norms. Given the chapter's focus on the challenge of balancing optimal youth outcomes, we also consider less than optimal interactions between dynamic elements in the talent development process, and potential negative experiences and outcomes amongst youth. Throughout, we consider future research directions, and conclude the chapter with a discussion of broader research considerations, as researchers, practitioners, administrators, and policy makers strive to facilitate the attainment and maintenance of the optimal talent-development (i.e., performance) and personal-development (i.e., PYD) balance.

The 'what': Personal engagement in activities

The first dynamic element highlighted within the PAF (Côté et al., 2016) involves one's personal engagement in activities. In this section we consider how time invested, training activities, and developmental trajectories may shape youths' sport experiences, asset development, and subsequent outcomes of performance and personal development.

Time invested in activities

Time invested in an activity has emerged as a defining feature of youths' performance and personal development outcomes, while also being one of the most contested constructs of talent development. Ericsson, Krampe, and Tesch-Römer's (1993) seminal research on expert performance suggests that extensive time (i.e., 10 years) is associated with expert level of performance in any domain (see Chapter 3, for example). Much research shows partial support for this theory, as time invested in sport training has been positively associated with expert performance (Baker & Young, 2014); however, research in developmental psychology shows a more ambiguous relationship between time in extra-curricular activities and youths' personal development (Larson, Hansen, & Moneta, 2006; Simpkins, Ripke, Huston, & Eccles, 2005). Within youth sport specifically, high investment has been associated with positive outcomes including higher scores in identity, initiative, time management, positive relationships, adult networks, social capital, and diverse peer relationships (Strachan, Côté, & Deakin, 2009; Wilkes & Côté, 2010), alongside more negative outcomes such as physical and emotional exhaustion, increased stress, social isolation, less family integration, fewer links to community, and a unidimensional self-concept (Kirk, Carlson, Burke, Davis, & Glover, 1997a; Kirk, O'Connor, Carlson, Burke, Davis, & Glover, 1997b; Strachan et al., 2009; Tofler, Stryer, Micheli, & Herman, 1996; Wilkes & Côté, 2010). These negative associations align with other work in developmental psychology, showing that extensive time in any one activity can be associated with an increase in risk behaviours such as aggression, alcohol, and drug use (e.g., Busseri, Rose-Krasnor, Willoughby, & Chalmers, 2006).

Type of activities

Mixed associations between time investment and personal development are likely related at least in part to *how* time is spent within sport programmes – or type of activities. Ericsson and colleagues' (1993) conceptualization of deliberate practice (i.e., effortful training focused towards a goal with little inherent enjoyment) has served as a foundation for extensive research on high performance sport over the past two decades; however, there is much debate about the simplicity of the relationship between deliberate practice training and high performance sport, with some research suggesting a more balanced inclusion of play-based training may be necessary (e.g., Baker, Cobley & Fraser-Thomas, 2009; Fraser-Thomas, Côté, & Deakin, 2008a; Strachan, Côté, & Deakin, 2011). One recent conceptualization of talent development proposes benefits in youths' engagement in four diverse activity types, which facilitate four aligning forms of learning (Vierimaa et al., 2016). Specifically, Vierimaa and colleagues (2016) first acknowledge that youth are often driven by external values such as performance, and thus engage in coach-led deliberate practice, facilitating the development of sport specific skills; this process is termed *rational learning*, and is described as systemic, logical, and efficient in nature. However, Vierimaa and colleagues (2016) also suggest that children and youth engage in intrinsically motivated self-directed 'deliberate play', whereby the physical, social, and emotional unpredictability of their environment fosters their adaptability; this process is termed *creative learning*, and is characterized by flexibility, experimentation, and novelty. In between these two opposing approaches, emotional learning and informal learning are also proposed. *Emotional learning* occurs when youth are driven by internal values, but led by adults, resulting in 'play-practice'; this process is characterized by the integration of playful fun activities into structured training sessions. Finally, *informal learning* occurs when youth are once again driven by internal values, but in this case lead themselves in activities aimed at improving skill development; this process involves 'spontaneous practice' and allows for creativity, without perceptions of adult directive or judgment. While these four forms of activities and learning offer an interesting multifaceted framework to examine high performance sport training, the deliberate practice lens remains a dominant framework of examination in talent development.

Developmental trajectories

When considering personal engagement in activities, youths' time investment and training approach inform youths' overall developmental trajectories within sport. The Developmental Model of Sport Participation (DMSP; Côté, 1999; Côté & Fraser-Thomas, 2016) is an empirically based model, which proposes differing paths of sport development, leading to differing outcomes related to performance and personal development. Specifically, two diverse approaches are proposed to form the foundation of youths' trajectories towards sport expertise:

sampling and specializing (see Chapter 9). Sampling involves children trying out different sports and activities throughout childhood (i.e., up to approximately age 12), while specializing involves children focusing almost exclusively on one sport from a young age, with minimal involvement in other sports or activities. While research shows both sampling and specializing have the potential to lead to elite performance (e.g., Baker et al., 2009; Baker & Young, 2014; Fraser-Thomas et al., 2008a), early specialization has been associated with negative outcomes related to personal development including physical injuries (DiFiori et al., 2014; Law, Côté, & Ericsson, 2007), dropout (Fraser-Thomas et al., 2008a; Wall & Côté, 2007), and burnout (Strachan et al., 2009), once again highlighting the potential of one outcome (i.e., personal development) being compromised in the pursuit of another (i.e., performance).

In sum, factors associated with young athletes' activity engagement (i.e., time, type, and trajectory) inform one key dynamic element of youths' experiences (i.e., the 'what'), which in turn may foster youths' asset development, and subsequent performance and personal development. To date, limited research has examined these specific relationships collectively. The construct of time is particularly noteworthy, given its inherent position within definitions of development (Bronfenbrenner, 1977, 2005; Lerner, 2002). Larson (2000) argued that concerted engagement and effort directed towards a goal over time are essential ingredients in facilitating developmental assets. One study of over 1,100 children and youth further accentuates the interdependent complexity of these factors (Zarrett, Lerner, Carrano, Fay, Peltz, & Li, 2008). Zarrett and colleagues found that youth who were highly involved in sport and other extracurricular activities (i.e., samplers with high time investment) scored highest on the 5Cs; however, no consideration was given to performance outcomes in this study. As such, it appears further research is necessary to better understand the 'what' of both performance and personal development processes, by placing greater focus on the dynamic interactions within the time–training–trajectory triangle.

The 'who': Quality relationships

The second dynamic element highlighted within the PAF (Côté et al., 2016) – quality relationships – constitutes the 'who' of the developmental process. In this section, we explore how relationships with coaches, parents, siblings, and peers may shape youths' sport experiences, asset development, and subsequent outcomes of performance and personal development.

Coaches

It is likely that coaches have the most complex challenge in facilitating a balanced approach to talent development and PYD, given deeply rooted social and cultural beliefs within sport that performance success sometimes comes at the expense of athletes' personal development and well-being (Miller & Kerr, 2002). For example, a study by Stirling and Kerr (2008) found that elite female swimmers believed that enduring emotional abuse was part of the progression to an elite level; they did not question the abuse, but rather accepted it as the norm. Research has concurrently reported incidences of elite youth sport coaches belittling, humiliating, shouting, scapegoating, rejecting, isolating, threatening, ignoring, intimidating, and favouring their athletes, suggesting this behaviour is often perceived as part of the climate necessary to achieve success (Fraser-Thomas & Côté, 2009; Gervis & Dunn, 2004; Holt, Tamminen, Tink, & Black, 2009).

In recent years, however, there has been growing conceptualization of successful coaching as optimizing performance *and* personal development. In particular, Côté and Gilbert (2009) proposed an integrative definition of coaching effectiveness and expertise, conceptually grounded in coaching and PYD literature (see Chapter 20). While little research has empiri-cally tested this specific approach, Gould and colleagues' (2007) examination of award-winning football coaches (i.e., recognized for both their performance records and development of young people) lends support to these principles. Coaches in this study were highly motivated to win, but players' personal development was also at the forefront of coaches' priorities, resulting in life skills and other performance enhancement strategies being viewed through an integrated lens. Other studies in high performance settings show a few consistent means by which coaches balance talent development with PYD outcomes including: (a) creating an autonomy-support-ive climate (i.e., including athletes in decision-making, creating opportunities for initiative-development, holding athletes to expectations), (b) engaging athletes in meaningful relationships (i.e., being caring, communicating effectively, knowing each athlete as an individ-ual), (c) creating a task-oriented environment (i.e., focusing on learning and improvement, motivating athletes to put forward their best effort), (d) being a model (e.g., demonstrating respect, modelling appropriate values), and (e) using teachable moments (i.e., to teach life skills, facilitate transfer) (Fraser-Thomas & Côté, 2009; Gould et al., 2007; Holt et al., 2009; Strachan et al., 2011; Trottier & Robitaille, 2014).

Parents

Parents also face the challenge of balancing the facilitation of their child's pursuit of success with optimal personal development. Like coaches, parents' intended goals for their child's development do not always appear in line with their actual behaviours, or consequences of their behaviours (Dorsch, Smith, Wilson, & McDonough, 2015; Schwab, Wells, & Arthur-Banning, 2010). This is commonly seen through parents' provision of tangible, instructional, or emotional support. For example, parents may perceive their behaviours to be supporting their child's talent development (e.g., enrolling their child in additional training sessions, adjusting the family lifestyle, providing performance-related instructional feedback), but their children may in fact interpret these behaviours as pressuring or negative, and thus a hindrance to their optimal personal development (e.g., Keegan, Spray, Harwood, & Lavallee, 2010; Fraser-Thomas, Côté, & Deakin, 2008b).

As a whole, empirical research suggests parents play constructive and supportive roles in youths' sport development, but high prevalence of negative parental influences are concerning and warrant discussion (Gould, Lauer, Rolo, Jannes, & Pennisi, 2008). In particular, parents have been found to offer negative (or negatively perceived) feedback, serve as poor role models (e.g., of emotional regulation, values of sportspersonship), control their child's behaviours, create an environment of unhealthy dependence (e.g., parents packing their child's sporting equipment), and even protect their child from conflict (i.e., in turn, inhibiting their development of coping skills) (Lauer, Gould, Roman, & Pierce, 2010; Tamminen & Holt, 2012). Coakley (2006) suggested that while parents are assumed to be well intentioned, they may lose perspective of how to best foster their child's development as they become caught up in their child's success. Given parents' time and financial investment in their child's sport, these findings may not be surprising (Kirk et al., 1997a, 1997b), yet further attention is warranted in cases where children feel indebted to their parents as a reaction to the sacrifice they have made for their sport involve-ment (Fraser-Thomas & Côté, 2009; Harwood & Knight, 2009; Wolfenden & Holt, 2005).

In contrast to evidence that some youth sport parents may (unintentionally) consider their child's performance success ahead of their personal development, there is also emerging evidence suggesting that the high performance sport environment may offer an optimal context for parents to facilitate youths' personal development (PYD). Specifically, the time investment (e.g., travel to and from training and competition) and stresses (e.g., highs and lows) of high performance sport create a context ripe for parent–child bonding, and special relationships (Côté, 1999; Fraser-Thomas & Côté, 2009; Lauer et al., 2010; Tamminen & Holt, 2012). As such, through sport, youth often experience unconditional care, comfort, and understanding from their parents, while also engaging in "intelligent conversations" (e.g., optimism and coping skills during adverse times). Further, suggestions that parents and coaches take an integrative team approach to athlete development (Camiré, Trudel & Bernard, 2013) appear largely overlooked at the high performance level, as parent–coach partnerships do not appear to be the norm, with coaches often perceiving (or preferring) parents' roles in tangential roles such as financial support, fundraising, and preparing youth for training (Strachan et al., 2011). Parents may, however, influence high performing athletes' PYD through their expectations, role modelling, and engagement (Holt et al., 2009; Lauer et al., 2010). Specifically, parents may instil values and work ethic in their children, model humility and respect towards others, take responsibility for their actions, stress appropriate sportspersonship, demonstrate effective communication, model emotional control, teach life skills, and facilitate self-awareness and resilience (Holt et al., 2009; Lauer et al., 2010). Moving forward, one of the key areas that remains poorly understood is *how* parents parent (Roberts, 2012), and this appears to be particularly relevant when examining parents' balancing of their child's talent and PYD in high performance sport.

Siblings

Sibling relationships have received minimal research attention in connection with both performance and PYD. Early work highlighted family disruptions in the name of athletes' needs (e.g., relocating the family to attend national training centres, eating family meals while in transfer to training) as potentially concerning for siblings (Côté, 1999; Kirk et al., 1997a). Often, siblings of high performers receive less time, attention, and fewer resources from parents – in the form of tangible support (e.g., time, financial) and emotional support, with parents finding it challenging or impossible to treat all children equally (Harwood & Knight, 2009; Wolfenden & Holt, 2005). Further, if one child in the family finds a sport niche and begins to demonstrate talent while another child does not reach the same level of performance, feelings of jealousy, rivalry, and resentment may emerge (Fraser-Thomas et al., 2008b).

Despite these concerns, sibling relations may indirectly enhance the development of talent, while also facilitating optimal PYD. Specifically, older siblings can serve as role models in youths' introduction of sport, with a recent study amongst Canadian and Australian athletes finding an over-representation of elite athletes among later born children with older siblings who had participated in sport (Hopwood, Farrow, MacMahon, & Baker, 2015). It has been suggested that siblings influence each other's talent development (even more than peers and teammates) through emotional and information support, and sometimes even through motivation to outperform each other (Blazo, Czech, Carson, & Dees, 2014; Davis & Meyer, 2008; Fraser-Thomas et al., 2008b). Recent work also highlights that sport can bring together siblings, creating a sense of 'team family' with a shared identity, healthy values and attitudes, and strong sense of work ethic and discipline (Trussell, 2012). Future research should focus on whole family dynamics, particularly parental and sibling dyads and bi-directional relationships (Taylor & Collins, 2015). Many questions remain regarding how siblings can optimize youths' talent and personal development in sport, but also how youths' high performance sport involvement may optimize or create dysfunction within sibling and broader family dynamics.

Peers

Relationships with peers in elite sport are sometimes likened to those with family, given the extensive time spent with teammates and the enduring nature of friendships (Fraser-Thomas & Côté, 2009; Wilkes & Côté, 2010). It follows that youths' friendships with teammates are complex, particularly when considered through the lens of performance and personal development. For example, young athletes often must compete against their teammates (i.e., for position on the team), which creates a context ripe with rivalries, jealousy, infighting, boasting, teasing, and poor sportspersonship (Fraser-Thomas et al., 2008b; Keegan et al., 2010, Patrick et al., 1999, Strachan et al., 2011). Further, greater alcohol and drug use, and greater engagement in binge drinking among collegiate athletes suggests peers in sport contexts may negatively influence each other to engage in high-risk behaviours (Hildebrand, Johnson & Bogle, 2001).

Despite negative potential influences among peers, one study concluded peers were the most important influence in the process of life skill development (Holt et al., 2009). Through interactions with teammates, youth learn social and psychological skills, gain leadership opportunities, and enhance their work ethic, with these skills being maintained into adulthood (Fraser-Thomas & Côté, 2009; Gould, Dieffenbach, & Moffatt, 2002; Holt et al., 2009; MacPhail & Kirk, 2006). Additionally, through high performance sport, youth can develop unique friendships with different aged peers, whereby older veterans act as mentors, models, and leaders to younger athletes, while creating a sense of belonging to a wider community (Bruner, Munroe-Chandler, & Spink, 2008; Fraser-Thomas et al., 2008b; Fraser-Thomas & Côté, 2009). Essentially, sport friendships, built upon common interests and goals, tend to be grounded by youth who understand each other, and act as genuine supporters of each other through similar lived experiences (MacPhail & Kirk, 2006). Thus, while teammates can serve as facilitators of performance and personal development, more work is required to unpack the contexts and processes by which they play the optimal roles for youth striving to achieve both of these goals. Specifically, research is warranted focusing on how indirect peer influences may contribute to youths' performance and personal development.

The 'where': Appropriate settings

The third dynamic element highlighted within the PAF (Côté et al., 2016) – appropriate settings – constitutes the 'where' of developmental processes. In this section, we explore how programmes' contexts may shape youths' sport experiences, asset development, and subsequent outcomes of performance and personal development. We draw upon the National Research Council and Institute of Medicine's (NRCIM; Eccles & Gootman, 2002) eight proposed features of positive developmental settings to guide our discussion: (1) physical and psychological safety, (2) appropriate structure, (3) supportive relationships, (4) opportunities to belong, (5) positive social norms, (6) support for efficacy and mattering, (7) opportunities for skill building, and (8) integration of family, school, and community efforts. The NRCIM postulates that when programmes successfully target more features, elements work in collaboration, and programmes facilitate higher rates of PYD. However, sport organizations have varying objectives and foci, resulting in different emphases (Eccles & Gootman, 2002), with only one study, to our knowledge, exploring the NRCIM's eight setting features specifically in high performance youth sport (Strachan et al., 2011). As some of the eight features relate to the two other key elements discussed above (i.e., personal engagement in activities, quality relationships), we focus in this section on only four of the setting features: opportunities for skill building, physical and psychological safety, integration of school and community, and appropriate structure.

Opportunities for skill building

A fundamental assumption of youth sport contexts is that they offer opportunities for young people to develop skills – these skills include physical, technical, and tactical sport skills typically associated with performance, but are also often assumed to include personal, social, and life skills tied to PYD. The processes by which sport skills are taught and learned has been extensively studied in pedagogical and educational literature (e.g., Wulf, 2007), but until recently, little work has focused on how 'life skills' (i.e., assets, characteristics, and skills that are facilitated/developed through sport and utilized outside of sport in general life; Gould & Carson, 2008) are taught and learned. This has led to an emerging area of research focused on transfer of life skills from the sport to non-sport settings.

Turnnidge, Côté, and Hancock (2014) explained two key approaches of life skill transfer in sports. First, programmes may use an explicit approach, whereby sport environments are intentionally designed to teach life skills and the transferability of life skills to other contexts, often utilizing specific lessons or modules administered by adult leaders (e.g., Sports United to Support Education and Recreation; Teaching Personal and Social Responsibility, The First Tee; Danish, 2002; Hellison, 2003; Weiss, 2006). Such programmes appear to place primary importance on developing the person before the athlete, which explains at least in part, why this approach has been studied (and likely observed) only minimally in high performance sport settings. In contrast, an implicit approach encourages youths' physical, social, and personal skills development through the sport setting without the use of specific programming, lessons or modules focused on promoting life skills or transfer (Turnnidge et al., 2014). Within this approach, coaches act as key figures in transfer facilitation, by utilizing strategies such as taking advantage of teachable moments, holding athletes accountable to high expectations, creating opportunities for mentoring and volunteering, serving as role models, promoting leadership and conflict resolution skills, and encouraging athletes to reflect on life skill development in their sport setting (Allen, Rhind, & Koshy, 2015; Camiré, Trudel, & Forneris, 2012; Flett, Griffes, & Lauer, 2013); however, these findings emerge primarily from non-elite contexts. The few studies that have examined implicit transfer in high performance contexts highlight coaches' use of similar above mentioned strategies, and also suggest underlying processes of the elite sport context may be conducive to PYD facilitation, either due to the inherent elements of commitment, challenge, discipline, work ethic, responsibility, and time management required for involvement at the elite level, or the extensive time spent in the sport, as opportunities exist to develop problem solving skills, navigate complex relationships, and engage in goal setting and leadership (Fraser-Thomas & Côté, 2009; Gould et al., 2007; Trottier & Robitaille, 2014; Strachan et al., 2011).

Thus, in addition to providing opportunities for the development of physical and technical skills necessary to yield high performance youth athletes, the high performance context also appears to have the potential to foster personal development through an implicit approach to teaching life skills. However, it remains unclear whether explicit transfer could also be an effective means of facilitating PYD in high performance sport, and if so, what this approach might 'look like' with regard to curricula and pedagogical approaches. Further, a question that persists within coaching, parental, administrative, and research circles, relates to the responsibilities of coaches (and particularly high performance coaches), in facilitating youths' PYD, and whether the goals of PYD are in fact divorced from the reality of (high performance) coaching (Cushion, Armour, & Jones, 2003). Clearly, more research is necessary to enhance understanding of *how* young athletes in high performance sport settings advance within their sport, while simultaneously developing personal and social skills, and transferring these skills into non-sport settings.

Physical and psychological safety

Another setting feature warranting attention in high performance sport pertains to youths' physical and psychological safety. While athletes' safety is often assumed to be a paramount consideration in youth settings, physical safety is often compromised, as evidenced by the risk of concussion and high rates of overuse injuries among early specializing youth athletes (DiFiori et al., 2014; Emery, Hagel, Decloe, & Carly, 2010; Fridman, Fraser-Thomas, McFaull, & Macpherson, 2013). While some degree of risk is assumed with all sport participation, overuse injuries are estimated to be as high as 68% in some youth sports. Subsequently, the American Medical Society for Sports Medicine offered a position statement cautioning that youths' early high investment in sport be carefully considered, as it may have a long-term influence on athletes' success (as a result of injury risk) (DiFiori et al., 2014). Recently implemented policies, protocols, and rule changes are also reflective of increased awareness and concern for youths' health (e.g., Hockey Canada, 2013; Ontario Ministry of Education, 2014).

Notwithstanding rising recognition of physical safety concerns in youth sport, less attention has been given to psychological safety. As outlined above, there is some research associating youths' participation in high performance environments to negative outcomes such as injury, dropout and burnout (DiFiori et al., 2014; Fraser-Thomas et al., 2008a, 2008b; Law et al., 2007; Strachan et al., 2009; Wall & Côté, 2007), and although limited in scope, links have also been made between high performance sport to issues of mental health. For example, there is evidence of a greater incidence of eating disorders in high performance athletes (Sundgot-Borgen & Torstveit, 2004). Additionally, collegiate athletes experience greater pressure and anxiety than non-athletes, indicating a greater risk for depression (Etzel, Watson, Visek, & Maniar, 2006; Maniar, Chamberlain, & Moore, 2005). Currently, evidence remains mixed regarding whether the stress associated with high performance sport optimizes coping skills by preparing athletes to manage non-sport stressors, or further exacerbates athletes' challenges (Fraser-Thomas & Côté, 2009; Hudd et al., 2000; Scully, Kremer, Meade, Graham, & Dudgeon, 1998; Tamminen, Holt, & Neely, 2013). The argument could be made that the increased structure and coach supervision of high performance sport could actually create a safer environment for youth experiencing mental health challenges.

Until recently, mental illness among high performance athletes received little attention, perhaps in part due to the misconception that mentally tough athletes could not become mentally ill (e.g., Baum, 2005; Dean & Rowan, 2013; Markser, 2011; Reardon & Factor, 2010). More recently however, a growing number of high performance athletes have shared their stories of battling mental illness (e.g., Olympians Clara Hughes and Ian Thorpe; professional tennis players Mardy Fish and Rebecca Marino), leading to more public discussions regarding the mental health of high performance athletes (e.g., Alexander, 2014; Stroumboulopoulos, 2012). Striking the balance in optimizing talent and personal development may be particularly difficult in cases of mental health challenges, as evidenced by Rebecca Marino, as she announced her early retirement from professional tennis due to clinical depression; she stated that she needed to "put the person before the athlete" (Brady, 2013). Despite growing public discourse, research in this area remains limited, leaving many questions regarding how to assure youths' psychological safety, while concurrently optimizing their talent development.

Integration of school and community

Another feature of PYD settings that appears somewhat underdeveloped in high performance sport relates to the integration of school and community. High performance coaches in

Strachan and colleagues' (2011) study indicated school administrators often misunderstood sport programmes, leading to poor communication and negative rapport; however, on a more personal level, school peers (i.e., classmates) have been found to facilitate youth athletes' performance and personal development, by acting as athletes' confidence builders and supporters given their more distanced position from sport, in turn contributing to youths' unique identity as athletes (Fraser-Thomas et al., 2008b; Gould et al., 2002; MacPhail & Kirk, 2006).

Strachan et al.'s (2011) study found youths' integration within their community was perceived relatively favourably by coaches, with athletes engaging in various community events, in turn raising programmes' visibility, funds, and status within communities. Coaches did not appear however to reflect upon the reciprocity of school or community relations, as they focused primarily on how these entities could best meet their programmes' needs, rather than how programmes could 'give back' to schools or communities. In order to better understand the relationship between high performance sport programmes and communities, it may be appropriate to focus first on smaller communities. Previous research has not only found that high performance athletes are over-represented in smaller communities, but also that youth in smaller communities have higher personal asset scores (Côté, MacDonald, Baker, & Abernethy, 2006; Fraser-Thomas, Côté, & MacDonald, 2010; Imitiaz, Hancock, Vierimaa, & Côté, 2014). However, questions regarding why and how smaller communities are providing more appropriate environments for programme–community relationship building remain unanswered. As Strachan et al. (2011) conclude, 'integration of the community … is a promising avenue to pursue in endorsing the growth of positive youth within an elite sport context' (p. 29).

Appropriate structure

Finally, it is important to consider organizational structures that may influence youths' performance and personal development. The pyramid analogy suggests high performance sport greatly depends on broad-based participation, requiring focus on athlete entrance, retention, and advancement (Green, 2005). However, amateur sports face many systematic and organizational challenges. In one Canadian study, national and provincial sport organizations were often found to prioritize elite performance, and subsequently, depend heavily on resource-strapped local sport clubs to provide a full range of programming at the grassroots level (Livingston & Tirone, 2012). These findings were reinforced in another Canadian study, where community sports clubs played a facilitative role in youths' continued sport participation into adulthood and advancement to higher levels, by providing a range of programming options to meet all athletes' needs (Wolman & Fraser-Thomas, 2014). Thus, there could be benefit in greater collaboration between sport organizations and community level programmes, to facilitate youths' collective talent development and personal development, through enhanced athlete recruitment, commitment, and support through life and athletic transitions.

Finding the balance moving forward

We began this chapter with conceptualizations of talent development and PYD. While in the past, talent has been primarily constructed through a physiological lens, models are increasingly embracing a more holistic view of talent development, which also considers psychological and social constructs (Cobley, 2016; Harwood & Johnston, 2016; Vierimaa et al., 2016). Our review suggests PYD is a more central consideration within talent development than in years past, but that an optimal balance between performance and personal development outcomes in youth sport settings has not yet become a reality, and there remains conflict between these two goals.

Below, we focus on three of the many issues we feel warrant further examination, exploration, and attention moving forward.

Navigating performance and personal development

First, it may be important to begin at the end, with outcomes, as many questions remain around the constructs of performance and personal development in youth sport. Within this chapter, we conceptualized talent development as an evolving multifaceted construct, and PYD as a strengths-based approach, but there is no singularly accepted definition of PYD through sport within the literature (Holt, Deal, & Smyth, 2016). We believe conceptualizations should continue to evolve, with particular consideration to rapidly changing social patterns and trends among the youth demographic (Roberts, 2012). Questions for consideration include: How will changing social structures (e.g., technology) influence the next generation of youths' activity engagement, relationships, and primary settings? What are the life skills that high performance sport programmes should be striving to facilitate and transfer in this changing social landscape? How is a strengths-based approach currently conceptualized, and does this conceptualization align with today's youth?

To answer these questions, research must adopt a revised lens of inquiry. When conducting this review drawing upon the PAF (Côté et al., 2016), we observed a trend of research exhibiting a 'silo' mentality; research examining performance outcomes focused largely on youths' engagement in activities (time, type, trajectory), and research examining personal development outcomes focused largely on quality relationships (coaches, parents, siblings, peers). While this was observed as a general trend, and certainly not exclusively the case, the consideration of independent sets of variables when studying each outcome nonetheless exacerbates the perception that performance and PYD cannot be mutually attained. As such, researchers should embrace a more holistic approach to factors of activity engagement, relationships, and settings, in turn facilitating greater understanding of how to optimally balance performance and personal development. Our review also highlights the need for more studies simultaneously examining performance and personal development outcomes, to allow a better understanding of the bidirectional and reciprocal facets of these outcomes. Researchers have begun to address the question: How can high performance sport facilitate PYD? However, researchers have rarely addressed the question: Can PYD facilitate high performance, and if so, how? Finally, while in principle there is value in embracing evolving and expanding models of talent development, it is important to acknowledge the risk that accompanies such change; incorporation of 'all things' within a single model has the potential to dilute the understanding of specific factors.

Acknowledging and understanding mental illness in high performance sport

Second, in gauging the potential for balance between talent development and PYD, it was inevitable that we also consider negative outcomes associated with high performance sport. Our review yielded several concerning outcomes in connection with high performance sport, some of which are considered clinical psychological issues (e.g., anxiety, depression, eating disorders; Etzel et al., 2006; Maniar et al., 2005; Fraser-Thomas & Côté, 2009; Sundgot-Borgen & Torstveit, 2004). Until recently, discussion of mental illness in high performance sport was scarce. While open conversations by high-profile elite athletes are an important first step in acknowledging the existence of athletes' mental health challenges, more understanding is critical to advance discussions around the performance–personal development balance. Specifically, research should focus on capturing prevalence rates of mental illness (e.g., depression, anxiety, eating disorders, addiction disorders) among high performance athletes compared to recreational athletes and non-athletes, exploring factors within the sporting environment that may be contributing to mental illness, and considering how to optimally support athletes struggling with these illnesses throughout and following their sport careers. Longitudinal designs will be vital to a comprehensive understanding, given fluctuations throughout athletes' talent and personal developmental trajectories. In bringing our discussion full circle, it would be particularly interesting to explore the potential role of PYD in managing mental health issues in elite sport settings, and how this may in turn optimize athletes' performance (see Chapter 24).

Social and cultural considerations

Finally, it is important to acknowledge a key limitation of our reviewed research, namely that studies examining performance and personal development have focused on a very narrow segment of the youth population. While some sport organizations are facilitating broader based participation through the pyramid approach to talent identification and development (Green, 2005), participation, particularly at an elite level, remains more prevalent and accessible among youth of higher socio-economic status (Kirk et al., 1997a; Vandermeerschen, Vos, & Scheerder, 2014). Additionally, research focused on PYD in sport has been conducted almost exclusively in Canada, the United States, and the United Kingdom, further restricting our lens of investigation and understanding, and raising some questions regarding the cultural relevance of the PYD approach. These limitations are in line with historical trends, as sport psychology has been criticized for its failure to consider culture, whereby athletes' identities are examined through an over-simplified lens, leading to misguided or biased findings (Blodgett, Schinke, McGannon, & Fisher, 2015; Duda & Allison, 1990; Ryba & Wright, 2005, 2010). In moving research and practice forward, it is essential that potential differences in how individuals experience high performance sport and PYD be considered. Cultural sport psychology, an emerging field, offers an effective lens to do so, allowing youths' multiple intersecting discourses of gender, race, ethnicity, sexuality, nationality, and socio-economic status to be recognized and acknowledged (Blodgett et al., 2015). Enhanced comprehension of youth who are often marginalized or excluded within sport participation and performance research, will undoubtedly shift our conceptualization of youths' engagement in activities, quality relationships, and appropriate settings, leading to the continued evolution of more effective sport development frameworks, that come closer to balancing talent development and PYD.

References

Alexander, B. (2014, February 22). After the gold: Olympic medalists struggle with real life. *NBC News.* Retrieved from www.nbcnews.com/storyline/sochi-olympics/after-gold-olympic-medalists-struggle-real-life-n35561

Allen, G., Rhind, D., & Koshy, V. (2015). Enablers and barriers for male students transferring life skills from the sports hall into the classroom. *Qualitative Research in Sport, Exercise and Health,* 7(1), 53–67.

Baker, J., Cobley, S., & Fraser-Thomas, J. (2009). What do we know about early sport specialization? Not much! *High Ability Studies,* 20(1), 77–89.

Baker, J., & Young, B. (2014). 20 years later: Deliberate practice and the development of expertise in sport. *International Review of Sport and Exercise Psychology,* 7(1), 135–157.

Baum, A. L. (2005). Suicide in athletes: A review and commentary. *Clinics in Sports Medicine,* 24(4), 853–869. Retrieved from www.sportsmed.theclinics.com/issues?issue_key=S0278-5919%2805%29X0016-3

Blazo, J. A., Carson, S., Czech, D. R., & Dees, W. (2014). A qualitative investigation of the sibling sport achievement. *The Sport Psychologist,* 28, 36–47.

Blodgett, A. T., Schinke, R. J., McGannon, K. R., & Fisher, L. A. (2015). Cultural sport psychology research: Conceptions, evolutions, and forecasts. *International Review of Sport and Exercise Psychology, 8*(1), 24–43.

Brady, R. (2013). Rebecca Marino and learning to put the person before the athlete. *Globe and Mail Online.* Retrieved from www.theglobeandmail.com/sports/more-sports/rebecca-marino-and-learning-to-put-the-person-before-the-athlete/article9003243/

Bronfenbrenner, U. (1977). Toward an experimental ecology of human development. *American Psychologist, 32*, 513–531.

Bronfenbrenner, U. (2005). The bioecological theory of human development. In U. Bronfenbrenner (ed.), *Making human beings human: Bioecological perspectives on human development* (pp. 3–15). Thousand Oaks, CA: Sage.

Bruner, M. W., Munroe-Chandler, K. J., & Spink, K. S. (2008). Entry into elite sport: A preliminary investigation into the transition experiences of rookie athletes. *Journal of Applied Sport Psychology, 20*, 236–252.

Busseri, M. A., Rose-Krasnor, L., Willoughby, T., & Chalmers, H. (2006). A longitudinal examination of breadth and intensity of youth activity involvement and successful development. *Developmental Psychology, 42*(6), 1313.

Camiré, M., Trudel, P., & Bernard, D. (2013). A case study of a high school sport program designed to teach athletes life skills and values. *The Sport Psychologist, 27*(2), 188–200.

Camiré, M., Trudel, P., & Forneris, T. (2012). Coaching and transferring life skills: Philosophies and strategies used by model high school coaches. *Sport Pychologist, 26*(2), 243–260.

Coakley, J. (2006). The good father: Parental expectations and youth sports. *Leisure Studies, 25*, 153–163.

Cobley, S. (2016). Talent identification and development in youth sport. In K. Green & A. Smith (eds), *Routledge Handbook of Youth Sport* (pp. 476–491). New York: Routledge.

Côté, J. (1999). The influence of the family in the development of talent in sports. *The Sport Psychologist, 13*, 395–417.

Côté, J., Bruner, M., Erickson, K., Strachan, L., & Fraser-Thomas, J. (2010). Athlete development and coaching. In J. Lyle & C. Cushion (eds) *Sport coaching: Professionalism and practice* (pp. 63–79). Oxford: Elsevier.

Côté, J., & Fraser-Thomas, J. (2016). Youth involvement and positive development in sport. In P. R. E. Crocker (ed.), *Sport psychology: A Canadian perspective* (3rd ed., pp. 256–286). Toronto: Pearson Prentice Hall.

Côté, J., & Gilbert, W. (2009). An integrative definition of coaching effectiveness and expertise. *International Journal of Sports Science and Coaching, 4*(3), 307–323.

Côté, J., Macdonald, D. J., Baker, J., & Abernethy, B. (2006). When "where" is more important than "when": Birthplace and birthdate effects on the achievement of sporting expertise. *Journal of Sports Sciences, 24*(10), 1065–1073.

Côté, J., Strachan, L., & Fraser-Thomas, J. (2008). Participation, personal development, and performance through youth sport. In N. L. Holt (ed.), *Positive youth development through sport* (pp. 34–45). Routledge: New York.

Côté, J., Turnnidge, J., & Evans, M. B. (2014). The dynamic process of development through sport. *Kinesiologia Slovenica, 20*(3), 14–26.

Côté, J., Turnnidge, J., & Vierimaa, M. (2016). A personal assets approach to youth sport. In K. Green & A. Smith (eds), *Routledge Handbook of Youth Sport* (pp. 243–255). New York: Routledge.

Cushion, C. J., Armour, K. M., & Jones, R. L. (2003). Coach education and continuing professional development: Experience and learning to coach. *Quest, 55*(3), 215–230.

Damon, W. (2004). What is positive youth development? *Annals of the American Academy of Political and Social Science, 591*, 13–24.

Danish, S. J. (2002). *SUPER (Sports United to Promote Education and Recreation) program leader manual* (3rd ed.). Richmond, VA: Life Skills Center, Virginia Commonwealth University.

Davis, N. W., & Meyer, B. B. (2008). When sibling becomes competitor: A qualitative investigation of same-sex sibling competitive in elite sport. *Journal of Applied Sport Psychology, 20*(2), 220–235.

Dean, C., & Rowan, D. (2013). The social worker's role in serving vulnerable athletes. *Journal of Social Work Practice: Psychotherapeutic Approaches in Health, Welfare and the Community, 28*(2), 219–227.

DiFiori, J. P., Benjamin, H. J., Brenner, J., Gregory, A., Jayanthi, N., Landry, G. L., et al. (2014). Overuse injuries and burnout in youth sports: A position statement from the American Medical Society for Sports Medicine. *Clinical Journal of Sport Medicine, 24*(3), 3–20.

Dorsch, T. E., Smith, A. L., Wilson, S. R., & McDonough, M. H. (2015). Parent goals and verbal sideline behaviour in organized youth sport. *Sport Exercise, and Performance Psychology, 4*(1), 19–35.

Duda, J. L., & Allison, M. T. (1990). Cross–cultural analysis in exercise and sport psychology: A void in the field. *Journal of Sport & Exercise Psychology, 12*(2), 114–131.

Eccles, J. S., & Gootman, J. A. (2002). *Community programs to promote youth development.* Washington, DC: National Academy Press.

Emery, C. A., Hagel, B., Decloe, M., & Carly, M. (2010). Risk factors for injury and severe injury in youth ice hockey: A systematic review of the literature. *Injury Prevention, 16,* 113–118. doi: 10.1136/ip.2009.022764

Ericsson, K. A., Krampe, R. T., & Tesch-Römer, C. (1993). The role of deliberate practice in the acquisition of expert performance. *Psychological Review, 100,* 363–406.

Etzel, E. F., Watson, J. C., Visek, A. J., & Maniar, S. D. (2006). Understanding and promoting college student-athlete health: Essential issues for student affairs professionals. *Journal National Association of Sport Physical Education, 43*(3), 518–546.

Flett, M. R., Gould, D., Griffes, K. R., & Lauer, L. (2013). Tough love for underserved youth: A comparison of more and less effective coaching. *Sport Psychologist, 27*(4), 325–337.

Fraser-Thomas, J., & Côté, J. (2009). Understanding adolescents' positive and negative developmental experiences in sport. *The Sport Psychologist, 23*(1), 3–23.

Fraser-Thomas, J., Côté, J., & Deakin, J. (2005). Youth sport programs: An avenue to foster positive youth development, *Physical Education and Sport Pedagogy, 10,* 19–40. doi: 10.1080/1740898042000334890

Fraser-Thomas, J., Côté, J., & Deakin, J. (2008a). Examining adolescent sport dropout and prolonged engagement from a developmental perspective. *Journal of Applied Sport Psychology, 20,* 318–333. doi: 10.1080/10413200802163549.

Fraser-Thomas, J., Côté, J., & Deakin, J. (2008b). Understanding dropout and prolonged engagement in adolescent competitive sport. *Psychology of Sport and Exercise, 9,* 645–662. doi: 10.1016/j.psychsport.2007.08.003.

Fraser-Thomas, J., Côté, J., & MacDonald, D. J. (2010). Community size in youth sport settings: Examining developmental assets and sport withdrawal. *PHEnex Journal, 2*(2), 1–9.

Fraser-Thomas, J., & Strachan, L. (2015). Personal development and performance? Exploring positive youth development in elite sport contexts. In J. Baker, J. Fraser-Thomas, & P. Safai (eds), *Health and elite sport: Is high performance sport a healthy pursuit?* (pp. 15–32). New York: Routledge.

Fridman, L., Fraser-Thomas, J., McFaull, S., & Macpherson, A. (2013). Epidemiology of sports-related injuries in children and youth presenting to Canadian emergency departments from 2007 to 2010. *BMC Sports Science, Medicine and Rehabilitation.* doi: 10.1186/10.1186/2052-1847-5-30.

Gervis, M., & Dunn, N. (2004). The emotional abuse of elite child athletes by their coaches. *Child Abuse & Neglect, 26,* 697–714.

Gould, D., & Carson, S. (2008). Life skills development through sport: Current status and future directions. *International Review of Sport and Exercise Psychology, 1,* 58–78.

Gould, D., Collins, K., Lauer, L., & Chung, Y. (2007). Coaching life skills through football: A study of award winning high school coaches. *Journal of Applied Sport Psychology, 19*(1), 16–37.

Gould, D., Dieffenbach, K., & Moffatt, A. (2002). Psychological characteristics and their development in Olympic champions. *Journal of Applied Sport Psychology, 14,* 172–204.

Gould, D., Lauer, L., Rolo, C., Jannes, C., & Pennisi, N. (2008). The role of parents in tennis success: Focus group interviews with junior coaches. *The Sport Psychologist, 22,* 18–37.

Green, B. C. (2005). Building sport programs to optimize athlete recruitment, retention, and transition: Toward a normative theory of sport development. *Journal of Sport Management, 19*(3), 233–253.

Harwood, C., & Johnston, J. (2016). Positive youth development and talent development: Is there a best of both worlds? In N. Holt (ed.) *Positive youth development through sport* (2nd ed., pp. 113–125). New York: Routledge.

Harwood, C., & Knight, C. J. (2009). Understanding parental stressors: An investigation of British tennis parents. *Journal of Sport Sciences, 27*(4), 339–351.

Hellison, D. (2003). *Teaching responsibility through physical activity* (2nd ed.). Champaign, IL: Human Kinetics.

Hildebrand, K. K., Johnson, J. D., & Bogle, K. (2001). Comparison of patterns of alcohol use between high school and college athletes and non-athletes. *College Student Journal, 35*(3), 358–365.

Hockey Canada (2013). *Hockey Canada's 94th Annual General Meeting concludes in Charlottetown, PEI; body checking rule change approved.* Retrieved from www.hockeycanada.ca/en-ca/news/agm-concludes-in-charlottetown

Holt, N. L., Deal, C. J., & Smyth, C. L. (2016). Future directions for positive youth development through sport. In N. Holt (ed.), *Positive youth development through sport* (2nd ed., pp. 229–240). New York: Routledge.

Holt, N. L., & Neely, K. C. (2011). Positive youth development through sport: A review. Revista Iberoamericana de Psicologia de Ejercicio y el Deporte Ibero. *American Journal of Sport Psychology, 6*, 299–316.

Holt, N. L., Tamminen, K. A., Tink, L. N., & Black, D. E. (2009). An interpretive analysis of life skills associated with sport participation. *Qualitative Research in Sport and Exercise, 1*(2), 160–175. doi:10.1080/19398440902909017

Hopwood, M. J., Farrow, D., MacMahon, C., & Baker, J. (2015). Sibling dynamics and sport expertise. *Scandinavian Journal of Medicine in Science and Sport, 25*(5), 724–733. doi: 10.1111/sms.12387

Hudd, S. S, Dumlao, J., Erdmann-Sager, D., Murray, D., Phan, E., Soukas, N., & Yokozuka, N. (2000). Stress at college: Effects on health habits, health status, and self esteem. *College Student Journal, 34*(2), 217–222.

Imitiaz, F., Hancock, D. J., Vierimaa, M., & Côté, J. (2014). Place of development and drop-out in youth ice hockey. *International Journal of Sport and Exercise Psychology, 12*(3), 234–244.

Keegan, R., Spray, C., Harwood, C., & Lavallee, D. (2010). The motivational atmosphere in youth sport: Coach, parent and peer influences on motivation in specializing sport participants. *Journal of Applied Sport Psychology, 22,* 87–105.

Kirk, D., Carlson, T., O'Connor, A., Burke, P., Davis, K., & Glover, S. (1997a). The economic impact on families of children's participation in junior sport. *Australian Journal of Science and Medicine in Sport, 29*, 27–33.

Kirk, D., O'Connor, A., Carlson, T., Burke, T., Davis, K., & Glover, S. (1997b). Time commitments in junior sport: Social consequences for participants and their families. *European Journal of Physical Education, 2,* 51–73.

Larson, R. (2000). Towards a psychology of positive youth development. *American Psychologist, 55*(1), 170–183.

Larson, R., Hansen, D., & Moneta, G. (2006). Differing profiles of developmental experiences across types of organized youth activities. *Developmental Psychology, 42*(5), 849–863. doi:10.1037/0012-1649.42.5.849.

Lauer, L., Gould, D., Roman, N., & Pierce, M. (2010). Parental behaviors that affect junior tennis player development. *Psychology of Sport and Exercise, 11,* 487–496.

Law, M. P., Côté, J., & Ericsson, K. A. (2007). Characteristics of expert development in rhythmic gymnastics: A retrospective study. *International Journal of Sport and Exercise Psychology, 5,* 82–103.

Lerner, R. M. (2002). *Concepts and theories of human development* (3rd ed.). Mahwah, NJ: Erlbaum.

Lerner, R. M., Lerner, J. V., Almerigi, J. Theokas, C., Phelps, E., Naudeau, S., et al. (2005). Positive youth development, participation in community youth development programs, and community contributions of fifth grade adolescents: Findings from the first wave of the 4-H study of Positive Youth Development. *Journal of Early Adolescence, 25,* 17–71.

Livingston, L. A., & Tirone, S. (2012). Understanding structural barriers in amateur sport and the participation of immigrants in Atlantic Canada. In S. C. Darnell, Y. Nakamura, & J. Joseph (eds), *Race and sport in Canada: Intersecting inequalities.* Toronto: Canadian Scholars' Press Inc.

MacPhail, A., & Kirk, D. (2006). Young people's socialization into sport: Experiencing the specializing phase. *Leisure Studies, 25,* 57–74.

Maniar, S., Chamberlain, R., & Moore, N. (2005). Suicide risk is real for student-athletes. *NCAA News, 42*(4,20).

Markser, V. Z. (2011). Sport psychiatry and psychotherapy: Mental strains and disorders in professional sports. Challenge and answer to societal changes. *European Archives of Psychiatry and Clinical Neuroscience, 261*(2), 182–185.

Miller, P. S., & Kerr, G. A. (2002). Conceptualizing excellence: Past, present, and future. *Journal of Applied Sport Psychology, 14,* 140–153.

Ontario Ministry of Education (2014). *Policy/Program Memorandum No. 158. School Board Policies on Concussion.* Retrieved from www.edu.gov.on.ca/extra/eng/ppm/158.pdf

Patrick, H., Ryan, A. M., Alfeld-Liro, C., Fredricks, J. A., Hruda, L. Z., & Eccles, J. S. (1999). Adolescents' commitment to developing talent: The role of peers in continuing motivation for sports and the arts. *Journal of Youth and Adolescence, 28,* 741–763.

Reardon, C. L., & Factor, R. M. (2010). Sport psychiatry: A systematic review of diagnosis and medical treatment of mental illness in athletes. *Sports Medicine, 40*(11), 961–980.

Roberts, G. C. (2012). Motivation in sport and exercise from an achievement goal theory perspective: After 30 years, where are we? In G. C. Roberts & D. C. Treasure (eds), *Advances in Motivation in Sport and Exercise* (pp. 5–58). Champaign, IL: Human Kinetics.

Roth, J., Brooks-Gunn, J., Murray, L., & Foster, W. (1998). Promoting healthy adolescents: Synthesis of youth development program evaluations. *Journal of Research on Adolescence, 8*, 423–459.

Ryba, T. V., & Wright, H. K. (2005). From mental game to cultural praxis: A cultural studies model's implications for the future of sport psychology. *Quest, 57*(2), 192–212.

Ryba, T. V., & Wright, H. K. (2010). Sport psychology and the cultural turn: Notes toward cultural praxis. In Ryba, T. V., Schinke, R. J., & Tenenbaum, G. (eds), *The cultural turn in sport psychology*. Morgantown, WV: Fitness Information Technology.

Schwab, K. A., Wells, M. S., & Arthur-Banning, S. (2010). Experiences in youth sports: A comparison between players' and parents' perspectives. *Journal of Sport Administration and Supervision, 2*(1), 41–51.

Scully, D., Kremer, J., Meade, M. M., Graham, R., & Dudgeon, K. (1998). Physical exercise and psychological well being: A critical review. *British Journal of Sports Medicine, 32*(2), 111–120.

Simpkins, S. D., Ripke, M., Huston, A., & Eccles, J. S. (2005). Predicting participation and outcomes in out-of-school activities: Similarities and differences across social ecologies. *New Directions for Youth Development, 105,* 51–69.

Stirling, A. E., & Kerr, G. A. (2008). Defining and categorizing emotional abuse in sport. *European Journal of Sport Science, 8*, 173–181.

Strachan, L., Côté, J., & Deakin, J. (2009). 'Specializers' versus 'samplers' in youth sport: Comparing experiences and outcomes. *The Sport Psychologist, 23,* 77–92.

Strachan, L., Coté, J., & Deakin, J. (2011). A new view: Exploring positive youth development in elite sport contexts. *Qualitative Research in Sport, Exercise and Health, 3*(1), 9–32. doi: 10.1080/19398441.2010.541483

Stroumboulopoulos, G. (2012). Interview with Clara Hughes. *George Stroumboulopoulos Tonight.* Retrieved from www.youtube.com/watch?v=KEvLL-u2f1w.

Sundgot-Borgen, J., & Torstveit, M. K. (2004). Prevalence of eating disorders in elite athletes is higher than in the general population. *Clinical Journal of Sport Medicine, 14*(1), 25–32.

Tamminen, K. A., & Holt, N. L. (2012). Adolescent athletes' learning about coping and the roles of parents and coaches. *Psychology of Sport and Exercise, 13*(1), 69–79.

Tamminen, K. A., Holt, N. L., & Neely, K. C. (2013). Exploring adversity and the potential for growth among elite female athletes. *Psychology of Sport and Exercise, 14,* 28–36.

Taylor, R. D., & Collins, D. (2015). Reviewing the family unit as a stakeholder in talent development: Is it undervalued? *Quest, 67,* 330–343.

Tofler, I. R., Stryer, B. K., Micheli, L. J., & Herman, L. R. (1996). Physical and emotional problems of elite female gymnasts. *New England Journal of Medicine, 335,* 281–283.

Trottier, C., & Robitaille, S. (2014). Fostering life skills development in high school and community sport: A comparative analysis of the coach's role. *The Sport Psychologist, 28,* 10–21. doi:10.1123/tsp.2012-0094

Trussell, D. E. (2012). Contradictory aspects of organized youth sport: Challenging and fostering sibling relationships and participation experiences. *Youth and Society,* 0044118X12453058.

Turnnidge, J., Côté, J., & Hancock, D. J. (2014). Positive youth development from sport to life: Explicit or implicit transfer? *Quest, 66*(2), 203–217. doi: 10.1080/00336297.2013.867275

Vandermeerschen, H., Vos, S., & Scheerder, J. (2014) Towards level playing fields? A time trend analysis of young people's participation in club-organised sports. *International Review for the Sociology of Sport.* doi: 10.1177/1012690214532450

Vierimaa, M., Erickson, C., & Côté, J. (2016). The elements of talent development in youth sport. In K. Green & A. Smith (eds), *Routledge handbook of youth sport* (pp. 464–475). New York: Routledge.

Wall, M., & Côté, J. (2007). Developmental activities that lead to drop-out and investment in sport. *Physical Education and Sport Pedagogy, 12*(1), 77–87.

Weiss, M. R. (2006). *The First Tee 2005 research summary: Longitudinal effects of the First Tee life skills educational program on positive youth development.* St. Augustine, FL: The First Tee.

Wilkes, S., & Côté, J. (2010). The developmental experiences of adolescent females in structured basketball programs. *PHENex Journal, 2*(2). Online. Retrieved from http://ojs.acadiau.ca/index.php/phenex/article/view/6/1162

Wolfenden, L. E., & Holt, N. L. (2005). Talent development in elite junior tennis: Perceptions of players, parents, and coaches. *Journal of Applied Sport Psychology, 17,* 108–126.

Wolman, L., & Fraser-Thomas, J. (2014). Exploring the continuity of sport participation: The role of community clubs in the sport development process. Poster presentation at *Canadian Society for Psychomotor Learning and Sport Psychology (SCAPPS)*. London, Canada.

Wulf, G. (2007). *Attention and motor skill learning.* Champaign, IL: Human Kinetics.

Zarrett, N., Lerner, R. M., Carrano, J., Fay, K., Peltz, J. S., & Li, Y. (2008). Variations in adolescent engagement in sports and its influence on positive youth development. In N. L. Holt (ed.), *Positive youth development through sport* (pp. 9–23). Routledge: New York.

28

HIGH PERFORMANCE SPORT AND ATHLETE HEALTH

Srdjan Lemez and Fieke Rongen

While there are many health benefits associated with involvement in high performance sport (e.g., superior lifespan longevity; Lemez & Baker, 2015), this chapter considers the health consequences. Many youth athletes pursue a career in high performance sport, often through involvement in elite youth or talent development programs. Despite its appeal, concerns have arisen regarding the health impact of this quest for high performance (e.g., Baker, Safai, & Fraser-Thomas, 2015). The purpose of this chapter is to review the immediate and long-term physical and psychosocial health outcomes in elite athletes. Such a review is important for identifying health risks associated with involvement in high performance sport and provides important implications for athlete development.

Physical health outcomes in active elite athletes

Musculoskeletal outcomes

The process of becoming an elite athlete is not a short one, as expert skill development typically reflects a manifestation of thousands of hours of intensive practice (Baker & Young, 2014). Consequently, over time, athletes become susceptible to overuse injuries, often reflected in areas of the musculoskeletal system that are most exposed to repetitive strain and/or trauma.

Perhaps unsurprisingly, soft tissue injuries in active elite athletes have been well-documented in limited-contact sports that are widely participated in such as soccer, collision and full-contact sports such as American football and rugby, and non-contact sports where movements are often repetitive (e.g., tennis). Beginning with limited-contact sports, substantial research has shown high prevalence and incidence of lower extremity injuries in elite soccer players, specifically sprains and contusions to thigh and ankle joint locations (e.g., Aoki, O'Hata, Kohno, Morikawa, & Seki, 2012), with previous injuries and short recovery periods serving as risk factors for re-injury in locations such as the knee (Waldén, Hägglund, & Ekstrand, 2006) and Achilles tendon (Gajhede-Knudsen, Ekstrand, Magnusson, & Maffulli, 2013). Similarly, in basketball, baseball, handball, and netball, there is a sizeable amount of evidence on negative health outcomes from participation. Basketball players have a high prevalence of ankle and knee injuries (e.g., McCarthy, Voos, Nguyen, Callahan, & Hannafin, 2013), while baseball players are susceptible to shoulder ailments, such as weakness of external rotators (Byram et al., 2010). As well, overuse has been found to produce ailments such as structural shoulder abnormalities and pain in handball players (e.g., Myklebust, Hasslan, Bahr, & Steffen, 2013), and back problems in netball players (e.g., Langeveld, Coetzee, & Holtzhausen, 2012).

In active full-contact competitors at the adult level, tackling has been a robust predictor of soft tissue injury for most elite rugby players, commonly arising in the lower extremities (Quarrie & Hopkins, 2008) and in older players, who typically experience higher injury risk (Rogalski, Dawson, Heasman, & Gabbett, 2013). In addition, the types of collision, playing position, and skill level have also been found to influence injury risk (e.g., Gabbett, Ullah, Jenkins, & Abernethy, 2012). A meta-analysis performed by Williams, Trewartha, Kemp, and Stokes (2013) corroborated previous literature findings that the lower limbs were most likely to get injured, while upper limb injuries were most severe. These common injury profiles and mechanisms also appear at the youth level, although injury incidence is lower in comparison to the senior elite rugby competition (Scase et al., 2012). In youth playing American football, for example, soft tissue injuries to the knee and ankle have been identified as the most common, with sprains and strains occurring more often than bone injuries or concussions (Kompel, Murakami, & Carrino, 2016).

Last, the locations of injury in non-contact sports such as tennis, volleyball, gymnastics, and rowing are generally specific to the musculoskeletal areas (over) used in the activity. Before an injury transpires, repetitive strain on muscles and joints predispose soft tissue to damage. For example, Moreno-Pérez, Moreside, Barbado, and Vera-Garcia (2015) reported that a glenohumeral internal rotation deficit of the dominant shoulder is a risk factor for shoulder injury in professional tennis players. Other examples include injuries to (a) the shoulder and knee in elite volleyball players (e.g., Augustsson, Augustsson, Thomeé, & Svantesson, 2006), including a prevalence of jumper's knee in youth with a high volume of volleyball training and match exposure (Visnes & Bahr, 2013), (b) foot and ankle in gymnasts (e.g., Chilvers, Donahue, Nassar, & Manoli, 2007), and (c) lower back in rowers (e.g., Winzen, Voigt, Hinrichs, & Platen, 2011).

While there is considerable evidence of injury incidence across all sports, such as shoulder injuries in elite cricketers (e.g., Saw, Dennis, Bentley, & Farhart, 2011), acute (e.g., ankle sprain) and overuse (e.g., stress fractures) injuries in elite junior figure skaters (Dubravcic-Simunjak, Pecina, Kuipers, Moran, & Haspl, 2003), and lower back and wrist/hand injuries in professional golfers (Grassmayr, Steinweg, Trainor, Ferdinands, & Vanwanseele, 2010), it is important to recognize how the role of early specialization may produce these higher rates of overuse injury in the musculoskeletal system over time. The manifestations of these injuries in active athletes are likely an amalgamation of past and present training and performance environments, and should be considered during the onset of more specialized forms of training. Likewise, athlete development programs will have to address these challenges in the short term during more sensitive periods of skill development, such as emphasizing fundamentals and proper technique as a form of injury prevention.

Overtraining and physical health

While musculoskeletal injuries are associated with both the short and particularly longer term increases in volume and intensity of training that accompany the pursuit of excellence (Myklebust & Bahr, 2005), other health concerns have also been identified. Overtraining, representing an unintended decrement in performance capacity resulting from a failure to recover from the accumulation of training and non-training stress (Budgett, 1998), is one key potential negative consequence of intensified regimes (see Chapter 25). It is important to distinguish overtraining from overreaching, which is a deliberate part of training necessary to produce performance improvements (Lehman, Foster, Gastmann, Keizer, & Steinacker, 1999). Overreaching is deemed to result in a short-term performance decrement that can be overcome through a brief period of recovery (i.e., few days or weeks; Kreider, Fry, & O'Toole, 1998). Overtraining, however, signifies an imbalance between training fatigue and non-training stressors and recovery (Matos & Winsley, 2007), where the helpful features of overreaching tip into unwanted harm from over-burden, with a recovery period that may take several weeks or months (Kreider et al., 1998). Overtraining is associated with a range of clinical symptoms comprising both physical health and psychological well-being. More specifically, overtraining is signalled by chronic fatigue and decreased performance (Meeuwsen et al., 2006), as well as mood disturbances, general apathy, loss of appetite, disturbed sleep, irritability and vulnerability to injury and illness (e.g., Birrer, Lienhard, Williams, Röthlin, & Morgan, 2013).

In terms of prevalence, 28% and 10% of US Olympic athletes competing at the Atlanta and Nagano Games, respectively, reported they were overtrained (e.g., Gould & Dieffenbach, 2002) and approximately 30% of Swiss elite athletes were classified as having been overtrained at least once in their career (Birrer et al., 2013). In regards to adult elite athletes, Matos and Winsley (2007) provided overtraining incidence rates ranging from 10% to 64% in individual sports and 33% to 50% in team sports. In relation to talent identification and particularly development, youth elite athletes have been suggested to often push themselves too far or hard, experience extreme tiredness on a regular basis, and never reach their full potential due to excessive training and inadequate recovery (e.g., Gould & Dieffenbach, 2002). In a review on trainability and overtraining in youth athletes, Matos and Winsley (2007) estimated a 30% prevalence of overtraining in this population, which they attributed to a combination of heavy training loads, insufficient recovery and restrained social support networks brought on by early specialization and intensification.

In addition to overtraining, during prolonged periods of intensive training and immediately following competitions, immune functioning can be suppressed in elite athletes (e.g., Ekblom, Ekblom, & Malm, 2006), which may place them at a higher risk for infections. For instance, while moderate training volumes are related to a decreased risk of upper respiratory tract infection, this risk increases significantly for high training volumes (Nieman, 1994). Research has shown that respiratory symptoms that are suggestive of asthma are common in athletes and indeed, the prevalence of asthma in the elite athlete population is relatively high, ranging from 3% to 23% in summer sports and 12% to 50% in winter sports (Carlsen et al., 2008). These findings lead Carlsen and colleagues (2008) to conclude that elite level athletes are at increased risk of asthma, particularly in endurance sports.

For young adolescents and adults, playing sport at a competitive level has also been linked to increased cardiovascular disease, although certain subgroups of athletes appear to be at greater risk (e.g., African American football players and linemen; e.g., Baron, Hein, Lehman, & Gersic, 2012). However, it has been argued that it is not sport but rather the culmination of intensive training in athletes with underlying cardiovascular disease or etiological abnormalities (e.g., genetic disorders such as hypertrophic cardiomyopathy) that results in increased risk (Ljungqvist et al., 2009). Given the rigorous training regimes of both youth and adult elite athletes, careful screening to rule out cardiovascular disorders such as hypertension, dysrhythmia, heart murmur, congenital heart disease or structural/acquired heart disease is vital (e.g., Ljungqvist et al., 2009).

All together, intensification of training is associated with a range of potential negative physical health outcomes. While these outcomes have been largely studied in active (adult) elite athletes, the above has aimed to highlight how similar concerns (may) apply to the intensified training regimes that often characterize elite youth sport involvement. Given the potential impact and wider consequences that conditions such as overtraining, infections and reduced immune functioning may have on the healthy and successful development of youth athletes, these concerns warrant particular attention within talent development systems.

Physical health outcomes in former elite athletes

Active elite athletes are often regarded as having superior health relative to the general population. However, after years of dedicating their lives to sport, the ability to sustain good health post-retirement can wane (e.g., Kuijt, Inklaar, Gouttebarge, & Frings-Dresen, 2012). In particular, the unique demands of their respective sport can impact the type and severity of deficiencies in physical functioning later in life. For example, sport can be classified according to its energy system demand; more specifically, they include: (i) endurance (aerobic sports), (ii) mixed (sports that require activation of both the aerobic and anaerobic energy systems), and (iii) power (anaerobic sports). Accordingly, longitudinal research in these three domains has generally focused on (i) cardiac benefits, (ii) osteoarthritis (OA), and (iii) cognitive impairments in former elite athletes, respectively.

Endurance sports

Similar to superior lifespan longevity outcomes (Lemez & Baker, 2015), former elite endurance sport athletes appear to have the most favourable physical health outcomes in later life compared to mixed and power sport athletes. For example, Bjørnstad and colleagues (2009) reported no evidence of harmful cardiac effects in top-level endurance athletes after a 15-year follow-up. Further, although Hagmar, Hirschberg, Lindholm, Schenck-Gustafsson, and Eriksson (2005) found mild cardiac enlargement in a group of post-menopausal former elite endurance athletes, there were no increases in wall thickness, and long-term training maintained high levels of cardiovascular fitness. The long-term persistence of cardiac changes (i.e., remodelling and function) was also noted in former Swiss professional cyclists, although their impact on long-term health is unclear (Luthi et al., 2008).

Importantly, while former elite cyclists have shown a prevalence of sinus node disease and arrhythmias (Baldesberger et al., 2008) and former elite swimmers a suppressed systemic and mucosal immunity (i.e., weaker ability to fight viruses and infections; Gleeson et al., 1995), overall morbidity is low in former endurance athletes, as evidenced by a low risk for ischemic heart disease and diabetes (Sarna, Kaprio, Kujala, & Koskenvuo, 1997) and absence of other types of diseases (e.g., no prevalence of amyotrophic lateral sclerosis (ALS) in former cyclists; Chiò et al., 2009).

Mixed sports

In former mixed sport athletes, OA has been consistently found to be a leading ailment in later life. Former elite soccer players have the most robust empirical evidence of OA in later life, particularly in the lower extremities, which correlates with the earlier reported preponderance of physical injuries sustained while active. For example, Kuijt and colleagues' (2012) systematic review found a high prevalence of knee and ankle OA in former elite players relative to the general population in each study (although only four studies were included). Unfortunately, OA does not appear to be exclusive to former soccer players, as research has shown a greater prevalence of OA in the ankles of former elite volleyball players (Gross & Marti, 1999), premature hip OA in former elite handball players (L'Hermette, Polle, Tourny-Chollet, & Dujardin,

2006), shoulder OA in former elite tennis players (Maquirriain, Ghisi, & Amato, 2006), and knee OA in former elite table-tennis players (Rajabi, Johnson, Alizadeh, & Meghdadi, 2012) compared to age- and sex-matched controls from the general population. Other research has documented a high risk for ALS (Chiò, Benzi, Dossena, Mutani, & Mora, 2005), which may be a result of repeated injury, noxious drugs (e.g., smoking cigarettes), and exposure to environmental toxins, such as pesticides (Beghi, 2013).

Power sports

Growing empirical evidence indicates former elite power sport athletes have the potential to experience the most severe health consequences. For example, the repercussions of repetitive head trauma have been at the forefront of recent media and social media coverage of American football players as a result of medical professionals identifying cases of brain damage in former athletes. Chronic traumatic encephalopathy (CTE), a neurodegenerative brain disease, has been identified as a primary by-product of long-term concussive and subconcussive injury in contact-sport athletes (e.g., Huber, Alosco, Stein, & McKee, 2016). Other negative long-term health consequences have also been found in these athletes. For example, in a study of retired professional American football players, prevalence of advanced subclinical atherosclerosis was similar to men from the general population who were overweight or obese (Hurst et al., 2010). Former power sport athletes also have a high prevalence of OA. For instance, former elite rugby players have a significant risk of knee OA (Deacon, Bennell, Kiss, Crossley, & Brukner, 1997), while former professional American football players, particularly linemen, have a high prevalence of ankle OA (Zinder, Guskiewicz, & Marshall, 2010). Additionally, former elite javelin throwers have been linked to degenerative changes in their throwing arm over time (Schmitt, Hansmann, Brocai, & Loew, 2001).

It is likely that a substantial portion of these physical health outcomes in former elite athletes, particularly those who participated in mixed and power sports, will elicit re-evaluations of athlete development and performance training models. In particular, as emerging findings continue to highlight longitudinal health risks of involvement in elite sport (e.g., Kuijt et al., 2012), there will be important implications and increased scrutiny as to how sport practitioners structure training environments at the youth levels. For example, new concussion policies and protocols are now regularly implemented in contact-based sports such as American football (e.g., emphasizing fundamentals such as proper tackling and avoiding full speed head-on blocking or tackling drills). As such, athletes will have to be trained and developed differently as the fear of injury and questions surrounding coaching competence to properly handle an injured athlete continue to rise. Going forward, it will be interesting to see how increased sensitivity of these longitudinal health risks may affect future participation rates in youth sports, particularly sports that expose children to potentially harmful health consequences incurred from physical play.

Psychosocial health outcomes in active elite athletes

For many athletes, retirement can mean financial and/or family concerns, struggling to transition out of sport and properly adjust their self-identity, or boredom after following a regimented schedule for years. Below, we highlight some of the more commonly reported negative psychosocial health outcomes, beginning with active elite athletes.

Burnout

Building on the earlier outlined concerns regarding overtraining, burnout is one of the key negative psychosocial health impacts associated with intensified or elite level sport participation. Coakley (1992) described it as a more severe consequence of the social conditions in elite sport and some scholars consider burnout to be the end-point and most severe outcome of the fatigue–overreaching–overtraining continuum (Kenttä, Hassmén, & Raglin, 2001). Burnout results from the athlete feeling unable to meet excessive demands, and is characterized by physical and emotional exhaustion, a reduced sense of accomplishment, and devaluing of sport participation (Lemyre, Roberts, & Stray-Gundersen, 2007). Common symptoms include poor sleep quality, lack of energy, chronic fatigue, loss of motivation, feelings of helplessness, depression and isolation, nausea and frequently being ill, problems concentrating and an unbalanced approach to life (e.g., Gould & Dieffenbach, 2003; Lemyre et al., 2007; see also Chapter 25).

Despite being highlighted as a key concern regarding the health of active youth and adult elite athletes, the prevalence of burnout has not been extensively researched. In particular, there is limited normative – large-scale survey – data available. The few studies that have explored burnout in athlete populations indicate a prevalence of between 1% to 5% (Gould & Dieffenbach, 2003) and 11% (Raedeke, 1997) in competitive swimming, 6% to 25% in rugby (Cresswell & Eklund, 2007), and 1% to 9% in elite Swedish athletes with 1% to 2% suffering from severe burnout (Gustafsson, Kenttä, Hassmén, & Lundqvist, 2007). Gustafsson and colleagues (2007) highlighted that the widespread burnout prevalence reported in these studies might be due to relatively small and homogenous samples, but it may also be due to different studies using different cut-off points to classify high levels of burnout.

Relating back to talent identification and development, burnout is argued to be prevalent in youth athletes who were, or had been, involved in intensive and competitive training regimes (e.g., Coakley, 1992). Early specialization has been linked to burnout (DiFiori et al., 2014) and youth athletes have been reported to be closer to the critical thresholds for burnout than adult elite athletes, suggesting they may be at higher risk (Lemyre et al., 2007). DiFiori and colleagues (2014) highlighted that the incidence of burnout in youth athletes is higher for females, in individual sports and for the highest-level competitors. Further, they emphasized that the psychological makeup of a youth athlete, such as the perceived psychosocial stress and pressure, may be a particularly strong predictor of burnout (DiFiori et al., 2014).

Athletic identity as a "cumulative" psychosocial risk factor

It has been argued that the social conditions and culture of elite sport is entrenched in a narrative that revolves around single-mindedness, a predominant focus on the sporting aspects of one's life, combined with a focus on winning and performance outcomes (e.g., Douglas & Carless, 2009). Emergence in such a culture has been associated with a number of additional negative effects on psychosocial health. In particular, it is associated with the development of an identity closely aligned to "athletic role," placing the development of a multifaceted well-rounded identity at risk (e.g., Wylleman & Lavallee, 2004). The development of a single-minded, exclusive (and narrow) identity can be seen as a potential negative psychosocial health outcome in itself. However, this type of identity is perhaps most aptly described as a psychosocial health risk factor, predisposing athletes to further detrimental consequences.

First, it has been associated with poor physical and mental health, including social isolation (Horton & Mack, 2000). Second, a strong athletic identity is linked to the development of obsessive passion, which consequently relates to the risk of overtraining and burnout (e.g.,

Coakley, 1992). Last, a strong and exclusive athletic identity is associated with inadequate coping, negative affect and disturbed mood when dealing with the inevitable, but commonly temporary, setbacks that accompany high-level sport (e.g., such as injury, performance slumps or failures; Stambulova, 2003).

The robust association between a strong and exclusive athletic identity and an overriding performance focus and "winning at all cost mentality" also poses additional problems, such as the willingness to self-sacrifice or self-harm (e.g., Theberge, 2008). In elite sport contexts, "No pain, no gain" narratives persist (e.g., Carless & Douglas, 2013), and athletes have reported regularly training and competing in pain (Thiel, Mayer, & Digel, 2010) as well as not allowing sufficient time to recover from injury and illness (Currie, Potts, Donovan, & Blackwood, 1999).

In exploring elite athletes' perspectives on health and injury, Theberge (2008) highlighted that while athletes were able to acknowledge they were generally pushing their bodies beyond what "may be healthy," this and the resultant injuries were portrayed as a normal and accepted part of elite sport. Further, long-term consequences did not feature heavily in their considerations and athletes spoke about their bodies as objects to be managed and health as a capacity that allowed them to perform in their respective sports.

At the developmental level, a survey of German elite youth athletes found that those athletes who (a) were highly involved in the elite sport system, (b) largely value sport at the expense of other life domains and (c) were perfectionists, were extremely willing to accept both physical and psychological risks (Schnell, Mayer, Diehl, Zipfel, & Thiel, 2014). Similarly, youth elite athletes involved in an elite sport school in Germany were shown to pay progressively more attention to nutrition and appearance (Beckmann, Elbe, Szymanski, & Ehrlenspiel, 2006). Indeed, disordered eating is a health-compromising behaviour associated with a strong identification with the sport, a willingness to win and "manage" the body as needed. In particular, sports where a high lean body to fat mass ratio are: (i) linked to improved performance, (ii) favoured aesthetically (e.g., gymnastics) or (iii) provide a competitive advantage (e.g., rowing, wrestling) can increase this risk (e.g., Sundgot-Borgen & Torstveit, 2010).

Athletes with stronger athletic identities appear more likely and more willing to engage in such health-compromising behaviours. The willingness to risk one's health can also be related to the "toxic jock" (Miller & Hoffman, 2009) side of athletic identity, often underpinned by masculinity values. In this instance, this refers to the social valuing of physical strength and size, aggressiveness, and assertiveness, values that reinforce "acting tough" in social situations, and "risk-taking and stoicism in the face of pain and injury" (Miller & Hoffman, 2009, p. 352). Strong identification with the jock identity (as opposed to an athlete identity) is associated with several health risk behaviours such as problem drinking and interpersonal violence (e.g., Miller, Melnick, Farrell, Sabo, & Barnes, 2006). It is important to note that none of these relationships emerged for those strongly identifying with the athlete identity. Further, whilst athlete identity was negatively correlated with depression and odds of a past-year suicide attempt, a strong jock identity was associated with increased odds of a suicide attempt (Miller & Hoffman, 2009). This highlights how the relationship between athletic identity and health risks is perhaps not as straightforward as once thought.

Nonetheless, at the developmental level in particular, the training volume, associated required sacrifices (e.g., time away from school, time away from friends or alternative activities) and a heavy performance focus can produce an environment where youth athletes may be susceptible to perceptions of a one-dimensional identity. Indeed, talented youth athletes have been reported to be at risk for developing a strong athletic identity (e.g., Mitchell et al., 2014). As identity development takes place throughout adolescence and early adulthood, it is likely to coincide with the time at which youth athletes commit to progressively more intensified and specialized training. Identity development, at the same time, is largely shaped through a process of socialization. Therefore, attention to how youth elite sport contexts and the practitioners working within these contexts may foster a "healthy" or "unhealthy" identification with the role of an athlete warrants further attention. In this light, questions around appropriate training volumes, how to balance sport and life, how to combine a performance focus with healthy athlete development and what is acceptable (or deemed expected) in the pursuit of excellence need answering in order to mitigate the risks surrounding identity development.

Mental health

Relatively little is known regarding mental disorders in elite athletes. In one of the rare studies in this area, Schaal and colleagues (2011) explored the mental health of high-level French athletes and found 17% had at least one ongoing or recent disorder. The leading mental health problem in their sample was generalized anxiety disorder (GAD; 6%) followed by non-specific eating disorders (4.2%) with depression affecting a much smaller percentage of athletes (3.6%). In a similar vein, Gulliver, Griffiths, Mackinnon, Batterham, and Stanimirovic (2015) recently investigated Australian elite athletes and found a surprising 46.4% of athletes to have been experiencing symptoms of at least one mental health problem. The leading mental health problems in their sample were eating disorders (28.2%), depression (27.2%), general psychological distress (16.5%), social anxiety (14.7%), GAD (7.1%), and panic disorder (4.5%; Gulliver et al., 2015). In regards to depression, other research has generally supported these findings that high-level athletes encounter depression at a similar or higher frequency than the general population (Reardon & Factor, 2010). Alarmingly, Hammond, Gialloreto, Kubas, and Davis (2013) found that a surprisingly high percentage – 68% – of elite level Canadian swimmers met criteria for a major depressive episode.

In line with findings in the general population, female athletes are more likely than male athletes to encounter psychopathology (Schaal et al., 2011). Yet, the above findings also highlight that the relationship between elite sport and mental health is not a straightforward one, and the specific constraints of different sports play a role in the development of some disorders. For example, athletes from aesthetic sports (e.g., gymnastics, synchronized swimming, and figure skating) showed the highest prevalence of GAD, whereas athletes from high-risk sports (e.g., sliding sports, motor sports and aerial sports) showed the lowest prevalence. Further, although the overall prevalence of anorexia and bulimia nervosa was comparable to the general population, the majority of eating disorders in this sample were classified as Eating Disorder-Not Otherwise Specific (EDNOS). A diagnosis of EDNOS would be given in those cases where symptoms did not meet all criteria for anorexia or bulimia or where symptoms were a mix of both. In addition, whereas in the general population the women to men ratio for dealing with eating disorders lies between 6:1 and 10:1 (Sundgot-Borgen & Torstveit, 2010), within the elite athletes sample this ratio was 2:1. Hence, within the athlete population both men and women are more equally affected, with eating disorders being most common for females in racing sports and males in combat sports. Gulliver and colleagues (2015) also noted that injured athletes had higher levels of depression and GAD. We can generally assume that more severe injuries sustained while active can exacerbate present psychosocial states. Thus, it is important not to underestimate the complexity of the underlying interactions between psychological and social factors that lead to negative health outcomes, and how it may influence athlete development and performance.

Aside from injury, elite combat sport athletes also typically reflect unique performance-related stressors. For example, Koral and Dosseville (2009) examined the effects of dieting and training for gradual and rapid weight loss for competition in elite judo athletes, and found that their psychological states were adversely affected, scoring significantly higher in confusion and tension measures relative to a control group. In another full-contact sport, elite rugby players were found to be exposed to a variety of stressors, such as injury concerns and mental and physical errors, although the effectiveness of their coping strategies varied greatly (Nicholls, Holt, Polman, & Bloomfield, 2006). Similarly, in a non-contact sport such as figure skating, psychosocial consequences such as disordered eating (Scoffier, Woodman, & d'Arripe-Longueville, 2011) have been reported.

The implications of mental health issues on athlete development are complex, and highlight a need for a more complete understanding of underlying mechanisms that contribute to its manifestation in athletes. For example, while the development of negative psychosocial outcomes may be initially associated with injury incidence, a variety of other factors can influence an athlete's present mental state, including their coping mechanisms to stress, severity of injury (e.g., minor vs career-ending), overtraining and tiredness leading to burnout, pressures of performance, disturbed sleep and diet. Therefore, while research indicates that injury is a strong predictor of a lower life quality in active elite athletes (e.g., Gulliver et al., 2015), knowledge of other unique and circumstantial psychosocial risk factors that develop and persist could be valuable in developing a comprehensive model of health/injury risk for athlete development and training programs.

Psychosocial health outcomes in former elite athletes

Adaptation in retirement

Ultimately, all elite athletes will have to deal with transitioning out of high performance sport. This change is characterized by a disruption of daily routines and activities that have often been self-defining (e.g., Wylleman, Alfermann, & Lavallee, 2004), and athletes report experiencing loss in terms of social networks, identity and public attention (Lally, 2007). Further, as athletes typically retire at a relatively young age, they need to pursue new career paths (Cosh, Crabb, & LeCouteur, 2013), and clearly, the ongoing transition process that athletes face when retiring from their athletic career can be challenging. Wylleman and colleagues (2004) highlighted that retiring athletes are vulnerable to psychological and emotional difficulties such as depression, identity crises, eating disorders, decreased self-confidence, social isolation and alcohol/substance abuse. However, some individuals encounter minimal, if any, side effects, and the "smoothness" of the transition varies across athletes.

That being said, research exploring these differences has identified several predictors for the *quality* of the transition (Park, Lavallee, & Todd, 2013). Three predictors have received particular attention: (i) the voluntary nature, or degree of choice over the decision to retire, (ii) athletic identity, and (iii) pre-retirement planning (e.g., Wylleman et al., 2004). First, when retirements are involuntary, particularly if sudden and unexpected, athletes encounter more difficulties. In the previous section, we highlighted that having a strong and exclusive athletic identity may be a psychosocial health risk factor for active elite athletes. This also applies to retiring athletes, where a strong athletic identity can render them ill-prepared for transitioning out of sport when this changeover occurs prematurely (due to de-selection or career ending injury; Alfermann, 2000), or naturally (end of career; e.g., Lally, 2007). Third, related to the second point, a strong athletic identity has been associated with identity foreclosure and particularly a lack of exploration of other roles, delayed or poor career development and planning (e.g., Park et al., 2013), and decreased willingness to engage in pre-retirement planning (Lally, 2007). Consequently, it is the more challenging transitions that are more likely to result in mental health problems, including identity loss and depression (e.g., Douglas & Carless, 2009; Lally, 2007). Given the large impact of both feelings of control and preparation for a smooth transition, this may have strong implications for awareness and incorporation of these factors within talent development systems. Ensuring that youth athletes are able to balance sport and other life demands, and develop holistically, including safeguarding their educational development and guaranteeing alternative career plans, may prove a key challenge for healthy athlete development.

Quality of life

To date, much of the existing investigations on the long-term psychosocial health outcomes and life qualities of former elite athletes have been performed by a team of Finnish researchers (e.g., Bäckmand, Kaprio, Kujala, & Sarna, 2001; Bäckmand, Kaprio, Kujala, Sarna, & Fogelholm, 2006; Bäckmand, Kaprio, Kujala, & Sarna, 2009), in which they highlight the importance of maintaining physical activity participation. For example, high engagement in physical activity has been found to have a protective effect against depression by decreasing anxiety and improving physical functioning (Bäckmand et al., 2009) in former elite athletes. Interestingly, we can extrapolate these findings to power sports as well; former elite athletes from this sport energy system were found to be more extroverted, generally more satisfied with life and less depressed relative to male referents from the general population (Bäckmand et al., 2001), and current physical activity protected against poor psychological functioning and negative daily functionality (Bäckmand et al., 2006).

As such, much of our current understanding appears to be highly influenced by whether the former athlete is able to sustain their involvement in physical activity. It is also important to note that physical health may moderate psychosocial health, although there has been limited research performed on athlete samples. Some examples of this research on psychophysical health in former athletes has found that those who experienced career-ending injuries reported reduced life satisfaction (Kleiber & Brock, 1992), in addition to experiencing bodily changes that were reported as decreasing global self-esteem and physical self-perceptions (Stephan, Torregrosa, & Sanchez, 2007).

Importantly, research should consider whether sport demands result in injuries that persist into adulthood, and consequently detract from later life physical activity involvement. As discussed earlier, physical health certainly plays a key role in an athlete's ability to engage in physical activity in later life, such as being affected by OA from participating in soccer or experiencing cognitive declines from participating in a full-contact sport such as American football. Simon and Docherty (2013) investigated this relationship in former Division I athletes and found that scores in physical function, depression, fatigue, sleep disturbances, and pain interference were significantly worse in the former athlete group than in non-athletes. Consequently, the former athletes reported more limitations during daily activity and exercise, in addition to more chronic and major injuries compared to non-athletes (Simon & Docherty, 2013). Further, Kerr and colleagues (2014) found an association between former concussion and greater risk of severe depression, higher levels of impulsivity, and aggression among former collegiate athletes. However, we need to be cautious when discussing causality, as situational factors may play a role in an athlete's struggle in retirement.

More long-term focused athlete development programs may be needed to foster improved life quality after retirement. More specifically, a short-term and performance-focused athlete development environment may not consider the longitudinal chronic and psychosocial damage that can occur from intensive training demands and pressures from early ages. The quality of life in former elite athletes appears to be marred by several potential confounders, such as the demands of the sport they previously competed in and engaging in negative health behaviours in early life that can lead to later life mental health problems. For example, a 30-year follow-up study of former Swedish-elite male power-sport athletes who used anabolic androgenic steroids in the past were found to have a high prevalence of other substance abuse and mental health problems, particularly depression and anxiety (Lindqvist et al., 2013). Therefore, investigating these nuances from early development will be important going forward as mental health awareness and adjustment in later life as a non-competitive athlete continues to gain attention in former elite competitors.

Conclusion

Decades of research has illuminated a multitude of factors that underpin health outcomes in elite athletes. In this chapter, we highlighted physical and psychosocial health concerns in active and former elite athletes; however, we must also consider the synergy of the social, emotional, and spiritual elements to adequately assess health through a more integrated and holistic approach. Reaching optimal health and wellness will positively impact an athlete's training and developmental environment. For example, sport practitioners who understand how one element of health affects another (e.g., the role of physical injury on emotional health) can create programs that are better suited for learning and growth in sport. In youth sport, performance-driven developmental environments may predispose participants to similar health problems as high performance competitors (e.g., musculoskeletal overuse injury). Thus, there is a need to understand how to minimize the accumulation of negative health practices in youth, which can have both immediate and longitudinal consequences for them as athletes (performance) as well as individuals (personal development). These issues of health also relate to the multi-dimensional talent identification process; a range of determinants of health, such as biological, economic, and environmental factors can affect how an athlete is evaluated from a young age. It is therefore important that future research continues to explore how interrelationships among these health factors relate to talent identification and athlete development from an early age, and its subsequent role on performance and later life well-being.

References

Alfermann, D. (2000). Causes and consequences of sport career termination. In D. Lavallee & P. Wylleman (eds), *Career transitions in sport: International perspectives* Morgantown, WV: Fitness Information Technology: 45–58.

Aoki, H., O'Hata, N., Kohno, T., Morikawa, T., & Seki, J. (2012). A 15-year prospective epidemiological account of acute traumatic injuries during official professional soccer league matches in Japan. *The American Journal of Sports Medicine*, 40: 1006–1114.

Augustsson, S. R., Augustsson, J., Thomeé, R., & Svantesson, U. (2006). Injuries and preventive actions in elite Swedish volleyball. *Scandinavian Journal of Medicine & Science in Sports*, 16: 433–440.

Bäckmand, H., Kaprio, J., Kujala, U., & Sarna, S. (2001). Personality and mood of former elite male athletes: A descriptive study. *International Journal of Sports Medicine*, 22: 215–221.

Bäckmand, H. M., Kaprio, J., Kujala, U. M., & Sarna, S. (2009). Physical activity, mood and the functioning of daily living. A longitudinal study among former elite athletes and referents in middle and old age. *Archives of Gerontology and Geriatrics*, 48: 1–9.

Bäckmand, H., Kaprio, J., Kujala, U. M., Sarna, S., & Fogelholm, M. (2006). Physical and psychological functioning of daily living in relation to physical activity. A longitudinal study among former elite male athletes and controls. *Aging Clinical and Experimental Research*, 18: 40–49.

Baker, J., Safai, P., & Fraser-Thomas, J. (2015). *Health and elite sport: Is high performance sport a healthy pursuit?* Routledge: London.

Baker, J., & Young, B. (2014). 20 years later: Deliberate practice and the development of expertise in sport. *International Review of Sport and Exercise Psychology, 7*: 135–157.

Baldesberger, S., Bauersfeld, U., Candinas, R., Seifert, B., Zuber, M., Ritter, M., … Attenhofer Jost, C. H. (2008). Sinus node disease and arrhythmias in the long-term follow-up of former professional cyclists. *European Heart Journal, 29*: 71–78.

Baron, S. L., Hein, M. J., Lehman, E., & Gersic, C. M. (2012). Body mass index, playing position, race, and the cardiovascular mortality of retired professional football players. *The American Journal of Cardiology, 109*: 889–896.

Beckmann, J., Elbe, A., Szymanski, B., & Ehrlenspiel, F. (2006). *Chancen und risiken: Vom leben im verbundsystem von schule und leistungssport. Psychologische, soziologische und sportliche leistungsaspekte* (Auflage 2006 ed.): Bundesinstitut für Sportwissenschaft, Bonn.

Beghi, E. (2013). Are professional soccer players at higher risk for ALS? *Amyotrophic Lateral Sclerosis & Frontotemporal Degeneration, 14*: 501–506.

Birrer, D., Lienhard, D., Williams, C. A., Röthlin, P., & Morgan, G. (2013). Prevalence of non-functional overreaching and the overtraining syndrome in Swiss elite athletes. *Sweizerische Zeitschrift für Sportmedizin und Sporttraumatologie, 61*: 23–29.

Bjørnstad, H. H., Bjørnstad, T. H., Urheim, S., Hoff, P. I., Smith, G., & Maron, B. J. (2009). Long-term assessment of electrocardiographic and echocardiographic findings in Norwegian elite endurance athletes. *Cardiology, 112*: 234–241.

Budgett, R. (1998). Fatigue and underperformance in athletes: The overtraining syndrome. *British Journal of Sports Medicine, 32*: 107–110.

Byram, I. R., Bushnell, B. D., Dugger, K., Charron, K., Harrell, F. E., & Noonan, T. J. (2010). Preseason shoulder strength measurements in professional baseball pitchers: Identifying players at risk for injury. *The American Journal of Sports Medicine, 38*: 1375–1382.

Carless, D., & Douglas, K. (2013). "In the Boat" but "Selling Myself Short": Stories, narratives, and identity development in elite sport. *Sport Psychologist, 27*: 27–39.

Carlsen, K. H, Anderson, S. D., Bjermer, L., Bonini, S., Brusasco, V., Canonica, W., … van Cauwenberge, P. (2008). Exercise-induced asthma, respiratory and allergic disorders in elite athletes: Epidemiology, mechanisms and diagnosis: Part 1 of the report from the Joint Task Force of the European Respiratory Society (ERS) and the European Academy of Allergy and Clinical Immunology (EAACI) in cooperation with GA2LEN. *Allergy, 63*: 387–403.

Chilvers, M., Donahue, M., Nassar, L., & Manoli, A. (2007). Foot and ankle injuries in elite female gymnasts. *Foot & Ankle International/American Orthopaedic Foot and Ankle Society [and] Swiss Foot and Ankle Society, 28*: 214–218.

Chiò, A., Benzi, G., Dossena, M., Mutani, R., & Mora, G. (2005). Severely increased risk of amyotrophic lateral sclerosis among Italian professional football players. *Brain: A Journal of Neurology, 128*: 472–476.

Chiò, A., Calvo, A., Dossena, M., Ghiglione, P., Mutani, R., & Mora, G. (2009). ALS in Italian professional soccer players: The risk is still present and could be soccer-specific. *Amyotrophic Lateral Sclerosis, 10*: 205–209.

Coakley, J. (1992). Burnout among adolescent athletes: A personal failure or social problem? *Sociology of Sport Journal, 9*: 271–285.

Cosh, S., Crabb, S., & LeCouteur, A. (2013). Elite athletes and retirement: Identity, choice and agency. *Australian Journal of Psychology, 65*: 89–97.

Cresswell, S. L., & Eklund, R. C. (2007). Athlete burnout: A longitudinal qualitative study. *The Sport Psychologist, 21*: 1–20.

Currie, A., Potts, S. G., Donovan, W., & Blackwood, D. (1999). Illness behaviour in elite middle and long distance runners. *British Journal of Sports Medicine, 33*: 19–21.

Deacon, A., Bennell, K., Kiss, Z. S., Crossley, K., & Brukner, P. (1997). Osteoarthritis of the knee in retired, elite Australian Rules footballers. *The Medical Journal of Australia, 166*: 187–190.

DiFiori, J., Benjamin, H., Brenner, J., Gregory, A., Jayanthi, N., Landry, G., & Luke, A. (2014). Overuse injuries and burnout in youth sports: A position statement from the American Medical Society for Sports Medicine. *British Journal of Sports Medicine, 48*: 1–15.

Douglas, K., & Carless, D. (2009). Abandoning the performance narrative: Two women's stories of transition from professional sport. *Journal of Applied Sport Psychology, 21*: 213–230.

Dubravcic-Simunjak, S., Pecina, M., Kuipers, H., Moran, J., & Haspl, M. (2003). The incidence of injuries in elite junior figure skaters. *The American Journal of Sports Medicine, 31*: 511–517.

Ekblom, B., Ekblom, O., & Malm, C. (2006). Infectious episodes before and after a marathon race. *Scandinavian Journal of Medicine and Science in Sports,* 16, 287–293.

Gabbett, T. J., Ullah, S., Jenkins, D., & Abernethy, B. (2012). Skill qualities as risk factors for contact injury in professional rugby league players. *Journal of Sports Sciences,* 30: 1421–1427.

Gajhede-Knudsen, M., Ekstrand, J., Magnusson, H., & Maffulli, N. (2013). Recurrence of Achilles tendon injuries in elite male football players is more common after early return to play: An 11-year follow-up of the UEFA Champions League injury study. *British Journal of Sports Medicine,* 47: 763–768.

Gleeson, M., McDonald, W. A., Cripps, A. W., Pyne, D. B., Clancy, R. L., & Fricker, P. A. (1995). The effect on immunity of long-term intensive training in elite swimmers. *Clinical and Experimental Immunology,* 102: 210–216.

Gould, D., & Dieffenbach, K. (2002). Overtraining, underrecovery, and burnout in sport. In M. Kellmann (ed.), *Enhancing recovery: Preventing underperformance in athletes* (pp. 25–35). Champaign, IL: Human Kinetics.

Gould, D., & Dieffenbach, K. (2003). Psychological issues in youth sports: Competitive anxiety, overtraining, and burnout. In R. M. Malina & M. A. Clark (eds). *Youth sports: Perspectives for a new century.* Monterey, CA: Coaches Choice: 149–170.

Grassmayr, M., Steinweg, J., Trainor, P., Ferdinands, R., & Vanwanseele, B. (2010). Injury prevalence in Australian professional golfers. *Medicine & Science in Sports & Exercise,* 42: 420–421.

Gross, P., & Marti, B. (1999). Risk of degenerative ankle joint disease in volleyball players: Study of former elite athletes. *International Journal of Sports Medicine,* 20: 58–63.

Gulliver, A., Griffiths, K. M., Mackinnon, A., Batterham, P. J., & Stanimirovic, R. (2015). The mental health of Australian elite athletes. *Journal of Science and Medicine in Sport,* 18: 255–261.

Gustafsson, H., Kenttä, G., Hassmén, P., & Lundqvist, C. (2007). Prevalence of burnout in adolescent competitive athletes. *The Sport Psychologist,* 21: 21–37.

Hagmar, M., Hirschberg, A. L., Lindholm, C., Schenck-Gustafsson, K., & Eriksson, M. J. (2005). Athlete's heart in postmenopausal former elite endurance female athletes. *Clinical Journal of Sport Medicine,* 15: 257–262.

Hammond, T., Gialloreto, C., Kubas, H., & Davis, H. (2013). The prevalence of failure-based depression among elite athletes. *Clinical Journal of Sport Medicine,* 23: 273–277.

Horton, R. S., & Mack, D. E. (2000). Athletic identity in marathon runners: Functional focus or dysfunctional commitment? *Journal of Sport Behavior,* 23: 101–119.

Huber, B. R., Alosco, M. L., Stein, T. D., & McKee, A. C. (2016). Potential long-term consequences of concussive and subconcussive injury. *Physical Medicine and Rehabilitation Clinics of North America.* doi: 10.1016/j.pmr.2015.12.007

Hurst, R. T., Burke, R. F., Wissner, E., Roberts, A., Kendall, C. B., Lester, S. J., … Khandheria, B. (2010). Incidence of subclinical atherosclerosis as a marker of cardiovascular risk in retired professional football players. *The American Journal of Cardiology,* 105: 1107–1111.

Kenttä, G., Hassmén, P., & Raglin, J. S. (2001). Training practices and overtraining syndrome in Swedish age-group athletes. *International Journal of Sports Medicine,* 22: 1–6.

Kerr, Z. Y., Evenson, K. R., Rosamond, W. D., Mihalik, J. P., Guskiewicz, K. M., & Marshall, S. W. (2014). Association between concussion and mental health in former collegiate athletes. *Injury Epidemiology,* 1: www.injepijournal.com/content/1/1/28

Kleiber, D. A., & Brock, S. C. (1992). The effect of career-ending injuries on the subsequent well-being of elite college athletes. *Sociology of Sport Journal,* 9: 70–75.

Kompel, A. J., Murakami, A., & Carrino, J. (2016). Imaging of American football injuries. In A. Guermazi et al. (eds), *Imaging in Sports-Specific Musculoskeletal Injuries,* 117–44. Switzerland: Springer.

Koral, J., & Dosseville, F. (2009). Combination of gradual and rapid weight loss: Effects on physical performance and psychological state of elite judo athletes. *Journal of Sports Sciences,* 27: 115–120.

Kreider, R. B., Fry, A. C., & O'Toole, M. L. (1998). Preface. In R. B. Kreider, A. C. Fry, & M. L. O'Toole (eds), *Overtraining in sport* (pp. vii–ix). Champaign, IL: Human Kinetics.

Kuijt, M. T. K., Inklaar, H., Gouttebarge, V., & Frings-Dresen, M. H. W. (2012). Knee and ankle osteoarthritis in former elite soccer players: A systematic review of the recent literature. *Journal of Science and Medicine in Sport/Sports Medicine Australia,* 15: 480–487.

L'Hermette, M., Polle, G., Tourny-Chollet, C., & Dujardin, F. (2006). Hip passive range of motion and frequency of radiographic hip osteoarthritis in former elite handball players. *British Journal of Sports Medicine,* 40: 45–49.

Lally, P. (2007). Identity and athletic retirement: A prospective study. *Psychology of Sport and Exercise,* 8: 85–99.

Langeveld, E., Coetzee, F. F., & Holtzhausen, L. J. (2012). Epidemiology of injuries in elite South African netball players. *South African Journal for Research in Sport, Physical Education and Recreation*, 34: 83–93.

Lehmann, M. J., Foster, C., Gastmann, U., Keizer, H., & Steinacker, J. (1999). *Overload, performance incompetence, and regeneration in sport*. New York: Plenum Press.

Lemez, S., & Baker, J. (2015). Do elite athletes live longer? A systematic review of mortality and longevity in elite athletes. *Sports Medicine – Open*, 1.

Lemyre, P. N., Roberts, G. C., & Stray-Gundersen, J. (2007). Motivation, overtraining, and burnout: Can self-determined motivation predict overtraining and burnout in elite athletes? *European Journal of Sport Science*, 7: 115–126.

Lindqvist, A. S., Moberg, T., Eriksson, B. O., Ehrnborg, C., Rosén, T., & Fahlke, C. (2013). A retrospective 30-year follow-up study of former Swedish-elite male athletes in power sports with a past anabolic androgenic steroids use: A focus on mental health. *British Journal of Sports Medicine*, 47: 965–969.

Ljungqvist, A., Jenoure, P., Engebretsen, L., Alonso, J. M., Bahr, R., Clough, A., ... Thill, C. (2009). The International Olympic Committee (IOC) Consensus Statement on periodic health evaluation of elite athletes March 2009. *British Journal of Sports Medicine*, 43: 631–643.

Luthi, P., Zuber, M., Ritter, M., Oechslin, E. N., Jenni, R., Seifert, B., ... Attenhofer Jost, C. H. (2008). Echocardiographic findings in former professional cyclists after long-term deconditioning of more than 30 years. *European Journal of Echocardiography*, 9: 261–267.

Matos, N., & Winsley, R. J. (2007). Trainability of young athletes and overtraining. *Journal of Sports Science & Medicine*, 6: 353–367.

Maquirriain, J., Ghisi, J. P., & Amato, S. (2006). Is tennis a predisposing factor for degenerative shoulder disease? A controlled study in former elite players. *British Journal of Sports Medicine*, 40: 447–450.

McCarthy, M. M., Voos, J. E., Nguyen, J. T., Callahan, L., & Hannafin, J. A. (2013). Injury profile in elite female basketball athletes at the Women's National Basketball Association combine. *The American Journal of Sports Medicine*, 41: 645–651.

Meeusen, R., Duclos, M., Foster, C., Fry, A., Gleeson, M., Rietjens, G., ... Urhausen, A. (2006). Prevention, diagnosis and treatment of the Overtraining Syndrome. ECSS position statement 'task force'. *European Journal of Sport Science*, 6(1), 1–14. doi: 10.1249/MSS.0b013e318279a10a.

Miller, K. E., & Hoffman, J. H. (2009). Mental well-being and sport-related identities in college students. *Sociology of Sport Journal*, 26: 335–356.

Miller, K. E., Melnick, M. J., Farrell, M. P., Sabo, D., Barnes, G. M. (2006). Jocks, gender, binge drinking, and adolescent violence. *Journal of Interpersonal Violence*, 21: 105–120.

Mitchell, T., Nesti, M., Richardson, D., Midgley, A., Eubank, M., & Littlewood, M. (2014). Exploring athletic identity in elite-level English youth football: A cross-sectional approach. *Journal of Sport Sciences*, 32: 1294–1299.

Moreno-Pérez, V., Moreside, J., Barbado, D., & Vera-Garcia, F. J. (2015). Comparison of shoulder rotation range of motion in professional tennis players with and without history of shoulder pain. *Manual Therapy*, 20: 313–318.

Myklebust, G., & Bahr, R. (2005). Return to play guidelines after anterior cruciate ligament surgery. *British Journal of Sports Medicine*, 39: 127–131.

Myklebust, G., Hasslan, L., Bahr, R., & Steffen, K. (2013). High prevalence of shoulder pain among elite Norwegian female handball players. *Scandinavian Journal of Medicine & Science in Sports*, 23: 288–294.

Nicholls, A. R., Holt, N. L., Polman, R. C. J., & Bloomfield, J. (2006). Stressors, coping, and coping effectiveness among professional rugby union players. *The Sport Psychologist*, 20: 314–329.

Nieman, D. C. (1994). Exercise, infection and immunity. *International Journal of Sports Medicine*, 15: 131–141.

Park, S., Lavallee, D., & Todd, D. (2013). Athletes' career transition out of sport: A systematic review. *International Review of Sport and Exercise Psychology*, 6: 22–53.

Quarrie, K. L., & Hopkins, W. G. (2008). Tackle injuries in professional Rugby Union. *The American Journal of Sports Medicine*, 36: 1705–1716.

Raedeke, T. D. (1997). Is athlete burnout more than stress? A commitment perspective. *Journal of Sport and Exercise Psychology*, 19: 396–417.

Rajabi, R., Johnson, G. M., Alizadeh, M. H., & Meghdadi, N. (2012). Radiographic knee osteoarthritis in ex-elite table tennis players. *BMC Musculoskeletal Disorders*, 13: 1–6.

Reardon, C. L., & Factor, R. M. (2010). Sport psychiatry: A systematic review of diagnosis and medical treatment of mental illness in athletes. *Sports Medicine*, 40: 961–980.

Rogalski, B., Dawson, B., Heasman, J., & Gabbett, T. J. (2013). Training and game loads and injury risk in elite Australian footballers. *Journal of Science and Medicine in Sport/Sports Medicine Australia*, 16: 499–503.

Sarna, S., Kaprio, J., Kujala, U. M., & Koskenvuo, M. (1997). Health status of former elite athletes. The Finnish experience. *Aging,* 9: 35–41.

Saw, R., Dennis, R. J., Bentley, D., & Farhart, P. (2011). Throwing workload and injury risk in elite cricketers. *British Journal of Sports Medicine,* 45: 805–808.

Scase, E., Magarey, M. E., Chalmers, S., Heynen, M., Petkov, J., & Bailey, S. (2012). The epidemiology of injury for an elite junior Australian Football cohort. *Journal of Science and Medicine in Sport/Sports Medicine Australia,* 15: 207–212.

Schaal, K., Tafflet, M., Nassif, H., Thibault, V., Pichard, C., Alcotte, M., … Toussaint, J. F. (2011). Psychological balance in high level athletes: Gender-based differences and sport-specific patterns. *PloS ONE,* 6: 1–9.

Schmitt, H., Hansmann, H. J., Brocai, D. R., & Loew, M. (2001). Long term changes of the throwing arm of former elite javelin throwers. *International Journal of Sports Medicine,* 22: 275–279.

Schnell, A., Mayer, J., Diehl, K., Zipfel, S., & Thiel, A. (2014). Giving everything for athletic success! Sports-specific risk acceptance of elite adolescent athletes. *Psychology of Sport & Exercise,* 15: 165–172.

Scoffier, S., Woodman, T., & d'Arripe-Longueville, F. (2011). Psychosocial consequences of disordered eating attitudes in elite female figure skaters. *European Eating Disorders Review: The Journal of the Eating Disorders Association,* 19: 280–287.

Simon, J. E., & Docherty, C. L. (2013). Current health-related quality of life is lower in former division 1 collegiate athletes than in non-collegiate athletes. *The American Journal of Sports Medicine,* 42: 423–429.

Stambulova, N. (2003). Symptoms of a crisis-transition: A grounded theory study. In Hassmén, N. (ed.), *Sipf Yearbook 2003.* Örebro, Sweden: Örebro University Press: 97–109.

Stephan, Y., Torregrosa, M., & Sanchez, X. (2007). The body matters: Psychophysical impact of retiring from elite sport. *Psychology of Sport and Exercise,* 8: 73–83.

Sundgot-Borgen, J., & Torstveit, M. K. (2010). Aspects of disordered eating continuum in elite high-intensity sports. *Scandinavian Journal of Medicine & Science in Sports,* 20: 112–121.

Theberge, N. (2008). "Just a normal bad part of what I do": Elite athletes' accounts of the relationship between health and sport. *Sociology of Sport Journal,* 25: 206–222.

Thiel, A., Mayer, J., & Digel, H. (2010). Gesundheit in Spitzensport. Eine Socialwissenschaftliche Analyse *[Health in elite sports. An analysis from a social science perspective].* Schorndorf: Hofmann-Verlag.

Visnes, H., & Bahr, R. (2013). Training volume and body composition as risk factors for developing jumper's knee among young elite volleyball players. *Scandinavian Journal of Medicine & Science in Sports,* 23: 607–613.

Waldén, M., Hägglund, M., & Ekstrand, J. (2006). High risk of new knee injury in elite footballers with previous anterior cruciate ligament injury. *British Journal of Sports Medicine,* 40: 158–162.

Williams, S., Trewartha, G., Kemp, S., & Stokes, K. (2013). A meta-analysis of injuries in senior men's professional Rugby Union. *Sports Medicine,* 43: 1043–1055.

Winzen, M., Voigt, H. F., Hinrichs, T., & Platen, P. (2011). Injuries of the musculoskeletal system in German elite rowers. *Sportverletz Sportschaden,* 25: 153–158.

Wylleman, P., Alfermann, D., & Lavallee, D. (2004). Career transitions in sport: European perspectives. *Psychology of Sport and Exercise,* 5: 7–20.

Wylleman, P., & Lavallee, D. (2004). A developmental perspective on transitions faced by athletes. In M. Weiss (ed.), *Developmental sport and exercise psychology: A lifespan perspective.* Morgantown, WV: Fitness Information Technology: 503–523.

Zinder, S. M., Guskiewicz, K. M., & Marshall, S. W. (2010). Prevalence of ankle osteoarthritis following a history of ankle sprain in retired professional football players. *Medicine & Science in Sports & Exercise,* 42: 608.

29

ISSUES OF MALTREATMENT IN HIGH PERFORMANCE ATHLETE DEVELOPMENT

Mental toughness as a threat to athlete welfare

Gretchen Kerr and Ashley Stirling

Searching for the key to performance success

For centuries, people have been fascinated with highly talented people and the means by which they actualize their potential. In this chapter, the topic of talent development in sport is briefly introduced with a focus on 'mental toughness' as a perceived requirement for athletic success. The topic of mental toughness and its relationship to high performance sport talent development is reviewed, critiqued, and proposed as a guise for athlete maltreatment with potentially harmful effects on athletes. This chapter concludes with recommendations for talent development strategies that are more consistent with healthy psychosocial development and learner-centred educational practices to advance both personal and performance success of high performance athletes.

Talent development in sport

Talent refers to the potential for success in a specific domain (Baker, Cobley, & Schorer, 2012). Extending this definition, 'talent development in sport' is considered the growth and advancement of potential for domain specific success. The identification and development of athletic talent has flourished as a field of study over the past 30 years. Determining the most effective and efficient ways to actualize athletic potential has been, and continues to be, a primary focus of attention for sport scientists, coaches, sport policy makers, and even parents. For sport scientists, including mental trainers, nutritionists, physiologists, biomechanists, and strength and conditioning specialists, understanding the complexities of talent development in athletes is the "cornerstone" of their work (Cobley, Schorer, & Baker, 2012, p. 1).

Within the significant body of literature on talent development in sport, researchers have expressed a consistent view that the process of realizing athletic talent is multifactorial. Some of the fundamental requirements needed to actualize athletic potentials include: physical capabilities; contextual considerations such as finances, coaching expertise and specific training resources; deliberate practice, and parental support; as well as psychological qualities such as motivation, enjoyment, and self-efficacy (Abbott & Collins, 2004; Côté, Baker, & Abernethy, 2007; Csikszentmihalyi, Rthunde, & Whalen, 1997).

The means by which athletic talent is nurtured have drawn attention and scrutiny, in part because much of the talent development process in sport occurs when athletes are young – in childhood and adolescence. In fact, concerns about the development of talent in young athletes have a long history and for the most part centre on the sequela of an over-emphasis on performance or winning outcomes. Orlick and Botterill (1975) for example, identified excessive levels of pressure and stress on young athletes to perform and to win as contributing to low self-esteem and attrition from sport. Substantial concerns have also been expressed about the singular identity that often develops with young, elite athletes and the implications that potentially arise from this one-dimensional identity. More specifically, the extensive commitments to sport required at elite levels necessitate exclusion from other activities and relationships, thus making young athletes more vulnerable to social isolation and difficulties coping with threats to their athletic identity such as performance set-backs and slumps, injuries, and retirement from sport (Douglas & Carless, 2006; Wylleman & Lavallee, 2004). Several authors have criticized the elite sport environment for its exploitation of young athletes (Coakley, 1992; David, 2005), including sexual abuse of athletes by their coaches (Brackenridge, 2001). The development of talent in sport therefore, is often a competitive, highly pressurized and demanding, ego-focused process (David, 2005; Rongen, Cobley, McKenna, & Till, 2015) that has the potential "to be (un)healthy and (in)humane" (Rongen et al., 2015, p. 33).

The cultural norms associated with elite sport have been identified as partially – or largely – responsible for unhealthy talent development processes. The 'performance narrative' or norms that encourage and reward those behaviours that are needed to achieve performance outcomes may contribute to talent development processes that are not aligned with the best interests of athletes. Some of these normative behaviours include a full commitment and dedication to the role and identity of an athlete, and organizing the lives of the athlete, the coach and parents around the athlete's performance-related needs (Christensen & Sorensen, 2009; Douglas & Carless, 2006). The performance narrative also includes the development and reinforcement of an athlete's abilities to tolerate pain, adversity, and high levels of pressure – commonly referred to as "mental toughness".

Mental toughness

Mental toughness has been defined in numerous ways including: the mindset behind sporting achievement (Sheard, 2010); "the psychological edge that enables an athlete to cope better than opponents with the demands of training, competition and the lifestyle of an athlete; being consistent, determined, focused, confident and in control under pressure" (Jones, Hanton, & Connaughton, 2002, p. 213); "a high sense of self-belief and an unshakable faith that they [athletes] can control their own destiny" (Clough, Earle, & Sewell, 2002, p. 38); and "a collection of values, attitudes, behaviors, and emotions that enable you to persevere and overcome any obstacle, adversity, or pressure experienced, but also to maintain concentration and motivation when things are going well to consistently achieve your goals" (Gucciardi, Gordon, & Dimmock, 2008, p. 278). Gordon and Gucciardi (2011, p. 144) stated: "Mentally tough athletes believe in their abilities, effectively manage their attentional focus, persevere through tough times, desire success, expect positive outcomes, effectively manage their emotions, and understand the sport context". As well, Jones and Moorehouse (2007) proposed a framework of mental toughness that consists of four pillars including: motivation, self-confidence, attentional focus, and coping with pressure. Alternatively, Clough et al. (2002) applied the psychological hardiness literature to articulate a 4Cs Model of Mental Toughness that included control, challenge, commitment and confidence.

Although specific definitions vary, there is general consensus that the individual character-istics associated with mental toughness consist of self-confidence, the ability to navigate adversity, drive and determination, the ability to manage stress, a sense of control, and a clear and singular focus. Generally speaking, mental toughness is an umbrella term used to separate those athletes who excel from those who do not.

Mental toughness as essential for talent development

Athletes, coaches, sport administrators, and the media consistently acknowledge the importance of mental toughness for talent development. Some have gone as far as to say that mental tough-ness is an *essential attribute* for success in sport (Sheard, 2010; Weiser & Theiel, 2014). Loehr (1986) for example, reported that a sample of elite athletes believed that at least 50% of supe-rior athletic performance resulted from mental toughness. Gould, Hodge, Peterson, and Petlichkoff (1987) reported that 82% of wrestling coaches rated mental toughness as the most important psychosocial determinant for athletic success. Further, most researchers believe that mental toughness is a quality or set of qualities that can be developed in young people given the appropriate circumstances and mental skills training (Crust & Azadi, 2010; Jones et al., 2002; Connaughton, Wadey, Hanton, & Jones, 2008; Gucciardi, Gordon, & Dimmock, 2009; Mahoney, Gucciardi, Ntoumanis, & Mallet, 2014). Given the prevailing view that mental toughness can be developed, exploring ways to do so has been a predominant focus of coaches and sport psychology consultants; in fact, Jones et al. (2002, p. 213) has gone as far as to say, "Because mental toughness is the very essence of sport psychologists' work with elite athletes, it presents an important, and challenging area of investigation."

Criticisms of the construct of mental toughness

Although the construct of mental toughness is popular in sport settings, it is not without its critics who have identified a lack of conceptual consistency, clarity or usefulness for academics (Crust, 2007). Jones et al. (2002) proposed that almost every desirable psychological quality has been deemed part of mental toughness at one time or another. Others have identified overlaps between mental toughness and such constructs as hardiness, resilience, and growth through adversity; in fact, Andersen (2011) suggested that mental toughness is a construct that has been in existence for almost 30 years and is simply an old concept dressed up in new clothes. Further, he criticizes the word 'toughness' as resonating with much of what is questionable in sport, including a macho, masculine, patriarchal and pathogenic culture (p. 69). The limited predic-tive value of mental toughness has also been identified; as many definitions depend upon comparisons with opponent(s) and the outcomes of competitions, mental toughness can only be determined in a post-hoc manner – that is, only after the win or successful performance (Andersen, 2011).

In addition to the criticisms of the definition of mental toughness itself, the vast literature on mental toughness is remarkably non-critical. The prevailing assumptions throughout the mental toughness literature are that mental toughness is not only desirable but required for successful performance and, moreover, that coaches, parents and sport science support staff can and should promote its development. Without a critical perspective however, the means by which mental toughness is developed are not necessarily considered, thus opening the door for the possibility of harmful sporting practices. Andersen (2011) supported this claim when he stated that there is a dark side to mental toughness development and this dark side remains rela-tively unexplored. In the next section, we question whether methods of developing mental toughness in athletes may involve inappropriate or unhealthy coaching practices. Moreover, we postulate that athletes may experience harm within the coach–athlete relationship as a result of coaching practices that are intended to enhance mental toughness.

Mental toughness as a threat to athlete welfare

Researchers have raised concerns about potential negative impacts of a focus on mental toughness development on athletes' physical health. For example, Crust (2008) cautioned that mental toughness may be associated with playing while injured, which may hinder the performance of the athlete or team and risk long-term physical harm. Others have suggested that a focus on mental toughness encourages athletes to self-sacrifice and self-harm (Douglas & Carless, 2006), to "act tough" and take risks when confronted with pain and injury (Miller & Hoffman, 2009). Further, Levy, Polman, Clough, Marchant, and Earle (2006) suggested that mentally tough athletes may appraise their injuries as being less severe and less likely to recur which in turn, may reduce compliance with rehabilitation and increase the risk of further injury.

Andersen (2011), in his brilliant chapter entitled, "Who's mental, who's tough and who's both?" questioned whether the promotion of mental toughness may also have negative influences on athletes' psychological health. More specifically, many of the qualities associated with the construct of mental toughness, if viewed through a critical lens, can be seen as problematic for an athlete's psychological health. As Andersen wrote, it is conceivable that an athlete who is determined, persistent, confident, and believes s/he can exercise a high degree of self-control, would feel pressure to maintain such characterizations, and thus be disinclined to admit vulnerability or to seek help when needed. Aspects of mental toughness including a "refusal to quit until the goal has been achieved" (Goldberg, 1998, p. 241), and promotion of a "never give up attitude when faced with difficult situations" (Connaughton, Thelwell, & Hanton, 2011, p. 145), may, in fact, be counterproductive to performance outcomes and the athlete's health. Instead, one could argue that psychological fortitude is better illustrated when athletes know when it is healthy or adaptable to stop pursuing the goal in question. Similarly, the quality of being solely focused on the athletic role that is so common in conceptualizations of mental toughness, may contribute to the well-documented problems of a singular identity and resultant lack of development of other relationships and areas of life (Wylleman, Rosier, & De Knop, 2015).

A major element of mental toughness is the ability to navigate adversity, including the abilities to cope with associated negative emotions, to recover from adverse experiences, and to learn and grow from such experiences. The process of talent development in sport inherently involves adverse experiences including acute and chronic injuries, performance disappointments and setbacks, not being selected for important teams, and the need to train and compete effectively in the face of negative life events that may occur outside of the sport realm. An important body of work on growth through adversity (Joseph & Linley, 2005, 2006; Linley & Joseph, 2011) highlights the significance of navigating adverse events for learning and personal growth. It is important to remember however, that this body of work stemmed from uncontrollable traumas such as survival from concentration camp experiences and natural disasters, and that this does not imply that for growth or talent development to occur in sport, such degrees of harm need to be inflicted or experienced. Instead, the pressing question for researchers and practitioners is how to best incorporate challenging experiences in developmentally appropriate ways that mitigate risk to well-being and are consistent with athlete welfare.

Further, the mental toughness quality of "an unshakable faith that they [athletes] can control their own destiny" (Clough et al., 2002, p. 38) is contradicted by the plethora of research documenting the significant power differential between coaches and athletes and the abuse some athletes have experienced at the hands of their coaches (Brackenridge, 2001; Burke, 2001). The potential for coaches to use their position of power in harmful ways in the spirit of developing mental toughness in athletes will be explored in the next section.

Mental toughness as a guise for harmful coaching practices

Researchers have written extensively about the important role of the coach in influencing athletes' health, performance, and the overall quality of the athletes' sport experiences (Jowett, 2003, 2005; Jowett & Cockerill, 2003; Jowett, Paull, Pensgaard, Hoegmo, & Riise, 2005). This potential for influence over athletes is attributable to the position of power held by the coach by virtue of age, knowledge, expertise, and access to resources (Tomlinson & Strachan, 1996) and has been likened to the power held by a master (Crosset, 1986), or a priest (Brackenridge, 2001). A coach's position of power may be used to facilitate athletes' performance, health and overall development as a person (Kidman, 2005); however, this power may also be used in harmful ways as documented through athletes' experiences of abuse in the coach–athlete relationship (Stirling & Kerr, 2009).

One form of athlete abuse that has recently drawn scholarly attention is emotional abuse, defined as "a pattern of deliberate non-contact behaviours by a person within a critical relationship role that has the potential to be harmful to an individual's emotional well-being" (Stirling & Kerr 2008, p.178). Important elements of this definition include a repeated pattern of behaviour, the potential for harm, and the occurrence of these behaviours within a critical relationship or a relationship in which one person depends upon the other for a sense of security, trust and fulfillment of needs (Crooks & Wolfe, 2007). A parent–child relationship is the most common example of a critical relationship, but the coach–athlete relationship may also be characterized as such. Emotionally abusive coaching practices occur frequently in sport (Alexander, Stafford, & Lewis, 2011; Gervis & Dunn, 2004) in various forms including: verbal comments such as yelling and degrading remarks, physical behaviours such as throwing objects for the purposes of intimidation, and the denial of attention and support (Stirling & Kerr, 2007).

When a sample of elite coaches were asked to account for their use of emotionally abusive coaching practices, they described what Stirling (2013) termed expressive reasons; more specifically, coaches claimed that the emotionally laden settings of sport training and competition aroused intense emotional responses and at times, they simply lost emotional control. The coaches in Stirling's study also reported that they engaged in emotionally abusive practices because they believed these coaching practices were effective as instructional tools, or what Stirling referred to as instrumental purposes. In this research, one coach stated he would yell and scream at athletes as a strategy to toughen up the players and help them perform well in sport. He felt that this coaching technique would not only lead to better sport performance, but would also enhance the mental fortitude of the athletes and prepare them for life outside sport. This was a technique that the coach had experienced as a former athlete and the coach had not thought about the potential negative implications of this behaviour until it was brought to his attention that a child dropped out of sport as a result of his actions.

> I remember this one kid – I called the kid to ask why he hasn't signed up for the next season and the father said to me, "Because of you he doesn't want to play soccer anymore." It was one of the most devastating comments I have heard. I can honestly tell you I was in tears. To say, "My kid doesn't want to play soccer anymore because of you." I felt like someone had just slapped me across the face because it was a shock to me – that whatever I did unintentionally caused the kid to not want to play

anymore. I wanted to make sure that it never happened again so I committed to myself to change ... Since then every time I open my mouth to say stuff to athletes I remember how important it is to say the right thing and to make sure that I never have that experience again.

(Stirling, 2013, p. 633)

Complementing this story, when athletes were asked to explain their previous experiences of emotional harm in sport, one athlete stated,

They [the coaches] would get so mad if people weren't working hard enough or if people weren't pulling out the times they expected us to hold on reps and stuff like that ... They would scream and swear at you and just say really rude things.

(Stirling, 2007, p. 72)

Similarly another athlete stated,

Coaches go on power trips. They think because they have authority and because kids will listen that they have the right to talk down to them or treat them badly ... They think that being a hard ass is using reverse psychology ... but really they have done nothing but traumatize people.

(Stirling, 2007, p. 71)

In another study that examined youth hockey players' interpretations of the use of punishment strategies in sport (Battaglia, 2015, p. 70), one athlete said, "Yelling can lead to mental toughness – like tough skin so it can make you better...". When asked why coaches may use punishment strategies, one athlete stated: "Punishments let you know how much you can handle ... there will always be ups and downs so from those experiences coaches may be pushing you to get mentally stronger and achieve bigger tasks" (Battaglia, 2015, p. 68). The use of exercise as punishment specifically, has purportedly been used for the purposes of toughening-up athletes mentally and physically. As one athlete stated,

Coaches use exercise as punishment because they want you to become stronger, physically stronger. Even mentally stronger because it gets in your head and you start thinking 'I need to do better. I need to work harder because I don't want to be punished.'

(Gurgis, 2015, p. 65)

If coaches use emotionally abusive practices for instrumental purposes or as a means to an end, perhaps they also used these practices as a vehicle by which to develop mental toughness. Supporting this assertion, Crust (2014) proposed that verbal abuse of athletes may occur in response to expectations for athletes to be mentally tough. Could it be therefore, that the development and reinforcement of mental toughness can disguise or legitimize harmful coaching practices?

Poisonous pedagogy

Using the development of mental toughness as a reason for the implementation of harmful instructional methods is consistent with the concept of poisonous pedagogy, a term originally used to refer to child-raising methods that are repressive and potentially harmful (Miller, 1980). As Alice Miller (1980) wrote in her book, *For Your Own Good*, poisonous pedagogy represents methods used to break the will of the child so the parent may ensure obedience, compliance, and pliability to conform to societal expectations. Some examples of the strategies used in poisonous pedagogy include: manipulation, scare tactics, humiliation, corporal punishment, coercion, ridicule, and withdrawal of attention. Such strategies are used in the spirit of the child's good, to teach the child life lessons such as the importance of being honest and patient, and to toughen-up the child for subsequent life experiences. Poisonous pedagogy is characterized by foundational assumptions that adults are the masters, similar to Crosset's master–slave analogy in sport. Further, parents/adults are assumed to deserve respect simply because of their positions and the character of a child is thought to be strengthened through obedience (Miller, 1980). Although this construct originated in the parenting literature, it has since been applied to the educational system, which as some have argued, also relies on student obedience and compliance.

It is not a far stretch to see the construct of poisonous pedagogy embedded in sport coaching. Previous researchers (Kerr & Stirling, 2012; Stirling & Kerr, 2014) have documented the normalization of emotionally abusive coaching practices; more specifically, some coaches, athletes and parents not only viewed emotionally abusive coaching practices as a normal part of sport training but went further to describe it as being necessary for the development of athletic talent. Similarly, Cushion and Jones (2006, p. 148) stated: "harsh, authoritarian and often belligerent coaching behaviour was viewed as a necessary aspect of preparing young players" by football coaches and athletes. Seifried (2010) advocated for the use of corporal punishment in sport, in the form of exercise as punishment; the premise of his position was that corporal punishment helps athletes understand and focus on the requisite behaviours for athletic success. The suggestion that corporal punishment should be used for the athletes' "own good" is, we believe, an example of poisonous pedagogy.

At the root of many questionable practices in sport, including emotionally abusive coaching behaviours, is the use of power to promote and ensure compliance and obedience by athletes (Brackenridge, 2001; Burke, 2001; Coakley, 1992). We posit that such practices constitute a form of poisonous pedagogy and one of the ways in which these practices are rationalized and accepted in sport coaching is through the promotion of mental toughness.

An athlete welfare approach to talent development

Based upon a critique of the construct of mental toughness and the supposition that efforts to develop mental toughness can cloak harmful coaching practices, we propose several recommendations. First, we suggest scholars and sport practitioners abandon the term "mental toughness." Not only is the construct nebulous, but it reinforces the performance narrative, the masculine culture, and win-at-all costs approach that are often associated with negative or harmful consequences for athletes (Andersen, 2011; Miller & Hoffman, 2009). Instead, we propose that the psychological characteristics associated with optimal performance within and outside of sport, such a managing stress and adversity, remain as areas of study within the talent development field but that these lines of inquiries are grounded in and framed by an athlete welfare approach. Such an approach prioritizes the athlete's holistic health and development, both in the present and in the long-term. Table 29.1 provides some examples of the ways in which questions about talent identification may be framed within an athlete welfare approach. Such questions may form the foundation for future research in the area of talent identification and may also guide the practice of coaches.

Table 29.1 Talent development within an athlete welfare framework

Self-confidence	• How can appropriate opportunities be provided for athletes to demonstrate their competencies and to experience success? • How might opportunities be provided to athletes to assume responsibility for their own learning, thus allowing them to experience the gratification that comes with achievements they feel they contributed to?
Dealing with adversity	• How can sufficient opportunities be provided for athletes to experience disappointments and failures within an environment of support? • How should skills of reflection and insight be encouraged to use adverse experiences as growth opportunities?
Managing stress	• How can a balance of overload and challenge experiences within an environment of support be provided?
Drive and determination	• How can opportunities for success, autonomy and relatedness be provided and supported? How can self-motivation be channelled and nurtured by others?
Sense of control	• How can opportunities be provided for athletes to self-reflect, evaluate their experiences, and have input into decisions that affect them?
Clear focus	• How can the ability to focus sufficiently on athletic development be encouraged while ensuring some balance in life with other relationships, pursuits and identities?

Clearly, the achievement of the objectives identified in Table 29.1 is contingent upon the roles of coaches and parents and an appropriate sharing of power between these adults and the athlete. The roles of significant adults in sport are consistently recognized as critical within the body of literature on talent development (Bloom, 1985; Côté, 1999; Csikszentmihalyi et al., 1997). An athlete welfare approach to talent development involves attention to the nature of the coach–athlete relationship, the ways in which power is shared, and the role of the coach. With such an approach, the relationship between the athlete and coach more closely represents a partnership in which power is shared in an age- and stage-appropriate manner. The coach's role is one of a facilitator or an expert guide; in this way, the coach assists the athlete with the process of self-reflection, discovery, and the development of autonomy. In an athlete welfare approach to talent development, the athlete is an active agent in his or her sport experience and the process of talent development is grounded in discovery-based learning, guided problem-solving, and autonomous learning. Autonomy-supportive coaching that involves the promotion of athletes' independence, decision-making and problem-solving abilities, internal motivation, and guided discovery is consistent with this view (Stebbings, Taylor & Spray, 2011). Moreover, the importance of exposure to, rather than protection from, challenging circumstances has been highlighted as opportunities for developing learning in general (Csikszentmihalyi et al., 1997) and talent development in sport more specifically (Crust & Clough, 2011). These behaviours are consistent with an athlete-centred approach to coaching and athlete development (Kidman, 2005).

Interestingly, these recommendations have been long recognized and implemented in the education sector. Empirical evidence from research in the field of education clearly indicates that an age- and stage-appropriate learner-centred approach benefits the teacher–learner relationship, facilitates student learning, and enhances the quality of the experiences for both the teacher and learner. The foundation of a learner-centred approach to education involves: a collaborative relationship between teacher and learner, promotion of self-direction through the use of questioning, presenting stage-appropriate challenges with concomitant support, and the enhancement of learning and self-awareness through self-reflection (Entwistle, 2012). Could it be that the performance-related ideology and insulated, self-regulated nature of sport has inhibited potential learning from other domains such as education? Perhaps a learner-centred approach to developing talent may not only protect athletes from harm but also enhance athletic success? These questions await further research.

Conclusion

Mental toughness is widely recognized as a constellation of characteristics that are critical for the development of talent in athletes. In spite of this view, the construct of mental toughness has been criticized as being nebulous and linked with the masculine cultural values of sport. The proposition of this chapter is that mental toughness can also be problematic as coaching practices used to develop mental toughness may threaten the welfare of athletes. More specifically, we propose that efforts to develop mental toughness in athletes can hide or excuse harmful coaching practices such as emotionally abusive coaching behaviours.

Recommendations are therefore made to abandon the construct of mental toughness and to adopt an athlete welfare approach to talent development. Such an approach is characterized by a collaborative partnership between the coach and athlete in which power is shared with the athlete in developmentally appropriate ways and the athlete contributes to decisions that affect him or her. Additionally, a coach who exemplifies an athlete welfare approach plays a facilitative role, encouraging and guiding the processes of self-awareness, self-discovery and development of autonomy in athletes.

And finally, we recommend that researchers and coaches lean more heavily on the foundational knowledge offered by the educational literature, including teaching and learning strategies that have been empirically derived and tested within educational settings. We posit that promoting a learner-centred approach to the development of talent in young people would go a long way to building a healthy coach–athlete relationship, keeping youth in sport, facilitating talent development in sport, and promoting psychosocial development of young people.

References

Abbott, A., & Collins, D. (2004). Eliminating the dichotomy between theory and practice in talent identification and development: Considering the role of psychology. *Journal of Sports Sciences, 22*, 395–408.

Alexander, K., Stafford, A., & Lewis, R. (2011). *The experiences of children participating in organized sport in the UK.* The University of Edinburgh/NSPCC Child Protection Research Unit.

Andersen, M. (2011). Who's mental, who's tough and who's both? Mutton constructs dressed up as lamb. In D. Gucciardi & S. Gordon (eds), *Mental toughness in sport: Developments in theory and research* (pp. 69–88). London: Routledge.

Baker, J., Cobley, S., & Schorer, J. (eds). (2012). *Talent identification and development in sport: International perspectives.* London: Routledge.

Battaglia, A. (2015). *Youth athletes' interpretations of punishment in hockey.* Unpublished Masters thesis. University of Toronto.

Bloom, B. (1985). *Developing talent in young people.* New York: Ballantine.

Brackenridge, C. (2001). *Spoilsports: Understanding and preventing sexual exploitation in sport.* New York: Routledge.

Burke, M. (2001). Obeying until it hurts: Coach-athlete relationships. *Journal of the Philosophy of Sport, XXVIII*, 227–240.

Christensen, M., & Sorensen, J. (2009). Sport or school? Dreams and dilemmas for talented young Danish football players. *European Physical Education Review, 15*(1), 115–133.

Clough, P., Earle, K., & Sewell, D. (2002). Mental toughness: The concept and its measurement. In I. Cockerill (ed.), *Solutions in sport psychology* (pp. 32–45). London: Thomson.

Coakley, J. (1992). Burnout among adolescent athletes: A personal failure or a social problem. *Sociology of Sport Journal, 9*, 271–285.

Cobley, S., Schorer, J., & Baker, J. (2012). Identification and development of sport talent: A brief introduction to a growing field of research and practice. In J. Baker, S. Cobley, & J. Schorer (eds), *Talent identification and development in sport. International perspectives*. London: Routledge.

Connaughton, D., Wadey, R., Hanton, S., & Jones, G. (2008). The development and maintenance of mental toughness: Perceptions of elite performers. *Journal of Sport Sciences, 28,* 699–716.

Connaughton, D., Thelwell, R., & Hanton, S. (2011). Mental toughness development: Issues, practical implications and future directions. In D. Gucciardi & S. Gordon (eds), *Mental toughness in sport: Developments in theory and practice*. London: Routledge.

Côté, J. (1999). The influence of family in the development of talent in sport. *The Sport Psychologist, 13,* 395–417.

Côté, J., Baker, J., & Abernethy, B. (2007). Practice and play in the development of sport expertise. In G. Tenenbaum & R. Eklund (eds), *Handbook of sport psychology*. Hoboken, NJ: Wiley.

Crooks, C., & Wolfe, D. (2007). Child abuse and neglect. In E. Mash & R. Barkley (eds), *Assessment of childhood disorders* (4th ed.). New York: Guilford Press.

Crosset, T. (1986). *Male coach-female athlete relationships*. Paper presented to Norwegian Confederation of Sport Conference on Coaching Female Top-Level Athletes. Sole, Norway, Nov. 15–16.

Crust, L. (2007). Mental toughness in sport: A review. *International Journal of Sport and Exercise Psychology, 5*, 270–290.

Crust, L. (2008). A review and conceptual re-examination of mental toughness: Implications for future researcher. *Personality and Individual Differences, 45*, 576–583.

Crust, L. (2014). Is mental toughness being used as a screen for bullying? Mental Toughness Research Group. http://mtough.org.uk/2014/10/23.

Crust, L., & Azadi, K. (2010). Mental toughness and athletes' use of psychological strategies. *European Journal of Sport Science, 10*, 43–51.

Crust, L., & Clough, P. (2011). Developing mental toughness: From research to practice. *Journal of Sport Psychology in Action, 2*, 21–32.

Csikszentmihalyi, M., Rthunde, K., & Whalen, S. (1997). *Talented teenagers: The roots of success and failure*. Cambridge: Cambridge University Press.

Cushion, C., & Jones, R. (2006). Power, discourse, and symbolic violence in professional youth soccer: The case of Albion Football Club. *Sociology of Sport Journal, 23*(2), 142–161.

David, P. (2005). *Human rights in youth sport: A critical review of children's rights in competitive sports*. New York: Routledge.

Douglas, K., & Carless, D. (2006). Performance, discovery, and relational narratives among women professional tournament golfers. *Women in Sport and Physical Activity Journal, 15*(2), 14–27.

Entwistle, H. (2012). *Child-centred education*. London: Routledge.

Gervis, M., & Dunn., N. (2004). The emotional abuse of elite child athletes by their coaches. *Child Abuse Review, 13*, 215–223.

Goldberg, A. (1998). *Sports slump busting: 10 steps to mental toughness and peak performance*. Champaign, IL: Human Kinetics.

Gould, D., Hodge, K., Peterson, K., & Petlichkoff, L. (1987). Psychological foundation of coaching: Similarities and differences among intercollegiate wrestling coaches. *The Sport Psychologist, 1*, 293–308.

Gordon, S., & Gucciardi, D. (2011). A strengths-based approach to coaching mental toughness. *Journal of Psychology in Action, 2*(3), 143–155.

Gucciardi, D., Gordon, S., & Dimmock, J. (2008). Towards an understanding of mental toughness in Australian football. *Journal of Applied Sport Psychology, 20*, 261–281.

Gucciardi, D., Gordon, S., & Dimmock, J. (2009). Evaluation of a mental toughness training programme for youth-aged Australian footballer: 1. A quantitative analysis. *Journal of Applied Sport Psychology, 21*, 307–323.

Gurgis, J. (2015). *Examining the use of punishment in sport as a cultural tool*. Unpublished Masters thesis. University of Toronto.

Jones, G., Hanton, S., & Connaughton, D. (2002). What is this thing called mental toughness? An investigation of elite sport performers. *Journal of Applied Sport Psychology, 14*, 205–218.

Jones, G., & Moorehouse, A. (2007). *Developing mental toughness: Gold medal strategies for transforming your business performance.* Oxford: Spring Hill.

Joseph, S., & Linley, P. (2005). Positive adjustment to threatening events: An organismic valuing theory of growth through adversity. *Review of General Psychology, 9,* 262–280.

Joseph, S., & Linley, P. (2006). Growth through adversity: Theoretical perspectives and implications for clinical practice. *Clinical Psychology Review, 26,* 1041–1053.

Jowett, S. (2003). When the "honeymoon" is over: A case study of a coach–athlete dyad in crisis. *The Sport Psychologist, 17,* 444–460.

Jowett, S. (2005). The coach–athlete partnership. *The Psychologist, 18*(7), 412–415.

Jowett, S., & Cockerill, I. M. (2003). Olympic Medallists' perspective of the athlete–coach relationship. *Psychology of Sport and Exercise, 4,* 313–331.

Jowett, S., Paull, G., Pensgaard, A. M., Hoegmo, P. M., & Riise, H. (2005). Psychology and the coach: Coach-athlete relationship. In J. Taylor & G. Wilson (ed.), *Applying sport psychology: Four perspectives* (pp. 153–170). Champaign, IL: Human Kinetics.

Kerr, G. A., & Stirling, A. E. (2012). Parents' reflections on their child's experiences of emotionally abusive coaching practices. *Journal of Applied Sport Psychology, 24*(2), 191–206.

Kidman, L. (2005). *Athlete-centred coaching: Developing inspired and inspiring people.* Riccarton: New Zealand Innovative Print Communications.

Levy A., Polman, R., Clough, P., Marchant, D., & Earle, K. (2006). Mental toughness as a determinant of beliefs, pain, and adherence in sport injury rehabilitation. *Journal of Sports Rehabilitation, 15,* 246–254.

Linley, P., & Joseph, S. (2011). Meaning in life and posttraumatic growth. *Journal of Loss and Trauma, 16,* 150–159.

Loehr, J. (1986). *Mental toughness training for sports: Achieving athletic excellence.* Lexington, MA: Stephen Greene Press.

Mahoney, J., Gucciardi, D., Ntoumanis, N., & Mallet, C. (2014). Mental toughness in sport: Motivational antecedents and associations with performance and psychological health. *Journal of Sport and Exercise Psychology, 36*(3), 281–292.

Miller, K., & Hoffman, J. (2009). Mental well-being and sport-related identities in college students. *Sociology of Sport Journal, 26*(2), 335–356.

Miller, A. (1980). *For your own good. Hidden cruelty in child-rearing and the roots of violence.* New York: Farrar, Straus, & Giroux.

Orlick, T., & Botterill, C. (1975). *Every kid can win.* Chicago, IL: Nelson Hall.

Rongen, F., Cobley, S., McKenna, J., & Till, K. (2015). Talent identification and development: The impact on athlete health. In J. Baker, P. Safai & J. Fraser-Thomas (eds), *Health and elite sport. Is high performance sport a healthy pursuit?* (pp. 33–51). London: Routledge.

Seifried, C. (2010). The misconception of corporal punishment: A rejoin to Albrecht's "Drop and give us 20, Seifried: A practical response to defending the use of punishment by coaches". *Quest, 62,* 218–223.

Sheard, M. (2010). *Mental toughness: The mindset behind sporting achievement.* London: Routledge.

Stebbings, J., Taylor, I. M., & Spray, C. M. (2011). Antecedents of perceived coach autonomy supportive and controlling behaviors: Coach psychological need satisfaction and well-being. *Journal of Sport and Exercise Psychology, 33*(2), 255–272.

Stirling, A. E. (2007). *Elite female athletes' experiences of emotional abuse in the coach athlete relationship.* Unpublished master's thesis, University of Toronto, Toronto, Ontario, Canada.

Stirling, A. E. (2013). Understanding the use of emotionally abusive coaching practices. *International Journal of Sports Science & Coaching, 8*(4), 625–639.

Stirling, A. E., & Kerr, G. (2007). Elite female swimmers' experiences of emotional abuse across time. *Journal of Emotional Abuse, 7*(4), 89–113.

Stirling, A. E., & Kerr, G. A. (2008). Defining and categorizing emotional abuse in sport. *European Journal of Sport Science, 8*(4), 173–181.

Stirling, A. E., & Kerr, G. A. (2009). Abused athletes' perceptions of the coach-athlete relationship. *Sport in Society, 12*(2), 227–239.

Stirling, A., & Kerr, G. (2014). Initiating and sustaining emotional abuse in the coach-athlete relationship: An ecological transactional model of vulnerability. *Journal of Aggression, Maltreatment and Trauma, 23*(2), 116–135.

Tomlinson, P., & Strachan, D. (1996). *Power and ethics in coaching.* National Coaching Certification Program, Ottawa, ON: Coaching Association of Canada.

Weiser, R., & Theil, H. (2014). A survey of "mental hardiness" and "mental toughness" in professional male football players. *Chiropractic and Manual Therapies, 22*(1), 106.

Wylleman, P., & Lavallee, D. (2004). A developmental perspective on transitions faced by athletes. In M. Weiss (ed.). *Developmental sport and exercise psychology: A lifespan perspective.* Morgantown, WV: Fitness Information Technology, pp. 503–523.

Wylleman, P., Rosier, N., & De Knop, P. (2015). Transitional challenges and elite athletes' mental health. In J. Baker, P. Safai, & J. Fraser-Thomas (eds), *Health and elite sport. Is high performance sport a healthy pursuit?* (pp. 99–116). London, UK: Routledge.

PART V

Emerging issues

30

THE ROLE OF ANALYTICS IN ASSESSING PLAYING TALENT

Bill Gerrard

The nature of analytics

Analytics is one of the current buzzwords that crops up in a wide range of contexts – business analytics, retail analytics, supply chain analytics, human resource analytics, and political analytics, to name but a few of the more frequent ones, and, of course, sports analytics. Analytics is data analysis to support decision making. It is analysis with purpose, motivated not by interesting questions but by practical questions, by questions asked by those in positions of responsibility within organisations who have to make decisions that will affect future performance. It is actionable insight, analysis that aims to make a difference, combining technical rigour with practical relevance.

Analytics (or data science) encompasses a wide range of analytical methods. Statistical analysis is at the core of analytics but other non-statistical techniques such as linear programming, cluster analysis and network analysis are all used to support decision making and so should properly be included in analytics. Indeed many would argue that analytics is just a new label for what we previously called operations research and management science. There is some substance to this argument. Ultimately what label we use is unimportant. The crucial point is that analytics (or data science or operations research or management science) is all about harnessing the power of data analysis to improve the effectiveness of decision-making processes. As will be argued in this chapter, analytics represents an evidence-based approach founded on the premise that decisions on the best course of action are more likely to be successful in terms of improved performance when all relevant available information is considered in a systematic manner rather than relying solely on intuitive judgment.

Analytics consists of the three Ds – data, domain and decisions. Effective analysts not only need analytical skills but must also understand the objectives of the decision makers and the context within which they are operating. Analytics is not just about applying analytical techniques to a data set. When new problems emerge, they are often ill-understood initially and need to be structured more formally by the analyst to determine what relevant analysis is possible, what data is required, and which analytical techniques are appropriate. These analytical decisions require that the analyst and the decision maker work together. The decision maker will usually have much more knowledge and experience of the specific context and the analyst needs to utilise this expertise. So analytics is an art and a science with the effective analyst combining both technical skills and interpersonal skills.

Organisations, even those in the same sector, vary hugely in the extent to which they employ analytics. Davenport and Harris (2007) propose a five-stage characterisation of the analytical capabilities of organisations. Stage 1 organisations are the analytically impaired organisations with negligible analytical capabilities. Stage 2 organisations have localised analytics with analytics used within a small number of departments to improve one or more functional activities. Stage 3 organisations have analytical aspirations in the sense of a strategic commitment to developing a distinctive analytical capability that will act as a source of competitive advantage but are only starting the process of developing the use of analytics across the organisation supported by an integrated database. Stage 4 organisations have built an organisation-wide analytical capability with analytics viewed as an important contributor to organisational success: Stage 4 organisations are differentiated from other organisations operating in the same sector by their extensive use of analytics but analytics is not yet the primary source of competitive advantage. Davenport and Harris reserve the accolade of 'analytical competitors' for Stage 5 organisations for which analytics has become the primary driver of organisational performance with an organisation-wide imperative to continually innovate analytically in order to stay ahead of competitors.

Re-interpreting the *Moneyball* story

Applying the Davenport and Harris analytical stages model to elite sports teams, it would be relatively uncontentious to claim that most teams at the start of the twenty-first century were Stage 1 or Stage 2 organisations, making little use of data analysis in any part of their organisation. If sports teams were doing any data analysis, it was likely to be in the business aspects of their operations. Analysis in the sporting operation was principally video analysis. There was little if any general awareness of the possibilities for sports analytics as a source of competitive advantage. All of that changed with the publication of *Moneyball: The Art of Winning an Unfair Game* by Michael Lewis (2003) and then its release as a Hollywood movie in 2011 with Brad Pitt in the starring role.

Moneyball is the story of the Oakland Athletics in Major League Baseball (MLB) and how, under the leadership of Billy Beane, their General Manager (who was promoted in October 2015 to Executive Vice President – Baseball Operations), they utilised insights from sabermetrics (i.e. the statistical analysis of baseball) to identify undervalued players. Oakland are a small-market team with a restricted budget who view analytics as a type of 'David' strategy by which resource-constrained organisations can compete effectively with resource-rich rivals. *Moneyball* focuses principally on the 2001 and 2002 seasons when the Oakland A's had one of the lowest player wage budgets in the MLB and only around a third of that of the New York Yankees yet in both seasons qualified for the post-season play-offs. Indeed under Beane the Oakland A's managed an incredible sequence of 16 winning seasons from 1999 to 2014 despite their small budget and regularly having to trade their best players.

So how did the Oakland A's create a sustainable competitive advantage using statistical analysis? The answer is that they took advantage of what economists call 'informational inefficiencies' in the MLB players' labour market (Hakes and Sauer, 2006). Informational efficiencies occur when market traders do not use the available information as effectively as they could to determine their valuations of whatever is being traded. There are numerous reasons why traders might be inefficient in their use of information. They may be using outdated information and failing to give enough weight to new information. They may have strong preconceptions about what drives value and may ignore any contrary information. Or it may be that traders are following conventional wisdom, a sort of 'pack mentality', basing their own valuations on what others consider to be the correct valuation. Whatever the causes of the informational inefficiencies, economists argue that the market process will lead these inefficiencies to be corrected over time. All it takes is one trader to realise that the available information could be used better and to make a profit from doing so. Other traders will observe that someone is gaining an advantage and try to imitate their success. Eventually the market as a whole will adopt this new more profitable approach to using the available information and the competitive advantage of the original innovator will be eliminated. At this point the market is said to be 'information-efficient' until of course a trader discovers a new way to do even better in the market, initiating the process of learning and market correction again. The phenomenon of informational inefficiencies occurs in all walks of life. Indeed economists would interpret the relative age effect in talent ID resulting in the over-representation in elite youth development programmes of those born early in the school year as a classic case of informational inefficiency with insufficient weight being given to relative age within a cohort (see Wattie, Schorer & Baker, 2015).

In professional team sports, the ultimate transformation process is to convert a financial budget into sporting performance – wages into wins. Teams with a restricted wage budget can only remain competitive with resource-richer rivals by being more efficient in how they spend their budget. They need to identify value-for-money players, that is, players who will contribute more to winning per dollar of wage spend. The Oakland A's were highly efficient in using the available information to identify value-for-money players. As *Moneyball* highlights, the Oakland A's differed from other teams in two main respects. First, they relied much less on the intuitive expert judgments of scouts as to who were the best prospects and put much more weight on the performance statistics of players. Second, the Oakland A's did not rely on the traditional performance statistics that other teams looked at but instead, based on the analysis of Bill James and other sabermetricians, they used different metrics that statistical analysis showed to be better predictors of winning percentages. In particular, in the case of hitters, the Oakland A's did not focus on batting and slugging averages that measured getting to base only by hitting. The Oakland A's used on-base percentage which included not only hits but also walks. Essentially conventional wisdom had been that walks resulted from pitcher error and hence no market value was attached to the batter's ability to judge which pitches to hit and which to leave. As a result, in the MLB players' labour market, an above-average propensity to be walked to base constituted the proverbial 'free lunch' since it was not factored into the market valuations of players. The Oakland A's took full advantage of this market inefficiency as the two sports economists, Hakes and Sauer, show in their 2006 study. Interestingly they also show that this particular source of competitive advantage more or less disappeared in 2004 after the publication of *Moneyball* and other teams became more aware of the market value inherent in batters with high on-base percentage, just as the market efficiency hypothesis in economics would predict. The Oakland A's then had to look elsewhere for hidden value in the market.

The potential competitive gain from analytics is the key message that the world of elite sport has taken from *Moneyball*, although many in the sports world remain unconvinced. However there has been much misinterpretation and misunderstanding of *Moneyball* particularly the implications for traditional scouting. People tend to forget that although *Moneyball* is based on a true story, both the book and especially the movie, represent a popularised, dramatically heightened account of the Oakland story. There are important differences between how the Hollywood A's managed by Brad Pitt operate and how the Oakland A's managed by Billy Beane operated. Crucially the Hollywood A's are portrayed internally as a highly dysfunctional organisation with Brad Pitt and his fictional analyst in continuous conflict with the scouts and the field manager. The message of the film is that data scientists can replace scouts with recruitment decisions based on algorithms rather than intuition and experience. The either/or, art-versus-science storyline works as a dramatic device but it does not represent the reality of the Oakland A's who retain their scouting network which is as extensive as any other MLB team. The difference with the Oakland A's is that they combine the evidence provided by the scouts with the evidence provided by the data scientists. The reality of the Oakland A's is much less dramatic than the Hollywood A's with scouts and data scientists working in tandem to provide a much more holistic input into the decision-making process. Billy Beane watches videos and goes to games to watch specific players, and combines his own subjective evaluations with those of his scouts and the metrics provided by his analysts. The message is not 'don't rely on your eyes' but rather 'don't rely *only* on your eyes', a subtle but crucial difference and one that is often misunderstood by proponents and critics alike.

The other misunderstanding of *Moneyball* is to see it as 'one-size-fits-all' solution to resource constraints in any professional team sport. At times the proponents of sports analytics give insufficient weight to the specific baseball context of *Moneyball* and hence underestimate the difficulties involved in transferring the insights into other sporting contexts, particularly the invasion (or territorial) sports such as the various codes of football, hockey, rugby and basketball (Gerrard, 2007). In the crudest form, the 'one-size-fits-all' approach leads to a time-wasting search for the Holy Grail of a performance metric in a specific sport that will be akin to on-base percentage in baseball and provide the key to discover hidden value in the sport's players' labour market. Two important features of the baseball context need to be appreciated. First, baseball as a striking-and-fielding game is relatively atomistic in the sense that at its core is the individualistic contest between the pitcher and the batter. There is relatively little tactical coordination required between players. This has the important consequence that the contributions towards game outcomes of individual players are highly separable and largely independent of each other. Second, baseball involves a very high degree of skill specialisation – pitchers pitch and batters bat – so that potentially the contribution of any individual player can be reduced to a single metric. Essentially the *Moneyball* story is about getting an advantage from not only using metrics, but from using better metrics. Specifically on-base percentage is a better metric for measuring the win contribution of batters than batting and slugging averages.

Moving into the invasion-territorial team sports involves a very different context. These sports seek to emulate the battlefield with an object (i.e. a ball or puck) having to be moved into enemy-defended territory. These games have a more complex structure with players in a team having to work together either in possession to gain territory to create and convert scoring opportunities (i.e., offense) or out of possession to protect their territory and prevent their opponents from scoring (i.e., defence). It follows that tactical coordination is fundamental to these types of team sports with players requiring to coordinate their individual actions and having to continually make spatial decisions in and out of possession as to where to position themselves, with these decisions crucially dependent on the positioning decisions of their teammates and their opponents. The importance of tactical coordination means that individual player contributions are much more interdependent and so the win contributions of individual players are much less separable.

The other important contextual difference is that in many invasion-territorial sports, player performance is multi-dimensional with individual players required to undertake a variety of different actions in offense and defence. The degree of specialisation by individual players varies across sports with association football (i.e., soccer) towards the 'generalist' end of the spectrum while American (gridiron) football is more towards the 'specialist' end of the spectrum. But, irrespective of the degree of individual specialisation, it follows that the invasion-territorial sports require an array of performance metrics to capture the multi-dimensional skill sets that individual players and teams require. Any summary player performance metric must be of necessity a composite player rating that is based on combining a set of skill-specific performance metrics. Unlike baseball there is no single skill-specific performance metric that can effectively capture an individual player's contribution to team performance and game outcome. So player rating systems in the invasion-territorial sports necessarily comprise two distinct problems, an identification problem of determining the most appropriate set of skill-specific performance metrics, and a composition (or weighting) problem of how to best combine the set of skill-specific performance metrics to construct a summary player performance rating. This goes way beyond *Moneyball*, which focuses mainly on the identification problem in the context of finding the single best metrics for the two core skills in baseball, pitching and batting. (Statistically, fielding is of minor importance as a systematic determinant of game outcomes.)

Expert judgment versus statistical analysis

The issues facing the development of a more analytical approach to talent ID and player recruitment decisions in the invasion-territorial team sports are not unique. Indeed there is a large body of decision research on the relative merits of expert judgment and statistical analysis as the basis for decisions on the best course of action in multivariate contexts. Dawes (1988) actually tracks the antecedents of this research right back to Benjamin Franklin in the eighteenth century, and Franklin's proposal of the method of 'prudential algebra' in which the reasons for and against each alternative course of action are identified and assigned a score of +1 or −1, respectively, with the recommended course of action having the highest net score. The findings of this research particularly over the last 60 years are remarkably consistent and very instructive for the specifics of how to most effectively utilise the contributions of coaches, scouts and data analysts.

The starting point for the modern research on expert judgment and statistical analysis as the basis for decision making is Paul Meehl's book, *Clinical versus Statistical Predictions: A Theoretical Analysis and Revision of the Literature* published in 1954. Meehl compared the findings of 20 different studies in a wide range of areas and discovered that statistical analysis always provided at least as good predictions of future outcomes, and in most cases significantly more accurate predictions, than the predictions of experts using their intuition and experience. Meehl's book, which he himself described as 'my disturbing little book', provoked considerable controversy at the time and led to further studies comparing the effectiveness of experts and algorithms. This research continues. But the overwhelming body of evidence points in one direction, namely, the superiority of algorithms over experts. When it comes to man versus machines in predicting the outcomes of different courses of action, it is as close to a unanimous verdict as could be expected in the real world. For example, Daniel Kahneman, a Nobel Prize winner and author of *Thinking, Fast and Slow* (2012) in which he surveys around 200 studies across a wide range of contexts, concludes that 60 per cent of these studies show that statistically-based algorithms produce more accurate predictions with the rest of the studies showing that algorithms are as good as the experts in the area. Dawes (1988) in his earlier review reached the same conclusion, stating that 'the finding that linear combination is superior to global judgment is strong; it has been replicated in diverse contexts, and no exception has been discovered' (p. 207). Yet despite this remarkable consistency in the conclusions – unparalleled in the social sciences where the multiple possible interpretations of behaviour usually means that alternative contending hypotheses continue to co-exist – Dawes laments that this research has had virtually no impact on practice with confidence in the superiority of expert judgment remaining unassailed.

The range of contexts covered by this research includes college admissions tutors predicting student performance, loan officers evaluating the likelihood of bankruptcy amongst firms applying for bank loans, clinical practitioners predicting survival rates of patients, marriage counsellors predicting marital stability, and parole officers predicting recidivism. A common finding in many of the studies is that unstructured interviews tend to lead to poorer decisions as information provided by metrics of past performance gets marginalised by interviewers who focus on the specific information that became a focal point in the interview but has limited predictive content relative to the whole body of data available prior to the interview.

It would be easy to conclude that the body of research supports Brad Pitt's approach of looking only at the data and ignoring the scouts. But this would be to ignore the intricacies of the decision-making process in multivariate contexts. In particular, Dawes himself, as well as comparing the relative effectiveness of expert judgment and statistical analysis, has also investigated what it is about statistical analysis that leads to more accurate predictions and better decisions. His paper on the subject (Dawes, 1979) has been described by Kahneman (2012) as 'the most important development in the field since Meehl's original work' (p. 226) and, paradoxically, shows the importance of the expert in effective decision making.

Dawes (1979) investigated what we have designated above as the composition (or weighting) problem. Given an identified set of predictors, Dawes first considered the predictive accuracy of models that use a statistically derived set of weightings to combine the individual predictors and then compared these with models that use non-statistically-derived weightings. The statistical models are called 'proper linear models' and use multiple regression analysis to derive the optimal weights. Dawes compared the predictive accuracy of these statistical models with what he called 'improper linear models' in which the weightings are either randomly selected from normal or rectangular distributions, or set to be equal (as in Franklin's prudential algebra method). Dawes undertook 20,000 simulations and found that randomly selected weightings worked almost as well as the optimal weightings produced by multiple regression analysis, and equal weightings worked even better.

The remarkable effectiveness of improper linear models, particularly the use of equal weights, recasts the algorithms-versus-experts debate in two ways. First, it emphasises the importance of the identification problem and being able to comprehensively identify all of the factors influencing the behaviour patterns and future outcomes with which the decision maker in a specific context is concerned. And this reasserts the importance of the expert in using their knowledge and experience of the specific context to identify the factors to be included in the algorithm. Second, when it comes to the role of statistical analysis, it shows that the most important contribution is the consistency with which information is combined across all the alternatives. The use of optimal weightings derived statistically, equal weights or some other weighting system is of secondary importance. Critically experts should not override algorithms with a special-case argument to impose different sets of weights in evaluating alternative options. It is the consistency of linear models, both proper and improper, that Dawes has shown to be critical to effective decision making.

> What can be concluded is that the procedure of looking first within each variable and then comparing across by some weighting system is superior to that of making global intuitive judgments across variables regarding each choice in isolation.
>
> *(Dawes, 1988, p. 222)*

Player rating systems with multiple performance metrics

As previously discussed, as soon as we move into the invasion-territorial team sports, there is a need to develop player rating systems that combine multiple performance metrics. Applying the findings from decision research, most prominently Meehl, Dawes and Kahneman, the key argument for using player rating systems is that they ensure consistency in the comparison of all players. The actual weightings used to combine the multiple performance metrics into an overall player rating is a secondary concern.

However, before downgrading the role of multiple regression analysis in constructing player rating systems, it is important to recognise the dual roles played by the estimated regression coefficients. So far, the discussion has focused on the role of the estimated regression coefficients in optimising the relative importance of the individual predictors of future performance. In this context formally optimising implies choosing estimated coefficients to create the line of best fit that minimises the sum of the squared deviations between the predicted and observed performance levels. The line of best fit optimises predictive accuracy relative to the sample data used to estimate the regression. Provided that the sample is representative, the estimated regression is applicable to the population as a whole. However, there is always the constant danger of data mining and overfitting where models of ever-increasing complexity with more and more predictors are developed to increase the goodness of fit for the sample data, but these models can become sample-specific and eventually begin to lose general applicability. This is one reason why improper linear models especially equal-weights models are often as accurate in their predictions as proper linear (i.e. regression) models. Using equal weights ensures consistency but avoids using weights that have been derived from one specific sample.

But regression coefficients play another role apart from optimising the relative importance of individual predictors. Regression coefficients also control for differences in the units of measurement across the predictors. This is an important consideration in player rating systems particularly when often the individual performance metrics are of two broad types with very different units of measurement. Performance metrics can often be categorised as either activity levels or success ratios. Activity levels are tally counts of the frequency with which a player has performed a specific action such as the number of attempted passes, the number of attempted tackles and the number of shots at goal. By contrast, success rates show the proportion of successful outcomes relative to the total number of attempts and are often reported as percentages. Pass completion, tackle success and shot accuracy are all examples of success ratios. Given the very different units of measurement involved in activity levels and success ratios, it follows that any useful player rating system must allow for these measurement differences as well as taking account of relative importance considerations.

So, even if the equal-weights approach is adopted to develop a player ratings system that combines a number of skill-specific performance metrics, this is insufficient on its own. The skill-specific performance metrics need to be standardised before being combined into a composite player rating. The most frequently used method of standardisation is Z-scores in which each performance metric is expressed as a deviation from its mean value divided by its standard deviation. An example of the use of Z-scores in sport is Severini (2015) who uses Z-scores to compare the top receiving performances in the NFL across seasons. So one way of implementing the equal-weights approach is to adopt a two-stage approach of first standardising the individual performance metrics using Z-scores and then adding together the Z-scores for each individual player to calculate an overall player rating.

In my own work in developing player rating and valuation systems in association football, I have used both proper and improper linear models. Gerrard (2001) proposes a measure of player and team quality that utilises weights derived from a regression analysis of football transfer fees. These estimated coefficients show the relative importance of the various indicators of playing quality as reflected in transfer fees as well as controlling for the different units of measurement. The indicators of playing quality include age, career league experience, current appearance rates, career and current scoring rates, international appearances, and the size and status of the player's current team. In contrast, I have developed an improper linear variant of the football transfer fees model called the *SOCCER TRANSFERS* player valuation system (Gerrard, 2004) in which the original regression model is consolidated into seven composite value predictors converted into a common logarithmic scale and then added together on an equal-weights basis.

The implications for talent ID and assessing the development of youth players are very clear. An effective player rating system must be comprehensive, which requires that it includes metrics that capture all of the relevant factors and these metrics must be combined in a consistent manner. The expertise of coaches and scouts is the crucial starting point for determining the relevant factors that are able to identify young talented players with the highest success probabilities of a career at the elite level of their sport. In this discovery phase, the analysts play a secondary role in formulating the precise metrics to measure the relevant factors as well as validating the degree to which these metrics are predictive of future career success. Having agreed the set of metrics to be used to identify young talented players and track their development progression, the analyst then has the task of developing a composite rating that brings together all of the metrics. The findings of decision research suggest that the rating system does not necessitate the use of sophisticated statistical multivariate techniques such as multiple regression. Simple can prove best. So long as the various metrics have been standardised to be directly comparable, simply adding them together may suffice. Standardisation could involve converting all of the metrics to the same point-scale or to Z-scores. A comprehensive player rating system constructed in this way will provide a basis for consistent comparisons between players and over time. And crucially the greater the involvement of the coaches and scouts in the initial discovery phase, the greater the likelihood of buy-in from the coaches and scouts in using the rating system to assist in their decision making. If used properly, a player rating system provides a first cut in reaching decisions about the future career potential of young players. There may be other, more intangible factors not directly included in the rating system that although difficult to measure are still important and need to be included in final decision. Crucially if such considerations are to be included they should be done so for all players in a similar fashion to maintain the consistency of the decision-making process.

Overcoming the clash of cultures in elite sports

Moneyball, particularly as depicted in the Hollywood movie, while highlighting the possibilities for data analytics in the player recruitment decisions in elite team sports, does so in a way that represents the data scientist as an alternative to the traditional scout. The clash of cultures, art versus science, man versus machine, creates the dramatic tension that runs throughout the movie with analytics ultimately winning the day, captured in the moment when the home run that seals the A's record-breaking 20-game winning streak is scored by a player recruited on the basis of his statistics in the face of opposition from the scouts. By reinforcing the stereotypes of the analyst who only knows the statistics taking on the scouts and coaches who know the game, *Moneyball* may have been counter-productive in persuading teams to be innovative in embracing analytics and becoming analytical competitors in the Davenport and Harris taxonomy. Indeed Hollywood followed up *Moneyball* with an anti-analytics baseball movie, *Trouble with the Curve*, starring Clint Eastwood in which traditional scouting triumphs by detecting a fundamental flaw in the batting technique of a first-round draft pick with great metrics as well as discovering a great pitching prospect for whom there is no data and so would never register on the analyst's radar.

Decision research does seem on first reading to side with the analytical approach to player recruitment and talent ID but, as this chapter has argued, the work of Dawes in particular supports what I call coach-led analytics and the need for teams to adopt an evidence-based approach that combines expert judgment and statistical analysis. As Pfeffer and Sutton (2006) put it, 'evidence-based management is conducted best not by know-it-alls but by managers who profoundly appreciate how much they do not know' (p. 72). Whether it is the coach who knows it all or the analyst who knows it all does not matter, neither is conducive to an evidence-based approach. Coach-led analytics utilises the coach (or scout) as the expert best able to identify a comprehensive set of player characteristics that predict future performance. But what Dawes shows is that expertise in the identification problem does not translate into expertise in the composition problem. Indeed expertise in identifying performance predictors often gets in the way of applying consistency in combining these performance predictors. Coaches and scouts have a tendency towards inconsistency by rating individual players individually, giving more weight to certain predictors for some players but not all. The evidence clearly shows that this subjective and selective application of algorithms is likely to diminish rather than enhance the effectiveness of the decision-making process. Hence the key lesson from decision research that algorithms whether statistically based or applying equal weights to standardised metrics are the best way to support decision makers. Effective decision making is an art and a science. Analytics has a key role to play in supporting coaching decisions but so too has the experience and expert judgment of the coaches and scouts. The most successful teams are likely to be those that can combine effectively both sources of input into the decision calculus.

References

Davenport, T. H., & Harris, J. G. (2007). *Competing on analytics: The new science of winning*. Boston: Harvard Business School Press.

Dawes, R. M. (1979). The robust beauty of improper linear models in decision making, *American Psychologist, 34*, 571–582.

Dawes, R. M. (1988). *Rational choice in an uncertain world*. San Diego, CA: Harcourt Brace Jovanovich.

Gerrard, B. (2001). A new approach to measuring player and team quality in professional team sports, *European Sport Management Quarterly, 1*, 219–234.

Gerrard, B. (2004). The measurement and valuation of player quality in association football. In J. J. Gouguet (ed.), *Professional sport after the Bosman Case: An international economic analysis* (pp. 143–164). Limoges, France: IASE/Pulim.

Gerrard, B. (2007). Is the Moneyball approach transferable to complex invasion team sports? *International Journal of Sport Finance, 2*, 214–230.

Hakes, J. K., & Sauer, R. D. (2006). An economic evaluation of the *Moneyball* hypothesis. *Journal of Economic Perspectives, 20*, 173–185.

Kahneman, D. (2012). *Thinking, fast and slow*. London: Penguin Books.

Lewis, M. (2003). *Moneyball: The art of winning an unfair game*. New York: Norton.

Meehl, P. (1954). *Clinical versus statistical predictions: A theoretical analysis and revision of the literature*. Minneapolis:, MN University of Minnesota Press.

Pfeffer, J., & Sutton, R. I. (2006). Evidence-based management. *Harvard Business Review*, Jan, 62–74.

Severini, T. A. (2015). *Analytic methods in sports*. Boca Baton, FL: CRC Press.

Wattie, N., Schorer, J., & Baker, J. (2015). The relative age effect in sport: A developmental systems model. *Sports Medicine, 45*, 83–94.

31

TALENT DEVELOPMENT
IN PARASPORT

Joseph Baker, Srdjan Lemez, Andy Van Neutegem, and Nick Wattie

While the origins of sport for persons with a disability can be traced to the Deaflympics in 1924, social and political attention to parasport is a relatively recent phenomenon. Since the 1960 Rome Games the number of athletes competing in the Paralympic Games has risen from 400 to 4,302 in the London 2012 Paralympic Games. Further, the number of countries has increased from 23 to 164. This increasing attention from athletes and the stakeholders involved, either directly or indirectly, with athlete development (e.g., coaches, trainers, and parents as well as from policy makers), is coupled with a concomitant increase in the need for evidence-based models of para-athlete development.

Unfortunately, the pace of research on factors affecting the development of exceptional athletes in parasport has been slow, particularly compared to that of able-bodied sport. A recent systematic review conducted by our research group (Dehghansai, Lemez, Wattie, & Baker, in press) highlighted that over the past 65 years only 21 studies have been conducted on the development of para-athletes. Of these, only five focused on issues of training, development, and/or skill acquisition. The conclusion of this review was that we have very little evidence to use to guide the creation of sport-specific models for use in parasport.

Instead, approaches from able-bodied sport have typically been adapted to parasport contexts. Although there may be some universals in athlete development between parasport and able-bodied sport domains, such as the importance of high-quality coaching and deliberate practice, other factors may be considerably different. Athlete development trajectories and guidelines for sport involvement in early stages of development are examples of factors that may be appreciably different due to the unique constraints of each domain. Further, able-bodied athlete development models focus on maturation-based staging and physiological driven 'windows of trainability' or sensitive periods that have little relevance to athletes with congenital or acquired disabilities. Finally, athlete development models address psycho-social-emotional development of able-bodied athletes, which do not explicitly acknowledge the unique constraints for para-athletes (see Case Study below) and therefore implicitly assume that the same challenges exist for athletes with and without disabilities. Very little attention, if any, is given to the unique psycho-social-emotional issues of being a Paralympic athlete. In the sections below, we discuss the factors affecting athlete development in parasport and highlight several important areas for future work.

Newell's Constraints Model

Newell (1986) identified three categories of constraints that interact to determine optimal coordination and control of any activity: performer (i.e., organismic), environmental, and task constraints. This interactive constraints model (typically displayed as three points of a triangle) has become highly influential for understanding the often complex interaction among variables that affect human performance, including sport performance and athlete development (see Rienhoff, Tirp, Strauss, Baker, & Schorer, 2016; Wattie, Schorer, & Baker, 2015). Given the unique collection of variables with the potential to affect talent development in parasport, the 'Newell triangle' provides a valuable framework for organizing and discussing these factors. It is important to note that the word 'constraint' is used in the Newell framework to represent factors that both limit/discourage *and* permit/encourage (see also Haywood & Getchell, 2009).

Performer constraints

For an optimal movement pattern to occur, the performer must successfully interact with both the environment and task. Performer constraints are mental and physical characteristics that are embodied in an individual, and have two general subdivisions: (i) structural constraints, which relate to body structure (e.g., height, weight, and body size), and (ii) functional constraints, which are behavioural characteristics (e.g., cognitive attributes such as motivation and focus, and emotional attributes such as anxiety) (Haywood & Getchell, 2009; Newell, 1986).

Structural constraints

For athletes with a disability, movement limitations due to a disability offer additional constraints that need to be considered. Adding to the complexity, there are varying degrees of disability that inhibit the movement patterns of athletes in different ways. For example, according to the International Wheelchair Basketball Federation rule book (2014), the total value of classification points of a team's five players on the court cannot exceed the 14-point limit, and the classification system ranges from 1.0 (e.g., unable to move their trunk in any of the planes of movement) to 4.5 (e.g., able to move their trunk in all planes of movement) ('Classification', 2016). As such, it is reasonable to assume that talent selection and development programmes in parasport encourage participation of individuals with disabilities that span from low to high functioning. As a result, high variability between bodily constraints is often typical of participants in youth parasport programmes, and athletes and coaches who seek to optimize their functional ability rather than manage their lack of function or disability avoid a 'deficit-oriented' perspective that may inhibit and de-emphasize skill acquisition and development possibilities within their domain.

A dynamical systems perspective is useful in understanding how movement develops and changes, and provides a valuable framework to describe the unique nuances in para-athletes' readiness for skill acquisition and talent development. Dynamical systems suggests that human movement is a highly complex collection of co-dependent sub-systems, such as respiratory-, skeletomuscular-, and perceptual-systems, composed of several interacting components, such as oxygen molecules and muscle tissue (e.g., St Clair, 2003). In a parasport context, the nature of the disability can have a large impact on how coordination and control emerges from the interaction between these interacting parts (i.e., degrees of freedom) during skill acquisition. For example, a common movement impairment in athletes with a disability is functional asymmetry (e.g., amputees), which can make maintaining balance difficult as the athlete oscillates more to correct their balance, and is problematic in sports such as swimming (e.g., balancing on the starting block) and running (e.g., upper-limb amputees often wear a prosthesis during running to promote better arm-to-leg balance) (Rice et al., 2011). While the nature of the impairment creates kinematic differences that typically produce a dominant side during participation, the sport itself can also accentuate certain structural constraints. For example, sitting height and arm length are beneficial to performance in sitting volleyball; thus, maneuverability is not the only individual constraint that is an important indicator to participation and performance.

In Pope and colleagues' (Pope, Breslin, Getchell, & Liu, 2012) discussion of how to use constraints to design developmentally appropriate movement activities for children with autism spectrum disorders, they highlight the effectiveness of using Newell's (1986) model as a framework to describe how physical educators can modify the task or the environment to promote enhanced movement, in spite of the inability to change an individual's structural constraints (e.g., height or hand size). This also applies to para-athletes; despite the perceived difficulty in establishing a systematic talent identification and development programme for a pool of individuals who differ physically, a model such as Newell's (1986) can provide a more structured approach for coaches (Pope et al., 2012). For example, a beginner entering an established parasport programme who contains a commonly observed structural constraint (e.g., spina bifida) will participate in a modified environment that best suits their goal-directed behaviour, irrespective of the degree of fundamental motor skill deficiency. In addition, attention has been drawn to the importance of seeing disabilities in a more inclusive conceptual environment (i.e., thinking of them as constraints rather than restraints, without viewing them as positive or negative; Getchell & Gagen, 2006). In turn, the focus for coaches, particularly at the youth level, should remain on skill development and ability rather than focusing on the differences that limit movement (see Davis & Broadhead, 2007).

Functional constraints

Although technological advances such as the evolution of adaptive devices have given persons with physical disabilities increased opportunities to participate in sport and recreational physical activity, internal constraining factors can also impede involvement and performance. Crawford and Godbey (1987) characterized these intrapersonal constraints as psychological attributes and states, such as stress and anxiety, that can negatively affect development. While coaches may overlook a para-athletes' behavioural makeup in favour of a more visible physical disability (e.g., amputation) as it relates to confounders in skill acquisition, Patterson (2001) highlighted that any form of constraint can be internalized as a limitation or barrier imposed on the performer that may lead to decreased or non-participation in an activity. Another example is individuals with disabilities may have lower self-reported health, and in some cases can be more susceptible to experiencing a number of negative health outcomes. From a talent identification perspective, this may decrease the available talent pool; from a talent development perspective, it may mean that some individuals have to overcome initial functional constraints at early stages of the athlete development process before they can go on to experience successful athletic development.

In essence, it can be argued that functional constraints can have a *more* severe impact on the success of talent selection and development programmes in parasport compared to structural constraints, where an individual's motivation to begin or maintain participation in parasport may be contingent on the availability of appropriate environments manipulated to enhance skill development. Further, while individual constraints may be the least modifiable constraint in Newell's (1986) model, functional constraints *can* be modified by coaches to a certain degree. For example, Rice and colleagues (2011) suggested that high performance is possible with increases in fitness, health, and mobility. In turn, by optimizing the practice environment to maximize the learner's functional abilities, an implicit byproduct may be the improvement of psychological attributes (e.g., motivation, self-esteem and self-reported health) that can support talent development. Thus, it is important to view structural and functional constraints as moderators of one another, rather than constraints that affect the individual dichotomously.

Task constraints

Task constraints relate to the goal of the task, and the rules (or other factors) that constrain possible responses. In all sports, there are specific rules and policies that regulate the types and amounts of specific behaviours demonstrated in competition. The most obvious constraint in parasport that makes it unique from non-parasport is the issue of classification. Classifications reflect the International Paralympic Committee's (IPC) objective 'to support and co-ordinate the ongoing development of accurate, reliable, consistent and credible sport focused classification systems and their implementation' (IPC, 2016a). More specifically, classification considers the relationship between an individual's disability and performance in a given sport. Because the demands of each sport are unique, classifications are sport-specific; a given impairment can affect an athlete's capacity to perform in different sports to a different extent. Ultimately, this means an athlete might meet the criteria to participate in one sport, but not another.

Individual sports

Classifications in Paralympic individual sports reflect the unique individual limitations that need to be accommodated. In some cases, this can be rather straightforward: for example, visual impairments in sports such as para-alpine skiing, para-Nordic skiing, blind golf, five-a-side football, and judo are classified as B1 (representing athletes who are considered totally or almost totally blind), and B3 (athletes with partial sight, with visual acuity of between 2/60 and 6/60) with a classification of B2 reflecting athletes with visual impairments between B1 and B3. Other forms of impairment, however, are more complicated: in para-athletics, impairments that affect an athlete's ability to control their body (e.g., ataxia, hypertonia) are classified according to an 8-level system ranging from T31 (i.e., the ability to propel a wheelchair but very little strength in arms, legs, and trunk as in severe quadriplegia) to T38, which reflects:

> … clear evidence of hypertonia, ataxia and/or athetosis on physical assessment that will affect running. Co-ordination impairment is mild to moderate and can be in one to four limbs. Co-ordination and balance are typically mildly affected, and overall these athletes are able to run and jump freely.
>
> *(IPC, 2016b)*

Athletes in classifications T31 to T34 compete in a sitting position while those in T35 to T38 compete standing.

Despite the varying levels of complexity in the systems used to classify athletes, they reflect awareness of how different levels of impairment uniquely affect an athlete's ability to perform a sport-related task, and the need to alter the rules around the task accordingly. These unique task constraints also have the potential to affect athlete selection and development. For instance, an athlete with a degenerative impairment (e.g., to vision or motor control) may find herself moving across classification systems throughout their development. As a result, models of athlete development and approaches to athlete selection need to consider these dynamics.

Team sports

Because classification of an athlete's impairment can vary so considerably, team sports have created rules to standardize the performance environment to prevent any team from taking advantage. Wheelchair basketball, for example, has established specific rules regarding the participation of players with different levels of ability. They use a standardized classification system (1 to 4.5 scale, with severity of disability reflected in lower scores) to determine the functional abilities of players on a team. In Paralympic competition, the number of points allowable on the court at one time (i.e., the sum of all classifications of the five players on court) cannot exceed a total of 14. Similar rules governing team makeup are found in several other team parasports including wheelchair rugby (a total of 8 points on the court at one time), sitting volleyball (restricted to one minimally disabled player on the court at a time), and 7-a-side football (each team of seven players must have one FT5 or FT6 player on the field at all times and is not allowed to have more than one FT8 players on the field).

These sport-specific constraints also affect a host of athlete selection and development outcomes. In addition to the general training and development issues noted above for individual sport athletes, there are unique team-based concerns. For example, a team who had a high degree of one type of classification would focus athlete selection initiatives elsewhere to 'round out' the team. Similarly, offensive and defensive strategies on a given team will need to reflect the specific abilities of team members.

Environmental constraints

Environmental constraints are those that generally do not change the nature of the task (i.e., specific sport). These include a range of factors such as the physical and sociocultural environment, and policies. Environmental constraints influence athletes themselves, their developmental environment, as well as athletes' communities, family and friends. While Newell (1986) conceded that environmental and task constraints are not necessarily mutually exclusive, we will attempt to restrict this discussion to environmental constraints on the development of athletes with a disability (largely from a Canadian perspective).

Socio-economic constraints are perhaps one of the most notable environmental constraints experienced by developing athletes (see Wattie and Baker, in press). It is generally recognized that high performance athlete development requires financial resources, including the discretionary time and resources to train and travel, purchase equipment, and hire specialist coaches. Research suggests that many high performance athletes come from households with higher family incomes (Beamish, 1990; Collins & Buller, 2003). For example, research suggests that nearly half of Canadian national team athletes in the 1980s come from families in the top 20% distribution of Canadian incomes, while approximately 10% of national team athletes emerge from families in the bottom 20% distribution of household income (Beamish, 1990). Without the necessary financial resources athletes may face a number of barriers to their development. While income inequality constrains both able-bodied athletes and para-athletes, social inequalities amongst populations with a disability are such that the probability of that constraint on para-athletes is greater.

Data from Statistics Canada describes the extent of the social inequality experienced by those with disabilities. In 2011, the employment rate of Canadians with disabilities was nearly 50%, compared 79% for Canadians without disabilities, and significant numbers of Canadians with disabilities reported that they have been refused employment because of their disability (Turcotte, 2014). Moreover, when employed, the average income of those with disabilities was approximately 16% less than the average income of a Canadian without disability (Jackson, 2010). The social inequality experienced by individuals with disabilities is not unique to Canada. Analyses of data from 49 countries in the World Health Survey conducted by the World Health Organization found that disability was more prevalent in the poorest wealth quintile within *all* countries (Hosseinpoor et al., 2013).

These trends are notable, particularly given that the cost of programmes and of accessing facilities has been reported as a significant barrier to training and physical activity for individuals with disabilities (Mulligan, Hale, Whitehead, & Baxter, 2012). In addition, the cost of specialized equipment for certain sports (e.g., wheelchair basketball) may also be prohibitive and has also been identified as a barrier (Mulligan et al., 2012).

A number of other environmental constraints may also create barriers for athletes with a disability. In their systematic review of barriers to physical activity, Mulligan et al. (2012) documented aspects of the physical environment and the social environment that constrain engagement in physical activity for individuals with disabilities. Common barriers in the physical environment included accessibility of facilities, lack of convenient accessible transportation, limited choice and availability of programmes, and lack of appropriate equipment for training. The social environmental constraints, which may ultimately influence the existence of environmental barriers, include a lack of expectation from others to be active and participate in programmes, as well as poor attitudes and lack of encouragement from people to be active (Mulligan et al., 2012). Both physical and social environmental barriers have been described as forms of discrimination, and the result of negative stereotypes about individuals with disabilities.

In a broad sense, the greater likelihood of income/employment inequalities among individuals with disabilities, combined with the physical and social environmental barriers (Mulligan et al., 2012), can result in social exclusion: exclusion from the chance to participate in and contribute to social and cultural activities (Raphael, 2010). From an athlete development perspective, these social inequalities may result in 'talent exclusion': exclusion from the potential talent pool of athletes. They may also create prohibitive barriers that cause exclusion during the talent development processes. Going forward it will be increasingly important to understand how social inequalities influence the development of athletes with a disability. Moreover, it will be important to understand the intersection of constraints, such as that between sex, race/ethnicity (individual constraints), social inequality (environmental constraint) and type of sport (task constraint). Similarly, given that environmental constraints such as income can influence the sequential formation of athletic skills (see Wattie and Baker, in press), it may be useful to consider whether social inequalities interact with individual constraints, such as whether athletes' disabilities are acquired or congenital, and the subsequent impact on the process of athlete development. Such multifactorial context-specific approaches will be necessary for complete theoretical and applied models of para-athlete development. In the section below, we examine how these constraints relate to the creation and utilization of an athlete development model.

Case study: Canadian wheelchair rugby

Wheelchair rugby is a relatively new Paralympic sport having been invented in Winnipeg in 1976. Originally, the sport was developed for people with spinal cord injury but now includes participants with a range of disabilities, including: quadruple amputation and neuromuscular disorders such as muscular dystrophy, cerebral palsy, and transverse myelitis. Its rise in worldwide popularity was initially driven by the award-winning documentary, *Murderball*; but, it is also an example of a sport that has continually evolved in response to the constraints that have been highlighted in Newell's (1986) model.

In 2008, the Canadian Wheelchair Sport Association (CWSA), the national sport organization for wheelchair rugby, developed its long-term player development model based on the generic 7-stage long-term athlete development model (LTAD) developed for Canadian sport (Balyi, Way, Higgs, Norris, & Cardinal, 2005), but including two different initial stages, Awareness and First Involvement. These two stages address the social and environmental influences on engagement in physical activities for people with disabilities. The model also provides 10 key factors that characterize the implementation principles of the player development model. These include: Physical Literacy, Specialization, Developmental Age, Sensitive Periods, Mental, Cognitive and Emotional Development, Periodization, Competition, Excellence Takes Time, System Alignment and Integration Continuous Improvement.

Although the LTAD is meant to have applicability to able-bodied athletes and athletes with disabilities, these factors may not be relevant to parasport since many of them have been based on sport science research for able-bodied athletes. Newell's (1986) three categories of constraints provide a useful framework for examining the relevancy of the LTAD model to development of athletes with a disability. From the perspective of Newell's *performer constraints* the factors of *Specialization, Development Age* and *Sensitive Periods* have little relevance to talent identification and development of athletes with a disability. Athletes with a congenital disability may not follow the same developmental patterns regarding physical maturation as a result of medication and/or different functional abilities related to the diagnosed medical condition. Athletes with acquired disabilities (e.g., traumatic injury or disease) may also not experience traditional patterns of development highlighted in the 7-stage athlete development pathway since they too may have different functional abilities as a result of different body composition (e.g., limb loss, vision loss) and emotional experiences as a result of assuming the label of a *disabled person*. These athletes may not have trainable sensitive periods like able-bodied athletes or have the maturation trajectory to specialize in sports, especially sports that have not been adapted or created for athletes with a disability.

Athletes with a disability may also not experience the social, emotional, and cognitive development patterns as able-bodied athletes. The person who has acquired a disability through a trauma or disease experiences a range of emotional trauma that differs from the able-bodied population. This is equally true for athletes with a congenital disability who may experience school differently and in many instances be excluded from regular physical activity and sport opportunities. Newell (1986) refers to the functional constraints related to behavioural characteristics such as motivation, focus, and anxiety. Although athletes with a disability may display many of the behavioural characteristics of an able-bodied athlete, the presence of a trauma or different lifespan development patterns is a common theme in the lives of athletes with a disability. The semiotics of society provide constant reminders that athletes with disabilities have different internal constraining factors that, if not acknowledged, can have limiting effects on the development of athletes with a disability.

Wheelchair rugby is a sport that features a complex system of classification that ascribes the athletes a 0.5, 1.0, 1.5, 2.0, 2.5, 3.0, 3.5 classification based on function levels (lowest functioning athletes is a 0.5 classification). Although the classification system may appear to be a facilitating mechanism to allow as many players possible to participate in an equitable manner, it does create a constraint in terms of the behaviours the athletes can display on the field of play. The sport requires 4 players per team that aggregate to a maximum of 8.0 classification points on the court. Although this allows for a range of functional abilities to participate, the potential to not have players within all ranges of classification may limit the type of line-ups (e.g., 3.5, 2.0, 1.5, 1.0 = 8.0 line-up points) that can be created to play. In many instances, a player is excluded from a game because there are not the necessary players with a specific classification to create a line-up. Wheelchair rugby continually seeks to recruit athletes with specific disabilities and functional abilities to develop effective line-ups. The recruitment focus is not limited to searching for players in each class but also to find players with specific body structures and biophysical performance characteristics. Recently, wheelchair rugby teams at the international level have focused recruitment on athletes with quadruple amputations since they possess the core abdominal muscles that athletes with spinal cord injuries do not possess, and therefore have considerable functional advantage related to executing performance tasks.

Wheelchair rugby in Canada has also focused its attention on tactical play at the international level to match an evolving game of high functioning athletes performing at the highest level within their classification. Newell's (1986) *task constraints* suggest that selection and development is constrained by the different abilities and that tactical strategy will need to reflect the specific abilities of team members. In Canada, recruitment is focused on athletes with physical characteristics that exceed notions of constraints embodied in a classification system. Recruitment strategies include targeting non-spinal cord injuries and specifically targeting athletes with a disability with a team sport background (ideally a contact team sport) to optimize tactical awareness of spacing and decision-making inherent in team sports.

Newell (1986) highlighted the role of environmental constraints influencing para-athlete's developmental environment as well as their communities. Wheelchair rugby in Canada developed its LTAD model around the management of a number of environmental constraints. Given the lack of applicability of the able-bodied 10 LTAD factors, wheelchair rugby chose to address the following environment constraints: funding, coaching, competition, equipment and facilities, sport science, sport support, personal support, and officials. These constraints were examined in Canadian wheelchair rugby's LTAD document, *Full Contact* (Canadian Wheelchair Sports Association, 2014). It addressed each pillar from the perspective of barriers to participation, which aligns with the findings of Mulligan et al. (2012) that documented common barriers to participation including accessibility of facilities, lack of convenient accessible transportation, limited choice of programmes, and lack of appropriate equipment for training. The CWSA has focused its attention on developing programmes such as *Podium Club* which provides funding to wheelchair rugby clubs in Canada to breakdown these physical and social barriers. This programme provides tiered funding in areas such as coaching, sport science, equipment, competition travel, training court access, and officials' training so that each club facilitates participation and provides aligned talent recruitment and development strategies. For example, clubs are invited to submit basic club development plans that focus on training athletes in the right environment with qualified coaches. Clubs that meet the nationally driven action-based criteria related to identified constraints (e.g., coaching) are given financial assistance to implement their club plans. The programme has been hugely successful in removing environmental constraints and growing support for the physical, emotional, and social development of wheelchair rugby athletes. Talent recruitment and development has also been stimulated through *Podium Club* as a result of incentives to provide brief scouting reports of club players based on targeted physiological testing parameters (e.g., 20 m sprint) and chair skill assessments.

Wheelchair rugby in Canada has evolved talent recruitment and development structures that address performer, task, and environmental constraints. Its starting point is to adopt athlete development pathways that are specific to the disability population groups that can play the sport through classification processes. It does not default to able-bodied athlete pathway models to develop and implement athlete development programming. As a sport, it acknowledges the structural constraints inherent in the athlete's disability as well as the environmental and societal constraints that shape engagement in the sport. At the world-class level, Canadian wheelchair rugby implements aggressive sport science and sport medicine protocols, and performance analytics to optimize player and team task performance. It implements a process of *gold-medal profiling* that seeks to identify, track and develop the key performer characteristics and attributes to deliver a podium competition result. It also provides a 'gold-medal standard' for training and competition environments to achieve podium outcomes. This approach uses the environmental, performer and task constraints to design developmentally appropriate training and competition activities at different stages in the athlete pathway. In doing so, Newell's (1986) model serves as a framework to enhance performance at specific stages of development of wheelchair rugby athletes. The process of *gold-medal profiling* provides a systematic and structured approach to coaching athletes with disabilities. The structural (functional abilities) and functional (behaviours) constraints are identified and acknowledged for each classification grouping; but, each constraint is addressed from the perspective of individualizing and optimizing a training programme to achieve world-class performance outcomes.

Wheelchair rugby has grown globally as a sport in terms of number of participants and popularity with the public. Since its first international tournament with three countries in Toronto in 1981 it has grown to 25 active countries competing world-wide under its own international federation, the International Wheelchair Rugby Federation. In Canada, a very deliberate approach has been taken in recent years to address its athlete development pathway from the perspective of managing or removing constraints to player development. Its approach reflects an understood difference in developing an athlete with a disability compared to able-bodied athletes; yet still employing a range of world-leading practices, similar to able-bodied sport, in sport science, sport medicine and coaching that optimizes the performance of wheelchair rugby athletes at the highest level of competition.

Concluding remarks: The need for considerable future research

The unique constraints of parasport necessitate the development or expansion of more comprehensive models of athlete selection and development. These models will need to be sufficiently nuanced to reflect the considerable diversity and variability in the trajectories to the highest levels of performance in parasport. For instance, understanding how trajectories of development differ between athletes with congenital versus acquired injuries is an obvious starting point but what about differences between athletes who acquire their injuries in childhood versus adolescence versus early adulthood? Relatedly, how do opportunities for sport involvement at different phases of development facilitate or impede athlete development?

In addition to questions unique to parasport contexts, understanding the similarities between para-athletes and their mainstream counterparts could be valuable to the development of comprehensive models of athlete development. While the relevance of high-quality training and practice seems clear, the value of diverse versus specialized sporting involvement is less so. Opportunities to participate in parasports are considerably fewer than mainstream sports and so the value and transfer of participation in other sports takes on different meaning. Similarly, the relevance of current initiatives like 'talent transfer' (see Chapter 32) might be greater in parasport where the number of sports and participants may be significantly lower than in high-participation-based sports. Finally, why do athletes with a disability drop out of sport? Given the small athlete populations in most parasport and the long-term benefits of maintaining physical activity and sport participation in those with functional impairments, understanding the factors affecting dropout are important.

The few areas identified above reflect a very superficial 'to do' list for future researchers in this area. Ultimately, continued evaluation of the issues affecting the selection and development of para-athletes will lead to a greater understanding of skill acquisition in general, and in parasport in particular. Considerable work is required in order to develop sophisticated, evidence-based models of athlete development across the range of parasports that reflect the sometimes extreme and oftentimes subtle differences between athletes on the road to sporting expertise.

References

Balyi, I., Way, R., Higgs, C., Norris, S., & Cardinal, C. (2005). *Canadian sport for life: Long-term athlete development* [Resource paper]. Vancouver, Canada: Canadian Sport Centres.

Beamish, R. (1990). The persistence of inequality: An analysis of participation patterns among Canada's high performance athletes. *International Review for the Sociology of Sport, 25*(2), 143–155.

Canadian Wheelchair Sports Association. (2014). *Full Contact: A Long-Term Athlete Development Model for Wheelchair Rugby in Canada*. Unpublished.

Classification. (2016). Wheelchair Basketball Canada. Retrieved April 23, 2016, from www.wheelchair-basketball.ca/the-sport/classification/

Collins, M., & Buller, J. (2003). Social exclusion from high performance sport: Are all talented young sports people being given an equal opportunity of reaching the Olympic podium? *Journal of Sport and Social Issues, 27*(4), 420–442.

Crawford, D. W., & Godbey, G. (1987). Reconceptualizing barriers to family leisure. *Leisure Sciences, 9,* 119–127.

Davis, W., & Broadhead, G. (2007). *Ecological task analysis and movement.* Champaign, IL: Human Kinetics.

Dehghansai, N., Lemez, S., Wattie, N., & Baker, J. (in press). A systematic review of influences on development of athletes with disabilities. *Adapted Physical Activity Quarterly.*

Getchell, N., & Gagen, L. (2006). Interpreting disabilities from a 'constraints' theoretical perspective: Encouraging movement for all children. *Palaestra, 22,* 20–53.

Haywood, K. M., & Getchell, N. (2009). *Life span motor development* (5th ed.). Champaign, IL: Human Kinetics.

Hosseinpoor, A., Williams, J., Gautam, J., Posarac, A., Officer, A., Verdes, E., ... Chatterji, S. (2013). Socioeconomic inequality in disability among adults: A multicountry study using the World Health Survey. *American Journal of Public Health, 103,* 1278–1286.

International Paralympic Committee (2016a). IPC Publications and documents. Retrieved May 3, 2016, from www.paralympic.org/the-ipc/publications

International Paralympic Committee (2016b). *Athletics classifications.* Retrieved May 3, 2016, from www.paralympic.org/athletics/classification

International Wheelchair Basketball Federation. (2014). *Official wheelchair basketball rules 2014.* Version 1. Retrieved October 25, 2016, from http://77.104.141.88/~iwbf2497/wp-content/uploads/2016/08/2014_IWBF_Rules_V2.pdf

Jackson, A. (2010). *Work and labour in Canada: Critical issues* (2nd ed.). Toronto: Canadian Scholar's Press.

Mulligan, H. F., Hale, L. A., Whitehead, L., & Baxter, G. D. (2012). Barriers to physical activity for people with long-term neurological conditions: A review study. *Adapted Physical Activity Quarterly, 29,* 243–265.

Newell, K. M. (1986). Constraints on the development of coordination. In M. G. Wade and H. T. A. Whiting (eds), *Motor development in children: Aspects of coordination and control* (pp. 341–361). Amsterdam: Martin Nijhoff.

Patterson, T. (2001). Constraints: An integrated viewpoint. *Illuminaire, 7,* 30–38.

Pope, M., Breslin, C. M., Getchell, N., & Liu, T. (2012). Using constraints to design developmentally appropriate movement activities for children with autism spectrum disorders. *Journal of Physical Education, Recreation and Dance, 83,* 35–40.

Raphael, D. (2010). *About Canada: Health and illness.* Halifax: Fernwood Publishing Company.

Reinhoff, R., Tirp, J., Strauss, B., Baker, J., & Schorer, J. (2016). The 'Quiet Eye' and motor performance: A systematic review based on Newell's constraints-led model. *Sports Medicine, 46,* 589–603.

Rice, I., Hettinga, F. J., Laferrier, J., Sporner, M. L., Heiner, C. M., Burkett, B., & Cooper, R. A. (2011). Biomechanics. In Y. Vanlandewijck and W. R. Thompson (eds), *The paralympic athlete: Handbook of sports medicine and science.* Chichester, UK: Wiley-Blackwell.

St Clair, G. (2003). Dynamical systems theory: A relevant framework for performance-oriented sports biomechanics research. *Sportscience, 7.*

Turcotte, M. (2014). Persons with disabilities and employment. Statistics Canada, Catalogue no. 75-006-X. Retrieved May 6, 2016 from: www.statcan.gc.ca/pub/75-006-x/2014001/article/14115-eng.htm

Wattie, N., & Baker, N. (in press). An uneven playing field: Talent identification systems and the perpetuation of participation biases in high performance sport. In R. Dionigi and M. Gard (eds), *Sport and physical activity across the lifespan: Critical perspectives*. Basingstoke, UK: Palgrave Macmillan.

Wattie, N., Schorer, J., & Baker, J. (2015). The relative age effect in sport: A developmental systems model. *Sports Medicine, 45*, 83–94.

32

THE STRUCTURED REPSYCHLING OF TALENT

Talent transfer

Tracy Rea and David Lavallee

Introduction

In sport, significant resources are dedicated to the development of large groups of athletes in the hope of producing elite performers. It has been estimated that the expenditure required to achieve an Olympic gold medal is about A\$37 million and A\$8 million per medal (Hogan & Norton, 2000). However, many identified athletes fail to reach their potential, which raises questions regarding the most effective and efficient use of resources to ensure optimal talent development, retention and ultimately successful athletic performance. If it were possible to minimize type II errors (e.g., those athletes who are already identified by the governing body and in the talent pathway but who do not successfully transition to senior level), this would enable sporting bodies and agencies to focus expenditure on developing a smaller number of athletes and offer more focused coaching and resources in their quest for elite performance.

For more than a generation, sporting bodies, to get ahead of other respective countries and win medals on the World stage, have unwittingly called for a new capacity of talent. This talent would have the ability not just to demonstrate certain characteristics needed to perform with distinction, they would also be able to step outside the specific demands of one sport to validate their own capabilities to more steadfast characteristics needed to transfer their 'talent' to another domain.

The use of talent transfer is becoming increasingly common within high performance sport to help support medal-winning potential (Vaeyans, Güllich, Warr, & Phillippaerts, 2009). For example, China moved Chen Zhong from basketball to taekwondo as early as 1995 and within five years she had been selected for the national team. Zhong went on to win gold at the 2000 Olympics where taekwondo made its debut as an Olympic sport. A high-profile talent transfer in the UK was Rebecca Romero who first won silver for Britain rowing the quadruple scull at the Athens Games in 2004 and then took up cycling in 2006, winning two golds for Great Britain at the 2008 Beijing Olympics.

Prevalent initiatives such as UK Sport/English Institute of Sports' Tall and Talented (2012), the Australian Institute of Sports' Second Chance and Sports Draft programmes, the Canadian Sport Institute's Podium Search (including Row to Podium and Pedal to the Medal) and Germany's Row4Tokyo and Zero to Hero, are indicative of the investment given to sporting bodies with the intention of creating as many chances as possible of medalling within targeted sports for future Olympic games. Collins, Collins, MacNamara and Jones (2014) analysed data from the 2010 and 2012 Olympic teams and found that from Australia, Canada, GB and USA, 174 (7.5%) athletes were identified as resulting from talent transfer. Furthermore, Collins et al. (2014) noted that Australia and the UK, who have made significant investments in their formal talent transfer initiatives, converted 8% of their Olympic athletes as transfers. These statistics suggest the notion of talent transfer may be worthwhile for sporting bodies hoping to maximize identification and development of sporting talent.

What is talent transfer?

There are varying definitions of what talent transfer is. Collins et al. (2014) defined talent transfer as a recently formalized and highly structured process used to identify and develop talented athletes by selecting individuals who have already succeeded in one sport and transferring them to another. Recently, MacNamara and Collins (2015) took this definition one step further by describing talent transfer as an athlete that has competed at international, national or state level in both their 'donor' (sport 1) and 'transfer' (sport 2) sport. In simple terms, transfers were considered as between *sports* rather than between *events* conducted under the same governing body and/or international federation. A common example is a switch from gymnastics to diving.

At its most basic level, talent transfer occurs when existing high performance athletes are targeted and their athletic skills are transferred to another sport. For example, the New Zealand National Athlete Transfer System specifically targets athletes with a proven track record of performance at the international level or at the highest standard nationally (High Performance Sport New Zealand, 2013). Jaime Nielson, for example, showed promise as an Olympic rower for New Zealand before the opportunity to switch came through BikeNZ, which was running a programme called 'Power to the Podium'. Such talent identification and development initiatives increase the probability of identifying athletes who can attain senior expertise by minimizing adolescent maturational issues, reducing talent development time frames, and maximizing return on the developmental investment already made in these older athletes (Gulbin & Ackland, 2009; Halson, Martin, Gardner, Fallon, & Gulbin, 2006). Subsequently, talent transfer athletes can experience success in their new sport in relatively short time frames.

Specifically, targeting athletes who feel as though they have more to give and/or are nearing retirement/have retired, are given a 'second chance' to switch sports and directly contribute to the success of achieving medals on the international stage. Conversely, as Vaeyans and colleagues (2009) suggest, the 'structured recycling of talent' (p. 1374) in programmes such as UK Sport's Girls for Gold: Army; Target Tokyo; Power2Podium: Skeleton; Girls4Gold: Canoeing; Fighting Chance: Battle4Brazil; and Paralympic Potential: Bring on Brazil (to name but a few) introduces a more proactive, systematic approach to delivering athletes already 'primed' for podium success.

Why do athletes transfer?

Lavallee and Wylleman (2000) noted that some athletes struggle with the loss of sporting identity after the transition of retiring, whether resulting from a normative transition (chosen retirement due to age) or a non-normative transition (through a career-ending injury). Results from Rea and Lavallee's (2015) study support this notion and illustrate three primary reasons as to why athletes chose to transition to another sport: 1) they were not achieving good enough results to compete at an international level within their previous sport; 2) they had a career-ending injury that forced them to reconsider their options; and/or 3) their sporting identity was a challenge to let go of and that most athletes still had 'more to give' or 'aspired for something more'. Evidently, this clear focus that a person is 'not quite finished yet' is a determining factor as to why athletes might choose to stay within the field of competitive sport (Rea and Lavallee, 2015). Katie O'Brien is an example of an athlete who had something more to give. O'Brien was identified through Cycling Canada's 'Pedal to the Medal' athlete identification programme. Previously she had been a 2014 Olympian in women's two-person bobsleigh. Within 10 months of dedicated track cycling training, O'Brien placed 12th at the 2015 World Track Cycling Championships.

Of course, informal talent transfer has occurred for some time, when abilities are noticed by coaches or through an athlete looking for a new challenge. In Rea and Lavallee's (2015) study, one athlete (who had a career-ending injury within their previous sport) identified a key person within the training environment as being the catalyst to them undertaking a talent transfer process. This was based on their expertise as a strength and conditioning coach, but having the knowledge of 'key markers' that have been used with other athletes, a conversation transpired that was the prompt needed for the athlete to pursue another sport.

If the switch to a new sport was prompted by a plateau in performance, or limited opportunities for further development (e.g., an athlete who participates in a non-Olympic sport who dreams of winning Olympic gold), transfer to a new sport may lead to attainment of greater success at a higher level. Interestingly, Team USA does not have a formalized talent transfer programme, yet similar to Australia (7.4%) and the United Kingdom (8.4%), 6.9% of athletes competing at the 2012 London Olympics 'switched' sports somewhere in their development (Collins et al., 2014). These results suggest that talent transfer would seem to be effective but perhaps not solely as a formal initiative (Collins et al., 2014).

How does talent transfer work?

Despite the increasing popularity of talent transfer amongst sporting bodies, there is little empirical evidence as to its efficacy or how it may be most efficiently employed. Below we identify six areas that support the process of talent transfer. We describe each below.

Previous sporting experience

The New Zealand National Athlete Transfer System specifically targets athletes with a proven track record of performance at the international level or at the highest standard nationally. The New Zealand Institute of Sport (High Performance Sport New Zealand, 2013) states there is now 'sufficient evidence showing that athletes can progress in a new sport in a significantly shorter timeframe. This is because athletes can transfer some of the skills (physical and mental), physiological attributes, and training ethic already required.' Therefore, rather than undertaking a programme targeted to a specific sport (i.e., Sporting Giants, 2010, for volleyball and basketball in UK Sport), the New Zealand Institute of Sport 'recommend one or more sports that best suit an athlete's potential and will support them to make an informed decision' (High Performance Sport New Zealand, 2013).

Prior sporting experience is a prerequisite when transferring between sports, whether that is through physiological similarities, for example, gymnastics to freestyle aerial skiing, or psychologically where the transference is about similar athletic traits such as mental toughness and the resilience to compete and train at the required level. Targeting athletes who have previously been a part of a world-class Olympic programme and who are 'medal-capable' can make the transfer considerably easier as the athlete understands what is necessary to train and compete on the world stage. Halson et al. (2006) described a 26-year-old female alpine skier with 5 years of international racing experience in the super giant slalom and downhill events who displayed an exceptional ability to produce power during a cycle ergometer 30-second sprint and was subsequently identified as one of 26 women with the potential to excel in the track cycling 500-m time trial event. Her previous sporting experience was evidently an advantage within her new sport.

Similarly, Bullock et al.'s (2009) study of talent identification in skeleton offered a unique opportunity to target existing high performance athletes to transfer into this sport. The ability to utilize existing high performance athletes' skills and competition experience gave them the capacity to exploit talent gaps at the World Cup level by possibly compressing the development time frame of these athletes. All 10 athletes chosen for this programme had achieved at least state-level representation in their previous sport and as a result, had already experienced training at high intensities and competing under intense pressure, which assisted them in coping with the new sporting environment.

Likewise, Hoare and Warr (2000) targeted 15- to 19-year-olds with a background in team ball sports or athletics to develop potential female soccer players. The authors decided to target athletes who had achieved success at a competitive level in a previous sport, based on the premise that athletes would have some existing attributes (a positive training ethic, as well as being competitive and athletic, amongst others) that may contribute to success in soccer. As such, they would be 'ready-made' athletes and attention could be focused on training them in the technical and tactical aspects of soccer (Hoare & Warr, 2000).

The three studies described above highlight the benefits of identifying athletes who already have a sporting background, especially for sporting bodies who can then justify the 'recycling of athletes' due to maximizing return on investments and resources that have been made over a number of years in the athletes' earlier sport. However few researchers have examined whether or how athletes transfer previous sporting experience to facilitate performance and adapt to a novel set of circumstances (Smeeton, Ward, & Williams, 2004). The study of talent transfer provides an interesting insight into those factors that enable skilled athletes to apply their existing knowledge to new experiences.

Age

Hand in hand with previous sporting experience is the age of an athlete when undertaking the talent transfer process. Bullock et al.'s (2009) findings support aggressive talent identification and talent transfer approaches that identified successful senior athletes aged 22.2 + 5.1 years. In support of this accelerated talent transfer approach, an Australian Sports Commission (2012) study revealed that of 256 athletes in the national or state institute system who transferred to a new sport, 72 (28%) represented Australia in their new sport in less than 4 years (Australian Sports Commission, 2012). These quick developers started the sport at which they attained senior national status at an age of 17.1 + 4.5 years, and on average had participated in three sports beforehand (Oldenziel, Gagné, & Gulbin, 2004). Rea and Lavallee (2015) also identified the age range of the athletes in their study as between 19 and 36 years and Collins et al. (2014) identified that 48.4% of transfers within their study occurred between the ages of 16 and 21, which they claimed could indicate an ideal bracket from which to recruit. Therefore, the less obvious, but notable benefit of talent transfer highlighted by these studies is the minimized adolescent maturational issues associated with talent development, as well as the athletes' previous sporting experience (as identified above). Conversely, a limitation of this late selection is that the number of athletes to draw from is also very small, which may limit the overall breadth of talent.

Physiological and psychological requirements/protocols

In the UK, there seem to be several sport science disciplines involved in talent transfer, with skill acquisition/motor control and physiology the most prevalent (UK Sport Talent Team, 2013). Formal initiatives use the systematic selection of athletes based on defined protocols (MacNamara & Collins, 2015). Typically, talent transfer initiatives screen a large number of athletes based on performance (athletic background and sporting history) variables before inviting selected athletes to a testing day where they complete a number of physiological and performance tests. For example, UK Sport's Power2Podium: Skeleton, was aimed at males and females aged 17–25 who were competing in any sport at a regional standard. Unlike UK Sport's (2016) Tall and Talented campaign, which specifically asked for minimum height requirements, Power2Podium: Skeleton advertised questions such as 'fast, powerful and strong?' as well as 'competitive and mentally tough?' to entice large numbers of athletes to apply. Using this approach, a number of physiological and psychological assessment methods may be utilized by sporting agencies to 'sift through' the scores of athletes applying. The specifics of how this is done, however, is still unclear and does not follow consistent criteria (at least none that have been made publicly known).

An example of this is Bullock et al.'s (2009) study where 26 athletes were recruited to a skeleton programme based on a variety of physical aptitude tests (30-m sprint), sport-specific skill assessments (similar sled push and loading ability: the lower body power traits) and subjective evaluations (being a team player: how the athletes interacted with fellow competitors during the camp). During the 7-month selection process, the hopefuls were whittled down to 4 athletes to make the national team. The use of 30-m sprint time as a primary selection characteristic may have initially acted as a 'filtering mechanism' to select 'already fast' athletes, but other factors – creative thinking, decision making, attention, self-confidence, motor skills and coach interaction (Williams & Reilly, 2000) were also considered for talent identification/selection. This suggests that the selection of appropriate talent should involve a multi-dimensional approach involving more than just physical performance (Abbot & Collins, 2004; Nieuwenhuis, Spamer & Van Rossum, 2002; Reilly, Williams, Nevill, & Franks, 2000; Staerck, 2003).

The challenge that sporting agencies have across the globe is that they are unwilling to share the assessment methods/protocol used within talent identification initiatives in case it gives another country or federation an advantage. As a result, there is no agreed definition nor model that could help sporting bodies follow a consistent framework. It is only through studies like Bullock et al. (2009) and Hoare and Warr (2000) that researchers are able to read and share information about the process.

Consequently, sports scientists will have an opinion on the fluctuating protocols that sports scientists and governing bodies decide to utilize for the testing phase(s) of a talent transfer (e.g., Collins et al., 2014). The assessments can be critiqued as there is no universal agreement. MacNamara and Collins (2015) identified a number of limitations with the initial screening and selection process. They claimed that psychosocial variables (such as resilience and coachability, amongst others) that are more challenging to identify/assess, should be an integral part of the initial section process. Van Yperen (2009) and Abbott and Collins (2004) both reasoned that talent transfer initiatives should consider whether potential transferees have the psycho-behavioural skills needed to successfully develop in the transfer environment. Abbot, Button, Pepping and Collins (2005) argued that initial screening of athletes typically does not account for these (psychosocial) process markers. Nevertheless, Morgan (1979) and Orlick and

Partington (1988) suggest psychological variables are a significant predictor of success (among a range of other physical and technical variables) and therefore should be a mandatory requirement in talent identification. Additionally, Vaeyans, Lenoir, Williams, and Philippaerts (2008) contended that as talent transfer programmes target athletes increasing in age, the population of successful athletes becomes more homogenous with respect to their physical and physiological profiles. Perhaps this should/could also be the case for psychological profiles where sports scientists know which traits to assess when selecting athletes. For instance, determination and commitment as described in Collins et al. (2014) study. British Shooting's Target Tokyo (UK Sport, 2020) campaign, in collaboration with UK Sport and the English Institute of Sport, saw shooters assessed on factors including their performance, commitment, motivation, coachability, learnability, skill acquisition and concentration (British Shooting, 2014). Similarly, the New Zealand Institute of Sport solicited athletes who were intrinsically motivated, had a strong work ethic, were passionate about succeeding and enjoyed competition, as well as being coachable, that is, prepared to listen to advice and try new skills (amongst other physiological requirements). UK Sport and the New Zealand Institute of Sport (amongst others), may have identified a talent confirmation phase that incorporates these psychological factors from the outset, even if the assessment is just qualitative in nature.

MacNamara and Collins (2015) noted that another limitation with the process of screening and selection is the combination of factors that demonstrably underpin the successful transfer, with 'success' defined as competing at World/Olympic level within their donor sport. Examples of gymnasts transferring to diving or even aerial skiing are obvious – Alisa Camplin and Lydia Lassila are two Australian gymnasts who successfully transferred to become Olympic aerial skiing gold medallists. However, as Rea and Lavallee (2015) identified, athletes do not always come from sports that are so clearly related; one of the athletes in their study was a club-level rugby player who, within four years of transferring to canoeing, went to the London 2012 Olympics. From the athlete's perspective, there was little (or no) obvious underlying rationale for a successful transfer in terms of physiological or anthropometrics, apart from height. The athlete was considered the 'dregs' of the Tall and Talented Rowing initiative and did not meet the criteria because at nearly 6'4" he was an inch too short of the 6'5" requirements (personal correspondence). Instead, they directed him to canoeing. Collins et al. (2014) also found that several successful transfer athletes lacked an obvious explanation from either a motor control or physiology perspective. Collins et al. (2014) suggested that they would not have been elected/recruited if the physiological standards currently in use had been applied to them. Rea and Lavallee (2015) identified that this athlete had other attributes that would have made him successful at rowing as much as canoeing, which raises the question regarding how many other athletes miss out on opportunities because of strict physical requirements?

Collins (2011: cited in Collins & MacNamara, 2012) argued that a large number of potentially talented performers may have been excluded from talent identification and transfer programmes due to poor identification measures. For example, high-profile athletes may not necessarily fail performance evaluation tests but there may have been (at the time) athletes who were marginally better but (they) could perhaps still achieve the criteria to secure selection for a talent transfer programme. Phillips, Davids, Renshaw, and Portus (2010) agreed that there is a large number of performers who are unsuccessful in transfer, or de-selected during identification, because of 'snapshot' approaches, on a small number of factors. MacNamara and Collins (2015) contend that identifying talent as a one-off anthropometric, physiological and performance snapshot (which most formal talent transfer programmes assess) means that some athletes may be overlooked who, at the time of testing, may not meet the prescribed standards, or predetermined profiles, but who may have the potential to develop in the future.

Thus, MacNamara and Collins (2015) argue that an exploration of the range of factors athletes perceive to support talent transfer would seem a logical step in providing an evidence base for applied initiatives or even improving their design and efficiency. Abbott and Collins (2004) state that in order to predict future accomplishments successfully, it is necessary to identify which characteristics indicate that an individual has the potential to develop in sport and become a successful senior athlete.

An integral element of talent transfer is that excellence in a sport is not idiosyncratic to a standard set of skills or physical attributes; it can be achieved in individual or unique ways through different combinations of skills, attributes and capacities (Feldman, 1986). In this manner, Gagné (1999) maintains that talent is understood to emerge from complex and unique choreographies between different groups of causal influences. Thus, there is clearly not a single genetic endowment underlying a talent domain, with neither talented nor untalented individuals emerging from genetically homogenous groups (Simonton, 2001).

Physiological and psychological requirements/protocols: Team sports

For a team-based approach to talent identification, Hoare and Warr (2000) used a quasi-applied research model based on anthropometric, physiological and skill attributes. Utilizing objective assessment methods that measure tactical and technical competence enables researchers to develop and validate testing protocols that would support the transfer of athletes into team sports.

Hoare and Warr (2000) acknowledged that it has not yet been possible to develop objective and ecologically valid tests of psychological determinants, unlike that of anthropometric and physiological characteristics. Similarly, there is considerable evidence of the importance of perceptual-cognitive attributes in successful players (McMorris & Beazeley, 1997; Williams & Davids, 1998), but little understanding of how to use these as part of the identification process.

Moreover, there are additional challenges using team-based assessment protocols. Vaeyans et al. (2008) noted that unlike sports where the majority of variance in performance may be accounted for by a relatively small number of characteristics, these approaches have proven problematic in the majority of fast-ball sports and team ball games. Thus, talent identification initiatives have previously focused on sports that are individual, repetitive and/or where success has been related to specific anthropometric and physiological attributes (such as cycling, rowing and skeleton).

There is acknowledgement within the research community (e.g., Hoare & Warr, 2000) that limited attempts have been made to embark on talent identification programmes with team sports because of the difficulty in quantifying a suitable amount of variance in performance. Research that has been published is still largely focused on anthropometric and physical performance characteristics (for example, Mohamed et al., 2009 – handball) despite acknowledgements that determinants of success are multifactorial (Hugg, 1994; Hoare, 2000).

With the lack of a holistic perspective (incorporating physiological and psychological determinants) to identifying talent, Pinder, Renshaw, and Davids (2013) argue that caution should be taken in emphasizing some sub-disciplines over others. Attempts to target isolated psychological characteristics in talent identification programmes have led to psychologists repeating the same errors as their physiology counterparts (e.g., Weissensteiner, Abernethy, Farrow & Gross, 2012). This issue is only exacerbated by the adoption of mono-disciplinary approaches to sport science support work and strengthens the need for a multidisciplinary and holistic approach (Renshaw, Oldham, Glazier and Davids, 2004).

Deliberate programming

Researchers continue to debate the elements essential for developing expertise (e.g., Baker & Davids, 2006; Tucker & Collins, 2012). However, most agree that expert-level performance is not possible without a long-term commitment to training and practice (e.g., Baker & Young, 2014; Starkes, 2000). This suggests it would be impossible for an athlete with less accumulated practice in a particular sport to fast-track or to perform at, or above the level of, individuals who started sport-specific deliberate practice earlier and maintained maximal levels of deliberate practice.

Bullock et al. (2009) use the definition of 'deliberate programming' (rather than deliberate practice as proposed by Ericsson, Krampe, & Tesch-Römer, 1993) to encompass other planned factors in addition to practice such as high-quality strategic planning, access to quality coaching, equipment, the best possible (and many) competitions, and technical, financial and sport science and medicine support to ensure athletes fulfil their potential. Using a deliberate programming model, their investigation explored the minimum exposure required for a novice selection athlete to reach an Olympic standard through intensified sport-specific training.

This supports the notion that adaptability and training experiences accumulated in many sports (within skeleton it was an accumulation of at least 15 years sporting experience in an array of sports) may be an alternative pathway to expertise (Baker, 2007; Coleman, 2007; Runco, 2007). The concept of talent transfer and the aim of achieving excellence through late specialization and rapid development requires further exploration in relation to Bullock et al.'s (2009) definition of deliberate programming. In support of this concept is Canadian Clara Hughes, who won multiple medals in both speed skating and cycling, at the summer (1996, 2000, 2012) and winter (2002, 2006, 2010) Olympics. Evidently, the accumulation of hours training in both sports worked in Hughes' favour as she continued to train and compete in both sports over a number of years.

Competition

As noted above in Bullock et al.'s (2009) study on skeleton, competition appears to be an important element of deliberate programming to ensure athletes fulfil their potential. The developmental time frame was short (14 months) and exposed athletes to competition within two weeks of starting the sport with four athletes competing against senior elite athletes (World Cup) within one sliding season (Bullock et al., 2009). However while deliberate practice theory does not support the value of competition for becoming an expert (Ericsson et al., 1993), Bullock et al. (2009) emphasized competition as an essential element for athlete development to enhance the ability to perform at the highest level.

Within two competitive seasons of deliberate practice, their athletes achieved top six rankings in World Cups and one individual competed at an Olympic Games, which suggests that fast-tracking and surpassing more experienced competitors is achievable with late specialization (Bullock et al., 2009). Others have similarly emphasized the importance of competition (e.g., Baker, Côté & Abernethy, 2003). In particular, Starkes (2007) noted that a component of expertise is the athlete's ability to reliably perform the skill in a competitive setting, rather than excelling as a 'practice player'.

Support services

This chapter has largely focused on formal talent identification programmes but there is little documentation stating the specific detail of support services (i.e., physiotherapy, strength and conditioning, nutrition, psychology, performance lifestyle) given to the athletes to help them succeed with the transfer to another sport. These would include World-class coaching and sports science and medicine support as part of a carefully planned training and competition programme, with the major goal of achieving selection and success for upcoming competitions. Rea and Lavallee (2015) identified that support services was one of three factors that athletes perceived as important for a successful transfer, including services such as (World-class) coaching and sports medicine as well as informal support mechanisms such as family, friends and partners.

Collins et al. (2014) also suggested that 'educated coaches' who have experience and understanding of the challenges faced by talent transfer athletes are an important element of the process. In Rea and Lavallee's (2016) study of one athletes' subjective experiences of a talent transfer process, access to high-quality coaching appeared to be an integral component in maximizing athlete development as well as the right environment to train and compete in to accelerate learning. In support of this, Bullock et al. (2009) acknowledged that a supportive and aggressive, but time-limited, learning environment was needed. Additionally this would be led primarily by a world-class coach with previous Olympic medal success who knew what it would take for a high performance programme to succeed. The athletes also had access to a team of sport scientists and practitioners on a daily basis to ensure an optimal daily training environment. These two combined factors (environment and coach) were needed to minimize mistakes and condense the time associated with the talent transfer process (Bullock et al., 2009).

Limitations

It has previously been suggested that talent transfer programmes are likely to be more successful in sports where the standard and international depth of competition is lower than in other sports (Baker, 2003; Hoare, 2000) and skeleton has been identified to be in this position (Bullock et al., 2009). For the United Kingdom (23.1%) and Australia (26.5%), the number of talent transfer athletes in their Winter Olympic squad (for Vancouver, 2010) suggests either that winter sports are more effective programmes to target (Collins et al., 2014) or that these countries were able to transfer athletes into sports where the talent pool is less competitive (MacNamara & Collins, 2011). As talent transfer initiatives expand and develop, the opportunities for continued growth could regress in terms of limited opportunities for individuals to compete at the highest level. For example, in skeleton a total quota of 50 athletes (30 for men and 20 for women) can compete at an Olympic Games based on World rankings. In contrast, with the International Olympic Committee limiting the number of events a cyclist can compete in (each nation is limited to one athlete per individual event: *The Guardian*, 2012), there could be fewer opportunities to develop athletes at the highest level as they simply cannot be selected based on availability of athletes per country, and sporting bodies cannot justify the investment.

Russell (1989) stated that the primary aim of talent identification is to recognize current participants with the greatest potential to excel in a particular sport. Within talent transfer programmes, targeting 'experienced' athletes to concentrate their efforts in a new sport, within a limited time period (perhaps to target an impending 'Games') means pursuing sports that are closed rather than open. As discussed above, the prediction of success is likely to be easier in more closed sports (rather than invasion games) because the movements are less affected by the environment and fewer components are likely to impact performance (Vaeyans et al., 2008). These constraints would likely explain why sporting agencies have invested more resources in talent identification models within sports such as cycling, rowing, canoeing, weightlifting and skeleton (Abbott, Collins, & Martindale, 2002).

However, countries like the UK have expanded talent transfer initiatives into more open sports for the 2016 Olympic Games in Rio, for example handball, boxing, and volleyball. The criteria on assessing physiological requirements needed for open sports is more challenging. Collins et al. (2014) expressed concern for the transition some athletes might have to make when joining a highly skilled sport, stating that 'the complexity faced by a player, a team games player, is so substantial that they need experience of that and the training in that' (p. 1627). The full effect of these newly targeted transfer programmes (e.g., UK Sport) have yet to be established for open/team sports. If a framework was created based on the length of time needed to 'upskill' an athlete in the technical requirements, there may be more opportunities of successful transfers between sports.

Conclusion

There is a significant lack of literature within sport exploring the best way to support athletes through the process of talent transfer. As there is no agreed-upon definition or theoretical framework of talent transfer, it is difficult to establish a baseline to evaluate and build our knowledge of what a successful talent transfer process might look like. Therefore it is difficult to inform and educate national governing bodies, coaches or individuals so that they can undertake this process for themselves. Until such a framework is constructed, researchers are left with independent findings from studies require replication and extension. As can be determined from the limited studies and references used within this chapter, our current understanding of talent transfer and its value for athlete development is limited.

Nevertheless, this chapter has noted several considerations for an athlete, or sporting body, wanting to undertake a talent transfer process including: (a) the influence of previous sporting experience, athlete age and support services; (b) similarities between donor and transfer sports; and (c) the value of deliberate programming and involvement in competition. While such proactive talent identification systems may never take over as the sole process of athlete recruitment, they offer an additional avenue of athlete recruitment in support of existing programmes and procedures.

References

Abbott, A., Button, C., Pepping, G-J., & Collins, D. (2005). Unnatural selection: Talent identification and development in sport. *Nonlinear Dynamics, Psychology and Life Sciences, 9*(1), 61–88.

Abbott, A., & Collins, D. (2004). Eliminating the dichotomy between theory and practice in talent identification and development: Considering the role of psychology. *Journal of Sports Sciences, 22*(5), 395–408.

Abbots, A., Collins, D., & Martindale, R. (2002). *Talent identification and development: An academic review.* Edinburgh: University of Edinburgh.

Australian Sports Commission (2012). News. Available at: www.clearinghouseforsport.gov.au/knowledge_base/high_performance_sport/athlete_pathways_and_development/athlete_talent_identification_and_talent_transfer

Baker, J. (2003). Early specialization in youth sport: A requirement for adult expertise? *High Ability Studies, 14*, 85–94.

Baker, J. (2007). Nature and nurture interact to create expert performers. *High Ability Studies, 18*, 57–58.

Baker, J., Côté, J., & Abernethy, B. (2003). Learning from the experts: Practice activities of expert decision-makers in sport. *Research Quarterly for Exercise and Sport, 74*, 342–347.

Baker, J., & Davids, K. (2006). Genetic and environmental constraints on variability in sport performance. In K. Davids, S. J. Bennett, & K. M. Newell (eds), *Movement system variability* (pp. 109–129). Champaign, IL: Human Kinetics.

Baker, J., & Horton, S. (2004). A review of primary and secondary influences on sport expertise. *High Ability Studies, 15*, 211–228.

British Shooting website (2014). Targeted talent. Available at http://britishshooting.org.uk/news/d=985 (Accessed: January 6, 2016).

Bullock, N., Gulbin, J. P., Martin, D. T., Ross, A., Holland, T., & Marino, F. (2009). Talent identification and deliberate programming in skeleton: Ice novice to winter Olympian in 14 months. *Journal of Sport Sciences, 27*(40), 397–404.

Coleman, L. J. (2007). Parts do not make a whole: Lumping expertise into one whole. *High Ability Studies, 18,* 63–64.

Collins, R., Collins, D., MacNamara, Á., & Jones, M. I. (2014). Change of plans: an evaluation of the effectiveness and underlying mechanisms of successful talent transfer. *Journal of Sports Sciences, 32*(17), 1621–1630.

Collins, D., & MacNamara, Á. (2012). The rocky road to the top: Why talent needs trauma. *Sports Medicine, 4*(11), 1–8.

Ericsson, K. A., Krampe, R. T., & Tesch-Römer, C. (1993). The role of deliberate practice in the acquisition of expert performance. *Psychological Review, 100,* 363–406.

Gagné. F. (1999). Nature or nurture? A re-examination of Sloboda and Howe's (1991) interview study on talent development in music. *Psychology of Music, 27,* 38–51.

Gulbin, J. P., & Ackland, T. (2009). Talent identification and profiling. In T. R. Ackland, B. C. Elliott, & J. Bloomfield (eds), Applied Anatomy and Biomechanics in Sport. (pp. 11–26). Champaign, IL: Human Kinetics.

Halson, S. L., Martin, D. T., Gardner, A. S., Fallon, K., & Gulbin, J. (2006). Persistent fatigue in a female sprint cyclist after a talent-transfer initiative. *International Journal of Sport Physiology and Performance, 1,* 65–69.

High Performance Sport New Zealand (2013). Talent Transfer. Available at: http://hpsnz.org.nz/athlete-transfer (Accessed: January 6, 2016).

Hoare, D. (2000). Predicting success in junior elite basketball players – the contribution of anthropometric and physiological attributes. *Journal of Science and Medicine in Sport, 3*(4), 391–405.

Hoare, D. G., & Warr, C. R. (2000). Talent identification and women's soccer: An Australian experience. *Journal of Sports Sciences, 18,* 751–758.

Hogan, K., & Norton, K. (2000). The price of Olympic gold. *Journal of Science and Medicine in Sport, 2,* 203–218.

Hugg, P. J. (1994). The selection of Australian youth soccer players based on physical and physiological characteristics. Unpublished master's thesis, University of Canberra.

Lavallee, D., & Wylleman, P. (2000). *Career transitions in sport: International perspectives.* Morgantown WV: Fitness Information Technology.

MacNamara, Á., & Collins, D. (2011). Development and initial validation of the psychological characteristics of developing excellence questionnaire. *Journal of Sport Sciences, 29,* 1273–1286. doi:10.1080/02640414.2011.589468

MacNamara, Á., & Collins, D. (2015). Second chances: Investigating athletes' experiences of talent transfer. *PLoS ONE 10* (11): e0143592. Doi:10.1371/journal.pone.0143592.

McMorris, T., & Beazeley, A. (1997). Performance of experienced and inexperienced soccer players on soccer specific tests of recall, visual search and decision making. *Journal of Human Movement Studies, 33,* 1–13.

Mohamed, H., Vaeyens, R., Matthys, S., Multael, M., Lefevre, J., Lenoir, M., & Philippaerts, R. (2009). Anthropometric and performance measures for the development of a talent detection and identification model in youth handball. *Journal of Sports Sciences, 27*(3), 257–266.

Morgan, W. P. (1979). Prediction of performance in athletics. In P. Klavora & J. V. Daniel (eds), *Coach, athlete and the sport psychologist* (pp. 173–186). Toronto: University of Toronto Press.

Nieuwenhuis, C. F., Spamer, E. J., & Van Rossum, J. H. A. (2002). Prediction function for identifying talent in 14–15 year old female field hockey players. *High Ability Studies, 13*(1), 21–33.

Oldenziel, K., Gagné, F., & Gulbin, J. (2004). Factors affecting the rate of athlete development from novice to senior elite: how applicable is the 10-year rule? Paper presented at the Athens 2004 Pre-Olympic Congress. Available at: www.cev.org.br/biblioteca/preolymp/download/ O.027.doc (05-20-2008).

Orlick, T., & Partington, J. (1988). Mental links to excellence. *The Sport Psychologist, 2,* 105–130.

Phillips, E., Davids, K., Renshaw, I., & Portus, M. (2010). Expert performance in sport and the dynamics of talent development. *Sports Medicine, 40*(4), 271–283.

Pinder, R. A., Renshaw, I., & Davids, K. (2013). The role of representative design in talent development: A comment on 'Talent identification and promotion programmes of Olympics athletes'. *Journal of Sports Sciences, 31*(8), 803–806.

Rea, T., & Lavallee, D. (2015). An examination of athletes' experiences of the talent transfer process. *Talent Development and Excellence, 7*(1), 41–67.

Rea, T., & Lavallee, D. (2016). *The subjective experience of a talent transfer athlete.* Manuscript submitted for publication.

Reilly, T., Williams, A. M., Nevill, A., & Franks, A. (2000). A multidisciplinary approach to talent identification in soccer. *Journal of Sport Science, 18*(9), 695–702.

Renshaw, I., Oldham, T., Glazier, P., & Davids, K. (2004). Around the world: Why applied sports scientists need a theoretical model of the performer. *The Sport and Exercise Scientist, 1,* 24.

Runco, M. (2007). Achievement sometimes requires creativity. *High Ability Studies, 18,* 75–77.

Russell, K. (1989). Athletic talent: From detection to perfection. *Scientific Periodical on Research and Technology in Sport, 9*(1), 1–6.

Simonton, D. K. (2001). Talent development as a multidimensional, multiplicative, and dynamic process. *Current Directions in Psychological Science, 10,* 39–43.

Smeeton, N. J., Ward, P., & Williams, M. (2004). Do pattern recognition skills transfer across sports? A preliminary analysis. *Journal of Sports Sciences, 22,* 205–213.

Sporting Giants (2010). Sporting giant's initiative. Available at: www.uksport.gov.uk/pages/sportinggiants (Accessed: January 6, 2016).

Staerck, A. (2003). The anthropometric and physical requirements of women's hammer throwing: The implications for talent identification. *Journal of Sports Science, 21*(4), 305–306.

Starkes, J. L. (2000). The road to expertise: Is practice the only determinant? *International Journal of Sport Psychology, 31,* 431–451.

Starkes, J. L. (2007). Plus ça change, plus c'est la même chose. *International Journal of Sports Psychology, 38,* 89–95.

Tall and Talented (2012). Tall and talent initiative. Available at: http://uksport.gov.uk/pages/talent-2016-tall-and-talented/ (Accessed: January 6, 2016).

The Guardian (2012). London 2012 rule changes likely to restrict GB cyclists' medal haul. Available at: www.theguardian.com/sport/blog/2012/feb/14/london-2012-rule-changes-cyclists (Accessed: January 6, 2016).

Tucker, R., & Collins, M. (2012). What makes champions? A review of the relative contribution of genes and training to sporting success. *British Journal of Sports Medicine, 46,* 555–561.

UK Sport Talent Team (2013). Frontline solutions. Available at: www.uksport.gov.uk/pages/frontline-solutions/ (Accessed: January 6, 2016).

UK Sport (2016). Previous campaigns: Tall and Talented. Available at: www.uksport.gov.uk/our-work/talent-id/previous-campaigns (Accessed: January 6, 2016).

UK Sport (2020). Target Tokyo. Available at www.uksport.gov.uk/news/2014/07/17/british-shooting-targeting-tokyo-with-new-talent-id-campaign (Accessed: January 6, 2016).

Vaeyans, R., Güllich, A., Warr, C., & Phillippaerts, R. (2009). Talent identification and promotion programmes of Olympic athletes. *Journal of Sports Sciences, 27*(13), 1367–1380.

Vaeyans, R., Lenoir, M., Williams, A. M., & Philippaerts, R. M. (2008). Talent identification and development programmes in sport: Current models and future predictions. *Sports Medicine, 38*(9), 703–714.

Van Yperen, N. W. (2009). Why some make it and others do not: Identifying psychological factors that predict career successes in professional adult soccer. *The Sport Psychologist, 23,* 317–329.

Weissensteiner, J. R, Abernethy, B., Farrow, D., & Gross, R. (2012). Distinguishing psychological characteristics of expert cricket batsmen. *Journal of Science and Medicine in Sport, 15*(1), 74–79.

Williams, A. M., & Davids, K. (1998). Visual search strategy, selective attention, and expertise in soccer. *Research Quarterly for Exercise and Sport, 69,* 111–128.

Williams, A. M., & Reilly, T. (2000). Talent identification and development in soccer. *Journal of Sports Sciences, 18,* 657–667.

33

TALENT POLICIES

Eivind Åsrum Skille, Cecilia Stenling and Josef Fahlén

What is government (sport) policy and how is it connected to talent selection and development?

During the past decades, sport as a policy domain has emerged on government agendas in a wide range of countries, including: *United Kingdom* (UK) (Coalter, 2007; Green, 2007a; Houlihan, 2005), *Switzerland* (Chappelet, 2010), *Spain* (Puig, Martinez, & Garcia, 2010), *the Netherlands* (Waardenburg, & van Bottenburg, 2013), *Norway* (Skille, 2009), *Sweden* (Fahlén & Stenling, 2015), *Venezuela* (López de D'Amico, 2012), *Japan* (Yamamoto, 2012), *Iran* (Dousti, Goodarzi, Asadi, & Khabiri, 2013), *New Zealand* (Sam, 2009), and *Australia* (Hoye & Nicholson, 2009). Recently, elite sport, elite *youth* sport, and talent policies have become key policy priorities for both governments and non-governmental organizations (Skille & Houlihan, 2014). But, what is talent policy? Our aim in this chapter is to develop some answers to this question. Many definitions of 'policy' centre on the state. Hill (1997), for example, defines policy as 'the product of the exercise of political influence, determining what the State does and setting limits to what it does' (p. 41). Thus, policy refers to both process ('exercise of political influence') and outcome ('the product of the exercise').[1] However, the state is not necessarily one unity where everybody agrees, as there may be many views across state politicians or bureaucrats (Houlihan, 1997). Moreover, the state is not the only actor within a policy field (Sabatier & Jenkins-Smith, 1999). This is particularly the case in the sport policy field where non-governmental sport organizations both have a stake in the making of government sport policy and formulate their own policies, including those pertaining to talent identification and development. These policies may be more or less in line with those outlined by the government (Fahlén & Sjöblom, 2012). In that sense, the *Oxford Thesaurus of English*'s definition of policy as a 'course or principle of action adopted or proposed by organization'[2] refers to policy as a principle of action set out by any type of organization, not solely governments.

Sport is a complex and contested policy domain consisting of different interests and stakeholders (Houlihan, 2001; Skille, 2010). A definition that covers this complexity is provided by Jenkins (1997). He views policy as a set of interrelated 'decisions taken by a political actor or group of actors concerning the selection of goals and the means of achieving them within a specified situation where these decisions should … be within the power of these actors to achieve' (p. 30). Here, several elements are identified: Decisions are interrelated (Green & Houlihan, 2005); decisions concern both means and ends (tools and objectives); 'the reference to 'political actors' signals issues of power' (Green & Houlihan, 2005, p. 12); and the actors (decision-maker) believe it is possible to achieve the defined goal. All of these elements reflect the complexity of the sport policy context of which talent policy is a part. The complexity increases with the fact that in addition to having a stake in the *making* of sport policy, non-governmental sport organizations such as National Olympic Committees, National Sport Confederations, National Sport Federations, and sport clubs, simultaneously play a prominent role as *implementers* of (government) sport policy. In some national contexts, as shown below, such organizations may be the sole implementers. Given that these organizations may not share the objective of government sport policy and that they exhibit a mutual variation in characteristics, a classic definition of policy implementation as a top-down, rational process (van Meter and van Horn, 1975) has little analytical value when it comes to sport policy implementation (Skille, 2008; Stenling, 2014a; Stenling & Fahlén, 2014). The issues and tensions related to the distinction between policy making and policy implementation and the relationship between the state and sport organizations will be important themes throughout this chapter.

With Jenkins' (1997) definition as a point of departure for understanding talent policy, we treat the question (what is talent policy?) by organizing the chapter as follows. We first discuss the rise of elite sport and talent development on the public policy agenda. Second, we describe how the institutional arrangements for talent policies vary across countries and regimes; including policy-making and makers, as well as how the administrative and financial structures for talent policies are set up. Third, we discuss how structural differences, combined with the cultural elements of the regimes, lead to an array of implications for working with talent policies. We conclude the chapter by returning to an overall question referring to Chapters 2 and 3 of this book (which provide different answers to the question: does talent exist?), and discuss whether talent policy exists.

The rise of talent identification and development on the government agenda

As initially mentioned, the past decades have witnessed a rise of sport on government agendas worldwide. Analogous to trends of deregulation, contracting-out and privatization, visible in many other societal domains (e.g., school, railway, television and radio broadcasting, postal service, telecom market), sport has increased its attraction among policy makers as a cost-efficient means for political reforms (Fahlén, Wickman, & Eliasson, 2014). This development has been fuelled by the increasing belief in sport as an instrument to achieve a wide array of societal objectives such as (immigrant and) social integration (Stenling, 2014b; Fahlén, 2015; Skille, 2009), public health (Aggestål & Fahlén, 2015; Skille, 2010), and social capital (Coalter, 2007). Two points should be emphasized from this development. First, the vast majority of the literature on 'sport as social good' shows that social policy goals are difficult or impossible to reach when sport is being used as a tool (e.g., Coalter, 2007). One reason is that implementers (sport organizations) do not necessarily share the goals set up by policy makers (public authorities). Second, and somewhat at odds with the first point, elite sport policy stands out as a policy domain where policy makers and implementers actually share the overall values, namely sport performance.[3]

Thus, with the exception of a few countries (e.g., Sweden and Norway where sport including elite sport, belongs to the voluntary sector, Fahlén & Stenling, 2015; Skille & Säfvenbom, 2011), international elite sport success has become *the* government sport policy priority (e.g., Green & Houlihan, 2011; Henry, Amara, Al-Tauqi, & Lee, 2005; Houlihan & Zheng, 2013). This development has been described as 'a global sporting arms race' (Bloyce & Smith, 2010;

De Bosscher, Bingham, Shibli, van Bottenburg & De Knop, 2008; Houlihan, 2001) denoting nations' struggle to improve their position on medal rankings in international championships. Scholars (Green & Oakley, 2001) have traced the origin of the global arms race to the 'soviet model' that was established during the interwar period and further developed and refined during 1970–1990 by the satellite states in the former Eastern bloc. East Germany is highlighted as the most distinct and successful example, at least in terms of the number of medals won at international championships (Green & Oakley, 2001). The East German dominance between 1952 and 1988 was nearly total. In the literature, this dominance is explained with reference to the elevated position of sport in that particular society, with sport being used as an instrument for claiming ideological superiority. Sport, in both voluntary sport clubs and the school system, was heavily regulated, which provided opportunities for systematic identification, testing and training of young talents. Identification was, in turn, heavily selective and connected to the cultural anchorage and popularity of each sport as well as based on the assessed potential to win medals. The latter was, and still is, calculated by comparing the international competition: the weaker the competition – the more reason to invest in that particular sport (Green & Oakley, 2001). In order to avail for further refinement of their qualities, living expenses were furnished by the state, which allowed the athlete to direct all focus at their sporting development. A dedicated focus at reaching the highest international levels simultaneously created room and need for trained coaches and teachers. This, in turn, entailed a rapid and widespread extension of vocational training programmes, a professionalization of the talent development trade (Houlihan, 2001).

At the time, these were all considered extraordinary measures. However, with the gradual professionalization and commercialization of sport, which followed on new ideological currents of the 1970s and 1980s, investments in elite sport and talent development also increased in the Western democracies (Green, 2007b). With increasing investments, there followed increased success; at least that is the popular explanation which, in turn, spurred processes of standardization and globalization spreading the intensification of elite sport investments and talent development ventures worldwide (Green, 2005; Green & Houlihan, 2011). Since then, the range of the extended sport policy and elite sport ventures have varied over time, and between the countries engaging in the arms race. However, the purpose and direction of them have been similar: identifying young talents, providing them with optimal resources for development, in order to win international competitions. In that sense, the elite sport policies and talent development systems of today, in the countries taking part in 'the global sporting arms race', are copies of the talent identification and development model that emerged during the glory days of the Soviet Union and Eastern bloc countries (Green & Oakley, 2001).[4] This process has, in turn, led to a homogenization of national elite sport systems since most nations, in more or less deliberate manners, tend to copy each other's recipes for success (De Bosscher, De Knop & van Bottenburg, 2009). Differences between them, when observable, are explained with references to each nation's specific history, socio-economic conditions and cultural profile (Henry et al., 2005; Houlihan, 2009; Houlihan & Green, 2008). Examples of such differences are the integration of sport in schools in many English-speaking countries (UK, USA, NZ), the tougher selections made in countries with large populations (Russia and China in technical, power demanding and endurance sports; USA in for example track and field; South American and South European countries in football/soccer), and the focus on sports with few technological prerequisites in some developing countries (typically running in African countries).

Parallel with an increased government interest for elite sport policy, there has been an increased academic interest. In terms of talent development policy, the common denominators observed in the so called SPLISS-studies (Sport Policy factors Leading to International Sporting Success, De Bosscher, De Knop, van Bottenburg & Shibli, 2006) are: government funded financial support to selected sports and athletes, 'especially those that are less "attractive" to the commercial market and the media' (p. 201); long-term investments; an instrumental approach to talent selection; well developed and structured educational systems for coaches; and, large financial investments. Generally speaking, the most successful nations spend the most resources, have the largest populations and the highest GDP per capita. Their larger populations allow them to be stricter in their talent selections, to send more participants to championships and to host more championships that tend to give them a so-called 'home advantage' due to increased investments made prior to, for example, a World Championship or the Olympic Games. Population size and GDP are the two most important explanatory factors for success, it is argued, and they account for 50 per cent of the medal tables at international events. Talent identification and talent development systems, support to coaches and cooperation with the research community, on the other hand, are identified as the most neglected development areas, thus the ones with the most potential for development in order to gain competitive advantages.

The incorporation of talent identification and development in the government machinery

Reflecting governments' low priority of sport in the past, sport policy issues have historically either been located within government departments whose responsibility is much broader than sport, such as departments of education or defence, or non-existent – or at least rather invisible – within the government machinery. However, as part of the 'global sporting arms race', many governments have established specialist departments dedicated to elite sport (Houlihan & Zheng, 2013) or allocated public funding to the establishment of such units within the voluntary sector. Nonetheless, as displayed by Andersen, Houlihan, and Ronglan (2015), there is variation in the role of the state across various countries' elite sport systems, with several broad types of systems identifiable. The totalitarian communist state, in which elite sport policy and talent policy are natural parts of the regime, is one type (covered in the historical part above). Two other types of systems are the state-led systems in Australia, New Zealand, and the UK, and the voluntary system found for example in the Nordic countries (Andersen et al., 2015).

In the former type, the incorporation of elite sport into the government machinery is especially prominent. For example, in Australia the poor performance in the 1976 Montreal Olympic Games and the increasing political awareness of the importance of providing public support to elite sport led the government to create the Australian Institute of Sport (AIS), a strategic high performance agency (Hoye & Nicholson, 2009, p. 231). The AIS 'links sports investment to performance targets and provides world-class expertise and services – ensuring Australia's current and emerging high performance athletes have access to the right support at the right time in their pursuit of excellence' (AIS, 2015a). In 2012, the AIS launched *Australia's Winning Edge*, a strategic plan for high performance sport 2012–2022 (developed in collaboration with key partners in the sport sector). *Australia's Winning Edge* sets out the ambition to move Australia 'from world class to world best' (AIS, 2015b) with international performance targets (Olympic medals, etc.) for Australia over the coming decades. An integral part of the current Australian sport strategy is performance budgeting with an investment model that links investments to 'high performance targets and greater accountability of national sporting organizations (NSOs) for governance and commercial performance' (Australian Sports Commission,

2012). Similarly, in 2001/2002 The New Zealand Sport Academy was established and the government set medal targets and made performance budgeting a part of its sport strategy for the first time (Sam, 2015). In 2011, Sport New Zealand created a subsidiary called High Performance Sport New Zealand (HPSNZ), which currently operates under a 2013–2020 strategic plan

> underpinned by three goals: (1) to achieve performance results as measured by medals, (2) to achieve system sustainability as measured by a percentage of clients that say it positively impacts performance and athlete/team world rankings and (3) to be recognized as a world leader.
>
> *(Sam, 2015, p. 20)*

In the UK, elite sport was largely non-interventionist until the mid-1990s. However, as part of the broader project of 'modernizing' government and its key partners (such as National Sport Federations) UK Sport, a specialist government agency, was created. UK Sport's primary function is to deliver elite sport success at Olympic Games; it operates under the slogan *No Compromise*, meaning that funds are allocated to National Sport Federations and sports that are most likely to deliver Olympic medals. This return-on-investment funding model also includes the withdrawal of public funds to National Sport Federations that fail to meet medal targets (Houlihan & Chapman, 2015).

Contrary to the state-led systems of Australia, New Zealand, and the UK, the primary actors of the elite sport systems in the Nordic Countries, which rely entirely on the voluntary sector for sport delivery, are National Sport Federations and National Olympic Committees that develop their own strategic plans. In these countries, the state allocates resources but otherwise keeps an arms-length relationship to the voluntary sport sector (Skille & Säfvenbom, 2011; Fahlén & Sjöblom, 2012). Thus, although the state's governance mode in these countries has changed towards increased goal-steering and accountability, the state's increased interest in sport has primarily been into sport's ability to contribute to social policy objectives, not elite sport (Fahlén & Stenling, 2015, Skille & Säfvenbom, 2011). In fact, the Swedish government recently withdrew its comparatively modest dedicated funding to elite sport. It is unlikely that an organization like the AIS (Australia), HPSNZ (New Zealand) or UK Sport (UK) would be created as part of the government bureaucracy in, for example, Sweden or Norway. While there are high performance institutes such as Olympiatoppen (Norway) and Bosön (Sweden) in these countries, they are subsections of the National Sport Confederations (which are fully voluntary organizations) and do not have the resource allocating or governing function that the AIS and similar institutes have.

The elite sport system in the Nordic Countries should however be seen as an exception in terms of the state's role in relation to (elite) sport and the strong position of large and cohesive popular movements relative to the state in these countries. As noted by Houlihan and Zheng (2013), within the context of the Nordic Countries' long-standing commitment to social democratic ideals such as equality and everybody's right to participate (i.e., sport-for-all), which in many ways is in contrast to the meritocratic values of high performance sport, prioritizing elite sport has always been sensitive. Thus, while the Danish government was instrumental to the establishment of Team Denmark in the mid-1980s (Hansen, 2012), the initiative was first and foremost underpinned by an accentuated need for addressing the social conditions of elite athletes, and not medal targets. Even so, the Danish example can be seen as illustrative of some kind of a middle course – between the state-led systems and the voluntary systems.

Working with talent selection and development during the global sporting arms race and under advanced performance regimes

The integration of elite sport, and thus talent identification and development policy, into the public administration of nation states has provided political decision-makers with real possibilities to influence the conditions constraining the implementation of such policies (Houlihan, 2009; Grix, 2009). Although the possibilities and ambitions vary, advanced liberal governing modes seem to permeate elite sport systems both in countries where policy making for elite sport is integrated in the government bureaucracy, and in countries where those who deliver elite sport are kept in the voluntary sector and at an arms-length from the state. Even in Sweden, a country whose sport system is focused at, and funded because of, its contributions to social policy objectives, one of the key performance indicators of the effectiveness of the government support to voluntary sport is *Sports' international competitiveness* (Fahlén & Sjöblom, 2012). This is measured by number of medals won in international championships, number of athletes with capacity to win medals, number of athletes in national talent development programmes and number of students in elite sport schools (high school/upper secondary school level).

What are the implications of working with talent selection and development under the current conditions? As shown above, the global sporting arms race has attracted a lot of attention from the scientific community. These contributions, perhaps best exemplified by the SPLISS-studies (De Bosscher et al., 2006), have often focused on identifying best-practices to provide practitioners with concrete and applied advice on how to design and implement successful and medal-winning elite sport policies. In the wake of such works, a more critical and inquisitive stream of studies has emerged, asking questions about the ramifications of a governance mode that is characterized by the use of targeted investments, contractual relations, and performance management, on the strategy and talent-policy-related operations of the organizations set to implement government sport policy objectives (e.g., Green, 2005, 2009; Green & Houlihan, 2004; Grix, 2009; Oakley & Green, 2001; Piggin, Jackson, & Lewis, 2009; Sjöblom & Fahlén, 2012; Sam, 2009; Skille & Houlihan, 2014; Steen-Johnsen & Hanstad, 2008).

A common feature in many of these studies is the effect of implementing organizations' push for legitimacy in the eyes of resource providers. While all policy areas are infused with questions of legitimacy, a distinguishing feature of elite sport as a public policy domain is that its legitimacy rests on its value for other policy areas. Elite sport, and by extension talent systems, are thus interesting and financially supported due to its capacity to deliver against other policy goals (Sam, 2009), such as financial growth linked to the bidding and hosting of national and international events, a country's international reputation and relations, and increased grassroots participation. However, the viability of this interlinking of elite sport with other policy-goals hinges on the delivery of elite sport success. It is not the practice of elite sport itself that drives up participation rates for example, it is the medals. At least, this seems to be the common understanding of policy-makers.

Therefore, in order to legitimize public resources to elite sport, the makers and implementers of elite sport policy are forced to make promises of a certain number of medals at the next championship. In order to win international medals in an ever increasing competition, increased funding is necessary (Green, 2009). With increased financial support follows increased monitoring. This phenomenon adds to the processes noted by Grix (2009): increased demands on effectiveness and cost efficiency, that is, increased government control. In practice, it leads to an increase in the measuring of results with 'medal per currency unit' as the instrument of control. How to use the resources provided to what means is defined by the state. Green (2005) showed how this forces sport organizations to professionalize management and leadership, to increase quality among coaches, and to bring about more accurate talent identification systems. This mechanism seems to be at work regardless of whether these would be the strategies the implementers would like to use when striving for increased competitiveness. Green and Houlihan (2004) made a similar observation: governments launch programmes that are disguised as providing sport organizations with more autonomy when in practice they increase government control through the imposition of external objectives and terms of reference. However, increased government control is not to be mistaken for increased government responsibility (Oakley & Green, 2001). Since the imposition of external objectives and terms of reference is often accepted without further argument, possible failures to reach the medal goals set up can be blamed on the receiving end, the sport organizations. Complaining about medal goals imposed on them has proven to be fruitless since resistance is immediately connected to resisting development. Not accepting resources is equally difficult since resources are most often short. The end result is that increased government control is welcomed since it involves increased resources.

Implementing organizations are thus pressured to commit to performance targets that are set by actors outside the field of sport (i.e., the government or its representative organs) (Piggin et al., 2009). Being forced to legitimize something that cannot be controlled (i.e., number of medals won), implementing organizations are held hostage by policy-makers (Sam, 2009). As a consequence, the ideas, values, and conditions underpinning the state's resource allocation tend to impregnate implementing organizations' (e.g., NSOs) strategic decisions regarding, for example, talent-identification criteria (e.g., Grix, 2009). Another consequence is that implementers (e.g., talent development officers and national team coaches) feel inclined to display legitimacy by using the same strategies, techniques and vocabulary as similar and competing organizations, in effect diminishing the competitive edge of the organization (Piggin et al., 2009). Yet another consequence of the development described in the preceding is the internal suppression of alternative voices and critics in elite sport organizations that threaten the continued financial support for the organization. Most representatives of implementing organizations are happy to agree on medal-targets or strategies prescribed by policy-makers, since such behaviour is likely to secure continued funding. In this context, dissidents, irrespective of how 'good' their ideas may be, are dismissed as resisting development because they endanger the benevolence of the policy-maker (Steen-Johnsen & Hanstad, 2008). In sum, a key implication of the governance mode presently permeating many elite sport systems is that it displaces conceptions of who are the primary and legitimate stakeholders of sport; influence and power over direction, priorities and values is moved from athletes, clubs, and federations, (i.e., from sport itself), to external interests such as politicians, governments and their representative organs (Grix, 2009).

Concluding remarks

In order to wrap up this chapter on talent policies, we take first one, then two steps back. Taking one step back, we conclude by revisiting the definition of policy launched in the chapter's introduction (Jenkins, 1997). In that respect, we have shown how talent policy consists of interrelated decisions, made by several actors that try to influence each other and the field of sport policy including the field of elite sport policy, and specifically in the field of talent policy. These actors can, broadly speaking, be divided in state governments and sport organizations. We have shown how policy for talent selection and development concerns both political goals and tools (ends and means), in which large variations across types of policy regimes are identified throughout history and across nation states today. In that respect, the relationship between policy makers (state governments) and implementers (state controlled versus voluntary sport organizations) is discussed. We have shown how talent policy – as any issue including political actors – indicates that power is in use. The power is often related to economic priorities. And we have shown how definitions and realizations of talent policy goals are interrelated, especially by pinpointing the challenge of and distinction between policy making and implementation. The latter underlines the complexity of the sport policy field which we have discussed throughout the chapter and which is treated further below.

Taking two steps back, we conclude this chapter by returning to the beginning of this Handbook, and paraphrase the questions and answers regarding whether talent exists. Thus, we ask: Does talent policy exist? More refined, we ask: 1) Does talent selection policy exist?; and 2) Does talent development policy exist? The simple answer is yes. However, as this chapter treats a number of issues, a more nuanced and appropriate answer would be no. There is not one talent policy; there are several talent policies, of which the emphasis on talent selection versus talent development may vary. Moreover, the answer to the question (Does talent policy exist?), in simple or refined forms, varies across specific sports. This specificity has not been treated in detail in this chapter and should be of interest for future research. What is treated in this chapter can be considered as an answer to a similar but still very different question: How is talent policy constructed within different cultural, social and political contexts? As cultural, social and political issues can – and do – change across time and space, we have presented the rise of talent policies and the various types of talent policies identifiable across nation states today. In that respect, we have merged cultural, social and political issues as representative for nation states, a point in which we suggest that future research could be more refined. Also, other aspects could be added to such analysis, not least the economic aspect.

All in all, our contribution to the field of talent research in sport, is that we have presented how various elite sport systems operate, with a particular focus on the distinction between policy making and policy implementation and on the relationship between the state and sport organizations. A key aspect of any elite sport system is the degree and type of government involvement. In this regard, the state-led systems found in countries such as the UK, Australia, and New Zealand are distinctly different from those in the Nordic countries which rely entirely on the voluntary sector for sport delivery. Another lesson learned is that all types of regimes of today, to higher or lesser degrees, relate to, or build on, the first rise of talent policies. Despite differences related to historical and political conditions, contemporary trends show that most nations seem to import or establish some version of the old East Bloc system combining it with modern (Western) economy and ideologies; thus there seem to be processes of homogenization across the types of regimes, driven by underlying mechanisms of professionalization and commercialization of sports. We conceive though, that such processes play out differently in different cultural, social, political (and economical) contexts, and that this is important insight for researchers into a broader area of talent identification and development in sport.

Notes

1   The process is often referred to as politics (Houlihan, 2000), a concept that will not be treated further here.
2   https://en.oxforddictionaries.com/definition/policy
3   The link made between mass sport with social goals and elite sport with performance goals, that is used to legitimate the budgets for elite sport, is the belief that elite sport generates mass sport.

Research shows, however, that there is no causal link between them (Nielsen, 2002; Hanstad & Skille, 2010; Vigor, Mean, & Tims, 2004).

4   Perhaps apart from the systematic doping of athletes (Green & Oakley, 2001).

References

Aggestål, A., & Fahlén, J. (2015). Managing sport for public health: Approaching contemporary problems with traditional solutions. *Social Inclusion, 3,* 108–117.

Andersen, S. S., Houlihan, B., & Ronglan, L. T. (2015). *Managing elite sport systems: Research and practice.* London: Routledge.

Australian Institute of Sport (AIS) (2015a). What is the AIS? Retrieved from www.ausport.gov.au/ais/about, August, 17, 2015.

Australian Institute of Sport (AIS) (2015b). Australia's Winning Edge: High Performance Strategy. Retrieved from www.ausport.gov.au/ais/australias_winning_edge, August, 17, 2015.

Australian Sports Commission (2012). Australia's Winning Edge 2012–2022. High performance investment principles. Retrieved from www.ausport.gov.au/__data/assets/pdf_file/0010/508465/High_performance_investment_principles.pdf, August, 17, 2015.

Bloyce, D., & Smith, A. (2010). *Sport policy and development.* London: Routledge.

Chappelet, J.-L. (2010). Switzerland. *International Journal of Sport Policy and Politics, 2*(1), 99–110.

Coalter, F. (2007). Sports clubs, social capital and social regeneration: 'Ill-defined interventions with hard to follow outcomes'? *Sport in society, 10*(4), 537–559.

De Bosscher, V., De Knop, P., van Bottenburg, M., & Shibli, S. (2006). A conceptual framework for analysing sports policy factors leading to international sporting success. *European Sport Management Quarterly, 6*(2), 185–215.

De Bosscher, V., Bingham, J., Shibli, S., van Bottenburg, M., & De Knop, P. (2008). *The Global Sporting Arms Race: An International Comparative Study on Sports Policy Factors leading to International Sporting Success.* Oxford: Meyer & Meyer Sport.

De Bosscher, V., De Knop, P., & van Bottenburg, M. (2009). An analysis of homogeneity and heterogeneity of elite sports systems in six nations. *International Journal of Sport Marketing & Sponsorship, 10*(2), 111–131.

Dousti, M., Goodarzi, M., Asadi, H., & Khabiri, M. (2013). Sport policy in Iran. *International Journal of Sport Policy and Politics, 5*(1), 151–158.

Fahlén, J. (2015). The corporal dimension of sports-based interventions: Understanding the role of embedded expectations and embodied knowledge in sport policy implementation. *International Review for the Sociology of Sport,* doi: 10.1177/1012690215607083.

Fahlén, J., & Sjöblom, P. (2012). Elitidrott i skilda världar: Den svenska elitidrottens existensvillkor. In J. Norberg & J. Pihlblad (eds). *För framtids segrar – En analys av det svenska elitidrottssystemet.* Stockholm: Centrum för idrottsforskning, 81–131.

Fahlén, J., & Stenling, C. (2015). Sport policy in Sweden. *International Journal of Sport Policy and Politics,* doi: 10.1080/19406940.2015.1063530.

Fahlén, J., Wickman, K., & Eliasson, I. (2014). Resisting self-regulation: An analysis of sport policy programme making and implementation in Sweden. *International Journal of Sport Policy and Politics,* doi: 10.1080/19406940.2014.925954.

Green, M. (2005). Integrating macro- and meso-level approaches: A comparative analysis of elite sport development in Australia, Canada and the United Kingdom. *European Sport Management Quarterly, 5*(2), 143–166.

Green, M. (2007a). Policy transfer, lesson drawing and perspectives on elite sport development systems. *International Journal of Sport Management and Marketing, 2*(4), 426–441.

Green, M. (2007b). Olympic glory or grassroots development? Sport policy priorities in Australia, Canada and the United Kingdom, 1960–2006. *The International Journal of the History of Sport, 24*(7), 921–953.

Green, M. (2009). Podium or participation? Analysing policy priorities under changing modes of sport governance in the United Kingdom. *International Journal of Sport Policy, 1*(2), 121–144.

Green, M., & Houlihan, B. (2004). Advocacy coalitions and elite sport policy change in Canada and the United Kingdom. *International Review for the Sociology of Sport, 39*(4), 387–403.

Green, M., & Houlihan, B. (2011). *Elite sport development: Policy learning and political priorities.* London: Routledge.

Green, M., & Oakley, B. (2001). Elite sport development systems and playing to win: uniformity and diversity in international approaches. *Leisure Studies, 20*(4), 247–267.

Grix, J. (2009). The impact of UK sport policy on the governance of athletics. *International Journal of Sport Policy and Politics, 1*(1), 31–49.

Hansen, J. (2012). The institutionalization of Team Denmark. In S. Andersen & L. T. Ronglan (eds), *Nordic elite sport: Same ambitions – different tracks*. Oslo: Norwegian University Press, 43–61.

Hanstad, D. V., & Skille, E. Å. (2010). Does elite sport develop mass sport? A Norwegian case study. *Scandinavian Sport Studies Forum, 1*, 51–68.

Henry, I., Amara, M., Al-Tauqi, M., & Lee, P. C. (2005). A typology of approaches to comparative analysis of sports policy. *Journal of Sport Management, 19*(4), 480–496.

Hill, M. (1997). *The policy process: A reader* (2nd ed.). London: Prentice Hall.

Houlihan, B. (1997). *Sport, policy and politics: A comparative analysis*. London: Routledge.

Houlihan, B. (2000). Politics and sport. In J. Coakley & E. Dunning (eds), *Handbook of sports studies*. London: Sage, 213–227.

Houlihan, B. (2001). *Sport policy and politics: A comparative analysis*. London: Routledge.

Houlihan, B. (2005). Public sector sport policy developing a framework for analysis. *International Review for the Sociology of Sport, 40*(2), 163–185.

Houlihan, B. (2009). Mechanisms of international influence on domestic elite sport policy. *International Journal of Sport Policy, 1*(1), 51–69.

Houlihan, B., & Chapman, P. (2015). Modernisation and elite sport development in the United Kingdom. In S. S. Andersen, B. Houlihan, & L. T. Ronglan (eds), *Managing elite sport systems: Research and practice* (pp. 31–47). London: Routledge.

Houlihan, B., & Green, M. (2008). *Comparative elite sport development: Systems, structures and public policy*. Oxford: Elsevier.

Houlihan, B., & Zheng, J. (2013). The Olympics and elite sport policy: Where will it all end? *International Journal of the History of Sport, 30*(4), 338–355.

Hoye, R., & Nicholson, M. (2009). Australia. *International Journal of Sport Policy and Politics, 1*(2), 229–240.

Jenkins, B. (1997). Policy analysis: Models and approaches. In M. Hill (ed.), *The policy process: A reader*. London: Prentice Hall, 30–38.

López de D'Amico, R. (2012). Policy in Venezuela. *International Journal of Sport Policy and Politics, 4*(1), 139–151.

Nielsen, K. (2002). Skaber elite bredde – og omvendt? In H. Eichberg & B. V. Madsen (eds), *Idrættens enhed eller mangfoldighet*. København: Klim, 213–222.

Piggin, J., Jackson, S. J., & Lewis, M. (2009). Telling the truth in public policy: An analysis of New Zealand sport policy discourse. *Sociology of Sport Journal, 26*(3), 462–482.

Puig, N., Martinez, J., & Garcia, B. (2010). Sport policy in Spain. *International Journal of Sport Policy and Politics, 2*(3), 381–390.

Sabatier, P. A., & Jenkins-Smith, H. C. (1999). The advocacy coalition framework: An assessment. In P. A. Sabatier (ed.), *Theories of the policy process*. Boulder, CO: Westview Press, 117–166.

Sam, M. P. (2009). The public management of sport: Wicked problems, challenges and dilemmas. *Public Management Review, 11*(4), 499–514.

Sam, M. (2015). 'Big brother' and caring sister: Performance management and the athlete's entourage. In S. S. Andersen, B. Houlihan, & L. T. Ronglan (eds), *Managing elite sport systems: Research and practice*. London: Routledge, 16–30.

Sjöblom, P., & Fahlén, J. (2012). Nationella elitidrottssystem och internationell konkurrenskraft: En forskningsgenomgång. In J. Norberg & J. Pihlblad (eds), *För framtids segrar – En analys av det svenska elitidrottssystemet*. Stockholm: Centrum för idrottsforskning, 59–79.

Skille, E. Å. (2008). Understanding sport clubs as sport policy implementers: A theoretical framework for the analysis of the implementation of central sport policy through local and voluntary sport organizations. *International Review for the Sociology of Sport, 43*(2), 181–200.

Skille, E. Å. (2009). State sport policy and the voluntary sport clubs: The case of the Norwegian Sports City Program as social policy, *European Sport Management Quarterly, 9*(1), 63–79.

Skille, E. Å. (2010). Competitiveness and health: The work of sport clubs seen from the perspectives of Norwegian sport club representatives. *International Review for the Sociology of Sport, 45*(1), 73–85.

Skille, E. Å. & Houlihan, B. (2014). The contemporary context of elite youth sport. The role of national sport organisations in the UK and Norway. In D. V. Hanstad, M. Parent & B. Houlihan (eds), *The Youth Olympic Games*. London: Routledge, 34–50.

Skille, E. Å., & Säfvenbom, R. (2011). Sport policy in Norway. *International Journal of Sport Policy and Politics, 3*(2), 283–293.

Steen-Johnsen, K., & Hanstad, D. V. (2008). Change and power in complex democratic organizations: The case of Norwegian elite sports. *European Sport Management Quarterly, 8*(2), 123–143.

Stenling, C. (2014a). Sport programme implementation as translation and organizational identity construction: the implementation of Drive-in sport in Swedish sports as an illustration. *International Journal of Sport Policy and Politics, 6*(1), 55–69.

Stenling, C. (2014b). The emergence of a new logic? The theorizing of a new practice in the highly institutionalized context of Swedish voluntary sport. *Sport Management Review, 17*(4), 507–519.

Stenling, C., & Fahlén, J. (2014). Same same, but different? Exploring the organizational identities of Swedish voluntary sports: Possible implications of sports clubs' self-identification for their role as implementers of policy objectives. *International Review for the Sociology of Sport,* doi: 10.1177/1012690214557103

van Meter, D. S. and van Horn, C. E. (1975). The policy implementation process. *Administration & Society, 6*(4), 445–488.

Vigor, A. Mean, M. And Tims, C. (2004). Introduction. In A. Vigor, M. Means and C. Tims (eds). *After the Gold Rush. A Sustainable Legacy for London.* London: IPPR and Demos, 1–30.

Waardenburg, M., & van Bottenburg, M. (2013). Sport policy in the Netherlands. *International Journal of Sport Policy and Politics, 5*(3), 465–475.

Yamamoto, M. Y-Y. (2012). Development of the sporting nation: sport as a strategic area of national policy in Japan. *International Journal of Sport Policy and Politics, 4*(2), 277–296.

34

CONCLUDING, BUT DEFINITELY NOT CONCLUSIVE, REMARKS ON TALENT IDENTIFICATION AND DEVELOPMENT

Jörg Schorer, Nick Wattie, Stephen Cobley, and Joseph Baker

At the Rugby Football Union symposium on Talent Identification and Development held at the UK's Royal Society in May 2013, Sir Leszek Borysiewicz, Vice-Chancellor of the University of Cambridge, concluded that the depth of knowledge on talent identification was not as advanced as necessary to make firm judgments about how to use the science to inform practice in this sport. While sport science is far younger than disciplines such as medicine or philosophy and should, therefore, be given a bit of leeway, this statement does highlight the need for, and importance of, high-quality evidence in order to make accurate decisions. At the conclusion of this Handbook, if we return to Sir Leszek's conclusion from 2013, we see that things have not changed significantly. While our understanding has advanced in certain key areas (as outlined in several of this text's chapters), there is still much to learn. Thankfully our authors have identified a number of important issues and questions that can be used to advance research in this field. We elaborate on these below and highlight a range of key areas for future research.

Future directions for talent identification research

1. The need to clarify what "talent" is and how it might be measured

A large part of the section on talent identification concerns a definition of talent, which has important implications for both models of talent identification and how this concept is investigated. There is currently no consensus definition of talent and because of this, discussions of what talent "is" occur regularly, such as in Chapter 5 in this Handbook, where Gagné's approach (see for example, Gagné, 2013) was used as the basis for the Australian sport strategy. In our opinion, continued discussion over how to operationalize "talent" stifles advancement in this field. That is not to say defining this concept is an easy task, but it is necessary for our field. One key future research direction is to determine the extent to which definitions of talent are domain-specific. Given the variations highlighted across sports and other domains of endeavor, not to mention that what constitutes talent changes over time as performances

466

continue to evolve, is a general, operational definition of talent possible? Although there are a range of ways this could be explored using systematic reviews, consensus/position statements, etc., one intriguing starting place would be to explicate the knowledge of top coaches (cf. Roth, 1996). Many times we hear coaches express that an athlete has something special without being able to elaborate what this special quality is. Determining the implicit or explicit knowledge coaches use in making talent selection decisions might be particularly useful in determining the depth and breadth of factors used to define talent.

2. What does "good" talent identification look like?

A second issue going forward will be to ascertain what constitutes a reasonable success rate in the long-term prediction of future high achievement. While a 100% success rate is clearly unobtainable given what seems like a near-infinite number of variables that can affect an athlete's development over the timeframes under examination, it might be valuable to have clear expectations of what constitutes a "good" versus a "weak" talent identification/selection program. For instance, in their evaluation of professional draft selections, Koz, Fraser-Thomas, and Baker (2012) found that 17% of the variance in games played (their measure of a player's value at the elite level) was explained by draft selection; but is 17% a reasonable (or exceptional) degree of success? Certainly it was statistically significant and superior to the other sports examined, but one could argue that those within the domain should set the ultimate value of a predictive statistic, not some predetermined convention of statistical relevance. Further, it may be valuable to create unique probabilistic estimates specific at the individual and context level (e.g., youth developmental athletes vs. athletes in the professional entry drafts). Given that talent identification involves several actors including, not only the athletes and coaches, but policy makers and parents (among others), it will be important to have a consistent definition of how success in talent identification and selection is determined (cf. Schorer, Rienhoff, Fischer & Baker, 2016).

3. Reducing the lag between research results and practical application

As noted by Büsch and Granacher (see Chapter 8 in this Handbook), we need to remember the end users of this research. Other chapters also stressed the need to test theoretical concepts and experimental findings in applied settings that are representative of the talent identification, development and competition environments. Unfortunately, much of the research conducted does not readily transfer to the applied world due to a range of factors such as publication in scholarly journals behind an expensive pay-wall, or presentation at academic conferences that are expensive and/or not widely publicized to those outside the research domain. This can lead to a significant time lag between when research is conducted and when it is utilized by coaches (if ever). Undoubtedly, part of this reticence on the part of scientists to be involved in the knowledge translation and application process is due to the limited performance metrics most scientists working in the academy have to use in order to demonstrate scholarly productivity (e.g., journal impact factors, citation counts, H-index, etc.). If practical application of this knowledge is socially important, it is important that universities and policy makers support it in various ways. This could include measuring applied articles in the same way as those published in top journals, and re-evaluating the value of working with athletes/teams in applied settings. It is also important for academics to overcome any reluctance to work in applied settings. Even the best advice given to practitioners is probabilistic given the unique constraints between athletes, and as such researchers face the uncomfortable reality that their best evidence-informed advice may not affect any positive change (or not affect positive change in the time expected by practitioners). This can be an uncomfortable reality for researchers used to producing academic work filled with tentative language (e.g., "these results *could* have implications for talent identification and development"). But the accuracy of talent identification and development will likely only improve as researchers and practitioners overcome these challenges by exchanging knowledge, and improving knowledge through cooperative and collaborative exchanges.

Future directions in talent development research

1. Continuing evolution of the value of deliberate practice

The frequent mention of "deliberate practice" in many of the chapters continues to emphasize the relevance of this concept to long-term success. Appropriately, there is critical discussion of this topic in Chapters 9 and 14 (among others). Recent discussions have also considered the potential negative effects of this kind training (see Chapter 9). However, the concept of deliberate practice emphasizes that there are other factors, beyond training volume, that need to be considered in understanding expert athlete development. Certainly, the chapter by Gorman and Renshaw (see Chapter 22) emphasizes that not all practice is created equal and that researchers have likely over-valued the importance of the quantity in practice regimes.

2. Talent development is multivariate and multi-disciplinary

The section on talent development illustrates the value of a multivariate approach to understanding this process. In the early years of research in this field, motor skill learning and resistance or endurance training were prominent topics. More recently, however, the range of research domains relevant to athlete development has increased considerably, now prominently featuring psychological skills, perceptual skills, and may soon include other domains like applied statistics and biomechanics of movement. The problem with these skills is that quite often they require either specialist or special equipment that is not accessible to many coaches and athletes. Given rapid improvements in online capabilities, one hope for the future is that low-cost options are developed that can be used to measure and interpret a range of variables making extensive training unnecessary.

3. The need for more comprehensive models

Another important issue that may not be firmly established in the perceptions of researchers and coaches is that development is a non-linear process. This was nicely described in Chapters 11 (Malina et al.) and 16 (Anderson and Mayo) where both argued there are different phases in an athlete's development. Sometimes an athlete may need a phase to consolidate their learning, during which time their peers show increases in performance. Currently, these consolidation phases are often considered as stagnation, but the opposite might be case. This work highlights a more general concern regarding the degree to which athlete development models (e.g., LTAD,[1] FTEM and/or DMSP, see Baker & Wattie, in press, for a comparison of these models) are generalizable across an athlete population (and talent pool) that is incredibly diverse (see Chapters 9 and 31). For example, the early diversification (participation in many sports/activities) advocated by the DMSP and LTAD is likely not possible for youth from low socioeconomic (SES) families, at least in systems where sport "involvement" is conceptualized as organized, "pay for use" sport. Similarly, there are unique developmental constraints for athletes with disabilities (see Chapter 31) and despite the inclusion of additional components to some models to address some of these different populations, there are significant questions as to whether these general and modified models sufficiently account for the constraints and processes of athlete development in different groups. Going forward it will be important to critically appraise the generalizability of athlete development models, and whether policies driven by such models reduce the efficiency of talent identification and development practices. In addition it will be important for us to learn what such models can teach us about existing social inequalities (SES, gender) that ultimately lead to biases in talent identification and development.

What is an optimal environment for athlete development and identification and can it be "created"?

One recent development within talent identification and development domains, which is reflected in this collection, has been a shift in focus towards designing an optimal environment to promote athlete development and skill acquisition. This emphasis has both broad macro and narrow micro implications, both of which have been excellently illustrated by authors in this handbook. At a broader level, evidence suggests researchers and practitioners need to consider the complete ecology of athlete development environments and integrations therein: coaches (see Chapter 20), sport clubs, culture, parents (see Chapter 13), teachers and school culture (see Chapter 19), as well as team dynamics and group cohesion (see Chapter 21). Larsen and Alfermann similarly stress the need to consider the influence of various environmental influences to understand dropout risk (see Chapter 23). At a more micro level, Gorman and Renshaw (see Chapter 22) present a detailed summary of numerous ways to design learning environments (practices) to optimize learning and motor skill acquisition.

But how can we help build optimal environments? While numerous chapters in this collection suggest ways to help better design athlete development environments, that question is also perhaps incomplete. Contemporary developmental theories stress the importance of considering the bidirectional interaction between individuals and the multiple facets of the environments in which they develop. As such, it might be more apt to ask, how can we help build an optimal environment *for particular learners in particular contexts*? In considering this question, there are some important issues to consider going forward.

Optimal environments for talent development

Given the importance of considering individual variability (see Chapter 11), unique environmental characteristics (see Chapters 14 and 19), and that development is the product of bidirectional interactions between an individual and their environment, one of the challenges is the extent to which an "optimal environment" is generalizable to different athletes. This challenge is not unique to sport. Henrich, Hein, and Norenzayan (2010) proposed that many assertions on human nature (psychology and behavior) have been based on research obtained from samples in "Western, Educated, Industrialized, Rich, and Democratic (WEIRD) societies" (p. 61). As a result, they suggest exercising caution when considering which theories and findings are generalizable beyond these contexts. It could be argued that the perspectives within this Handbook to some extent reflect predominantly WEIRD societies as well. Therefore, caution should perhaps also be used when deciding whether the "optimal characteristics of environments" are universal and generalizable. We would also suggest that optimal environments might differ between WEIRD societies as well, given the different historical and cultural realities.

Several popular examples of successful talent development environments exist, which would not qualitatively fit within the WEIRD classification: Kenyan marathon runners; baseball players from the Dominican Republic; the oft-mentioned soccer players from the favelas of Brazil. There are also exceptionally talented performers who have emerged from relatively resource poor environments *within* societies that are WEIRD at a macro level (e.g., boxers from low SES inner cities); there are societies within societies. As such, very different environments appear to have the capacity to be "optimal" in terms of producing high performance athletes, although perhaps for very different reasons.

This is not to suggest that recommendations for how to "build optimal developments" should be disregarded simply because the context is different. In some respects, non-WEIRD environments may be optimal for the same reasons that are described by research samples from WEIRD societies, despite qualitative differences between the two. For example, youth playing football in the favelas of Brazil may play in ways highly analogous to practices characterized by high contextual interference, which might optimize skill acquisition (see Chapter 18). Similarly, the cultural popularity of baseball in the Dominican Republic may create successful athlete talent development environments similar to those espoused by the holistic ecological approach. Both of these examples may also simply reflect highly engaged youth involved in high volumes of intrinsically motivated activities such as deliberate play, as well as intensive training. On the other hand, concepts like "purposeful stress/challenge" (see Chapter 24), and the generalizability of that pedagogical approach, needs to be explored. Is it possible to contrive stress/challenge, or to use the type of stress/challenge inherent to one environment (e.g., deprivation of resources and general life stress) in a different context where they are not naturally occurring? Going forward it will be important for researchers and practitioners to consider what environments are optimal, for whom, and why.

Additionally, it will also be important to embrace a lifespan developmental perspective when considering why certain environments are optimal. For example, aside from a few chapters (see Chapters 18 and 28), acknowledgement that athlete development continues after athletes reach the top level of their sport (international or professional) is limited in the literature. But development is a process that continues throughout the lifespan, and there has been little attention to how athletes continue to develop at the top level of their sport (i.e., what adaptations do they have to make to fitness or style of play as they age? Do they learn to "play smarter" as commonly believed?). Even within the career of an athlete there might be considerable variation, which is rarely considered (Baker, Koz, Kungl, Fraser-Thomas, & Schorer, 2013). On a related note, dialogues and research on young children often relates to important things like biases in talent identification (e.g., Wattie, Schorer & Baker, 2015), positive youth development (see Chapter 27) and health (see Chapters 25 and 26), with less attention to the process of skill formation (see Chapter 20). As such, the emphasis of talent development, including in this collection, seems to be predominantly on adolescent athletes. Members of our group have suggested elsewhere that a focus on the lifecycle formation of skills may be a useful way of considering how skills develop at different points throughout the entire process of athlete development (Wattie & Baker, in press), but these hypotheses remain to be tested.

These notions may also be relevant for talent transfer, a notion that has emerged in recent years, although in practice it is likely far from optimal. Our understanding of how an athlete successfully transfers from one sport to another is restricted by the limited number of studies in this area (see Chapter 32). In addition to being a relatively new area of research and practice, the isolationist and self-protective practice of encouraging athletes to commit to one sport may be limiting the impact of this strategy. Indeed, the pressure to draw and retain a large talent pool from which to identify and develop athletes may be creating a "tragedy of the commons" (Baker, Wattie & Schorer, 2016), essentially, wasting potential talent through either non-cooperative practices or lack of knowledge of the potential transferable characteristics from one sport to another. Of course optimizing the notion of talent transfer is no easy task, and there are a number of questions to consider going forward. For example, at what stage of development is it optimal to introduce talent transfer initiatives? Is it better to focus talent transfer initiatives in early phases of development where participant numbers are much larger or is it more useful to focus efforts on older athletes, who have more fully developed physical and cognitive characteristics indicative of those needed for transfer to other activities. For example, millions of high school basketball players in the United States are essentially de-selected from basketball development systems when they are not selected for college teams. These athletes could possibly be transferred to sports where similar qualities are valued, which could be particularly valuable for sports with lower levels of participation (e.g., handball in the US). Another issue for talent transfer researchers concerns the extent to which programs need to be modified to accommodate individuals coming into the system at later stages of development and with varying levels of skill. Understanding how skill acquisition trajectories and motivational processes are affected in the "transferred" athlete remain as rich areas for future exploration.

Optimal environments for talent identification

Perhaps less intuitive is the challenge of building an optimal environment for talent identification. While aspects of this challenge are explicitly addressed by Büsch and Granacher (see Chapter 8) as well as Gerrard (see Chapter 30) in their respective chapters on applied statistics and analytics, discussions about "building optimal environments" tend to gravitate toward talent development. Talent identification programs often consist of measuring anthropometrics and indicators of performance (such as entry draft combines). Other suggestions include adopting integrated multivariate and multidisciplinary approaches (see Chapters 18 and 30). But few discussions seem to be about how environments can be designed or built so that selectors make optimal decisions and ultimately increase the low efficacy talent identification programs (see Chapter 7). This includes how to design tryouts and selection camps, the integration of batteries of performance tests, and even the culture surrounding talent identification and the importance of long-term development over short-term performance. These appear to be potentially fruitful areas for future research.

Can we mitigate negative consequences while maximizing skill acquisition and athlete development?

As highlighted by many of the authors, ill health and injury can be critical limiting factors for athlete development and can have profound outcomes outside of sport. In particular, Pelka and Kellmann (see Chapter 25) as well as John and Carter (see Chapter 26) remind us that issues like burnout and overtraining, as well as chronic and acute injury, can be regular occurrences throughout athlete development. While progressive coaches should consider a proactive approach to optimally manage these events when they occur, we actually know very little about the prevalence and incidence of these issues across the extended timeframes necessary for long-term skill acquisition. A key area for future research is to track these processes longitudinally over development to determine (a) the prevalence of each of these issues and (b) their overall influence on athlete development to get an idea of the size and scope of these effects. Moreover, understanding the optimal balance between the physical and cognitive effort required for maximal training adaptations and the recovery necessary to make these adaptations and reduce injury risk is still largely guesswork. While some biomarkers have been identified, they are not widely used and require considerable replication through further research. Moreover, much of our understanding about the negative and positive effects of training stress has remained focused on physical forms of stress, arguably because these are more easily measured. However, cognitive and psychological stressors also contribute to the stress load an athlete is experiencing at any point in development (see Chapter 25). Farrow and Robertson (2016) recently explored these concepts, advocating a multi-faceted relationship between forms of stress, recovery and maximal development.

Similarly, Chapters 27 and 29 remind us that while sport has the potential for positive outcomes such as skill acquisition, positive youth development, and elite performance, it also has the potential for negative outcomes like emotional and physical abuse and compromised development if not programmed effectively. To complicate matters further, Chapter 24 by Collins and MacNamara highlights the potential value of difficult and challenging experiences. Currently, we have very little understanding of what elements of challenge/negative experiences best facilitate athlete development, and, more importantly, whether these outcomes can be promoted without the negative experience. As a result, an important area of future research will be to understand the process of walking the "knife-edge" between training that is challenging enough to elicit/develop an athlete's resiliency and skill acquisition, and training that constitutes abuse (see Chapter 29).

As noted in the section above, there has been very little examination of talent development after reaching peak performance, almost as if researchers have focused entirely on the journey to the destination without any thought to what happens after. Lemez and Rongen (see Chapter 28) emphasize that understanding the processes leading to elite performance is only part of the journey and that athletes can carry the developmental consequences of the elite training environment with them in their post-high-performance sport lives. Further work is also necessary here to promote greater knowledge about the relationships between early life training experiences and later life health and development outcomes.

Further issues in talent research

In summary, going forward there will be a need to consider talent identification and development from more perspectives—both of them in applied, theoretical and empirical research. It will, therefore, be necessary to conceptualize the athlete identification and development environments not as stable or immediate, but as dynamic settings with emergent characteristics and rates of change that are highly variable (akin to those of growth and maturation: see Chapter 11). Despite the questions offered by the authors of the chapters in this Handbook, there were some areas not covered herein that are important for an informed discussion. We present two brief examples to illustrate this, but are aware that there are several others.

Ethics of talent identification and development

Although we felt it was important to include a chapter discussing the ethical implications of talent identification and development in sport, we were ultimately unable to secure this contribution. This was unfortunate given that many of the trends highlighted in this Handbook warrant a thorough ethical discourse:

- Talent identification and development practices in many sports and countries target very young youth (e.g., Chapter 9);
- There are significant challenges to balancing the need to develop and produce elite performers while considering the development of healthy, well-adjusted individuals (see Chapters 25–29);
- The emergence of deliberate stress/challenge (e.g., "talent needs trauma," Collins & MacNamara, 2012) as a tool to optimize skill acquisition in developing athletes (see Chapter 24). How are these trends in talent identification and development balanced with the fiduciary duty that parents and coaches have toward youth athletes?
- What are the ethical implications of spending tremendous amounts of money on talent identification and development (as opposed to grassroots sport), as well as profiting from high performance youth sport?

Leaving aside larger social questions of whether money spent on talent identification and development initiatives is better spent here than in other areas of social need (e.g., recreational sport, healthcare, education, etc.), is it socially justifiable to focus on selecting and developing only those athletes who are considered talented? Should we try to provide optimal development for everyone to the extent this is possible given clear limitations in important resources such as high-quality coaching, training facilities and competition opportunities?

A related issue that we know very little about concerns the athletes who are de-selected from the system. Until an athlete is told that they are "talented" or "not-talented" they lie in a Schrödinger's cat-like state of "superposition" where they have the potential to be either. But, what happens after that key event? How does motivation, desire, interest, etc., change simply through being given that message? This question is perhaps most central to understanding and managing the most critical of all resources in sport (i.e., the athletes), but we have essentially no understanding of how this key event affects them at a personal level. Perhaps more importantly, is there a way to promote elite athlete development without compromising elements of positive youth development. Recent work by Hardy et al. (in press) suggests the most successful athletes (i.e., multiple medal winners) are selfish, ruthless and self-centered. How does this promote positive youth development? At the highest levels of sport, are they mutually exclusive concepts and which one should we be valuing as a society? These questions and concerns are not trivial and each could likely fill a volume with valuable discourse. We raise them simply as important discussion points for future scholars in this area.

Methodological issues in talent research and application

Further understanding of athlete identification and development may also be limited by the research methods most commonly used. For instance, most talent selections are done based on relative comparisons. In many cases, talent scouts compare qualitatively or quantitatively young athletes in specific areas and decide that the most talented are those with the best current values on the measures of interest. While this approach might be useful in sport systems like ice-hockey in North America or soccer in many European countries where there is a very high level of competition and development, in other sports a rather untalented youth may be considered talented simply because of the absence of more talented youth (e.g., a type of "big fish, little pond" effect). It would be valuable for future research to have points of reference in administered tests so that developing athletes worldwide could be compared to normative data for their sport. While we acknowledge the difficulty in creating such metrics, current advances in technology could help researchers and coaches develop these capabilities.

A second issue here is that the "expertise approach" is often taken to identify potential predictors for talent selection (cf. Hohmann, 2009). While it can be useful to look at current champions for a range of research questions, current high performance might be considerably different to the ultimate level of performance of developing athletes within the system when they reach expertise (cf. Baker, Wattie, & Schorer, 2016). For example, soccer in Germany used to have large, very strong players all over the field but in recent years the trend has shifted to smaller, more technical players on many positions, arguably because Spain was very successful with this approach. Such fluctuations in the ideal characteristics of talented athletes are difficult to predict, but remind us that talent selection is *not about predicting the current level of elite performance* but identifying those factors that predict the level of *performance necessary for future success at the elite level.* With this in mind, having coaches (and policy makers) think "outside the box" could be valuable.

A third concern is the continual lack of longitudinal research in this field (see Chapter 18 for exceptions). Given that talent identification and development aims to understand the skill acquisition process up to the highest level of attainment, the time span involved is obviously protracted. While a length of at least ten years is often proposed to reflect this timeframe (e.g., Ericsson, Krampe, & Tesch-Römer, 1993), research in sport (see Baker & Young, 2014, for a review) has shown that this duration is highly variable. In most sports this duration is longer than five years, which highlights several issues with most current work. First, funding for most research projects is limited to two to three years and, as a result, finding the resources needed to run a longitudinal project is extremely difficult. Second, although senior researchers typically oversee projects, most research today is conducted by PhD students, which limits a project's length to the duration of a PhD. Finally, important partners within most sports, such as national-level coaches, have limited-term contracts, which can result in turnover during the duration of the project with new coaches less interested in continuing the project. Therefore, the much-needed longitudinal work requires long-term partnerships where all sides see the value and reward from this type of work.

A final methodological concern is that our statistical approaches to talent research might be flawed. Quite often the performances from varying tests are taken together and the person with the best overall score is considered the most talented. Additionally, most of the current studies use group-based statistics that are based on the comparisons of means and some sort of deviation. While this might give us a trend of what characteristics are important overall, these approaches might miss individuals who are exceptional in certain key aspects, because they lack an overall great performance. For teams, and potentially also for individuals, outliers in one aspect might be of high value for future elite performances. Purely statistical approaches may not identify these individuals, although it is possible they might be seen by the "coach's eye" as someone with something special that is hard to define. On the one hand, future research efforts might try to find statistical solutions to identify such cases such as moving from group-based inferential statistics to a more personalized exploratory approach (e.g., Sedlmeier, 1996). On the other hand, it emphasizes the additional work to be done to understand the value of implicit decision-making done by successful coaches.

A road map to future work

We have tried to distill some of the questions that emerged from the Handbook with a view to highlighting the different ways that research and practice in talent identification and development can continue to progress. However, complicating matters further is that many of the issues and questions are not mutually exclusive. Indeed, as many of the chapters in this Handbook highlight, meeting these demands requires the integration of sport and non-sport environmental factors, the integration of multiple variables from multiple disciplines within the talent identification and development environments, as well as an understanding of variations in growth, maturation and development and how such factors affect immediate and long–term outcomes. In short, the challenge is to better understand a process that is dynamic, multifaceted, nonlinear, and heterogeneous!

In our first chapter, we stated that our intention was to provide a "state of the science" and that in our concluding chapter we would sketch for the reader a road map for future work. Below, we try to keep that promise, although perhaps more generally than we originally intended. Our initial intent for this chapter was to create a diagram that would summarize the whole book, reflecting the links and inter-connections between chapters; however, after reading each of the previous chapters, it became obvious that these "puzzle pieces" fit together in a variety of configurations. Moreover, we believe there are currently still important pieces missing. In order to assist in promoting a more comprehensive profile of the factors related to talent identification and athlete development, we have highlighted the following general concerns:

1   *Most of the research is isolated in its special discipline.*
When reading the different chapters, it became clear that there were obvious connections between different domains (e.g., sport psychology and biomechanics and how they could potentially interact); however, most research continues to be focused in a single discipline. Although part of this was somewhat artificial given how we instructed authors in certain chapters, this does reflect the reality that most researchers tend to focus on one field in their training and research. It is also possible that constraints on research funding in some countries place multidisciplinary approaches (e.g., a sport scientist looking at sport from various perspectives) at a disadvantage and therefore less attractive to researchers.

2   *The research is generally based on single cultures or single countries.*
Most research is conducted in one country typically with small samples of athletes. As Ford and Williams advocate in Chapter 9, it would be valuable to conduct studies of varying cultures to be able to compare and contrast results across different sport development systems. Intercultural studies have the great benefit of being able to determine the influence of varying environments on talent development and identification. Again, research funding for such projects can be difficult to acquire, but this would be a great step forward in our field.

3   *Investigations are typically sport-specific.*
Most research continues to evaluate single sports and our overall understanding of elite athlete development is largely based on a piecemeal approach of evaluating how individual studies might relate to sport as a whole. Similar to the point made above regarding the value of comparing multiple countries, contrasting across sports would also be beneficial to determine similarities as well as key differences. It is reasonable to assume that talent identification and development will have to be different for sports like figure skating, basketball and horse riding, but understanding those factors that are similar would also be valuable.

Taken together, a key next step would be to begin to build an international, interdisciplinary research collaboration that has the necessary contacts with practitioners in the field to develop a longitudinal study. From our point of view, this study should have elements that are similar over all sports and countries, as well as sport- and culturally-specific elements that help specific athlete populations. While this is just a vision for the future of our field, a deeper understanding of talent identification and development requires this type of next step.

Note

1   LTAD refers to both the Long-Term Athlete Development model and its current reincarnation, Canadian Sport for Life (CS4L).

References

Baker, J., Koz, D., Kungl, A. M., Fraser-Thomas, J., & Schorer, J. (2013). Staying at the top: Playing position and performance affect career length in professional sport. *High Ability Studies, 24*, 63–76.

Baker, J., & Wattie, N. (in press). Athlete development models. In C. Mallett and D. Gould (eds), *Sports coaching handbook*. Champaign, IL: Human Kinetics.

Baker, J., Wattie, N., & Schorer, J. (2016). *Compromising talent: Issues in identifying and selecting talent in sport.* Manuscript under review.

Baker, J., & Young, B. (2014). 20 years later: Deliberate practice and the development of expertise in sport. *International Review of Sport and Exercise Psychology, 7*, 135–157.

Collins, D., & MacNamara, Á. (2012). The rocky road to the top: Why talent needs trauma, *Sports Medicine, 42*, 907–914.

Ericsson, K. A., Krampe, R. T., & Tesch-Romer, C. (1993). The role of deliberate practice in the acquisition of expert performance. *Psychological Review, 100*, 363–406.

Farrow, D., & Robertson, S. (2016). *Development of a skill acquisition periodisation framework for high-performance sport.* Manuscript under review.

Gagné, F. (2013). The DMGT: Changes within, beneath, and beyond. *Talent Development and Excellence, 5*, 5–19.

Hardy, L., Barlow, M., Evans, L., Rees, T., Woodman, T., & Warr, C. (in press). Great British medallists: Psychosocial biographies of super-elite and elite athletes from Olympic sports. *Progress in Brain Research*.

Henrich, J., Heine, S. J., & Norenzayan, A. (2010). The weirdest people in the world? *Behavioral and Brain Sciences, 33*, 61–135.

Hohmann, A. (2009). *Entwicklung sportlicher Talente an Sportbetonten Schulen. Schwimmen – Leichtathletik – Handball*. Petersberg: Imhof.

Koz, D., Fraser-Thomas, J., & Baker, J. (2012). Accuracy of professional sports drafts in predicting career potential. *Scandinavian Journal of Medicine and Science in Sports, 22*, e64–e69.

Roth, K. (ed.). (1996). *Techniktraining im Spitzensport. Alltagstheorien erfolgreicher Trainer.* Köln: Strauß.

Schorer, J., Rienhoff, R., Fischer, L. & Baker, J. (2016). *Exploring the prognostic validity of talent selections in handball.* Manuscript under review.

Sedlmeier, P. (1996). Jenseits des Signifkanztest-Rituals: Ergänzungen und Alternativen. Methods of Psychological Research Online, 1, 41–63.

Wattie, N., & Baker, N. (in press). An uneven playing field: Talent identification systems and the perpetuation of participation biases in high performance sport. In R. Dionigi and M. Gard (eds), *Sport and physical activity across the lifespan: Critical perspectives*. New York: Macmillan.

Wattie, N., Schorer, J., & Baker, J. (2015). The relative age effect in sport: A developmental systems model. *Sports Medicine, 45*, 83–94.

INDEX

American football 229; injuries 395
American Medical Society for Sports Medicine 365, 385
American Youth Football 363
amplified diversity 202
Analytical Sports Career Model 169
analytics 423–4; analytical capabilities of organisations 424; culture clashes in elite sports 430–1; expert judgement vs. statistical analysis 427–8; player rating systems with multiple performance metrics 428–30; re-interpreting the *Moneyball* story 424–7
anatomical development 225, 228–9
Andersen, M. 411, 412
Anderson, D.L. and Rodriguez, A. 231
Anderson, James 241
ankle sprain 368–9, 371
anterior cruciate ligament (ACL) injury 368
Anterior Cruciate Ligament Injury-Risk-Estimation Quiz (ACL-IQ) *see* ACL-IQ test
anterior talofibular ligament 368–9
anthropometric qualities 99, 162, 238, 250, 254; longitudinal studies of 253; predictive of injury 255
anticipation skills 22, 23; visual 208–9, 213, 214–15
anxiety 257, 320; cognitive 304; natural learning 282; pre-competitive 304–5; somatic 304; survival 282
apophyseal overuse injury 373
apophysis, injuries of 372
applied motor learning: constraints-led approach 313–14; emotion 320; empirical research, lack of take-up 312; functional variability and individualizing motor skill learning 316–18; learner-regulated practice environments 318–19; metastability 315–16; optimal learning environments for skill development 312–18; problem-based coaching 313–14; representative learning design in the practice environment 319–20
applied statistics *see* statistics
appraisal(s): pre-competitive 304; primary 350; secondary 350
appropriate settings, PAF 383–6
ARC Linkage project 140
artefacts 276, 279
articular cartilage 370, 372, 374
artistic composition sports 157
athlete development 134–7; achieving a paradigm 136; continuation in 331, 332; continuous process 291; effective framework for 137; influences 288; IOC consensus statement 136–7; limitations of concepts and frameworks 135–6; longitudinal studies *see* longitudinal studies; matching with talented coaches 285; multi-factorial 251; My

Sporting Journey questionnaire 57, 139; outcomes 257–8; psychological tools and constructs 256; systems 2; *see also* 3D-AD athlete development model; FTEM Athlete Development Framework
athlete pathway 133–4; 3D-AD athlete development model 134, 135, 137, 139; athlete development, consolidated and unified view of 134–7; best practice through FTEM 139, 141–3; current state of 134; elite and mastery levels 139, 140, 143; foundational competencies, decline in 133; foundational levels 139, 140, 141; framework for understanding and managing 137–45; paradigm for understanding athlete development 136; pre-elite levels 139, 140, 142–3; trichotomy of 136; *see also* FTEM Athlete Development Framework
athletes: characteristics of 332; coordinative profiles 55; demands and expectations of 332; emerging 292–3; individualized movement patterns and techniques 316; juggling of competing demands 54; later-age transfer 91; and leadership 307–8; perception of coaches' behaviour 286; power differential with coaches 285, 413; practice and achievement 142; preference for different sports in the same category 197; psychological attributes 54; psychological makeup 329; psychological profiles of 54; reaction to low points 337; retention of 305; selection by coaches 287–9; services for 83; shifting priorities 331; talent transfer, approaches for identifying 55; *see also* elite athletes; pre-elite athletes; senior world-class athletes; youth athletes
athlete satisfaction 305
athlete-specific optimal techniques 244, 245
athlete support programmes 89
athletes with a disability: acquired disability 438; congenital disability 438; emotional trauma 438; environmental constraints 436–7; functional asymmetry 433–4; physical environment barriers 437; social environment barriers 437; structural constraints 433; talent exclusion 437
athlete welfare approach 415–17
athletic ability 70, 71
athletic identity 399–401, 402
athletic performance 15, 16
athletic talent, definition of 272
athletic talent development, definition of 272
athletic talent development environment (ATDE) working model 272, 273; definition and criterion of success 273–4; Seaside golf team 277–80; shared features 280; successful and less successful environments 274–80, 281; Wang kayak team 275–7